September 200[

MW01205090

TARBELL'S
KJV & NRSV
Lesson
Commentary

BASED ON THE INTERNATIONAL SUNDAY SCHOOL LESSONS

EDITOR: DR. DANIEL LIOY

COOK COMMUNICATIONS MINISTRIES CURRICULUM
COLORADO SPRINGS, COLORADO/PARIS, ONTARIO

TARBELL'S KJV & NRSV LESSON COMMENTARY © 2003 Cook Communications Ministries, 4050 Lee Vance View, Colorado Springs, CO 80918, U.S.A. All rights reserved. Printed in U.S.A. May not be reproduced without permission. Lessons based on International Sunday School Lessons: the International Bible Lessons for Christian Teaching, © 1998 by the Committee on the Uniform Series.

Editorial Manager: Douglas C. Schmidt

Editor: Daniel Lioy, Ph.D.

Designer: Robert de la Peña

Writers: Joseph Snider, Diana Stucky, David Jenkins, Phil Bence

Cover Design by Jeffrey P. Barnes

Cover photography © 1998 by Dan Stultz

All Scripture quotations are from the King James Version or the New Revised Standard Version of the Bible. Scripture quotations from THE NEW REVISED STANDARD VERSION OF THE BIBLE, © 1989 by the Division of Christian Education, National Council of the Churches of Christ in the United States of America, are used by permission. All rights reserved.

All Scripture quotations in the author's material, unless otherwise noted, are from the New Revised Standard Version of the Bible.

ISBN: 0-7814-3814-4

CONTENTS

SEPTEMBER, OCTOBER, NOVEMBER 2003
FAITH FACES THE WORLD

UNIT I: PUT FAITH INTO PRACTICE

UNIT II: LIVE IN HOPE

UNIT III: LIVE AS GOD'S CHILDREN

UNIT IV: LIVE WITH PURPOSE

DECEMBER 2003, JANUARY, FEBRUARY 2004
LESSONS FOR LIFE

UNIT I: A CHILD IS GIVEN

UNIT II: JOB: INTEGRITY IN TIMES OF TESTING

UNIT III: WISDOM FOR THE TIMES OF OUR LIVES

CONTENTS

■

A Word to the Teacher

In March 1850, the following advertisement appeared in a San Francisco newspaper: "Wanted: young, skinny, wiry fellows not over 18. Must be expert riders willing to risk death daily. Orphans preferred. Wages $25 per week. Apply to Central Overland Express."

The Pony Express wanted people who would put their jobs ahead of their lives, if necessary. The Pony Express went out of business a long time ago, but God is still looking for people such as you and me who are thoroughly committed to Christ. We must be willing to risk anything and everything for Him—even apparent failure by the world's standards.

As you teach the lessons presented in this year's edition of Tarbells, consider it an opportunity to share with others the new life you have in Christ. Give it your all, knowing that our Lord will be with you every step of the way!

Forever in His Service,

Dan Lioy

A Note of Appreciation

I would like to thank each of the lesson writers who contributed to this year's edition of Tarbells—Joseph Snider, Diana Stucky, Phil Bence, David Jenkins. If it wasn't for their hard work and dedication to providing quality material, this teaching resource would not be possible.

Sunday school materials from the following denominations and publishers follow the International Sunday School Lesson outlines (sometimes known as the Uniform Series). Because *Tarbell's KJV & NRSV Lesson Commentary* follows the same ISSL outlines, you can use *Tarbell's* as an excellent teacher resource to supplement the materials from these publishing houses.

Nondenominational:

Cook Communications Ministries—*Adult*

Echoes Sunday School Literature—*Adult*

Standard Publishing—*Adult*

Urban Ministries—*All ages*

Denominational:

Advent Christian General Conference—*Adult*

American Baptist (Judson Press)—*Adult*

Church of God in Christ (Church of God in Christ Publishing House)—*Adult*

Church of Christ Holiness—*Adult*

Church of God (Warner Press)—*Adult*

Church of God by Faith—*Adult*

National Baptist Convention of America (Boyd)—*All ages*

National Primitive Baptist Convention—*Adult*

Progressive National Baptist Convention—*Adult*

Presbyterian Church (U.S.A.) (Bible Discovery Series—Presbyterian Publishing House or P.R.E.M.)—*Adult*

Southern Baptist (Baptist Sunday School Board)—*All ages*

Union Gospel Press—*All ages*

United Holy Church of America—*Adult*

United Methodist Church (Cokesbury)—*All ages*

FAITH FACES THE WORLD

TRIALS AND TEMPTATIONS

BACKGROUND SCRIPTURE: James 1:1-18
DEVOTIONAL READING: 2 Corinthians 4:5-11

KEY VERSES: My brothers and sisters, whenever you face trials of any kind, consider it nothing but joy, because you know that the testing of your faith produces endurance. James 1:2-3.

KING JAMES VERSION

JAMES 1:1 James, a servant of God and of the Lord Jesus Christ, to the twelve tribes which are scattered abroad, greeting.

2 My brethren, count it all joy when ye fall into divers temptations;

3 Knowing this, that the trying of your faith worketh patience.

4 But let patience have her perfect work, that ye may be perfect and entire, wanting nothing.

5 If any of you lack wisdom, let him ask of God, that giveth to all men liberally, and upbraideth not; and it shall be given him.

6 But let him ask in faith, nothing wavering. For he that wavereth is like a wave of the sea driven with the wind and tossed.

7 For let not that man think that he shall receive any thing of the Lord.

8 A double minded man is unstable in all his ways. . . .

12 Blessed is the man that endureth temptation: for when he is tried, he shall receive the crown of life, which the Lord hath promised to them that love him.

13 Let no man say when he is tempted, I am tempted of God: for God cannot be tempted with evil, neither tempteth he any man:

14 But every man is tempted, when he is drawn away of his own lust, and enticed.

15 Then when lust hath conceived, it bringeth forth sin: and sin, when it is finished, bringeth forth death.

16 Do not err, my beloved brethren.

17 Every good gift and every perfect gift is from above, and cometh down from the Father of lights, with whom is no variableness, neither shadow of turning.

18 Of his own will begat he us with the word of truth, that we should be a kind of firstfruits of his creatures.

NEW REVISED STANDARD VERSION

JAMES 1:1 James, a servant of God and of the Lord Jesus Christ,

To the twelve tribes in the Dispersion:

Greetings.

2 My brothers and sisters, whenever you face trials of any kind, consider it nothing but joy, 3 because you know that the testing of your faith produces endurance; 4 and let endurance have its full effect, so that you may be mature and complete, lacking in nothing.

5 If any of you is lacking in wisdom, ask God, who gives to all generously and ungrudgingly, and it will be given you. 6 But ask in faith, never doubting, for the one who doubts is like a wave of the sea, driven and tossed by the wind; 7, 8 for the doubter, being double-minded and unstable in every way, must not expect to receive anything from the Lord. . . .

12 Blessed is anyone who endures temptation. Such a one has stood the test and will receive the crown of life that the Lord has promised to those who love him.

13 No one, when tempted, should say, "I am being tempted by God"; for God cannot be tempted by evil and he himself tempts no one. 14 But one is tempted by one's own desire, being lured and enticed by it; 15 then, when that desire has conceived, it gives birth to sin, and that sin, when it is fully grown, gives birth to death. 16 Do not be deceived, my beloved.

17 Every generous act of giving, with every perfect gift, is from above, coming down from the Father of lights, with whom there is no variation or shadow due to change. 18 In fulfillment of his own purpose he gave us birth by the word of truth, so that we would become a kind of first fruits of his creatures.

HOME BIBLE READINGS

Monday, September 1	2 Corinthians 4:5-10	*Persecuted, but Not Forsaken*
Tuesday, September 2	2 Corinthians 4:11-15	*Facing Death for Christ's Sake*
Wednesday, September 3	2 Corinthians 6:3-10	*A Great Endurance*
Thursday, September 4	1 Peter 4:12-19	*Suffering that Glorifies God*
Friday, September 5	James 1:1-8	*Faith Must Be Tested*
Saturday, September 6	James 1:9-12	*A Crown Awaits One Who Endures*
Sunday, September 7	James 1:13-18	*Temptations Come from Our Desires*

BACKGROUND

The author of James identifies himself in 1:1. He was James, the half brother of Jesus (Mark 6:3) and brother of Jude (Matt. 13:55). At first James had rejected Jesus as the Messiah (John 7:5), but later believed the truth about Him (1 Cor. 15:7). It is noteworthy that the author of James did not mention his familial relation to Jesus in this letter; instead, the sole claim of James to authority was his spiritual servanthood to the Messiah.

James became the leader of the Jerusalem church (Acts 12:17; 15:13; 21:18; Gal. 2:9, 12). He was also called James the Just because of his extraordinary godliness, his zeal for obedience to the law of God, and his singular devotion to prayer. He was martyred around A.D. 62 (according to the first century Jewish historian Josephus).

Though not universally agreed upon, the evidence is strong that James is one of the oldest books in the New Testament. Since the letter contains no specific references to time or events that would indicate a particular date (for example, the Jerusalem Council described in Acts 15; A.D. 49), one must consider the Jewish tone of the letter and the letter's accurate reflection of the general situation found in the early apostolic church. In A.D. 44, which is when Peter was released from prison and when Herod Agrippa II died, James became the leader of the Jerusalem church (12:5-23). In light of this, an early date of around A.D. 46 seems reasonable for this letter.

This epistle appears to have been a circular letter that was passed from church to church, with no specific geographical destination being pinpointed. Internal evidence strongly indicates that the original readership were Jewish Christians who were forced to live outside of Palestine (Jas. 1:1). This may have been as a result of Stephen's martyrdom (Acts 7; about A.D. 34). Another possibility is that it was due to the persecution under Herod Agrippa I (Acts 12; about A.D. 44).

James referred to his audience as *brothers and sisters* (1:2), which was a common designation among the first century Jews. Not surprisingly, then, James is Jewish in content. For example, the Greek noun translated *assembly* (2:2) is *synagoge*. Further, James contains more than 40 allusions to the Old Testament, as well as more than 20 to the Sermon on the Mount (Matt. 5—7).

Most of the recipients seem to have been poor and suffering from oppression imposed by their fellow Jews, among whom they were living. Evidently some of these Jewish Christians had been imprisoned and deprived of their possessions and livelihoods. Under such conditions, they fell into the clutches of worldliness, fought among themselves, favored the rich over the poor, and lost their original love for one another.

NOTES ON THE PRINTED TEXT

James, the half-brother of the Lord Jesus Christ, introduced himself with abject humility. James called himself simply *a servant of God and of the Lord Jesus Christ* (Jas. 1:1). James made no allusions to his family ties with the Lord and no reference to his authority in the church. Instead, James exalted Jesus by calling Him *Lord*, the title of deity, and *Christ*, the title of the anointed of God to redeem and reign.

The Dispersion (1:1) was a technical term in Jewish culture that alluded to the scattering of the Jews among the nation from the time of the Assyrian and Babylonian captivities in the Old Testament. The use of the expression in James is ironic, for these Jewish Christians had been scattered by persecution at the hands of antagonistic Jews. *The twelve tribes in the Dispersion* (1:1) thus refer to the Jewish Christians who had been scattered from Jerusalem where they possibly had been under the pastoral care of James.

James identified with the hardships his readers experienced as a result of persecution and expulsion from their homeland. He stood common sense on its head by urging them to consider *trials of any kind* (1:2) to be *nothing but joy*. He explained that joy is not found in the trial but in the patient endurance a person develops when faith stands firm through the test (1:3).

Consistent and patient endurance through the trials of life leads to personal maturity, to spiritual wholeness, and to sufficiency for every circumstance (1:4). *Mature* speaks to fitness and skill for the tasks of life; *complete* addresses the character traits needed to deal with adversity; and *lacking in nothing* points toward the ideal of never failing.

James urged his readers to ask God for the wisdom they needed to succeed against their trials (1:5). James assured his readers that God answers such prayers, for He is generous in giving wisdom and never holds a grudge against those who need additional prudence (Prov. 2:3-5). James promised that God always gives wisdom to those who ask for it (Jas. 1:5), but insisted that asking is a function of single-minded faith (1:6). To ask for God's wisdom without confidence in God's generosity exposes one's heart to a raging battle between forces of doubt and faith. James compared this internal conflict to opposing winds driving and tossing a wave of the sea. People of two minds are too unstable *in every way* (1:7-8) to use wisdom to endure the trials of life.

The Greek language of the New Testament used the same word to express the ideas of trial and temptation. James 1:2-8 addressed the concept of trial. Verses

12-18 deal with the idea of temptation. Interestingly, the same circumstance of life can involve both a trial and a temptation, that is, an opportunity to mature spiritually and a solicitation to sin. The point is that through every trying circumstance God intends to produce maturity and endurance in His children. He should not be blamed when a double-minded person fails to find wisdom and falls into sin.

James pronounced a blessing on *anyone who endures temptation* (1:12) and who stands *the test* of sin's seduction. The Lord Jesus views such endurance as evidence of a person's love for Him, and He rewards such endurance with *the crown of life*. Eternal life is the prize, the winner's laurels, the crowning blessing awarded Christians at the end of their race run by faith.

God never intends any situation to be a solicitation to sin (1:13). Evil can make no appeal to God's character, and He never desires a person to think or act contrary to righteousness. James did not explore the role of the devil in tempting people to sin. Instead, he focused on human desire as the enemy of faith, wisdom, and patient endurance in the trials and temptations of life (1:14).

Any strong desire that resists God's goals in the difficulties of life and lures a person toward its own goal is a source of sin (1:15). Such desire is an embryo that grows within a person's imagination until that imagination births sinful behavior. Sinful behavior then grows in a person's life until that corrupted life hatches its own destruction.

To connect God with sin is to be deceived, James maintained (1:16). Far from being a tempter, God is a giver. He is the direct or indirect source of *every generous act of giving* (1:17) and of *every perfect gift*. Two of His great gifts are wisdom (1:5) and eternal life (1:12, 18). Astronomers learn about the heavens by observing minute changes over long periods of time in the paths, phases, and brilliance of heavenly bodies. God, who created the changing heavens, never changes Himself, no matter how long one looks for the slightest variation (1:17).

James told his readers that the unvarying will and purpose of God is to give eternal life to believers through *the word of truth* (1:18) in order to present them as *a kind of first fruits of his creatures* (1:18). The Letter of James makes few direct references to Jesus. Accordingly, *the word of truth* that gives new birth is an indirect reference to the message of the death and resurrection of the Savior.

SUGGESTIONS TO TEACHERS

James wrote to Jewish Christians who had been driven from their homes, families, and country because of their faith in Jesus. James encouraged them to persevere in the face of trials, to seek wisdom from God to understand their difficulties, and to resist any urge to give up and accuse God of trying to destroy them.

1. THE JOY OF TRIALS. James never said that trials are situations to be enjoyed; yet he did say that God can use unpleasant, painful circumstances to produce joyous results in the lives of people who trust Him wholeheartedly. The corollary of James' teaching is that maturity, endurance, and deeply satisfying joy cannot be achieved apart from trying circumstances. Some aspects of these character traits can only be developed by trials.

2. THE GIFT OF WISDOM. Biblical wisdom consists of the intellectual, moral, social, and spiritual skills necessary for successful living. Wisdom springs from the fear of the Lord (Prov. 1:7; 9:10; 15:33). James promised that God gives wisdom generously to all who persist in asking for it. The context suggests James' readers needed wisdom to handle the trials of their lives. While everyone has occasional doubts—sometimes intense ones—James' double-minded person is characterized by persistent doubts that undermine the effectiveness of his or her faith in discovering and utilizing wisdom.

3. THE CROWN OF LIFE. In ancient cultures, crowns marked the highest levels of status in statesmanship, athletics, oratory, and other areas of achievement. James identified eternal life as the crown awarded the child of God who persists in overcoming temptation to sin. James did not mean that eternal life is earned by resisting temptation; rather, eternal life is the gift of God, given on the basis of Christ's sacrificial death on the cross for the sins of all people. Christians who live their lives by resisting sin demonstrate that they truly love the Lord, who will crown them with eternal life in heaven.

4. THE SOURCE OF TEMPTATIONS. James placed the responsibility for sinful thoughts and actions squarely on the shoulder of each sinner. He denied categorically that God ever traffics in sin or temptation. James ignored the external forces of the world and the devil and focused exclusively on passions as the entrance point for temptation into the human heart and spirit. Wanton passions are selfish and draw people to put their preferences above God's will. A short way down passion's path is sin, and at its end is the destruction of dreams, reputation, family, health, and life.

5. THE SOURCE OF ALL GIFTS. James insisted that God can't be blamed for sin and death. Instead, God is the source of all generous gifts and acts of giving. He is the author of His own great gifts to believers. He is the model and motive for all human generosity. When Jesus said, *"It is more blessed to give than to receive"* (Acts 20:35), He was underscoring the generosity of God. James wanted his readers to trust in God's goodness and grace in the midst of their trials and temptations.

FOR ADULTS

■ TOPIC: Endurance in God's Strength

■ QUESTIONS: 1. What attitude should believers have as they face *trials of any kind* (Jas. 1:2)? 2. What should believers do when they sense the need for wisdom? 3. Why are believers who endure temptation *blessed* (1:12)? 3. What are some trials you have recently experienced? How did you handle them? 4. What are some temptations you have recently experienced? How did you handle them? 5. Where was God in the midst of your trials and temptations?

■ **ILLUSTRATIONS:**

The Joy of Trials. The cocoon of the Emperor moth is flask-like in shape. To develop into a perfect insect, it must force its way through the neck of the cocoon by hours of intense struggle. Entomologists explain that this pressure to which the moth is subjected is nature's way of forcing a life-giving substance into its wings.

Feeling sorry for the moth, an observer said, "I'll lessen the pain and struggles of this helpless creature!" With small scissors he snipped the restraining threads to make the moth's emergence painless and effortless. But the creature never developed wings. For a brief time before its death it simply crawled instead of flying through the air on rainbow colored wings!

Sorrow, suffering, trials, and tribulations are wisely designed to grow us into Christlikeness. The refining and developing processes are oftentimes slow, but through grace, we emerge triumphant.

Crown of Life. In his commentary on James, William Barclay noted the following:

> In the ancient world the crown *(stephanos)* had at least four great associations. *(a)* The crown of flowers was worn at times of joy, at weddings and at feasts (cp. *Isaiah* 28:1, 2; *Song of Solomon* 3:11). The crown was the sign of festive joy. *(b)* The crown was the mark of royalty. It was worn by kings and by those in authority. Sometimes this was the crown of gold; sometimes it was the linen band, or fillet, worn around the brow (cp. *Psalm* 21:3; *Jeremiah* 13:18). *(c)* The crown of laurel leaves was the victor's crown in the games, the prize which the athlete coveted above all (cp. 2 *Timothy* 4:8). *(d)* The crown was the mark of honour and of dignity. . . . Wisdom provides a man with a crown of glory (*Proverbs* 1:9). . . . We do not need to choose between these meanings. They are all included.

Sinners Are Lazy. Charles "Tremendous" Jones, evangelist and motivational speaker, said, "The difference between success and failure is that successful people make themselves do what they hate to do and failures wait for their managers to make them do it or to do it for them."

Along the same lines he could have said that the difference between moral success and failure is that people who are moral successes make themselves say "no" to their sinful desires and "yes" to God's expectations, and people who are moral failures want somebody else to take the blame for their sins so they don't have to feel bad about doing whatever they wanted.

Watch What You Want. Two cars collided in a busy intersection. Both cars were demolished, but the drivers miraculously escaped without injury. One driver said to the other, "Look at our cars! They're ruined, but we're okay. That has to mean something. Don't you agree?"

"Yeah, I guess it might," the second driver said, still dazed.

"You're a man, and I'm a woman," the first driver went on. "That has to mean something. Maybe we're to become friends, get married, and be together for the rest of our lives. Don't you agree?"

The man was a little more interested in this development. "Yeah. Could be."

"Oh look, the woman said. This has to mean something. My car's demolished, but the bottle of wine I bought is okay. Maybe we're supposed to celebrate. Don't you agree?"

The man really liked this idea. He broke the seal on the wine, took a long pull straight from the bottle and handed it back to the women. "That's good. You have some."

"No," she said, closing the bottle, "I think I'll just wait for the police."

| FOR YOUTH | ■ **TOPIC:** Facing Ups and Downs
■ **QUESTIONS:** 1. What does the testing of our faith produce? |

2. Why is it wrong to be filled with doubt when we ask God for wisdom? 3. Why is it incorrect to claim that God is the source of our temptations? 4. What are some ways we can handle trials that come to us? 5. What are some ways we can handle temptations that we experience?

■ **ILLUSTRATIONS:**

The Reward of Endurance. Once upon a time in a land far away lived a band of minstrels who traveled from town to town performing their songs and plays for a few rich and a lot of poor people. Hard times came, audiences dwindled, and income dried up. After a string of particularly dismal one-night stands in small market towns, the troupe met to discuss performing in a dreary mill town.

"I see no reason to open tonight," a juggler tossed out. "It looks like snow. No one will come."

"I agree," a singer chimed in. "Last night we performed for a handful. This town makes that one look lively. Let's return our advance fee and cancel."

"How can anyone do his best for so few?" frowned a clown. Then he turned to an old friend sitting on the bench beside him. "What do you think, Laertes?"

The old man didn't move for a moment as though he hadn't heard. Then he stood, turned, and scanned the faces of his fellow-performers. "You are discouraged," he said at last. "So am I. But we will go on tonight. We will do the best show we can. It's not the fault of those who come to see us that others do not. We don't punish our fans by canceling. We reward them with our best."

The old man sat down. Nobody said anything. Nobody got excited. But they did the show. They did the best show they had done in weeks, for the smallest audience ever. After the last prop was packed, the old man held up an elegant scroll and motioned for attention. The troupe gathered around, the old man broke the seal, unrolled the parchment, and read in his rich voice, "Thank you for a beautiful performance. Well done." The old spellbinder paused, collected them with his eyes, and whispered into the expectant hush, "Your King."

Beware of Peer Pressure. A biologist conducted an experiment with "processional caterpillars," a species marked by strong follow-the-leader tendencies. The experimenter lined up caterpillars head-to-tail all the way around a big clay pot in which one of the caterpillars' favorite foods grew. Legs churned, backs undulated, and dozens of caterpillars followed one another around the pot for a full week. Not one caterpillar broke ranks to grab a quick bite from the beckoning plant. Instead, they slowed and died, one by one, from exhaustion and starvation. The survivors kept circling until there were none.

It's hard to break ranks with group leaders at school, in the neighborhood, or even at church who are going in the wrong direction. But when you should, you must. Follow God's wisdom. Follow Jesus. The results are better. So is the view. Who wants to go through life looking at the back ends of caterpillars?

God Wants Your Best. The farmer had just been in the barn boasting about the breakfast his wife had made for him that morning—ham and eggs. After the farmhands left, a pig and a chicken got into a heated argument about whether the hen house or the pigsty had made the greater contribution to the blue-ribbon breakfast. The chicken argued that the eggs, sunny side up, had been the featured food and that everything else—ham, potatoes, biscuits and gravy, juice, and coffee—played supporting roles. The pig argued that the ham was the tastiest, best smelling, and most nutritious part of the breakfast.

The debate went on for hours, until a barnyard council was held under the jurisdiction of a cranky owl who didn't like being wakened to make a ruling in broad daylight. The barn owl listened patiently to the claims of the chicken and the pig. When they were done, the owl sat in thought so long, the animals began to think he had drifted back asleep. Finally he stirred himself and ruled: "The eggs, splendid as they were, must be ruled a contribution to the breakfast, while the ham, also of high quality, involved total commitment to the breakfast. The pig wins."

No matter how hard life gets, no matter how tempting sin seems, don't be satisfied with contributing a bit of your time and effort to God. Make a total commitment.

Accept Responsibility. A police officer pulled over a car that had been weaving in and out of several lanes of traffic. He approached the driver-side door of the car and addressed the man who waved to him cheerily. "Sir," the officer said, "I need you to step out of the car and blow into this breathalyzer tube."

The driver replied, "Sorry, officer, I can't do that for you. I'm a severe asthmatic. If I do that I'll have a bad asthma attack."

"Okay," the policeman went on, "but you'll have to come down to the station and give us a blood sample."

"Oops. I can't do that either. I'm a hemophiliac. If I do that, I'll bleed to death."

In irritation, the officer ordered, "Out of the car. You'll have to walk this white line."

"Nope. Can't do that either," said the driver.

"Why?" the policeman shot back.

"Because I'm drunk. If I do that, I'll fall down!"

Be quicker than this drunk in admitting your sins. Take your sins more seriously than he did. Make it your aim not to transgress against the Lord.

FAITH AND ACTION

BACKGROUND SCRIPTURE: James 1:19—2:26; 5:7-20
DEVOTIONAL READING: Matthew 7:21-27

2

KEY VERSE: Be doers of the word, and not merely hearers who deceive themselves. James 1:22.

KING JAMES VERSION

JAMES 1:22 But be ye doers of the word, and not hearers only, deceiving your own selves.

23 For if any be a hearer of the word, and not a doer, he is like unto a man beholding his natural face in a glass:

24 For he beholdeth himself, and goeth his way, and straightway forgetteth what manner of man he was.

25 But whoso looketh into the perfect law of liberty, and continueth therein, he being not a forgetful hearer, but a doer of the work, this man shall be blessed in his deed.

26 If any man among you seem to be religious, and bridleth not his tongue, but deceiveth his own heart, this man's religion is vain.

27 Pure religion and undefiled before God and the Father is this, To visit the fatherless and widows in their affliction, and to keep himself unspotted from the world. . . .

2:8 If ye fulfil the royal law according to the scripture, Thou shalt love thy neighbour as thyself, ye do well:

9 But if ye have respect to persons, ye commit sin, and are convinced of the law as transgressors. . . .

14 What doth it profit, my brethren, though a man say he hath faith, and have not works? can faith save him?

15 If a brother or sister be naked, and destitute of daily food,

16 And one of you say unto them, Depart in peace, be ye warmed and filled; notwithstanding ye give them not those things which are needful to the body; what doth it profit?

17 Even so faith, if it hath not works, is dead, being alone. . . .

5:13 Is any among you afflicted? let him pray. Is any merry? let him sing psalms.

14 Is any sick among you? let him call for the elders of the church; and let them pray over him, anointing him with oil in the name of the Lord:

15 And the prayer of faith shall save the sick, and the Lord shall raise him up; and if he have committed sins, they shall be forgiven him.

16 Confess your faults one to another, and pray one

for another, that ye may be healed. The effectual fervent prayer of a righteous man availeth much.

NEW REVISED STANDARD VERSION

JAMES 1:22 But be doers of the word, and not merely hearers who deceive themselves. 23 For if any are hearers of the word and not doers, they are like those who look at themselves in a mirror; 24 for they look at themselves and, on going away, immediately forget what they were like. 25 But those who look into the perfect law, the law of liberty, and persevere, being not hearers who forget but doers who act—they will be blessed in their doing.

26 If any think they are religious, and do not bridle their tongues but deceive their hearts, their religion is worthless. 27 Religion that is pure and undefiled before God, the Father, is this: to care for orphans and widows in their distress, and to keep oneself unstained by the world. . . .

2:8 You do well if you really fulfill the royal law according to the scripture, "You shall love your neighbor as yourself." 9 But if you show partiality, you commit sin and are convicted by the law as transgressors. . . .

14 What good is it, my brothers and sisters, if you say you have faith but do not have works? Can faith save you? 15 If a brother or sister is naked and lacks daily food, 16 and one of you says to them, "Go in peace; keep warm and eat your fill," and yet you do not supply their bodily needs, what is the good of that? 17 So faith by itself, if it has no works, is dead.

5:13 Are any among you suffering? They should pray. Are any cheerful? They should sing songs of praise. 14 Are any among you sick? They should call for the elders of the church and have them pray over them, anointing them with oil in the name of the Lord. 15 The prayer of faith will save the sick, and the Lord will raise them up; and anyone who has committed sins will be forgiven. 16 Therefore confess your sins to one another, and pray for one another, so that you may be healed. The prayer of the righteous is powerful and effective.

HOME BIBLE READINGS

BACKGROUND

The Epistle of James can be compared to a braided rope. An idea emerges in a passage and then drops out of sight as other thoughts take their turns. Soon the first idea weaves its way to the top again, only to submerge and reappear. The relationship of belief and behavior is one of the strands of James' "rope." That explains why several passages must be considered to explore faith and action.

To comprehend the Scripture text for this week's lesson, it would be helpful to consider some background about mirrors, religious law, and oil in the first century world. When James compared the Word of God to a *mirror* (Jas. 1:23), he did not have in mind a piece of glass with a silvered backing. A mirror was a highly polished metal surface, usually brass. You didn't glance at a mirror as you ran out the door, for looking at oneself in a mirror couldn't be done quickly. You had to look carefully and study your reflection to notice anything significant about your appearance. The care required to use an ancient mirror is part of what makes it remarkable that the person in James' illustration forgot so quickly what he took great pains to find out.

Paul had such a mirror in mind when he wrote, *For now we see in a mirror, dimly* (1 Cor. 13:12). The image was dim and distorted, not because of poor lighting or the deterioration of the silvering on the back of glass. A polished metal mirror reflected a useful image, but not the kind of image we associate with modern mirrors.

James wrote to Jewish Christians, so his emphasis on the law is one they understood. In James, law represents the moral demands of Christian faith. He was not laying down for his readers a legal basis for salvation; rather, he was establishing the ethical basis for sanctification. William Barclay observed, "The difference between James and Paul is a difference in starting point. Paul starts with the great basic fact of the forgiveness of God which no man can earn or deserve; James starts with the professing Christian and insists that a man must prove his Christianity by his deeds. We are not saved by deeds; we are saved *for* deeds."

Finally, the oil mentioned in James 5:14 was medicinal, rather than salvific, in nature. The Greek participle translated *anointing* is not the religious verb *chrio* but rather the everyday verb *aleipho*. Also, the liquid was olive oil, a universal remedy for various ailments. James expected Christians who got sick to summon their church leaders. He also expected the elders to apply medicinal oil, but to depend on God to heal the sick person, in response to believers' prayers more than in response to their use of medicine.

NOTES ON THE PRINTED TEXT

Be doers of the word (Jas. 1:22) may be the key verse of the Letter of James. "The call to 'do what it says' lies at the center of all that James teaches" (Burdick, *The Expositors Bible Commentary*). The verse concludes by warning readers not to be *merely hearers who deceive themselves.* People with an intellectual assent to the concepts of Scripture may deceive themselves about their relationship with God. James said those people are like individuals who carefully study their faces in their mirrors but immediately forget what they saw when they walk away (1:23-24).

The illustration of the mirror communicates the illogic of a professed faith that doesn't affect behavior. The purpose of studying your face in the mirror is to correct any defects in your appearance. Anything else is vanity, a character defect. Similarly, the purpose of studying God's Word is to correct any defects in our manner of life. Anything else is vanity, a theological defect.

God's Word is *the perfect law* (Jas. 1:25). It is *law* in the sense of the moral standard for life, rather than as a set of rules to keep to earn God's favor. It is *perfect* in the sense that Scripture leads a person to the meaning of human existence. This goal is expressed in the phrase *law of liberty.* The moral standard of God's Word frees a person from bondage to sin and makes possible a full and joyous life.

That full and joyous life is available to those who *persevere* in living out what they learn from looking into *the perfect law, the law of liberty.* Those who strive to be doers of the Word and not mere hearers *will be blessed in their doing.* God's hand of favor rests on them.

The Greek word translated *religious* (1:26) refers to the ceremonies and rituals or worship. James insisted that religion is about the pattern of one's life rather than the pattern of one's liturgy. He identified three behaviors that denote *religion that is pure and undefiled before God* (1:27). They are constructive speech, care for the needy, and personal purity (1:27-28).

A Christian can achieve a life of harmony and excellence by obeying God's *royal law* (2:8). James quoted Leviticus 19:18, *"You shall love your neighbor as yourself."* This is "the supreme law that is the source of all other laws governing human relationships" (NIV *Study Bible*). "It is a law fit for those who are royal, and able to make men royal" (Barclay). The royal law commands our speech, our compassion for the needy, and our rejection of the impurity of the world.

James commended loving our neighbor and condemned favoring the wealthy and despising the poor (Jas. 2:9). Anyone who favors the rich and powerful over the poor and weak sins. That makes the sinner a lawbreaker. The lawbreaker has transgressed the entire law code, not just a single statute.

James then addressed the situation in which someone might assert that he or she has a private faith that does not engage in public deeds (2:14). In the question *Can faith save you?*, the Greek noun translated *faith* has a definite article, indicating the particular kind of faith that produces no good deeds. The grammar of the Greek question expects a negative answer.

James illustrated the absurdity of inactive faith by imagining someone telling a half-naked, starving fellow-Christian to be happy, get warm, and eat heartily (2:15-16). Words, which are all that professed faith consists of, are worthless in the face of the real issues of life. *So faith by itself, if it has no works, is dead* (2:17).

Deeds of faith include more than compassionate care of the needy. Prayer, praise, and confession are important acts of faith (5:13-16). Prayer is the response of faith to *suffering* (5:13), and *songs of praise* is the response of faith to pleasant circumstances of life.

One of the most common forms of suffering people encounter is sickness. Faith should prompt believers to appeal to the elders of the church to pray for them while anointing them with olive oil. Faith should prompt the elders to pray for them *in the name of the Lord* (5:14). The prayer offered in faith will *save the sick* (5:15). That is a general principle, to which there are many exceptions. *The Lord will raise them up*. God may use medicine as a means. He may also respond to prayer. In either case, God gets the glory for healing the ailing believer.

Sometimes sin is involved in sickness. Prayers for forgiveness of confessed sins always avail. Therefore, James exhorted his readers, *Confess your sins to one another, and pray for one another* (5:16). Confession and prayer extends beyond the elders to involve the entire church, that is, *to one another*. Healing probably has spiritual as well as physical overtones in verse 16. *The righteous* is a group of people synonymous with those of active faith. Their prayers of faith possess spiritual power and produce tangible effects.

SUGGESTIONS TO TEACHERS

James always connected truth and behavior. Scripture was to be obeyed, not just formulated into propositions for analysis and assent. He stood in the line of the theology of the Old Testament in which law, or "torah," meant instruction for living and wisdom meant skill in living. James reflected the stance of Christ, who said, *"Everyone then who hears these words of mine and acts on them will be like a wise man who built his house on rock. . . . And everyone who hears these words of mine and does not act on them will be like a foolish man who built his house on sand"* (Matt. 7:24, 26).

1. HEARING AND DOING. James believed that the Word of God has not been heard until it has been obeyed. Comprehending the meaning of the Word in the abstract without making concrete application of it is dangerous. A person can deceive himself or herself into thinking intellectual agreement with the Word impresses God.

2. LAW AND LIBERTY. When Paul wrote about the law, he had in mind an approach to salvation based on the efforts of the flesh to achieve the righteousness of God. James used the term "law" to represent God's moral principles inherent in human character and relationships. From James' perspective, living in harmony with God's law spiritually liberates believers, while living in opposition to God's law produces bondage to sin.

3. FAITH AND ACTIONS. James denied that inactive faith is real faith within the body of Christ. James "indicates that it is not the right kind of faith. It is not living faith, nor can it save" (Burdick). At the same time, the actions prompted by faith do not save. Faith in Christ alone saves. Actions validate the vitality of a person's saving faith.

4. PRAYER AND HEALING. James presented prayer as an action of faith. Prayers of petition, praise, and confession evidence living faith in the God to whom they are addressed. James emphasized prayer for the sick because it shows dependence on God for healing, even when medicine is employed.

FOR ADULTS

■ TOPIC: Faith Means Action!

■ QUESTIONS: 1. Why is it important to *be doers of the word* (Jas. 1:22)? 2. How did James define true religion? 3. What is the nature of saving faith? 4. What are some ways faith is seen to be at work in your life? 5. What steps can you take to strengthen your faith in Christ?

■ **ILLUSTRATIONS:**

Active Faith. An old boatman painted the word "faith" on one oar of his boat and "works" on the other. He was asked his reason for this. In answer, he slipped the oar with "faith" into the water and rowed. The boat, of course, made a very tight circle. Returning to the dock, the boatman then said, "Now, let's try 'works' without 'faith' and see what happens." The oar marked "works" was put in place and the boatman began rowing with just the "works" oar. Again the boat went into a tight circle, but this time in the opposite direction.

When the boatman again returned to the wharf, he interpreted his experiment in these strong and convincing words: "You see, to make a passage across the lake, one needs both oars working simultaneously in order to keep the boat in a straight and narrow way. If one does not have the use of both oars, he or she makes no progress either across the lake nor as a Christian."

The Folly of Fine Feelings. Barclay, in his commentary on James, noted the following:

It is a fact that every time a man feels a noble impulse without taking action, he becomes less likely ever to take action. In a sense it is true to say that a man has no right to feel sympathy unless he at least tries to put that sympathy into action. An emotion is not something in which to luxuriate; it is something which at the cost of effort and of toil and of discipline and of sacrifice must be turned into the stuff of life.

Effective Praying. A tornado was coming. All the people, family and those working on the farm, had hurried into the tornado shelter. They were huddled together in a dark room with the winds howling and rattling the only door that everybody had come through. The wind was blowing in such a fierce way that they were afraid that the door would come off as it shook from the wind. If that happened, they could be sucked out into the tornado.

An old preacher was praying with great oratorical effects in the midst of this violent storm, crying out, "Send us the spirit of the children of Israel, the children of Moses, the children of the promised land."

At this, an old man with less oratory but more directness lifted his voice and prayed loudly, "Lord, don't send nobody. Come Yourself! This ain't no job for none of them children."

FOR YOUTH

■ TOPIC: Faith Equals Action!
■ QUESTIONS: 1. What do you think is the *law of liberty* (Jas. 1:25)? 2. What is wrong with faith that produces no good works? 3. How should believers handle episodes of suffering? 4. How can you demonstrate your faith in concrete ways? 5. How has the power of prayer been demonstrated in your life?

■ ILLUSTRATIONS:

Faith Lets God Lead. A scientist once compared black holes in outer space to invisible dance partners. Black holes are stars that have collapsed into concentrations of matter so dense that their gravity prevents the escape of light. The scientist likened the universe to a dance floor, with the ladies in white dresses representing visible matter and the men all in black representing "dark" matter. If the lights are turned down, all that can be seen is the white of the ladies; and yet we know the men are there because of the pattern of the ladies' movements. Unseen partners lead them.

God is Spirit and invisible to the physical sense of sight. Faith sees God and dances with Him. Faith in action reveals God's presence to everyone who sees Him leading the believers across the floor of life.

Sin, Sickness, and Prayer. Cable television mogul Ted Turner is a vocal critic of Christianity. At a banquet in Orlando, Florida, Turner was given an award by the American Humanist Association for his work on behalf of the environment and world peace in 1990. When he addressed the audience, Turner said he had had a strict Christian upbringing and had at one time considered becoming a missionary. "I was saved seven or eight times," he said. But he said he became disenchanted with Christianity after his sister died, despite his prayers. Turner said the more he strayed from his faith, "the better I felt." (*Spokesman-Review*, May 1, 1990).

Ted Turner tried to control God. He wasn't submitting if God's will differed from his. Turner felt better when he decisively rejected God's control. At the same time, Turner lost the opportunity to pray in times of trial and sickness. He has chosen to reject God's most precious blessings associated with faith.

Confession and Prayer. When the famous preacher Norman Vincent Peale was a boy, he found a big, black cigar on the sidewalk. Young Peale slipped into an alley and lit up. It tasted horrible, but it made him feel very grown up. Then he saw his father coming for him. Quickly he put the cigar behind his back and tried to act casually.

Desperate to divert his father's attention, Norman pointed to circus posters pasted to the buildings lining the alley. "Can I go, Dad? Please, let's go when it comes to town."

His father's reply taught Norman a lesson he never forgot. "Son," he answered quietly but firmly, "never make a petition while at the same time trying to hide a smoldering disobedience" (John Lavender, *Why Prayers Are Unanswered*).

Confession of sin clears the air between us and our heavenly Father. We stay on good terms with Him when we quit trying to hide our sins and appear better than we are.

FAITH AND WISDOM

BACKGROUND SCRIPTURE: James 3
DEVOTIONAL READING: Colossians 1:3-14

3

KEY VERSE: Who is wise and understanding among you? Show by your good life that your works are done with gentleness born of wisdom. James 3:13.

KING JAMES VERSION

JAMES 3:1 My brethren, be not many masters, knowing that we shall receive the greater condemnation. 2 For in many things we offend all. If any man offend not in word, the same is a perfect man, and able also to bridle the whole body. 3 Behold, we put bits in the horses' mouths, that they may obey us; and we turn about their whole body. 4 Behold also the ships, which though they be so great, and are driven of fierce winds, yet are they turned about with a very small helm, whithersoever the governor listeth. 5 Even so the tongue is a little member, and boasteth great things. Behold, how great a matter a little fire kindleth! 6 And the tongue is a fire, a world of iniquity: so is the tongue among our members, that it defileth the whole body, and setteth on fire the course of nature; and it is set on fire of hell. 7 For every kind of beasts, and of birds, and of serpents, and of things in the sea, is tamed, and hath been tamed of mankind: 8 But the tongue can no man tame; it is an unruly evil, full of deadly poison. 9 Therewith bless we God, even the Father; and therewith curse we men, which are made after the similitude of God. 10 Out of the same mouth proceedeth blessing and cursing. My brethren, these things ought not so to be. 11 Doth a fountain send forth at the same place sweet water and bitter? 12 Can the fig tree, my brethren, bear olive berries? either a vine, figs? so can no fountain both yield salt water and fresh.

13 Who is a wise man and endued with knowledge among you? let him shew out of a good conversation his works with meekness of wisdom. 14 But if ye have bitter envying and strife in your hearts, glory not, and lie not against the truth. 15 This wisdom descendeth not from above, but is earthly, sensual, devilish. 16 For where envying and strife is, there is confusion and every evil work. 17 But the wisdom that is from above is first pure, then peaceable, gentle, and easy to be intreated, full of mercy and good fruits, without partiality, and without hypocrisy. 18 And the fruit of righteousness is sown in peace of them that make peace.

NEW REVISED STANDARD VERSION

JAMES 3:1 Not many of you should become teachers, my brothers and sisters, for you know that we who teach will be judged with greater strictness. 2 For all of us make many mistakes. Anyone who makes no mistakes in speaking is perfect, able to keep the whole body in check with a bridle. 3 If we put bits into the mouths of horses to make them obey us, we guide their whole bodies. 4 Or look at ships: though they are so large that it takes strong winds to drive them, yet they are guided by a very small rudder wherever the will of the pilot directs. 5 So also the tongue is a small member, yet it boasts of great exploits.

How great a forest is set ablaze by a small fire! 6 And the tongue is a fire. The tongue is placed among our members as a world of iniquity; it stains the whole body, sets on fire the cycle of nature, and is itself set on fire by hell. 7 For every species of beast and bird, of reptile and sea creature, can be tamed and has been tamed by the human species, 8 but no one can tame the tongue—a restless evil, full of deadly poison. 9 With it we bless the Lord and Father, and with it we curse those who are made in the likeness of God. 10 From the same mouth come blessing and cursing. My brothers and sisters, this ought not to be so. 11 Does a spring pour forth from the same opening both fresh and brackish water? 12 Can a fig tree, my brothers and sisters, yield olives, or a grapevine figs? No more can salt water yield fresh.

13 Who is wise and understanding among you? Show by your good life that your works are done with gentleness born of wisdom. 14 But if you have bitter envy and selfish ambition in your hearts, do not be boastful and false to the truth. 15 Such wisdom does not come down from above, but is earthly, unspiritual, devilish. 16 For where there is envy and selfish ambition, there will also be disorder and wickedness of every kind. 17 But the wisdom from above is first pure, then peaceable, gentle, willing to yield, full of mercy and good fruits, without a trace of partiality or hypocrisy. 18 And a harvest of righteousness is sown in peace for those who make peace.

BACKGROUND

The Letter of James is more practical than doctrinal in character; nevertheless, the epistle contains strong theological statements. For example, God is *the Father of lights, with whom there is no variation* (1:17), meaning that He is the Creator and is unchangeable. Jesus is *our glorious Lord* (2:1), a reference to His deity. James asserted that Christ is coming again (5:7-8), and when He does, He will judge all of humanity (5:9).

James wrote with a passionate desire for his readers to be uncompromisingly obedient to the Word of God. He complemented Paul's emphasis on justification by faith with his own emphasis on true faith demonstrating itself in spiritual fruitfulness. While Paul left the church an eloquent legacy of teaching about grace and faith (often in response to those who were slavishly legalistic), the contribution of James to the balanced Christian life would be an emphasis on real faith producing authentic deeds.

James has been variously considered an epistle, a sermon (to be read aloud in churches), a form of wisdom literature, a prolonged discourse, and a moral exhortation. These categories are not mutually exclusive, and there are elements of all these forms in James. The letter has a markedly Jewish flavor and refers frequently to the Old Testament. The literary structure of parallelism is used (1:9-10), along with direct, pungent statements on wise living (reminiscent of Proverbs and the prophet Amos), concrete images drawn from nature, and groups of sayings that have a clear similarity to the style of Jesus.

Like other wisdom literature found in Scripture, James, though relying at times on observation and study, made greater use of introspection and meditation. The author focused on the enduring aspects of the human condition. He examined the world around him, and under the guidance of the Spirit drew conclusions about human nature and living in a way that is pleasing to God.

A consistent characteristic of James is its practical advice and teaching on how to navigate skillfully through the twists and turns of life. Though the wisdom statements found in the letter are practical, they are not superficial or external, for they contain moral and ethical elements that stress upright living that flows out of a right relationship with God. In fact, from beginning to end, such biblical wisdom is sourced in God for its ideas, methods, and morals.

NOTES ON THE PRINTED TEXT

James assumed that his Jewish Christian readers would hold the office of teacher in high regard and warned them against coveting such honor in case they were neither gifted nor called by God to fill such a role (Jas. 3:1). The first reason James gave for cautioning his readers about teaching is that teachers will be held accountable by God to a high standard in final judgment. Jesus had said, *"The scribes and the Pharisees sit on Moses' seat; therefore, do whatever they teach you and follow it; but do not do as they do, for they do not practice what they teach. . . . But woe to you, scribes and Pharisees, hypocrites! For you lock people out of the kingdom of heaven. For you do not go in yourselves"* (Matt. 23:2-3, 13).

James acknowledged that all people *make many mistakes* (Jas. 3:2). The Greek word rendered *mistakes* means "to stumble" and was used as a euphemism for sinning. James asserted that stumbling in speech was inevitable. Only a perfect person can keep from sinning verbally. That verbally perfect person would have no trouble reining in any other sin of the flesh.

James introduced two quick analogies to illustrate the power of speech to control the course of life. He compared the tongue—small body part that it is—with the bit that controls a massive horse (3:3) and the rudder that steers a huge ship (3:4). In both cases a master uses something small to control something large in the face of other forces—the will of the horse and the winds in the ship's sails. The tongue is as controlling as the bit or the rudder (3:5). Sadly, it seems not to yield to the will of its human master.

Instead, the tongue is a great power run amok. It is a wildfire that sets ablaze everything around it (Jas. 3:6). The tongue is *a world of iniquity* that defiles the whole person, represented by his or her body. All evil in the world seems to spring from the human tongue and set fire to *the cycle of nature*, "the whole of life and living" (Barclay). Although the tongue seems to serve no human master, it does serve the purposes of hell and hell's master.

James illustrated the uncontrollable and deadly character of the human tongue and its speech by means of a contrastive analogy about taming wild animals (3:7-8). The biggest and the most ferocious beasts have been tamed by humans; however, the tiny tongue restlessly resists all human efforts to tame it, and its poison is more virulent than that of any creature.

The human tongue—representing human speech—shows its deadly nature in its erratic and inconsistent behavior. It can strike at any time. One moment it blesses God; the next it curses a human made in God's image (3:9). James despaired that the same mouth could spout blessings and cursings in almost the same breath. Such inconsistency does not occur in the natural world. A spring gives either fresh or brackish water, not one now and the other later. Fruit trees and vines bear their natural harvests, never unnatural ones. The tongue, by contrast, is perverse (vss. 10-12).

James began his third chapter by warning against a hasty, ill-advised desire to be a teacher in the church. He then explored the dangers a teacher faces in controlling the tongue, the chief instrument of instruction. In verse 13, James began considering two sources of wisdom that can motivate a teacher. These two wisdoms help explain why the tongue is sometimes devastating and sometimes edifying.

James began by asking who the truly wise person is and answering his own question. The true sage lives a good life, the deeds of which are characterized by gentleness (3:13). There is a false wisdom abroad in the world that values self-assertion. This wisdom is selfish, ambitious, and boastful (3:14). This is not the wisdom God gives when we ask for it (1:5). This "wisdom" fits the fallen values of this earth. It has nothing of God's Spirit in it. Any spirits associated with this wisdom are demonic (3:15).

Teaching, speaking, or living motivated by self-assertive "wisdom" leads to *disorder and wickedness of every kind* (3:16). Envy lies at the heart of much self-protective speech and behavior. Envy fears that someone is ahead of me and has more than I do. This fear generates divisiveness and turmoil. By contrast, *the wisdom from above* (3:17), which God gives, leads to *peace* (3:18).

The sage concerned with moral and spiritual excellence takes his or her eyes off of self and pursues peace. This sage is gentle rather than harsh, is willing to take second place rather than grasp for power, and is merciful rather than brutal. Such wisdom promotes righteousness—right relations with God and right relations with other people. Such righteousness promotes the harmony and happiness of peace.

SUGGESTIONS TO TEACHERS

In the first lesson of this unit, we studied about the role of wisdom in dealing with the trials and temptations of life. In this week's lesson, we are looking at the role of wisdom as the controlling factor in speech and life. Apart from God's wisdom, we are helpless to counter the destructive effects of sin and the Fall on our relationships with God and other people.

1. POWERFUL SPEECH. Leaders in the church will give an account for how they handle the authority they exercise. Perhaps the greatest burden a teacher bears is the responsibility to govern his or her tongue. Our words wield enormous power in the lives of those to whom we speak. The little tongue may be the most powerful member of the body.

2. DEVASTATING SPEECH. Thoughtless or malicious speech lays waste to lives, reputations, and careers like a fire consuming a forest and leaving it a blackened, smoking wasteland. No human power is able to exercise effective, lasting control over the tongue.

3. INCONSISTENT SPEECH. The tongue can alternately bless and curse, build up and tear down. Its potential for good is limitless; so is its power for evil. The Jekyll and Hyde nature of human speech is unparalleled in the natural world where animate and inanimate beings have consistent characters. The tongue is frightening in its power, destructive capacity, and inconsistent, unpredictable character.

4. TWO WISDOMS. There are two wisdoms at work in the world. They reveal themselves in radically different ways of behaving. Their contrast explains the schizophrenia of our speech. The wisdom of the earth is based on envy, expresses itself in selfish ambition, and results in turmoil and sin. Its spiritual nature is demonic. The wisdom from above is based on purity, expresses itself in sweet reasonableness, and results in peace and righteousness. Its spiritual nature is godly.

For many Christians, the concept of righteousness might seem too abstract to understand. This difficulty is decreased as they grow in their appreciation of what it means to live in a holy, or morally pure, manner.

People are considered righteous when their personal and interpersonal behavior are in harmony with God's will as it is revealed in Scripture. The righteous person willingly serves the Lord (Mal. 3:18), takes delight in Him (Ps. 33:1), and gives thanks to Him for His mercy and love (140:13). The righteous are blessed by God (5:12) and upheld by Him (37:17).

The righteous may experience hardships and trials in life, but God promises to help them through their difficulties (Ps. 34:19). No matter how severe their afflictions might be, the Lord will never forsake them (37:25) or allow them to fall (55:22). The prospect for the righteous is joy (Prov. 10:28) and the way of the Lord is their strength, or refuge (vs. 29). The Lord promises to be with them in their darkest moments (11:8) and to be a refuge for them in death (14:32).

FOR ADULTS

■ **TOPIC:** Living Wisely

■ **QUESTIONS:** 1. Why did James encourage caution in becoming a teacher of Scripture? 2. What power did James say the tongue has? 3. What is the difference between worldly wisdom and divine wisdom? 4. How can we use our speech to promote good? 5. How can we cultivate godly wisdom in our lives?

■ **ILLUSTRATIONS:**

Bite Your Tongue. The story goes that a hotheaded woman told John Wesley, "My talent is to speak my mind." Replied Wesley, "God wouldn't care a bit if you would bury that talent."

Caution: Words at Work. Once upon a time, in Victorian England, the smooth-tongued statesman William Gladstone escorted a noted beauty to dinner. The next evening, Benjamin Disraeli—Gladstone's oratorical rival—dined next to the same elegant lady. When asked her opinion of the two political titans, the woman replied thoughtfully: "When I left the dining room after sitting with Mr. Gladstone, I thought he was the cleverest man in England. But after sitting next to Mr. Disraeli, I thought I was the cleverest woman in England."

Words and Anger Burn. In the spring of 1894, the Baltimore Orioles went to Boston to play a routine baseball game. But what happened that day was anything but routine.

The Orioles' John McGraw got into a fight with the Boston third baseman. Within minutes all the players from both teams had joined in the brawl. The warfare spread to the grandstands. Among the fans the conflict went from bad to worse. Someone set fire to the wooden stands and the entire ballpark burned to the ground. Not only that, but the fire spread to 107 other Boston buildings as well (*Our Daily Bread*).

Folly of Selfish Wisdom. Two Texans were trying to impress one another with their ranches. One asked the other, "What's the name of your spread?"

The second rancher boasted, "Why, it's the Rocking R, ABC, Flying Q, Circle C, Bar U, Staple Four, Box D, Rolling M, Rainbow's End, Silver Spur Ranch."

The first rancher was impressed. "Go-olly! What a handle! How many head of cattle do you run?"

"Actually, not many," the second rancher admitted. "Very few survive the branding."

Sow Seeds of Peace. Ramsey MacDonald, a former prime minister of England, once discussed the possibility of lasting peace with a fellow government official. This expert on foreign affairs marveled at the prime minister's idealism. He remarked cynically, "The desire for peace does not necessarily ensure it."

MacDonald replied, "Quite true. Neither does the desire for food satisfy your hunger, but at least it gets you started toward a restaurant."

FOR YOUTH

■ TOPIC: Watch Your Tongue!

■ QUESTIONS: 1. What words of caution did James offer regarding the tongue? 2. What harm did James say could come through the inappropriate use of speech? 3. Why should we shun ungodly forms of wisdom? 4. Why is it sometimes hard for people to control their speech? 5. What can we do promote peace through the things we say?

■ **ILLUSTRATIONS:**

A Time to Speak. Albert Einstein was asked to say a few impromptu words at a dinner given in his honor at Swarthmore College. He stood and said, "Ladies and gentlemen, I am very sorry, but I have nothing to say," and sat down. Shortly he rose again and added, "If I do have something to say, I'll come back."

Six months later, Einstein wired the president of Swarthmore to say, "Now I have something to say," Another dinner was hosted, and Einstein made a notable speech.

Heated Words. A waitress carrying a two-gallon container of dressing to the salad bar paused for a second while coming through the swinging doors from the kitchen. Bad idea. The doors whacked her backside, knocked her forward, and launched two gallons of dressing over a well-dressed customer. It was 12:30 on a Sunday afternoon. Where had a guy in a suit and tie come from at 12:30 on Sunday afternoon?

The customer leaped to his feet with dressing oozing from his hair, covering his glasses, coating his face, drenching his jacket, shirt, tie, and trousers, and puddling around his smeared shoes. Two gallons of it.

The diner spluttered and swore. Then he found his tongue. "You're so stupid! I can't believe you could do such a stupid, stupid thing. This is a brand-new suit. It cost me $300. I want to see the manager!"

The shaken waitress hurried off to get the manager, who remembered his training and asked blandly, "Is there a problem?"

The man ranted, "Is there a problem? She's ruined my $300 suit. It's brand new. I want a new suit!"

The manager says, "We'll be glad to get your suit cleaned. We are terribly sorry about this dreadful accident."

"No! No!" the man objected. "I don't want my suit cleaned. I want a brand new suit. I demand a check for $300 right here and now."

To avoid a bigger scene, the manger went to his office, and wrote out a check for $300. Restaurant employees wiped off as much salad dressing as they could, and the irate diner fumed out the door with his check.

Where had a guy in a suit and tie come from at 12:30 on Sunday afternoon? I wonder what the sermon topic was?

Selfish Wisdom. Two friends were camping in the woods. They woke up one morning to see and hear an obviously irritated grizzly bear coming down the hillside toward them. One man reached for his shoes and frantically started tying them. His friend said, "What are you doing? Do you honestly think you can outrun a grizzly bear?"

"No," the first guy said as he rose to go. "I don't have to. I just need to outrun you."

The Power of Peace. Christmas Eve 1914 brought an eerie halt to the carnage of World War I on the western front. Trenches lay within 50 miles of Paris. The war was only five months old but had killed or wounded 800,000 combatants. What would happen Christmas Day?

British soldiers raised Merry Christmas signs. Here and there, sounds of carols wafted from both lines. Frequently unarmed British and German soldiers left their trenches against the orders of their superiors and met in no-man's land to sing, talk, and exchange candy and cigars. At one spot, an impromptu soccer game broke out, and the German team won three to two.

In some places, the Christmas truce stretched on through the next day. Neither army wanted to fire the first shot. But new troops kept arriving, eager for battle, and fighting resumed from the English Channel to the Swiss Alps. The high command of both armies ordered that further "informal understandings" with the enemy be treated as treason.

FAITH AND ATTITUDES

BACKGROUND SCRIPTURE: James 4:1—5:6
DEVOTIONAL READING: 1 Peter 5:1-6

KEY VERSE: Humble yourselves before the Lord, and he will exalt you. James 4:10.

4

KING JAMES VERSION

JAMES 4:1 From whence come wars and fightings among you? come they not hence, even of your lusts that war in your members?

2 Ye lust, and have not: ye kill, and desire to have, and cannot obtain: ye fight and war, yet ye have not, because ye ask not.

3 Ye ask, and receive not, because ye ask amiss, that ye may consume it upon your lusts.

4 Ye adulterers and adulteresses, know ye not that the friendship of the world is enmity with God? whosoever therefore will be a friend of the world is the enemy of God.

5 Do ye think that the scripture saith in vain, The spirit that dwelleth in us lusteth to envy?

6 But he giveth more grace. Wherefore he saith, God resisteth the proud, but giveth grace unto the humble.

7 Submit yourselves therefore to God. Resist the devil, and he will flee from you.

8 Draw nigh to God, and he will draw nigh to you. Cleanse your hands, ye sinners; and purify your hearts, ye double minded.

9 Be afflicted, and mourn, and weep: let your laughter be turned to mourning, and your joy to heaviness.

10 Humble yourselves in the sight of the Lord, and he shall lift you up. . . .

13 Go to now, ye that say, To day or to morrow we will go into such a city, and continue there a year, and buy and sell, and get gain:

14 Whereas ye know not what shall be on the morrow. For what is your life? It is even a vapour, that appeareth for a little time, and then vanisheth away.

15 For that ye ought to say, If the Lord will, we shall live, and do this, or that.

16 But now ye rejoice in your boastings: all such rejoicing is evil.

17 Therefore to him that knoweth to do good, and doeth it not, to him it is sin.

NEW REVISED STANDARD VERSION

JAMES 4:1 Those conflicts and disputes among you, where do they come from? Do they not come from your cravings that are at war within you? 2 You want something and do not have it; so you commit murder. And you covet something and cannot obtain it; so you engage in disputes and conflicts. You do not have, because you do not ask. 3 You ask and do not receive, because you ask wrongly, in order to spend what you get on your pleasures. 4 Adulterers! Do you not know that friendship with the world is enmity with God? Therefore whoever wishes to be a friend of the world becomes an enemy of God. 5 Or do you suppose that it is for nothing that the scripture says, "God yearns jealously for the spirit that he has made to dwell in us"? 6 But he gives all the more grace; therefore it says,

"God opposes the proud,
    but gives grace to the humble."

7 Submit yourselves therefore to God. Resist the devil, and he will flee from you. 8 Draw near to God, and he will draw near to you. Cleanse your hands, you sinners, and purify your hearts, you double-minded. 9 Lament and mourn and weep. Let your laughter be turned into mourning and your joy into dejection. 10 Humble yourselves before the Lord, and he will exalt you. . . .

13 Come now, you who say, "Today or tomorrow we will go to such and such a town and spend a year there, doing business and making money." 14 Yet you do not even know what tomorrow will bring. What is your life? For you are a mist that appears for a little while and then vanishes. 15 Instead you ought to say, "If the Lord wishes, we will live and do this or that." 16 As it is, you boast in your arrogance; all such boasting is evil. 17 Anyone, then, who knows the right thing to do and fails to do it, commits sin.

BACKGROUND

There are a couple of points of Jewish background that make James 4 clearer. The first is the Old Testament perspective that Israel was the bride of the Lord (Isa. 54:5; Jer. 3:20). Whenever Israel lapsed into idolatry, the nation was guilty of adultery against the Lord (Exod. 34:15-16). The prophets viewed such infidelity as an abhorrent violation of Israel's covenant with the Lord (Deut. 31:16).

At the Lord's command, the prophet Hosea married a prostitute named Gomer and suffered through the anguish of her adultery and self-degradation. This illustrated to Israel how her faithlessness wounded the heart of God and jeopardized her future (Hos. 1:2; 3:1). Jesus described the Pharisees and Sadducees as *an evil and adulteress generation* (Matt. 16:4).

The New Testament adopted the imagery of the Old Testament when speaking about the church as the bride of Christ (2 Cor. 11:1-2; Eph. 5:24-32; Rev. 19:7; 21:9). In 2 Corinthians 11:3, Paul expressed concern that the betrothed of the Lord might be led astray into infidelity.

James 4:13 refers to a merchant selecting a target city in which to invest a year of his life in order to make a fortune. This scene would be familiar to first century Jews. There was a large mobile Jewish merchant class that provided capital and entrepreneurial spirit around the Mediterranean basin. Roman roads and shipping made travel relatively easy and safe. Greek culture and language linked people at the eastern end of the Mediterranean Sea. Virtually every major city of the area had a sizeable Jewish community.

NOTES ON THE PRINTED TEXT

James 4 probes further into the human heart for the source of the conflicts described in chapter 3. *Conflicts and disputes* (4:1) are strong words that suggest full-blown wars between bitter enemies rather than tiffs between friends. Antagonisms between Christians are the spillover of wars inside them. Those wars are battles based on *cravings*, that is, hedonistic desires or lusts.

These lusts are not necessarily sexual. Anything we covet for our pleasure fills the bill. James said his readers wanted things badly enough to murder for them (4:2). This is the "murder" of hatred described by Jesus in the Sermon on the

Mount (Matt. 5:21-22). Such hateful covetousness produces disputes and conflicts, which can never provide the coveter what he craves.

James told his readers that, to start with, they didn't have what they wanted because they didn't pray (Jas. 4:2). In fact they wouldn't get it when they did pray because the motive of their prayers boiled down to hedonistic pleasures (4:3).

Then James called his readers *adulterers* (Jas. 4:4). The spiritual values reflected in their covetousness indicated they had abandoned God as their covenant partner and given allegiance to *the world*.

James identified another kind of double-mindedness that Christians seem to want at their worst moments—friendship with God and friendship with the world. James harked back to the dictum of Jesus that a person can't serve two masters and asserted that any friend of the world is an enemy of God. By way of evidence, James pointed out the foul mouths and quarrelsome behavior of those who were trying to have it both ways.

James referred to the teaching of Scripture when he noted that *"God yearns jealously for the spirit that he has made to dwell in us"* (4:5). The idea that God is a jealous God is a repeated Old Testament concept (Exod. 20:5; 34:14). Jealousy is an appropriate emotion for a husband whose spouse has committed adultery. James impressed on his readers that God burns with jealousy in order that His Spirit alone should live within and control the words and actions of His covenant people.

Since God makes such an exclusive demand on the love and loyalty of His people, He lavishes grace on them to enable them to respond (Jas. 4:6). James quoted Proverbs 3:34 as evidence that God's grace is always available to those who humbly submit to Him. The other side of that proverb is that *God opposes the proud* (Jas. 4:6). Pride leads one back to friendship with the world and spiritual infidelity.

James taught that repentance and humility are requisites for receiving God's grace. Ten imperative verbs dot the Greek text of 4:7-10. The first two form a complementary pair: submit to God and resist the devil (4:7). Submission is the act of accepting God's will in the place of mine. When God's will rules my life, I can successfully resist the devil and see him flee. Jesus did it in the wilderness by quoting God's Word to the devil (Matt. 4:1-11). Peter also commanded such resistance (1 Pet. 5:9).

As the devil retreats, one can draw still nearer to God and find Him approaching from His side (Jas. 4:8). This new proximity invites new purification. Both hands and heart—signifying actions and motives—need to be cleansed because we are sinners in a sinful world. Despite our best efforts, we live *double-minded* lives—submitting to God in our better moments and submitting to the world and devil in our worse ones. When we yield to the devil, we must *lament and mourn and weep* (4:9). It is a mistake to shrug off the evil we do.

We must face our sin and repent with godly sorrow. Laughter and joy can only be restored by mourning and dejection when we sin against God. When we lower ourselves before our Lord in repentance, He lifts us up and renews our joy (4:10).

Christians should humbly submit to God's will and resist every urge to depend on asserting our own wills. James warned against such arrogance by means of the example of the self-assured businessman who has mapped out his time, chosen his activities, and set his goals for an entire year with no reference to God (4:13).

No human can see into the future, and life is fragile and transitory (4:14). Arrogant planning denies these truths. Proper planning acknowledges that every scheme is contingent on the will of God (4:15). Such planning acknowledges that God has the last word about whether we will be alive tomorrow.

Our saying *"If the Lord wishes"* is not invoking a magic formula to manipulate God. It is the expression of an attitude of submission and dependence. James assumed his readers were guilty of arrogant planning and called on them to stop such sinning and adopt the right attitudes (4:16-17).

SUGGESTIONS TO TEACHERS

There are four sections to this week's Scripture text, and they group into two contrasting sets of verses. The first two sections contrast worshiping pleasure and worshiping God. The second two sections contrast confidence in God's plans with confidence in our own plans. In James 1:8, the writer was concerned that his readers were double-minded in the sense of wavering between faith and doubt. In 4:8, he was concerned that they were double-minded in the sense of wavering between trusting God and trusting the world.

1. WORLDLY ANTAGONISM. The same Greek noun is translated *cravings* (4:1) and *pleasures* (4:3). It is the term from which the English word "hedonism" derives. James forcefully stated that our cravings for pleasure and happiness easily take the place in our hearts and minds that belongs only to God. When they do, we find ourselves in antagonistic relationships with people who might block our pleasures and happiness.

2. SPIRITUAL ADULTERY. Devotion to our desires is a worldly attitude and, therefore, *friendship with the world* (4:4). God will not accept a rival for the devotion of His covenant people. He expects undivided loyalty and provides His grace to enable us to be true to Him.

3. SUBMISSIVE CONFIDENCE. This rapid fire set of commands gives substance to the idea of humility introduced in James 4:6. Humility involves choosing God over the devil and then choosing to be intimate with God. Humility realizes that intimacy with God demands moral purity and is willing to repent to experience it. Just as Jesus promised (Matt. 23:12), self-abasement leads to exaltation by God.

4. ARROGANT CONFIDENCE. We live in a culture obsessed with planning and goal setting. "If you can visualize it, you can achieve it," is a mantra of our age. James taught that all planning and goal setting must be tentative. It must be contingent on God's will. Only His will is deserving of the trust and confidence our culture teaches us to place in our plans and goals.

FOR ADULTS	■ TOPIC: Humility Is Next to Godliness

■ **TOPIC:** Humility Is Next to Godliness

■ **QUESTIONS:** 1. What was the origin of the conflicts and disputes to which James referred? 2. In what way does God give grace to the humble? 3. Why is it important to relate to God with an attitude of humility? 4. How can believers submit all their plans to God? 5. Why is God displeased when we go through our lives with an attitude of arrogance?

■ **ILLUSTRATIONS:**

Dueling Desires. The groom was handsome and hardworking; the bride was beautiful and very bright. Hans and Hilda seemed a match made in heaven. But some people in the village worried. "He's the most stubborn man I know," one observed. "She always has to have her way," another said.

After the wedding feast, the newlyweds collapsed into chairs on opposite sides of their cottage. "I'm exhausted," Hans sighed. "Oh no," he added, "the last guest left the front door ajar. Darling, will you close the door? There's a draft."

"Why me?" Hilda asked. "I've been on my feet all day too. You close it."

For five minutes Hans and Hilda glared at one another. Then Hilda had an idea. "I don't want to get up and shut the door, and you don't want to get up and shut the door. Fine. The first one to speak has to get up and shut the door. How about it?"

"Fine," Hans said and shut his mouth.

Two hours after Hans and Hilda began their silent contest, a pair of thieves passing with a cart noticed the open front door and peeked in. The house seemed deserted, so they started carrying out everything that was loose. They even rolled up the rugs, but neither Hans nor Hilda moved or spoke.

The thieves thought the newlyweds were mannequins and stripped them of watches, rings, and wallets. Neither would make the first move or sound. All night long Hans and Hilda sat in stony silence in their ransacked home. In the early morning the constable on patrol stuck his head in the open door and asked if everything was all right. Neither answered.

"Where's your furniture? Why won't you move or speak?" the officer shouted. Finally in desperation, the policeman raised his hand to slap Hans.

"Don't you lay a finger on my new husband," Hilda cried out.

Hans jumped up. "I won," he shouted. "Now go close that door, woman!"

When we have to have our way, we find ourselves in conflict with the people who mean the most to us, and we usually don't get what we want. Strong desires can prove to be treacherous things. They don't deliver what we think they are promising us.

It's Okay to Tell Him. The stoic Vermont farmer was sitting on the porch with his wife of 47 years. That evening the idea slowly but surely formed in his mind that he was a very fortunate man to be married to such a hardworking, even-tempered woman. He sat there a long time trying to figure out what to say. He had never demonstrated much affection or gratitude in his whole life. Finally he said with his clipped New England twang, "Wife, you've been such a wonderful woman that there are times when I can hardly keep from telling you."

Sometimes we treat God like that. He is so loyal and loving and we take Him for granted for so long that we can't figure out what to say. Don't take Him for granted for so long that you become unfaithful.

Humility's Perspective. Several years ago, shortly after Tom Brokaw was promoted to co-host the "Today" show, he was picking up some things in Bloomingdale's. That promotion capped a series of career advances that started with NBC in Omaha and progressed through Los Angeles and Washington, D.C., to New York. Brokaw noticed a man watching him closely and prepared for some fan adoration. Finally the man stepped up, pointed, and said, "Tom Brokaw, right?"

"Right," Brokaw nodded.

"You used to do the morning news on KMTV in Omaha, right?"

Brokaw was impressed with how much the fan knew about him. "That's right."

"I knew it the moment I spotted you," the tourist went on. After a pause, he asked, "Whatever happened to you?"

Humility recognizes that we aren't as impressive as we might like to think we are.

FOR YOUTH

■ **Topic:** Tough Choices

■ **Questions:** 1. In what ways can Christians become embroiled in disputes and conflicts with one another? 2. What does it mean to be a friend with the world? 3. Why is it arrogant to make plans without submitting them to the will of God? 4. What can believers do to cultivate an intimate relationship with God? 5. How can we, as Christians, refrain from sinful forms of boasting?

■ **Illustrations:**

Where Conflict Comes From. One day the lion was feeling especially good about himself, so he set out to feed his ego. He approached the bear and asked, "Who is king of the jungle?"

"Why you are, of course," the bear answered quickly.

The lion roared his approval and stalked off to find the tiger. "Who's the king of the jingle?" he demanded.

"Everyone knows that you are," the tiger said with a low bow.

The lion checked the tiger's name from his list and went looking for the elephant. "Who is king of the jungle?" the lion snarled at the hulking pachyderm.

The elephant, who suffered from a painfully inflamed tusk, grabbed the lion with her trunk, whirled him around six times in the air, slammed him against a tree, dribbled him on the ground, held him under the surface of the waterhole five minutes, and tossed him contemptuously under a bush.

The lion—battered and bruised—struggled to his unsteady feet. "Look," he said, "just because you don't know the answer, you don't have to get mean about it."

When we focus on ourselves and what makes us happy, we end up in conflict with other people doing exactly the same thing. Everybody can't get his or her own way at the same time.

Loyal Love. A college man took a portrait of his new girlfriend to a photography studio. He wanted copies of her picture so he could post them at strategic places at school and at home. When the studio owner removed the photograph from its frame, he noticed an inscription on the back: "My dearest John, I love you with all my heart. I love you more and more each day. I will love you forever and ever. I am yours for all eternity." It was signed, "Marsha." Beneath the signature was a P.S.: "If we ever break up, I want this picture back."

God expects greater faithfulness than that.

Humble Yourself. The naval officer long had dreamed of commanding a battleship. Finally he was given command of the newest and proudest battleship of the fleet. One stormy night, as the ship plowed toward harbor, the captain was on duty on the bridge when he spotted a strange light closing with his ship.

Immediately the captain ordered his signalman to flash the message, "Alter your course ten degrees to the south." Almost instantly the reply came, "Alter your course ten degrees to the north."

Determined to take a backseat to no one, the captain sent this message: "Alter course ten degrees. I am the captain." The reply: "Alter your course ten degrees. I'm seaman third class Jones."

Infuriated, the captain grabbed the signal lamp and flashed, "Alter your course. I'm a battleship." Back came: "Alter your course. I'm a lighthouse."

The captain had to face facts, swallow his pride, and take appropriate action to arrive safely in harbor. We too have to be willing to face our needs and respond to God's warnings and humbly receive His grace.

If God Wills. A young woman filled with hopes for the future flew from Fresno, California, to Pullman, Washington, for an interview at the Washington State University School of Veterinary Medicine. She had advance reservations for a rental car and a motel room so she could quickly prepare for her interview that afternoon. Upon landing, she went to the rental car agency's desk, intending to pay for the car with her credit card. To her disbelief, her credit card was refused and she had no other form of payment with her.

Sobbing hysterically, she blubbered her story over the airport payphone to her roommate back in California. While she poured out her heart over the phone, a stranger who must have overheard the whole scene at the car rental booth tapped her on the shoulder, gave her a one hundred dollar bill, and walked away into the surging crowd.

The student made her interview. Washington State accepted her into the School of Veterinary Medicine. The woman wrote a touching letter of thanks to her anonymous benefactor and mailed it to Ann Landers, wrote gladly included it in her column.

This woman's plans fell apart because she had no control over the future and because human life is fragile. But God's will was for her good, and something better than her plan emerged. And she was grateful.

CALLED TO BE GOD'S PEOPLE

BACKGROUND SCRIPTURE: 1 Peter 1:1—2:10
DEVOTIONAL READING: Leviticus 19:1-10

KEY VERSES: As he who called you is holy, be holy yourselves in all your conduct; for it is written, "You shall be holy, for I am holy." 1 Peter 1:15-16.

KING JAMES VERSION

1 PETER 1:3 Blessed be the God and Father of our Lord Jesus Christ, which according to his abundant mercy hath begotten us again unto a lively hope by the resurrection of Jesus Christ from the dead, 4 To an inheritance incorruptible, and undefiled, and that fadeth not away, reserved in heaven for you, 5 Who are kept by the power of God through faith unto salvation ready to be revealed in the last time. . . .

13 Wherefore gird up the loins of your mind, be sober, and hope to the end for the grace that is to be brought unto you at the revelation of Jesus Christ; 14 As obedient children, not fashioning yourselves according to the former lusts in your ignorance: 15 But as he which hath called you is holy, so be ye holy in all manner of conversation; 16 Because it is written, Be ye holy; for I am holy. 17 And if ye call on the Father, who without respect of persons judgeth according to every man's work, pass the time of your sojourning here in fear: 18 Forasmuch as ye know that ye were not redeemed with corruptible things, as silver and gold, from your vain conversation received by tradition from your fathers; 19 But with the precious blood of Christ, as of a lamb without blemish and without spot: 20 Who verily was foreordained before the foundation of the world, but was manifest in these last times for you, 21 Who by him do believe in God, that raised him up from the dead, and gave him glory; that your faith and hope might be in God. . . .

2:4 To whom coming, as unto a living stone, disallowed indeed of men, but chosen of God, and precious, 5 Ye also, as lively stones, are built up a spiritual house, an holy priesthood, to offer up spiritual sacrifices, acceptable to God by Jesus Christ. . . .

9 But ye are a chosen generation, a royal priesthood, an holy nation, a peculiar people; that ye should shew forth the praises of him who hath called you out of darkness into his marvellous light: 10 Which in time past were not a people, but are now the people of God: which had not obtained mercy, but now have obtained mercy.

NEW REVISED STANDARD VERSION

1 PETER 1:3 Blessed be the God and Father of our Lord Jesus Christ! By his great mercy he has given us a new birth into a living hope through the resurrection of Jesus Christ from the dead, 4 and into an inheritance that is imperishable, undefiled, and unfading, kept in heaven for you, 5 who are being protected by the power of God through faith for a salvation ready to be revealed in the last time. . . .

13 Therefore prepare your minds for action; discipline yourselves; set all your hope on the grace that Jesus Christ will bring you when he is revealed. 14 Like obedient children, do not be conformed to the desires that you formerly had in ignorance. 15 Instead, as he who called you is holy, be holy yourselves in all your conduct; 16 for it is written, "You shall be holy, for I am holy."

17 If you invoke as Father the one who judges all people impartially according to their deeds, live in reverent fear during the time of your exile. 18 You know that you were ransomed from the futile ways inherited from your ancestors, not with perishable things like silver or gold, 19 but with the precious blood of Christ, like that of a lamb without defect or blemish. 20 He was destined before the foundation of the world, but was revealed at the end of the ages for your sake. 21 Through him you have come to trust in God, who raised him from the dead and gave him glory, so that your faith and hope are set on God. . . .

2:4 Come to him, a living stone, though rejected by mortals yet chosen and precious in God's sight, and 5 like living stones, let yourselves be built into a spiritual house, to be a holy priesthood, to offer spiritual sacrifices acceptable to God through Jesus Christ. . . .

9 But you are a chosen race, a royal priesthood, a holy nation, God's own people, in order that you may proclaim the mighty acts of him who called you out of darkness into his marvelous light.
10 Once you were not a people,
    but now you are God's people;
once you had not received mercy,
    but now you have received mercy.

Monday, September 29	Deuteronomy 7:6-11	*God's Treasured Possession*
Tuesday, September 30	Leviticus 19:1-5	*People Led by a Holy God*
Wednesday, October 1	1 Peter 1:1-7	*New Birth into a Living Hope*
Thursday, October 2	1 Peter 1:8-12	*People of a Glorious Joy*
Friday, October 3	1 Peter 1:13-21	*Disciplined and Holy People*
Saturday, October 4	1 Peter 1:22—2:3	*People Longing for Spiritual Milk*
Sunday, October 5	1 Peter 2:4-10	*God's Own People*

BACKGROUND

The author identified himself as *Peter, an apostle of Jesus Christ* (1 Pet. 1:1). That he is the well-known apostle of the Gospels and Acts is confirmed by both internal and external evidence. The author described himself as a *witness of the sufferings of Christ* (5:1), and there are numerous echoes of Jesus' teaching and deeds in the epistle. Parallels of thought and phrase between 1 Peter and the apostle's speeches in Acts lend further support for the letter's Petrine authorship.

The external attestation of 1 Peter as a genuine letter of the apostle is widespread, early, and clear; nevertheless, linguistic and historical objections have been raised in the last two centuries. The Greek of 1 Peter is said to be too polished and too influenced by the Septuagint (an ancient Greek translation of the Old Testament) to have come from an uneducated Galilean fisherman such as Peter (Acts 4:13). Also, the persecutions alluded to in 1 Peter (4:12-19; 5:6-9) reputedly reflect a situation later than Peter's lifetime.

None of these criticisms is decisive against Peter's authorship. In response to the linguistic objection, one could note that first-century Galilee was bilingual (Aramaic and Greek), and it is quite possible that a commercial fisherman would have known the language of commerce. Also, the description of Peter and John as *uneducated and ordinary men* (Acts 4:13) may refer only to their lack of formal training in the Scriptures. Moreover, the 30 years that elapsed between Peter's days as a fisherman and the time the epistle was written would have provided ample opportunity for him to improve his proficiency in Greek. Furthermore, Silvanus' possible role as secretary (1 Pet. 5:12) could account for the smoother style of 1 Peter as compared to 2 Peter.

According to 1 Peter 5:13, the apostle was in *Babylon* when he wrote the letter. Various identifications have been suggested, including a military outpost in Egypt, the ancient Mesopotamian city itself, and Rome. Several lines of evidence favor Rome. Mark, who was with Peter when he wrote, is known to have been with Paul in Rome (Col. 4:10; Philem. 24). In the early church, Rome was often seen as the epitome of the godless world system code-named *Babylon* (Rev. 17:5, 9). The uniform testimony of early church history is that Peter was in Rome at the end of his life.

If Rome is the place of origin, 1 Peter was probably composed in between A.D. 62–64. This date is established by the fact that Peter's writings show familiarity with Paul's prison epistles. Also, early church tradition maintains that Peter was crucified upside down in Rome in A.D. 68 at the latest.

It is clear that the Jewish and Gentile readership in the northern and western parts of Asia Minor were suffering persecution for their faith; but nothing in the letter indicates official, legislative persecution or requires a date of composition later than the early 60s. The sufferings these Christians endured were common to first-century believers. These included insults (4:4, 14) and slanderous accusations of wrongdoing (2:12; 3:16). Beatings (2:20), social ostracism, sporadic mob violence, and local police action may have been involved as well.

NOTES ON THE PRINTED TEXT

Peter opened his letter with a benediction embracing God as Father and Jesus Christ as Lord (1 Pet. 1:3). Peter praised the Father for *a new birth into a living hope . . . and into an inheritance that is imperishable* (1:3-4). The hope that lives within every Christian is based on Jesus' resurrection, for it guarantees resurrection and eternal life for His followers.

The inheritance of believers awaits in heaven where nothing can harm it, pollute it, or diminish its glory (1:4). While Christians wait in confident hope for their inheritance, God watches over them with all the resources of His power (1:5). On their part, Christians exercise faith in God's provision for this glorious *salvation ready to be revealed in the last time.*

The *last time* is not a vague future era; rather, it is the period that began with the day of Pentecost and continues until the return of Christ. Believers in Christ must live as citizens of the last time. Thus, our minds need to be geared toward *action* (1:13). Our thinking needs to be sober. Our hope should be fixed on the inheritance Jesus will lavish on us at His return.

More than thinking is affected by an expectation of the Lord's return. We are to be *obedient children* (1:14) of our heavenly Father. Once we obeyed—or conformed to—the desires of our flesh in the dark ignorance of sin. Here we find Peter's thoughts aligning with Paul, who advocated transformed minds in order to stave off conformity to the world (Rom. 12:1-2).

The evil world may conform to fleshly passions, but Peter urged holiness as the standard for Christian behavior (1 Pet. 1:15). Peter quoted one of God's primary commands in Leviticus when he wrote, *"You shall be holy, for I am holy"* (1:16; see Lev. 11:44-45; 19:2; 20:7). William Barclay noted, "The [Greek] word for *holy* is *hagios* whose root meaning is *different"* (*Letters of James and Peter*). Holiness indicates a person belongs to God and has consecrated himself or herself to godly behavior.

The same God whom we appeal to as our Father is the one who will serve as impartial Judge of our behavior (1 Pet. 1:17). We live in hope, and we *live in rev-*

erent fear. This is not a cringing terror of God; rather, it is the worshipful response of a mere mortal overwhelmed by the glorious power and holiness of God.

Christians live as exiles in this world. They are resident aliens because God has ransomed them from the futile course of fallen human existence at the cost of the life of His Son (1:17-19). Nothing so ultimately worthless as silver or gold could ransom sinners. It took the precious blood of Christ, the perfect Lamb of God, to atone for our sins.

There is a timelessness to God's redemptive work. Redemption was eternally planned before creation occurred, but it wasn't revealed until the last days for the benefit of all who believe in Christ (1:20). Our faith focuses first on Christ, the sacrificial Lamb, and then on God who raised Christ from the dead. We look to the Father for the same kind of life and glory (1:21).

Peter declared that Jesus is a *living stone* (2:4) who has been rejected by the builders of God's old covenant people, but has become the cornerstone for a new building (Ps. 118:22). That spiritual edifice is constructed of other *living stones* (1 Pet. 2:5), namely, Christians. They form the temple in which God's Holy Spirit dwells. The living stones of this temple are also its priests who offer *spiritual sacrifices acceptable to God through Jesus Christ.* These sacrifices include our bodies (Rom. 12:2), our praise (Heb. 13:15), and our good deeds (13:16).

In 1 Peter 2:9, the apostle applied a number of Old Testament labels to God's New Testament people. We are *a chosen race*, *a royal priesthood*, and a *holy nation.* As *God's own people*, we are to be heralds spreading the good news that God's *mighty acts* can deliver people out of the kingdom of darkness into the kingdom of light.

Finally, Peter applied to the church the language Hosea applied to Israel (Hos. 1:9-10; 2:23). Once we were scattered in the darkness; now we are united in the light as God's people (1 Pet. 2:10). Once we were objects of God's wrath; now we are recipients of His mercy. God's promises belong to His new covenant people as a community of faith, as a people built into a spiritual house on the living cornerstone of their Savior and Lord.

SUGGESTIONS TO TEACHERS

Peter called on his readers to praise the Father and Son for a redemption that was planned in eternity past, was anticipated by Israel's prophets, and climaxed with the redemptive work of Christ and His resurrection. Jesus is the guarantee of our hope for an eternal inheritance in heaven.

1. CALL TO SALVATION. Peter opened his epistle with a description of the salvation God provided in Christ. Salvation is a broad term in the New Testament. It can mean initial deliverance from the penalty of sin, also known as justification (Titus 3:5). It can refer to the lifelong process of turning from sin to righteousness in daily living, also known as sanctification (1 Cor. 1:18). It can mean the reception of the full benefits of redemption at our death or at the Second Coming, also

known as glorification (Rom. 13:11). All three of these ideas are found in 1 Peter 1:3-5—justification (1:3), sanctification (1:5*a*), and glorification (1:5*b*). The only appearance of the term *salvation* in this passage has the third meaning, glorification.

2. CALL TO CHARACTER. Peter's concern was with renewed thinking and behaving. Before trusting in Christ, we followed our passions and lived in ignorance of God's ways. Now we are to obey God's call to be holy. One side of holiness is propositional: we belong to God and His ownership makes us different. The other side of holiness is behavioral: we accept the challenge to live consistently with the character of God who owns us.

3. CALL TO REVERENCE. God is our gracious, merciful, and heavenly Father, but He is also our impartial Judge. We live as resident aliens in this world, looking forward to receiving our true inheritance in another country, namely, heaven. We live to please the Ruler of heaven, who is our Creator and Lord. He has arranged our ransom from the hostile powers of this world. His Son has paid a ransom that only He was qualified to pay. We can look forward with confidence to sharing in the resurrection and glory of Christ.

4. CALL TO COMMUNITY. Peter wanted his readers to know that they were the covenant people of God. With Christ as the cornerstone, the church forms a living dwelling for God on earth where spiritual sacrifices are offered continually. This community of faith is not a closed one. Its priests proclaim to the world that God continually calls people from the darkness of sin to the light of salvation.

FOR ADULTS

■ TOPIC: Called to New Life

■ QUESTIONS: 1. What is the living hope to which believers have been called? 2. Why is holiness so paramount for believers? 3. In what sense are New Testament believers the covenant people of God? 4. How can we cultivate holiness in our lives? 5. What can we do to proclaim God's mighty acts to the unsaved?

■ ILLUSTRATIONS:

My Inheritance in Heaven. The children gathered in front of the sanctuary for the children's sermon. The pastor sat on the platform steps, which placed him near eye level with his youngest parishoners. He talked earnestly in simple language to the children about being good and going to heaven. At the end of his talk, the pastor asked, "Where do you want to go?"

The little voices chorused, "HEAVEN!"

"And what must you be to get to Heaven?" the pastor asked.

"Dead!" the boys and girls yelled.

The children missed their pastor's point. But they were correct that the full inheritance of the Christian will be realized in the life to come.

The Blood of a Lamb. A documentary on sheep and shepherds included a segment about orphan sheep. A ewe will normally have one lamb. Some ewes die during the birthing process and leave orphan lambs.

One might think that it would be simple to place an orphan with another ewe, but sheep will only accept their own offspring. In this case, the shepherd will take a lamb that has newly died and remove its hide. He will wrap the hide like a wool sweater around the orphan lamb and place it with the ewe whose lamb died. The mother then accepts the orphan as her own lamb.

Jesus, the spotless Lamb of God, gave His life by shedding His precious blood on the cross, so that we, who are lost, can be accepted as God's very own children.

Bridge Builder. The concept of priesthood can be an unfamiliar one to Protestant Christians. William Barclay offers an interesting insight from the Latin term for priest. "The Latin word for priest is *pontifex*, which means *bridge-builder*; the priest is the man who builds a bridge for others to come to God; and the Christian has the duty and the privilege of bringing others to that Saviour whom he himself has found and loves" (*The Letters of James and Peter*).

Proclaim His Mighty Acts. In September 1985, lifeguards at a New Orleans municipal pool celebrated the first summer in memory without a drowning. Two hundred people, including 100 certified lifeguards, jammed the pool deck and splashed in the water to party. When the festivities broke up, the four lifeguards on duty found a fully dressed body in the deep end of the pool. They tried to revive him, but it was too late. The man had drowned surrounded by lifeguards celebrating their successful season.

The church is a dwelling place for the Lord made up of living stones who must proclaim the mighty saving acts of God so that unsaved people can cross over from death to life. It would be tragic to keep celebrating in worship without evangelizing those who stand on the sidelines watching.

FOR YOUTH

■ Topic: Called to Something Big

■ Questions: 1. For what is God to be praised concerning our salvation? 2. What did Jesus' atoning sacrifice accomplish for us? 3. In what sense are we God's royal priesthood? 4. What aspect of Christian service do you believe God has called you to? 5. How might you discipline your mind and body for service to Christ?

■ Illustrations:

Discipline Your Mind. A man observed a woman in the grocery store with a three-year-old girl in her basket. As they passed the cookie section, the little girl asked for cookies and her mother refused. The little girl immediately began to whine and fuss, and the mother said quietly, "Now Monica, we just have half of the aisles left to go through. Don't be upset. It won't be long."

Soon they came to the candy aisle, and the little girl began to shout for candy. And when the girl was told she couldn't have any, she began to cry. The mother said, "There, there, Monica, don't cry. Only two more aisles to go, and then we'll be checking out."

When they got to the checkout stand, the little girl immediately began to clamor for gum and burst into a terrible tantrum upon discovering there'd be no gum purchased. The mother patiently said, "Monica, we'll be through this checkout stand in five minutes and then you can go home and have a nice nap."

The man followed them out to the parking lot and stopped the woman to compliment her. "I couldn't help noticing how patient you were with little Monica," he began.

Whereupon the mother said, "I'm Monica. My little girl's name is Tammy."

Sometimes we need to keep reminding ourselves of our hope and awaiting inheritance so we can discipline ourselves to live as God wants us to in the face of the pressures and temptations of the world.

My Inheritance. Martha was one of the dearest folks in Pastor Jim's church, and she was dying. Pastor Jim faced Martha across her small living room wondering what words of comfort he could share with her. Martha read his concerned look and said, "Don't look so glum. I have lived a long life. The Lord has been good. I'm ready to go. Don't you know that?"

"Yes, but I still wish it wasn't so," Pastor Jim said.

Martha ignored that and plowed ahead with what was on her mind. "I do want to talk about my funeral. I been thinking about it, and this is what I want."

Martha had her hymns and Scripture passages picked out. She had some stories she wanted told. When it seemed that they had covered just about everything, Martha paused, looked at her pastor with a twinkle in her eye, and added, "One more thing, preacher. When they bury me, I want my old Bible in one hand and a fork in the other."

"A fork?" Pastor Jim was sure he had heard everything, but this caught him by surprise. "Why do you want to be buried with a fork?"

"I must have gone to a thousand pitch-in church suppers through the years," Martha explained. "At every one of those dinners, when it was time to clear the dishes, somebody would say, 'Be sure and save your fork.' I knew dessert was coming! Not a cup of Jello or pudding or even a dish of ice cream. You don't need a fork for that. It meant the good stuff, like chocolate cake or cherry pie! When they told me I could keep my fork, I knew the best was yet to come!"

"You tell them that at my funeral. Oh, they can talk about all the good times we had together. That would be nice. But when they walk by my casket and look at my pretty blue dress, I want them to turn to one another and say, 'Why the fork?'"

"That's when you say, 'Martha wants you to know the best is yet to come. She just got hers.'"

Our full inheritance may be future, but it inspires hope for daily living right now.

Proclaim His Mighty Acts. Josh McDowell tells of a "headhunter" who located and hired corporate executives for various firms. The headhunter said, "When I get an executive that I'm trying to hire for a client, I like to disarm him. I offer him a beverage, take my coat off, undo my tie, throw up my feet and talk about baseball, football, family—whatever—until he's all relaxed. When he's off guard, I lean over, look him square in the eye and say, 'What's your purpose in life?' It's amazing how top executives fall apart at that question."

"Well, I was interviewing this fellow one time. Had him all disarmed, with my feet up on his desk, talking about football. I leaned up and said, 'What's your purpose in life, Bob?' And he said, without blinking an eye, 'To go to heaven and take as many people with me as I can.' For the first time in my career, I was speechless."

That's not a bad purpose statement for every Christian. Peter says it should be a purpose statement for the whole church.

BE A GOOD EXAMPLE

BACKGROUND SCRIPTURE: 1 Peter 2:11—5:14
DEVOTIONAL READING: Galatians 5:16-25

KEY VERSE: Conduct yourselves honorably . . . so that, though they malign you as evildoers, they may see your honorable deeds and glorify God when he comes to judge. 1 Peter 2:12.

KING JAMES VERSION

1 PETER 2:11 Dearly beloved, I beseech you as strangers and pilgrims, abstain from fleshly lusts, which war against the soul; 12 Having your conversation honest among the Gentiles: that, whereas they speak against you as evildoers, they may by your good works, which they shall behold, glorify God in the day of visitation. . . .

3:13 And who is he that will harm you, if ye be followers of that which is good? 14 But and if ye suffer for righteousness' sake, happy are ye: and be not afraid of their terror, neither be troubled; 15 But sanctify the Lord God in your hearts: and be ready always to give an answer to every man that asketh you a reason of the hope that is in you with meekness and fear:

16 Having a good conscience; that, whereas they speak evil of you, as of evildoers, they may be ashamed that falsely accuse your good conversation in Christ. 17 For it is better, if the will of God be so, that ye suffer for well doing, than for evil doing. . . .

4:7 But the end of all things is at hand: be ye therefore sober, and watch unto prayer. 8 And above all things have fervent charity among yourselves: for charity shall cover the multitude of sins. 9 Use hospitality one to another without grudging. 10 As every man hath received the gift, even so minister the same one to another, as good stewards of the manifold grace of God. 11 If any man speak, let him speak as the oracles of God; if any man minister, let him do it as of the ability which God giveth: that God in all things may be glorified through Jesus Christ, to whom be praise and dominion for ever and ever. Amen. . . .

5:8 Be sober, be vigilant; because your adversary the devil, as a roaring lion, walketh about, seeking whom he may devour: 9 Whom resist stedfast in the faith, knowing that the same afflictions are accomplished in your brethren that are in the world.

10 But the God of all grace, who hath called us unto his eternal glory by Christ Jesus, after that ye have suffered a while, make you perfect, stablish, strengthen, settle you.

NEW REVISED STANDARD VERSION

1 PETER 2:11 Beloved, I urge you as aliens and exiles to abstain from the desires of the flesh that wage war against the soul. 12 Conduct yourselves honorably among the Gentiles, so that, though they malign you as evildoers, they may see your honorable deeds and glorify God when he comes to judge. . . .

3:13 Now who will harm you if you are eager to do what is good? 14 But even if you do suffer for doing what is right, you are blessed. Do not fear what they fear, and do not be intimidated, 15 but in your hearts sanctify Christ as Lord. Always be ready to make your defense to anyone who demands from you an accounting for the hope that is in you; 16 yet do it with gentleness and reverence. Keep your conscience clear, so that, when you are maligned, those who abuse you for your good conduct in Christ may be put to shame. 17 For it is better to suffer for doing good, if suffering should be God's will, than to suffer for doing evil. . . .

4:7 The end of all things is near; therefore be serious and discipline yourselves for the sake of your prayers. 8 Above all, maintain constant love for one another, for love covers a multitude of sins. 9 Be hospitable to one another without complaining. 10 Like good stewards of the manifold grace of God, serve one another with whatever gift each of you has received. 11 Whoever speaks must do so as one speaking the very words of God; whoever serves must do so with the strength that God supplies, so that God may be glorified in all things through Jesus Christ. To him belong the glory and the power forever and ever. Amen. . . .

5:8 Discipline yourselves, keep alert. Like a roaring lion your adversary the devil prowls around, looking for someone to devour. 9 Resist him, steadfast in your faith, for you know that your brothers and sisters in all the world are undergoing the same kinds of suffering. 10 And after you have suffered for a little while, the God of all grace, who has called you to his eternal glory in Christ, will himself restore, support, strengthen, and establish you.

Monday, October 6	Romans 12:9-18	*Be Zealous in Serving God*
Tuesday, October 7	1 Peter 2:11-17	*Conduct Yourselves Honorably*
Wednesday, October 8	1 Peter 3:8-12	*Don't Repay Evil for Evil*
Thursday, October 9	1 Peter 3:13-22	*Be Ready with a Gentle Defense*
Friday, October 10	1 Peter 4:1-6	*Live by the Will of God*
Saturday, October 11	1 Peter 4:7-11	*Maintain Love for One Another*
Sunday, October 12	1 Peter 5:7-14	*Keep Alert, Resist the Devil*

BACKGROUND

Peter wrote to encourage persecuted and bewildered Christians and to exhort them to stand fast in their faith (1 Pet. 5:12). To that end he repeatedly turned their thoughts to the joys and glories of their eternal inheritance (1:3-13; 4:13; 5:1, 4) and instructed them about proper Christian behavior in the midst of unjust suffering (4:1, 19). While addressed primarily to persecuted believers, the principles of this letter apply to all suffering, regardless of the cause, provided it is not occasioned by one's own sin.

On the basis of the epistle, Peter has with justice been called the "apostle of hope." Yet the accent falls not on wishful thinking, but on present help. The central exhortation of the entire letter can be summed up in the phrase "trust and obey." No biblical writer shows the connection between faith and conduct in a clearer manner than does Peter. For the apostle, practice was the most important thing.

The conduct Peter described was the result of a life reclaimed by the perfect power of Christ. The Savior has redeemed believers (1:18-19); He upholds and guides them (1:8; 2:25); and He will reward them (5:4). Jesus is both the model and the goal of the redeemed life. Consequently, believers may move forward on the pilgrim way, confident that the end will rise up to meet them with joy and salvation (2:11; 4:13-14).

In terms of literary style, this letter is written in fine Greek and refers often to the Old Testament. The tone is warm, pastoral, and full of encouragement. The epistle is predominantly rhetorical and didactic in nature.

Some critics have argued that the theology of 1 Peter is too much like that of Paul. Supposedly the letter reflects Paul's thought rather than experiences of the earthly life of Christ, as one might expect from Peter, one of Jesus' closest disciples. In response, it is perfectly understandable why Peter's letter would reflect ideas similar to those found in the writings of Paul, for the two men knew each other well. Peter had Paul's letters (2 Pet. 3:15-16), and both men were under the guidance of the Spirit when they wrote. Thus, finding Pauline concepts in 1 Peter is not a strong argument that Peter could not be the author.

The epistle can be divided into three main sections. In part one (1:1—2:12), Peter discussed the salvation and sanctification of the believer. The apostle stressed that the future hope of redemption in Christ encouraged believers to endure present trials, to pursue holiness, to love one another unconditionally, to nourish their souls on God's Word, and to abstain from sinful desires.

In part two (2:13—3:12), Peter discussed the believer's submission in various contexts, including the government, business, marriage, and all of life. In part three (3:13—5:14), Peter discussed the sufferings experienced by Christians. The apostle emphasized the need for godly conduct, related Christ's example of suffering, and stressed how various groups within the church should serve one another in the midst of suffering.

NOTES ON THE PRINTED TEXT

Peter called on his readers to live blamelessly. He stated his case negatively and then positively. Negatively, he urged them *to abstain from the desires of the flesh* (1 Pet. 2:11). Christians hold citizenship in the kingdom of heaven, so we are *aliens*. We are passing through, so we are *exiles*, or strangers on earth. *The desires of the flesh*—both carnal and malicious—attack the integrity and peace of our souls.

Positively, Peter commanded, *Conduct yourselves honorably* (2:12). *Honorably* translates one of the Greek words for "good." *Kalos* connotes the idea of esthetic good or excellence. Peter urged a lifestyle so winsome and faultless before those who want to criticize us that they cannot. Jesus said, *"Let your light shine before others, so that they may see your good works and give glory to your Father in heaven"* (Matt. 5:16).

By means of a rhetorical question, Peter asserted that, as a rule, no one will set out to harm a person who is truly zealous for doing good (1 Pet. 3:13). But when, as an exception to the rule, suffering for righteous behavior occurs, God's blessing follows (3:14). The world dreads undeserved suffering, but Christians are not intimidated by injustice. We call *Lord* (3:15) one who saved us by suffering unjustly. When we sanctify Him in our hearts, we can explain our own hope for deliverance and blessing even as we face our own unjust suffering.

When we are challenged harshly to defend our faith, we are to do so in the spirit of Christ—gently and respectfully, not combatively and angrily (3:16). A clear conscience is a prerequisite for bearing unjust suffering. If we are called names and accused of doing evil when we are guilty, nothing is gained. But if we are maligned when innocent, our accusers may recognize their hypocrisy and repent because of their shame. If God wills that our unjust suffering accomplish good for others, we should accede to His will even though it is unpleasant (3:17).

Peter anticipated the return of the Lord and gained a sense of urgency from its nearness (4:7). The apostle said that contemplating the Lord's return would give us clarity of mind and self-discipline, which in turn will increase the effectiveness of our prayers. Peter saw this life of urgent prayer resulting in a life of diligent service. He thus urged an active love for all the saints (4:8). As Proverbs 10:12

says, love overlooks the faults of others. Love also remembers how much God has forgiven us (1 Cor. 13:5-7; Eph. 4:32).

Gracious hospitality is a concrete expression of love (1 Pet. 4:9). The early church depended on the hospitality of its members for meeting places and for housing missionaries and traveling teachers. Hospitality recognizes that my home and my food belong to God (4:10). If we all act as stewards of what He has given us individually, everyone benefits from the whole spectrum of His gracious gifts to the church.

The general idea of gracious gifts narrows to the specific idea of spiritual gifts—divine enablements given by the Spirit of God for the edification of the church (4:11). Peter divided spiritual gifts into two broad categories: speaking and serving. Both kinds of gifts must be taken seriously and exercised with care. One who exercises a speaking gift must prepare and present what he or she says as *the very words of God.* One who exercises a serving gift must act as though he or she had access to *the strength that God supplies.* In either case, there should be no careless, half-hearted exercise of gifts.

Also, there should not be any careless, half-hearted Christian living. The church must be disciplined and alert in the face of the devil's relentless search for easy prey among spiritually lazy Christians (5:8). Although the devil is like a powerful lion, he can be resisted by Christians (5:9). We do not resist the devil in our own strength; rather, we do so through steadfast faith in God. God's indwelling Spirit exercises greater strength in us than the devil exercises in the world around us (1 John 4:4).

Peter promised that suffering at the hands of wicked people for doing right will be temporary, even in the unlikely event that it lasts an earthly lifetime (1 Pet. 5:10). God, who possesses all grace, has called us *to his eternal glory in Christ.* God, Himself, makes faithful sufferers four promises. He will make better than new any damage done us. He will make us impervious to any harm. He will make us stronger than any foe. He will put an eternal foundation under us.

SUGGESTIONS TO TEACHERS

The old adage rightly claims that actions speak louder than words. The best witness for Jesus Christ is a large dose of an attractive, faithful Christian life interpreted by a few words. The worst witness for Jesus Christ is a large dose of carefully-chosen, persuasive words contradicted by a small but fatal dose of selfish hypocrisy. Peter taught, and the early church successfully practiced, how to suffer undeserved persecution. Eventually the church flourished and the Roman empire shriveled. Around the world today, many Christians face suffering as acute as that facing Peter's readers.

1. LIVE BLAMELESSLY. It has been observed that in lower income churches, the hymnody tends toward "This world is not my home; I'm just a passing through," while in higher income churches, it tends toward "This is my Father's world." Until God comes to judge the world, it is under the sway of the devil. God's people hold citizenship in His "not yet" kingdom. As we act as His subjects, our behavior will appeal to the image of God latent in unbelievers. The witness of an honorable life is invaluable.

2. SUFFER RIGHTEOUSLY. Our Lord Jesus set the pattern for righteous suffering. Our suffering is never atoning as His was, but it is an eloquent component of the witness of a blameless life. Righteous suffering will lead to questions about the Christian hope that survives such hardship. Gentle, loving explanations of the Gospel on top of righteous suffering is a potent witness for Christ.

3. SERVE DILIGENTLY. The Christian life is a disciplined one. It begins with active love. In the eighteenth century, Greek scholar Johann Albrecht Bengel called it "vehement love" (Barclay, *The Letters of James and Peter*). This love shares hearth and home, and shares every aspect of God's grace so that more can benefit from that grace. This love motivates the wholehearted exercise of verbal and non-verbal spiritual gifts within the church.

4. PERSEVERE VICTORIOUSLY. The disciplined Christian recognizes that behind all human foes ultimately stands the spiritual foe, the devil, who slanders believers. The devil is angry, hateful, and bent on destruction. He cannot be resisted by human strength but by human faith in God. Paul expressed it this way when he wrote, *I consider that the sufferings of this present time are not worth comparing with the glory about to be revealed to us* (Rom. 8:18).

FOR ADULTS	■ TOPIC: Be a Good Example

■ **QUESTIONS:** 1. How should believers respond to suffering? 2. How can believers maintain love for one another in the midst of suffering? 3. How can believers successfully resist the attacks of the devil? 4. What are some hardships that you or other believers are experiencing for Christ? 5. How can Christians support and encourage one another through these difficult times?

■ **ILLUSTRATIONS:**

You Can Too. As you drive up the steep, winding road to the Cave of the Winds near Colorado Springs, you suddenly come to a narrow passageway between high rock walls through which it looks as though the car cannot possibly go. But facing you is a sign which says: "Yes, you can! Millions of others have." And so, driving carefully through, you soon come to a wider roadway.

So many times we face seemingly insoluble problems and impossible situations. But we can know that God is able to open ways before us that are now hidden from our view. We may hear God's message to us: "Yes, you can! Millions of others have gone this way. Be of good cheer. Trust in the Lord and go ahead!"

We face the same suffering that our brothers and sisters through all times have faced and in all places are facing. Like them, we can make it through these ordeals in the strength that the Lord provides.

Growing Through Suffering. An old dog fell into his owner's well. The farmer felt sorry for his four-legged friend but decided that neither the dog nor the well was worth the trouble of saving. Instead he planned to bury the old dog in the well and put him out of his misery.

The farmer began shoveling, and the old dog put up a pitiful yowling. As the farmer kept throwing dirt down on his back, the dog had a brainstorm. Every time a shovel load of dirt landed on his back, he shook it off and stepped up onto it. "Shake it off and step up! Shake it off and step up! Shake it off and step up!" he repeated to encourage himself.

It hurt, and it went on and on. The old dog fought panic, as he kept shaking it off and stepping up. Finally, battered and exhausted, the old dog stepped triumphantly over the wall of that well. What seemed as though it would bury him actually lifted him up, all because of the way he handled his adversity.

Discipline your mind. Put your faith in God's care for you. Resist the devil. Live in hope of your eternal inheritance, and your good deeds will lead others to give glory to your Father in heaven.

Gifts of Service. An old man came to the back door of a house some college students were renting. The old man's eyes were glassy from drink, and greasy stubble bristled on his lined face. He clutched a wicker basket holding a few wilted vegetables. He bid the students a good morning and offered his produce for sale. They made a quick purchase to get rid of the old guy.

That backfired. He treated them as regular customers. Soon he had a name—Mr. Roth—and an address—an old shack on the edge of town. And he wasn't drunk. Cataracts made his eyes blurry. Soon they didn't mind when Mr. Roth would shuffle in, wearing two mismatched right shoes, and pull out his harmonica. With glazed eyes set on a future glory, he'd puff out old gospel tunes and talk about vegetables and Jesus.

One day, Mr. Roth exclaimed, "The Lord is so good! I came out of my shack this morning and found a bag full of shoes and clothing on my porch."

"That's wonderful, Mr. Roth!" the students said, "We're happy for you."

"You know what's even more wonderful?" he asked. "Just yesterday I met some people that could use them."

Mr. Roth had a gift of service and he used it in the strength God supplied him.

■ **TOPIC:** You Are an Example
■ **QUESTIONS:** 1. In what sense are Christians aliens and exiles on earth? 2. What is the best way for believers to handle suffering?

3. Why does God permit the devil to attack believers? 4. How can we show kindness to others when we are in distress? 5. Why is it important for us to remain committed to God when we are feeling overwhelmed by our circumstances?

■ **ILLUSTRATIONS:**

Thanks for Everything. In an early episode of *The Simpsons*, Bart was asked to say grace at dinner. He said, "Dear God, we paid for all this stuff ourselves, so thanks for nothing."

Wrong! Doesn't that boy get it? Nothing is ours. We're stewards of money and things that God entrusts to us. We might never say what Bart said, but sometimes we act as though we feel that way. Let's be more aware that our possessions are actually God's and we should use them for His glory.

Use It or Lose It. Writer Robert Fulghum tells about meeting a young American traveler in the airport in Hong Kong. Her backpack bore the scars and dirt of some hard traveling. It bulged with mysterious souvenirs of seeing the world.

The woman sat in the airport quietly crying. Fulghum imagined some lost love or the sorrow of giving up adventure for college classes. Then she began to sob— a veritable flood of tears.

The woman was not quite ready to go home, she said. She had run out of money. She had spent two days waiting in the airport on standby with little to eat and too much pride to beg. She had finally been called for a flight, it was about to leave, and she had lost her ticket.

Fulghum and a nice older couple from Chicago comforted the girl. They offered to take her to lunch and to talk to the powers that be at the airlines about some remedy. She stood up to go with them, turned around to pick up her belongings, and shrieked. Fulghum wondered what new disaster had struck, but it was her ticket. In despair she had been sitting on her ticket for three hours.

"Like a sinner saved from the very jaws of hell," writes Fulghum, "she laughed and cried and hugged us all and was suddenly gone. Off to catch a plane for home and what next. Leaving most of the passenger lounge deliriously limp from being part of her drama" (Fulghum, *Uh Oh*). The woman had been sitting on her ticket the whole time.

Too often we overlook or ignore the gifts God has given us. Those gifts benefit everyone around us and make our lives interesting and creative. We may be sitting around bored and certain we're missing out on everything fun in life. Maybe it's because we're sitting on our "ticket" to the best that life has for us—the gift or gifts that bring God's grace into our own lives and the lives of everybody around us.

Responding to Hardship. A girl griped to her dad about how hard things were for her right then. "As soon as I solve one problem," she said, "another one comes up. I'm tired of struggling." Her dad was a hotel chef. He took her to the kitchen where he filled three pots with water and placed each on a high fire. Soon the pots came to a boil. In one he placed carrots, in the second, eggs, and in the last, ground coffee beans. He let them sit and boil, without saying a word.

The daughter waited impatiently, wondering what point her father was trying to make. After a while, he went over and turned off the burners. He fished out the carrots and placed them in a bowl. He pulled the eggs out and placed them a bowl. He poured the coffee into a bowl. Turning to her he asked, "Kiddo, what do you see?"

"Carrots, eggs, and coffee," she replied.

He brought her closer and asked her to feel the carrots. She did and noted that they were soft. He then asked her to examine an egg. She peeled the shell from a hard-boiled egg. Finally, he asked her to sip the coffee. She smiled as she tasted its rich flavor.

She asked, "What's your point, Dad?" He explained that each of the foods had faced the same adversity—boiling water—but each reacted differently. The carrot went in strong and hard, but after being subjected to the boiling water, it softened and became weak.

The egg had been fragile. Its thin outer shell had protected its liquid interior, but after sitting through the boiling water, its inside hardened.

The ground coffee beans were unique, however. Boiling water changed the carrots and the eggs, but the coffee changed the water.

He asked his daughter, "When adversity knocks on your door, which are you?"

Grow in Faith

BACKGROUND SCRIPTURE: 2 Peter 1
DEVOTIONAL READING: Ephesians 3:14-21

KEY VERSE: His divine power has given us everything needed for life and godliness, through the knowledge of him who called us by his own glory and goodness. 2 Peter 1:3.

KING JAMES VERSION

2 PETER 1:3 According as his divine power hath given unto us all things that pertain unto life and godliness, through the knowledge of him that hath called us to glory and virtue:

4 Whereby are given unto us exceeding great and precious promises: that by these ye might be partakers of the divine nature, having escaped the corruption that is in the world through lust.

5 And beside this, giving all diligence, add to your faith virtue; and to virtue knowledge;

6 And to knowledge temperance; and to temperance patience; and to patience godliness;

7 And to godliness brotherly kindness; and to brotherly kindness charity.

8 For if these things be in you, and abound, they make you that ye shall neither be barren nor unfruitful in the knowledge of our Lord Jesus Christ.

9 But he that lacketh these things is blind, and cannot see afar off, and hath forgotten that he was purged from his old sins.

10 Wherefore the rather, brethren, give diligence to make your calling and election sure: for if ye do these things, ye shall never fall:

11 For so an entrance shall be ministered unto you abundantly into the everlasting kingdom of our Lord and Saviour Jesus Christ.

12 Wherefore I will not be negligent to put you always in remembrance of these things, though ye know them, and be established in the present truth.

13 Yea, I think it meet, as long as I am in this tabernacle, to stir you up by putting you in remembrance;

14 Knowing that shortly I must put off this my tabernacle, even as our Lord Jesus Christ hath shewed me.

15 Moreover I will endeavour that ye may be able after my decease to have these things always in remembrance.

NEW REVISED STANDARD VERSION

2 PETER 1:3 His divine power has given us everything needed for life and godliness, through the knowledge of him who called us by his own glory and goodness. 4 Thus he has given us, through these things, his precious and very great promises, so that through them you may escape from the corruption that is in the world because of lust, and may become participants of the divine nature. 5 For this very reason, you must make every effort to support your faith with goodness, and goodness with knowledge, 6 and knowledge with self-control, and self-control with endurance, and endurance with godliness, 7 and godliness with mutual affection, and mutual affection with love. 8 For if these things are yours and are increasing among you, they keep you from being ineffective and unfruitful in the knowledge of our Lord Jesus Christ. 9 For anyone who lacks these things is nearsighted and blind, and is forgetful of the cleansing of past sins. 10 Therefore, brothers and sisters, be all the more eager to confirm your call and election, for if you do this, you will never stumble. 11 For in this way, entry into the eternal kingdom of our Lord and Savior Jesus Christ will be richly provided for you.

12 Therefore I intend to keep on reminding you of these things, though you know them already and are established in the truth that has come to you. 13 I think it right, as long as I am in this body, to refresh your memory, 14 since I know that my death will come soon, as indeed our Lord Jesus Christ has made clear to me. 15 And I will make every effort so that after my departure you may be able at any time to recall these things.

Background

This epistle says it was written by Simon Peter (2 Pet. 1:1), and several things in the letter support the claim. The author refers to his own imminent death in terms that recall Jesus' words to Peter (2 Pet. 1:14; see John 21:18-19). The author claims to have been an eyewitness of Jesus' transfiguration (2 Pet. 1:16-18; see Matt. 17:1-8). And the author implies a connection between 1 Peter and 2 Peter (3:1).

There are remarkable similarities in the vocabulary of the two letters. For instance, the salutation is essentially the same in each epistle. The author uses similar words in both letters. Both Petrine letters also refer to the same Old Testament event (1 Pet. 3:18-20; 2 Pet. 2:5).

The differences in themes explain the reason for differences in emphases, such as why one letter teaches that the Second Coming is near, and one deals with its delay. First Peter, ministering especially to suffering believers, focuses on the imminency of Christ as a means of encouraging the believers. Second Peter, dealing with scoffers, emphasizes the reasons why that imminent return of Christ has not yet occurred.

Given Peter's authorship, the letter must have been written just before his death in A.D. 67–68. The reference to the apostle's imminent death in 1:14 suggests a time near the end of his life. If 3:1 refers to 1 Peter, the date of composition for 2 Peter must be sometime after A.D. 63–64. A date between A.D. 65–67 is therefore plausible.

The place of origin of 2 Peter is uncertain. Rome is the most likely suggestion, given the apostle's location there in 1 Peter (5:13) and the tradition that he was martyred there under Nero. Since 2 Peter 3:1 refers to 1 Peter, this would indicate that the recipients for both epistles are the same, namely, Gentile and Jewish Christians living in Asia Minor. Word of their difficulties with false teachers had reached the apostle in Rome, and he dispatched 2 Peter to them to encourage them and warn them about the dangers they faced.

Notes on the Printed Text

Peter assured his readers that the power of God was available for every aspect of their outer behavior and inner character (2 Pet. 1:3). The resources of this divine power come to Christians through their full knowledge of God. God has called believers through His inner excellence and His outer excellence.

The Holy Spirit brings to bear in our lives the full impact of God's glory and goodness, and we realize that *his precious and very great promises* (1:4) are ours in Christ. When we take possession of the promises contained in the Bible, we can avoid the moral and spiritual decay of the world system caused by a greedy pursuit of fleshly desires. At the same time, we conform progressively to the image of Christ and better reflect the divine character.

On the basis of the heavenly resources available to them, Peter urged his readers *to make every effort* (1:5) to climb a ladder of virtues whose bottom rung is faith and whose top rung is love. Faith should have excellence of conduct added to it. The Greek term rendered *goodness* doesn't focus on the moral quality of our behavior as much as its nobility and the courage that produced it.

Excellence should have *knowledge* added to it. This is the knowledge that guides faith and goodness into action. Knowledge should have *self-control* (1:6) added to it. Secular Greek literature treated self-control as a cardinal virtue. The New Testament mentions it only three times (Acts 24:25; Gal. 5:23; 2 Pet. 1:6), preferring to focus on the control the Holy Spirit exercises in our lives. Even in Galatians 5:23, *self-control* is the result of the Spirit's activity. Since Peter viewed these virtues as springing from God's *precious and very great promises* (2 Pet. 1:4), self-control depends on the Spirit here, too.

Self-control should have *endurance* (1:6) added to it. Endurance is the ability to deal through time with difficult circumstances without anger or frustration. Endurance should have *godliness* added to it. *Godliness* translates the very complex Greek term *eusebeia*, which means to "look in two directions. The man who has *eusebeia* always correctly worships God and gives him his due; but he always correctly serves his fellow-men and gives them their due" (Barclay, *The Letters of James and Peter*).

Godliness should have *mutual affection* (1:7) added to it. *Mutual affection* translates the Greek noun *philadelphia*. It is the love of friendship based on common interests and personal attraction. In conclusion, mutual affection should have *love* added to it. *Love* is the selfless, sacrificial commitment to the welfare of the beloved that reflects the love of God. Love is the goal of all Christian maturity because *God is love* (1 John 4:8).

Peter assured his readers that if they kept developing these Christian virtues, their knowledge of the *Lord Jesus Christ* (2 Pet. 1:8) would always issue in an effective and fruitful Christian life. The virtues of this list are to be cultivated simultaneously rather than sequentially.

Peter warned against undisciplined, complacent Christian living by saying that those who don't work at these virtues are living myopically at best, or blindly at worst (1:9). When we aren't advancing in Christian virtues, we become insensitive to the immense spiritual distance between our former sins and our present sanctity. That makes us vulnerable to temptation and sin.

However, if we keep developing these Christian virtues, we cooperate with and affirm God's call and choice directed at us (1:10). The path of increasing virtue leads directly into the future *eternal kingdom of our Lord and Savior Jesus Christ* (1:11). Effective, fruitful living assures a lavish welcome into the presence of God at the end of life.

Because Peter wanted his readers to enter God's presence triumphantly, he assured them he would repeatedly remind them of the basic truths of effective, fruitful living (1:12). He knew he was covering familiar ground, but he intended to repeat the truth in order to keep it alive in their memories (1:13). Peter knew his time was short before he would go to his rich welcome into the eternal kingdom (1:14).

Before Peter died, he intended to make every possible effort to make his apostolic witness to the Gospel and its implications for effective, fruitful living available so that his readers could have their memories refreshed again and again (1:15). The letters of 1 and 2 Peter are the fruits of the apostle's efforts. The Gospel of Mark has been regarded from the time of the church fathers as Peter's testimony about Jesus as reported by John Mark under Peter's tutelage. It too may be part of Peter's legacy to keep our memories alert to the knowledge of Jesus.

SUGGESTIONS TO TEACHERS

This week's lesson text offers Peter's summary of the Christian life. It abounds with references to knowledge and knowing, truth, and memory or recollection. Peter looked at the knowledge of God and Christ as more than intellectual assent. To know God and Christ was to believe in them and live for them with all one's heart, mind, and strength.

1. BASIS OF FAITH. Knowing God means getting acquainted with the glory of His character and the excellence of His deeds among humanity. God's *glory and goodness* (2 Pet. 1:3) form the basis for faith in *his precious and very great promises* (1:4) in the Bible. Those promises form the basis for the confidence that a life of corruption can be exchanged for a life reflecting *the divine nature*.

2. PATH OF FAITH. Peter linked several virtues leading from initial faith to ultimate love. They may be logically sequential, but in practice they develop simultaneously. You don't necessarily master one before attempting the next. We are not to be timid but bold in our confidence that Christ will reproduce His character in us.

3. GOAL OF FAITH. God has called His children to be effective and fruitful in living out their knowledge of Jesus Christ. Faith clearly sees that goal and the path to it. We must not shut our eyes or turn them myopically to the things of the world near at hand; otherwise, we will stumble into ineffective and fruitless living. The goal is to live effectively and fruitfully for the Savior.

4. REMINDER TO FAITH. Peter knew that established Christians don't need new truth as much as they need motivation to put foundational truth into action.

He committed the rest of his life to reminding his first century readers—and Christians ever since and into the future—to hold onto the basis of faith, to walk the path of faith, and to pursue the goal of faith.

FOR ADULTS

■ TOPIC: Growing in Faith

■ QUESTIONS: 1. What does God's divine power provide for believers? 2. What is the basis for growing in the Christian virtues that Peter listed? 3. Why did Peter want to continue reminding his readers of their hope in Christ? 4. What can believers do to ensure they are spiritually maturing? 5. How can believers fight the tendency to forget the truths of the faith?

■ ILLUSTRATIONS:

Unprepared Teacher. A couple of years ago, a local newspaper reported a bomb scare in a church in western Kentucky. The police dispatcher received a 911 call around 6:30 P.M. one Sunday evening from the youth minister, who stated that there was a bomb in the sanctuary.

The Kentucky State Police patrol cars and bomb disposal experts promptly arrived. After evacuating the building, they searched the church and found no explosive device on the premises. This made the police suspicious, and so they quizzed the youth pastor. Eventually, they learned that the bomb threat was a hoax. The young man confessed that he had called 911 that Sunday night. It seems that he was scheduled to preach that evening and was not prepared. Because of his prank, no worship service was held that evening.

Being unprepared for the time when Christ returns will not bring police charges or personal embarrassment to us. Nevertheless, we will miss out on all the spiritual joy associated with the advent of the Savior. Peter's emphasis on faith and maturity thus is for all of us to take seriously.

Know Thyself. The antiquated steam engine chugged slowly through the countryside on its unimportant branch line. The only passenger in one car was a nervous notions salesman who was new to his territory and the train. More or less suddenly, the train lurched to a halt. The salesman called to the conductor, who explained that there was a cow on the track.

Five minutes later, the train puffed into motion and creaked a few more miles down the track before wheezing once more to stop. "Just a temporary delay," the conductor said before the salesman could complain. "We'll be on our way in a moment."

Not to be robbed of his change to gripe, the salesman asked, "What is it now? Did we catch up with that cow again?"

How many of Peter's virtues did the salesman fail to display to the conductor? How many should we cultivate in our walk with Christ?

Work on Yourself. A prosperous young Wall Street broker of a century ago met and fell in love with a rising young actress of gentility and dignity. He frequently escorted her about town and wanted to marry her. Being a cautious man, he decided that, before proposing marriage, he should have a private investigating agency check her background and present activities. After all, he reminded himself, I have both a growing fortune and my reputation to protect against a marital misadventure.

As a further precaution against notoriety, the young man requested that the agency not reveal his identity to the investigator making the report on the actress. In due time the investigator's report arrived. It said the actress had an unblemished past, a spotless reputation, and her friends and associates were of the best repute. The report concluded, "The only shadow in this sunny picture is that she is often seen around town in the company of a young broker of dubious business practices and principles."

■ TOPIC: Everything You Need
■ QUESTIONS: 1. What are some of the precious promises God has given to us in Scripture? 2. How can believers avoid becoming spiritually nearsighted? 3. Why is it important for believers to affirm the truth of Christ's second coming? 4. How can believers strive to maintain self-control in their lives? 5. How has trusting in Jesus for salvation made a tangible difference in your life?

■ **ILLUSTRATIONS:**

Free Virtue Download. The maker of all human beings is recalling all units manufactured, regardless of make or year, because of a serious defect in the primary component of the heart. A malfunction occurred in the original prototype units code named Adam and Eve, resulting in the reproduction of the same defect in all subsequent units. This defect is technically termed "Substantial Internal Non-morality," or more commonly SIN, and is primarily symptomized by loss of moral judgment.

The manufacturer, who is neither liable nor at fault for this defect, is providing factory authorized repair and service, free of charge to correct this pernicious defect. The number for the recall station in your area is: P-R-A-Y-E-R. Once connected, please upload your burden of SIN by pressing REPENTANCE. Next, download J-E-S-U-S into the heart drive. No matter how big or small the SIN defect is, the JESUS repair will replace it with (1) faith, (2) goodness, (3), knowledge, (4) self-control, (5) endurance, (6) godliness, (7) mutual affection, and (8) love.

Please see the operating manual, HOLY BIBLE, for further details on the use of these fixes.

Brand Name Spirituality. Legend has it that Alexander the Great once was called to discipline a foot soldier whose behavior in battle had bordered on cowardice. His commander wanted to know how severely to punish him.

Alexander the Great walked up to the accused soldier and stood toe to toe with him. "What is you name, boy?" asked the general.

"Alexander," the young soldier almost whispered.

The general stood a long time, struggling to master his rage. With ice and steel in his voice, Alexander the Great said quietly, "You change your conduct in battle or you change your name. Do I make myself clear?"

The soldier squeaked, "Yes, sir!" Alexander the Great turned on his heel and strode away.

We bear the name of Jesus. We need to live up to that name.

From Beyond the Grave. The entertainment world suffered a huge loss with the passing of the writer of the novelty song, "The Hokey Pokey." The loss was especially difficult for the immediate family. They were summoned by the morticians to help put their dearly beloved in his coffin. They'd put his left leg in, and, well, you know the rest.

Peter wanted to extend his ministry from beyond the grave, and God had him record his witness as an apostle in two letters and—through John Mark—in the Gospel of Mark. Let Peter's reminders keep you on your toes spiritually.

TRUST GOD'S PROMISE

BACKGROUND SCRIPTURE: 2 Peter 3
DEVOTIONAL READING: Hebrews 10:19-25

KEY VERSES: Beloved, while you are waiting for these things, strive to be found by him at peace, without spot or blemish; and regard the patience of our Lord as salvation. 2 Peter 3:14-15.

KING JAMES VERSION

2 PETER 3:3 Knowing this first, that there shall come in the last days scoffers, walking after their own lusts, 4 And saying, Where is the promise of his coming? for since the fathers fell asleep, all things continue as they were from the beginning of the creation. 5 For this they willingly are ignorant of, that by the word of God the heavens were of old, and the earth standing out of the water and in the water: . . .

7 But the heavens and the earth, which are now, by the same word are kept in store, reserved unto fire against the day of judgment and perdition of ungodly men.

8 But, beloved, be not ignorant of this one thing, that one day is with the Lord as a thousand years, and a thousand years as one day.

9 The Lord is not slack concerning his promise, as some men count slackness; but is longsuffering to us-ward, not willing that any should perish, but that all should come to repentance. 10 But the day of the Lord will come as a thief in the night; in the which the heavens shall pass away with a great noise, and the elements shall melt with fervent heat, the earth also and the works that are therein shall be burned up.

11 Seeing then that all these things shall be dissolved, what manner of persons ought ye to be in all holy conversation and godliness, 12 Looking for and hasting unto the coming of the day of God, wherein the heavens being on fire shall be dissolved, and the elements shall melt with fervent heat? 13 Nevertheless we, according to his promise, look for new heavens and a new earth, wherein dwelleth righteousness. 14 Wherefore, beloved, seeing that ye look for such things, be diligent that ye may be found of him in peace, without spot, and blameless. 15 And account that the longsuffering of our Lord is salvation. . . .

17 Ye therefore, beloved, seeing ye know these things before, beware lest ye also, being led away with the error of the wicked, fall from your own stedfastness. 18 But grow in grace, and in the knowledge of our Lord and Saviour Jesus Christ. To him be glory both now and for ever. Amen.

NEW REVISED STANDARD VERSION

2 PETER 3:3 First of all you must understand this, that in the last days scoffers will come, scoffing and indulging their own lusts 4 and saying, "Where is the promise of his coming? For ever since our ancestors died, all things continue as they were from the beginning of creation!" 5 They deliberately ignore this fact, that by the word of God heavens existed long ago and an earth was formed out of water and by means of water, . . .

7 But by the same word the present heavens and earth have been reserved for fire, being kept until the day of judgment and destruction of the godless.

8 But do not ignore this one fact, beloved, that with the Lord one day is like a thousand years, and a thousand years are like one day. 9 The Lord is not slow about his promise, as some think of slowness, but is patient with you, not wanting any to perish, but all to come to repentance. 10 But the day of the Lord will come like a thief, and then the heavens will pass away with a loud noise, and the elements will be dissolved with fire, and the earth and everything that is done on it will be disclosed.

11 Since all these things are to be dissolved in this way, what sort of persons ought you to be in leading lives of holiness and godliness, 12 waiting for and hastening the coming of the day of God, because of which the heavens will be set ablaze and dissolved, and the elements will melt with fire? 13 But, in accordance with his promise, we wait for new heavens and a new earth, where righteousness is at home.

14 Therefore, beloved, while you are waiting for these things, strive to be found by him at peace, without spot or blemish; 15 and regard the patience of our Lord as salvation. . . .

17 You therefore, beloved, since you are forewarned, beware that you are not carried away with the error of the lawless and lose your own stability. 18 But grow in the grace and knowledge of our Lord and Savior Jesus Christ. To him be the glory both now and to the day of eternity. Amen.

Monday, October 20	Hebrews 10:19-25	*Hold Fast to Our Hope*
Tuesday, October 21	1 Corinthians 1:4-9	*God Is Faithful*
Wednesday, October 22	2 Corinthians 1:18-22	*In Christ, It Is "Yes"*
Thursday, October 23	Isaiah 55:8-12	*God's Word Shall Not Return Empty*
Friday, October 24	2 Peter 3:1-7	*Where Is the Promise?*
Saturday, October 25	2 Peter 3:8-13	*God Is Not Slow*
Sunday, October 26	2 Peter 3:14-18	*Regard God's Patience as Salvation*

BACKGROUND

Second Peter was written to believers being threatened by false teaching from within their congregations (2:1). The frauds evidently were using Christian liberty as a license to sin, especially to commit sexual immorality (2:14). In addition, they were guilty of denying the Lord (2:1), despising authority and slandering celestial beings (2:10), and scoffing at the second coming of Christ (3:3-4).

As an antidote, Peter stressed the truth and ethical implications of the Gospel. In particular, the apostle underscored the importance of holy living. Peter traced the motivation for leading a holy life back to the imminent return of Christ and the punishment and rewards that Jesus will bring.

The letter groups these teachings into five different themes. First, Peter asserted his own authority and the authority of the apostles' teaching. Their instruction would help the readers of 2 Peter to distinguish truth from error. Second, the recipients of this letter were having trouble establishing the connection between following Christ and leading a holy life. Peter thus reiterated to them that Christian discipleship meant putting away all kinds of immorality.

Third, the apostle warned his readers not to imitate the arrogance of the false teachers, who were slandering spiritual beings. Fourth, to encourage his readers to persevere and remain faithful to the truths of the faith, Peter depicted the day of the Lord, which would result in a new heaven and new earth.

Fifth, toward the end of his letter, Peter encouraged his readers to be patient. God had good reasons for delaying Christ's return and the fulfillment of His prophetic program. The day of the Lord had been delayed, but it was still imminent. For this reason, they were to vigilantly watch their belief and practice so that they would not be deceived by falsehood.

NOTES ON THE PRINTED TEXT

Peter reminded his readers that the first line of defense against false teachers is an awareness that the last days will be characterized by scoffers who delight in cynical jest about the most important truths of life and godliness (2 Pet. 3:3). In Peter's day the truth being mocked was the idea of the personal, bodily return of Christ as Judge of all.

The false teachers pointed to the fact that *our ancestors* (3:4) had died without seeing the Savior's return. Some think Peter was referring to the Old Testament patriarchs, who never saw the Messiah. Another possibility is that Peter was talking about the deaths of people belonging to the first generation of Christians.

The scoffers deliberately forgot a key truth, namely, that God, by means of His powerful command, had long ago made the *heavens* (3:5) and the *earth*. The latter He brought up *out of water* and *by means of water*. Peter pointed to the great Flood in Noah's day as proof that the apparent delay in Christ's second coming did not imply a lack of fulfillment (3:6).

The account of the Flood (Gen. 6—9) proved the inevitability of the divine judgment and testified to God's patience. Even more importantly, the biblical record was evidence of the reliability of God's promise. The seeming delay of Jesus' return simply meant that God had reserved judgment for a future date. It thus was absolutely certain that on the day of judgment, the *godless* (2 Pet. 3:7) will perish and *the present heavens and earth* will be consumed by *fire*.

Peter borrowed from the language of Psalm 90:4 to show that the false teachers failed to understand God's unique time perspective. Since God is not subject to the same time limitations as His creatures, a thousand years would seem to Him to be no more than *one day* (2 Pet. 3:8).

God, of course, is not merely outside of time. He is also in control of it; thus, the delay between the Ascension and Second Coming is intentional. In fact, God's delay is redemptive, reflecting His desire to see others *come to repentance* (3:9). Thus, what some have interpreted as *slowness* is really an act of mercy that has allowed the lost to hear and respond to the Gospel.

While the time between Jesus' two comings is a merciful delay, it is not indefinite. Peter warned that *the day of the Lord* (3:10) will come without warning, like a thief. At that time of judgment, *the heavens will pass away with a loud noise*; also, there will be great heat that melts the elements.

The truth concerning the day of the Lord has immediate relevance for believers. First and most importantly, it is an incentive for *holiness and godliness* (3:11). Peter urged believers to regard Jesus' return with practical anticipation, rather than useless speculation.

Second, an awareness of Jesus' return is to be a motivation for evangelism. Though believers cannot change the Father's timing (Matt. 24:36), they can cooperate with the Father's plan by spreading the Good News. In that sense, believers can help hasten *the coming of the day of God* (2 Pet. 3:12).

Peter again declared that, in the time of divine judgment, God will set *the heavens . . . ablaze* and dissolve the elements *with fire*. This truth does not cause believers to despair, for they are looking forward to a *new heavens and a new earth* (3:13). This pristine world will be the dwelling place of righteousness.

Peter urged his readers to make every effort to live in a holy manner. Their desire was to be morally pure and blameless in their conduct and living at peace with God at the Savior's return (3:14).

Peter was urging his audience to take a different view than that of the false teachers concerning the delay of Christ's return. The apostle explained that *the patience of our Lord* (3:15) was meant to give the lost time to be saved. In the midst of this redemptive purpose, believers were to pray for the unsaved and herald the Gospel.

Peter did not want his readers to be *carried away* (3:17) by the errors of wicked people who had infiltrated the church. Thus, the apostle issued one final warning to Jesus' followers to keep their guard up. If they remained vigilant, they would retain their spiritual balance.

Ultimately, of course, it was the grace and knowledge of *our Lord and Savior Jesus Christ* (3:18) that would prevent believers from stumbling over false teaching. Peter rightly declared that all glory and honor belonged to Christ *both now and to the day of eternity.*

SUGGESTIONS TO TEACHERS

Jesus promised and angels confirmed that He would return bodily to the earth at a future time (Matt. 24:30-31; Acts 1:11). The New Testament writers understood that the return of Christ will mark the end of this age and the beginning of the kingdom of God (1 Thess. 4:16-17; 5:1-2; 2 Pet. 3:10; Rev. 19:11-16; 21:1-4). Peter addressed the promised return of Jesus because false teachers were challenging its truthfulness.

1. THE CHALLENGE TO THE PROMISE. Century after century, scoffers have posed the same objections to the teaching that Jesus will return some day. Generations have come and gone, they say, and Jesus hasn't returned; therefore, He isn't coming. Everything is as it has always been from the beginning of time, they say; therefore, Jesus' return isn't going to break the pattern. Scoffers want Christians to feel self-conscious or presumptuous for imagining that Jesus might do something in their time that He hasn't done for past generations.

2. THE PROOF OF THE PROMISE. Peter demonstrated several logical and biblical fallacies in the reasoning of the scoffers who deny that Jesus will return bodily. Peter argued in favor of the return of a sovereign Lord, operating outside the confines of time, with the best interests of His creatures in mind, and having a commitment to dealing with the effects of the Fall on creation and humankind.

3. THE IMPLICATIONS OF THE PROMISE. The Bible does not present theology as an intellectual exercise. There are behavioral implications for God's truth. Peter presented compelling arguments for holiness and godliness from the fact that the day of the Lord will come as a thief in the night. We cannot know when Jesus will return, but we can live in such a way that we affirm His return and His reign over the new heavens and earth.

4. THE RESPONSE TO THE PROMISE. While believers wait for the Lord, we should strive to imitate Jesus in peace, purity, and patience. We should seek to build lasting stability in our lives by growing in grace and the knowledge of Christ. Second Peter ends as it began with an emphasis on the transforming knowledge of God and His Son Jesus (1:2-3, 5, 8; 3:18).

<table>
<tr><td>

FOR ADULTS

</td><td>

■ TOPIC: Being Faithful to Promises

■ QUESTIONS: 1. Why did false teachers scoff at the truth of Jesus'

</td></tr>
</table>

return? 2. How did Peter address their arguments? 3. What did Peter say believers should be doing as they wait for Jesus' return? 4. What are some ways believers can affirm the truth of Jesus' return? 5. How can believers strive to remain faithful to God's promises in Scripture regarding the Second Coming?

■ ILLUSTRATIONS:

Scoffers Beware! Friday at quitting time, Jim said, "Boss, have you got any extra work I can do tonight?'

"Sure," Jim's boss replied, "but I can't pay you overtime."

"That's okay," Jim answered. "I just don't want to go home."

"Why not?" his boss asked.

"Well," Jim admitted, "I've been in the doghouse since last night."

"Uh-oh," his boss interjected. "What did you do to deserve that?"

"I honestly don't know," Jim shrugged. "It must be one of those woman things. I was minding my own business relaxing in front of the TV. My wife comes in and asks, 'What's on the TV?' I swear all I said was, 'Dust!' She's been mad ever since!"

Jim's wife failed to see any humor in her husband's dig at her housekeeping. God gets more than a little miffed at teachers in the church who go by His Son's name and scoff at the teachings of the Bible.

Avoid Scoffers. Despite the "Do Not Touch" signs, a museum was having no success in keeping patrons from touching—and soiling—priceless furniture and art. But the problem evaporated overnight when a clever museum employee replaced the signs with ones that read: "Caution: Wash Hands after Touching!"

Peter, and other New Testament writers, advise us to stay away from false teachers, for they distort and deny the sense of God's Word. If you have to deal with them, at least cleanse your mind and heart afterward.

First Things First. A traveler lost in the deserts of North Africa crawled up to the tent of a Bedouin and croaked, "Water."

The Bedouin appeared and replied sympathetically, "I am sorry, sir, but I have no water. However, would you like a nice necktie?" With this, he brandished a collection of exquisite silken neckwear.

"You fool," gasped the man. "I'm dying! I need water!"

"Well, sir," replied the Bedouin, "If you really need water, there is a tent about two miles south of here where you can get some, but you really should take one of these ties."

The parched traveler summoned sufficient strength to drag himself to the second tent. He collapsed at the entrance. Another Bedouin, this one dressed in a costly tuxedo, appeared at the door and enquired, "May I help you, sir?"

"Water," The traveler croaked weakly.

"I am very sorry sir, but you cannot come in here without a tie!!" the doorman said and turned on his heel.

The false teachers mentioned in 2 Peter thought they could have Christian liberty without repentance and renewal. They thought they could scoff at Jesus, live in sin, and go to heaven in the end. They were wrong.

Grace and Good Works. Christmas decorations will soon go up and right after Thanksgiving you'll hear:

> You better watch out, you better not cry,
> You better not pout, I'm telling you why,
> Santa Claus is coming to town.

> He's making a list, checking it twice,
> Gonna find out who's naughty and nice,
> Santa Claus is coming to town.

> He sees you when you're sleeping.
> He knows when you're awake.
> He knows when you've been bad or good,
> so be good *for goodness' sake*.

As a kid, I never liked that song. You can't fool Santa. He knows it all. Well, great! Then he knows I lied about scratching the car with my bike. He knows I hit my sister. He knows I was cussing up a storm with my friends down the street. He knows it all. That's just great! What chance do I have for a decent Christmas present now? I might as well just keep on being bad.

Was Peter saying Christians have to be good for goodness' sake or the day of the Lord would catch them like a thief in the night and fix them good? That's how some people look at it. Jesus is coming back. You had better watch out. You had better be good, because He knows it all. You had better be ready, prepared, faithful, and loving, because there's no fooling Him.

That notion misses the point of the grace of God. Ephesians 2:8-10 tells us that we cannot be good enough to earn God's favor. Instead, He gives us the gift of eternal life when we believe in Jesus; and through our knowledge of His Son, He recreates us in Christ so that we can be good.

■ TOPIC: Live Patiently and Faithfully

■ QUESTIONS: 1. What attitude did the false teachers have concerning the truth of Jesus' return? 2. How did Peter describe the second coming of Christ? 3. How did Peter want believers to live as they awaited Jesus' return? 4. What should be our attitude concerning the truth of Jesus' coming? 5. Why is it important for us to live in a holy manner as we anticipate the Second Coming?

■ ILLUSTRATIONS:

Let Sleeping Dogs Lie. Upon entering a little country store, a stranger noticed a sign reading, "Danger! Beware of Dog" posted on the glass door. Inside, he noticed a harmless old hound dog asleep on the floor besides the cash register. He asked the store manager, "Is that the dog folks are supposed to beware of?"

"Yep, that's him," the store manager replied.

The stranger couldn't help but be amused. "That certainly doesn't look like a dangerous dog to me. Why in the world would you post that sign?"

"Because," the owner replied, "before I posted that sign, people kept tripping over him."

You may not think that cults and off-the-wall teachings look dangerous. They may seem harmless enough. But leave them alone. They may not eat you alive, but they can make you stumble.

Time Is Relative. Mary was so excited that John had asked her out on a date. She was ready 20 minutes early. It disappointed her that he wasn't on time. By the time he was 30 minutes late, she was angry with John. After an hour, Mary was angry with herself for caring in the first place. She took off her makeup, put on her pajamas, gathered all the junk food in the pantry, and sat down to watch television with the dog. As her favorite show was coming on, the doorbell rang. It was John.

He stared at her wide-eyed. "I'm two hours late, and you're still not ready?"

John is without excuse, and Mary is blameless unless she clobbers him or sics the dog on him. However, don't let Jesus' return sneak up on you. He didn't name a day or hour. Be ready all the time.

Judgment Is Coming. A burglar broke into a house and began to pilfer the silver from the dining room. Out of the dark a voice said, "Jesus is watching you."

The burglar froze in terror for a second. When nothing happened, he resumed his theft. The voice spoke again: "Jesus is watching you."

The burglar waited in the dark for five minutes. No one moved. No one spoke. Cautiously, the burglar lifted the tea service and lowered it into his bag. It clinked and the voice said, "Jesus is watching you."

This time the burglar saw a dark shape in the corner. When he approached, he realized it was a birdcage. He removed the cover to find a parrot. He was so relieved when he saw the parrot. What's your name?" he asked.

The parrot replied "Moses."

"What kind of person names a parrot Moses?" the burglar wondered out loud.

The parrot replied, "The same kind of person that named a Rottweiler 'Jesus.'"

Fiery Judgment. Legend has it that a fire-and-brimstone preacher outdid himself one Sunday in a sermon about judgment day. As he neared the conclusion of his message, he painted a vivid word picture for his congregation of weeping and wailing and especially the gnashing of teeth.

A little old lady in the front row, whose hearing was gone, turned to her neighbor and said loudly in what she thought was a whisper, "I'm glad I don't have any teeth any more."

The preacher pointed at her and said sternly, "Madam, teeth will be provided."

Divine judgment is no laughing matter. It cannot be avoided with feeble excuses or a note from the dentist. Judgment is avoided through a saving relationship with Jesus, which leads to a life lived in anticipation of His return to rule.

ENJOY FELLOWSHIP WITH GOD

BACKGROUND SCRIPTURE: 1 John 1:1—3:10
DEVOTIONAL READING: Ephesians 5:1-10

KEY VERSE: If we walk in the light as he himself is in the light, we have fellowship with one another, and the blood of Jesus his Son cleanses us from all sin. 1 John 1:7.

KING JAMES VERSION

1 JOHN 1:5 This then is the message which we have heard of him, and declare unto you, that God is light, and in him is no darkness at all. 6 If we say that we have fellowship with him, and walk in darkness, we lie, and do not the truth: 7 But if we walk in the light, as he is in the light, we have fellowship one with another, and the blood of Jesus Christ his Son cleanseth us from all sin.

8 If we say that we have no sin, we deceive ourselves, and the truth is not in us. 9 If we confess our sins, he is faithful and just to forgive us our sins, and to cleanse us from all unrighteousness. 10 If we say that we have not sinned, we make him a liar, and his word is not in us.

2:1 My little children, these things write I unto you, that ye sin not. And if any man sin, we have an advocate with the Father, Jesus Christ the righteous: 2 And he is the propitiation for our sins: and not for ours only, but also for the sins of the whole world.

3 And hereby we do know that we know him, if we keep his commandments. 4 He that saith, I know him, and keepeth not his commandments, is a liar, and the truth is not in him. 5 But whoso keepeth his word, in him verily is the love of God perfected: hereby know we that we are in him. 6He that saith he abideth in him ought himself also so to walk, even as he walked. . . .

15 Love not the world, neither the things that are in the world. If any man love the world, the love of the Father is not in him. 16 For all that is in the world, the lust of the flesh, and the lust of the eyes, and the pride of life, is not of the Father, but is of the world. 17 And the world passeth away, and the lust thereof: but he that doeth the will of God abideth for ever. . . .

29 If ye know that he is righteous, ye know that every one that doeth righteousness is born of him.

3:1 Behold, what manner of love the Father hath bestowed upon us, that we should be called the sons of God: therefore the world knoweth us not, because it knew him not.

NEW REVISED STANDARD VERSION

1 JOHN 1:5 This is the message we have heard from him and proclaim to you, that God is light and in him there is no darkness at all. 6 If we say that we have fellowship with him while we are walking in darkness, we lie and do not do what is true; 7 but if we walk in the light as he himself is in the light, we have fellowship with one another, and the blood of Jesus his Son cleanses us from all sin. 8 If we say that we have no sin, we deceive ourselves, and the truth is not in us. 9 If we confess our sins, he who is faithful and just will forgive us our sins and cleanse us from all unrighteousness. 10 If we say that we have not sinned, we make him a liar, and his word is not in us.

2:1 My little children, I am writing these things to you so that you may not sin. But if anyone does sin, we have an advocate with the Father, Jesus Christ the righteous; 2 and he is the atoning sacrifice for our sins, and not for ours only but also for the sins of the whole world.

3 Now by this we may be sure that we know him, if we obey his commandments. 4 Whoever says, "I have come to know him," but does not obey his commandments, is a liar, and in such a person the truth does not exist; 5 but whoever obeys his word, truly in this person the love of God has reached perfection. By this we may be sure that we are in him: 6 whoever says, "I abide in him," ought to walk just as he walked. . . .

15 Do not love the world or the things in the world. The love of the Father is not in those who love the world; 16 for all that is in the world—the desire of the flesh, the desire of the eyes, the pride in riches—comes not from the Father but from the world. 17 And the world and its desire are passing away, but those who do the will of God live forever. . . .

29 If you know that he is righteous, you may be sure that everyone who does right has been born of him. 3:1 See what love the Father has given us, that we should be called children of God; and that is what we are. The reason the world does not know us is that it did not know him.

HOME BIBLE READINGS

BACKGROUND

Neither the Epistles of John nor the Gospel of John identify their author. Church fathers as early as Irenaeus in the second century attributed them to John the beloved disciple of Jesus, the son of Zebedee, and the brother of James. The earliest citations of John's works are found in writings from western Asia Minor around Ephesus where the apostle John ministered in the later years of his life. John's authorship of these books has been universally accepted into the modern era, and even many critical scholars find the evidence compelling.

First John reflects a date of composition late in the first century, probably between A.D. 85 and 95. John addressed his readers from the perspective of an elderly man, calling them *little children* (2:1). In 2 and 3 John, the apostle referred to himself as *the elder* (2 John 1; 3 John 1). The false teaching addressed in John's epistles also reflects ideas characteristic of a later date rather than an earlier one in the apostolic period.

In John's day, Ephesus was an ancient city that prided itself as the cultural center of the province of Asia. That culture was thoroughly Hellenistic and included many forms of revived paganism that tried to bring together different strands of religious thought, old and new, eastern and western. John's letters reflect a struggle between the truth of God's Word and some heretical teachings within the churches around Ephesus that threatened to divide the congregations.

The proponents of the heretical teachings seem to have agreed that *God is light* (1 John 1:5). They accepted Christ as a heavenly being, but denied His humanity (4:2). They believed the Gospel freed them from the presence of sin (1:8). They assumed they were free from any further practice of sin (1:10). They did not make a connection between their belief and their behavior. They were neither gracious nor loving (3:14-17). They were involved in missionary activity to expand their sect (2 John 10).

The new sect had been a part of the church around Ephesus. By the time John wrote his first letter, it had separated from the church and had begun rivaling it (1 John 2:19). The apostle summoned the members of the church to resist the sect that wanted to divorce faith and life. One must walk in the light; one must live in love; and to abide in God is to obey His commands.

NOTES ON THE PRINTED TEXT

John opened his first letter with claims to be an eyewitness of the life of Jesus (1 John 1:1-4). John could assert, in contrast to the false teachers in Ephesus, that his message came from Jesus (1:5) The burden of that message was *that God is light*. Light, as a metaphor for God, stresses the ideas of splendor, power, truth, revelation, and purity. Light also makes an ethical demand. Anyone who associates with the Light must disassociate from the darkness, for sin has no place in the presence of God.

In 1 John 1:6, 8, and 10, the apostle introduced three claims inherent in the message of the false teachers. They each begin with the words, *If we say that*. The first claim asserted that the light of God's nature does not require personal purity (1:6). The false teachers apparently felt the sins of their bodies did not affect the purity of their spirits. John affirmed that living outside the truth—a synonym for light—is a form of lying.

John's response to the false teachers' first claim was that, because God is light, we should *walk in the light* (1:7). We can fellowship with God individually and corporately only by adopting His character. Only in the purity of God's light can we expect to experience the ongoing cleansing from daily sin by *the blood of Jesus*.

The second claim of the false teachers was that they did not sin when they walked in the darkness (1:6). They were dead to sin as a principle of life. Their spirits were pure. John said these teachers deluded themselves. It wasn't sin as a principle, but truth as a principle that they were dead to.

John's response to this second claim of the false teachers was that confession is essential for dealing with the sins we commit (1 John 1:9). Confession moves our sins from the dark into the light, where the blood of Jesus can cleanse them (1:7). Faithfulness and justice are aspects of the light of God's character that come into play when He forgives sins.

The third claim of the false teachers went beyond the second claim and asserted they no longer committed any sins (1:10). John's response was that such a claim flew in the face of God's Word, which says all people sin (Eccl. 7:20; Isa. 53:6; Rom. 3:23). John's response to this third claim of the false teachers was that, even though we all sin, we should make it our goal not to sin (1 John 2:1).

Sin is not a spiritually inconsequential event, as the false teachers alleged. Sin needs a remedy. John insisted that Christians have *an advocate*, a defense attorney in the courtroom of heaven, who speaks to God the Father on their behalf. That defense attorney is *Jesus Christ the righteous*. The Son of God, who is righteousness personified, stands up for believers who *walk in the light* (1:7) but lapse into *sin* (2:1).

By shedding His blood, Jesus became *the atoning sacrifice* (2:2) that appeases God's righteous wrath against sin and that cleanses the guilt of sin from the lives of believers. Jesus' sacrifice expiated the sins of every person who will ever live, and is appropriated by those who trust in Him for salvation.

The topic in 1 John 1:5—2:2 is fellowship with God, namely, how to enter into and maintain a relationship with the Father and His Son. In 2:3, the topic changes to knowing God, that is, how to reach the deepest levels of communion with the Father and His Son. John asserted that the short answer to that question is to *obey his commandments*. The false teachers separated knowing God and living morally and righteously (2:4).

John regarded obedience to God's Word as the primary evidence that a person loves God (2:5). In other words, the litmus test for knowing and loving God is imitation of God (2:6). The Greek verb rendered *abide* occurs several times in 1 John, usually in the idea of abiding in the Father or His Son. To abide in the Father and His Son means to live in union and harmony with them. Abiding includes imitating, that is, walking *just as [Jesus] walked.*

Abiding in the Father demands a break with the walk of the world. You cannot love the Father and love *the world* (2:15). *The world* here does not mean the world of people (John 3:16) or the creation known as the world (17:24). *The world* (1 John 2:15) is the evil system that corrupts the course of human events under the influence of the devil (5:19).

The devil's world system corrupts people through three primary attitudes: *the desire of the flesh, the desire of the eyes, the pride in riches* (2:16). Those three attitudes translate roughly into selfishness, greed, and vain status seeking (Barker, *Expositor's Bible Commentary*). The flesh is selfish; the eyes are greedy; and pride is a strutting peacock.

The world and these three henchmen *are passing away* (2:17). The false teachers and their deceived followers will suffer their end with the world. All *who do the will of* the Father—those who walk in the light, obey His Word, and abide in His Son—*live forever*. Because God is *righteous* (2:29), those who have been *born of him* demonstrate their relationship by upright behavior.

Being called *children of God* (3:1) is a rare privilege. Bearing this label demonstrates *the love the Father has given us*. The world thinks Christians are saddled with oppressive rules and standards because godliness is antithetical to selfishness, greed, and vain status seeking. Since the world misunderstood Jesus (John 1:5, 10), the world will also misunderstand *the children of God* (1 John 3:1).

SUGGESTIONS TO TEACHERS

John had enjoyed direct fellowship with Jesus. John taught his readers they could have that same fellowship by responding to the eyewitness testimony of those apostles. Fellowship with the Father and His Son is not abstract or theoretical. It is concrete and behavioral.

1. WALK IN THE LIGHT. God radiates glory, purity, and truth into the lives of His spiritual children. We need to live our lives in God's light and allow His light to transform us. If we avoid His light in favor of the darkness of the world, our fellowship with the Father and His Son will be interrupted. If we open our lives every day to God's light, it will expose our sins and we will experience the daily cleansing from our sins by Christ's blood.

2. CONFESS YOUR SINS. God's light will make our sins hateful to us, but we will sin. When we do, Jesus Christ defends us to the Father on the basis of His blood shed to appease God's wrath and wash away our guilt. We acknowledge the reality of our sins and our responsibility for them through the act of confession to God and the people we hurt. If we conceal our sins, deny our sins, or ignore our sins, we walk out of God's light into the darkness of the world. This breaks our fellowship with the Father and His Son.

3. OBEY GOD'S WORD. In the theology of the apostle John, to know God, to abide in God, and to love God are all synonymous expressions for obeying God. We who say we know and love the Father and the Son *ought to walk just as he walked* (1 John 2:6). We know the Father because the Son has shown Him to us (John 1:18; 14:8-11). The example and commands of Jesus provide the blueprint for our obedience of God (14:21).

4. LOVE NOT THE WORLD. No one can serve two masters (Matt. 6:24). The devil works through the allures of the world (1 John 5:19) to draw believers away from fellowship with God into fellowship with the world. We are not ignorant of the devil's schemes (2 Cor. 2:11). He uses selfishness, greed, and vain status seeking to appeal to our sinful natures and seduce us from fellowship with the Father and His Son.

We have to recognize the incompatibility of the darkness of the world and God's light. We need to remind ourselves that fellowship with the world leads to judgment, while fellowship with the Father and His Son leads to eternal life. We also need to remind ourselves that, when we live as children of God, we will receive the same treatment from the children of the world that Jesus did.

FOR ADULTS

■ TOPIC: Enjoy Fellowship

■ QUESTIONS: 1. What did John mean when he said that *God is light* (1 John 1:5)? 2. Why is it wrong for Christians to deny the presence of sin in their lives? 3. Why is it wrong to love the evil world system? 4. How can believers cultivate their fellowship with God? 5. How can Christians encourage unbelievers to turn to Jesus in faith and enjoy fellowship with Him?

■ ILLUSTRATIONS:

Confession Works. Confession of sin involves more than asking God to forgive your sins. When you admit you have done wrong, you may need to correct the wrong.

During the Welsh Revivals of the nineteenth century, as people sought to be filled with the Spirit, they did all they could to confess their wrongdoing and to make restitution. This unexpectedly created serious problems for the shipyards along the coast of Wales. Over the years workers had stolen all kinds of things, from wheelbarrows to hammers. As workers sought to be right with God, they returned what they had taken, with the result that the shipyards of Wales were overwhelmed with huge piles of returned tools. Several of the yards put up signs that read, "If you have been led by God to return what you have stolen, please know that the management forgives you and wishes you to keep what you have taken."

Vain Status Seeking. In Plutarch's *Characters*, the Roman writer described "pride in riches" (Greek *alazon*) like this:

> The *Alazon* is the kind of person who will stand on the mole [pier] and tell perfect strangers what a lot of money he has at sea, and discourse of his investments, how large they are, and what gains and losses he has made, and as he spins his yarns he will send his boy to the bank—his balance being but a shilling. If he enjoys company on the road, he is apt to tell how he served with Alexander the Great, how he got on with him, and how many jeweled cups he brought home; and to discuss the Asiatic craftsmen, how much better they are than any in Europe—never having been away from Athens. He will say that he was granted a free permit for the export of timber, but took no advantage of it, to avoid ill-natured gossip; and that during the corn-shortage he spent more than fifteen hundred pounds in gifts to needy citizens. He will be living in a rented house, and will tell anyone who does not know the facts that this is the family residence, but he is going to sell it because it is too small for his entertainments.

The Way of the World. Some time ago, a newspaper in Tacoma, Washington, carried the story of Tattoo, the basset hound. Tattoo didn't intend to go for an evening run, but when his owner shut his leash in the car door and took off with Tattoo still outside the vehicle, he had no choice.

A motorcycle officer named Terry Filbert noticed a passing vehicle with something that appeared to be dragging behind it. As he passed the vehicle, he saw the object was a basset hound on a leash.

"He was picking them up and putting them down as fast as he could," said Filbert. He chased the car to a stop, and Tattoo was rescued, but not before the dog reached a speed of twenty to twenty-five miles per hour, and rolled over several times. The dog was fine but asked not to go out for an evening walk for a long time.

If you befriend the world, it will take you for a ride that wears you out and rolls you over. And, if you aren't rescued by the Savior (through faith in Him), your life will end in eternal gloom.

■ **TOPIC:** Live in Light

■ **QUESTIONS:** 1. What does it mean to have fellowship with God? 2. Why is it important for Jesus to cleanse us from our sins? 3. Why is it important to obey God's commands? 4. How can we encourage others to live in God's light? 5. Why is it important for us to confess our sins to God?

■ **ILLUSTRATIONS:**

Walk This Way. Back in the late 1980s, Meryl Streep starred in *Ironweed*. She played a ragged derelict who died in a cheap motel room. For more than half an hour before that scene was filmed, Streep hugged a bag of ice cubes in an attempt to discover what it was like to be a cold, clammy corpse. When the cameras came on, she just lay there as Jack Nicholson's character cried and shook her limp body.

Streep lay there for take after take and in between takes, too. One of the crew members got scared and went the director and said, "What's going on? She's not breathing!"

When the director looked at her, he saw no signs of life, but he kept the camera rolling. After the scene was done and cameras were off, Meryl Streep still didn't move. It took ten minutes for her to emerge from the semi-conscious state she had sunk into. The director was amazed and said, "Now that's acting! That is an actress!"

Meryl Streep identified so closely with death that she took on its character. The challenge of the Christian life is to identify so totally with Jesus that we take on His character. The great difference is that we are identifying with life—abundant life—not death.

Confess Now. Nearly 200 years ago, the great Charles Finney was the best-known American evangelist. Once during a series of meetings in Rochester, New York, Finney had a strange experience. The chief justice of the supreme court of New York sat in one of the upper balconies of the church. As he listened to Finney preach, he thought, *That man is speaking the truth. I ought to make a public confession of Jesus Christ.*

Another voice in his head told him he was an important person who didn't need the humiliation of going forward like an ordinary sinner. The attorney knew he would talk himself out of doing what he should if he sat there very long. So he left his seat, went down the stairs, and headed down the aisle—all while Finney kept preaching away. The judge stepped onto the platform, tugged on the evangelist's sleeve and announced, "If you will call for decisions for Christ now, I am ready to come."

The time to confess is the instant we know something is sin.

There's Always a Catch. A high-spirited cowpoke was riding his horse into town one day when he spied a hunched over old farm hand plodding along on a mule.

Deciding to have a little fun, the cowboy drew his six-shooter and ordered the old man down off his mule. "Dance, clodbuster!" the cowpoke shouted and started firing bullets into the ground near the old man's feet. The cowboy roared with laughter as the old guy shuffled and hopped. Then the unamused field hand sauntered to his mule and pulled a shotgun from under his pack. The cowboy's revolver was now empty.

"Did you ever kiss a mule long and hard on the mouth?" the old man drawled.

The suddenly subdued cowboy said, "No, but I've always wanted to."

Sometimes the world offers selfish, greedy, status seeking actions that seem like such a good idea at the time. But they don't last. In the end, there's a price to pay. Often you never see it coming until it's too late.

LOVE ONE ANOTHER

BACKGROUND SCRIPTURE: 1 John 3:11—4:21
DEVOTIONAL READING: 1 Corinthians 13:1-13

KEY VERSE: Beloved, since God loved us so much,
we also ought to love one another. 1 John 4:11.

KING JAMES VERSION

1 JOHN 3:11 For this is the message that ye heard from the beginning, that we should love one another. . . .

14 We know that we have passed from death unto life, because we love the brethren. He that loveth not his brother abideth in death.

15 Whosoever hateth his brother is a murderer: and ye know that no murderer hath eternal life abiding in him.

16 Hereby perceive we the love of God, because he laid down his life for us: and we ought to lay down our lives for the brethren. . . .

4:7 Beloved, let us love one another: for love is of God; and every one that loveth is born of God, and knoweth God.

8 He that loveth not knoweth not God; for God is love.

9 In this was manifested the love of God toward us, because that God sent his only begotten Son into the world, that we might live through him.

10 Herein is love, not that we loved God, but that he loved us, and sent his Son to be the propitiation for our sins.

11 Beloved, if God so loved us, we ought also to love one another.

12 No man hath seen God at any time. If we love one another, God dwelleth in us, and his love is perfected in us.

13 Hereby know we that we dwell in him, and he in us, because he hath given us of his Spirit.

14 And we have seen and do testify that the Father sent the Son to be the Saviour of the world.

15 Whosoever shall confess that Jesus is the Son of God, God dwelleth in him, and he in God.

16 And we have known and believed the love that God hath to us. God is love; and he that dwelleth in love dwelleth in God, and God in him.

NEW REVISED STANDARD VERSION

1 JOHN 3:11 For this is the message you have heard from the beginning, that we should love one another. . . .

14 We know that we have passed from death to life because we love one another. Whoever does not love abides in death. 15 All who hate a brother or sister are murderers, and you know that murderers do not have eternal life abiding in them. 16 We know love by this, that he laid down his life for us—and we ought to lay down our lives for one another. . . .

4:7 Beloved, let us love one another, because love is from God; everyone who loves is born of God and knows God. 8 Whoever does not love does not know God, for God is love. 9 God's love was revealed among us in this way: God sent his only Son into the world so that we might live through him. 10 In this is love, not that we loved God but that he loved us and sent his Son to be the atoning sacrifice for our sins. 11 Beloved, since God loved us so much, we also ought to love one another. 12 No one has ever seen God; if we love one another, God lives in us, and his love is perfected in us.

13 By this we know that we abide in him and he in us, because he has given us of his Spirit. 14 And we have seen and do testify that the Father has sent his Son as the Savior of the world. 15 God abides in those who confess that Jesus is the Son of God, and they abide in God. 16 So we have known and believe the love that God has for us.

10

Monday, November 3	1 Corinthians 13:1-7	*Love Believes, Hopes, Endures*
Tuesday, November 4	1 Corinthians 13:8-13	*Love Never Ends*
Wednesday, November 5	1 John 3:11-17	*Lay Down Your Life for Another*
Thursday, November 6	1 John 3:18-24	*Love in Truth and Action*
Friday, November 7	1 John 4:1-7	*Love Is from God*
Saturday, November 8	1 John 4:8-12	*God Is Love*
Sunday, November 9	1 John 4:13-21	*We Love Because God Loved Us*

BACKGROUND

While 1 John has traditionally been regarded as a letter, it lacks key distinguishing features of an epistle (for example, a salutation, introductory greeting, and final greeting); nevertheless, John addressed his readers as *my little children* (2:1). He seemed to be writing to a specific group of people with whom he had a close relationship. Thus, in its basic purposes of admonition and instruction, 1 John is similar to most of the New Testament letters.

This epistle does not yield naturally to a structural outline. Nevertheless, one is discernable. The prologue (1:1-4) introduces the incarnate Word of Life, Jesus Christ. This is followed by material dealing with walking in the light as God's children (1:5—2:27), practicing righteousness as God's children (2:28—4:6), and showing unconditional love as God's children (4:7—5:12). The letter ends with the epilogue (5:13-21).

The language of this letter is not difficult or technical, but the ideas expressed are profound. For example, the writer said that God has been revealed in Christ in order to communicate eternal life to those who believe. God is light, truth, and love. Each of these characteristics is the subject of some meditation, but always in connection with the development of corresponding virtues in believers.

The ideals of purity and love that are held out to the reader are gifts of God, communicated from His self-revelation in Christ. At the same time, these ideals are real for believers when they are lived out. This reality is possible through being born again and through the forgiveness of sin.

Whereas the Gospel of John was written to bring people to faith in Christ (20:30-31), 1 John insists that one must confess that Christ has come in the flesh (4:2). Second John 7 likewise identified as deceivers those who did not confess the incarnation of the Messiah. The letters therefore are concerned with correcting a false belief about Christ that was spreading in the churches.

From this emphasis on the incarnation, it can be assumed that the opponents held to the divinity of Christ but either denied or diminished the significance of His humanity. Their view might be an early form of Docetism (from the Greek verb *dokeo*, which means "to seem"), the heresy that emerged in the second century and that claimed Jesus only seemed to be human.

According to early church tradition, another form of heresy that John might have attacked was led by a man named Cerinthus. He contended that Christ's spirit descended on the human Jesus at His baptism but left Him before His crucifixion. John wrote that the Jesus who was baptized at the beginning of His ministry was the same person who was crucified on the cross (1 John 5:6).

In light of the circumstances of the epistle, the apostle emphasized that a person's behavior was naturally a result of that person's belief. John taught that those who are truly born again have been given a new nature, which gives evidence of itself in obedience to God and love for others.

The apostle wrote to bring back the fellowship and joy that were missing from the church (1:3-4). He sought to help his readers live in spiritual victory rather than in defeat (2:1). John endeavored to expose the deceivers among his readers as well as remind the latter about the truth they needed to embrace (2:26; 4:1-3). The apostle wanted to reassure believers of the certainty of their salvation (5:13).

NOTES ON THE PRINTED TEXT

In 1 John, the Greek word rendered *love* appears numerous times. Quite a few of the occurrences are in 4:7—5:3. John summarized all he had to say about love when he indicated that mutual compassion among the members of the Body of Christ was the aim of the Gospel *message you have heard from the beginning* (3:11).

The presence of love among Christians is evidence that conversion has occurred (3:14). Love is an attribute of those who possess eternal life, while hatred is an attribute of those who have opted for eternal death. In fact, those *who hate a brother or sister* (3:15) spread death to others, for to hate is to murder. Those who possess eternal life do not spread death. Conversely, those who spread death do not possess eternal life.

John went on to explain how the good news about the sacrificial death of Jesus as a payment for sins was motivated by love and should result in love among believers in Jesus. Christ set the pattern for sacrificial love when *he laid down his life for us* (3:16). We know love because we know what Jesus did on our behalf. We can identify true love in ourselves and others by comparing it to the love of Jesus. As John noted, *everyone who loves is born of God and knows God* (4:7).

Christlike love is not innate to people. It is innate to God, for *God is love* (4:8). When John called his readers *beloved* (4:7) and urged them to *love one another*, he knew that his love and their love had to come *from God*. Earlier John had connected the presence of love and the presence of eternal life (3:14). In 4:7, the apostle claimed that *love* evidenced not only new birth but also mature knowledge of God. On the other hand, anyone who is unloving is ignorant of God's character and God's way of dealing with people (4:8).

John spelled out in greater detail how God revealed His love through His Son. First, the Son entered human experience by means of His incarnation (4:9). The goal of Jesus' incarnation was that people might receive eternal life. Accordingly, the atonement had to follow the incarnation. Jesus became *the atoning sacrifice for our sins* (4:10). Jesus' death appeased the wrath of God aroused by sin and washed away human guilt. Here we see that God initiated love and we responded.

There was no Christlike love in humanity until God demonstrated it for us. There were glimpses of such love throughout the Old Testament, but the full demonstration was seen in Jesus' sacrificial death. By way of analogy, we are to love as Jesus did (4:11). We are to be willing to lay down our lives for our fellow Christians in the little demands of everyday life and in the ultimate demands of extreme circumstances.

God is spirit and not visible to human sight (4:12); however, God has a way of making His presence known. In these last days, He revealed Himself through His incarnated Son (Heb. 1:2). Additionally, God reveals Himself through the loving deeds of His spiritual children. God, in a sense, incarnates Himself in our acts of love. *God lives in us* (1 John 4:12) as we love. John insisted that God's love *is perfected in us*. God intends that the fullest expression of His love on earth come through the united love of all His redeemed people around the globe.

Such a grand objective cannot be realized apart from divine enablement. We can reveal God's love as we abide in Him and He abides in us (4:13). The Holy Spirit works to achieve this reciprocal abiding by dwelling in God's people as His gift to them.

John and the other apostles had borne eyewitness testimony to the Father's activity through the Son, especially that He is the *Savior of the world* (4:14). The result was that many had confessed Jesus as the *Son of God* (4:15) and as their Savior. This set in motion the mutual abiding of God in redeemed people and people in God. Ultimately, then, we experience God's love in Christ. Therefore, we know His love and we believe that He is *love* (4:16). We imitate His love and thereby share in His life and open our lives to His presence and control.

SUGGESTIONS TO TEACHERS

John believed that love between believers in Jesus is a major outcome of faith in Him as the Son of God and the Savior of the world. Jesus taught this truth to His disciples in the upper room on the night before His death when He said, *"I give you a new commandment, that you love one another. Just as I have loved you, you also should love one another. By this everyone will know that you are my disciples, if you have love for one another"* (John 13:34-35).

1. A MATTER OF LIFE AND DEATH. The presence of Christlike love indicates the presence of the life of God in a person. The absence of such love indicates the presence of death in a person. Anyone who hates others is condemned as a murderer by Jesus' teaching in the Sermon on the Mount (Matt. 5:21-22). Sacrificial love is not optional for a child of God. It should not be regarded as something extraordinary. Sacrificial love should be the norm.

2. A MATTER OF KNOWING GOD. Sacrificial love is a normal character trait of God. It is not a normal character trait of human beings. People learn to love sacrificially when they share in the life of God through spiritual rebirth. Jesus modeled this sacrificial love when He died on the cross as the atoning sacrifice for our sins. As we comprehend the love of Jesus and the love of His Father, we will be changed by love so that we can love sacrificially as well.

3. A MATTER OF SHOWING GOD. A small part of the world once glimpsed God by seeing the love of His incarnate Son. Now God wants the whole world to see Him through the sacrificial love His adopted children show one another. God is spirit and invisible to human sight. His abiding presence can be seen through our Spirit-empowered lives of love. The testimony of eyewitnesses has set in motion a fellowship between God and those of us who have never seen Him. His love makes Him real to us, and our love makes Him real to one another.

FOR ADULTS

■ **TOPIC:** Love One Another

■ **QUESTIONS:** 1. What is the message John said had been heard from the beginning? 2. What does it mean to love in a Christlike way? 3. In what sense is God love? 4. Why is it important for believers to love one another sacrificially? 5. How can believers improve the way they show Christlike love to one another?

■ **ILLUSTRATIONS:**

Building with Love. An older carpenter prepared to retire. He told the contractor he worked for about his plans to stop building and to enjoy a more leisurely life with his wife and extended family. He would miss the paycheck, but he needed to retire. They could get by.

The contractor was sorry to see his good worker go and asked whether he would build just one more house as a personal favor. The carpenter agreed, but in time it was easy to see that his heart wasn't in his work. He grew careless and took shortcuts on quality. It was an unfortunate way to end his career. When the carpenter finished the house, the contractor handed him the front-door key. "This is your house," the contractor said. "It's my gift to you in appreciation for all your dedicated work."

If the carpenter had known he was building his own house, he would have done it all so differently. We build our lives every day by the way we express God's love to those around us. Our love should be like the love of Jesus—only the highest quality—so that our lives will be like His, too.

Love Sacrifices for Others. During the Great Depression of the 1930s, thousands of displaced people wound up in tent cities in California where they had gone searching for nonexistent jobs. One day a man and woman worked their way through one of these tent cities inviting boys and girls to go to Sunday school. They invited a ten-year-old girl whose father was an alcoholic and whose older sisters were prostitutes. The girl herself likely was headed toward necessity-driven prostitution. But this couple came the next Sunday and took the ragged little girl to church. After church, they took her home with them and fed her. Week after week they showed her love. Eventually the girl came to know Christ as Savior.

Three of that girl's sons served as pastors. As the twenty-first century moves along, three of her grandchildren pastor churches. Other descendants teach Sunday school and lead worship as musicians. The nameless couple in California invested a lot of time in a ragged child many would have ignored. Who knows whether this couple's sacrifice seemed great or small at the time? They loved a neglected child and changed the course of one branch of a family tree.

Hate Kills. When Elizabeth Barrett married the famous poet Robert Browning, her parents were so upset that they disowned her. She and her husband settled far from England in Florence, Italy. Elizabeth loved her mother and father and pursued reconciliation with them. Several times a month she wrote expressive, loving letters.

After ten years of no response, a package came from Elizabeth's parents. It was a happy moment for her as she opened it. Inside she found all of the letters she had sent—unopened. Like her husband, Elizabeth Barrett Browning was a poet. Her letters seeking reconciliation were eloquent. But her parents never read them. What must have happened in the soul of Elizabeth when she felt the full impact of her parents' cruelty and rejection? Did it feel like death?

Love's Cost-Benefit Analysis. "We become vulnerable when we love people and go out of our way to help them," declared wealthy industrialist Charles Schwab after winning a nuisance lawsuit at age 70. Given permission by the judge to speak to the audience, he made the following statement: "I'd like to say here in a court of law, and speaking as an old man, that nine-tenths of my troubles are traceable to my being kind to others. Look, you young people, if you want to steer away from trouble, be hard-boiled. Be quick with a good loud 'no' to anyone and everyone. If you follow this rule, you will seldom be bothered as you tread life's pathway. Except you'll have no friends, you'll be lonely, and you won't have any fun!" Schwab's point is that love may bring heartache, but it's worth it! God's point is that love costs, but it pays divine dividends.

FOR YOUTH

■ **TOPIC:** A Love-Filled Life

■ **QUESTIONS:** 1. What does it mean to love another? 2. How is the new birth connected with showing Christlike love? 3. Why did the Father send His Son into the world? 4. Who are some people you know that need the unconditional love of Christ? 5. Why is it so hard at times for us to be Christlike in our compassion to others?

■ **ILLUSTRATIONS:**

Love Gives Life. During their second month of nursing school, the student nurses walked into a class and faced a pop quiz. Most students breezed through the early questions. Then one by one they reacted in confusion to the last item on the quiz. It read: "What is the first name of the woman who cleans this building?" The students thought this was some kind of joke. They had seen the cleaning woman. She was tall, dark-haired, and in her 50s, but how could they know her name? Most left the last item blank when they handed in their quiz papers.

At the end of class, one brave nurse asked if the last question would count toward the quiz grade. "Absolutely," said the professor. "In your careers you will meet many people. All are significant. They deserve your attention and care, even if all you do is smile and say hello." By day's end all the nurses knew that the cleaning lady was named Dorothy.

The student nurses learned a lesson in humility. The cleaning lady felt as though she were the most important person in the school. Love lifted her from obscurity to first-name friendship with everyone.

Laying Down Your Life. Author and lecturer Leo Buscaglia once was asked to judge a contest to identify and reward the most caring child in the area. Buscaglia selected a four-year-old child, whose next-door neighbor was an elderly gentleman who had recently lost his wife. Upon seeing the man cry, the little boy went into the old gentleman's yard, climbed onto his lap and just sat there. When his mother asked him what he had said to the neighbor, the little boy said, "Nothing. I just helped him cry" (Jack Canfield and Mark Victor Hansen, *A 3rd Serving of Chicken Soup for the Soul*).

Christlike love probably makes more little sacrifices than big ones. Sometimes we miss the most important acts of love because we think love must make dramatic sacrifices. Love pays attention to who needs what and tries to help.

Love One Another. After an accident in which she lost her arm, a girl named Jamie refused to go to school or church for an entire year. Finally the young teen thought she could face her peers. In preparation, her mother called her Sunday school teacher and asked that he not call attention to Jamie. The teacher promised, but when he got sick one Sunday and had to call a substitute, he forgot to tell the second teacher. At the conclusion of the lesson that day, which was about inviting friends to church, the substitute led the class in doing the hand motions to the familiar children's poem:

Here's the church.
Here's the steeple.

Open the doors.

See all the people.

Jamie's eyes filled with tears. A 13-year-old boy realized how she must be feeling. He knelt beside her. With one hand apiece, they made the church, steeple, and people. Jamie laughed, and the boy felt like a hero. What was heroic was recognizing Jamie's pain—when no one else noticed—and carrying it for her for five minutes.

Share God's Life. The article "What Good Is a Tree?" in *Reader's Digest* says that when the roots of trees begin to mingle, a strange fungus grows among them. This fungus facilitates an interaction among the roots of the trees—even between trees of dissimilar species. A whole forest may be linked together. If one tree has access to water, another to nutrients, and a third to sunlight, the trees have the means to share with one another. Love certainly isn't a fungus, but it has the ability to link God's people together and disperse the life of God among them.

LIVE WITH CONFIDENCE

BACKGROUND SCRIPTURE: 1 John 5
DEVOTIONAL READING: Romans 5:1-11

KEY VERSE: This is the testimony: God gave us
eternal life, and this life is in his Son. 1 John 5:11.

KING JAMES VERSION

1 JOHN 5:1 Whosoever believeth that Jesus is the Christ is born of God: and every one that loveth him that begat loveth him also that is begotten of him.

2 By this we know that we love the children of God, when we love God, and keep his commandments.

3 For this is the love of God, that we keep his commandments: and his commandments are not grievous.

4 For whatsoever is born of God overcometh the world: and this is the victory that overcometh the world, even our faith.

5 Who is he that overcometh the world, but he that believeth that Jesus is the Son of God?

6 This is he that came by water and blood, even Jesus Christ; not by water only, but by water and blood. And it is the Spirit that beareth witness, because the Spirit is truth.

7 For there are three that bear record in heaven, the Father, the Word, and the Holy Ghost: and these three are one.

8 And there are three that bear witness in earth, the Spirit, and the water, and the blood: and these three agree in one.

9 If we receive the witness of men, the witness of God is greater: for this is the witness of God which he hath testified of his Son.

10 He that believeth on the Son of God hath the witness in himself: he that believeth not God hath made him a liar; because he believeth not the record that God gave of his Son.

11 And this is the record, that God hath given to us eternal life, and this life is in his Son.

12 He that hath the Son hath life; and he that hath not the Son of God hath not life.

13 These things have I written unto you that believe on the name of the Son of God; that ye may know that ye have eternal life, and that ye may believe on the name of the Son of God.

14 And this is the confidence that we have in him, that, if we ask any thing according to his will, he heareth us:

15 And if we know that he hear us, whatsoever we ask, we know that we have the petitions that we desired of him.

NEW REVISED STANDARD VERSION

1 JOHN 5:1 Everyone who believes that Jesus is the Christ has been born of God, and everyone who loves the parent loves the child. 2 By this we know that we love the children of God, when we love God and obey his commandments. 3 For the love of God is this, that we obey his commandments. And his commandments are not burdensome, 4 for whatever is born of God conquers the world. And this is the victory that conquers the world, our faith. 5 Who is it that conquers the world but the one who believes that Jesus is the Son of God?

6 This is the one who came by water and blood, Jesus Christ, not with the water only but with the water and the blood. And the Spirit is the one that testifies, for the Spirit is the truth. 7 There are three that testify: 8 the Spirit and the water and the blood, and these three agree. 9 If we receive human testimony, the testimony of God is greater; for this is the testimony of God that he has testified to his Son. 10 Those who believe in the Son of God have the testimony in their hearts. Those who do not believe in God have made him a liar by not believing in the testimony that God has given concerning his Son. 11 And this is the testimony: God gave us eternal life, and this life is in his Son. 12 Whoever has the Son has life; whoever does not have the Son of God does not have life.

13 I write these things to you who believe in the name of the Son of God, so that you may know that you have eternal life.

14 And this is the boldness we have in him, that if we ask anything according to his will, he hears us. 15 And if we know that he hears us in whatever we ask, we know that we have obtained the requests made of him.

HOME BIBLE READINGS

BACKGROUND

As an eyewitness of the events of Jesus' ministry, death, and resurrection, John bore testimony to all he saw so that his readers could enjoy fellowship with the Father, the Son, and the community of believers in Jesus (1 John 1:1-3). This week's lesson text develops the concept of "testimony" introduced in 1:2. John supplied several witnesses in keeping with Old Testament laws of evidence. Two of John's witnesses, *water and blood* (5:6) in the life of Jesus, strike modern readers as odd.

The Old Testament law required two or three witnesses to establish the judicial certainty of a matter. *Only on the evidence of two or three witnesses shall a charge be sustained* (Deut. 19:15). This principle was especially important in capital cases. *A person must not be put to death on the evidence of only one witness* (17:6).

When the witnesses who testified against Jesus at His trial could not provide a unified testimony (Mark 14:55-59), He should have been released on the basis of the Mosaic law. In the church, Paul prescribed this standard for handling charges against elders. *Never accept any accusation against an elder except on the evidence of two or three witnesses* (1 Tim. 5:19).

John presented three witnesses to the person and work of Jesus: *the Spirit and the water and the blood* (1 John 5:8). There are various ways to understand this verse. Some equate the *water* and the *blood* with two ordinances: baptism and the Lord's Supper. Others connect the passage with the spear thrust into the side of Jesus and the blood and water that came out of the wound (John 19:34-35).

Another view finds a link to Christ's birth in the *water* (1 John 5:6) and to His death in the *blood*. The most widely held view makes the water and the blood references to Christ's baptism and death. Support for this notion is found in the fact that Jesus began His earthly ministry with His baptism and He ended it with His crucifixion.

John insisted that the witness of Jesus' baptism and death testified to different conclusions than those proposed by the false teachers the apostle was combating. Jesus had recognized His redemptive mission long before His baptism (Luke 2:41-52). At His baptism, the descending Spirit and the Father's voice from heaven did not mark the arrival of the Son in human flesh, but the beginning of the road to the cross (3:21-22). On the cross, the Son of God shed His blood for the sins of the world (Mark 15:39). Until Jesus returns, the Spirit of God will continue to testify through the water and the blood in the Christian observances of baptism and the Lord's Supper.

NOTES ON THE PRINTED TEXT

As John wound down his epistle, he encouraged his readers to build their Christian lives around the virtues of faith, love, and obedience. Faith involves a body of content and a relationship with God and His children (1 John 5:1-2). The necessary content of faith is that *Jesus is the Christ* (5:1). That simple statement in the context of 1 John includes the truth of Jesus' incarnation, His atonement, His bodily resurrection, and His future return.

The relationship of faith begins with new birth into the family of God and matures into love of God and His children shown by obedience to God's commands (5:2). Love demonstrates two things in this text. Love for God's children is evidence of love for their heavenly Father (5:1), and love for God is also evidence of love for His children (5:2). This intertwined reasoning is true because love for God expresses itself in obedience to His command to lay down our lives for one another (3:16-18).

John insisted that God's commands *are not burdensome* (5:3). In fact, sacrificial love is very difficult, but difficult does not necessarily equal burdensome. After all, Jesus said that His yoke is easy and His burden light (Matt. 11:30). The yoke of obedient discipleship is easy because it is shared; but it is still a yoke. The burden—another symbol for the same obedient life—is light because the Lord bears it with us. God's assistance flows through all who are born of Him so that we conquer *the world* (1 John 5:4).

Our initial victory over the world comes through the faith that leads to new birth. Our daily victory over the world comes through the faith that continually confesses *that Jesus is the Son of God* (5:5). Victory over the world is initial escape from the devil's control (5:19) and ongoing conquest of sinful patterns represented by *the desire of the flesh, the desire of the eyes, the pride in riches* (2:16).

The confession that *Jesus is the Son of God* (5:5) challenged the views John attributed to *the antichrist* (2:22). The latter entity insisted that the Son of God could never take on flesh and suffer as Jesus did on the cross.

The arrival of Jesus as the Savior of the world was marked by two major events, represented by *water and blood* (5:6). The baptism of Jesus and the crucifixion of Jesus bore witness to His deity and His divine mission. The baptism was validated by the descending Spirit and the voice of the Father (Luke 3:22). The crucifixion was validated as the atonement for our sins by the resurrection and ascension of Jesus (1 Pet. 1:18-21).

The Holy Spirit affirms the testimony of the *water and blood* (1 John 5:6). Because *the Spirit is the truth*, His testimony can be trusted. In fact, *there are three that testify* (5:7). The Spirit, the water, and the blood are in total harmony about the full humanity and full deity of Jesus (5:8). The God-man is the one whose life, death, and resurrection move us to faith, love, and obedience.

The false teachers could produce nothing more than *human testimony* (5:9) to support their theories about Jesus, and many people believed them. John insisted that he, as an apostle and eyewitness, conveyed the superior *testimony of God.* John appealed to his readers to recognize *in their hearts* (5:10) the testimony of God concerning Jesus.

John summarized God's testimony about Jesus this way: *eternal life* (5:11)—namely, fellowship with the Father, Son, and people of God—flows from a relationship with Jesus, who is God's Son. To have a relationship with the Son is to have life, while to miss that relationship is to miss life (5:12).

In 5:13-15, John listed and briefly developed three certainties of new life in Christ. The first is that those *who believe in the name of the Son of God* (5:13) can know they have eternal life. Jesus is the Son of God. Eternal fellowship with the Father through the Son is not a philosophical speculation or a vague hope. It is a certainty for people of faith.

Second, John insisted that we can be bold to *ask anything according to [God's] will* (5:14), and know that He is paying attention to our petitions. Jesus taught in the Lord's Prayer that His disciples should pray for the perfect expression of God's will on earth (Matt. 6:10); and in the garden of Gethsemane, Jesus modeled submission to the Father's will by dying on the cross for humanity's sins (Mark 14:36).

The third certainty is that, when God hears our prayers, which accord with His will, *we have obtained the requests made of him* (1 John 5:15). The challenge of this verse is not to discover how to get God to do things for us; rather, it is to synchronize the passion of our hearts with the passion of God—through faith, love, and obedience—so that we are fully submissive to the will of God in our lives.

SUGGESTIONS TO TEACHERS

A confident life is one of fellowship with the Father, the Son, and God's people (1 John 1:1-3). In the last chapter of his first epistle, the apostle summarized the qualities a person needs to respond to God, the evidence a person should accept, and the attitudes that characterize eternal life in fellowship with God.

1. THREE VIRTUES. Faith accepts that Jesus is truly human and truly divine. Love obeys God and sacrifices itself for God's children. Obedience produces a life that overcomes the world. These three virtues are the heart of John's practical theology of Christian living.

2. THREE WITNESSES. Tertullian (A.D. 150–222) is the earliest known interpreter who suggested water and blood in 1 John 5:6-8 refer to the baptism and death of Jesus (Barker, *Expositor's Bible Commentary*). Jesus' baptism was important because He identified completely with all sinful people, who needed to accept John the Baptist's message of repentance. Jesus showed His full humanity when He accepted that baptism, even though He was sinless. Jesus was the spotless Lamb of God who shed His blood for the sins of the world (1 Pet. 1:19). The Holy Spirit continually testifies about Jesus and exalts Him (John 16:14).

3. THREE CERTAINTIES. John claimed that he wrote his first epistle so that his readers could know they had eternal life (1 John 5:13). To be certain about that is to remove life's greatest concern. Where will we spend eternity? The second certainty is that God hears every prayer offered according to His will. This assures us that He pays attention to us. The third certainty is that God grants every prayer uttered according to His will. This assures us that we can partner with God in bringing His kingdom to earth. A life lived by these certainties is a confident one indeed!

FOR ADULTS

■ **TOPIC:** Live with Confidence

■ **QUESTIONS:** 1. Why is it important to believe that Jesus is the promised Messiah? 2. Why is it important to obey God's commands? 3. Why is it important to affirm the full deity and full humanity of Jesus? 4. How can we avoid making obedience to God an intolerable burden? 5. How can we help other believers recognize the assurance of salvation they have in Christ?

■ **ILLUSTRATIONS:**

Keep Your First Love. Jerome, the sixth-century translator of the Latin Vulgate, related that the apostle John, when he became old, used to go among the churches around Ephesus, everywhere repeating the words, "Little children, love one another." John's disciples, wearied by the constant repetition, asked him why he always said this. "Because," the apostle replied, "it is the Lord's commandment; and if it only be fulfilled, it is enough." John knew that the greatest truth was most apt to be forgotten because it often gets taken for granted.

Obedience Builds Character. In the eleventh century, King Henry III of Bavaria grew tired of court life and the pressures of being a monarch. He made application to Prior Richard at a local monastery, asking to be accepted as a contemplative and spend the rest of his life in the monastery. "Your Majesty," said Prior Richard, "do you understand that the pledge here is one of obedience? That will be hard because you have been a king."

"I understand," said Henry. "The rest of my life I will be obedient to you, as Christ leads you."

"Then I will tell you what to do," said Prior Richard. "Go back to your throne and serve faithfully in the place where God has put you."

When King Henry died, a statement was written: "The King learned to rule by being obedient." When we tire of our roles and responsibilities, it helps to remember that God has planted us in a certain place and told us to be a good accountant or teacher or mother or father. Christ expects us to be faithful where He puts us, and when Jesus returns, we'll rule together with Him.

Connecting to God. Lawrence of Arabia visited Paris with some Arab friends after World War I. He showed them all the sights of the City of Light, but what fascinated them most were the faucets in their hotel room. They spent hours turning it on and off. They marveled that all they had to do was turn the handle, and they could get all the water they wanted.

When the time came to leave, Lawrence found his guests in the bathroom trying to detach the faucet. They explained, "It is very dry in Arabia. What we need are faucets. If we have them, we will have all the water we want." Lawrence had to explain that the effectiveness of the faucets lay in their connection to the pipeline.

Prayer is effective when it is connected to the will of God and draws power from that divine will.

Thy Will Be Done. The Bible scholar F.B. Meyer preached in London, England, at the same time as Charles Spurgeon and G. Campbell Morgan. They were all great preachers, but Spurgeon's and Morgan's churches were both bigger than Meyer's. He confessed being a bit envious of them.

So Meyer prayed, asking God to tell him what to do about this troubling jealousy. He sensed God instructing him to pray for both Spurgeon and Morgan, that their churches would prosper and that more and more people would come to them.

Meyer didn't want to pray that way, but he knew he should obey the Lord. He prayed diligently that Spurgeon's and Morgan's churches would grow. In the end Meyer insisted, "Their churches grew so much in answer to my prayers, that they overflowed. The overflow," he said, "filled my church."

FOR YOUTH
■ TOPIC: Confident Living
■ QUESTIONS: 1. Why is loving God's children an important thing to do? 2. To what does the Spirit testify? 3. How is it possible for believers to pray to God with boldness? 4. How has God lately answered your prayers to Him? 5. How has God recently enabled you to witness for Him to your peers?

■ **ILLUSTRATIONS:**

Love Me Tender. In the nineteenth century, British Prime Minister William Gladstone announced in the House of Commons the death of Princess Alice, daughter of Queen Victoria. Gladstone related how Princess Alice's small daughter had become gravely ill with diphtheria. The physicians had told the princess not to kiss her daughter at the peril of her own health. As her child struggled to breathe, princess Alice had taken the little one into her arms to keep her from choking to death. Rasping and wheezing, the child begged, "Momma, kiss me!" Alice kissed her daughter. She contracted diphtheria and some days thereafter she died, and the prime minister made his announcement.

Real love forgets self. Real love forgets danger. Real love doesn't count the cost.

Routine Obedience. The preacher said, "We think giving our all to the Lord is like taking a thousand dollar bill and laying it on the table. 'Here's my life, Lord. I'm giving it all.'"

"But the reality for most of us is that God sends us to the bank and has us cash in the thousand dollar bill for quarters. We go through life putting out 25 cents here and 50 cents there. We listen to the neighbor kid's troubles instead of saying, 'Get lost.' We go to a committee meeting instead of doing what we want to do. We give a cup of water to a shaky old man in a nursing home instead of hanging out with our friends. Usually giving our life to Christ isn't glorious. It's done in all those little acts of love, 25 cents at a time. It would be easy to go out in a flash of glory; it's harder to live the Christian life little by little over the long haul."

The preacher is right.

God Pays Attention. A man's wife died and suddenly he was mother and father to a six-year-old son. After the funeral, the father and son went home, both feeling alone and lost. That night as they prepared for bed, the boy asked, "Daddy, may I sleep in your room tonight, too?"

Neither one could go to sleep. They tossed and turned until late in the night. Finally, the little boy said, "Daddy, are you looking at me? Because if you are, I think I can go to sleep."

The father answered, "Yes son, I'm looking at you."

The little boy relaxed and fell asleep. After a while the father got out of bed, walked over to the window, and pulled back the curtain. He looked up into the starry sky and said, "Father, are You looking at me? Because if You are, I think I can rest and be at peace."

Thy Will Be Done. One night a father heard his young daughter speaking, although she was alone in her room. The door was ajar, so that he could see that she was kneeling beside her bed in prayer.

Interested to find out how his little girl would talk to God, the father paused outside the girl's door and listened. After tuning in to her speech, the father was puzzled to hear her reciting the alphabet: "A, B, C, D, E, F, G . . ." The girl went all the way through the alphabet three or four times. The father didn't want to interrupt her, but soon curiosity got the best of him and he broke into the prayer.

"Honey," he asked, "what are you doing?"

"I'm praying, Daddy."

"Well, why are you praying the alphabet?"

"I started my prayers, but I wasn't sure what to ask for. I decided to just say all the letters of the alphabet and let God put them together however He thinks best."

REMAIN LOYAL

BACKGROUND SCRIPTURE: 2 and 3 John
DEVOTIONAL READING: John 15:1-8

KEY VERSE: Beloved, do not imitate what is evil but imitate what is good. Whoever does good is from God; whoever does evil has not seen God. 3 John 11.

KING JAMES VERSION

2 JOHN 4 I rejoiced greatly that I found of thy children walking in truth, as we have received a commandment from the Father.

5 And now I beseech thee, lady, not as though I wrote a new commandment unto thee, but that which we had from the beginning, that we love one another. 6 And this is love, that we walk after his commandments. This is the commandment, That, as ye have heard from the beginning, ye should walk in it.

7 For many deceivers are entered into the world, who confess not that Jesus Christ is come in the flesh. This is a deceiver and an antichrist. 8 Look to yourselves, that we lose not those things which we have wrought, but that we receive a full reward. 9 Whosoever transgresseth, and abideth not in the doctrine of Christ, hath not God. He that abideth in the doctrine of Christ, he hath both the Father and the Son. . . .

3 JOHN 3 For I rejoiced greatly, when the brethren came and testified of the truth that is in thee, even as thou walkest in the truth. 4 I have no greater joy than to hear that my children walk in truth. 5 Beloved, thou doest faithfully whatsoever thou doest to the brethren, and to strangers; 6 Which have borne witness of thy charity before the church: whom if thou bring forward on their journey after a godly sort, thou shalt do well: 7 Because that for his name's sake they went forth, taking nothing of the Gentiles. 8 We therefore ought to receive such, that we might be fellowhelpers to the truth.

9 I wrote unto the church: but Diotrephes, who loveth to have the preeminence among them, receiveth us not. 10 Wherefore, if I come, I will remember his deeds which he doeth, prating against us with malicious words: and not content therewith, neither doth he himself receive the brethren, and forbiddeth them that would, and casteth them out of the church. 11 Beloved, follow not that which is evil, but that which is good. He that doeth good is of God: but he that doeth evil hath not seen God.

NEW REVISED STANDARD VERSION

2 JOHN 4 I was overjoyed to find some of your children walking in the truth, just as we have been commanded by the Father. 5 But now, dear lady, I ask you, not as though I were writing you a new commandment, but one we have had from the beginning, let us love one another. 6 And this is love, that we walk according to his commandments; this is the commandment just as you have heard it from the beginning—you must walk in it.

7 Many deceivers have gone out into the world, those who do not confess that Jesus Christ has come in the flesh; any such person is the deceiver and the antichrist! 8 Be on your guard, so that you do not lose what we have worked for, but may receive a full reward. 9 Everyone who does not abide in the teaching of Christ, but goes beyond it, does not have God; whoever abides in the teaching has both the Father and the Son. . . .

3 JOHN 3 I was overjoyed when some of the friends arrived and testified to your faithfulness to the truth, namely how you walk in the truth. 4 I have no greater joy than this, to hear that my children are walking in the truth.

5 Beloved, you do faithfully whatever you do for the friends, even though they are strangers to you; 6 they have testified to your love before the church. You will do well to send them on in a manner worthy of God; 7 for they began their journey for the sake of Christ, accepting no support from non-believers. 8 Therefore we ought to support such people, so that we may become co-workers with the truth.

9 I have written something to the church; but Diotrephes, who likes to put himself first, does not acknowledge our authority. 10 So if I come, I will call attention to what he is doing in spreading false charges against us. And not content with those charges, he refuses to welcome the friends, and even prevents those who want to do so and expels them from the church.

11 Beloved, do not imitate what is evil but imitate what is good. Whoever does good is from God; whoever does evil has not seen God. 12 Everyone has testified favorably about Demetrius, and so has the truth itself. We also testify for him, and you know that our testimony is true.

HOME BIBLE READINGS

BACKGROUND

Second and Third John were written shortly after John's first letter. They respond to problems associated with the same false teaching the apostle addressed in 1 John. Second John anticipated the arrival of traveling false teachers at outlying churches around Ephesus and encouraged true believers to refuse hospitality to them. Third John was sent to a church in which key leaders resented and resisted the authority of the apostle John. John felt concern that such a church was ripe for heresy.

In these two brief epistles, John refers to himself *as the elder* (2 John 1; 3 John 1). That title hearkened back to the historic leaders in the Jewish community. It identified the writer as a current authority in local church affairs. John probably chose "elder" over the more commanding title "apostle" to press his case on the less threatening basis of his advanced years and his long involvement with the group of churches around Ephesus.

Second John was addressed to *the elect lady and her children* (2 John 1) and concluded with greetings from *the children of your elect sister* (13). Are *the elect lady* (1) and her *sister* (13) women of stature in the church or symbols for two churches? Are *the children* physical offspring of literal women or spiritual off-spring of the Gospel? The Greek word translated *lady* (1) is the feminine form of "lord." It's a formal title, not a mere synonym for "woman." This favors literal women of noble birth or character.

However, the letter is not a deeply personal note to an individual but a general exhortation meant for a group. In verses 1 through 7 and verse 13, all occurrences of the Greek pronoun rendered *you* are singular in number. In verses 8 through 12, all occurrences of *you* are plural. It seems probable that John was addressing a church and its members under the metaphor of a noblewoman and her offspring.

Third John is populated with a cast of characters about whom nothing is known beyond what can be inferred from the epistle: Gaius (1), Diotrephes (9), and Demetrius (12). Gaius was a common Roman name. Diotrephes and Demetrius were Greek names. Demetrius was more common because a series of kings of ancient Macedon had carried the name. At least two other New Testament figures bear the name Gaius (Gaius from Derbe, Acts 19:29; 20:4; and Gaius from Corinth, Rom. 16:23; 1 Cor. 1:14). The silversmith who started a riot in Ephesus because Paul and Silas were preaching the Gospel was named Demetrius (Acts 19:24, 38). There is no reason—other than sharing common names—to connect either Gaius or the Ephesian Demetrius from 30 years earlier with the Gaius and Demetrius in 3 John.

NOTES ON THE PRINTED TEXT

John wrote his last two epistles to encourage his readers to live lives focused on love and obedience. When he wrote *the elect lady* (2 John 1), he could say he *was overjoyed to find some of [her] children walking in the truth* (4). *Walking in the truth* (2 John 4; 3 John 4) was John's shorthand expression for believing in the full deity and full humanity of Jesus, loving God and His children, and obeying His commands. John had to acknowledge that only some of the members of this congregation walked in the truth.

Therefore, John felt the need to repeat his favorite admonition to the churches: *let us love one another* (2 John 5). As he had noted in 1 John 2:7, the apostle stated that this commandment had been around since the Gospel was first proclaimed (John 13:34). Once again John defined love for God as keeping His commandments (2 John 6).

John regretted to inform the church he was writing that *many deceivers have gone out into the world* (7) from the mother church in Ephesus. These false teachers denied the full humanity of Christ, teaching that Jesus was the best of people. Supposedly, Jesus had served as the vessel for the Christ from His baptism to shortly before His crucifixion. Any such false teacher John consistently labeled *the deceiver and the antichrist.*

John wanted all Christians to lead purposeful lives and guard against false teachers (8). The apostle did not want the members of this church to lose the benefits and blessings of the Christian life for which John and others had labored so long in preaching the Gospel and teaching sound doctrine. John's desire as *the elder* (1) was to see all the members of the churches *receive a full reward* (8) at the second coming of Christ.

John was concerned that not all who claimed the name of Christ had truly come to know Him in a saving way. The apostle envisioned those who, when they were taught about Christ, did not make their spiritual homes in the truth. Instead, they went beyond the bounds of truth and pitched their spiritual tents on heretical ground (9). Such counterfeit believers did not possess the eternal life that consists of fellowship with the Father, Son, and community of true believers.

Third John was written to an individual named Gaius (1), a leader in an unidentified church perhaps somewhere near Ephesus. John wrote to Gaius in response to a report from traveling evangelists who had returned to John at Ephesus from the church Gaius led (3). The apostle commended Gaius for *your faithfulness to the truth.* John found it his supreme joy *to hear that my children are walking in the truth* (4).

Specifically, John commended Gaius for providing generous hospitality to the traveling evangelists from Ephesus when they were in his area (5). Gaius had faithfully cared for the evangelists, even though they were total strangers to him when they first met. The evangelists had been so impressed with Gaius' kindness that they had told the Ephesian church about him (6). John counted on Gaius to provide hospitality for these same evangelists who were returning. Perhaps they carried the letter we know as 3 John. The apostle urged Gaius to furnish the means for them to go to their next destination.

The evangelists were totally dependent on the support of those they served *for the sake of Christ* (7). They accepted *no support from non-believers*. They depended on Christians like Gaius who lived purposeful lives by walking in the truth. John editorialized that all Christians *ought to support such people, so that we may become co-workers with the truth* (8). Believers who invest their resources and time into the ministries of effective servants of Christ share in the results and blessings of those ministries.

John turned from commending Gaius and addressed some pointed criticism at Diotrephes. John apparently had written an earlier apostolic letter to the church, Diotrephes had suppressed it, and it had not been read (9). John did not fault Diotrephes in terms of his theology about Jesus. He was not an antichrist. Diotrephes' fault was personal: he *likes to put himself first.*

Diotrephes was proud and intent on keeping control of his congregation at all costs. John accused Diotrephes of spreading lies about him and refusing to give John's representatives an audience in his church (10). Diotrephes had gone so far as to excommunicate those in his church who supported the evangelists from John.

John intended to visit the congregation and expose the power politics of Diotrephes. The apostle urged Gaius to pursue a different path of service in his church (11). If he was to pursue a purposeful Christian life, he must not *imitate what is evil but imitate what is good.*

Purposeful Christians should follow the examples of people who pursue moral excellence. Diotrephes was a mentor whose evil example should be shunned. Those who devote themselves to good reveal by their lives that they belong to God. Those who devote themselves to evil reveal by their lives that they have no relationship with God.

SUGGESTIONS TO TEACHERS

John, now an aged apostle, appealed to his spiritual children as *the elder* (2 John 1; 3 John 1). He commended devotion to truth, love, and obedience where he found it and urged those slipping away from this devotion to return to their first allegiance to Christ.

1. BE LOVING. The first article of the truth of the Gospel, as far as John was concerned, is that we should *love one another* (2 John 5). In his Gospel and in the

Epistle of First John, the apostle defined love as sacrificing one's self for the welfare of a fellow human being (John 15:13; 1 John 3:16). John reminded those who walked in love to keep to that path.

2. BE ON GUARD. If the command to love was the positive note in all of John's letters, the negative note in them was a warning against teachers who denied the full humanity of Jesus. John feared that his labor in starting these congregations would be in vain if the members turned to a false view of Christ's person and work. The apostle pictured the truth about Christ as a target. False doctrines about the Son of God are arrows that fly beyond the target and miss the mark of salvation.

3. BE HOSPITABLE. John commended Gaius for hosting the evangelists the apostle had sent to clarify the truth about Jesus. John reported that Gaius' reputation in the home church had soared and appealed to him to treat the next batch of evangelists the same way. The apostle reminded his readers that all who support missionaries share in the blessings of their spiritual harvest.

4. BE HUMBLE. In addition to doctrinal conflict, John faced division caused by the desire of some for personal power. The apostle urged his readers to follow the example of Christians who are submissive to the authority of God's Word, rather than those who will abuse their position and other believers in order to stay in control.

■ TOPIC: Remain Loyal

■ QUESTIONS: 1. What does it mean to walk in the truth? 2. Why is it important to abide in the teaching of Christ? 3. Why should believers support those who serve as missionaries? 4. How can believers remain loyal to the truth? 5. Why are being people of integrity important for Christians to maintain?

■ ILLUSTRATIONS:

Love Builds Up. Edward Steichen, who eventually became one of the world's most renowned photographers, almost gave up on the day he shot his first pictures. At age 16, young Steichen bought a camera and took 50 photos. Only one turned out—a portrait of his sister at the piano.

Edward's father thought that was a poor showing. But his mother insisted that the photograph of his sister was so beautiful that it more than compensated for 49 failures. Her encouragement convinced the youngster to stick with his new hobby. He stayed with it for the rest of his life, but it had been a close call. What tipped the scales? Love spotted excellence in the midst of a lot of failure.

"Goat Leaders." Martin Luther once claimed, "We need goat sense." He reached that conclusion after seeing two goats meet on a path on a mountain ledge. He had expected to see the two male goats square off in a battle for dominance. Instead, one of them lay down and allowed the other to pass over him. That was practical and constructive humility. Luther recognized such humility as a rare but needed commodity among church leaders.

Don't Abuse Power. One day, in 1888, Alfred Nobel picked up the morning newspaper and read his obituary. His brother had passed away, but an over-zealous reporter had failed to check the facts. The obituary presented Alfred Nobel as the inventor of dynamite, an armaments manufacturer, and a merchant of death.

Because Nobel received this unusual opportunity to see his life as others did, he resolved to accentuate his desire for peace. He arranged that the income from all of his fortune would fund an award for those persons who did the most for the cause of peace. Today we remember Alfred Nobel, not as an arms merchant, but as the founder of the Nobel Peace Prize.

Don't Focus on Evil. A man came to a minister to be counseled. He had lost money and said, "I've lost everything."

Minister: "Oh I'm sorry to hear you have lost your faith."

Man: "No, I've not lost my faith."

Minister: "Well then I'm sorry to hear you have lost your character."

Man: "I didn't say that. I still have my character."

Minister: "I'm sorry to hear you have lost your assurance of salvation."

Man: "I didn't say that either. I haven't lost my assurance of salvation."

Minister: "You have your faith, your character, and your assurance of salvation. It seems to me that you've lost none of the things that really matter."

Do not spend your energies on what is evil; instead, spend your energies on what is good (3 John 11).

FOR YOUTH

■ TOPIC: Walk This Way

■ QUESTIONS: 1. What was it about John's readers that filled him with joy? 2. What was it that religious frauds denied concerning Christ? 3. How can believers be co-workers with ministers of the Gospel? 4. What difference has the truth of the Gospel made in your life? 5. How has the love of God in Christ transformed your view of the unsaved?

■ **ILLUSTRATIONS:**

Love "Fits" the Beloved. Richard Selzer noted the following on the results of a surgery he performed: "I stand by the bed where a young woman lies, her face postoperative, her mouth twisted in palsy, clownish. A tiny twig of facial nerve, the one to the muscles of her mouth, has been severed. She will be thus from now on. To remove a tumor in her cheek, I had to cut that little nerve.

"Her young husband is in the room. He stands on the opposite side of the bed, and together they seem to dwell in the evening lamplight, isolated from me. Who are they, I ask myself, he and this wry-mouth that I have made, who gaze at and touch each other so generously, greedily? The young woman speaks.

"'Will my mouth always be like this?' she asks. 'Yes,' I say, 'it will. It is because the nerve was cut.'

"She nods and is silent, but the young man smiles. 'I like it,' he says. 'It's kind of cute.'

"All at once I know who he is. I understand and lower my gaze. One is not bold in an encounter with a god. Unmindful, he bends to kiss her crooked mouth and I [am] so close I can see how he twists his own lips to accommodate to hers, to show her that their kiss still works" *(Mortal Lessons: Notes on the Art of Surgery)*.

Real Leaders Aren't Proud. Daniel Boone explored the great wilderness of Kentucky and Tennessee. It was Boone who marked the Wilderness Road that brought settlers into the new land west of the Appalachians. He often wandered over vast areas of forest, living off the land and dodging arrows. Once he was asked if he had ever been lost. Boone replied, "No." He claimed he had never been lost, but he did admit that he was "a mite confused once for three or four days."

Boone was gently joking, but he showed a common trait of tough guys (and gals). We don't like to be wrong. It's hard to admit errors, but godly leaders will. They aren't leading for praise on earth. They are leading for a heavenly "Well done" that is based on faithfulness, rather than performance.

Real Leaders Serve. The story goes that many years ago a well-dressed rider on horseback came across a squad of soldiers trying to move a heavy piece of timber. A corporal stood by, barking out orders, but the timber was too heavy for the squad.

"Why don't you help them?" asked the man on the horse.

"Me? Why, I'm their officer, sir!"

Dismounting, the stranger took his place with the soldiers. "Now, all together, boys. Heave!" he said. And the big piece of timber slid into place. The stranger mounted his horse and addressed the corporal.

"The next time you have a piece of timber for your men to handle, corporal, send for the Commander-in-Chief."

The horseman was President George Washington.

MAINTAIN STEADFAST FAITH

BACKGROUND SCRIPTURE: Jude
DEVOTIONAL READING: Galatians 6:1-10

KEY VERSES: Keep yourselves in the love of God; look forward to the mercy of our Lord Jesus Christ that leads to eternal life. And have mercy on some who are wavering. Jude 21-22.

KING JAMES VERSION

JUDE 3 Beloved, when I gave all diligence to write unto you of the common salvation, it was needful for me to write unto you, and exhort you that ye should earnestly contend for the faith which was once delivered unto the saints. 4 For there are certain men crept in unawares, who were before of old ordained to this condemnation, ungodly men, turning the grace of our God into lasciviousness, and denying the only Lord God, and our Lord Jesus Christ. . . .

8 Likewise also these filthy dreamers defile the flesh, despise dominion, and speak evil of dignities. . . .

10 But these speak evil of those things which they know not: but what they know naturally, as brute beasts, in those things they corrupt themselves. . . .

12 These are spots in your feasts of charity, when they feast with you, feeding themselves without fear: clouds they are without water, carried about of winds; trees whose fruit withereth, without fruit, twice dead, plucked up by the roots; 13 Raging waves of the sea, foaming out their own shame; wandering stars, to whom is reserved the blackness of darkness for ever. . . .

16 These are murmurers, complainers, walking after their own lusts; and their mouth speaketh great swelling words, having men's persons in admiration because of advantage. 17 But, beloved, remember ye the words which were spoken before of the apostles of our Lord Jesus Christ; 18 How that they told you there should be mockers in the last time, who should walk after their own ungodly lusts. 19 These be they who separate themselves, sensual, having not the Spirit. 20 But ye, beloved, building up yourselves on your most holy faith, praying in the Holy Ghost, 21 Keep yourselves in the love of God, looking for the mercy of our Lord Jesus Christ unto eternal life. 22 And of some have compassion, making a difference: 23 And others save with fear, pulling them out of the fire; hating even the garment spotted by the flesh.

NEW REVISED STANDARD VERSION

JUDE 3 Beloved, while eagerly preparing to write to you about the salvation we share, I find it necessary to write and appeal to you to contend for the faith that was once for all entrusted to the saints. 4 For certain intruders have stolen in among you, people who long ago were designated for this condemnation as ungodly, who pervert the grace of our God into licentiousness and deny our only Master and Lord, Jesus Christ. . . .

8 Yet in the same way these dreamers also defile flesh, reject authority, and slander the glorious ones. . . . 10 But these people slander whatever they do not understand, and they are destroyed by those things that, like irrational animals, they know by instinct. . . . 12 These are blemishes on your love-feasts, while they feast with you without fear, feeding themselves. They are waterless clouds carried along by the winds; autumn trees without fruit, twice dead, uprooted; 13 wild waves of the sea, casting up the foam of their own shame; wandering stars, for whom the deepest darkness has been reserved forever. . . .

16 These are grumblers and malcontents; they indulge their own lusts; they are bombastic in speech, flattering people to their own advantage.

17 But you, beloved, must remember the predictions of the apostles of our Lord Jesus Christ; 18 for they said to you, "In the last time there will be scoffers, indulging their own ungodly lusts." 19 It is these worldly people, devoid of the Spirit, who are causing divisions. 20 But you, beloved, build yourselves up on your most holy faith; pray in the Holy Spirit; 21 keep yourselves in the love of God; look forward to the mercy of our Lord Jesus Christ that leads to eternal life. 22 And have mercy on some who are wavering; 23 save others by snatching them out of the fire; and have mercy on still others with fear, hating even the tunic defiled by their bodies.

13

Home Bible Readings

Monday, November 24	Isaiah 26:1-6	*The Steadfast Are Kept in Peace*
Tuesday, November 25	Isaiah 26:7-13	*O Lord, We Wait for You*
Wednesday, November 26	Psalm 112:1-8	*The Righteous Have Steady Hearts*
Thursday, November 27	Revelation 3:7-13	*Keep My Word*
Friday, November 28	Galatians 6:1-10	*Don't Give Up in Doing Right*
Saturday, November 29	Jude 1-13	*Contend for the Faith*
Sunday, November 30	Jude 16-25	*Build Up Your Faith*

Background

Jude is an Anglicized form of the Greek name Judas, which was the Greek version of the Hebrew name Judah. Judas was a younger brother of James who wrote the epistle bearing his name. Both were half-brothers of Jesus (Matt. 13:55; Mark 6:3). Neither brother drew attention to his family tie to the Lord (Jas. 1:1; Jude 1). Both called themselves Jesus' servants.

Although Jude follows the letters of Peter and John in the New Testament, it precedes most or all of them in time of composition. Jude 4-18 and 2 Peter 2:1-22 are so similar that one relied directly on the other or both used a third source that no longer exists. Most New Testament scholars think Peter relied on Jude. If that is so, Jude had to be written long enough before Peter's death in the late A.D. 60s to have been recognized as authoritative. Assuming Jude precedes 2 Peter, it may have been written about A.D. 65.

Jude made extensive use of Old Testament allusions. This may indicate he wrote to an audience in Palestine. The false teachers Jude warned against seem to have interpreted the doctrine of salvation by grace to imply that carnal sins were acceptable or even desirable as stimulants for more grace (Jude 4). The false teachers John's epistles combated held false views about the full humanity and full deity of Christ. Jude's (and 2 Peter's) false teachers seem primarily to have tried to join the gracious Gospel of Christ to immorality.

False teachers appeared early in the life of the church. In Paul's letters, he often referred to opponents directly or indirectly. When we read those passages describing the way Paul saw the Gospel being distorted in the A.D. 50s, we find similarities to what Jude wrote about. It is easy to want both forgiveness from God and license to go on sinning. Paul and Jude knew that such a view missed the point of a transforming relationship with Father, Son, and Holy Spirit (Rom. 6:1-2; Eph. 5:8-10; Jude 4).

Notes on the Printed Text

Jude had begun to write an epistle about *the salvation we share* (Jude 3). Something, however, changed Jude's plans. Perhaps he received disturbing news about the arrival of false teaching. Perhaps he came to realize that he needed to address an ongoing problem concerning religious frauds. At any rate necessity compelled Jude to change his plans and coin the phrase *contend for the faith.*

Contend means to wrestle with all one's might to guard the common body of doctrine *entrusted to the saints* by God's Spirit through the apostles. Jude's use of *the faith* as a body of doctrine finds parallels in other New Testament passages, and the concept goes back to Pentecost (Acts 2:42; Gal. 1:23; 1 Tim. 4:6).

Jude regarded the false teachers troubling the churches he addressed as *intruders* (Jude 4) who had infiltrated the Christian community by stealth. These frauds were not novices at teaching error. They had been at it for a long time, and all along had been *designated for this condemnation as ungodly.* They perverted God's gracious forgiveness of transgressions into a license to sin willfully with no consequences. Jude regarded this as a denial of *our only Master and Lord, Jesus Christ.* Believers are saved from sin to serve Jesus as *Master and Lord.*

Jude insisted that these false teachers indulged in carnal pleasures to the same extent that the residents of Sodom and Gomorrah had (7-8). They were *dreamers* (8) who claimed visions as their authority for indulging in sexual sins, for rejecting the authority of the moral demands of the Scripture and apostolic teaching, and for speaking against angels.

Jude regarded the slandering of angelic beings by the false teachers as evidence of their ignorance (10). The area of expertise for these frauds was self-indulgent sin. They did whatever came naturally to their carnal natures, *like irrational animals.* They were heading for self-destruction.

Jude used five metaphors to describe the presence of these false teachers in Christian churches. First, they were ugly pimples on the beautiful face of their *love-feasts* (12). These were early church dinners that centered around the observance of the Lord's Supper.

Second, the frauds were like wind-blown clouds that promised refreshing rain but then vanished without delivering a drop. Third, they were like trees at the end of autumn that were doubly useless, for they had given no fruit that season and wouldn't in the future due to lack of any roots.

Fourth, the charlatans were like surf crashing ashore. They were similar to a froth of sinful passion that littered the beach with stinking jetsam (13). Fifth, they were like *wandering stars,* the ancients' term for the planets, which were unreliable guides for navigating the sea of life. Such deficient guides must themselves end up utterly and hopelessly lost.

Jude called special attention to the speech of the false teachers as indicative of their self-indulgence (16). They were whiners and complainers, much as ancient Israel had been in its dealings with Moses (1 Cor. 10:10). The frauds boasted about themselves and made inflated claims about their teachings (Jude 16). They knew how to flatter and manipulate gullible people to get what they wanted.

To escape the influence of the false teachers, Jude's *beloved* (17) friends needed to focus on the sober, simple, but sure words *of the apostles of our Lord Jesus*

Christ. The apostles' warning against false teachers contained three elements. First, the false teachers would arrive *in the last time* (18). Second the false teachers would be *scoffers*. Third, they would promote an immoral lifestyle.

These false teachers undoubtedly thought they were spiritually superior, but Jude said they were *worldly people* (19). They claimed visions from God (8), but Jude judged them *devoid of the Spirit* (19). They thought they were creating a caste of advanced Christians, but Jude labeled them as an undesirable divisive element.

In contrast to the worldly false teachers, Jude called on his readers to fortify their *most holy faith* (20). In contrast to the frauds who were devoid of the Spirit, Jude urged his readers to *pray in the Holy Spirit*. In contrast to the divisive religious charlatans, Jude encouraged his readers to abide *in the love of God* (21).

Jude closed his epistle with an appeal for mercy toward brothers and sisters ensnared by them. The model for their mercy had to be *the mercy of our Lord Jesus Christ*. Jude urged his readers to show mercy in three ways to different groups of believers under the influence of the false teachers. Those who were *wavering* (22) in doubt needed gentleness and compassion to woo them from error. Those who were ready to defect to the false teachers required forceful, quick action to rescue *them out of the fire* (23).

Those deeply involved and corrupted by the false teaching were not beyond recall. Believers need to approach them with *fear* lest the rescuers be defiled by their wicked practices. The rescue, if one should occur, would come because of strong faith, prayer in the Spirit, and the love of God.

SUGGESTIONS TO TEACHERS

Christian faith, at a personal level, is a spiritual affirmation that God has revealed Himself in Christ, who died to atone for our sins. The Christian faith, at a corporate level, consists of the body of truth about God, humankind, and salvation revealed by God in the Bible. It should be the goal of every Christian to be steadfast in personal and corporate faith. Jude focused primarily on corporate faith.

1. RECOGNIZE ERROR. Jude knew that the best way to recognize a counterfeit is to become very familiar with the genuine article. He appealed to his readers to get in excellent spiritual condition so that they could *contend for the faith that was once for all entrusted to the saints* (Jude 3). If they knew the Gospel backwards and forwards, they could spot an intruder on sight.

2. RECOIL FROM ERROR. People steadfast in their commitment to the faith pull back from the worthlessness of false teachers. They try to prevent disharmony in the fellowship of believers. They avoid and warn about people who make empty promises and display fruitless lives. They confront blatant immorality and steer the immature away from those who would lead them astray.

3. RESPOND TO ERROR. Steadfast faith contrasts sharply with error in character and behavior. Error is self-centered, vain, and destructive; steadfast faith is Christ-centered, holy, and constructive. Error has no contact with the power of God's Spirit; steadfast faith has constant prayerful contact with God's Spirit (Rom. 8:26-27; Gal. 4:6; Eph. 6:18). Error establishes a pecking order that destroys unity; steadfast faith expresses the love of God in such a way that unity is maintained in Christ.

4. RESCUE FROM ERROR. *The mercy of our Lord Jesus Christ* (Jude 21) compels people of steadfast faith to try to rescue fellow believers ensnared in error. Some can be convinced by calm reasoning. Others must be confronted sharply. Those deeply enmeshed in error must be approached with great caution, lest the rescuer be swept away with the victim in the tidal wave of sin.

FOR ADULTS

■ TOPIC: Maintain Steadfast Faith

■ QUESTIONS: 1. Why must believers contend for the faith? 2. What danger do religious frauds pose to the Christian faith? 3. What is the connection between what people believe and how they live? 4. How can believers encourage one another in the faith? 5. How can believers work together to bring the lost to saving faith?

■ ILLUSTRATIONS:

Know What You Believe. As a young man, Walter P. Chrysler worked as a master mechanic on a railroad. When Chrysler was 35 years old, he borrowed $5,000 and purchased his first automobile. It was a four-door Locomobile. The car was delivered to his hometown in Iowa and towed—not driven—to a barn at the Chrysler home.

For three months Walter Chrysler studied that car without ever attempting to drive it. He took his $5,000 Locomobile apart, spread the pieces on newspapers, and made sketches of them. Then Chrysler put the car back together. His theory was that he had to understand that car before he could drive it.

Most of us would benefit from a similar study of the basics of our Christian faith.

Shine in the Dark. One day in 1789, the sky over Hartford, Connecticut, darkened ominously. In the Connecticut House of Representatives, some of the state legislators gathered at windows and began to talk about the end of the world. Quelling a clamor for immediate adjournment, the Speaker of the House rose and said, "The Day of Judgment is either approaching or it is not. If it is not, there is no cause for adjournment. If it is, I choose to be found doing my duty. Therefore, I wish that candles be brought" (Robert P. Dugan, Jr., *Winning the New Civil War*).

Jude taught that the best defense against false teaching in these last days is a brightly shining faith.

Have Mercy. According to a fictional Hebrew story, one of the patriarchs was sitting outside his tent one evening when he saw an old man, weary from age and journey, coming toward him. The patriarch rushed out, greeted him, and invited him into his tent. There he washed the old man's feet and gave him food and drink.

The old man immediately began eating without saying any prayer or blessing. So the patriarch asked him, "Don't you worship God?"

The old traveler replied, "I worship fire only and reverence no other god."

When the host heard this, he became incensed, grabbed the old man by the shoulders, and threw him out of his tent into the cold night air.

When the old man had departed, God called to his friend and asked where the stranger was. The patriarch replied, "I forced him out because he did not worship You."

God answered, "I have suffered him these 80 years, though he dishonors me. Could you not endure him one night?"

FOR YOUTH

■ TOPIC: Keep the Faith

■ QUESTIONS: 1. What do you think Jude meant when he said concerning his readers that *certain intruders have stolen in among you* (Jude 1:4)? 2. Who were the *dreamers* (8) who defiled *the flesh*, rejected *authority*, and slandered *the glorious ones*? Why were they of concern to Jude? 3. How was it possible for those who were *devoid of the Spirit* (19) to cause *divisions* among God's people? 4. What actions did Jude recommend for us, as believers, to take in guarding against false teaching? 5. What types of people do you think need the correction from false teaching that Jude talked about in his letter?

■ ILLUSTRATIONS:

Something to Cheer About. It was a mild October afternoon in 1982, and Badger Stadium in Madison, Wisconsin, was packed. Over 60,000 die-hard Wisconsin fans watched their beloved football team take a beating from Michigan State. Even as the score became more and more lopsided, bursts of cheering kept erupting in the stands at moments that seemed to have nothing to do with the game.

Seventy miles away from Badger Stadium, the Milwaukee Brewers were beating the Saint Louis Cardinals in game three of the 1982 World Series. Many of the Badger faithful were listening to portable radios and celebrating something besides what was happening right in front of their eyes.

In many ways that is a fairly accurate description of what the Christian life is like. Even if there were conflict and confusion in our church, we should see by faith the victory that is ours in Christ.

Liberty: Use Responsibly. At the end of December 2000, a strange accident occurred in a Montreal hospital. A 73-year-old patient, in full control of her mental faculties lit a cigarette in her room. She had been instructed not to, both in writing and by word of mouth, because she was hooked to an oxygen supply. A small explosion and fire greeted the woman's ill-advised attempt to smoke.

The patient suffered minor burns. One hospital worker suffered burns to the hands while dousing the flames. Several patients were moved to another area of the hospital. The smoker was put in intensive care, minus her cigarettes and lighter.

A hospital spokesperson said that under the Charter of Rights and Freedoms, the hospital did not have the right to remove the patient's lighter until after the accident occurred. "We can't take away personal belongings," he said. "It's not a prison." Needless to say, the 73-year-old patient's name was not disclosed to the press.

Christ has set us free, but we are not to use our freedom as an excuse to sin. We'll still get burned if we dabble in what Scripture condemns.

Make a Difference. In the biography *Scully*, there is an account of a conversation between Steven Jobs, the founder of Apple Computer, and John Scully, who at the time was president of Pepsi. Jobs was attempting to recruit Scully for the top job at Apple, and he asked Scully, "Do you want to spend the rest of your life selling sugared water or do you want a chance to change the world?"

Jude challenged his readers to make a difference by knowing and living their faith in such a vibrant way that what the false teachers were peddling would seem like sugared water by comparison.

Modern Heretics. A youth worker boarded an airplane in Sacramento, California, for a flight to San Diego to attend a national youth ministry conference. He had fastened his seat belt, made sure his chair was in the full upright position, locked his tray table, and properly stowed his luggage when two well-dressed Ally McBeal look-alikes took the seats between him and the aisle.

The youth worker really did try to read his magazine, but it was rather tame compared to the young women's conversation. They talked about the club scene and what they enjoyed drinking. They moved on to discuss their intimate relationships with men, both single and married.

Then it turned into a gripe session. "Why do guys have such a hard time committing?" one asked. "And why don't they ever leave their wives like they promise to?" the other complained.

The young women talked about work for a while, and about the time the youth worker thought he could focus on his reading, one of them said, "But you know, if it wasn't for church, my life would fall apart." The women had the youth worker's full attention.

"Wow, you go to church too?" the second girl asked. "I know exactly how you feel. If it wasn't for church, I don't know where I'd be."

"Yeah," the first girl said, "if I miss more than two weeks of church everything in my life goes nuts."

The plane started its descent into San Diego and everything got quiet as the girls gathered their belongings.

Someone doesn't have to be a false teacher to disconnect faith and life. Too often, our relationship with Christ and our attendance in church is a religious "fix" that soothes our conscience for the sinful things we did the week before.

LESSONS FOR LIFE

SAMUEL: A CHILD DEDICATED

BACKGROUND SCRIPTURE: 1 Samuel 1—2:10; Luke 1:46-55
DEVOTIONAL READING: 1 Samuel 1:9-18

KEY VERSES: For this child I prayed; and the LORD has granted me the petition that I made to him. Therefore I have lent him to the LORD; as long as he lives, he is given to the Lord. 1 Samuel 1:27-28.

KING JAMES VERSION

1 SAMUEL 1:20 Wherefore it came to pass, when the time was come about after Hannah had conceived, that she bare a son, and called his name Samuel, saying, Because I have asked him of the LORD. . . .

26 And she said, Oh my lord, as thy soul liveth, my lord, I am the woman that stood by thee here, praying unto the LORD.

27 For this child I prayed; and the LORD hath given me my petition which I asked of him:

28 Therefore also I have lent him to the LORD; as long as he liveth he shall be lent to the LORD. And he worshipped the LORD there.

2:1 And Hannah prayed, and said, My heart rejoiceth in the LORD, mine horn is exalted in the LORD: my mouth is enlarged over mine enemies; because I rejoice in thy salvation.

2 There is none holy as the LORD: for there is none beside thee: neither is there any rock like our God.

3 Talk no more so exceeding proudly; let not arrogancy come out of your mouth: for the LORD is a God of knowledge, and by him actions are weighed.

4 The bows of the mighty men are broken, and they that stumbled are girded with strength.

5 They that were full have hired out themselves for bread; and they that were hungry ceased: so that the barren hath born seven; and she that hath many children is waxed feeble.

6 The LORD killeth, and maketh alive: he bringeth down to the grave, and bringeth up.

7 The LORD maketh poor, and maketh rich: he bringeth low, and lifteth up.

8 He raiseth up the poor out of the dust, and lifteth up the beggar from the dunghill, to set them among princes, and to make them inherit the throne of glory.

NEW REVISED STANDARD VERSION

1 SAMUEL 1:20 In due time Hannah conceived and bore a son. She named him Samuel, for she said, "I have asked him of the LORD."

26 And she said, "Oh, my lord! As you live, my lord, I am the woman who was standing here in your presence, praying to the LORD. 27 For this child I prayed; and the LORD has granted me the petition that I made to him. 28 Therefore I have lent him to the LORD; as long as he lives, he is given to the LORD."

She left him there for the LORD.

2:1 Hannah prayed and said,

"My heart exults in the LORD;
  my strength is exalted in my God.
My mouth derides my enemies,
  because I rejoice in my victory.
2 "There is no Holy One like the LORD,
  no one besides you;
  there is no Rock like our God.
3 Talk no more so very proudly,
  let not arrogance come from your mouth;
for the LORD is a God of knowledge,
  and by him actions are weighed.
4 The bows of the mighty are broken,
  but the feeble gird on strength.
5 Those who were full have hired themselves out
    for bread,
  but those who were hungry are fat with spoil.
The barren has borne seven,
  but she who has many children is forlorn.
6 The LORD kills and brings to life;
  he brings down to Sheol and raises up.
7 The LORD makes poor and makes rich;
  he brings low, he also exalts.
8 He raises up the poor from the dust;
  he lifts the needy from the ash heap,
to make them sit with princes
  and inherit a seat of honor.

BACKGROUND

The book of 1 Samuel is the record of the establishment of the monarchy in Israel, although it opens with the account of a very unhappy woman named Hannah. Elkanah, her husband, is mentioned first, but the principal focus of the opening chapters is on Hannah.

Elkanah actually had two wives, indicating that polygamy was both permitted and practiced among the Israelites. For a man to have a son to continue the family name was very important in that society. Thus, when the first wife did not produce a male child, the man would often choose a second wife. This may have happened with Elkanah. The obvious problems produced by polygamous marriages developed in the rivalry between Elkanah's two wives, Peninnah and Hannah. The result was the inevitable family conflicts and Hannah's extreme unhappiness. Though our Western society does not sanction polygamy, often some of the similar problems surface in second and third marriages when former spouses are still living.

Hannah, Elkanah's first wife, was not able to have children. In ancient times, barrenness was considered a sign of God's disfavor. In the case of Hannah, she felt great disappointment because she could not bear her husband a son. Hannah's frustration was made worse by the taunts that came from Elkanah's second wife, Peninnah, who had borne him children, and who *used to provoke [Hannah] severely, to irritate her, because the Lord had closed her womb* (1:6).

Once a year the family went to Shiloh to worship and sacrifice to God. Shiloh was about 16 miles east of Elkanah's home in Ramah. Shiloh was the central place of worship for the Israelites because the tabernacle containing the ark of the covenant was located there. The festival the family attended probably was the Feast of Tabernacles, which was celebrated in the fall. In keeping with the ritual, Elkanah gave portions of meat to each member of the family; but to show his special favor toward Hannah, Elkanah gave her *a double portion, because he loved her* (1:5).

Elkanah's extraordinary kindness to Hannah still did not relieve her sorrow and humiliation. At first she could not eat (1:7). Later she went to the entrance of the tabernacle where the priest Eli sat (1:9). There Hannah wept and prayed (1:10). She promised God that, if He would give her a son, she would give the child back to the Lord, vowing that she would never cut his hair (1:11).

Because Hannah did not pray audibly but only moved her lips, the priest *said to her, "How long will you make a drunken spectacle of yourself? Put away your wine"* (1:14). Hannah explained to Eli that she was not drunk but deeply burdened because of her plight (1:15-16). Eli then told Hannah to *"go in peace"* (1:17). Eli assured Hannah that God had heard her prayer and that He would grant her request. No doubt Hannah shared with Elkanah the good news that Eli had affirmed her request of the Lord. The record states that *the LORD remembered her* (1:19), and the promised child was *conceived* (1:20).

NOTES ON THE PRINTED TEXT

We can only imagine the joy Hannah and Elkanah experienced during the months before the promised child was born. No word is recorded about Peninnah, the second wife of Elkanah, who had gloated because of Hannah's barrenness. Though Hannah had chafed because of Peninnah's taunts, she now was vindicated by the grace of God. Like the elder brother in Jesus' parable of the prodigal son (Luke 15:11-32), Peninnah seemed to fade from the picture.

No mention is made of any problems Hannah encountered during her pregnancy. Surely she walked the mountaintops of ecstasy during those months! Because God miraculously healed Hannah's barren womb, the child arrived at the precise moment he was due. With no hesitation, Hannah *named him Samuel, for she said, "I have asked him of the LORD"* (1 Sam. 1:20).

The time was near for the annual family visit to Shiloh. Elkanah's entire household went, except for Hannah and Samuel. She determined to keep him near to her until he was weaned (1:21-23). In those ancient times, a child was breast-fed for two or three years before he or she was allowed to spend extended periods of time away from home. After the child was weaned, Hannah *brought him to the house of the LORD at Shiloh; and the child was young* (1:24). There, according to the promise Hannah had made (1:11), Samuel would serve the Lord in the tabernacle.

After the proper sacrifices had been offered, *[Elkanah and Hannah] brought the child to Eli* (1:25). Hannah reminded Eli that she was the woman who had prayed to the Lord earlier (1:26). Hannah joyfully exclaimed to Eli, *"the LORD has granted me the petition that I made to him"* (1:27). Hannah told Eli that she had *"lent [the child] to the LORD"* (1:28). The Hebrew word translated "lent" does not imply a temporary arrangement; rather, Hannah stated clearly to Eli that Samuel would be dedicated to the Lord *"as long as he lives."*

While Hannah stood before Eli to dedicate Samuel to the Lord, Hannah spontaneously began to pray (2:1-10). Her beautiful expression of praise was the climax of her act of worship. Although the record states that Hannah *"prayed"* (2:1), her prayer is generally referred to as "the Song of Hannah." It is very similar to other ancient Old Testament hymns, such as the Song of Moses (Exod. 15:1-18), the Song of Deborah (Judg. 5:1-31), and the Song of David (2 Sam. 22:2-51).

Mary's song (Luke 1:46-55) is very similar to Hannah's, in that it contains many of the themes expressed in Hannah's song. Some Bible authorities consider Hannah's song the "seedplot" for Mary's song. Both songs begin in the same way. Hannah and Mary became pregnant miraculously, though Mary's conception was the result of a far greater miracle than Hannah's. Also, each presented her firstborn son to the Lord at the sanctuary (Hannah at the central sanctuary at Shiloh and Mary at the temple in Jerusalem). Hannah's song of thanksgiving and praise came after the birth of Samuel, whereas Mary sang her song at the home of Elizabeth before Jesus was born.

The Hebrew people often expressed what they believed about God in their psalms and they sang them in the course of their worship. Hannah's song includes most of the Israelites' basic worship themes. In the first verse of her song (1 Sam. 2:1), Hannah praised God for the great blessing she had received, *"because I rejoice in my victory."* The first line, *"My heart exults in the LORD,"* is completed in the third line, *"my mouth derides my enemies."* What Hannah felt in her heart she expressed in the words of her mouth. Hannah concluded her opening praise by emphasizing that God had proved Himself to be holy, and *"there is no Rock like our God"* (2:2) upon whom one could rest in confidence.

Hannah expressed the boldness of her faith in God by challenging His enemies because of their unfounded pride and arrogance. Hannah underscored the fact that the Lord, as *"a God of knowledge"* (2:3), sees and knows everything. All of His actions are weighed in accordance with His holiness and found to be just.

Hannah brought her song to a thrilling climax when she declared that God is able to overturn the wicked. *"The bows of the mighty are broken"* (2:4) and their victims withstood them in God's strength. *"Those who were full"* (2:5) found that their bread was not enough, and the *hungry* were satisfied. The *barren* woman was exalted and able to bear children, while she who had borne *many children* became weak and unable to continue her childbearing.

In 2:6-8, Hannah's song indicates what she had implied in 2:4-5. God indeed *"kills and brings to life"* (2:6). He *"makes poor and makes rich"* (2:7), and gives honor to those who have been abused. Hannah's discovery was that God has a way of reversing circumstances that appear unchangeable (2:8). When we experience true worship as Hannah did, we find that God will vindicate His people in the midst of what appear to be impossible circumstances.

SUGGESTIONS TO TEACHERS

Hannah's life had been difficult. Although she knew her husband loved her dearly, she was not fulfilled. The reason is that Hannah had not been able to do what every wife longed to do in those ancient times—bear her husband a child.

No doubt Hannah had prayed many times for God to heal her barrenness. She was filled not only with disappointment, but also with grief. She felt that life had not been fair to her. Finally Hannah could resist no more. She poured out her heart to God and made a most unusual promise. If God would be gracious to her and make it possible for her to have a son, Hannah would do something for God.

Some of your students may have had a great disappointment in their lives. Frustration, resentment, and bitterness may have kept them from a close relationship with God. Hannah's account provides an opportunity to help them enter a new and rewarding relationship with God.

1. REMEMBERING THE PROMISE. Hannah doubtlessly experienced sheer ecstasy from the time she conceived until the time her child was born; yet she did not forget the promise she made to the Lord. Even the name Hannnah gave the child, "Samuel" (which means "name of God"), proved that Hannah knew God's hand was in it all. We might pray for physical healing. Excellent physicians might prescribe appropriate medicine and we recover. Do we recognize the reality of God's healing power through medical science as well as apart from it? Do we remember to give Him the glory for answered prayer?

2. REFLECTING THE JOY. The months of happiness and anticipation before Samuel was born no doubt changed Hannah's physical appearance. No longer was she sad and cast down, as she had been during the yearly family visits to Shiloh. She probably needed to remind the priest Eli who she was! Although Hannah had come to keep the promise she had made—to dedicate Samuel to the Lord—Hannah reflected great joy. The promises we make to God must never be taken lightly. We, too, experience a continual joy in our relationship with God when we keep our pledges to Him.

3. PRAISING THE LORD. How did Hannah demonstrate her gratitude to God for what He had done? Hannah offered her prayer of thanksgiving as a beautiful song in which she glorified God's holiness, trustworthiness, mercy, and justice. We should take care that we regularly offer praise to God and celebrate the gracious ways in which He deals with people and situations.

FOR ADULTS

■ TOPIC: Dedicating to God

■ QUESTIONS: 1. What were some of the factors that made life difficult for Hannah? 2. What was the significance of Hannah's choice of "Samuel" for her son's name? 3. After Samuel was weaned, what did Hannah do that proved her faithfulness to the Lord? 4. What important lessons had Hannah learned about God that she disclosed in her prayer? 5. How can we find great joy in keeping the promises we make to God?

■ ILLUSTRATIONS:

A Forgotten Promise. Jim was an excellent machinist and had worked diligently for many years for a large machine shop in town. Creative by nature, Jim one day completed a project he had been working on for a long time. It was a simple tool that made it possible for him to perform a certain function in his work with machines with much greater speed and accuracy.

The owner of the machine shop was very impressed and urged Jim to secure a patent for his invention. Two wealthy businessmen in town offered to finance the production of the tool and the advertising campaign. The result was that a large industrial concern offered Jim an unbelievable amount of money for the patent.

Jim and his family were active church members. He counseled with his pastor and assured him that the new wealth would not affect his relationship with the Lord or the church. The tragic reality is that Jim and his family became more and more involved in activities they could not afford. Eventually Jim's unwise use of his money took its toll. He faced bankruptcy, and his children, now teenagers, became rebellious and demanding. Also, Jim's wife filed for a divorce.

One day it dawned on Jim what he had done. He remembered the promise he had made to God and to his pastor. He invited the pastor to visit with the family. Jim confessed his sins before God, his family, and his pastor. The family was reunited. Despite the fact that the family's lifestyle was once again simple, a renewed joy was evident among the parents and children. God was once more the center of their lives, and they were ready to praise and glorify Him.

A Song in the Heart. Jericho is a small village located at the foot of Mount Diablo in the central part of the island of Jamaica. On the outskirts of the village is a small English Baptist church. Since there is no electricity in the area, the church is lighted at night by kerosene lanterns brought by the parishioners when they come to worship.

Every pew in the tiny building was filled on the first night I stood to preach. When the people sang, I noted that no one held a hymnbook. The music director called out the number of a psalm. It was a psalm of repentance, and in a mournful, minor key, the congregation began to repeat its words. They sang with great fervor, many with tears coursing down their cheeks. When the participants finished, the leader called the number of another psalm, this time a hymn of praise. The expressions on the faces of the people changed as they enthusiastically lifted their voices in worship to God.

After the service, the pastor explained to me that the Book of Psalms was their primary hymnal. "We memorize the psalms and hide their words in our hearts. Many of the psalms are prayers, and when we repeat them, we feel that we are communicating with God in a very special way. Many of the people here tonight walked several miles down forest trails to come to church. They come in family groups, and repeat the psalms all the way from their homes to the church. Not only are they in a spirit of worship when they arrive, but also they feel the protective presence of God as they sing His words."

The pastor's comments reminded me of Hannah's song of praise to God. Now, when I read a psalm recorded in Scripture, I find myself wanting to sing it to the glory of God.

The Master's Touch. We watched the aged potter as he put the shapeless lump of clay on his ancient, foot-propelled wheel. He slammed the clay hard against the surface of the spinning device. His hands caressed the lump. He took water from another container and sprinkled it on the clay. Then, slowly, his deft and skilled fingers began to move as he shaped the lump.

The artisan cupped his hands around the material and it began to rise. A slight pressure here and there gave shape and form to the object. There, in a matter of minutes, stood a tall and graceful vase.

Then came the final touch. The potter made an almost imperceptible move with his fingers and delicate leaves appeared on the side of the vase. A seemingly useless lump of clay had been transformed into a graceful vessel that would be used to hold beautiful flowers.

What an expression of God's incomparable handiwork! Similarly, Hannah was transformed by the Master's touch to bring glory to Him through her life.

FOR YOUTH

■ TOPIC: I'm Yours, God
■ QUESTIONS: 1. What factors had made life difficult for Hannah? 2. How did Hannah disclose her faith in God in the name she chose for her son? 3. With what expression did Hannah begin her prayer to God, after she presented Samuel to the priest Eli? 4. What great truth about God's dealings with people did Hannah express in 1 Samuel 2:6-8? 5. Why is it sometimes difficult for us to dedicate ourselves fully to God?

■ ILLUSTRATIONS:

A Reward for Luther. Luther was a sophomore when he transferred to our school. He was small for his age and very shy. His clothes were worn and patched, but always clean. He was a loner. He brought his lunch every day and sat by himself.

Soon some of the boys began to taunt and harass Luther. He tried to ignore them, but the situation only became worse. Bob, who was an excellent athlete, a good student, and a leader in his class, saw what was happening. He went out of his way to befriend Luther. He began bringing his lunch and sitting with Luther at noon. He soon discovered that Luther's lunch usually consisted of an apple and very little else. Bob asked his mother to prepare an extra sandwich and a few more treats than usual. He would act as if he was not hungry enough to eat two sandwiches and insist that Luther take one. At first, Luther declined, but Bob could tell that Luther really wanted the sandwich. Finally he accepted it.

Slowly, Luther began to talk. His father had died two years before, and his mother was the sole support for the family. They had moved several times in order for her to find work.

Luther had been a good baseball player in his former school. But when the guys chose sides, Luther would always be the last one chosen. Bob learned that Luther was a good pitcher. He persuaded the coach to let Luther pitch one day at practice. Soon the coach recognized Luther's natural ability, and began grooming him as one of the team's starting pitchers.

Slowly, Luther's personality began to change. During his senior year, his excellent pitching led his team to a district championship. Amid cheers after the game, the team put Luther on their shoulders and carried him to the locker rooms. The school bullies who had tried to make Luther a target for their insults were now silent. Luther had been vindicated. Luther was a hero.

Hannah suffered harassment from Peninnah; but in the end, God's blessings upon Hannah vindicated her and brought joy and reward.

Inching up the Curtain. Missionary Clarence Jones once said that "if God had suddenly shown me everything He was going to do in the years to come, I would have said, 'Wait a minute, Lord; You've got the wrong man!' But God inched up the curtain just a little bit at a time and said, 'Take a look and take a step.'"

That's the way God built a courageous faith in Hannah. It's also the way He works in our lives. Hannah learned to trust God one day at a time. She experienced dark valleys of discouragement, but through it all God was cultivating and testing her faith. Here we see that faith grows by single steps, not by gigantic hurdles.

The Real Test. Henry had felt for a long time that God wanted him to devote his life to vocational Christian service. He talked with missionaries who had worked with the underprivileged in remote places in the world. The haunting faces of the children he had seen on television gripped his heart.

When Henry finished high school, he enrolled in a Christian college. He told his professors where he felt God was calling him. A local church established a mission point in an extremely poor neighborhood among immigrants who had only recently come to America. Henry was asked to spend one day a week working with the children.

After a couple of weeks, Henry told his professor that God had called him to work overseas, not among people who lived in America. Ten years later, Henry was still drifting from one job to another. He discovered that he had not truly given himself to God as Hannah had given her child to the Lord. The anticipated adventure had been more appealing than the reality of a truly committed, hands-on involvement.

JOHN: FORERUNNER OF JESUS 2

BACKGROUND SCRIPTURE: Luke 1:5-80
DEVOTIONAL READING: Isaiah 40:3-11

KEY VERSE: "You, child, will be called the prophet of the Most High;
for you will go before the Lord to prepare his ways." Luke 1:76.

KING JAMES VERSION	NEW REVISED STANDARD VERSION

KING JAMES VERSION

LUKE 1:67 And his father Zacharias was filled with the Holy Ghost, and prophesied, saying,

68 Blessed be the Lord God of Israel; for he hath visited and redeemed his people,

69 And hath raised up an horn of salvation for us in the house of his servant David;

70 As he spake by the mouth of his holy prophets, which have been since the world began:

71 That we should be saved from our enemies, and from the hand of all that hate us;

72 To perform the mercy promised to our fathers, and to remember his holy covenant;

73 The oath which he sware to our father Abraham,

74 That he would grant unto us, that we being delivered out of the hand of our enemies might serve him without fear,

75 In holiness and righteousness before him, all the days of our life.

76 And thou, child, shalt be called the prophet of the Highest: for thou shalt go before the face of the Lord to prepare his ways;

77 To give knowledge of salvation unto his people by the remission of their sins,

78 Through the tender mercy of our God; whereby the dayspring from on high hath visited us,

79 To give light to them that sit in darkness and in the shadow of death, to guide our feet into the way of peace.

80 And the child grew, and waxed strong in spirit, and was in the deserts till the day of his shewing unto Israel.

NEW REVISED STANDARD VERSION

LUKE 67 Then his father Zechariah was filled with the Holy Spirit and spoke this prophecy:

68 "Blessed be the Lord God of Israel,
   for he has looked favorably on his people and
      redeemed them.

69 He has raised up a mighty savior for us
   in the house of his servant David,

70 as he spoke through the mouth of his holy
      prophets from of old,

71 that we would be saved from our enemies and
      from the hand of all who hate us.

72 Thus he has shown the mercy promised to our
      ancestors,
   and has remembered his holy covenant,

73 the oath that he swore to our ancestor Abraham,
   to grant us 74 that we, being rescued from the hands
      of our enemies,
might serve him without fear, 75 in holiness and
      righteousness
   before him all our days.

76 And you, child, will be called the prophet of the
      Most High;
   for you will go before the Lord to prepare his ways,

77 to give knowledge of salvation to his people
   by the forgiveness of their sins.

78 By the tender mercy of our God,
   the dawn from on high will break upon us,

79 to give light to those who sit in darkness and in
      the shadow of death,
   to guide our feet into the way of peace."

80 The child grew and became strong in spirit, and he was in the wilderness until the day he appeared publicly to Israel.

Monday, December 8	Isaiah 40:3-11	*Prepare the Way of the* LORD
Tuesday, December 9	Luke 1:5-11	*An Angel Appears to Zechariah*
Wednesday, December 10	Luke 1:12-17	*The Promise of a Son*
Thursday, December 11	Luke 1:18-25	*Elizabeth Conceives*
Friday, December 12	Luke 1:57-66	*John Is Born*
Saturday, December 13	Luke 1:67-75	*Zechariah Prophesies*
Sunday, December 14	Luke 1:76-80	*John Will Be God's Prophet*

BACKGROUND

In last week's lesson, we learned how God made it possible for Hannah to conceive a child in her old age. She demonstrated her faithfulness by dedicating the child, Samuel, to the Lord. Samuel became a judge, a priest, and a prophet among God's people (1 Sam. 1:27-28).

In this week's lesson, we will move more than ten centuries past the time Samuel was born. Once again we will encounter a godly man whose wife was barren. Whereas Elkanah was a layman who was a strong spiritual leader of his family (1:3), Zechariah was a priest dedicated to serving God in the temple in Jerusalem (Luke 1:5). He belonged to one of 24 classes of priests who served in the temple in Jerusalem.

Luke began this account (and his entire Gospel) like a true historian by setting the time as precisely as possible: *In the days of King Herod of Judea.* When King Herod ruled, Judea included all that was considered Palestine in Jesus' day.

Zechariah's wife was Elizabeth, who was *a descendant of Aaron,* the first high priest and the brother of Moses. For Zechariah to be married to a woman who descended from the first high priest was indeed special.

Luke was careful to note that both Zechariah and Elizabeth *were righteous before God* (1:6). They were not sinless, though the desire of their hearts was to serve God and to live *blamelessly according to all the commandments and regulations of the Lord.* But because Elizabeth was *barren* (1:7), they lived in shame, for she could not bear her husband a son.

The dream of every priest was to serve once during his lifetime at the golden altar of burnt incense in the Jerusalem temple. It just so happens that Zechariah had been chosen by lot for this special honor (1:8-9). It was during this great moment in his life that an *angel of the Lord* (1:11) appeared to Zechariah and told him his prayer had been heard (1:13). His wife, Elizabeth, would bear him a son *"and you will name him John."* The angel also described John's ministry and the kind of person he would be. He would possess *"the spirit and power of Elijah"* (1:17) and he would *"make ready a people prepared for the Lord."*

Amazingly, Zechariah expressed his doubt about the possibility of Elizabeth's bearing him a son (1:18). Zechariah's doubting caused him to be unable to speak until after the child was born (1:20).

Six months after Elizabeth conceived, *the angel Gabriel was sent by God* (1:26) to Nazareth, where he announced to a *virgin* (1:27) named Mary that she would conceive and bear a son, "*and you will name him Jesus*" (1:31). Mary's child would "*be called the Son of the Most High*" (1:32). Mary was shocked to learn that she would bear a child, for she was still *a virgin* (1:34). Gabriel explained that "*The Holy Spirit will come upon you, and the power of the Most High will overshadow you*" (1:35). For this reason, Mary's child would be *holy* and called the *Son of God*. This miraculous conception would occur, "*For nothing [is] impossible with God*" (1:37).

Since the angel had told Mary that her relative Elizabeth had also conceived "*in her old age*" (1:36), Mary quickly left Nazareth and traveled south to the home of Zechariah and Elizabeth. There Mary would share with them, in the form of a beautiful song (1:46-55), her good news. Mary stayed with Elizabeth for three months and *then returned to her home* (1:56).

When John was born (1:57), Elizabeth's relatives urged her to name the child *Zechariah after his father* (1:59). Apparently, Zechariah had somehow communicated to Elizabeth what an *angel* (1:11) had declared concerning the child's name (1:13). Elizabeth, in turn, told those with her what the child's name would be (1:60). They, however, insisted on asking Zechariah (1:62), who wrote on *a writing tablet* (1:63) that the name would be *John*. At that moment Zechariah was able to speak, and he gave glory to God (1:64). When the news spread (1:65), the question everyone asked was, "*What then will this child become?*" (1:66).

NOTES ON THE PRINTED TEXT

The Holy Spirit spoke through Hannah (1 Sam. 2:1-10) and Mary (Luke 1:46-55) in the form of songs of praise to God for the miraculous way He had dealt with them. Likewise Zechariah *was filled with the Holy Spirit* (1:67) when he spoke concerning God's blessings that were to come upon Israel.

The Holy Spirit did not permanently dwell within the Old Testament saints as He does now within believers since the day of Pentecost (Acts 4:31). Thus, it was a unique experience when the Spirit periodically came upon believers prior to Pentecost and spoke God's message through them.

For instance, Elizabeth was filled with the Holy Spirit when Mary visited her, and the child *leaped in her womb* (Luke 1:41) in recognition of the Christ child already conceived within Mary. Because the Spirit controlled Elizabeth, she knew that Mary was not only her relative, but also the most blessed of all women (1:42). Elizabeth also knew that the baby in Mary's womb was her *Lord* (1:43).

Despite Zechariah's earlier doubts concerning the angel's promise that his wife would bear him a son, God continued to lead Zechariah on his spiritual journey. For instance, at the time of John's birth, Zechariah functioned as a prophet as well as a priest, for *he spoke this prophecy* (1:67). Zechariah's prophecy stated both a truth already revealed (1:68-75) and foretold the role John would serve regarding the coming Messiah (1:76-79).

Zechariah began with a doxology in which he praised God because "*he has looked favorably on his people and redeemed them*" (1:68). "*Looked favorably*" can also mean "looked after." Jesus used the same word, which is translated "*took care of*" in Matthew 25:36.

Zechariah next noted that God expressed His concern for His people when He delivered them from Egyptian slavery. Also, "He "*redeemed them*" (Luke 1:68) from sin and its consequences. He even provided an unforgettable object lesson for their redemption in the Passover event, which focused on the blood placed on the doorposts of their homes (Exod. 12:23).

Zechariah continued his praise by stating that God had "*raised up a mighty savior for us*" (Luke 1:69). The Greek phrase translated "*a mighty savior*" literally means "a horn of salvation." The "horn" referred to often in the Old Testament symbolized a destructive power, for it pictured the horn of various wild animals (1 Kings 22:11; Ps. 22:21; 75:5; Dan. 8:5-7).

God, by destroying and scattering the enemies of His people, became "*a mighty savior*" (Luke 1:69) for them. Zechariah was careful to point out that this Savior would come from "*the house of his servant David,*" which was part of the tribe of Judah, and not from Zechariah's tribe, the tribe of Levi. Zechariah was pointing toward Jesus, whose death on the cross would overthrow the power of Satan and deliver believers from their sins. Jesus, of course, was born of Mary, and thus belonged to the tribe of Judah.

Zechariah must have believed in the divine inspiration of God's Word, for he clearly stated that God "*spoke through the mouth of his holy prophets*" (1:70). The prophets were *holy* because they were set apart to be instruments through whom God would communicate with humankind. Zechariah emphasized that God spoke through these prophets "*from of old.*" The coming Messiah was the focus, both directly and indirectly, of all the prophets, from Abraham to John the Baptist.

Zechariah extended his statement in 1:69 concerning the coming of "*a mighty savior*" by stating that, because of Jesus' coming, "*we would be saved from our enemies and from the hand of all who hate us*" (1:71). The primary emphasis here was not a political freedom from the tyranny of Rome, but a spiritual freedom from Satan and the powers of darkness.

God keeps His pledges in that "*he has shown the mercy promised to our ancestors*" (1:72). The message of the prophets pointing to a coming Savior caused Zechariah's *ancestors* to have hope. A merciful God would not allow their hope to be in vain.

When God acts after a long delay, the Scriptures state that He *remembered* (1:72). This does not mean that He had forgotten His covenant and His promises. Instead, Zechariah referred to the whole of God's covenant, beginning with "*our ancestor Abraham*" (1:73). It is a holy covenant because it came from God and would be carried out by Him.

In light of these truths, God's people are able to *"serve him without fear"* (1:74). They do so in *"holiness and righteousness"* (1:75). *Holiness* speaks of our relationship with God through faith in Jesus Christ, while *righteousness* has to do with how we respond to others. We are to serve God *"all our days,"* striving to be consistent in our witness before the world.

Beginning with 1:76, Zechariah prophesied concerning John the Baptist. More important to Zechariah than himself or his child is what was going to be accomplish through *"the Lord"* and His mighty work of grace. Concerning Zechariah's child, he would be *"the prophet of the Most High"* and *"give knowledge of salvation"* (1:77) to those who heard him. John's message would prompt the people to seek *"the forgiveness of their sins."*

Zechariah praised God for His *"tender mercy"* (1:78). Perhaps as Zechariah spoke about *"the dawn from on high,"* he had in mind the words of the prophet Malachi, who announced, *But for you who revere my name the sun of righteousness shall rise, with healing in its wings* (Mal. 4:2).

The coming Messiah, like the rising sun, would *"give light to those who sit in darkness"* (Luke 1:79). The *darkness* pictures danger, fear, and hopelessness with no help in sight. *Light* represents the true knowledge of God. Those who had sat in despair in the darkness were now standing and ready to follow the Savior, who would *"guide our feet into the way of peace."*

John grew up like any normal child (1:80). But because God's hand was upon him, he was strong in spirit and had superior moral and spiritual qualities. No doubt John's life *in the wilderness* provided an opportunity for the Spirit to mold his thinking and prepare him for his mission as the herald of the coming Messiah.

SUGGESTIONS TO TEACHERS

From the moment of Adam's sin in the Garden of Eden, God's plan for the salvation of the lost has been unfolding on schedule. Even Satan's efforts to thwart the coming of the Savior were unsuccessful. The climax of God's preparation for His Son's entrance into this hostile world came with the preaching of John the Baptist, the herald and forerunner of Jesus.

As He often did, God used the unusual and unexpected to manifest His great power. For instance, John was born to a childless couple far past the normal age of childbearing. The response of the priest Zechariah, John's father, to God's amazing grace was Zechariah's submission to the Holy Spirit, who prophesied a thrilling message through him.

1. A VOICE FOR GOD'S SPIRIT. Despite the fact that Zechariah initially doubted the message of the angel that he and his wife Elizabeth would have a child in their old age, God used the aged priest as a mouthpiece for His Spirit. God continues to use imperfect messengers through whom to proclaim His good news to a sinful world. Although God temporarily disciplined Zechariah for his unbelief, God undoubtedly continued to use him to demonstrate his commitment to the

Lord. God can speak through His people in different ways. Some can share their faith with eloquence, while others have great difficulty speaking. Those who live a consistent Christian life in the world are allowing God's Spirit to manifest divine love through them.

2. A MESSAGE OF HOPE. Zechariah praised God because He was raising up a Savior from the lineage of David, as He had promised. This confirmed the faithful preaching of the prophets of old. God moved to provide salvation for sinners because of His grace, not because of humankind's worthiness. The long centuries of despair for God's people might have caused many of them to think that God had abandoned them. The Spirit reminded them, through Zechariah, that the Lord would keep His promise of a coming Savior because of the covenant He had made with their ancestors.

Some believers today may struggle with a sense of hopelessness, convinced that their sins are beyond God's willingness to forgive. The message of hope God has given us to proclaim is that He is able and willing to save sinners because of His great love for them in Christ.

3. A LIGHT IN THE DARKNESS. John came to understand that his role in life was to be transparent so that the Savior might be revealed. John's message of repentance would not be pleasant for people to hear. This remained true, even though the authority of the Spirit of God through which John spoke would seize the hearts of the people.

The light of Christ, which shines in the world's darkness of sin, is sufficient to bring conviction upon those who allow it to pierce their hearts. It is always the message that is most important, not the messenger. For instance, John's message was to point the people away from him and to the Lamb of God. Forgiveness of sin would only come after a genuine repentance from sin.

FOR ADULTS

■ **TOPIC:** Preparing the Way

■ **QUESTIONS:** 1. How was Zechariah able to prophesy words of hope and promise to the people? 2. Why was it important for Zechariah to emphasize that the Savior would be of the lineage of David? 3. What was the *holy covenant* (Luke 1:72) that God had made with His people? 4. What was the message John would proclaim to the people? 5. How can we become more willing to let God speak through us to communicate the good news of salvation to those in our sphere of influence?

■ **ILLUSTRATIONS:**

Realizing a Dream. Many years ago, Rudy Atwood was the pianist for Charles E. Fuller's radio program the *Old Fashioned Revival Hour*. Atwood's improvisations of hymns and gospel music were fabulous. My family always listened to the *Old Fashioned Revival Hour* on Sunday mornings before we left home for

Sunday school and church. Also, my piano teacher knew how much I was fascinated by Atwood's playing, for I often would mimic his piano stylings in my limited way.

One day I read in the newspaper that Atwood and the *Old Fashioned Revival Hour* quartet were coming to the city auditorium for a one-night concert in our southeast Texas city. My heart skipped a beat. My "impossible dream" was to be able to see Atwood in person and hear him play.

My piano teacher knew someone who was instrumental in engaging the quartet for our town, and without my knowing it, made arrangements for me to sit on the stage, in the wings, just a few feet from the piano. I felt as if I was in heaven! At last, I realized my "impossible dream." But more importantly, God used that opportunity to confirm my calling into Christian ministry.

When Zechariah was chosen to serve in the temple, he, too, realized a dream every priest cherished, but few were able to experience. He did not know that a life-changing event awaited him.

Divine Cultivation. The long winter was over. The farmer, weary from the endless years of raising one crop after another, looked across his fields. The dead, tangled brush was matted on the ground. The earth was packed by the winter rains and snows. Suddenly, the task seemed too great. He refused to plow his fields this year.

On the adjoining farm, the farmer's neighbor stood observing his own fields. He saw the same scene—the dried, matted weeds and the hard earth. But the neighbor also saw, in his mind's eye, the waving, golden grain that would stand proudly on that land as it had season after season through the long years. So the neighbor hitched up his horses and began the arduous task of cultivation. Soon the soil was broken up, the furrows were straightened, and the seed was planted. In the summer, the harvest came as the golden grain waved in the wind.

The calloused, sinful hearts of God's people must have looked like the hard, weed-infested land after a long winter, but God did not walk away. In a manner of speaking, He plowed the field and cultivated the hearts of the people. The coming of John the Baptist was one way that God prepared them for the coming of His Son.

The Role of the Herald. In ancient times, direct communication between a king and his subjects was often impossible. These rulers used special people, called heralds, to deliver messages and orders, and to announce decisions and events. If the king and his royal entourage planned to visit a particular city, elaborate preparations were made.

For instance, the road leading to the city was specially prepared so that it would be a straight path on which the king's carriage would ride smoothly without having to negotiate dangerous curves, deep descents, or steep hills. The official herald would precede the king, sometimes by several days. He would enter the city and proclaim to the people that the monarch was coming. The herald would do so with great urgency in his voice. It was a rare and cherished privilege for a city to host the king's presence.

John the Baptist was the herald for the coming Messiah. John, too, approached his task with great urgency. If the people were truly to receive the Messiah, they must repent of their sins. Their hearts must be cleansed in order to receive the King of kings and Lord of lords. In a sense, every believer is a herald of the Savior, who desires to occupy the hearts of all who will trust in Him.

FOR YOUTH

■ **TOPIC:** A Leading Role

■ **QUESTIONS:** 1. What was the difference between the miracles involved in John's and Jesus' births? 2. What was more important to Zechariah than merely having a son in his old age? 3. As *"the prophet of the Most High"* (Luke 1:76), what would John do? 4. In what way was John different from Jesus in his growing up years? 5. What can we do to ensure that our role in life is the one God has for us?

■ **ILLUSTRATIONS:**

Paul Revere's Midnight Ride. Every school boy and girl should know the account of Paul Revere, the American patriot who, in 1775, carried news to Lexington that the British troops were approaching. He called the people of the countryside to arms.

On a borrowed horse, Revere road through the town in the middle of the night, crying out to the sleeping people, "The British are coming! The British are coming!" News had come that General Thomas Gate, the British commander-in-chief of the Massachusetts Bay Colony, had been instructed to enforce order among the colonists. So he ordered his lieutenant to proceed with a detachment of 700 men to destroy the supplies of the colonists in Concord and to arrest the patriot leaders, Samuel Adams and John Hancock.

What if Revere, when he arrived in town on that April night, had walked quietly up to each door, tapped lightly, and apologetically told the occupant that it was rumored that some British soldiers might be moving in their direction? On the contrary, Revere rode through the town shouting at the top of his voice! Lamps were lighted, windows flung open, people poured into the streets, and they were mobilized in moments. Why? It's because Revere heralded impending danger and disaster, and the people responded accordingly.

What Are You Hearing? A man from rural east Texas was visiting his friend in the city of New York. As they walked down a crowded street, the visitor said, "I hear a cricket." "A cricket?" the New Yorker chirped. "No way! You could never hear a cricket in all of this noise! It's the noon hour, and people are all around us. Horns are honking and taxis are squealing around corners. There's no way you could be hearing a cricket!"

"Yes, but I'm sure I do," muttered the east Texan. He walked over to a shrub in a large cement planter by the curb of the street. He dug beneath the leaves and found the cricket he had heard. His friend was astounded. The Texan assured him that his ears were no different from anyone else's. "It simply depends on what you are listening for. Here, let me show you." He took several coins from his pocket and slammed them on the concrete sidewalk. People walking for several yards in both directions stopped and turned their heads. "You see what I mean? It all depends on what you are listening for."

In the desert of Judea, John the Baptist would listen for the voice of God. John would hear it, and he would spend the rest of his life pointing others to Christ. What are you hearing?

In the Worst of Times. An old, weathered tombstone stands in a centuries-old cemetery in England. The name chiseled in the stone is unknown, save, no doubt, to the family to which the deceased belonged. Beneath the name and birth and death dates is inscribed this epitaph with a powerful message: "In the worst of times, he did the best of things."

In the worst of times, God prepared a herald for the coming of His Son. The pagan Romans occupied Palestine. God's people lived in physical and spiritual bondage. John was true to God's calling in his life, and "in the worst of times, he did the best of things." In fact, John fulfilled the mission God had designed for him.

JESUS: GOD WITH US

BACKGROUND SCRIPTURE: Matthew 1:18-25
DEVOTIONAL READING: John 14:6-14

KEY VERSE: "Look, the virgin shall conceive and bear a son, and they shall name him Emmanuel," which means, "God is with us." Matthew 1:23.

KING JAMES VERSION

MATTHEW 1:18 Now the birth of Jesus Christ was on this wise: When as his mother Mary was espoused to Joseph, before they came together, she was found with child of the Holy Ghost.

19 Then Joseph her husband, being a just man, and not willing to make her a publick example, was minded to put her away privily.

20 But while he thought on these things, behold, the angel of the Lord appeared unto him in a dream, saying, Joseph, thou son of David, fear not to take unto thee Mary thy wife: for that which is conceived in her is of the Holy Ghost.

21 And she shall bring forth a son, and thou shalt call his name JESUS: for he shall save his people from their sins.

22 Now all this was done, that it might be fulfilled which was spoken of the Lord by the prophet, saying,

23 Behold, a virgin shall be with child, and shall bring forth a son, and they shall call his name Emmanuel, which being interpreted is, God with us.

24 Then Joseph being raised from sleep did as the angel of the Lord had bidden him, and took unto him his wife:

25 And knew her not till she had brought forth her firstborn son: and he called his name JESUS.

NEW REVISED STANDARD VERSION

MATTHEW 1:18 Now the birth of Jesus the Messiah took place in this way. When his mother Mary had been engaged to Joseph, but before they lived together, she was found to be with child from the Holy Spirit.

19 Her husband Joseph, being a righteous man and unwilling to expose her to public disgrace, planned to dismiss her quietly. 20 But just when he had resolved to do this, an angel of the Lord appeared to him in a dream and said, "Joseph, son of David, do not be afraid to take Mary as your wife, for the child conceived in her is from the Holy Spirit. 21 She will bear a son, and you are to name him Jesus, for he will save his people from their sins." 22 All this took place to fulfill what had been spoken by the Lord through the prophet:

23 "Look, the virgin shall conceive and bear a son,
   and they shall name him Emmanuel,"
which means, "God is with us." 24 When Joseph awoke from sleep, he did as the angel of the Lord commanded him; he took her as his wife, 25 but had no marital relations with her until she had borne a son; and he named him Jesus.

Monday, December 15	John 14:1-5	*Believe in God, Believe in Christ*
Tuesday, December 16	John 14:6-10	*Know Christ, Know the Father*
Wednesday, December 17	John 14:11-15	*I Am in the Father*
Thursday, December 18	John 14:16-20	*Christ in God, Us in Christ*
Friday, December 19	Isaiah 7:10-17	*Isaiah Prophesies Immanuel*
Saturday, December 20	Luke 2:1-7	*Jesus Is Born*
Sunday, December 21	Matthew 1:18-25	*Prophecy Fulfilled*

BACKGROUND

Matthew's Gospel has been called the bridge between the Old and New Testaments because it helps us understand the relationship between the old and new covenants. For instance, several times Matthew refers to some historical fact by making a statement similar to this: *Then was fulfilled what had been spoken through the prophet* (2:17). This suggests to us that the birth, death, and resurrection of Christ fulfilled the Old Testament prophecies concerning God's plan for the salvation.

Ancient Jewish writers, such as Matthew, believed that the best way to begin to tell the account of a person's life was to present his or her genealogy. Matthew thus began his Gospel with the statement, *An account of the genealogy of Jesus the Messiah, the son of David, the son of Abraham* (1:1).

Verse 17 explains that Jesus' genealogy, as Matthew presented it, comprises three sections of 14 generations each. Not every ancestor of the Savior appears in the list; yet as the descendant of Abraham and David—two of Israel's most esteemed ancestors—Jesus unquestionably qualifies as the nation's Messiah. Matthew wanted to show that the progress of biblical history had reached its fulfillment with the coming of the Savior.

The incarnation of Jesus—namely, God the Son coming to earth as a human being—is the central event of the opening chapter of Matthew's Gospel. He related the account of Jesus' miraculous conception and birth in a simple but heart-gripping style. Reading 1:18-25 will reassure a believer that the writer of these words was totally convinced that every detail of Jesus' incarnation was factual. Matthew did not attempt to throw a veil of mystery around Jesus' birth. Certainly there is a great mystery involved in what took place in the humble home of a young woman in Nazareth; yet Matthew's faith in the utter truth of the event was such that there was no shadow of doubt in his words.

Concerning ancient Jewish marriages, they consisted of three steps. First, a man and a woman became engaged when their two families agreed to the arrangement. The second step came when a public announcement was made and the couple became betrothed (*engaged*, 1:18). This formal agreement between couples planning to be married was taken much more seriously than modern-day engagements. It was considered legally binding and could be broken only by death or divorce. The relationship would not be physically consummated until after the couple was married. This comprised the third and final step in the process.

We can only imagine what Joseph must have felt when Mary *was found to be with child* (Matt. 1:18). Joseph initially did not know that Mary's offspring was *from the Holy Spirit*. According to Jewish law, if a woman broke the second step of the betrothal process by being intimate with another man, she faced serious consequences. The fiance had a right to divorce her, and the religious authorities could have the lawbreakers stoned to death (Deut. 22:23-24).

Joseph was faced with the social stigma attached to what he thought Mary had done; but Joseph, *being a righteous man* (Matt. 1:19), was *unwilling to expose [Mary] to public disgrace. Joseph thus *planned to dismiss her quietly.* However, before Joseph could enact his plan, God miraculously intervened.

Thus, *just when [Joseph] had resolved* (1:20) to end his betrothal to Mary, *an angel of the Lord appeared to [Joseph] in a dream.* Angels are spirit beings created by God to serve Him and to function as His messengers (Heb. 1:14). In addition to good angels, there are also fallen ones. The latter are under Satan's control and do his bidding. In the case of Joseph, a good angel appeared to him. Joseph's attitude toward Mary was reversed when the angel revealed to him that *the child conceived in [Mary] is from the Holy Spirit* (Matt. 1:20).

NOTES ON THE PRINTED TEXT

Matthew began his Gospel by recording *the genealogy of Jesus* (1:1). Matthew then presented the actual historical facts concerning how Jesus was miraculously conceived and born. The Gospel of Luke also discusses this event. Together the accounts of both Gospels provide the clear facts about the incarnation of the Messiah. Upon their records this great doctrine of Christianity has been established.

Matthew's emphasis is on the manner in which Jesus was born. His birth took place *in this way* (Matt. 1:18). Because He was *the Messiah,* His coming to earth as a human being would be unique. The way in which Adam came into the world was awesome (Gen. 2:7); but Jesus' entrance upon the human scene was far more amazing.

Matthew was not writing to those who knew nothing about Jesus' birth. The fact of His virginal conception apparently was already well known and fully accepted among the early believers. Matthew thus mentioned neither the exact time nor place of this event. However, we can infer from Luke 1:26 that the locale was *a town in Galilee called Nazareth.*

Mary and Joseph decided to enter into a legally binding arrangement by becoming *engaged* (Matt. 1:18). If Mary and Joseph were of the ages typical for marriage in their time and place, she was in her early teens and he was somewhat older. The couple must have dreamed about what their life together would be like; yet neither of them could have imagined the extraordinary privilege and responsibility that would be theirs—the rearing of God's Son.

Matthew clearly stated that Mary became pregnant before she and Joseph *lived together*. Mary evidently did not tell Joseph that she had conceived a child *from the Holy Spirit*. Mary learned this from *the angel Gabriel* (Luke 1:26). He also revealed that Mary's *relative Elizabeth in her old age has . . . conceived a son* (1:36).

Upon learning this, Mary *set out and went with haste* (1:39) to visit with Elizabeth and share her good news. Mary left the matter of her pregnancy in God's hands and thus showed her total reliance upon Him. This was all the more courageous on Mary's part, for she had no way of proving her faithfulness to Joseph or to anyone else in Nazareth. Also, Mary surely knew that she could face social stigma for her pregnancy.

Joseph was *a righteous man* (Matt. 1:19), and this guided him in his decision making. Perhaps like Zechariah and Elizabeth, Joseph was *living blamelessly according to all the commandments and regulations of the Lord* (Luke 1:6). The Greek word translated *righteous* (Matt. 1:19) described Joseph's heart as well as his conduct. Out of devotion to God, Joseph decided not to consummate his marriage vows with Mary when he discovered that she was pregnant. Joseph's response to this discovery tells us something else about him. Apparently there was no outburst of anger. Joseph's love for Mary was such that he refused *to expose her to public disgrace*; instead, Joseph *planned to dismiss her quietly*.

The Lord miraculously intervened by dispatching His *angel* (1:20). This celestial being would help Joseph understand the importance of what had taken place. Whereas the angel appeared to Joseph *in a dream* (1:20), Luke states that an angel *came to* (Luke 1:28) Mary, delivered his message, and *departed from* (1:38) Mary.

The angel addressed Joseph as the *son of David* (Matt. 1:20). Matthew's genealogy listed Joseph as a descendant of the royal house of David. Now Joseph must prove himself to be a true son of David, who would have faith to believe that the promise of a Messiah was about to be fulfilled.

The angel's message to Joseph removed all of his concerns. The angel's statement, *"for the child conceived in her is from the Holy Spirit,"* explained in the clearest way the great mystery of the Incarnation. Notice that the angel did not attempt to discuss the scientific details of how the virginal conception of Jesus took place. This is the way of divine inspiration. Truths the human mind could never completely fathom are expressed in direct and completely adequate terms.

The angel was careful to tell Joseph that Mary would *bear a son* (1:21). Zechariah had also been told that Elizabeth would bear him a son (Luke 1:13), and Abraham moreover learned that his wife Sarah would bear him a son (Gen. 17:19).

This child Mary would bear was not Joseph's offspring; nevertheless, he was *to name him Jesus, for he will save his people from their sins* (Matt. 1:21). Joseph would be the legal father of this child. Incidentally, the name *Jesus* means "The

Lord saves." This observation reminds us that the Father would redeem the lost through His Son.

Matthew not only described the virgin birth, but also provided scriptural support for this unique event. It ultimately fulfilled what Isaiah the prophet had foretold long ago (1:22). Verse 23 quotes Isaiah 7:14, which says *the young woman is with child and shall bear a son, and shall name him Immanuel.* When translated, *Emmanuel* (Matt. 1:23) means *"God is with us."* This implies that the sovereign, eternal Lord would be miraculously conceived in *the virgin*, and thereby become human and dwell among people.

When Joseph awoke from his dream, he acted immediately to carry out the angel's orders (1:24). Despite what others in Nazareth might think, Joseph took Mary to be *his wife.* Joseph abstained from marital relations with her until the child was born, *and he named him Jesus* (1:25) as the angel had commanded.

SUGGESTIONS TO TEACHERS

The English word "promise" comes from a Latin term that means "to send forth." This suggests that a promise given, either written or orally, becomes the basis for expecting something to develop or happen. For instance, God promised that humanity, through the Second Adam (Rom. 5:12-20)—Jesus Christ—would triumph over the forces of sin, death, and Satan (Gen. 3:15; Rom. 16:20). Through the long centuries, that promise was kept alive. Though people often break promises, God is faithful to keep His pledge (Heb. 6:13-17). He did so when, in a most unusual and unexpected way, He sent His Son, *Emmanuel* (Matt. 1:23), to be *"God . . . with us."*

1. THE DILEMMA OF A RIGHTEOUS MAN. Being a devout, upright Jew, Joseph possibly embraced the hope of his people for a Messiah to deliver them from the bondage they had experienced from Rome. Joseph was not prepared for the way God would choose to keep His promise to send a Savior. Nevertheless, Joseph was willing to obey God's instructions. Often God chooses to accomplish His purposes in our lives in unusual and unexpected ways.

2. THE MESSAGE OF THE ANGEL. The angel first addressed Joseph's fear. He most likely was afraid of the social stigma and other negative consequences that could befall Mary, whom Joseph deeply loved. The angel's explanation was opposed to human logic and reason, yet Joseph accepted by faith what he could not fully comprehend within himself. The angel told Joseph all he needed to know in order to fulfill the purpose God had planned for him, Mary, and her unborn child.

3. THE FULFILLMENT OF PROPHECY. Matthew confirmed the message of the angel by referring to Isaiah's prophecy that *"the virgin shall conceive and bear a son, and they shall name him Emmanuel"* (Matt. 1:23). This was yet another evidence that God keeps His promise. The waiting period may at times seem long and dark, but God's promises to us will never be broken.

■ **TOPIC:** Believing God's Promise

■ **QUESTIONS:** 1. How did the Jews view the engagement period between a man and woman? 2. How did Matthew discuss the miraculous conception of Jesus? 3. In what ways did Joseph demonstrate his upright character in the situation involving Mary? 4. How did Matthew link the virgin birth to the Old Testament? 5. How can Christians be involved in the fulfillment of God's promise to provide a Savior to redeem the lost from their sin?

■ **ILLUSTRATIONS:**

The Unseen Player. Many years ago the *London Observer* carried the following fictitious story. A family of mice lived all their lives in a large piano. In their piano world came the music of that instrument, filling all the dark spaces with sound and harmony.

At first, the mice were impressed by the music. They drew comfort and wonder from the thought that there was someone who made the music, though the music-maker was invisible to them. Yet whoever he was, he was above them, yet close to them. The mice loved to think of this person as the Great Player whom they could not see.

Then one day a daring mouse climbed up inside the piano and returned to his fellow mice. He had found out how the music was made! Wires were the secret. Tightly stretched wires of different lengths trembled and vibrated. The mice thus had to revise all their old beliefs. None but the most conservative of them could believe in the Unseen Player.

Later another mouse explorer discovered hammers that danced up and down on the wires. This was a more complicated theory, but it proved that they lived in a purely mechanical world. Thus the Unseen Player came to be thought of by the mice as only a myth. Despite all that, the pianist, the Unseen Player, continued to play.

This is the way it has been through the ages concerning the miraculous birth of Jesus. Critics have tried to destroy the credibility of His virginal conception, claiming that it is only a lovely myth, a story with much symbolism, but no literal truth. Yet today the light of God's truth shines brighter than ever on our Lord's amazing birth and on the sinless life He lived in order to redeem us from our sins.

God's Signature. H.B. London, in his newsletter, *The Pastor's Weekly Briefing,* told about the death of a close friend named Carl Gaede, an outstanding architect. He had won many prestigious awards for his church buildings across the country. Because of his creative skills, he was able to leave his "signature" behind him. People who never knew Gaede personally see his buildings, worship in the sanctuaries he designed, and are blessed by the beauty and uniqueness of those structures.

Our signature is that unique something about us that causes others to remember us. It is the legacy we leave behind us. God the Son left His signature in the world when, in the fullness of time, He stepped out of heaven and, in the form of a little baby, became Immanuel, "God with us." His signature was His everlasting love poured into flesh and blood that never knew sin.

Making Preparation. When our orthodox Jewish friends celebrate Passover, they set a place at the table for Elijah, for they expect him to return to earth at any time to announce that the Messiah is coming. Thus, with the greatest care, they make preparation for the Savior's advent.

What kind of preparation are we making to celebrate the marvelous fact that the Messiah has, indeed, already come? Has our preparation consisted only of festive decorations and the placing of gifts under a tree? What about our spiritual preparation? Do we understand something of the fantastic preparations God made from eternity past for the coming of His Son? Have we prepared our hearts and minds to properly celebrate His birth?

■ **TOPIC:** The Perfect Christmas Gift

■ **QUESTIONS:** 1. How did Mary's engagement to Joseph differ from a couple's engagement today? 2. What did Joseph's decision not to expose Mary to public disgrace tell us about him? 3. What did the angel tell Joseph about the baby conceived in Mary's womb? 4. Why did Matthew think it was important to include a prophecy from Isaiah in his account of the conception of Jesus? 5. How has God proven faithful to you in the keeping of His promises?

■ **ILLUSTRATIONS:**

Someone to See and Touch. A little boy was afraid to sleep alone. He did not like the darkness, and he could not stand the idea that he was in his bed, his room, all by himself. His mother tried to console him by reminding him that he was not alone and that God would be with him to protect him at all times. The little boy thought about this truth for a while. Then he said, "But I need somebody in here who has skin on him!"

God knew that we would be that way and that we could never conceive the fact He is *Spirit* (John 4:24). The Lord also knew that we could never feel secure with the reality of His presence until His Son appeared in time "with skin on him" (in a manner of speaking).

The First Creche. A legend has it that in December of 1223, Francis of Assisi was on his way to preach in the village of Greccio, Italy. As he walked, he pondered how he could bring home to the poor illiterate peasants the real meaning of Christmas. He wanted the account of the Savior's birth to live in their hearts.

Suddenly Francis had an idea. He would recreate the manger scene for his audience. First, he went to a friend in the village, and between them they fashioned the first creche, or nativity scene. Then, when the peasants came to the church on Christmas eve, they stopped in amazement and fell on their knees in adoration. There they saw a live donkey and ox. They also noticed real people playing the parts of Joseph, Mary, and the shepherds. Moreover, in a crude manger lay a representation of the infant Jesus.

Francis proceeded to tell the onlookers the wonderful account of the birth of Christ. This enabled the peasants to feel as if they were actually in ancient Bethlehem. This experience helped them never to forget the message of hope and gladness they heard that night.

Failing to See the Obvious. For most of us, celebrating Christmas has been a part of our lives from our earliest memory. Year after year we trim Christmas trees, affix garlands and wreaths throughout the house, sing the beloved carols, and exchange gifts. Sometimes, however, in the midst of our annual festivities, we pass by the obvious. We miss the miracle of the holiday.

Several years ago, in the fall of the year, my son took me in his car to the top of a small mountain just east of our town. I had passed this mountain for years and knew that it was there, but never paid any attention to it. The leaves were every shade of scarlet and yellow and brown.

My son said, "Let's get out of the car, Dad." He pointed across the valley below, and the many lush colors nearly took my breath away. Every fall this fabulous splash of color had been there, but I had not seen it! Let's not lose the miracle of Christmas beneath the tinsel and lights and wrapping paper.

JESUS GREW IN GOD'S FAVOR

BACKGROUND SCRIPTURE: Luke 2:40-52

DEVOTIONAL READING: John 5:19-24

KEY VERSE: Jesus increased in wisdom and in years, and in divine and human favor. Luke 2:52.

4

KING JAMES VERSION

LUKE 2:40 And the child grew, and waxed strong in spirit, filled with wisdom: and the grace of God was upon him.

41 Now his parents went to Jerusalem every year at the feast of the passover.

42 And when he was twelve years old, they went up to Jerusalem after the custom of the feast.

43 And when they had fulfilled the days, as they returned, the child Jesus tarried behind in Jerusalem; and Joseph and his mother knew not of it.

44 But they, supposing him to have been in the company, went a day's journey; and they sought him among their kinsfolk and acquaintance.

45 And when they found him not, they turned back again to Jerusalem, seeking him.

46 And it came to pass, that after three days they found him in the temple, sitting in the midst of the doctors, both hearing them, and asking them questions.

47 And all that heard him were astonished at his understanding and answers.

48 And when they saw him, they were amazed: and his mother said unto him, Son, why hast thou thus dealt with us? behold, thy father and I have sought thee sorrowing.

49 And he said unto them, How is it that ye sought me? wist ye not that I must be about my Father's business?

50 And they understood not the saying which he spake unto them.

51 And he went down with them, and came to Nazareth, and was subject unto them: but his mother kept all these sayings in her heart.

52 And Jesus increased in wisdom and stature, and in favour with God and man.

NEW REVISED STANDARD VERSION

LUKE 2:40 The child grew and became strong, filled with wisdom; and the favor of God was upon him.

41 Now every year his parents went to Jerusalem for the festival of the Passover. 42 And when he was twelve years old, they went up as usual for the festival. 43 When the festival was ended and they started to return, the boy Jesus stayed behind in Jerusalem, but his parents did not know it. 44 Assuming that he was in the group of travelers, they went a day's journey. Then they started to look for him among their relatives and friends. 45 When they did not find him, they returned to Jerusalem to search for him. 46 After three days they found him in the temple, sitting among the teachers, listening to them and asking them questions. 47 And all who heard him were amazed at his understanding and his answers. 48 When his parents saw him they were astonished; and his mother said to him, "Child, why have you treated us like this? Look, your father and I have been searching for you in great anxiety." 49 He said to them, "Why were you searching for me? Did you not know that I must be in my Father's house?" 50 But they did not understand what he said to them. 51 Then he went down with them and came to Nazareth, and was obedient to them. His mother treasured all these things in her heart.

52 And Jesus increased in wisdom and in years, and in divine and human favor.

BACKGROUND

Much of Jesus' growth and development from infancy to adulthood is difficult for us to fathom. This is because Jesus was truly human as well as truly divine. Also, neither His body nor His spirit was touched by sin. As a human being, Jesus grew in physical strength and in mental understanding, yet He was completely unhindered by those sinful influences that affect all of us who are descendants of Adam. Jesus' body and spirit responded to His heavenly Father much as a bud drinks in the sunshine and rain and grows into a beautiful and perfect blossom.

The Scripture passage immediately preceding this week's lesson text is the account of Jesus' presentation *to the Lord* (Luke 2:22). According to Jewish custom, a woman who had given birth to a male child was unclean for seven days, or until the child was circumcised. For 33 days afterward, she was not allowed to touch *any holy thing, or come into the sanctuary* (Lev. 12:4). Then she had to come to the temple to be purified in the proper way. It was in connection with this ritual that Mary and Joseph brought Jesus to *Jerusalem* (Luke 2:22).

The Mosaic law also stipulated that every firstborn son had to be presented to the Lord and redeemed or bought back from Him for the price of five shekels (Num. 18:15-16). It was during this visit to the temple that Joseph, Mary, and Jesus met Simeon, who spoke prophetically about the Messiah (Luke 2:34-35). Then Anna, upon seeing Jesus, *began to praise God and to speak about the child to all who were looking for the redemption of Jerusalem* (2:38). No doubt the meeting with Simeon and Anna was another one of those mysteries Mary *pondered . . . in her heart* (2:19).

Luke states that Joseph and Mary *returned to Galilee, to their own town of Nazareth* (2:39). Luke, however, neither mentioned the events recorded in Matthew 2 nor any specific event that may have happened until Jesus was 12 years old. We assume that Joseph and Mary had children of their own during this time, for the Scriptures mention four of Jesus' half-brothers, *James and Joseph and Simon and Judas* (Matt. 13:55) and His *sisters* (13:56).

Luke was careful to note how Jesus grew and developed during this time (Luke 2:40). We can only imagine what an unusual situation existed in Joseph's home during those years. Was there sibling rivalry? Did these children, who were born with a sin nature (as all of us are), resent Jesus' perfect life and consistently godly conduct? How did Mary and Joseph deal with such problems in the home? These are issues that Scripture does not address. Despite this, the Bible sheds much light on the way in which Jesus related to His heavenly Father during the early years of the Savior's life.

NOTES ON THE PRINTED TEXT

Luke's statement concerning the physical development of Jesus compares with those made about other children whom God had chosen to serve a special role in His plan. For instance, concerning Samson, the author of Judges wrote, *The boy grew, and the LORD blessed him* (Judg. 13:24). Also, concerning Samuel it is written, *the boy Samuel grew up in the presence of the LORD* (1 Sam. 2:21). A further word about Samuel is even more closely related to Luke's words about Jesus: *Now the boy Samuel continued to grow both in stature and in favor with the Lord and with the people* (2:26). Moreover, Luke wrote about John the Baptist, *the child grew and became strong in spirit* (Luke 1:80).

This information indicates that Jesus' physical development was like any other healthy child. The writer of Hebrews supports this inference in his statement that Jesus *in every respect has been tested as we are, yet without sin* (Heb. 4:15). In order to identify with us in every way (except for sin), Jesus' physical growth from infancy to adulthood was a natural process.

Luke, being a physician by training, took special note of the physical maturation of Jesus, noting that *the child grew and became strong* (Luke 2:40). Luke knew, as a student of medical science, that the human body is a divine masterpiece in the way it is formed and how it grows. And concerning Jesus, because He was a carpenter's apprentice to Joseph, He needed physical strength to handle the tools of that trade. Jesus' townsfolk must have known about His carpenter's skills, for they said concerning Him, *Is not this the carpenter, the son of Mary* (Mark 6:3).

Luke moreover emphasized that Jesus was *filled with wisdom* (Luke 2:40). The wording of the text indicates that this development was an ongoing process. Jesus' wisdom was more than mere intellectual knowledge. It included the ability to use the knowledge He acquired to the best advantage.

Luke noted that *the favor of God was upon [Jesus]*. The Greek word rendered "favor" is also translated "grace" in the New Testament. Here, however, it is used in the wider sense of God's blessing. Because Jesus was human as well as divine, during His earthly life He depended on His heavenly Father for all things, just as we do. But Jesus was sinless, and God's favor upon Him was for reasons unique to His earthly life and ministry.

During Jesus' childhood, Joseph and Mary regularly attended the Passover festival in Jerusalem (2:41). In ancient times, every Jewish male was expected to attend the feasts of Passover, Pentecost, and Tabernacles in holy city (Exod. 23:14-17; 34:23; Deut. 16:16). When the Jews were dispersed throughout the known world because of persecution, most of them could not return to Jerusalem each year to attend these festivals. Some Jews, however, had the means to attend. Women were not required to attend, though many did. Because Mary went each year with Joseph, we can infer that Jesus grew up in a very devout home.

About the age of 12, a Jewish boy became "a son of the (divine) law" (that is, a *bar mitzvah*). This meant he pledged to learn and to obey the commandments of God. Similarly today, a Jewish boy spends his twelfth year studying the *Torah* (a Hebrew word normally translated "law") with rabbis and other Jewish scholars and teachers. Also, it is the dream of every Jewish boy to celebrate his *bar mitzvah* at Jerusalem's Western Wall. This is that portion of the retaining wall of the temple mount on which the sanctuary stood before the Romans destroyed the city in A.D. 70. In light of this information, we can understand why Jesus, while at *the festival* (2:42), spent time *sitting among the teachers, listening to them and asking them questions* (2:46).

People who attended Passover from far distances traveled in groups or caravans for safety. Women and children usually traveled at the front of the caravan and the men brought up the rear. At the age of 12, Jesus could have been with either group. Perhaps Mary and Joseph assumed that Jesus was with the other children. But He was so absorbed in His time at the temple that He remained behind while the caravan left (2:43). The group had traveled *a day's journey* (2:44) before Mary and Joseph began searching for Jesus among their relatives and friends.

When Jesus' parents were unable to find Him, they returned to Jerusalem (2:45). Finally, *after three days they found him* (2:46). Mary and Joseph had traveled with the caravan one day north toward Galilee, and it required a day for them to return to Jerusalem. Then they spent a day searching throughout the city for Jesus.

Around the temple were beautiful and spacious porches that provided excellent places for teaching. Mary and Joseph probably found Jesus in one of these locations with the teachers of the law. He was listening to them and asking them questions. Both the questions asked and the answers Jesus gave were such that *all who heard him were amazed at his understanding and his answers* (2:47).

When Jesus' parents found Him, it was Mary who addressed Him (2:48). There was surprise and frustration in Mary's words. This was the natural response of a mother who temporarily had lost her child. Jesus' answer showed that He had a clear understanding of the relationship between Himself and His Father. Throughout Jesus' public ministry, He referred to this relationship again and again. Jesus knew that He was one with His Father. For instance, Jesus' statement to Mary, *"Did you not know that I must be in my Father's house?"* (2:49), revealed that Jesus knew His life was on a divine schedule.

Mary and Joseph, it turns out, did not understand what Jesus meant (2:50). Despite this, *he went down with them and came to Nazareth, and was obedient to them* (2:51). In this way, Jesus set a wonderful example of obeying His parents.

Also, as the days passed, Mary *treasured all these things in her heart.* Moreover, during the days that followed, *Jesus increased in wisdom and in years, and in divine and human favor* (2:52). In other words, He kept growing stronger and wiser, for God was preparing Him for His redemptive work that lay ahead.

SUGGESTIONS TO TEACHERS

Little is known about Jesus' life from His presentation as an infant in the temple until He was 12 years old. We also have few details about what happened to Him up until the time He began His public ministry. Nevertheless, we can glean much from what is both said and implied in Scripture concerning Jesus' early life. By way of example, the Father, in His wisdom, chose for His Son to be born as an infant and to grow physically, mentally, spiritually, and socially in a normal way, except that He was without sin. Thus, as Jesus increased in God's favor, He modeled the kind of life we should strive to live.

1. LAYING THE FOUNDATION. Jesus did not live a pampered life on earth. For instance, carpentry in ancient times was a physically demanding occupation. Thus, as Jesus learned this trade from Joseph, the Savior developed a strong body in order to handle the demands of the trade.

At the same time, Jesus studied the Scriptures in the local synagogue, and God gave Him wisdom to understand the Old Testament. Because Jesus was God's beloved Son and without sin, the Father's unlimited favor was upon Him. Christian parents should seize every opportunity, with God's help, to influence their children for Christ during the early years of their lives.

2. PREPARING FOR MINISTRY. Jesus no doubt looked forward with great anticipation to attending the Passover festival in Jerusalem with His parents. Perhaps it was as He anticipated being recognized as a full-fledged member of the Jewish community that He sat at the feet of the teachers of the law in the temple.

Jesus not only benefitted from this experience, but also made an unforgettable impression upon the religious scholars because of the wisdom He displayed in His answers. A consistent exposure to God's Word and Christian teaching will help create a desire in a child's heart to know more about the Lord.

3. WAITING FOR GOD'S TIME. Jesus, at the age 12, was fully aware of His unique identity. He was also committed to obeying His heavenly Father. Jesus thus continued to honor His earthly parents by submitting to them. Also, after Jesus returned with them to their home in Nazareth, the Savior continued to grow physically toward adulthood.

Jesus' fellow townsfolk became increasingly aware of His dedication to God and desire to obey His commandments. It was also more and more evident that the grace of God was upon Jesus' life. Young people sometimes become impatient in their desire to break away from their home ties; but a loving Christian home atmosphere can help them develop the patience they need to wait for God's leading in their lives.

FOR ADULTS

■ **TOPIC:** Learning to Grow

■ **QUESTIONS:** 1. What is the difference between the way in which God's favor was manifested to Jesus and the way it is often shown to us? 2. How might Jesus have anticipated attending the Passover festival with His parents in Jerusalem? 3. In ancient times, what was the spiritual significance of a Jewish boy's twelfth birthday? 4. What caused the teachers of the law to be so impressed with the way Jesus responded to them? 5. What can parents learn from Jesus' childhood regarding the rearing of their own children?

■ **ILLUSTRATIONS:**

The Carpenter's Apprentice. What kind of tools and wood did Joseph use in his carpenter's shop in Nazareth? Archaeologists have discovered certain hand tools, most of which would be familiar to carpenters today.

To lay out the design of a building there was a ruler, a square, a straightedge, a chalkline, a plumbline, a level, and a marker or scriber. Different local woods were used for building—oak, pine, cypress, and sycamore fig. For special projects, such as furniture and kitchen utensils, there would be walnut, cedar, and olive wood. Axes were found along with large saws for ripping boards. Also excavated were primitive hatchets, mallets, chisels, planes, knives, and the axes used to smooth and fashion the planks.

Because Nazareth in Jesus' day was a small village with limited building projects, Joseph and Jesus might have worked also in Sepphoris, four miles northeast of Nazareth. Sepphoris was the Roman capital of Galilee during the first century. In any case, Jesus grew physically strong as He worked alongside Joseph and learned from him the skills of carpentry.

The Attractiveness of Christianity. The Society of Friends (Quakers) has a list of rules called "intentions" that have to do with a person's relationship with other people. One commitment is "to share myself with my household (an hour daily in relaxed conversation)."

Jesus undoubtedly had a winsome and loving personality at home as a child with His family. Moreover, as He grew, He *increased in wisdom and in years, and in divine and human favor* (Luke 2:52). We can be sure that Jesus did not stand among the teachers in the temple with an overbearing confidence, but with an eager, open mind and a humble spirit. He showed such a winsome respect for the leaders in the temple that *all who heard him were amazed at his understanding and his answers* (2:47).

The Freedom of Choice. Doug and Dan were fraternal twins; also, their parents were committed Christians and devoted to their church. The father and mother saw to it that their twin boys were in Sunday school and church from the time they were preschoolers.

Over the years, the parents watched the personalities of the twins develop. Doug was sensitive, kindhearted, and obedient, while Dan was stubborn, insensitive, and disobedient toward his parents. Often he had to be disciplined because of his insolence, whereas Doug rarely needed correction. Both boys were exposed to the same parental love and Christian influence.

Dan's teenage years were stormy and defiant, while Doug was solid and consistent in his faith. He loved his brother Dan and did all that he could to help him. Doug developed into a dependable, Christian man. He and Dan had a choice before them—to follow their parents' teaching and example or choose their own path. In the case of Jesus, He responded favorably to the teaching of Mary and Joseph.

For Youth

■ **Topic:** Growing in Mind, Body, and Spirit

■ **Questions:** 1. In what ways did Jesus grow during His adolescent years in Nazareth? 2. Why was Jesus' heavenly Father continually pleased with Him? 3. Why was the Passover festival so important to the Jews in ancient times? 4. How would you describe Jesus' attitude as He listened to the teachers in the temple and asked them questions? 5. How can a consistent faith in God help you grow in mind, body, and spirit?

■ **Illustrations:**

The Master Teacher. The old potter sat at his ancient wheel, pedaling it with his feet to make it spin. Beside him sat a young boy, his face eager and his eyes fastened on the potter's hands. The potter thrust a shapeless lump of clay in the center of the wheel. He felt the texture of the clay and gently began to move his fingers across its surface. Then he stopped the wheel, took the lump from it, and handed it to the lad.

The artisan rose from his stool and motioned for the boy to be seated. Barely able to reach the treadle, the boy began to spin the wheel. He placed the lump on the wheel, but not in the center. The results were disastrous! Patiently, the potter showed his young student the importance of centering the clay on the wheel. Then, step by step, he went through the process of molding a simple vase.

Though the boy's first attempt was quite primitive, he soon learned the basic steps. Because he sat with a master potter, he was well on his way to learning this ancient art. Jesus, as a youth, recognized the men in the temple as wise students of Scripture. He listened to them carefully and thereby grew in wisdom.

Lost! Little Bob was six years old. He had gone with his parents to a large department store in town that had a fabulous toy section. They left him with the toys while they shopped several aisles away. After a while, Bob decided to rejoin his parents. He looked down one aisle and then another, and assumed they had forgotten about him! But Bob knew the way home. He quickly left the store, walked several blocks until he was out of the shopping area, and found the street that led about 10 blocks to his home. An older woman asked Bob whether he was lost, and he blurted, "No! I'm going home!" The woman then asked whether Bob would like for her to walk with him. Bob agreed that it would be nice.

In the meantime, Bob's parents had panicked and notified the police, who began a frantic search through the downtown area. A dozen officers, several squad cars, and a helicopter were dispatched. Meanwhile, Bob's parents decided to drive home to see whether a friend had intercepted Bob and had driven him home. To the parent's great delight and relief, they found Bob sitting in the swing on their front porch with his new friend. Bob's parents' joy at finding him softened their words of correction.

Mary and Joseph were "lost from Jesus," but He was not lost, for He was in His Father's house.

The Path to Spiritual Growth. Ben and Ralph were both high school seniors. They had been invited by one of their friends to attend a youth activity at his church. Somewhat reluctantly, they agreed. Many of the young people were their peers in high school. The church youth reached out to Ben and Ralph and made them feel welcome and comfortable by inviting the two to Sunday school.

One day Ben and Ralph asked for an appointment with the pastor and expressed their desire to trust in Christ. Afterward, they said to the pastor, "We do not come from Christian homes. We do not know anything about the Bible. Would you help us learn how to study it?" The pastor gladly agreed, and began meeting regularly with the two youths. They were eager learners, and the pastor watched them grow spiritually because of their regular exposure to the Word of God.

Jesus, as a boy, loved God's Word, and it was reflected in His desire to study and learn its teachings.

Integrity in the Midst of Suffering

BACKGROUND SCRIPTURE: Job 1—2:10
DEVOTIONAL READING: Romans 8:18-25

KEY VERSE: Shall we receive the good at the hand of God, and not receive the bad? Job 2:10.

KING JAMES VERSION

JOB 2:1 Again there was a day when the sons of God came to present themselves before the LORD, and Satan came also among them to present himself before the LORD.

2 And the LORD said unto Satan, From whence comest thou? And Satan answered the LORD, and said, From going to and fro in the earth, and from walking up and down in it.

3 And the LORD said unto Satan, Hast thou considered my servant Job, that there is none like him in the earth, a perfect and an upright man, one that feareth God, and escheweth evil? and still he holdeth fast his integrity, although thou movedst me against him, to destroy him without cause.

4 And Satan answered the LORD, and said, Skin for skin, yea, all that a man hath will he give for his life.

5 But put forth thine hand now, and touch his bone and his flesh, and he will curse thee to thy face.

6 And the LORD said unto Satan, Behold, he is in thine hand; but save his life.

7 So went Satan forth from the presence of the LORD, and smote Job with sore boils from the sole of his foot unto his crown.

8 And he took him a potsherd to scrape himself withal; and he sat down among the ashes.

9 Then said his wife unto him, Dost thou still retain thine integrity? curse God, and die.

10 But he said unto her, Thou speakest as one of the foolish women speaketh. What? shall we receive good at the hand of God, and shall we not receive evil? In all this did not Job sin with his lips.

NEW REVISED STANDARD VERSION

JOB 2:1 One day the heavenly beings came to present themselves before the LORD, and Satan also came among them to present himself before the LORD. 2 The LORD said to Satan, "Where have you come from?" Satan answered the LORD, "From going to and fro on the earth, and from walking up and down on it." 3 The LORD said to Satan, "Have you considered my servant Job? There is no one like him on the earth, a blameless and upright man who fears God and turns away from evil. He still persists in his integrity, although you incited me against him, to destroy him for no reason." 4 Then Satan answered the LORD, "Skin for skin! All that people have they will give to save their lives. 5 But stretch out your hand now and touch his bone and his flesh, and he will curse you to your face." 6 The LORD said to Satan, "Very well, he is in your power; only spare his life."

7 So Satan went out from the presence of the LORD, and inflicted loathsome sores on Job from the sole of his foot to the crown of his head. 8 Job took a potsherd with which to scrape himself, and sat among the ashes.

9 Then his wife said to him, "Do you still persist in your integrity? Curse God, and die." 10 But he said to her, "You speak as any foolish woman would speak. Shall we receive the good at the hand of God, and not receive the bad?" In all this Job did not sin with his lips.

Monday, December 29	Romans 8:18-23	*Present Suffering and Future Glory*
Tuesday, December 30	Romans 8:24-28	*All Things Work Together for Good*
Wednesday, December 31	Romans 8:29-33	*God Is for Us*
Thursday, January 1	Romans 8:34-39	*Nothing Can Separate Christ's Love*
Friday, January 2	Job 1:1-5	*Job Was Upright*
Saturday, January 3	Job 1:13-22	*Job Kept Integrity in Suffering*
Sunday, January 4	Job 2:1-10	*Job Would Not Curse God*

BACKGROUND

In some respects the Book of Job is a long answer to a pointed question: if God is the sovereign Lord of the universe, then why does He allow suffering to come to the godly and good fortune to the wicked? For Job, thinking about this question moved into a consideration of the nature of God. In the face of Job's multiple calamities, he was forced to examine the foundations of his faith and to scrutinize his concept of the Lord.

Thus Job found himself struggling with this issue as well as with his counselors' traditional answers to it. Their primary view, stated and discounted throughout the book, was that human suffering is a direct result of sin. They believed that God punishes the wicked in this life by sending affliction, and He rewards the righteous in this life by providing blessings.

Such a view, however, did nothing to clear up Job's perplexity, since he knew he was a righteous man and had done nothing to earn the suffering he was having to endure. In reality, Job was afflicted in numerous ways as a test of his faithfulness to the Lord; nevertheless, Job was oblivious to the fact that he was the object of that test—one God Himself had permitted after being challenged by Satan.

Concerning when the book was written, no conclusive evidence has been found determining the date of Job. Some have suggested an early time period because of the fact that the book makes no mention of the patriarchs, the 12 tribes of Israel, or Moses.

This leads some to believe that the book was written in the time before Moses (about 1566–1446 B.C.). If so, then Job is the oldest book of the Bible. As such, it offers us insight into people's conceptions of God before they possessed written revelation.

Some Bible scholars propose much later dates for the writing of Job. Some say it was written during the reign of Solomon (970–930 B.C.), while others are far more general, saying it was written sometime between the times of Moses and Ezra.

Whatever view is taken, the writer undoubtedly was a skillful poet from the covenant community. While the numerous details in Job indicate that the events occurred during the patriarchal era, the literary evidence suggests that the book was written sometime later during an era when wisdom flourished.

NOTES ON THE PRINTED TEXT

In the prologue to the Book of Job (chaps. 1—2), six short but key scenes set the stage for Job's debate with his friends and his ultimate encounter with God (described later). The fourth scene (2:1-6), which divulges Satan's second challenge to God, begins with the mention of *the heavenly beings* (2:1). This phrase refers to the angels, who are superior to humans in power and intelligence. According to the Book of Job, these celestial entities periodically presented themselves before God, though we know little about the gatherings.

In the scenes of the celestial assembly, only one heavenly being, other than God Himself, is identified. This entity is referred to in Hebrew only by his title, which means "the adversary." In English he is called *Satan*. This character is one of the *heavenly beings* who serve under and report to the Lord.

The Lord asked Satan *"Where have you come from?"* (2:2). The adversary, in response, stated he had been going all over *"the earth."* Satan offered no report of what he had done to Job or of Job's response to his actions; but God showed that He knew about what had transpired by reminding the evil one about Job's blamelessness.

Verse 3 piles on one virtue after another in describing this person's integrity, including *blameless* and *upright*. The sense is that Job was distinguished among his peers. He not only revered God but also shunned evil, being a person of genuine virtue. Even Satan's attempts to harm Job could not cause him to deter from the path of uprightness.

The adversary, of course, disagreed with God's evaluation of Job's integrity. Satan cynically retorted that Job, like anyone else, was willing to sacrifice his family's *skin* (2:4) in order to save his own. The devil argued that, if God permitted him to attack Job's own *bone* (2:5) and *flesh,* then Job would give in and *curse* God.

God agreed to allow Satan to do what he proposed, but with one restriction: *"spare [Job's] life"* (2:6). Job likely had enjoyed excellent health and had never suffered any significant physical pain. For a person to come to mature adulthood blessed with good health and then experience the unspeakable suffering that came to Job is horrible beyond words.

Job suffered *loathsome sores . . . from the sole of his foot to the crown of his head* (2:7). We do not know the exact disease that afflicted Job. Some have said that he was covered with boils, while others suggest some form of leprosy. Still others believe it was elephantitis, which causes almost unbearable pain and disfigures one hideously.

In any case, Job *took a potsherd with which to scrape himself* (2:8). This ancient practice of scraping one's skin with a piece of broken pottery not only relieved the terrible itching, but also would remove the infected matter. While Job was scraping himself, he *sat among the ashes.* Ashes often were associated with sacrifices, mourning, and fasting. Also, putting ashes on one's head and sitting in ashes expressed grief, humiliation, and repentance. Moreover, an ash heap was perhaps the most sterile place a person with sores could sit. Here we see that total suffering had come to Job—physically, psychologically, socially, and spiritually. The ordeal seemed worse than death itself.

Job's wife apparently lacked the spiritual commitment and faith in God that Job demonstrated. Of course, Job's wife did not know the limitation God had placed on Satan in regard to his dealings with Job. On a human level we can sympathize with Job's wife as she observed her husband's deplorable condition.

"Do you still persist in your integrity?" (2:9), Job's wife asked him. Her words seem to have dripped with sarcasm, inferring that all of Job's righteous living had resulted in this terrible end. Chrysostom, the archbishop of Constantinople, explained that Satan did not destroy Job's wife along with his children so that the devil could use her as one of his tools against Job. Augustine labeled Job's wife as "the devil's advocate" who tempted her husband, and John Calvin called her "the embodiment of Satan."

"Curse God, and die," Job's wife said to him. To curse God in ancient times was a way of denying Him. Job's reply was masterful. He told his wife that she spoke *"as any foolish woman would speak"* (2:10). Job was not referring to intellectual foolishness, but to the kind of religious apostasy David had in mind when he wrote, *Fools say in their hearts, "There is no God"* (Ps. 14:1).

By Job's answer, we can see that he believed that his wife was speaking inappropriately. In contrast to this was the wisdom of Job: *"Shall we receive the good at the hand of God, and not receive the bad?"* (Job 2:10). In other words, Job was willing to receive with humility whatever God allowed to come into his life, whether good or bad. He maintained the same trust in God that he had evidenced after his first test (1:20-22). In this way, Job proved that God's confidence in him was well placed.

SUGGESTIONS TO TEACHERS

One fact we can be sure of is that we shall all suffer at one time or another and in one way or another. Our experiences of suffering often come unannounced and catch us off guard. The way in which we cope with these felling blows will be determined by the strength of our faith and the depth of our commitment to God. Though Job struggled as his trials continued and became more intense, he never abandoned his faith in God.

1. GOD KNOWS HIS PEOPLE. One of the marvels of our heavenly Father is that He knows us completely. Being the eternal God, He has our total lives spread out before Him, from beginning to end. He rejoices when we are strong, and He understands and is ready to help us when we falter.

2. GOD PROTECTS HIS PEOPLE. God knew the limits of Job's faith and endurance, and He placed a barrier beyond which Satan could not go in his attacks on Job. Though God allows trials and testings to come into our lives that almost seem impossible to endure at times, He knows our breaking point. He will not permit a temptation that is beyond our ability, in Him, to bear (1 Cor. 10:13).

3. GOD GIVES WISDOM TO HIS PEOPLE. Job loved his wife, and she had borne ten children whom Job loved with all of his heart. His wife's shocking suggestion surely was one of the most painful experiences Job could have. Yet, despite that terrible blow, God gave Job wisdom to answer his wife, even while he was suffering in the midst of a situation he could in no way understand. God has promised wisdom to His people that will help them endure overwhelming situations that come into their lives (Jas. 1:5).

FOR ADULTS

■ TOPIC: Holding Firm in Suffering
■ QUESTIONS: 1. What did Satan request as he came before God in heaven ? 2. Why do you think God asked Satan whether he had considered Job? 3. How had Satan misjudged Job in the accusation the devil brought against him? 4. What was inappropriate about the remarks Job's wife made to him in the midst of his suffering? 5. What example did Job provide for God's people when they find themselves in the midst of unexpected and intense suffering?

■ **ILLUSTRATIONS:**

How to Handle Troubles. Three women were talking about how they had handled worry and trouble in their lives. One said, "I have had lots of troubles. I have lain awake nights wrestling with them. Then I discovered that those things that worried me most never happened!" The second woman said, "I was once told that we carry 'three bags of troubles'—those we really have, those we had in the past, and those we are sure we are going to have."

The third lady chuckled and said, "Right now, I can't seem to remember my troubles. The Lord said for us to cast all our cares on Him. He gives me strength for each day's work, and helps me over the hard places. At night, by the time I've finished thanking Him for His goodness, I'm always so tired that I just fall asleep."

Taking Our Blessings for Granted. Novelist Somerset Maugham kept a cracked earthenware cup on the mantel in his plush London home. When someone asked him about that ugly, broken centerpiece among all of the beautiful objects of art there, he explained: "During the First World War, on a troop ship crossing the ocean, our rations of water were reduced to just one cup a day. I drank my ration of water from that cup, and I keep it on the mantel as a reminder that I can never take my blessings for granted."

Job had the same attitude toward life. In his prosperity, he did not forget to praise God for His blessings. And when these were taken away, Job eventually learned that the Lord still remained with him through his ordeals.

How God "Tempers" Us. Pastor J. Allen Blair tells the account of a certain blacksmith who had given his heart to Christ. One day a friend approached him and asked, "Why is it that you have so much trouble? I have been watching you since you became a Christian. You seem to have twice as many trials and troubles as you had before. I thought that when a person gave himself to God, his troubles were over!"

The blacksmith thought for a moment, and then said, "God saves us for something more than to have a good time. He chooses a certain task for us, and then He must temper us, as I am tempering this steel, to perform that task in life. That's where the trials and testings come in. They are painful, and we cannot always understand them. But we can be sure that God will give us the strength to bear them, if we will let Him."

FOR YOUTH

■ **TOPIC:** Holding Fast in Tough Times
■ **QUESTIONS:** 1. Why do you think the angels seemed to come periodically before the Lord? 2. What sort of relationship do you think exists between God and Satan? 3. What lesson do we learn from the fact God refused to allow Satan to kill Job? 4. How would you describe Job's wife? 5. Can you think of a time in your life when God gave you strength to bear an unexpected crisis?

■ **ILLUSTRATIONS:**

The Danger of Overconfidence. In Harold Begbie's *Twice-Born Men*, he tells the story of "O.B.D."—"Old Born Drunk"—who comes to Christ from the gutters of London through the ministry of the Salvation Army. He gets his name "O.B.D." because no one ever remembers seeing him sober. After his conversion he never drinks again. When someone asks whether alcohol continued to be O.B.D's "thorn in the flesh," he answers that he had no desire to drink, but the miracle was that "God had to deliver him from his pipe."

Paul warned us, *"So if you think you are standing, watch out that you do not fall"* (1 Cor. 10:12). Satan always probes for our weaknesses, just as he was searching for the weak spot in Job's character.

The Gold Ring. Cory was a college freshman. Through his high school years, he was deeply involved in the youth group in his church. His last two summers before college, he had worked in Christian camps for young children. Because of his outgoing personality, he made friends quickly in college.

One night, following a football game, three fellow students asked Cory to go with them for a late-night snack. When they stopped at a roadside café, one of the boys retrieved a carton of beer from the trunk of the car. When Cory refused to accept a can, the other boys began to pressure him. "Just one drink! What will it hurt? So you've never tried it—you need to know what it's like!"

Cory wanted very much to be accepted. He was about to weaken when he felt the plain, gold ring on the little finger of his right hand. His mother had given it to him the day he left home. His mother said, "Cory, when you are tempted to do something wrong, feel this ring. It will remind you that I am praying for you daily." Cory's resolve was strengthened and he was able to resist the temptation. Because of Job's strong faith in God, he too was able to resist the "easy way out" (as the saying goes) of his terrible dilemma.

Serving God with One Hand. Sarah was a high school senior and had won many music awards as a pianist. A major university had offered her a full scholarship to study piano in its school of music. During the summer following her graduation from high school, Sarah was involved in an automobile accident. One of her hands was so badly mangled that it had to be removed.

Sarah's Sunday school teacher dreaded visiting her in the hospital. How would Sarah respond to this tragedy? Would she be bitter? To the teacher's surprise, Sarah met her with a smile. Sarah's eyes sparkled as she told her Sunday school teacher that God knew her future, and apparently it was not His plan for her to perform. But Sarah could teach. She would train other young people to play the piano. Just as Job *did not sin with his lips* (2:10) because of his great loss, so Sarah determined to glorify God with her life regardless of what had happened to her.

INTEGRITY IN SEEKING GOD

BACKGROUND SCRIPTURE: Job 9:32-35; 13:20-24; 19:25-27; 23:10-12
DEVOTIONAL READING: Psalm 26:1-12

KEY VERSE: I would speak to the Almighty, and
I desire to argue my case with God. Job 13:3.

KING JAMES VERSION

JOB 9:32 For he is not a man, as I am, that I should answer him, and we should come together in judgment.

33 Neither is there any daysman betwixt us, that might lay his hand upon us both.

34 Let him take his rod away from me, and let not his fear terrify me:

35 Then would I speak, and not fear him; but it is not so with me. . . .

13:20 Only do not two things unto me: then will I not hide myself from thee.

21 Withdraw thine hand far from me: and let not thy dread make me afraid.

22 Then call thou, and I will answer: or let me speak, and answer thou me.

23 How many are mine iniquities and sins? make me to know my transgression and my sin.

24 Wherefore hidest thou thy face, and holdest me for thine enemy? . . .

19:25 For I know that my redeemer liveth, and that he shall stand at the latter day upon the earth:

26 And though after my skin worms destroy this body, yet in my flesh shall I see God:

27 Whom I shall see for myself, and mine eyes shall behold, and not another; though my reins be consumed within me. . . .

23:10 But he knoweth the way that I take: when he hath tried me, I shall come forth as gold.

11 My foot hath held his steps, his way have I kept, and not declined.

12 Neither have I gone back from the commandment of his lips; I have esteemed the words of his mouth more than my necessary food.

NEW REVISED STANDARD VERSION

JOB 9:32 For he is not a mortal, as I am, that I
  might answer him,
 that we should come to trial together.
33 There is no umpire between us,
 who might lay his hand on us both.
34 If he would take his rod away from me,
 and not let dread of him terrify me,
35 then I would speak without fear of him,
 for I know I am not what I am thought to be. . . .
13:20 Only grant two things to me,
 then I will not hide myself from your face:
21 withdraw your hand far from me,
 and do not let dread of you terrify me.
22 Then call, and I will answer;
 or let me speak, and you reply to me.
23 How many are my iniquities and my sins?
 Make me know my transgression and my sin.
24 Why do you hide your face,
 and count me as your enemy? . . .
19:25 For I know that my Redeemer lives,
 and that at the last he will stand upon the earth;
26 and after my skin has been thus destroyed,
 then in my flesh I shall see God,
27 whom I shall see on my side,
 and my eyes shall behold, and not another.
 My heart faints within me! . . .
23:10 But he knows the way that I take;
 when he has tested me, I shall come out like gold.
11 My foot has held fast to his steps;
 I have kept his way and have not turned aside.
12 I have not departed from the commandment of
   his lips;
 I have treasured in my bosom the words of
   his mouth.

6

BACKGROUND

The question of Job's authorship had been debated for centuries, and no one has come up with evidence for his or her answer that satisfies everyone. The main reason for this uncertainty is that the book itself neglects to identify its author. In fact, the complexity of its language makes it difficult even to determine a specific period of time within which the book was written.

Bible critics tend to view Job as a work of fiction. Some conjecture an Israelite took a foreign epic and made it stylistically palatable for a Hebrew audience. Others suggest the book was pieced together by a number of people over an extended period of time.

In contrast to such critical theories, one long-held view maintains that Job was indeed a historical person, and that he wrote the book himself sometime after his ordeal. If this is the case, the account of an encounter between God and Satan in the prologue of the book could have come to Job only by divine revelation.

Another traditional view holds that, while Job was a historical person, someone else wrote his account. Some think the writer personally knew Job and made keen observations and carefully recorded the poetic speeches. Others suggest the writer lived some years after Job and put his account together in poetic form based on what he knew about the historical person. Whatever view is taken, it is evident that the author was both divinely inspired and possessed of poetic genius.

Concerning Job himself, a number of interesting and illuminating facts about him can be obtained from Scripture. The Bible reveals that he was a spiritually mature person (Job 1:1, 8; 2:3). He was also the father of many children (1:2; 42:13) and the owner of many herds (1:3; 42:12).

Scripture portrays Job as a wealthy and influential man (1:3), a priest to his family (1:5), and a loving, wise husband (2:9). He was both a person of prominence in community affairs (29:7-11) and someone known for his benevolence (29:12-17; 31:32). In addition, Job was a wise leader (29:21-24) and a grower of crops (31:38-40).

As we study Job, we will discover that the book is not so much about suffering as it is about God's sovereignty and wisdom. Unknown to Job, the true purpose of his ordeal was to demonstrate in the face of Satan's challenge that he could stand as a supreme display of God's saving might. By remaining faithful to God under such distressing circumstances, Job demonstrated that true wisdom is rooted in God.

The wisdom setting of Job can be inferred from the counsel provided by Eliphaz, Bildad, and Zophar. As these three friends tried to comfort Job, they presented the conventional wisdom of their day in a variety of speeches. These remarks turn out to be little more than a string of proverbs. When Job opposed his friends, he was also opposing some of wisdom's basic assumptions.

Most significantly, Job rejected the conventional view that the world is orderly and that everything is arranged according to just principles. His tragedy was not just, for his upright and virtuous life did not result in good fortune. He was a living testimony to the fact that tragic things can happen to godly people.

The argument of Job's friends was that he must have sinned to deserve such suffering. This contention underscores the poverty of this particular aspect of their wisdom teaching. Job also rejected the idea that wisdom is to be sought from tradition. If his three friends represented the teachings of tradition, he wanted nothing to do with it (12:2-3).

NOTES ON THE PRINTED TEXT

After Job's first speech (Job 3), the book proceeds with three rounds of speeches. Each friend speaks in turn and is answered by Job. As the first round begins (4:1—14:22), Eliphaz the Temanite defended the traditional wisdom view of an orderly world (chaps. 4—5). In particular, he maintained that, in this just and orderly world, righteousness is rewarded and wickedness is punished. Eliphaz expressed this view as an attempt to comfort Job.

Job's second friend, Bildad the Shuhite, discarded all pretenses at offering comfort (chap. 8). His whole purpose was to defend the traditional wisdom teachings that had been passed from generation to generation. Bildad concluded that Job's children must have been wicked since they died (8:4). In fact, if Job were really pure, he would also not be suffering (8:6). Job's experience of injustice was unimportant to Bildad, especially when compared with the time-honored teachings of *bygone generations* (8:8).

Job's third friend, Zophar the Naamathite, flatly stated that Job deserved his suffering. In fact, Job was getting off easy (11:6). Much of Zophar's council asserted that God is too mysterious for Job, a mere mortal, to understand (11:7-8). While this was true, Zophar undercut the impact of his own argument by his confidence that he, also a mere mortal, was able to explain the ways of God to Job.

In the midst of Job's ordeal, he focused his attention on God, especially His immensity. Job realized that God is not a finite, mortal creature. Thus, it was impossible for Job to *answer* (9:32) God as if the two were in some sort of legal dispute. Because God is infinitely holy, it was impossible for Job, a fallen person, *to come to trial together* with God. The sense of the verb *come* with *to trial together* means "to confront one another in court" (see Ps. 143:2). In other words, Job could not put God on trial and expect to win his case.

In light of this realization, Job longed for an *umpire* (Job 9:33) between them. The idea is one of a mediator who could bring together God and Job, render a just verdict, and thereby settle their dispute. Job, however, realized that there was no arbitrator who would be able to *lay his hand on us both* so that the matter of Job's innocence could be brought to a conclusion.

Job was not looking for a mediator, as Christ would become, to forgive his sins. Rather Job sought for someone who would recognize his innocence and speak for him before God. Job felt that if God would only relieve him of his pain for a little while, he would be able to gather his wits enough to make his defense (9:34).

Job was also aware of God's overwhelming majesty. To stand in the presence of the Almighty would surely render Job speechless. Job knew that the perfect holiness of God would terrify him, and he would be in no condition to plead his case. Nonetheless, he still resisted the idea that he was an evil person and thus deserved what had happened to him, *for I know I am not what I am thought to be* (9:35).

Only grant two things to me (13:20), Job said. First, he wanted relief from his suffering; second, he did not want to be overwhelmed by the majesty of God (13:21). If God met these two preconditions, Job would respond to what God said, and God could respond to what Job said (13:22). In essence, Job was calling for a court to convene in which he would be either the defendant or the prosecutor.

If any self-righteousness had tainted Job's soul, a breakthrough came when he asked God, *How many are my iniquities and my sins?* (13:23). Job had dismissed the accusations of his friends. But could he be blind about himself? Could he indeed be guilty of sins that caused his suffering? Job pleaded with God to *make me know my transgression and my sin.*

Job felt as if God was hiding His face (13:24). This was a metaphorical way to indicate the withdrawal of God's favor or the outpouring of His wrath (Pss. 27:9; 30:7; Isa. 54:8). There are times when God hides His face to make Himself aloof (Job 34:29). Tragically, Job concluded that God considered him an enemy.

As Job reflected on his situation, he declared in faith that his *Redeemer* (19:25) lived. The focus here is not on God as one's Savior; rather, Job was thinking of the Lord as his defender who would vindicate him of wrongdoing. Although Job sensed he was going to die, he was confident God would acquit him before his accusers.

Job realized that his disease was destroying his body and that, after death, his *skin* (19:26) would be *destroyed*. Nevertheless, he was confident that in his *flesh* he would *see God*. This means Job would witness his vindication. Job faced the prospect of death with faith, not fear. He had the courage to admit that his body would one day decay in the ground. Nevertheless, he genuinely believed in the afterlife and that he would behold God with *my eyes* (19:27). Here we find Job's faith rising to an unparalleled level and anticipating the New Testament doctrine of the resurrection of the righteous.

Job was convinced that God *knows the way that I take* (23:10). Job was also assured that, *"when [God] has tested me, I shall come out like gold."* In other words, despite the accusations of Job's detractors, his integrity would be affirmed and his innocence vindicated. Job declared that he had faithfully followed God's *steps* (23:11). Thus, despite Job's suffering, he could affirm, *I have treasured in my bosom the words of his mouth* (23:12).

In reflecting on what has been said, we note that, when calamity struck Job and his family, he and his three friends wrestled with the question of whether God was fair. His friends took the view that God was punishing him, that he must have done something wrong to deserve such evil. Job disagreed, not only because he felt certain of his own integrity, but also because the wicked actually seemed to prosper, not suffer (12:6).

This realization, though, only brought Job back to the original question concerning God's fairness. If the wicked prosper, where is justice in the world? Job concluded that the seemingly easy life of the wicked was very temporary and that sooner or later it would all fall apart (27:13-23). Job maintained that, in the end, God would humble the proud, enable those with integrity to inherit their possessions, and thereby established justice. Thus He is indeed fair (36:6; 37:23-34).

SUGGESTIONS TO TEACHERS

Job could not understand why disasters had come into his life. He had recognized God in his daily living and had worshiped Him in sincerity and truth. Job also had been faithful in prayer and in modeling a righteous life before his family and those in his world.

Now, the strong spiritual foundation Job always had taken for granted was crumbling. The God who had been so real to Job seemed to be far away. The words of his friends were inadequate, and Job's own reasoning gave him no answers. He thus determined to search for God, whom he believed could help him unravel the mystery of what was happening in his life.

1. THE AGONY OF MISUNDERSTANDING. When Job looked at his life, his first response was, in so many words, "What have I done to deserve this?" He felt that, if he could speak with God, he could prove his innocence. Job was certain he could convince God that he was not worthy of the accusations others had brought against him. No one seemed willing to plead Job's case before God. Human nature is still the same. When tragedy strikes, we are baffled and we want to justify ourselves before God.

2. THE CRY FOR DELIVERANCE. Job was sure that if God would interrupt the flow of his troubles, he would be able to enter into dialogue with God. Job was willing to listen to what God had to say, or present his case and wait for God to answer. Job made a first step toward recognizing his sins. A necessary first step toward God and deliverance from our spiritual emptiness is an admission of our sinfulness.

3. RECOGNIZING A LIVING LORD. Through all of the darkness and confusion of his despair, Job made an amazing discovery—his God was alive and would vindicate him. Furthermore, Job was convinced that, after his body had perished, he would one day dwell with God. This is the eternal truth that enables a Christian to weather life's worst storms and even face death. Our living Lord stands above the most devastating crises we face in life.

4. WAITING FOR THE FINISHED PRODUCT. God revealed to Job the reasons behind the painful tests and trials he endured. Because of them, the dross would be burned away from Job's life. He would come forth eventually like gold that had been subjected to the fires of the furnace. As we hold to the everlasting truths in God's Word and strive daily to keep His commandments, we, too, shall stand before Him one day as pure gold.

<table>
<tr><td>

FOR ADULTS

</td><td>

■ **TOPIC:** Seeking God in Times of Trial

■ **QUESTIONS:** 1. What were the barriers that Job felt were keeping him from coming before God? 2. Why did Job feel that he

</td></tr>
</table>

needed an arbitrator between him and God? 3. In what way did Job see God as his Redeemer? 4. What did Job feel would be the final outcome of the testings God had allowed in his life? 5. How do believers feel when they emerge from a very difficult experience with a clearer understanding of God's will for their life?

■ **ILLUSTRATIONS**

Shining Brightest. A beautiful carving of the Lord's Supper, cut out of mother-of-pearl, was given to a pastor. The pastor took it to a jeweler to have it mounted. He told the jeweler that he thought it would best be suspended against a light so that all of its colors and beautiful figures could be seen. But the practiced eye of the jeweler caused him to say, "No, this must be mounted against something dark." Sorrow, grief, and pain in the world are often that against which the virtues and graces of life shine brightest.

One Small Step. Perhaps the most famous statement made that relates to humankind's first visit to the moon came from the mouth of Astronaut Neil Armstrong. His first words upon stepping from his spaceship upon the surface of the moon were: "One small step for man; one giant step for mankind."

Extended periods of trouble and crisis are extremely oppressive. The darkness of despair seems to close in, and the steps we take are extremely small. Often it seems that we take one step forward and three backwards. Job was having this kind of experience until, suddenly, God allowed him to see beyond and above his present dilemma. We can imagine him shouting, "I know that my Redeemer lives!" A new day dawns for us when, in the midst of our darkness, God breaks through with His eternal truth.

The Shield of Integrity. One dictionary defines integrity as "being of sound moral principle, uprightness, honesty, and sincerity." Such was the life Job had lived before God and the world. Job's integrity was like a shield that was able to deflect the accusations of his enemies and the flaming missiles of Satan. This shield is comparable to that of the Roman soldier in the first century A.D. It was a large, oblong-shaped object made out of two sections of wood that were glued together. The arrows of the enemy would sink into the wood and the fire would be extinguished. Such was a picture of Job's unwavering integrity.

FOR YOUTH ■ **TOPIC:** Stand by Me
■ **QUESTIONS:** 1. How did Job see himself in relation to God? 2. What two things did Job beg God to do for him? 3. How did Job face the prospect of death? 4. How did Job perceive his relationship with God? 5. How can we be certain that we are following in the way God would have us walk?

■ **ILLUSTRATIONS:**

No One Likes Me! Human reason often is our worst enemy. Charles Shultz, the creator of the comic strip *Peanuts*, often produced very familiar scenes of human situations. On one occasion, Charlie Brown, the hero of the comic strip, visited Lucy's outdoor stand because he was convinced that no one liked him. Lucy told him to look on the bright side of things. "Cheer up, Charlie Brown. You have lots of friends." Charlie's face brightened and he said to Lucy, "I do? I do?" As Charlie walked away saying to himself, "I do! I have lots of friends!", Lucy taunted him in her typical, sarcastic way. "Name one," she said.

Job was convinced that no one seemed to care for him; and he struggled desperately to find a reason why these things had happened to him that had so isolated him.

Seeing Beyond the Surface. Martin transferred to our high school in the middle of the fall semester. He was a victim of spastic paralysis. He shuffled along as he walked, sometimes swinging his legs and arms in an exaggerated fashion. He carried a handkerchief because he could not control the saliva that drooled from his mouth. He spoke with slurred speech.

During the first weeks Martin was in school, most of the students avoided him. He would try to talk with his fellow students whose lockers were adjacent to his. They would speak, but then they would quickly walk away from him. Most considered him retarded, and wondered why he had been enrolled in the mainstream classes.

Then one day Martin stood before his English class to give a book report. His teacher had offered to allow him to give his report to her privately, but he insisted on speaking before the class. Though his speech was halting, it was understandable. The students were stunned at the excellent report Martin gave. They discovered that they had jumped to wrong conclusions about him. They had not looked beyond the surface. They discovered that Martin had a brilliant mind, and soon he became a favorite among his classmates.

The Tunnels of Life. Corrie ten Boom once said, "When a train goes through a tunnel and it gets dark, you don't throw away the ticket and jump off. You sit still and trust the engineer." Johnny was 14 years old and was en route to visit his grandparents in Switzerland. He had flown nonstop from New York to Geneva. There a travel agent had helped him transfer to a train on which he would ride to his final destination in the Oberland region of central Switzerland.

Johnny had a window seat on the train, and had enjoyed the fabulous scenery—the beautiful lakes, the towering, snow-covered Alps, and the quaint Swiss villages with their colorful flowers and chateaus. Then came the first tunnel. As the train entered the tunnel, suddenly it became pitch dark. In a moment, the train stopped. No one spoke. There was not a glimmer of light. There had been a temporary interruption in the electrical system that drove the train.

Johnny almost panicked. "Are we going to get off? How can we see how to walk? What is going to happen?" In a few moments, the lights came on in the train, the journey resumed, and it wasn't long until they emerged from the tunnel into a burst of sunlight.

Job had entered a dark tunnel. We, too, have experiences in life that are frightening. But there is a heavenly engineer who controls the train and who will safely bring us through.

INTEGRITY IN EVERYDAY LIFE

BACKGROUND SCRIPTURE: Job 27:2-6; 31
DEVOTIONAL READING: Psalm 15:1-5

KEY VERSES: As long as my breath is in me and the spirit of God is in my nostrils, my lips will not speak falsehood, and my tongue will not utter deceit. Job 27:3-4.

KING JAMES VERSION

JOB 27:2 As God liveth, who hath taken away my judgment; and the Almighty, who hath vexed my soul;

3 All the while my breath is in me, and the spirit of God is in my nostrils;

4 My lips shall not speak wickedness, nor my tongue utter deceit.

5 God forbid that I should justify you: till I die I will not remove mine integrity from me. . . .

31:5 If I have walked with vanity, or if my foot hath hasted to deceit;

6 Let me be weighed in an even balance, that God may know mine integrity.

7 If my step hath turned out of the way, and mine heart walked after mine eyes, and if any blot hath cleaved to mine hands;

8 Then let me sow, and let another eat; yea, let my offspring be rooted out. . . .

13 If I did despise the cause of my manservant or of my maidservant, when they contended with me;

14 What then shall I do when God riseth up? and when he visiteth, what shall I answer him?

15 Did not he that made me in the womb make him? and did not one fashion us in the womb? . . .

24 If I have made gold my hope, or have said to the fine gold, Thou art my confidence;

25 If I rejoiced because my wealth was great, and because mine hand had gotten much; . . .

28 This also were an iniquity to be punished by the judge: for I should have denied the God that is above.

NEW REVISED STANDARD VERSION

JOB 27:2 "As God lives, who has taken away my right,
and the Almighty, who has made my soul bitter,
3 as long as my breath is in me
and the spirit of God is in my nostrils,
4 my lips will not speak falsehood,
and my tongue will not utter deceit.
5 Far be it from me to say that you are right;
until I die I will not put away my integrity
from me." . .
31:5 "If I have walked with falsehood,
and my foot has hurried to deceit—
6 let me be weighed in a just balance,
and let God know my integrity!—
7 if my step has turned aside from the way,
and my heart has followed my eyes,
and if any spot has clung to my hands;
8 then let me sow, and another eat;
and let what grows for me be rooted out." . . .
13 "If I have rejected the cause of my male or
female slaves,
when they brought a complaint against me;
14 what then shall I do when God rises up?
When he makes inquiry, what shall I answer him?
15 Did not he who made me in the womb
make them?
And did not one fashion us in the womb?" . . .
24 "If I have made gold my trust,
or called fine gold my confidence;
25 if I have rejoiced because my wealth was great,
or because my hand had gotten much; . . .
28 this also would be an iniquity to be punished
by the judges,
for I should have been false to God above."

Monday, January 12	Psalm 141:1-8	*My Eyes Are Turned toward You*
Tuesday, January 13	Psalm 119:121-128	*I Direct My Steps*
Wednesday, January 14	Psalm 15:1-5	*The Righteous Walk Blamelessly*
Thursday, January 15	Job 27:2-6	*Job Declares His Integrity*
Friday, January 16	Job 31:3-8	*Let God Know My Integrity*
Saturday, January 17	Job 31:13-23	*Job Defends Himself*
Sunday, January 18	Job 31:24-28	*Job Declares His Loyalty to God*

BACKGROUND

Job is one of the most highly praised literary works known to humankind. The beauty of the original in Hebrew may well put the book in a class by itself. Job includes such poetic genres as laments, hymns, proverbs, oracles, and legal disputations. This material is characterized by an economy of expression in which transitions are often omitted and the relationship of ideas is left for the reader to determine.

Parallelism is also a prominent literary feature in the book. The writer states an idea and then immediately expresses it again in different words. The concepts of the two lines correspond more or less closely, and the analogous parts of parallel lines help to explain each other. The idea is that two lines together define a concept more clearly, forcefully, or vividly than one alone.

As for the structure of Job, it consists of a prose framework in the prologue (Job 1—2) and epilogue (42:7-17), in between which is the poetic body of the book (3:1—42:6). This central section consists of Job's opening lament (chap. 3) and closing discourse (chap. 27), in between which are three cycles of speeches. There is also an interlude on wisdom (chap. 28), which is then followed by several monologues (29:1—42:6).

Whereas the prologue and epilogue portray Job as a patient saint who righteously endured suffering, the dialogue-dispute section shows him as one who longed for fair treatment by God. This tension between the patient and impatient Job shows him to be a person who struggled with his emotions and feelings.

As we study Job, we find that his friends repeatedly challenged him to become better acquainted with the ways of God, especially if Job wanted to bring an end to his ordeal. While the wisdom of the three is questionable, there is little doubt that they knew the Lord. This is based on a candid examination of their speeches, which strongly suggest they genuinely feared God.

This is an intriguing observation, given the period in history when these events are believed to have occurred. No one knows the exact date when Job lived, but many view him as a contemporary of Abraham (about 2000 B.C.). If that is so, then it appears that Job and Abraham were not the only ones who were aware of God in that day. At least four others families (including that of Elihu; 32:1) worshiped the Lord. Thus, even in that day, God had His people among the nations.

Notes on the Printed Text

Job's friends had maintained that God was punishing Job for his sin, and he responded by declaring his innocence. In fact, Job made a vow by the living God, which means Job was staking God's life on the credibility of his words (Job 27:2). Job then accused God of denying him justice. Supposedly *the Almighty* did this by afflicting Job unfairly. The sufferer's ordeal, in turn, left his *soul* feeling embittered. Put another way, his entire life was vexed by anguish.

Despite how Job felt, he refused to depart from the path of virtue. Job declared that he would remain upright in conduct as longed as he lived. After all, he realized that *"the spirit of God in . . . [his] nostrils"* (27:3) came from the Lord. Thus, in submission to God, his Creator, Job vowed that his lips would never *"speak falsehood"* (27:4). The verb rendered *utter* means "to mumble" or "to meditate." The implication is that Job would not communicate deceitful things, no matter how quiet or subtle; instead, he would only speak the truth.

Despite the discouraging words of his friends, Job staunchly refused to concede they were correct in their accusations against him. Job was so convinced of his innocence that he vowed to affirm, not deny, his *integrity* (27:5) until he died.

Numerous times in these verses Job used the personal pronouns "I," "me," and "my." Like a battered giant, Job stood his ground, maintaining that he was innocent and that his suffering was unjust. *"My heart does not reproach me"* (27:6), Job declared. Martin Luther translated this statement in verse 6, *"My conscience bites me not in respect of my whole life."*

Job's defensive posture is woven tightly into the fabric of chapter 31. In vivid terms, he sought to demonstrate his innocence once and for all by explaining how he had refrained from committing acts of wickedness and how he had performed deeds of righteousness.

Here we see that Job's ordeal caused him to make a sweeping inventory of his inner life. One of the areas he evaluated was his attitude toward women and how he handled his own sexual desires (31:1). He viewed lust as a serious moral failure (31:11) and spoke of it in the same context with the following vices: falsehood and deceit (31:5); oppression of slaves (31:13-15); mistreatment of the poor (31:16, 19-20); abuse or neglect of widows (31:16, 18); taking food out of the mouths of starving orphans (31:17-18, 21); rejoicing over the misfortunes of others, even if they are one's enemies (31:29-30); trusting in wealth rather than in God (31:24); and hypocrisy (31:33-34).

It is clarifying to note that Job, in declaring his practice of avoiding lustful stares, used a term—rendered *virgin* in 31:1—that was sometimes used of pagan goddesses. This is one fact that has led some to conclude that Job was, at least secondarily, swearing he did not participate in the worship of fertility goddesses. Such often involved lewd practices; thus Job would have been declaring his innocence of immorality as well as idolatry.

There were numerous fertility goddesses worshiped throughout the ancient world. These were known by various names, including Astarte, Anat, Ashtoreth, Ishtar, and the Queen of Heaven. Deuteronomy 16:21, in particular, records a warning to the Hebrew people against worshiping the goddess Asherah.

In light of what has been said, we can more readily understand why Job deplored the idea that he would *"have walked with falsehood"* (Job 31:5). *Falsehood* translates a Hebrew word that means "desolate, hollow, lying, or vain." The idea is that Job had been honest in his daily living.

Job, in a manner of speaking, wore no mask of falsehood to conceal wrongdoing. No contradiction existed between what was within and what was seen without in Job's life. He had not *"hurried to deceit"* in an effort to mislead others in any way.

Job, in a sense, was declaring that, should he have done these things (which he avowed he had not), then let God not spare him. Job was willing to place his integrity on *"a just balance"* (31:6), namely, on scales that had not been tampered with. The balance of justice was considered by the ancients to be the final judgment. On those perfect scales, Job declared, *"let God know my integrity!"*

Job avowed that he had not *"turned aside from the way"* (31:7), referring to the way of uprightness set forth by God. The phrase *"turned aside"* also means "swerved," in other words, a sweeping departure from a straight line. The idea is that Job had not veered from the path of integrity and virtue.

Job's *heart* had also been focused in the proper direction; in fact, it had not *"followed [his] eyes"* to do that which was wrong. He even challenged anyone to examine him, to see *"if any spot has clung to my hands ."* The Hebrew word translated "spot" can mean that which is blackened, or blackens, for soot would cling to one's hands. Job may also have had an accusation of thievery in mind, suggesting, as we would say today, that he did not have "sticky fingers."

Job completed his list of specific allegations that might be brought against him by saying that, if he was guilty of any wrongdoing, *"then let me sow, and another eat"* (31:8). We might paraphrase this as follows: "I will do the planting and be perfectly content to let another reap the harvest." Job would even be willing to *"let what grows for me be rooted out."* Again, we might paraphrase this as follows: "If, then, some of that which is sown should not be taken, I will not claim it. Let it be uprooted and tossed aside."

Job turned from denying personal sins to examine his relationship with his *"male or female slaves"* (31:13). Job well may have been the wealthiest man in his locale before tragedy struck. He probably owned many slaves. But he had not been a ruthless slave owner. He claimed to be sensitive to their rights as human beings. He even recognized their right to bring a *complaint* against him and expect justice.

In 31:14, the verb *rises up* means "to confront in judgment," while *makes inquiry* refers to Gods intervention for blessing or cursing. The idea is that, if Job had been unfair to his servants, God would call him to account for his actions and punish him with calamity.

Here we see that, contrary to the common attitude toward slavery in ancient times, Job believed that all human beings deserve to be treated humanely. He declared that the same God *"who made me in the womb [made] them"* (31:15). In other words, God shows no favoritism, and any wrong Job may have committed against others would be a sin against God.

Job's wealth certainly included *gold* (31:24) and *fine gold*; but, contrary to the conduct of many wealthy people of his day, Job had not placed his *trust* in gold. He had not *rejoiced* (31:25) because his *"hand had gotten much."* If Job had been guilty of any of these sins, then he *"would have been false to God above"* (31:28). In God's eyes, Job would have been a hypocrite, pretending to be that which he was not.

SUGGESTIONS TO TEACHERS

Job counted his personal integrity as being so important that he was willing to explore every possible area of life in which he might have sinned against God and people. Job also valued the personal testimony of his daily life, and was determined to keep it pure. Satan delights in catching believers off-guard and causing them either to compromise in some gray area of morality or ethics, or to blunder into some obvious wrongdoing in a moment of weakness.

1. DEALING WITH CIRCUMSTANCES. Job's friends, however well-intentioned they may have been in the beginning, had become increasingly judgmental toward him in their long, impassioned speeches. Though veiled at first, their accusations that Job had sinned became more and more painful. They were looking at circumstances—Job's sufferings—and applying them to their incorrect understanding of how God deals with His people. We, too, are sometimes guilty of judging others on the basis of the circumstances we see. Others, in turn, might judge us on the same basis.

2. SEARCHING OUR HEARTS. Job must have been weary with the haranguing of his friends, especially as their painful words added to his suffering. So earnestly did Job want to keep himself pure before God and the world around him that, in the midst of his own lack of understanding, he began to search his heart. One by one, he explored various wrong actions and attitudes. An excellent practice for all of us is to regularly search our hearts lest we fall into some trap of Satan and allow our testimony for Christ to give an uncertain sound. Consider, for example, what Paul wrote to the believers at Corinth: *But if we judged ouselves, we would not be judged* (1 Cor. 11:31).

3. ANSWERING TO THE ULTIMATE JUDGE. Human judges, despite their best efforts, sometimes make incorrect decisions. Job knew that he had been improperly accused and misjudged by his friends, who had come to comfort him. At times others may jump to flawed conclusions and judge us unfairly. We may be accused of some wrongdoing based on tragic circumstances. Job knew, as we must, that no one can be *"false to God above"* (Job 31:28), for He is the ultimate Judge. This reminds us of what Paul said to Timothy: *I have kept the faith* (2 Tim. 4:7). The time for the apostle's homegoing was fast approaching, and he was about to stand before God. Paul, like Job, had searched his heart and was confident he had remained a person of integrity before the Lord.

FOR ADULTS

■ TOPIC: Maintaining Integrity in Daily Living

■ QUESTIONS: 1. How did Job demonstrate that his personal integrity in his daily life was extremely important to him? 2. Despite the accusations of his friends, what did Job refuse to do? 3. What was the *"just balance"* (Job 31:6) in which Job was willing to be weighed? 4. How did Job see himself in relation to the male and female slaves he owned and who served him? 5. What can we do to maintain our personal integrity in our everyday living?

■ ILLUSTRATIONS:

Maintaining the Right Attitude. A young man in his mid-twenties, convicted of a crime he did not commit, was sentenced to spend ten years in the state penitentiary. He, his attorney, and his family knew that he was innocent. Nonetheless extenuating circumstances seemed to point directly toward him, and the judge and jury felt that the conviction was right.

The young man was a Christian, and he continued to believe that God would vindicate him. He prayed, read his Bible, and met regularly with his pastor, his family, and his attorney. In time, the truth surfaced, and the guilty person came forward to confess to the crime. The wrongly accused young man was released and his reputation was vindicated. Instead of lashing out when we are wrongly accused, the best course of action is to allow God, who knows our hearts, to vindicate us.

Ancient Courtroom Procedure. In the ancient courts of law, two things were always required. First, the prosecutor made a statement concerning the charge that was being brought against the defendant. Second, the defendant made a statement in rebuttal of the charge brought against him. The order of the procedure was that the prosecutor first stated his case and then the defendant his. Job's fellow human beings had delivered their charges against him, but they were not Job's true prosecutors. Job reversed the order and stated his case first, and then waited for God, the only true Judge, to answer him.

True Repentance. The great mathematician Copernicus revolutionized the thought of humankind about the universe. His famous treatise, *The Revolution of the Heavenly Bodies*, was printed just in time to be placed in his arms as he lay dying in the spring of 1543. Yet this person, who had given to humanity a new conception of the universe, saw himself before God, not as an astronomer or a scholar, but as a sinner. Today, on his grave you can read the epitaph that he chose for himself: "I do not seek a kindness equal to that given to Paul; nor do I ask the grace granted to Peter; but that forgiveness which Thou didst give to the robber— that I earnestly pray."

FOR YOUTH

■ **TOPIC:** Living with a Clear Conscience

■ **QUESTIONS:** 1. What was the most important thing to Job in regard to his life before the world? 2. What was Job willing to do to demonstrate to his accusers that he was innocent of the charges they brought against him? 3. Despite Job's former wealth and position, how did he show that he treated others humanely? 4. What was Job's attitude toward his wealth? 5. What should you do first when you feel that others have falsely accused you of some wrongdoing?

■ **ILLUSTRATIONS:**

Accepting Circumstances. Jim, a high school senior, suffered permanent spinal damage when he dived into a shallow pool and struck his head on the bottom. He was paralyzed from his waist down. He had been his school's football quarter-back, and had already had scholarship offers from several major universities.

At first, Jim was bitter. Next to his home was a vacant lot where younger boys often played football. He refused to allow his parents to roll his wheelchair to the porch when the boys were playing. He could not bear to watch them, with their strong, young bodies, engaging in the sport he loved so much.

One night as Jim lay in his bed surrounded by self-pity, he began to pray for God to help him. When Jim awoke the next morning, he felt a strong desire to watch the boys play. He asked his father to roll his wheelchair to the edge of the lot. Because Jim had been the boys' hero in the past, they swarmed him. "Coach us!" they cried. "Show us how to play right!" Jim began to help them. As the days passed, his self-pity melted away. He had accepted the circumstances in his life, and he found that he could help others regardless of his own situation.

Repentance and Faith. In the laboratory of the great chemist Faraday, a worker accidentally dropped a very valuable silver cup into a tank of strong acid. He and the other workers stood over the tank and watched the cup disintegrate.

Faraday, however, saw what had happened and poured a chemical into the tank. The silver fell to the bottom and was recovered. The shapeless mass was sent off again to the silversmith to be refashioned into the beautiful cup it once had been. Likewise, repentance can release the grace of God and move Him to forgive and recover what has been lost and restore it to its former usefulness and beauty in our lives.

Making Improper Judgments. Once a student rose to read in his classroom, and he held his book in his right hand. His teacher told him to take the book with the other hand, but the student continued to read, holding the book in his right hand. Again the angry teacher thundered at him to take the book in his left hand. "I cannot, sir," the student peeped, as he brought an empty sleeve from behind his back. The students booed the teacher, but the next moment they cheered when the teacher earnestly apologized to the student. Lips that move and do not speak, sleeves that have no arm within them—this is life. We should know the facts before we dare to pass judgment on others.

INTEGRITY IN GOD'S PRESENCE

BACKGROUND SCRIPTURE: Job 38:1-7; 40:7-9; 42:1-6

DEVOTIONAL READING: Isaiah 6:1-8

KEY VERSE: I had heard of you by the hearing of
the ear, but now my eye sees you. Job 42:5.

KING JAMES VERSION

JOB 38:1 Then the LORD answered Job out of the whirlwind, and said,

2 Who is this that darkeneth counsel by words without knowledge?

3 Gird up now thy loins like a man; for I will demand of thee, and answer thou me.

4 Where wast thou when I laid the foundations of the earth? declare, if thou hast understanding.

5 Who hath laid the measures thereof, if thou knowest? or who hath stretched the line upon it?

6 Whereupon are the foundations thereof fastened? or who laid the corner stone thereof;

7 When the morning stars sang together, and all the sons of God shouted for joy? . . .

40:7 Gird up thy loins now like a man: I will demand of thee, and declare thou unto me.

8 Wilt thou also disannul my judgment? wilt thou condemn me, that thou mayest be righteous?

9 Hast thou an arm like God? or canst thou thunder with a voice like him? . . .

42:1 Then Job answered the LORD, and said,

2 I know that thou canst do every thing, and that no thought can be withholden from thee.

3 Who is he that hideth counsel without knowledge? therefore have I uttered that I understood not; things too wonderful for me, which I knew not.

4 Hear, I beseech thee, and I will speak: I will demand of thee, and declare thou unto me.

5 I have heard of thee by the hearing of the ear: but now mine eye seeth thee.

6 Wherefore I abhor myself, and repent in dust and ashes.

NEW REVISED STANDARD VERSION

JOB 38:1 Then the LORD answered Job out of the whirlwind:

2 "Who is this that darkens counsel by words without knowledge?

3 Gird up your loins like a man,
  I will question you, and you shall declare to me.

4 "Where were you when I laid the foundation of
    the earth?
  Tell me, if you have understanding.

5 Who determined its measurements—surely you
    know!
  Or who stretched the line upon it?

6 On what were its bases sunk,
  or who laid its cornerstone

7 when the morning stars sang together
  and all the heavenly beings shouted for joy?" . . .

40:7 "Gird up your loins like a man;
  I will question you, and you declare to me.

8 Will you even put me in the wrong?
  Will you condemn me that you may be justified?

9 Have you an arm like God,
  and can you thunder with a voice like his?" . . .

42:1 Then Job answered the LORD:

2 "I know that you can do all things,
  and that no purpose of yours can be thwarted.

3 'Who is this that hides counsel without
    knowledge?'
Therefore I have uttered what I did not understand,
  things too wonderful for me, which I did not know.

4 'Hear, and I will speak;
  I will question you, and you declare to me.'

5 I had heard of you by the hearing of the ear,
  but now my eye sees you;

6 therefore I despise myself,
  and repent in dust and ashes."

Home Bible Readings

Background

In stepping back from our study of Job, we are benefited by noting the intense suffering this saintly person experienced. He enduring the following: painful boils from head to toe (2:7, 13; 30:17); severe itching and irritation (2:7-8); intense grief (2:13); loss of appetite (3:24; 6:6-7); agonizing discomfort (3:24); insomnia (7:4); worm and dust infested flesh (7:5); continual oozing of boils (7:5); hallucinations (7:14); decaying skin (13:28); shriveling up (16:8; 17:7; 19:20); severe halitosis (19:17); relentless pain (30:17); raging fever (30:30); and dramatic weight loss (33:21).

It is also helpful to note that, before his troubles, Job had been an advocate for the poor (29:12-17). But his enormous wealth and power in his community may have distanced him from their pain. Though he was aware of their plight, he had never experienced it for himself.

Then a series of disasters struck, and suddenly Job was reduced to poverty. As a result, the poor were no longer just a class of people that needed help, but fellow sufferers with whom Job shared a common ordeal. With a new perspective, he began to identify with slaves who feared unjust treatment from their masters (31:13). And he now understood what widows and orphans felt when they were forced to go without food, clothing, and shelter while watching others live in luxury (31:16-21). Job realized that people are basically the same, and that possessions and power have nothing to do with their fundamental humanity.

With respect to the final chapters of the book, God's emergence out of a whirlwind gave Job an answer to all his questions: trust the Lord regardless of the present circumstances. For Job to achieve godly wisdom, he had to simply trust in the almighty, infinite Creator, whose wisdom and ways were far beyond what he could imagine. In the end, all Job's understanding, reason, and doubt had to give way to faith.

In addition to teaching about God's nature and human suffering, the experience of Job brings to light a number of other truths, including the following: there are matters going on in heaven with God that believers know nothing about, yet these matters affect their lives; even the best effort at explaining the issues of life can be useless; God's people do suffer, and bad things happen all the time to good people, so one cannot judge a person's spirituality by his or her successes or painful circumstances; though God seems far away, perseverance in faith is a most noble virtue, for the Lord is good and believers can safely leave their life in His hands; believers in the midst of suffering should not abandon God, but rather draw near to Him, so that out of this fellowship can come His comfort, even if there is no explanation for the hardship; and suffering may be intense, but it will ultimately end for the righteous, and God will spiritually bless them in abundance.

NOTES ON THE PRINTED TEXT

Job had complained about God being silent and aloof in the midst of his distress. Finally, the Lord answered (Job 38:1); but He did not appear in a vision, but rather spoke to Job out of a whirlwind not unlike the one that had killed Job's children (1:18-19). The storm is a common accompaniment for a divine manifestation (Ezek. 1:4; Nah. 1:3; Zech. 9:14).

No indication is given that Job actually saw the Lord, only that he heard God's voice. We can imagine how taken aback Job must have been. He probably did not expect God to speak to him in such a direct manner.

The Lord initiated His speech by reminding Job of how he had questioned God's sense of justice. Though Job never cursed God, he had reached a point during his ordeal when the Lord seemed to be his enemy rather than his protector and provider. God immediately set him straight, asking him a rhetorical question that proved Job did not understand the divine plan for ordering the universe.

Job had presumed to question God's wisdom and purpose, even though the sufferer could only do so in *"words without knowledge"* (Job 38:2). God thus told Job to *"gird up your loins"* (38:3), an idiom that refers to taking the hem of a long garment or robe and pulling it up between one's legs and tucking it into the front of one's belt. This permitted easier and free movement of the legs.

The Lord was commanding Job to prepare himself for a divine interrogation. This process would help Job to discover something about God's true nature. This approach was entirely appropriate, for Job had posed questions of his own, especially as he wondered aloud how God exercised His justice.

God asked Job where he had been when the divine *"laid the foundation of the earth"* (38:4). Humankind had not even been created. God then asked Job, *"Who determined [the earth's] measurements—surely you know!"* (38:5). God moreover asked Job about the earth's *cornerstone* (38:6). God furthermore spoke about a magnificent heavenly celebration *"when the morning stars sang together and all the heavenly beings shouted for joy"* (38:7), signaling the formation of the earth.

Again God spoke to Job *out of the whirlwind* (40:6) and told him to brace himself *"like a man"* (40:7) so that the Lord could question Job and receive his answers. Already Job had begun to see that he was *"of small account"* (40:4) before God.

In 40:8, the Lord asked whether Job was going to *"put [God] in the wrong?"* In other words, was Job trying to make himself appear innocent by accusing God of unfairness? Job had not gone so far as to curse God, but Job had certainly called into question God's integrity, especially for allowing Job to suffer for no apparent reason. It was one thing for Job to claim his own integrity, but it was another matter altogether to nullify God's righteousness in the process.

God answered His own questions with more questions (40:9-14), with each one portraying attributes of God. In an almost mocking tone, God sought to adjust Job's attitude by asking him whether he thought he had *"an arm like God"* (40:9) and a voice of *"thunder."* Job would come to see that he had assumed the role of being God's critic, which was almost like making himself equal or superior to the Lord.

When God had finished speaking, it was Job's turn to respond (42:1). He replied simply, without trying to indulge in fancy rhetoric, that he understood the message of God's speeches. For instance, Job said, *"I know that you can do all things"* (42:2). Here we find Job confessing to the omnipotence of God. Never again would Job question God's power.

Job was convinced that none of God's plans and purposes *"can be thwarted."* Though Job was not saying that he now understood the affliction that God had allowed to come upon him, he realized that it was all in accord with God's plan. In genuine humility, Job confessed that he had *"uttered what [he] did not understand, things too wonderful for [him]"* (42:3). Job admitted freely that he had presumed to give his opinion about things that lay beyond his ability to understand, things about which he should have been in awe.

Job repeated God's injunction for him to listen and respond to His questions (42:4). Job then confessed that he previously only had an indirect and incomplete knowledge of the Lord. Now, in this encounter with the divine, Job had seen God with his own *eye* (42:5). This does not mean Job had seen the Lord in a vision; rather, Job simply meant that this experience of God was real and personal.

Job concluded with the statement, *"I despise myself"* (42:6). This means he abhorred what he had said. He admitted that, in comparison with God, his own knowledge, self-assessment, and arguments were nonsense. He thus was willing to repent, sitting on dust and ashes, which was the custom followed by those who were in deep grief. Job had discovered the presence of God, whose righteousness included a dimension of love and caring for Job he had never known before.

SUGGESTIONS TO TEACHERS

Job was a godly person before calamity struck in his life. In fact, God had described him as being *"a blameless and upright man who fears God and turns away from evil"* (Job 1:8). In a manner of speaking, Job was God's "exhibit number one" of a righteous person living in the midst of an evil world.

In contrast to others in his day, Job did whatever he could to please God. Nevertheless, Job's relationship with God had room for considerable growth. Thus, God brought Job through a process in which the Lord prepared him to know the divine more deeply.

1. EXAMINING WHO WE ARE. No doubt Job was an astute person in the ways of the world, for God had blessed him materially. And spiritually, Job recognized the importance of God in his life. But Job's understanding of God was far from complete. For instance, Job dared to challenge the way God was doing things. God reminded Job of His greatness in creation, and Job began to see who he really was in relation to the Lord. A certain amount of self-confidence is good for all of us, but it can get out of control to the point that we think we are as wise as God. It is good always to remember who we are in relation to God.

2. LEARNING WHO GOD IS. To know that God is sovereign and that His sovereignty is always tempered with His love, is one of the greatest discoveries a human being can make. Occasionally, like Job, we feel that what is happening to us is unfair. We cannot see how God can be glorified through the circumstances of the moment. Realizing that God is all-powerful and merciful will enable us to accept in our lives even those situations which, to us, have neither rhyme nor reason.

3. CHERISHING OUR RELATIONSHIP WITH GOD. Once we examine who we are and learn more about who God is, our relationship with Him becomes all the more precious. In the place of getting "answers" for the mysteries that plague our lives, we find contentment in trusting God in the midst of our overwhelming circumstances. He, in turn, helps us to see that He does all things well.

FOR ADULTS	■ **TOPIC:** Encountering God

■ **QUESTIONS:** 1. Why do you think God chose to answer Job *out of the whirlwind* (Job 38:1)? 2. What was God's purpose in confronting Job with questions about the creation? 3. In what ways had Job questioned God's fairness and integrity? 4. What happened in Job's relationship with God that caused Job to repent? 5. How is it possible for us to grow in our knowledge of God when tragedy strikes?

■ **ILLUSTRATIONS:**

Conceiving the Greatness of God. The uniqueness of humankind, as God has made us, lies in the fact that we are aware of the existence of the universe and of its divine Creator. This is not true in the animal kingdom. For instance, you cannot convince a dog of such facts.

A dog, of course, has a certain degree of intelligence. It experiences emotion. It has will power, at least to a point. It may even be said that a dog has "faith" in its master. But no dog can believe anything beyond its immediate consciousness, namely, that which it feels and senses and sees. In fact, no animal can grasp the idea of a universe or of God. Only people can do this, which underscores the greatness and dignity of the Lord.

God's Inconceivable Love. In His speaking to Job about the majesty of His creation, God revealed His love for undeserving humankind. The poet Faber expressed it like this:

"How Thou canst think so well of us,
And be the God Thou art,
Is darkness to my intellect,
But sunshine to my heart."

G. Campbell Morgan, in thinking about God's inconceivable love for us, rephrased Faber's poem like this:

"And Thou *dost* think so well of us,
Because of what Thou art,
Thy love illumines my intellect,
And fills with fear my heart!"

God Is in Control! A philosopher once said, "Whatever man can undo, man can do." After hearing this, a friend of mine said, "I'd like to break an egg over his head and say, 'Now, you do what I have undone.'" This sentiment is expressed in the nursery rhyme of Humpty-Dumpty's fall: "All the king's horses and all the king's men could not put him back together again!" God wanted Job to know, beyond any doubt, that the Lord is in control of the world. People can, through their sin, spawn death and destruction, but only God can put the world back together again.

TOPIC: Standing before God

QUESTIONS: 1. How do you think Job might have felt when God confronted him with questions about the mysteries of His creation? 2. What was God's ultimate purpose in interrogating Job? 3. What knowledge of God did Job have before his encounter with the divine? 4. What was the turning point in Job's experience that caused him to repent? 5. What must we do in order to know that God is real and that He cares about all that happens in our lives?

ILLUSTRATIONS:

The Creator of All Things. In Defoe's story of the shipwrecked Robinson Crusoe, he showed how Crusoe was able to make his house and his clothes. He planted and harvested his own grain for food, and killed animals for his meat. Eventually he appeared to have everything anyone could want. Everything he did was the work of one, poor, untrained, shipwrecked man. Robinson Crusoe, however, did not create out of nothing. Without the raw materials that God had created, he would have died.

With all of their intelligence, people could not have made the planet on which they live. God wanted Job to come to the same conclusion.

Everyone Has Seen It. In 1998, the movie *Titanic* outperformed all the other movies at the box office. One reason is that teenagers went to the movie over and over again. Exit surveys showed that many of those in attendance were repeat customers. In the junior high age group, a child who had not seen the movie was simply out of the loop, a situation that most students want to avoid. Erica and Elene, both 14, had seen the movie five times. Asked why they could see it repeatedly, they responded simply because their friends were all seeing it.

Youth want to belong to something, whether it is a club or a group that has seen a movie. Jesus has called you to be one of His disciples. Accept His invitation and join the group. Also, get involved and make a difference!

A Knowledge of God. Long ago the richest man in the world, Croesus, once asked one of the wisest men in the world, Thales, "What is God?" Thales asked for a day in which to think about his answer. Then he asked for another day, and another, and another. The longer he thought about it, the more difficult it became to give an answer. Tertullian, an early Christian leader, said of Thales: "There is the wisest man in the world, and he cannot tell you who God is. But the most ignorant Christian knows God, and is able to make Him known to others."

A TIME FOR ALL THINGS

BACKGROUND SCRIPTURE: Ecclesiastes 3:1-15
DEVOTIONAL READING: Psalm 1:1-6

KEY VERSE: For everything there is a season, and a time for every matter under heaven. Ecclesiastes 3:1.

KING JAMES VERSION

ECCLESIASTES 3:1 To every thing there is a season, and a time to every purpose under the heaven:

2 A time to be born, and a time to die; a time to plant, and a time to pluck up that which is planted;

3 A time to kill, and a time to heal; a time to break down, and a time to build up;

4 A time to weep, and a time to laugh; a time to mourn, and a time to dance;

5 A time to cast away stones, and a time to gather stones together; a time to embrace, and a time to refrain from embracing;

6 A time to get, and a time to lose; a time to keep, and a time to cast away;

7 A time to rend, and a time to sew; a time to keep silence, and a time to speak;

8 A time to love, and a time to hate; a time of war, and a time of peace.

9 What profit hath he that worketh in that wherein he laboureth?

10 I have seen the travail, which God hath given to the sons of men to be exercised in it.

11 He hath made every thing beautiful in his time: also he hath set the world in their heart, so that no man can find out the work that God maketh from the beginning to the end.

12 I know that there is no good in them, but for a man to rejoice, and to do good in his life.

13 And also that every man should eat and drink, and enjoy the good of all his labour, it is the gift of God.

14 I know that, whatsoever God doeth, it shall be for ever: nothing can be put to it, nor any thing taken from it: and God doeth it, that men should fear before him.

15 That which hath been is now; and that which is to be hath already been; and God requireth that which is past.

NEW REVISED STANDARD VERSION

ECCLESIASTES 3:1 For everything there is a season, and a time for every matter under heaven:

2 a time to be born, and a time to die;
a time to plant, and a time to pluck up what is planted;

3 a time to kill, and a time to heal;
a time to break down, and a time to build up;

4 a time to weep, and a time to laugh;
a time to mourn, and a time to dance;

5 a time to throw away stones, and a time to gather stones together;
a time to embrace, and a time to refrain from embracing;

6 a time to seek, and a time to lose;
a time to keep, and a time to throw away;

7 a time to tear, and a time to sew;
a time to keep silence, and a time to speak;

8 a time to love, and a time to hate;
a time for war, and a time for peace.

9 What gain have the workers from their toil? 10 I have seen the business that God has given to everyone to be busy with. 11 He has made everything suitable for its time; moreover he has put a sense of past and future into their minds, yet they cannot find out what God has done from the beginning to the end. 12 I know that there is nothing better for them than to be happy and enjoy themselves as long as they live; 13 moreover, it is God's gift that all should eat and drink and take pleasure in all their toil. 14 I know that whatever God does endures forever; nothing can be added to it, nor anything taken from it; God has done this, so that all should stand in awe before him. 15 That which is, already has been; that which is to be, already is; and God seeks out what has gone by.

BACKGROUND

Ecclesiastes presents the reflections of a man who boldly faced the complex questions of life, only to conclude in the end that true meaning and joy come from God. The human author prefaced his treatise with the statement *Vanity of vanities, . . . vanity of vanities! All is vanity* (Eccl. 1:2). Indeed, he carried this sentiment throughout the book.

The answer to this cry of despair does not become clear until the book's conclusion, in which the writer declared that, to discover meaning and wisdom, people must *Fear God, and keep his commandments* (12:13). In fact, everything in Ecclesiastes must be seen within the framework of these opening and closing statements. From this perspective the book proves to be a brilliant, inspired discourse that should encourage believers to work diligently toward a God-centered view of life.

The author of Ecclesiastes examined the things that human beings live for, including wisdom, pleasure, work, progress, and wealth; and yet, no matter what they attempt to attain in life, they all meet the same destiny—they die and are forgotten by others. In that way, the author did not try to hide the futility that people face. Indeed, he emphasized that all the goals of human beings have limitations—even wisdom. Thus it is useless for them to seek to master their own destiny.

There is, however, an underlying hope in the book. Although every human striving will eventually fail, God's purposes will never fail. Through the experience of one who seemed to have tried everything, the author concluded, based on his faith in the Lord, that God had ordered life according to His own purposes. Therefore, the best thing a person can do is to accept and enjoy life as God has given it.

NOTES ON THE PRINTED TEXT

The *Teacher* (Eccl. 1:1) had already lamented how life was meaningless when viewed apart from God. He had described how life occurred in a vicious cycle, repeating itself again and again. Now he was ready to take another look at living and dying, this time seeing some semblance of order and meaning because of God's dominion.

The Teacher introduced God's plan for living by stating that *for everything there is a season* (3:1). The word translated "season" can also refer to an event or an activity. The author was convinced that God has an overarching plan for the world and humankind and works according to His will. People cannot change God's plan, and they cannot always understand all that God does or allows.

In light of God's sovereign ordering of events, people are wise to take life day by day as a gift from God, realizing that there is *a time for every matter under heaven*. The believers' responsibility is to ask God to help them discern the right time for the right action.

When this happens, everything will be *suitable for its time* (3:11), and believers will come to see that God's will is reasonable and perfect, even though they may not completely understand it. This reminds us of a similar teaching in the New Testament. Paul declared that Christians are *created in Christ Jesus for good works, which God prepared beforehand to be our way of life* (Eph. 2:10).

In his treatise, the Teacher recorded a list of major activities in which human beings engage during the course of their lives. Most of the statements in Ecclesiastes 3:2-8 are obvious in their meaning and require no elaborate explanation. What we find here are 14 pairs of opposites. In Hebrew speech, mentioning opposites together expressed totality. Thus these 14 pairs stand for all the activities of life.

The Teacher began by noting that God has set boundaries for life, in that there is *a time to be born, and a time to die* (3:2). Contemporary issues of morality and ethics have complicated this straightforward statement. Also, advances in medical knowledge seem to give humanity the ability to live an increasing number of years; yet, according to Scripture, the boundaries for life and death are set by God.

A time to plant, and a time to pluck up what is planted (3:2) focuses on activity that is at first creative and then destructive in nature. Next comes *a time to kill, and a time to heal* (3:3). The Teacher was not condoning premeditated murder. Perhaps he was suggesting that we must wrestle for God's wisdom during times when we are confronted with aggression. Today, in consideration of Jesus' teachings concerning our attitude toward our enemies (Matt. 5:21-26, 38-48), there may be times when accommodation is the best solution to a problem.

Tears and laughter (Eccl. 3:4) are an inevitable part of life. Here we find the Teacher covering the range of human emotions—both private and public. Grieving is not forbidden, for, as Paul wrote to the Thessalonians, we do not *grieve as others do who have no hope* (1 Thess. 4:13). Also, the shedding of tears plays an important role in the human therapeutic process. Moreover, happiness expressed in laughter provides an emotional balance in the course of one's life.

The Teacher, as a builder (Eccl. 2:4-6), knew when *to throw away stones* (3:5) and when *to gather stones together.* For instance, unwanted rocks must be cleared away before a field can be planted or a foundation laid. Just as people in ancient times knew there was *a time to embrace*, they also knew when outward expressions of affection were inappropriate.

Acquiring things and giving things up are a part of life (3:6), as is removing worn cloth and sewing on new patches (3:7). People with common sense seem to know the importance of keeping quiet until the proper time comes *to speak. Love* (3:8) and *hate* are also inescapable in life, as long as we love and hate the proper things. Thus, from birth and death to the waging of *war* and the seeking for *peace*, the Teacher discussed the major events that take place in the normal course of life.

The human author reached a rather stark conclusion: *What gain have the workers from their toil?* (3:9). His point was that life is really beyond human control. Our task is to trust God to help us navigate through seemingly overwhelming circumstances that we cannot change (3:10).

The Teacher affirmed that God *has made everything suitable for its time* (3:11). Despite the frustrations of life, we can maintain an overall positive attitude toward God's sovereignty in what we experience. At the same time, God *has put a sense of past and future* (3:11) in our *minds* so that we are concerned about where life is leading us. We are not only concerned about specific things that happen to us in time, but we also want to know what outcome these events will have in the future.

We have to acknowledge that such matters defy our comprehension. Thus, in the midst of life's uncertainties, the Teacher directed God's people t*o be happy and enjoy themselves as long as they live* (3:12). Simple things ·such as food, drink, and the privilege of labor are blessings from God (3:13). Verses 14-15 summarize the previous declarations, with the added reminder that past and future are in God's control.

SUGGESTIONS TO TEACHERS

The words of the Teacher, when taken from the world's point of view, might appear fatalistic, as if humankind lives on a treadmill whose actions are always predictable and void of excitement and anticipation. But when considered from God's point of view, we can see a natural rhythm God has built in to the matters of life. Because life is not left to chance, we can find meaning and purpose in the most common, everyday events.

1. APPRECIATING GOD'S CONCERN. Because God is all-knowing, He is aware of everything that occurs. He sees the end from the beginning, and because of His involvement in His creation, He controls the times and seasons of life. Despite our sinful nature, God continues to love us so much that He demonstrates His concern by setting reasonable boundaries in our lives.

2. OBSERVING GOD'S INVOLVEMENT. God is wonderfully involved in those matters of life we tend to take for granted—like birth and death, planting and harvesting, tears and laughter, and grief and comfort; yet, within these life experiences with their beginnings and endings, God grants us latitude for growth, enjoyment, and discovery. He takes the monotony of life and changes its ugliness into beauty, and its meaninglessness into purpose.

3. ACCEPTING GOD'S PROVISION. God desires that His people find enjoyment in life. Also, He wants us to see His hand in life's simplest activities. Food and drink, which we take for granted, are gifts from God. The privilege of work, of occupying ourselves with productive labor, is likewise a great blessing. Indeed, God has provided for our every need, if only we would trust in Him.

■ **TOPIC:** The Seasons of Life
■ **QUESTIONS:** 1. What role does God take in the ordering of life's events? 2. What place does birth and death as well as happiness and pain have in the unfolding drama of life? 3. What benefit is there to laboring and toiling throughout one's life? 4. Why is it best to order the priorities of one's life around God's will and precepts? 5. How can we encourage our loved ones to make God the center of their life?

■ **ILLUSTRATIONS:**

The Appointed Hour. God's Word tells us that there is *a time to be born, and a time to die* (Eccl. 3:2). After the Battle of Bull Run, Captain Imboden asked Stonewall Jackson, who had received a painful wound in the battle, "General, how is it that you can keep so cool and appear so utterly insensible to danger in such a storm of shell and bullets as rained about you when your hand was hit?"

"Captain," answered Jackson in a grave and reverential manner, "my religious belief teaches me to feel as safe in battle as in bed. God has fixed the time for my death. I do not concern myself about that, but to be always ready no matter when it may overtake me." Then, after a pause, he added, "That is the way all people should live, and then all would be equally brave."

Gathering Stones. Most of the soil in Israel is filled with limestone and basalt rocks. When farmers prepare the ground for cultivation, they must first clear the land of these rocks. Piles of rocks along the periphery of a cultivated field is a common sight. After they have gathered these stones from the soil, they then take the larger ones and build a low, stone fence around the garden plot. The stone-gathering time is difficult and lengthy. The fields with stone fences give evidence that a gathering of *stones* (3:5) has first taken place.

A Time to Love. Just before Leonardo da Vinci began work on his famous *Last Supper* painting, he had a violent quarrel with a fellow artist. So enraged and bitter was da Vinci that he determined to paint the face of his enemy, the other artist, as the face of Judas Iscariot. Thus he could take revenge on his enemy by exposing his likeness to all of those in succeeding generations who would see his painting.

The face of Judas was one of the first that da Vinci finished, and everyone could recognize it as the face of the painter with whom he had quarreled. But when da Vinci came to paint the face of Christ, he could make no progress. Something seemed to be holding him back, frustrating his best efforts.

Finally da Vinci came to the conclusion that the thing that was frustrating him was the fact he had painted his enemy into the face of Judas. Da Vinci painted out the face of Judas and started anew on the face of Jesus, and this time with the success that the ages have acclaimed.

That incident is a striking parable of the Christian life. You cannot at one and the same time be painting the features of Christ into your own life and painting another face with the colors of enmity and hatred.

FOR YOUTH

■ **TOPIC:** Feel the Rhythm

■ **QUESTIONS:** 1. What do you think the Teacher meant when he said there is *a time to plant, and a time to pluck up what is planted* (Eccl. 3:2)? 2. In what circumstances might weeping be appropriate? When would merriment be appropriate? 3. When Solomon spoke of seeking and losing (3:6), what do you think he had in mind? 4. Why is it often so difficult to remain at peace with loved ones and friends? 5. What should we do when the circumstances in which we find ourselves do not make sense to us?

■ **ILLUSTRATIONS:**

How Long Is a Good Life? Jimmy was 14 years old. He had the wrinkled, shriveled body of an 80-year-old man. He was a victim of progeria, a rare genetic disorder, especially found in early childhood. Jimmy's mind was sharp, and he had a radiant faith in Christ. He knew that his life expectancy was very short.

Until Jimmy's body became too weak to travel, he spoke to youth groups in churches and to civic organizations about the progression of his illness and about his Christian faith. He was featured on national television, and news magazines carried his story. He received thousands of cards and letters. Many youth were led to faith in Christ because of Jimmy's testimony.

Jimmy repeatedly said that he knew his life on earth would be short, and that God had appointed him a time to die. Nonetheless his faith was radiant, and when he died a few weeks before his fifteenth birthday, he said to his loved ones around his bed, "It's been a great ride. I'll see you in heaven!"

The time between Jimmy's birth and his death was relatively brief. But it was a full life, especially because he considercd himself "on mission" for God. There is indeed a time to die. Only God knows the date.

Caught Red-Handed. He'd been sneaking money out of the register at the fast-food restaurant—five dollars here, ten dollars there, never much at a time, and not very often. Now he was caught, and it added up to more than three hundred dollars. He and his manager were in a booth in the back corner. Would the lad go to jail? What would his parents say?

The manager asked questions and the adolescent answered them. He forgot the excuses he'd cooked up and just told what he'd done. It took a long time, and when it was over, the manager stared at the tabletop. He finally looked up and said, "If I don't press charges and if I don't fire you, can I trust you in the future?"

"What?" was all the young man could stammer.

"You'll have to pay the money back, and you'll have to tell your parents and bring me a note from them that says you did," the manager went on. "You see, you're not the first to pull a stunt like this. I did pretty much the same thing, and my manager said he thought I was truly sorry and ready for some grace of God. I think you are too. What about it?"

A Time to Pluck Up. The last grape harvest was finished. The luscious, green arbors that had covered the hillside were beginning to show the results of the early winter cold. The vineyard keepers came with their shears to do their job. Almost ruthlessly, they snipped and cut until the gnarled vines were ugly and, to the untrained eye, hopelessly injured.

Surely the plants would never send their vines and tendrils upward to entwine about the trellises again, nor would they produce the succulent grapes. Yet the veteran vineyard keepers knew that such radical treatment was necessary, if the vines would produce another harvest the next season.

Indeed, there is *a time to pluck up what is planted* (Eccl. 3:2). The pruning process is often necessary in the spiritual realm, especially as God deals with His children by cutting away what is unnecessary and even harmful so that good fruit can be borne.

A TIME TO REMEMBER

BACKGROUND SCRIPTURE: Ecclesiastes 11:7—12:8

DEVOTIONAL READING: Psalm 143:1-8

KEY VERSE: Remember your creator in the days of your youth, before the days of trouble come. Ecclesiastes 12:1.

KING JAMES VERSION

ECCLESIASTES 11:7 Truly the light is sweet, and a pleasant thing it is for the eyes to behold the sun:

8 But if a man live many years, and rejoice in them all; yet let him remember the days of darkness; for they shall be many. All that cometh is vanity.

9 Rejoice, O young man, in thy youth; and let thy heart cheer thee in the days of thy youth, and walk in the ways of thine heart, and in the sight of thine eyes: but know thou, that for all these things God will bring thee into judgment.

10 Therefore remove sorrow from thy heart, and put away evil from thy flesh: for childhood and youth are vanity.

12:1 Remember now thy Creator in the days of thy youth, while the evil days come not, nor the years draw nigh, when thou shalt say, I have no pleasure in them;

2 While the sun, or the light, or the moon, or the stars, be not darkened, nor the clouds return after the rain:

3 In the day when the keepers of the house shall tremble, and the strong men shall bow themselves, and the grinders cease because they are few, and those that look out of the windows be darkened,

4 And the doors shall be shut in the streets, when the sound of the grinding is low, and he shall rise up at the voice of the bird, and all the daughters of musick shall be brought low;

5 Also when they shall be afraid of that which is high, and fears shall be in the way, and the almond tree shall flourish, and the grasshopper shall be a burden, and desire shall fail: because man goeth to his long home, and the mourners go about the streets:

6 Or ever the silver cord be loosed, or the golden bowl be broken, or the pitcher be broken at the fountain, or the wheel broken at the cistern.

7 Then shall the dust return to the earth as it was: and the spirit shall return unto God who gave it.

8 Vanity of vanities, saith the preacher; all is vanity.

NEW REVISED STANDARD VERSION

ECCLESIASTES 11:7 Light is sweet, and it is pleasant for the eyes to see the sun.

8 Even those who live many years should rejoice in them all; yet let them remember that the days of darkness will be many. All that comes is vanity.

9 Rejoice, young man, while you are young, and let your heart cheer you in the days of your youth. Follow the inclination of your heart and the desire of your eyes, but know that for all these things God will bring you into judgment.

10 Banish anxiety from your mind, and put away pain from your body; for youth and the dawn of life are vanity.

12 Remember your creator in the days of your youth, before the days of trouble come, and the years draw near when you will say, "I have no pleasure in them";

2 before the sun and the light and the moon and the stars are darkened and the clouds return with the rain;

3 in the day when the guards of the house tremble, and the strong men are bent, and the women who grind cease working because they are few, and those who look through the windows see dimly; 4 when the doors on the street are shut, and the sound of the grinding is low, and one rises up at the sound of a bird, and all the daughters of song are brought low; 5 when one is afraid of heights, and terrors are in the road; the almond tree blossoms, the grasshopper drags itself along and desire fails; because all must go to their eternal home, and the mourners will go about the streets; 6 before the silver cord is snapped, and the golden bowl is broken, and the pitcher is broken at the fountain, and the wheel broken at the cistern, 7 and the dust returns to the earth as it was, and the breath returns to God who gave it. 8 Vanity of vanities, says the Teacher; all is vanity.

10

Monday, February 2	Psalm 63:1-8	*I Have Beheld Your Power and Glory*
Tuesday, February 3	Psalm 77:4-10	*I Consider the Days of Old*
Wednesday, February 4	Psalm 77:11-15	*I Will Remember Your Wonders*
Thursday, February 5	Psalm 143:1-8	*I Think about All Your Deeds*
Friday, February 6	Ecclesiastes 11:1-5	*God's Work Is a Mystery*
Saturday, February 7	Ecclesiastes 11:6-10	*Youth Is Fleeting*
Sunday, February 8	Ecclesiastes 12:1-8	*Remember Your Creator*

BACKGROUND

King Solomon, who reigned over Israel for 40 years (about 970–930 B.C.), traditionally has been identified as the author of Ecclesiastes. The strongest evidence for this is that the author—who called himself *the Teacher* (12:8), translated from the Hebrew word *qoheleth* (traditionally rendered "Preacher")—initially referred to himself as *the son of David, king in Jerusalem* (1:1). After a poetic interlude about the meaninglessness of life, the author made the same reference again—*I, the Teacher, when king over Israel in Jerusalem* (1:12). This person would seem to be no other than Solomon.

Certain scholars, however, argue that any king of Judah might have been identified this way. They think there is evidence that the Hebrew of Ecclesiastes comes from a later period of time than the tenth century B.C. Also, they contend that many of the opinions in the book could not have come from Solomon.

Some Bible critics suggest that the book may have had as many as three authors. The first of the three authors, they say, was a pessimist who wrote an impious draft of the book. Then a second author, who was an orthodox Jewish believer, added more religiously proper views to the writings of the first author. Finally, according to these scholars, a third writer added a series of proverbs to what already had been written by the previous two individuals.

Nevertheless, too many factors—such as the book's unity of style, theme, and purpose—strongly suggest that Ecclesiastes had a single author who wrestled with various approaches to life and living. Thus highly respected Bible commentators such as Gerhard von Rad have concluded that a single author for the book "is now well established and widely accepted." Noting that the writer of Ecclesiastes was a king, and that he was evidently quite wise, the bulk of evidence seems to point out that Solomon, was, in fact, the sole author of the book.

NOTES ON THE PRINTED TEXT

Job, Proverbs, and Ecclesiastes make up the wisdom literature of the Bible. These books can be distinguished from the rest of the Old Testament in the way in which they present divine truth. Though the wisdom writers relied on observation and study, they made greater use of introspection and meditation than other Hebrew authors.

The sages commented little about Israel's history, politics, geography, kings, and laws. Instead, the wisdom writers focused on the enduring aspects of the human condition. The sages examined the world around them, and under the guidance of the Spirit drew conclusions about human nature and living in a way that is pleasing to God.

With respect to the Book of Ecclesiastes, as *the Teacher* (12:8) evidently ealized that he was coming to the end of his words, he began to move into his closing statements. At this point in his instruction, he looked back to his youth at the beginning of his life and then ahead to old age at the end. He taught that young people should enjoy their lives while the light of the sun is still bright and *sweet* (11:7) to them. No one knows how long the sun's light will shine on his or her life; therefore, all people should seek to *rejoice* (11:8) in the *many years* of life God gives them.

A sense of urgency is evident in the Teacher's adomonition to his readers. With respect to the blessings that come with each new day, people *should rejoice in them all*, remembering that *the days of darkness will be many*. In view of this, it is all the more imperative to heed the commandment the author wrote earlier in his treatise: *Whatever your hand finds to do, do with your might* (9:10).

The Teacher advised the young to *let your heart cheer you in the days of your youth* (11:9). Also, young people were encouraged to *follow the inclination of your heart and the desire of your eyes.*

At first glance, this advice may seem to be advocating hedonism (idolizing pleasure), or at least giving youth a license for immorality; but that was certainly not the Teacher's intent. He tempered his advice with a reminder that we are accountable before God. He *will bring you into judgment.* The Teacher also realized that many temptations await young people. Thus they must learn when to say "no" and when to say "yes." Ultimately, anything that harms one's mind or body must be avoided (11:10).

Because age takes its toll on the body and the mind, we are admonished to *Remember your creator in the days of your youth* (12:1). The natural excitement of youth fades as the passing years bring their physical and emotional burdens, causing one to say, *"I have no pleasure in them."* Individuals have these negative experiences in varying degrees, of course, for some people are able to retain their zest for life well into old age. In any case, the Teacher urged youth not to wait until the end of their life to cultivate their faith in God, for He wants to involve us as coworkers with Him throughout our existence.

The Teacher also compared the advance of life to the rhythm of the seasons. There is *the sun and the light* (12:2), followed by *the moon and the stars;* and soon they give place to *the clouds* and *the rain.* The time of youth, with its carefree existence, is like the spring and summer. But the autumn and winter come with the cold rains and the dark clouds of old age.

The approaching years so weaken the body that the arms and legs *tremble*

(12:3), the body is *bent*, and the eyes see only *dimly*. The *doors* (12:4) that are *shut* may symbolize deafness that often comes with old age. *The sound of grinding* could refer to an older person chewing food in a toothless mouth, and the fact that *one rises up at the sound of a bird* may characterize the elderly person who sleeps poorly and awakens at the first chirping of the birds. The lovely voices of *all the daughters of song* do not move the elderly, for they have grown hard of hearing.

In 12:5, there is a mixture of real experiences and those that are metaphorical. Old people often are *afraid of heights* and of *terrors . . . in the road*. The blossoming of the *almond tree* probably points to the white hair of advanced age, and the elderly person often shuffles along as *the grasshopper drags itself* and its natural *desire fails*. Finally one dies and goes to his or her *eternal home*, while the *mourners* wait outside to wail during the funeral procession.

Light and water appear often as biblical symbols. The *silver cord* (12:6) held the *golden bowl* or lamp. When the cord was *snapped*, the bowl fell and was *broken*, thus putting out the lamp. Also, when *the pitcher is broken at the fountain, and the wheel is broken at the cistern,* water cannot be drawn. All that is left is for the physical body to perish, and as *dust returns to the earth as it was* (12:7). The glimmer of hope in this sad recital is that *the breath* that made the physical body alive *returns to God who gave it.*

The Teacher repeated the theme with which he began his treatise, namely, that *all is vanity* (12:8). The word rendered *vanity* originally denoted breath or vapor. It can to signify, figuratively speaking, futility, meaninglessness, and emptiness. In Ecclesiastes, both meanings are evident. The Teacher concluded that, from our limited human perspective, life often seems futile and brief, with no lasting significance. Nevertheless, the light of hope, often like a flickering candle, remains alive in the heart of those who have trusted in and obeyed the Lord (12:13-14).

SUGGESTIONS TO TEACHERS

In the closing section of Ecclesiastes, the Teacher came to the end of his philosophical treatise on the futility of life without God. Throughout the book, the writer spoke about the vanity of godless living. He urged his readers both to enjoy the common activities of everyday living and to serve the Lord faithfully. The twilight years of life provide an ideal time to remember the goodness and mercy of God in the simple things we usually take for granted.

1. A WORD TO THE YOUNG. The years of life can be compared to the times of the day—the morning hours when the sun is bright and life seems exciting, the heat of the day when the pressures of living bear down, and the gathering shadows of the evening that point toward the sunset of life. The Teacher's advice was to take advantage of the years of one's youth and relish the blessings and enjoyment they bring. At the same time, be aware that God will hold us accountable for the way in which we have conducted ourselves.

2. A REMINDER TO THE AGED. Be aware that the time will come when the things that seemed very important in the earlier years of life begin to lose their appeal. The natural weaknesses that accompany old age will demand increased attention. The eyes will grow dim, the ears will become hard of hearing, and the mere task of living will seem more and more like a burden. Remembering the joyful days of youth when the body was strong and the spirit was alive will lessen the heaviness of heart and enable one to grow old gracefully.

3. AN ANTICIPATION OF REUNION WITH GOD. Despite the fact that so many things the Teacher said were sobering, he did not end his book with a fatalistic view of life. It's true that the physical body will inevitably return to the dust from which it was made; but the writer noted that death is not the end of one's existence. The spirit that enlivened one's physical body will return to the God, who breathes life into every person. From the New Testament we learn that God *gives us the victory* (1 Cor. 15:56) over the *sting of death* through *our Lord Jesus Christ*.

<table>
<tr><td>

FOR ADULTS

</td><td>

■ **TOPIC:** Change Comes to All

■ **QUESTIONS:** 1. Why did the Teacher urge his readers to rejoice

</td></tr>
</table>

in the years of life God gives? 2. Why does life sometimes seem so fleeting? 3. How did the writer depict the onslaught of old age? 4. What happens to one's body and spirit at death? 5. How can we be good stewards of the blessings in life we receive from God?

■ **ILLUSTRATIONS:**

The Importance of "Dark Light." Artists make much of the importance of light and shadows in a painting. In fact, they have a term for it which they borrowed from the Italians. It is *chiaroscuro*, which means "dark light." The skill of a painters' technique is their ability to combine light colors and dark colors on their canvas. If they paint only in bright colors, then there is no contrast with which to emphasize the brightness of their subject. They must have the dark colors in order to cause the observer to focus on the object of their painting. Likewise, the brightness of life's blessings often are brought into our awareness more vividly when the darkness of the storm clouds has settled about us for a season.

The Beauty of Remembering. Miss Tilly was nearing her ninetieth birthday. She was a tiny lady, always neatly dressed. She insisted that her hair was combed and secured in a bun at the back of her head. A single strand of pearls hung about her neck. On the shoulder of her blouse was a beautiful cameo pin that had belonged to her mother. She sat near the entranceway of the convalescent center, and had a perpetual smile and a cheerful word for everyone who passed by.

If a fellow resident of the center seemed sad, Miss Tilly would make it her business to speak with him or her and give a cheery word. If you stopped to chat with her, she would always tell you in the course of the conversation, however brief, that her son might be coming that day to visit with her. She would point out that she had worn her prettiest dress—one that he had sent her for Christmas. Then she would add, "He was such a beautiful child. He was smart, too. He played all of the sports in high school, and graduated from the university." Then Miss Tilly would tell some incident involving her son that was a vivid part of her memory.

Actually, the son lived in a faraway state and was able to come only rarely to visit his mother. But she remembered those youthful days when he was growing up. They brightened her life and gave her hope to continually anticipate his coming.

Getting the Best of Death. Henry Frances Lyte, a curate of the Church of England, died on November 20, 1847. He had worn himself out laboring in the slums of London. When he died, his family found the almost illegible manuscript of a poem he had written during his last days. It is now a hymn that is sung around the world: "Abide with me: fast falls the eventide; The darkness deepens; Lord, with me abide! When other helpers fail, and comforts flee, Help of the helpless, O abide with me." Lyte was a man whose faith in Christ enabled him "to get the best of death," and this hymn he left behind has helped many others to gain that same victory.

FOR YOUTH	■ **TOPIC:** Now Is the Time

■ **TOPIC:** Now Is the Time

■ **QUESTIONS:** 1. Why is it important to remember the brevity of life when one is young? 2. How is it possible to *banish anxiety from [one's] mind* (Eccl. 11:10)? 3. What are some ways we can remember our *creator in the days of [our] youth* (12:1)? 4. In what sense can life be described as filled with *vanity* (12:8)? 5. How can we make the most of life when it seems filled with disappointment?

■ **ILLUSTRATIONS:**

Forgiveness All the Way. The pastor's little boy had spent the whole afternoon at the mall with his mom. As time passed, the bored boy got in more and more trouble—wanting this, running off, trying to get coins out of the fountain in front of a store. In the car on the way home, the lad could tell he was in for it. He thought he'd try theology. "When we ask God to forgive us when we're bad, He does, doesn't He?"

"Yes, He does," replied the boy's mother.

"And when He forgives us, He buries our sins in the deepest seas, doesn't He?" the boy pressed on.

"Yes, that's what the Bible says," his mother snapped with evident impatience.

She knew her son was hoping to avoid discipline.

"Well," the boy added, "I've asked God to forgive me, but I bet when we get home, you're going fishing for those old sins. Aren't you?"

Sin does have its unavoidable consequences in our lives, but when God forgives, He forgives all the way.

Carpe Diem (Seize the Day). Edwin Booth, the great American actor, once wrote to Adam Badeau, General Grant's secretary and biographer, "Be brave and struggle, but do not set your heart on anything in this world. If good comes to you, take it and enjoy it; but be ready always to relinquish it without a groan."

That is good advice. We should remember that life, at its best, is fragile. We can get "things" that are enjoyable, but they will pass away. Our human relationships in time are brief in comparison with eternity. Thus we should "seize the moments" God grants us and use them in ways that glorify Him. By doing this, we will enrich our lives on this earth and lay up eternal treasures in heaven.

Keep My Memory Green! In Charles Dickens' story, "The Haunted Man," he tells about a chemist who sat before his fireplace one day with unhappy memories. Suddenly a phantom appeared and offered to take his memory away. The troubled man immediately accepted the offer. Thereafter he not only was a man without any memory, but he also had the ability to take the memories of others away from them.

Life, however, became for the chemist an even greater disappointment. So great was his misery and the misery he caused to come to others that he begged the phantom to restore his memory. The story ends with a grateful prayer from the man who could cherish memories again, "Lord, keep my memory green!" How wonderful it is to be able to remember our Creator and all of His blessings to us while we are young.

A TIME FOR LOVE

BACKGROUND SCRIPTURE: Song of Solomon 2:8-13; 7:10-12; 8:6-7
DEVOTIONAL READING: Jeremiah 31:1-5

KEY VERSE: Set me a seal upon your heart, as a seal upon your arm; for love is strong as death, passion fierce as the grave. Song of Solomon 8:6.

KING JAMES VERSION

SONG OF SOLOMON 2:8 The voice of my beloved! behold, he cometh leaping upon the mountains, skipping upon the hills. 9 My beloved is like a roe or a young hart: behold, he standeth behind our wall, he looketh forth at the windows, shewing himself through the lattice. 10 My beloved spake, and said unto me, Rise up, my love, my fair one, and come away. 11 For, lo, the winter is past, the rain is over and gone; 12 The flowers appear on the earth; the time of the singing of birds is come, and the voice of the turtle is heard in our land; 13 The fig tree putteth forth her green figs, and the vines with the tender grape give a good smell. Arise, my love, my fair one, and come away. . . .

7:10 I am my beloved's, and his desire is toward me. 11 Come, my beloved, let us go forth into the field; let us lodge in the villages. 12 Let us get up early to the vineyards; let us see if the vine flourish, whether the tender grape appear, and the pomegranates bud forth: there will I give thee my loves. . . .

8:6 Set me as a seal upon thine heart, as a seal upon thine arm: for love is strong as death; jealousy is cruel as the grave: the coals thereof are coals of fire, which hath a most vehement flame. 7 Many waters cannot quench love, neither can the floods drown it: if a man would give all the substance of his house for love, it would utterly be contemned.

NEW REVISED STANDARD VERSION

SONG OF SOLOMON 2:8 The voice of my beloved!
  Look, he comes,
leaping upon the mountains,
  bounding over the hills.
9 My beloved is like a gazelle
  or a young stag.
Look, there he stands
  behind our wall,
gazing in at the windows,
  looking through the lattice.
10 My beloved speaks and says to me:

"Arise, my love, my fair one,
  and come away;
11 for now the winter is past,
  the rain is over and gone.
12 The flowers appear on the earth;
  the time of singing has come,
and the voice of the turtledove
  is heard in our land.
13 The fig tree puts forth its figs,
  and the vines are in blossom;
  they give forth fragrance.
Arise, my love, my fair one,
  and come away." . . .
7:10 I am my beloved's,
  and his desire is for me.
11 Come, my beloved,
  let us go forth into the fields,
  and lodge in the villages;
12 let us go out early to the vineyards,
  and see whether the vines have budded,
whether the grape blossoms have opened
  and the pomegranates are in bloom.
There I will give you my love. . . .
8:6 Set me as a seal upon your heart,
  as a seal upon your arm;
for love is strong as death,
  passion fierce as the grave.
Its flashes are flashes of fire,
  a raging flame.
7 Many waters cannot quench love,
  neither can floods drown it.
If one offered for love
  all the wealth of his house,
  it would be utterly scorned.

Monday, February 9	Psalm 18:1-6	*I Love You, O Lord*
Tuesday, February 10	Deuteronomy 6:4-9	*A Commandment to Love God*
Wednesday, February 11	John 15:8-12	*Love Others as Christ Loves Us*
Thursday, February 12	John 15:13-17	*No Greater Love*
Friday, February 13	Jeremiah 31:1-5	*God's Everlasting Love*
Saturday, February 14	Song of Solomon 2:8-13	*A Song of Love*
Sunday, February 15	Song of Solomon 7:10-12 8:6-7	*Love Is Strong as Death*

BACKGROUND

According to 1 Kings 4:32, King Solomon composed 1,005 songs. Many Bible scholars assume that the Song of Solomon (sometimes called the Song of Songs) is one of these. Whereas the songs of Solomon probably covered a broad range of themes, this ballad is specifically about love. It portrays love's subtlety and mystery, its beauty and pleasures, and its captivation and enchantment. It reveals the romantic feelings of a woman and a man.

The Song of Solomon also portrays the power of love. In fact, in this poem the power of love is shown to rival the strength of death itself. Thus one of the main lessons to be learned from a study of the Song of Solomon is that God intends for powerful love to be a hallmark of a marital relationship.

Those who accept Solomon as the composer of this ballad point out that the title refers to Solomon by name (1:1). In fact, his name appears many times throughout the book (1:5; 3:7, 9, 11; 8:11-12). In this light many Bible scholars suggest that Solomon most likely wrote this poem to celebrate his wedding to one of his wives.

Those scholars who reject Solomon's authorship of the book say that the real author used Solomon's name to give prestige to his work. They follow various lines of reasoning to prove that Solomon could not have written the ballad, such as pointing to the presence of some rare words. These lines of reasoning are not convincing to most conservative scholars.

When was the Song of Solomon written? For those who accept Solomon as the composer, the answer is straightforward. He wrote the poem somewhere in the middle of the tenth century B.C. This is based on the fact that Solomon's reign extended from about 970 to about 930 B.C.

Both the Jewish and Christian faiths have held the Song of Solomon in high esteem, though perhaps no other book of the Old Testament has been subjected to so many different interpretations. There are three basic approaches.

The Song of Solomon has often been taken as *allegorical*. In this interpretation, the lovers in this ballad are viewed not as historical figures but as symbolic characters. Jewish interpreters who took the allegorical approach have seen the characters as representing God and Israel, while Christian interpreters have seen them representing Christ and the church.

A somewhat related interpretation sees the Song of Solomon as *typological*. In other words, the characters in this poem are accepted as historical, but their love is also take to illustrate the love God has for His people. Christians have seen in the love relationship between the young bride and groom the love that Jesus, the Bridegroom, has for His bride, the church.

The *natural* or *literal* interpretation takes the Song of Solomon at its face value, thus making the ballad portray an actual case of romantic love. (This is the view adopted here.) Of course, this interpretation does not preclude the author's use of metaphorical language, in which a word or phrase that ordinarily designates one thing is used to designate another. Thus, when the author referred to physical appearance, he may also have been focusing on character, personality, and so on.

There is no clear plot in the Song of Solomon as there would have be in a play or a story. Interpreters have therefore suggested several different story lines. This publication takes the view that the poem shows the love between King Solomon and one of his wives. The poem contains a cluster of five meetings in which the lovers pass through courtship, their wedding, the consummation of their love in marriage, and later occasions in which they renew their love. According to this analysis of the action, there are three sources of the speeches in the ballad: the bride, her attendants, and the groom.

NOTES ON THE PRINTED TEXT

The *Song of Songs* (S. of S. 1:1) is a collection of brief poems about love and marriage. The 117 verses of this ballad make some of the most well-known love poetry in all of world literature. Throughout these poems are words from three sources. First is the young Shulammite bride who talked about her love boldly and openly, reflecting the innocence of the love between Adam and Eve in the Garden of Eden (Gen. 2:24-25). Second is the groom, apparently King Solomon, who candidly expressed his joy and admiration of his new bride. Third is the bride's friends, namely, a group of young Jewish maidens.

Beginning in Song of Solomon 2:8, there is a scene change in the ballad, even though the young Shulammite woman was still speaking. Just before this change in the scene, the maiden and her betrothed seem to have been together. Now they were apart.

The girl was at home, and she saw the young man approaching as if he were *leaping upon the mountains, bounding over the hills* (2:8). The woman sees his deep desire to be with her like the energy of a *gazelle* (2:9) or *a young stag*. The gazelle belongs to the antelope family, and is a small, swift-footed, and graceful animal. It has large, bright eyes and spirally-twisted horns that point backward. Both the *gazelle* and *young stag* are surefooted. Thus, the girl's lover comes to her, and even rough, difficult terrain will not stop him.

The girl's house has a wall around it for privacy and protection. The suitor stands behind the wall, and the young woman knows he is there because she heard his voice and saw him coming over the hills. Discreetly and respectfully, the girl's *beloved* stands *behind our wall, gazing in at the windows*. These were only openings in the wall. They were covered by a *lattice*, namely, cross-hatched bars that provided both privacy and ventilation.

With tender words, the suitor urged the girl to *arise* (2:10) and *come away* with him. With poetic beauty, the groom beckoned his fair darling to join him in the forest, where springtime had made everything fresh (2:11). Not only was the weather now dry and warm, but *the flowers* (2:12) were blooming and the *turtledove* had returned from its winter migration. The *fig tree* (2:13) was producing its fruit, and the fragrance of the *vines* as they produced their blossoms filled the air. The setting seemed perfect, and the suitor repeated his call to his bride, *Arise, my love, my fair one, and come away.*

As we move forward in the ballad, the Shulammite woman and Solomon have married. In 7:1-9, the groom offered his most complete description of his new wife, praising her from foot to head. Then, in response to her husband's praise of her, the young wife offered adoration of her own. The bride expressed her commitment with the words, *I am my beloved's* (7:10). She admitted to their mutual affection when she added, *his desire is for me.*

Obviously, the Shulammite woman felt a sense of safe vulnerability in her love for Solomon. Their desire for each other was mutual. In fact, she was forthright enough to suggest they go out together in public. She wanted the two of them to retreat to the *fields* (2:11)—no doubt because she came from the country. The young bride also recommended staying overnight in the *villages* along the way. Having grown up in villages and vineyards (1:6), she wanted to share with her new husband a place where she felt at home.

In this natural setting, the Shulammite woman believed the two of them would be able to celebrate their love surrounded by *vines* (7:12) and *grape blossoms* and *pomegranates . . . in bloom.* All of these elements of nature symbolize the fullness and joy of their marriage union.

In the closing portion of the ballad, the newlyweds are portrayed as returning to the city from the countryside. The young maidens saw them first and announced their arrival (8:5). The wife was apparently *leaning* on her husband, not because she was weak or tired, but because she wanted to be close to him.

The bride recalled how she roused her lover *under the apple tree*. In the ancient Near East, physical intimacy was often expressed in connection with the mention of fruit trees, probably because of the trees' association with fertility. The Shulammite woman, rather than going to her mother's home—a desire she had earlier expressed (3:4; 8:2)—had gone with the groom to the home his *mother* (8:5).

At this location the couple vowed their eternal *love* (8:6) for each other. The wife asked her husband to *set me as a seal upon you heart, as a seal upon your arm*. In ancient times, an engraved seal was used to signify ownership. Possession of another person's seal indicated that the possessor had as much right to the owner's property as the owner himself. In this context the wife was saying that she wanted to seal her claim on her husband.

In what many consider the high point of the ballad, the young bride stated that *love is strong as death, passion fierce as the grave*. Her declaration of affection continued when she said that vast floods could not *quench love* (8:7). Furthermore, if one truly in love were asked to exchange love for material *wealth*, the offer would be rejected without hesitation. In short, love is not for sale.

SUGGESTIONS TO TEACHERS

Whatever we think of the parallel made between the lovers of the Song of Solomon and Christ and the church, we can receive the overarching message of God's love in our own lives. In this ballad, the bride called the husband to lasting love and contentment. In the Book of Revelation, the Spirit and the bride called for anyone who is thirsty to come (22:17). We are the thirsty ones, and God calls us to respond to His invitation to love Him with all our heart, mind, and soul. If we respond by running to Him in faith, He will quench our thirst with everlasting life and blessings.

1. THE PROPER APPROACH TO COURTSHIP. Solomon painted a picture of true chivalry as he described the manner in which the suitor approached the maiden whom he desired to court. He did not approach her presumptuously, but courteously asked whether he might spend time with her. Because of the way the Shulammite woman described Solomon's conduct, we can be sure that she was favorably impressed. They had passed through the winter of adjusting to each other. Now the cold winds and rain were gone and the springtime had arrived. It was time to move forward in the relationship.

2. THE ADJUSTMENT TO MARRIAGE. The period of courtship was completed. Friends of the bride and groom had shown their excitement and concern for the couple. The marriage had taken place and it was time for the honeymoon. The hectic pace that accompanies courtship and preparations for marriage can be physically and emotionally exhausting for any newly wedded couple. They must spend time alone, getting to know each other. They do so in the midst of God's blessing on their lives.

3. THE PERMANENCY OF THE RELATIONSHIP. It seems that with each passing generation, the marriage vows become less and less significant. The soaring divorce rate reflects the lack of seriousness with which the marriage vows are taken. In contrast, the young couple in our biblical poem are so deeply in love and consider their vows so seriously that they are convinced no amount of earthly wealth could replace it (S. of S. 8:7). The young woman wanted her beloved to let her be as a seal upon his heart (8:6), as if one would affix an official seal to a document. The strength of their relationship was in their love for one another. Not even the raging waters could extinguish their affection.

■ TOPIC: The Joy and Wonder of Love

■ QUESTIONS: 1. How did the Shulammite woman describe her suitor in Song of Solomon 2:8-9? 2. What indications of mutual affection are evident from the statements recorded in 2:10-13? 3. How strong was the desire of the bride and groom for one another? 4. What did the bride think would quench the love she and her husband had for each other? 5. How can married couples keep the ardor of their affection vibrant throughout the years of marriage?

■ ILLUSTRATIONS:

Advice to a Young Woman. Clarence E. Macartney gave the following advice to a young woman desiring to be married. It appears in the form of five "don'ts":

Don't marry an unbeliever.

Don't marry a man of bad habits.

Don't marry a man with room for himself and no one else.

Don't marry a "peacock" man, a conceited man.

Don't marry a man of low moral standards.

Permanent Vows. Vows to a marriage partner, like our vows to the Lord, are meant to be kept. With almost half of all marriages in the United States failing and ending, we are called to remember that the commitment to one's spouse is modeled on God's commitment to us through Christ. God has vowed to stay with us, caringly, faithfully, and permanently. In turn, we as husbands and wives give our word to the Lord, to one another, and to the public that we will remain together caringly, faithfully, and permanently.

Tragically, many enter into the marriage relationship along the lines indicated in a cartoon in *The Wall Street Journal* (May 11, 1999). A prospective bride and groom are shown standing before a pastor, with the husband-to-be asking, "Do you have a ceremony less drastic than marriage?"

The Unbreakable Covenant. He owned a small-town newspaper, which was published once a week. He was an excellent writer and journalist. His wife was a dedicated schoolteacher, greatly admired by her students and respected by their parents. The years passed, and the time for retirement came. The owner sold his newspaper, and his wife retired from the schoolroom. They returned to live in the town where they were born.

Less than a year after the couple moved to their new home, the wife began to show tell-tale signs of Alzheimer's disease. To the dismay of her husband, it progressed rapidly. His devotion to her was such that he adjusted, almost daily, to her mental deterioration.

Eventually it was necessary for the husband to place his wife in a convalescent center. He stayed with her. When it became necessary, he fed her every meal, bite by bite. His adult children tried to persuade him to move home and visit with his wife less often. But he refused, reminding them about the marriage vows he and their mother had taken. For more than 50 years they had enjoyed deeply each other's company. He held her hand and wept softly as she slipped away one day. Only a few months later he, too, died. The story of the undying love of this couple became a legend in that small town.

<table>
<tr><td rowspan="2">FOR YOUTH</td><td>■ TOPIC: What Does Love Have to Do with It?</td></tr>
<tr><td>■ QUESTIONS: 1. What signs of affection did the woman and her suitor display toward each other? 2. What opinion did the couple</td></tr>
</table>

have for one another? 3. What was the nature of the commitment that existed between the wife and her husband? 4. What was the extent of the love the couple had for each other? 5. How is it possible to tell the difference between love and lust?

■ **ILLUSTRATIONS:**

An Appeal for Common Courtesy. The young woman had grown up observing the courteous way in which her father treated her mother. He never failed to go around to the passenger side of the car and open the door for her. She had never heard him raise his voice at her mother even when they were having a disagreement. He bought her flowers at the appropriate time, and never forgot her birthday or their wedding anniversary.

Time came for the young woman's first date. The suitor drove up to the front of her home. She watched discreetly from a window. He did not get out of his car for a few moments. Then he lightly tapped on his horn. After awhile, he sounded two long blasts on the horn. Eventually he came to the door and was barely able to conceal his impatience because she had not responded to his car horn.

The young woman's parents knew the boy's mother and father, and they knew he was basically a good person. Obviously he had not witnessed, or been taught, common courtesy. When the two youths left for the date, the boy asked the girl why she had not come out of the house. She gave him a lesson in common courtesy that she had learned through observation. Because he thought so highly of her, he listened carefully. On the next date, he was a true gentleman. He came to the door and went inside for a brief visit with her parents. He opened the car door for her to get in and was there to help her get out. He became one of the most chivalrous young men in high school!

Key to Happiness. Most people generally assume that being single and living the carefree life of a young swinger is truly happy. There appear to be no responsibilities or duties except to oneself. Numerous studies, however, have demonstrated that faithfully married people live happier lives than those who are single.

Most recently, Wayne State sociologists Steven Stack and J. Ross Eshleman studied 18,000 adults in 17 industrialized countries including Japan, Canada, Australia, and Europe, and they concluded that couples living in faithful marriages were happier than couples who were cohabiting together, and much happier than singles.

The First Kiss. The young man and woman about to be married had come from devoted Christian homes. They had met at a Christian youth training center where she was a clerical worker and he an officer in charge of planning for the recreational activities in which the young men would be involved.

The young man had first contacted the girl's father, without her knowledge, and asked permission to court her. This was the method he chose by which to discover whether the possibility of marriage would be within God's will. The father consented, and the courtship began. After nearly a year, the suitor asked the girl to marry him.

When the two came to their pastor for counseling, the young man told the pastor that they were reserving their first kiss for the "bridal kiss" at the close of the marriage ceremony. He asked that the pastor announce to the congregation that this was indeed their "first kiss," and it would make their wedding all the more memorable. This was the young man's way of showing great consideration and sensitivity toward his bride.

A TIME FOR COURAGE

BACKGROUND SCRIPTURE: Esther 3—4
DEVOTIONAL READING: Psalm 27:1-8

KEY VERSE: I will go the to king, though it is against
the law: and if I perish, I perish. Esther 4:16.

KING JAMES VERSION

ESTHER 3:2 And all the king's servants, that were in the king's gate, bowed, and reverenced Haman: for the king had so commanded concerning him. But Mordecai bowed not, nor did him reverence. 3 Then the king's servants, which were in the king's gate, said unto Mordecai, Why transgressest thou the king's commandment? . . .

5 And when Haman saw that Mordecai bowed not, nor did him reverence, then was Haman full of wrath. 6 And he thought scorn to lay hands on Mordecai alone. . . .

4:7 And Mordecai told him of all that had happened unto him, and of the sum of the money that Haman had promised to pay to the king's treasuries for the Jews, to destroy them. 8 Also he gave him the copy of the writing of the decree that was given at Shushan to destroy them, to shew it unto Esther, and to declare it unto her, and to charge her that she should go in unto the king, to make supplication unto him, and to make request before him for her people. 9 And Hatach came and told Esther the words of Mordecai. 10 Again Esther spake unto Hatach, and gave him commandment unto Mordecai; 11 All the king's servants, and the people of the king's provinces, do know, that whosoever, whether man or woman, shall come unto the king into the inner court, who is not called, there is one law of his to put him to death, except such to whom the king shall hold out the golden sceptre, that he may live: but I have not been called to come in unto the king these thirty days. 12 And they told to Mordecai Esther's words. 13 Then Mordecai commanded to answer Esther, Think not with thyself that thou shalt escape in the king's house, more than all the Jews. 14 For if thou altogether holdest thy peace at this time, then shall there enlargement and deliverance arise to the Jews from another place; but thou and thy father's house shall be destroyed: and who knoweth whether thou art come to the kingdom for such a time as this? 15 Then Esther bade them return Mordecai this answer, 16 Go, gather together all the Jews that are present in Shushan, and fast ye for me, and neither eat nor drink three days, night or day: I also and my maidens will fast likewise; and so will I go in unto the king, which is not according to the law: and if I perish, I perish.

NEW REVISED STANDARD VERSION

ESTHER 3:2 And all the king's servants who were at the king's gate bowed down and did obeisance to Haman; for the king had so commanded concerning him. But Mordecai did not bow down or do obeisance. 3 Then the king's servants who were at the king's gate said to Mordecai, "Why do you disobey the king's command?" . . .

5 When Haman saw that Mordecai did not bow down or do obeisance to him, Haman was infuriated. 6 But he thought it beneath him to lay hands on Mordecai alone. . . .

4:7 and Mordecai told him all that had happened to him, and the exact sum of money that Haman had promised to pay into the king's treasuries for the destruction of the Jews. 8 Mordecai also gave him a copy of the written decree issued in Susa for their destruction, that he might show it to Esther, explain it to her, and charge her to go to the king to make supplication to him and entreat him for her people.

9 Hathach went and told Esther what Mordecai had said. 10 Then Esther spoke to Hathach and gave him a message for Mordecai, saying, 11 "All the king's servants and the people of the king's provinces know that if any man or woman goes to the king inside the inner court without being called, there is but one law—all alike are to be put to death. Only if the king holds out the golden scepter to someone, may that person live. I myself have not been called to come in to the king for thirty days." 12 When they told Mordecai what Esther had said, 13 Mordecai told them to reply to Esther, "Do not think that in the king's palace you will escape any more than all the other Jews. 14 For if you keep silence at such a time as this, relief and deliverance will rise for the Jews from another quarter, but you and your father's family will perish. Who knows? Perhaps you have come to royal dignity for just such a time as this." 15 Then Esther said in reply to Mordecai, 16 "Go, gather all the Jews to be found in Susa, and hold a fast on my behalf, and neither eat nor drink for three days, night or day. I and my maids will also fast as you do. After that I will go to the king, though it is against the law; and if I perish, I perish."

12

BACKGROUND

Unlike the books of Ezra and Nehemiah, conservative scholars are undecided about who wrote the Book of Esther. From the circumstances and tone of the book, it seems the original writer was a patriotic Jew. He was intimately familiar with the following: the particulars surrounding the imperial court of the Persian king Ahasuerus (or, Xerxes I ; 486–465 B.C.; a powerful and capable ruler); the physical features of Susa, the capital city; the king's winter palace in that city; and general Persian customs and culture.

The author's description of Mordecai's reputation gives the impression of someone who is looking back on events that had already occurred (Esth. 10:2-3). Extra-biblical sources suggest that Mordecai did not hold the office of prime minister after the reign of Ahasuerus. Perhaps a Jew who was familiar with Mordecai (for example, a personal assistant within the palace) gathered the information and compiled the material for this book sometime shortly after the reign of Ahasuerus (that is, between 465–450 B.C.).

The Book of Esther may be divided into three parts. The first section deals with the *plight* of the Jews (1:1—3:15). Through the course of events, enemies plot for the execution and extinction of the Jewish people. The second section deals with the *plan* of the Jews (4:1—5:14). Through the intervention of Mordecai and Esther's appeal to the king, the deliverance of God's people is set in motion. The third section deals with the *preservation* of the Jews (6:1—10:3). Haman's plot is overturned and God's people are rescued from potential slaughter.

At the beginning of Esther, the Jews faced the threat of doom. At the end of the book they experienced the triumph associated with deliverance. In the midst of persecution there was impending ruin for the Jews. God, nevertheless, remained in control. He preserved His people by providing an incredible release from danger. Throughout all the events of the book, God miraculously displayed His care.

NOTES ON THE PRINTED TEXT

Officials of the king had assembled a group of virgins for his harem. Mordecai was present at the king's gate at this time (Esth. 2:19). He was an important palace official within Susa. In accordance with Mordecai's previous instructions, Esther had not told anyone about her Jewish nationality and family background. The Jewess remained obedient to Mordecai even after she was no longer under his care (2:20).

Around the time when Mordecai was present at the king's gate, two officials became angry with Ahasuerus and plotted to murder him (2:21). Mordecai, however, found out about the scheme. He informed Queen Esther, who relayed the information to the king in Mordecai's name (2:22). The report was investigated and validated. As a result, both the guilty officials were executed by hanging from a tree. The entire incident was noted in the official records in the presence of the king (2:23).

After these events, Ahasuerus selected Haman to be the second most powerful official within the Persian Empire. He was an Agagite and possibly a descendent of the Amalekites (3:1). First Samuel 15 contains the account of a decisive battle fought between the armies of Israel under King Saul and the Amalekites, led by King Agag. Through the prophet Samuel, God had told Saul to exterminate all of the Amalekites. From the days of Moses they had been bitter and harassing enemies of God's people. But Saul spared King Agag. As a result, the Amalekites continued to be a thorn in the side of God's people. The aim of these Amalekites was to annihilate the Jews. Haman clearly shared this goal.

The manner in which Ahasuerus deferred to Haman later in the Book of Esther indicates that his position was like that of Joseph in Egypt, who served as second in command to Pharaoh. The king was so impressed with Haman that he commanded that *all the king's servants who were at the king's gate* (3:2) bow down and do *obeisance* (an attitude of respect or reverence) to Haman.

Mordecai, however, refused to revere Haman. There was no justification for Mordecai's behavior based on the Mosaic law (in other words, misplaced worship; Exod. 20:4) or scriptural precedent (Gen. 23:7; 33:3; 44:14; 1 Sam. 24:8; 2 Sam. 14:4; 1 Kings 1:16). Perhaps Mordecai's disobedience was based on the animosity that existed between the Jews and the Amalekites. Mordecai, motivated by a strong sense of patriotism, defied Haman because he was an enemy of God's people and ultimately a menace to their existence (Esth. 3:10; 7:6; 8:1; 9:10, 24).

The king's servants noticed Mordecai's belligerent conduct regarding Haman and asked him why he refused to obey *"the king's command"* (3:3). Undoubtedly, Mordecai could not bring himself to bow before one who was descended from the Amalekites, the bitter enemies of the Jews. When Mordecai's peers *spoke to him day after day* (3:4), he refused to *listen to them*.

Mordecai's peers finally *told Haman* about Mordecai's insubordination to determine whether this behavior was permissible or intolerable. When Haman verified what he had learned, he *was infuriated* (3:5). The Hebrew word rendered *infuriated* means "filled with anger." Mordecai's actions threatened Haman's inflated ego. Thus he became obsessed with the determination to retaliate against Mordecai.

When Haman was *told who Mordecai's people were* (3:6), Haman spurned the idea that killing this rebel would be sufficient. Haman determined that *all the Jews* living within the Persian Empire had to die, perhaps as a fitting punishment for Mordecai's insolence. Haman's anger drove him to devise a scheme whereby all of the Jews in the Persian Empire would be exterminated.

In the *twelfth year of King Ahasuerus* (3:7), the court astrologers and magicians cast a lot for Haman to determine when to exterminate the Jews. The lot fell on the last month of the Jewish calendar, giving Haman about 11 months to establish and implement his plan. He next presented his case to the king, and the monarch readily agreed and issued the decree (3:8-13). The edict was then dispatched to all of the provinces giving orders to annihilate all of the Jews in one day (3:14-15).

When Mordecai learned about the decree, he began to go through the city streets dressed in sackcloth and ashes (the clothing of mourning) and wept loudly (4:1-3). Esther's maids told her what Mordecai was doing, and she sent one of her attendants to find out from him what was happening (4:4-6).

Mordecai then reviewed the details of *all that had happened to him* (4:7). He even stated the enormous sum of money that Haman would place in the royal treasury for those who helped massacre the Jews. Mordecai also gave the official *a copy* (4:8) of the king's decree. Mordecai asked the queen to go into the king's presence and seek his favor and mercy concerning her fellow Jews.

The official explained to Esther the situation and she in turn sent back a reply to Mordecai (4:9-10). Esther reminded him that her life would be placed in jeopardy if she did what he had requested. The king might execute her for trying to seek an interview with him without being specifically summoned. The king would only spare Esther's life (in other words, clear her of guilt) if he held out his *golden scepter* (4:11) and granted her permission to see him. She reasoned that this possibility was remote, for the king had not summoned her into his presence for almost a month.

When Esther's servants communicated her response to Mordecai (4:12), he sent back a frank reply. He reminded her that even she was not immune from the king's decree (4:13). Mordecai's next words acknowledged the control of God over the course of events. If Esther chose to remain silent, the Lord would find another way to release them from their distress and rescue them from their potential destruction. He also would permit Esther and her ancestral line to be wiped out of existence. Mordecai suggested that the queen's royal position was permitted by God to resolve the present crisis. The Lord, in His providence, wanted to use Esther and Mordecai to bring about the miraculous deliverance of His people (4:14).

Esther again responded to Mordecai through her attendants (4:15). Her reply was a sterling display of devotion to God and commitment to His people. Her bravery was a demonstration of living trust in the Lord, especially at a critical time for the Jewish people.

Esther requested that Mordecai assemble all the Jews living in Susa and make the crisis a matter of fasting (and possibly prayer). The queen asked that her fellow Jews would abstain from food or water for three full days. She and her female attendants would likewise do the same. After this, she would break with Persian regulations by requesting an audience with the king. She resigned herself to the possibility of losing her life over this decision (4:16). Esther's attendants notified Mordecai, and he responded by heeding the queen's instructions (4:17).

SUGGESTIONS TO TEACHERS

Courage has been defined as an attitude of facing and dealing with anything recognized as dangerous, difficult, or painful instead of withdrawing from it. All of us face problems and situations in life that require courage in one degree or another. Occasionally we must face extremely challenging situations alone. Sometimes the issue is controversial, and friends and loved ones may discourage us or be critical of what we feel we must do. God often wanted those whom He chose to perform difficult tasks for Him to be courageous. He promised them He would be with them and provide the required strength at the moment of their need.

1. A TIME FOR CIVIL DISOBEDIENCE. As in the case of Mordecai and the apostles of Jesus, a time may come when our spiritual convictions force us to choose between obeying a humanly constructed law or the law of God. Of course, such a stand does not permit us becoming violent. Nevertheless, as with Mordecai, a firm stand for what we believe is the proper thing to do may result in others harming us. This possibility is especially strong in places where Christianity is despised. We should thank God daily for the religious freedoms we enjoy in our country.

2. THE RESULT OF HATRED. Hated is a devastating emotion, for when it festers within us, it becomes increasingly difficult to control. Often hatred has deep roots that may lie dormant for a long time before they produce their deadly fruit. Such was the case with Haman. His hatred for the Jews was ignited when he learned that Mordecai, who refused to bow before him, was a Jew. Misunderstandings, unresolved, can develop into hostilities that lay the groundwork for a simmering hatred. Hatred can drive us to do unreasonable and irrational things. Such a pattern was obvious in the downhill path Haman took as his hatred for Mordecai and the Jews exploded.

3. AN ACT OF COURAGE. Mordecai's courageous refusal to bow before Haman no doubt was reflected in the attitude of Esther, whose life was influenced by her godly uncle. Godly parents and relatives can be role models of courage before their children. These character traits are absorbed in subtle and progressive ways. Esther's respect for Mordecai was such that she was willing to risk her life and throw herself at the mercy of the king. God honored her act of courage and it saved her people from annihilation. The results of our acts of courage may not be as dramatic, but they can accomplish much for the glory of God and for the blessing of others.

<table>
<tr><td>

FOR ADULTS

</td><td>

■ TOPIC: Courage to Risk All

■ QUESTIONS: 1. Who were the servants at the king's gate in Susa?
2. Why do you think the king's servants asked Mordecai again and

</td></tr>
</table>

again for the reason he refused to bow down before Haman? 3. What was it that intensified Haman's vindictive attitude toward Mordecai? 4. What do you think Mordecai said to Esther that made her determine to approach the king, unbidden, on behalf of her people? 5. How did you feel at times in your life when you needed God's strength and courage to face issues and circumstances, even when others misunderstood you?

■ ILLUSTRATIONS:

The Holocaust. The Holocaust was the systematic destruction of more than six million Jews by the Nazis before and during World War II. Unbelievable stories of courage and faith on the part of many surviving Jews have been preserved and handed down from generation to generation.

In February, 1946, a Jewish rabbi arrived in New York. Among those who welcomed him in the New York harbor was an American G. I. From the Ninth Army, which had liberated the rabbi and others when they were fleeing from a death train in a German forest near Magdeburg. The G. I. pointed out with great pride the Statue of Liberty. He told the rabbi: "On its pedestal is an inscription written by a Jewish-American poet, Emma Lazarus: 'Give me your tired, your poor, your huddled masses yearning to breathe free.'" The G. I. translated the words into Yiddish for the rabbi's benefit.

The rabbi, who was one of the first Holocaust survivors to arrive in America after the war, listened and wiped a tear from his eye. "My friend, the words you have just translated for me are indeed beautiful. We, the few survivors coming to these shores, are indeed poor, tired, and yearning for freedom. We are remnants, a trickle of broken individuals who search for a few moments of peace in this world. We survived, 'one of a city, and two of a family.'"

Truth-Speaking Martyr. Some refer to Harry T. Moore as America's first civil rights martyr. Moore campaigned for justice and equality for African Americans in obscure towns in Florida before and immediately after World War II. At that time, Florida was third in the nation in lynchings. The Ku Klux Klan had infested the ranks of local politicians, business people, and police officers. Florida state officials were not sympathetic to civil rights complaints. Moore quickly acquired the reputation of being a "troublemaker" during the late 1930s and 40s.

This brave man sued to get equal pay for African American teachers, started voter registration drives, and fired off letters to the governors about the latest atrocity against African Americans. Unlike later civil rights leaders, Moore had no national media to publicize his cause. And he did not have the support of people from the north to finance him. Nevertheless, because Moore believed fervently in equality and democracy, he spoke the truth despite the presence of threats.

Like many other spokespersons of truth, Harry Moore paid with his life. He was killed in a bombing attack on Christmas Day, 1951. His death, however, was not in vain. Because of Moore's courageous efforts, Florida's African American voter registration was years ahead of that in the other southern states.

Amazing Courage. Wellington, the British general and statesman, used to speak about what he called "three o'clock in the morning" courage. What a person thinks and does when things are at their worst makes or mars one's future. Bitter disappointment, broken trust, and the fading of cherished hopes can bring about a crisis for everyone. Ultimately, we must either choose hate, bitterness, and despair, or have the courage to choose the way of forgiveness and endurance.

FOR YOUTH

■ TOPIC: Stand Up!
■ QUESTIONS: 1. Concerning what we know about Haman, how would you describe his personality? 2. Why do you think Mordecai refused to bow down before Haman? 3. What caused Haman's hatred to progress to the point where he decided to destroy the Jewish people living throughout the Persian Empire? 4. How would you describe Esther's response to Mordecai's request? 5. Why is it sometimes hard for us to stand up for our convinctions in front of our peers?

■ ILLUSTRATIONS:
The Price of Acceptance. John was a freshman in high school. He wanted desperately to be accepted by some of his older peers. He was a good athlete and looked older than his 15 years. A couple of junior boys who lived in his neighborhood invited John to "hang out" with them one Saturday night. He finally persuaded his parents to let him go with them.

The boys had not driven far until one of them produced a six-pack of beer and began to pass the cans around. John did not drink, and had not thought alcohol would be involved in their outing. He refused to take a can. The older boys tried to entice him to drink.

When the group stopped at a service station for gas, John told them he had to make a call. He called his father to come and get him. At midnight the telephone rang, and it was the parents of one of the boys who thought John was in the group. There had been a terrible accident and one of the boys was killed. The price of acceptance was almost too costly for John.

Four at the Pole. "See You at the Pole" has become an annual event on many public school campuses. At the beginning of a new school year, Christian students gather early one morning around the school's flag pole for a brief time of prayer for their school, its administration and teachers, and for each other.

When the program was first introduced, it did not meet with much success in some places. At one high school, only four students arrived for the event on an early fall morning. The four of them surrounded the flagpole, joining hands as they prayed and sang gospel choruses. Some of the students arriving ignored them, others deliberately walked far away from the pole, and some heckled them and made fun of them. Insulting remarks were made to them in the halls. But they refused to reciprocate with hostility.

During the course of the year, several youth came to the four and asked their forgiveness for not supporting them. Even some of the hecklers apologized. The next year, the number more than quadrupled. During the third year, more than a hundred young people gathered around the pole. That same year a Fellowship of Christian Athletes was organized on campus. The courage of "the four at the pole" paid off.

Risk-taking. Bob sat beside his pastor's desk one day. He was visibly shaken and disturbed. As an all-state high school basketball player, Bob had been offered scholarships to play basketball at several colleges and universities. He came from a family of meager means; thus he had to depend on scholarship assistance and educational grants in order to attend college.

One large university had offered Bob a full scholarship, everything paid, with a small stipend for spending money. A small Christian college in a nearby town where he had visited older friends who were students there had also offered him a scholarship. It was not nearly as enticing financially as the one from the larger school.

The previous weekend Bob had visited on the campus of the larger school and had stayed in the athletic dorm. He was exposed to a level of partying and drinking he had never seen before. He was fascinated by the school and the opportunities he would have there, both academically and athletically. He tried to convince himself that he would not have to take part in the fast social life of most of the students he had met. On the other hand, Bob remembered the good feeling he had had at the smaller Christian school. He and his pastor prayed, and he became convinced that the risk he would be taking in the larger school would be too great; thus he chose to accept the offer from the smaller school.

Mordecai could have "gone through the motions" in bowing down to Haman and would have fared much better in the kingdom; but he chose not to take that risk and remained true to his deeper convictions.

A Time to Celebrate

Background Scripture: Esther 8—9
Devotional Reading: Psalm 98:1-9

Key Verse: For the Jews there was light and gladness, joy and honor. Esther 8:16.

KING JAMES VERSION

ESTHER 8:3 And Esther spake yet again before the king, and fell down at his feet, and besought him with tears to put away the mischief of Haman the Agagite, and his device that he had devised against the Jews. 4 Then the king held out the golden sceptre toward Esther. So Esther arose, and stood before the king, 5 And said, If it please the king, and if I have found favour in his sight, and the thing seem right before the king, and I be pleasing in his eyes, let it be written to reverse the letters devised by Haman the son of Hammedatha the Agagite, which he wrote to destroy the Jews which are in all the king's provinces: 6 For how can I endure to see the evil that shall come unto my people? or how can I endure to see the destruction of my kindred? 7 Then the king Ahasuerus said unto Esther the queen and to Mordecai the Jew, Behold, I have given Esther the house of Haman, and him they have hanged upon the gallows, because he laid his hand upon the Jews. 8 Write ye also for the Jews, as it liketh you, in the king's name, and seal it with the king's ring: for the writing which is written in the king's name, and sealed with the king's ring, may no man reverse. . . .

9:18 But the Jews that were at Shushan assembled together on the thirteenth day thereof, and on the fourteenth day thereof; and on the fifteenth day of the same they rested, and made it a day of feasting and gladness. 19 Therefore the Jews of the villages, that dwelt in the unwalled towns, made the fourteenth day of the month Adar a day of gladness and feasting, and a good day, and of sending portions one to another. 20 And Mordecai wrote these things, and sent letters unto all the Jews that were in all the provinces of the king Ahasuerus, both nigh and far, 21 To stablish this among them, that they should keep the fourteenth day of the month Adar, and the fifteenth day of the same, yearly, 22 As the days wherein the Jews rested from their enemies, and the month which was turned unto them from sorrow to joy, and from mourning into a good day: that they should make them days of feasting and joy, and of sending portions one to another, and gifts to the poor. 23 And the Jews undertook to do as they had begun, and as Mordecai had written unto them.

NEW REVISED STANDARD VERSION

ESTHER 8:3 Then Esther spoke again to the king; she fell at his feet, weeping and pleading with him to avert the evil design of Haman the Agagite and the plot that he had devised against the Jews. 4 The king held out the golden scepter to Esther, 5 and Esther rose and stood before the king. She said, "If it pleases the king, and if I have won his favor, and if the thing seems right before the king, and I have his approval, let an order be written to revoke the letters devised by Haman son of Hammedatha the Agagite, which he wrote giving orders to destroy the Jews who are in all the provinces of the king. 6 For how can I bear to see the calamity that is coming on my people? Or how can I bear to see the destruction of my kindred?" 7 Then King Ahasuerus said to Queen Esther and to the Jew Mordecai, "See, I have given Esther the house of Haman, and they have hanged him on the gallows, because he plotted to lay hands on the Jews. 8 You may write as you please with regard to the Jews, in the name of the king, and seal it with the king's ring; for an edict written in the name of the king and sealed with the king's ring cannot be revoked." . . .

9:18 But the Jews who were in Susa gathered on the thirteenth day and on the fourteenth, and rested on the fifteenth day, making that a day of feasting and gladness. 19 Therefore the Jews of the villages, who live in the open towns, hold the fourteenth day of the month of Adar as a day for gladness and feasting, a holiday on which they send gifts of food to one another.

20 Mordecai recorded these things, and sent letters to all the Jews who were in all the provinces of King Ahasuerus, both near and far, 21 enjoining them that they should keep the fourteenth day of the month Adar and also the fifteenth day of the same month, year by year, 22 as the days on which the Jews gained relief from their enemies, and as the month that had been turned for them from sorrow into gladness and from mourning into a holiday; that they should make them days of feasting and gladness, days for sending gifts of food to one another and presents to the poor. 23 So the Jews adopted as a custom what they had begun to do, as Mordecai had written to them.

13

HOME BIBLE READINGS

BACKGROUND

As we enter this week's lesson, Haman's plans to exterminate the Jews seemed to be progressing as planned. There was a reversal of fortunes, however, when the king honored Mordecai and ordered Haman to be hanged on the gallows he intended for Mordecai's execution.

Especially noteworthy is the information contained in Esther 7. While Ahasuerus and Haman were dining with Esther, the king again asked her what she wanted from him. The queen implored Ahasuerus to spare her life and that of her people, explaining that they had been bartered away (by means of the bribe Haman offered) to be slaughtered. She would not have bothered the king if the Jews had been sold as slaves (7:1-4).

When Ahasuerus asked who would do such a thing, Esther fingered Haman. Filled with rage, the king went into the palace garden. In the monarch's absence, Haman kneeled before Esther and begged her to save his life. Somehow he lost his balance and stumbled onto the couch where Esther was reclining. Just then Ahasuerus returned, saw what was happening, and accused Haman of trying to assault his queen in his own palace (7:5-8).

The king's servants covered Haman's head. Then Harbonah, one the king's personal servants, noted the gallows Haman had built to hang Mordecai. Ahasuerus ordered that Haman be hanged on the tower, and when this was done, the king's anger was appeased (7:9-10).

NOTES ON THE PRINTED TEXT

Although Haman was no longer a threat to the Jews, the king's decree against them remained in force. God used Esther and Mordecai to get Ahasuerus to issue a new set of decrees in which he permitted the Jews to defend themselves. They commemorated their victory over their enemies by establishing the Feast of Purim.

Esther 3:7 reveals that, in March or April of 474 B.C., the court astrologers and magicians cast a lot for Haman to determine when the extermination of the Jews was to take place. "Pur" was the Babylonian word for lot, and "purim" is the plural form. Chapter 9:18-32 reveals that the Feast of Purim became one of the traditional Jewish feasts established by God's people. The Jews normally observed this sacred holiday between February and March (that is, the month of Adar). The festival involved a day of joyous celebration, feasting, and giving of presents. It was intended to remind the Jews of their remarkable deliverance as a people during the time of Esther.

According to 8:1-2, the king gave Esther all that had belonged to Haman. Ahasuerus also made Mordecai one of his highest officials and gave him the ring Haman had worn. Esther then put Mordecai in charge of Haman's property. After that, Esther entered the king's chambers and *fell at his feet, weeping and pleading with him* (8:3) on behalf of her people, the Jews, who were still under the death sentence.

Moved by Esther's display of concern for her people, *the king held out his golden scepter* (8:4) to her. The situation now was different from the previous time the king had extended his scepter to Esther (5:2). On that occasion, Esther risked her life to come into the king's presence uninvited. This time she had already made her emotional appeal before the king. His gesture in extending his scepter was an indication that Esther should rise from her prostrate position and continue to speak to him.

After expressing the proper courtesies to the king, Esther begged him to *"revoke the letters devised by Haman"* (8:5), which had ordered the destruction of *"the Jews who are in all the provinces of the king."* Esther showed that she was not self-serving in her request, for her grief was not just because she, too, faced the possibility of death. More importantly, she could not *"bear to see the destruction"* (8:6) that was about to come on her people.

The king was moved by Esther's sincere expression of distress and sorrow. He reminded her and Mordecai that he had executed Haman and had given his estate to Esther (8:7). Also, Mordecai had been elevated to prime minister of the kingdom and wore the king's signet ring. Thus the king told Esther and Mordecai that they had his permission to *"write as you please with regard to the Jews, in the name of the king"* (8:8). Whatever decree they wrote in favor of the Jews would stand, for it would be *"written in the name of the king and sealed with the king's ring."* Like the first edict Haman had written, this second one, the king reminded them, *"cannot be revoked."*

The new edict was proclaimed in the provinces and cities of the kingdom that *the Jews were to be ready on that day to take revenge on their enemies* (8:13). The Jews were filled with joy. Feasting and celebrations were the order of the day. Such an impact did this reversal of roles concerning the Jews have on the empire that many of the people, for fear of their lives, claimed to be Jews themselves (8:16-17).

The Jews who lived in Susa, the capital city, *gathered on the thirteenth day and on the fourteenth, and rested on the fifteenth day, making it a day of feasting and gladness* (9:18). The author added these words to explain that the Jews living in the city kept the Feast of Purim on the fifteenth day of Adar. Those living in the rural areas observed it on the fourteenth day (9:19). Apparently the Jews in Susa were permitted two days to kill their enemies, whereas the Jews living elsewhere had only one day to carry out their defense. Thus they celebrated the feast on the fourteenth of Adar.

Mordecai *recorded these things and sent letters* (9:20) to his fellow Jews throughout the provinces of Persia. In the letters he recorded the events of the past days, particularly that the Jews in Susa, after overcoming their enemies, rested on the fifteenth of Adar, while the Jews in the other provinces rested on the fourteenth of the month. Those days both groups kept as times of rejoicing.

Mordecai further stated that they were to observe these days of rejoicing *year by year* (9:21). Adar was to be remembered as the month during which *the Jews gained relief from their enemies* (9:22). In addition to this, they were to send *gifts of food to one another and presents to the poor*. When the Jews in the provinces received Mordecai's letter instructing them to establish an annual feast of rejoicing to commemorate their deliverance from their enemies, they *adopted as a custom what they had begun to do* (9:23).

SUGGESTIONS TO TEACHERS

In life threatening situations, adults are prone to think of themselves first and others last. Esther and Mordecai responded differently to their circumstances. They were more concerned for the welfare of their people than for their own well being. They are role models for us as we encounter terrifying situations.

1. FACING LIFE'S CHALLENGES. In the midst of difficult circumstances, it might be easy for believers to feel discouraged and frustrated. Be sure to remind your students how God enabled His people in the Old Testament to prevail in the most difficult situations.

2. GOD'S PERFECT TIMING. Believers sometimes can become impatient when they do not receive the recognition they think they deserve. Encourage your students to look at life from an eternal perspective. Even if others fail to notice all the good things they have done, God is not ignorant of their deeds. In due time, He will bestow His heavenly riches on them in Christ.

3. EXPRESSING FORGIVENESS. The jealously and pride that brought down Haman can unexpectedly trip up even the mature Christian. It is easy to magnify real or imagined slights and to strike back at them. Instead of seeking revenge, believers are to forgive those who wrong them. Although forgiving offenses is never easy, God can give His people the strength to do what is right.

FOR ADULTS

■ **TOPIC:** Feasting and Sharing

■ **QUESTIONS:** 1. What was the difference between the gesture of the king in extending his scepter to Esther the first time and the second time? 2. Why was Esther so distressed about the edict promoted by

Haman? 3. Why did the Jews of Susa celebrate victory over their enemies on the fifteenth day of Adar, while the Jews in the other provinces celebrated on the fourteenth day of the month? 4. What specific activities were to accompany the Jews' time of feasting? 5. What are some practical ways that we can show gratitude to God for our victory in Christ?

■ ILLUSTRATIONS:

Just Do Something! The syndicated news column that gives advice to readers who write to Ann Landers is more popular today than when it began many decades ago. Tens of thousands of readers write in each month asking for advice for the problems that confront them.

One time Ann Landers was asked what the most dominant theme was that characterized the letters that readers would ask her advice upon. She replied that, easily, the most dominant problem that her readers faced was fear. People are afraid of everything, she said, afraid of losing their health, their wealth, and their friends or loved ones. And most of all, she went on, they are afraid to do anything about it. They need someone to tell them not to be afraid, and to take action in the direction that they should go.

A Reason to Run Away. Martin Luther wrote a small book about the affairs of everyday life; it was simply called "Table Talk." One of his humorous anecdotes was a true story of a soldier in the Turkish war. When an officer was preparing his men for a coming battle with overwhelming odds against them, he said, "Whoever shall die today will soon be sitting down to supper with the Lord in Paradise." The soldier ran away from the battle before it had barely begun. When asked to give an account for his cowardly retreat he said, "I do not wish to have supper with Christ today; you see, I'm fasting."

Beginning with Extended Prayer. Martin Luther decided very early in his ministry that prayer was the main source of his daily power and direction. Though he had tremendous responsibilities, and met with many people each day, he once said: "I have so much to do, that I cannot get on without three hours a day of praying."

David Yongi Cho, pastor of the world's largest church (750,000 members in Seoul, Korea), also determined that the commitment to early morning prayer must remain his top priority. He says that the demands of pastoring such a large church require at last three to four hours of prayer each day to give him the wisdom and endurance to lead such a huge congregation.

FOR
YOUTH

■ TOPIC: Let's Party!

■ QUESTIONS: 1. What was the function of the king's scepter in ancient times? 2. How did Esther and Mordecai face the threat against their people? 3. What was the significance of the city of Susa? 4. What did the Jews observe on the fourteenth and fifteenth days of Adar? 5. What are some things God has recently done for you for which you can give Him thanks?

■ ILLUSTRATIONS:

She Kept the Color for Herself. The Russian empress, Elizabeth Petrovna, daughter of Peter the Great, had a strange love for the color pink. She was so in love with this color that she issued a decree that made it a capital crime for any other woman to wear clothing of this hue. It didn't matter whether the garment was a visible outward type or one worn underneath other clothing—it was a crime to wear pink. This was an odd breakdown in this woman's priorities, for in all other matters of the state she was known to be a strong advocate against the death penalty. But, in this unique instance, any woman found wearing the color pink was subject to mutilation or deportation to Siberia, or both. From this we see that some people are selfish beyond description.

Expressing Gratitude. When Robinson Crusoe was shipwrecked on his lonely island, he wrote two columns, which he called the evil and the good. He was cast on a desolate island, but still alive, not drowned, as all his shipmates were. He was separated from humankind and banished from human society, but he was not starving. He had no clothes, but he was in a hot climate where he didn't need them. He was without means of defense, but he saw no wild beasts, such as he had seen on the coasts of Africa. He had no one to speak to, but God had sent the ship so near to the shore that he could get out of it all things necessary for his wants. Crusoe thus concluded that there was not any condition in the world so miserable, but there was something to be thankful for.

The Bravest Were Honored. Plutarch was a famous Greek philosopher and biographer who lived in the first century A.D. He once spoke about the selfish ambition of those soldiers who fought in the Athenian wars. In their quest for military recognition (that would almost certainly lead to material wealth), the soldiers knew no bounds.

In one of his biographies, Plutarch described an event that happened when the Athenian soldiers, after a battle with Xerxes, came to the Isthmus. They were each invited to write down the names of two soldiers that had especially distinguished themselves in battle. The most valiant among them would receive many rewards. Interestingly, each soldier wrote his own name in the first place, and a soldier named Themistocles in the second place.

JESUS FULFILLS HIS MISSION (PASSION NARRATIVES)

LOVE AND BETRAYAL

BACKGROUND SCRIPTURE: Matthew 26
DEVOTIONAL READING: Psalm 55:12-22

KEY VERSES: [Jesus said] "Truly I tell you, one of you will betray me." And they became greatly distressed and began to say to him one after another, "Surely not I, Lord?" Matthew 26:21-22.

KING JAMES VERSION

MATTHEW 26:3 Then assembled together the chief priests, and the scribes, and the elders of the people, unto the palace of the high priest, who was called Caiaphas,

4 And consulted that they might take Jesus by subtilty, and kill him.

5 But they said, Not on the feast day, lest there be an uproar among the people.

6 Now when Jesus was in Bethany, in the house of Simon the leper,

7 There came unto him a woman having an alabaster box of very precious ointment, and poured it on his head, as he sat at meat.

8 But when his disciples saw it, they had indignation, saying, To what purpose is this waste?

9 For this ointment might have been sold for much, and given to the poor.

10 When Jesus understood it, he said unto them, Why trouble ye the woman? for she hath wrought a good work upon me.

11 For ye have the poor always with you; but me ye have not always.

12 For in that she hath poured this ointment on my body, she did it for my burial.

13 Verily I say unto you, Wheresoever this gospel shall be preached in the whole world, there shall also this, that this woman hath done, be told for a memorial of her.

14 Then one of the twelve, called Judas Iscariot, went unto the chief priests,

15 And said unto them, What will ye give me, and I will deliver him unto you? And they covenanted with him for thirty pieces of silver. . . .

20 Now when the even was come, he sat down with the twelve.

21 And as they did eat, he said, Verily I say unto you, that one of you shall betray me.

22 And they were exceeding sorrowful, and began every one of them to say unto him, Lord, is it I?

23 And he answered and said, He that dippeth his hand with me in the dish, the same shall betray me.

24 The Son of man goeth as it is written of him: but woe unto that man by whom the Son of man is betrayed! it had been good for that man if he had not been born.

25 Then Judas, which betrayed him, answered and said, Master, is it I? He said unto him, Thou hast said.

NEW REVISED STANDARD VERSION

MATTHEW 26:3 Then the chief priests and the elders of the people gathered in the palace of the high priest, who was called Caiaphas, 4 and they conspired to arrest Jesus by stealth and kill him. 5 But they said, "Not during the festival, or there may be a riot among the people."

6 Now while Jesus was at Bethany in the house of Simon the leper, 7 a woman came to him with an alabaster jar of very costly ointment, and she poured it on his head as he sat at the table. 8 But when the disciples saw it, they were angry and said, "Why this waste? 9 For this ointment could have been sold for a large sum, and the money given to the poor." 10 But Jesus, aware of this, said to them, "Why do you trouble the woman? She has performed a good service for me. 11 For you always have the poor with you, but you will not always have me." 12 By pouring this ointment on my body she has prepared me for burial. 13 Truly I tell you, wherever this good news is proclaimed in the whole world, what she has done will be told in remembrance of her."

14 Then one of the twelve, who has called Judas Iscariot, when to the chief priests 15 and said, "What will you give me if I betray him to you?" They paid him thirty pieces of silver. . . .

20 When it was evening, he took his place with the twelve, 21 and while they were eating, he said, "Truly I tell you, one of you will betray me." 22 And they became greatly distressed and began to say to him one after another, "Surely not I, Lord?" 23 He answered, "The one who has dipped his hand into the bowl with me will betray me. 24 The Son of Man goes as it is written of him, but woe to that one by whom the Son of Man is betrayed! It would have been better for that one not to have been born." 25 Judas, who betrayed him, said, "Surely not I, Rabbi?" He replied, "You have said so."

Monday, March 1	Psalm 55:12-17	*The Psalmist Mourns a Friend's Betrayal*
Tuesday, March 2	Psalm 55:18-22	*A Friend Violates a Covenant*
Wednesday, March 3	Psalm 69:6-14	*Zeal for Your House*
Thursday, March 4	Matthew 26:1-13	*A Woman Pours Ointment on Jesus*
Friday, March 5	Matthew 26:14-19	*Judas Agrees to Betray Jesus*
Saturday, March 6	Matthew 26:20-25	*Jesus Announces His Upcoming Betrayal*
Sunday, March 7	Matthew 26:31-35	*Peter Promises Not to Desert Jesus*

BACKGROUND

Jesus knew the hour had come for the end of His earthly ministry. Matthew said that after Jesus revealed the distant future (His return; Matt. 24—25) to His disciples, He warned them again about His immediate future: He would be crucified (26:1-2). The religious leaders were busy plotting Jesus' death, but first a woman in Bethany, where He was staying during the Passover week, would symbolically anoint Him with costly perfume. Her action would show her love for Jesus (26:6-13), just as He would then show His love for the disciples as He celebrated His last supper with them. But not all of them loved Him, for one of them would betray Him (26:14-16).

Why did Judas betray Jesus? We have only sketchy background details about Judas from the Gospel accounts. His surname "Iscariot" may refer to his hometown, either Kerioth of Moab or Kerioth-hezron in southern Judah. If the latter is true, he would be the only Judean among the disciples, and Judeans looked down upon Galileans. Another suggestion is that Judas's name is a Semitic version of the Latin word *sicarius,* the name for a radical Zealot who carried a dagger, but there is no evidence in the Gospels that he was a Zealot. His name always appears last in the lists of the apostles (Matt. 10:4; Mark 3:19; Luke 6:16), no doubt reflecting the writers' hatred of what he did. John, in fact, says Judas was a thief.

As the treasurer for Jesus and the disciples, Judas regularly pilfered money (John 12:4-6; 13:29). John tells about Mary anointing Jesus (John 12:1-8), an account that some scholars believe is the same as the anointing by the unnamed woman in Matthew 26. If so, Judas is the one who loudly protested Mary wasting expensive oil on Jesus. *"For this ointment could have been sold for a large sum, and the money given to the poor"* (26:9). That comment, John 12:6 says, merely reflected Judas's greed.

One motive, then, for Judas's betrayal could have been greed. After all, he took 30 pieces of silver from the religious leaders to betray Jesus (Matt. 26:14-16). Only when he saw Jesus being tried for execution did Judas fully realize what he had done (27:3-10). Another theory is that Judas was very patriotic; he betrayed Jesus when he realized that the Lord was not going to establish an earthly kingdom, or Judas hoped that the betrayal would cause Jesus to immediately establish His kingdom. Still another possibility (see John 13:2, 27) is that Satan deceived Judas into betraying Jesus, but Judas still remained fully responsible for his actions.

Whatever Judas's reason for betraying Jesus, Matthew 27:3 says Judas *repented* of his act, but then he attempted to atone for his own sin. He tried to give back the betrayal money, but the religious leaders ridiculed him. In despair, Judas hung himself, an act described in vivid detail by Peter in the Book of Acts (1:16-20). The chief priests then used this "blood money" (so to speak) to buy a field to bury the indigent poor, fulfilling Old Testament prophecy (Matt. 27:6-10).

NOTES ON THE PRINTED TEXT

Matthew 12:14 records that some of the religious leaders started plotting to kill Jesus early in His ministry, shortly after He healed the man with the withered hand on the Sabbath. Jesus challenged their teachings throughout Passover week, calling them blind guides and hypocrites (chap. 23).

The Jewish historian Josephus says that *Caiaphas* (26:3) was the high priest from about A.D. 18–36, the son-in-law of Annas, who had been removed as high priest by the Romans in A.D. 15. Since Caiaphas lasted as high priest for 18 years, we can presume he was shrewd both with the Romans and the other religious leaders; he was the one who suggested that Jesus should die for the good of the nation (John 11:49-50). Opposition to Jesus among the leaders grew after the raising of Lazarus (12:9-11), but the crowds at Passover liked the prophet from Nazareth, and a disturbance in His favor would not set well with the Romans (Matt. 26:4-5).

Simon the leper (Matt. 26:6) is not mentioned elsewhere in Scripture, but since he was hosting a dinner for Jesus, it is likely that the Lord had healed Simon some time earlier. How he relates to Mary, Martha, Lazarus, and the account of Mary anointing Jesus (John 12:1-8) is unclear. The account in John shares details with Matthew and Mark, but the account in Luke about a sinful woman anointing Jesus at the house of Simon the Pharisee is noticeably different (Luke 7:36-50). Mark identifies *the very costly ointment* (Matt. 26:7) the woman poured out of the alabaster jar as nard (Mark 14:3), a perennial herb whose strong perfume is extracted from its root. Mark also tells just how costly the perfume was, about 300 denarii, a year's wages in Jesus' time (14:5).

Was the anger of the disciples (Matt. 26:8-9) at the woman's anointing of Jesus really because they were thinking only about the poor? John identifies Judas as the person who was upset because he would not be able to steal part of the money from selling the perfume (John 12:4-6). That would help explain why Judas then went to the religious leaders and said, *"What will you give me if I betray him to you?"* (Matt. 26:15).

Jesus' comment that *"you always have the poor with you"* (26:11) should not be taken as an excuse for not helping the poor. Instead, Jesus reminds us that we will continually have opportunities to help those who are less fortunate, something He modeled in His ministry (26:10).

While Judas or some of the other disciples may have misjudged the woman's actions, Jesus understood what she did. She both anointed Him as the Messiah ("the anointed one") and prophetically *"prepared [Him] for burial"* (26:12). Unlike so many others, including Jesus' disciples, the woman seemed to see that Jesus would suffer as the Messiah-king. His death, and especially His resurrection, would truly be the *"good news"* (26:13) the world desperately needed.

The woman's sacrificial act of love contrasts sharply with Judas's cold-hearted betrayal (26:14-15). The Gospels imply that money motivated Judas's betrayal. However, *thirty pieces of silver* (26:15) seems like a small payment for betraying such a wanted man. It amounted to 120 denarii, about four months' wages. Many have pointed out that this amount was the price of a slave (Exod. 21:32; Zech. 11:13), and Matthew said later that the price was the fulfillment of prophecy (Matt. 27:9-10).

Though Jesus knew what Judas was going to do, Judas was still welcomed among the disciples at the Last Supper (26:20). All of them were reclining around the table when the Lord suddenly announced, *"One of you will betray me"* (26:21). Judas was eating with the person he would betray, an unthinkable thing to do in Middle Eastern culture. Eating with someone meant you were friends and would not hurt that person.

Interestingly, by comparing the Gospel accounts, it seems that the disciple reclining to the right of Jesus when He made His announcement was John (John 13:23), while the one on Jesus' left could have been Judas. Jesus dipped a piece of unleavened bread into the sauce on the table for the Passover meal and then handed it to Judas (13:26). The left side of the banquet host was the place of honor. Imagine allowing the person who you knew would betray you to sit next to you! Was Jesus still trying to "reach out" to Judas in love even that night?

Whether or not that is true, Jesus' final hours had already been *written of him* (Matt. 26:24). The Son of Man would suffer, as Isaiah had prophesied centuries before (Isa. 53), and His betrayal would come at the hands of one of His closest friends (Matt. 26:21, 25). Certainly, *"it would have been better for that [person] not to have been born"* (26:24).

SUGGESTIONS TO TEACHERS

While we may be shocked at what Judas did to Jesus and say to ourselves, *I would never do that,* each of us could find some of own character traits in this account of love and betrayal.

1. HAVE YOU EVER BEEN JEALOUS? Some of the religious leaders hated Jesus' popularity and the way He constantly pointed out their hypocrisy and vanity. What would you think about someone who pointed out your faults to you at every turn?

2. HAVE YOU EVER BEEN JUDGMENTAL? The disciples often jumped to conclusions and misjudged people and situations. They were going to keep the children away from Jesus, and they were shocked that rich people did not have a direct ticket to heaven. They even thought that this woman who anointed Jesus was wasting her time and money. How often do we see people and situations in just the opposite way that Jesus does?

3. HAVE YOU EVER WANTED WHAT YOU DIDN'T HAVE? Judas seemed to have been a greedy person who would sell out his own friend for money. However, there may have been other things Judas wanted that he would never get from Jesus. Jesus was not the way to money, but He was also not the way to fame or power. Jesus would not usher in an earthly kingdom with Judas as one of its chief officers. When we see being a Christian as anything but the way of self-sacrifice and service, we are starting to see Jesus through the eyes of Judas.

4. HAVE YOU EVER ACTED WITH UNCONDITIONAL LOVE? The woman defied custom and convention to show how much she loved Jesus. When was the last time you told Jesus that you would serve Him unconditionally, no matter what others thought or said?

FOR ADULTS

■ TOPIC: Love and Betrayal

■ QUESTIONS: 1. Why were the chief priests and others trying to arrest Jesus secretly? 2. What did the woman, who poured the costly ointment on Jesus, show us about true love? 3. Why were the disciples upset over the woman's actions? 4. What character traits did Judas demonstrate in these verses? 5. What character traits of Judas can you recognize in yourself?

■ **ILLUSTRATIONS:**

Real Love Can Cost. Jesus had to let Judas make his own decisions, even it if cost Jesus His very life. Parents are often put in a similar position, especially as their children reach adulthood. Our close friends have a daughter who became totally uncontrollable, and when she was 16, she moved out of their house—and in with her 22-year-old boyfriend. Our friends felt betrayed, angry, and like failures as parents; however, they also knew forcing their daughter to stay would be just as destructive to their relationship with her. They had to let her make her own mistakes and deal with the coming costs and consequences. They prayed that the Christian values she had learned as a child, and seen demonstrated in their home, would bring her back and heal their relationship with her. That is what happened, but it took several years and lots of tears and forgiveness.

The Closest People Hurt You the Most. Rhonda (not her real name) knows what it means to be betrayed. She is working hard to keep her home together and raise her three kids. While her children stay with her grandparents part of the evening, she is going back to college at night to finish her nursing degree. When her classes end, she works the all-night shift at a senior care center. At five in the morning she runs home from work in time to feed the kids breakfast and shuttle them off to school. Then it's off to bed for a few hours' sleep before picking up the kids and starting the process all over again.

Rhonda's husband once helped her with her dreams of being a nurse. "He said he loved me and supported my getting a degree," she says, "but then I found him one day in the arms of my best friend. He was lonely, he said. I filed for a divorce. They're now living together, and the kids and I are trying to make the best of a bad situation. You know, the people closest to you are the ones who can hurt you the most." Jesus knew that, too.

The View Ahead. We had been married three months, and my husband had just finished his graduate degree. As we looked for employment beyond his temporary teaching job, he saw an ad for a small-town newspaper editor, something he would love to do, and in a town not far from where our families lived. We met the owner of the paper for dinner, and by the time dinner was over, the owner had offered my husband the job, which he would start as soon as he finished teaching two months later. Imagine our surprise a couple of weeks later when we picked up an issue of that newspaper and read a column by the new editor, who was not my husband. When my husband called the owner, he said gruffly, "I never promised you anything in writing, and I decided I could not wait for you."

For a while we were devastated, but then we did what everyone does who is betrayed—look ahead. God must have some reason for this painful experience. As it turned out, my husband found a teaching position in another state, and that distance proved to be a blessing when family problems came up shortly thereafter that could have torn at our marriage if we had lived closer. The distance helped us strengthen our marriage and depend on each other even more.

Jesus saw beyond Judas's betrayal to what was ahead. He had already told His disciples about the future just days before He was betrayed (Matt. 24—25). Only by focusing on what's ahead, and by knowing that He has great things planned for us, can we see beyond the pain of betrayal.

For Youth	■ TOPIC: Betraying a Friend

■ QUESTIONS: 1. Who tried to arrest Jesus, and why? 2. Why did the woman pour a costly perfume on Jesus? 3. Who was upset about what the woman did? 4. What do we know about the kind of person Judas was? 5. Have you ever betrayed someone you love? Why?

■ **ILLUSTRATIONS:**

A Betrayal. Judas eventually realized what a terrible thing he had done by betraying Jesus, but by the time he did, it was too late to undo what he had done. Being betrayed by a friend is not something we easily forget or forgive. I still remember a time in high school when I had written a note to one of my friends, Monica, about Jill (another friend) and who she was wanting to date. When Jill found out that I had shared this "highly private" information with Monica, she was furious with me. When I tried to apologize and ask for Jill to forgive me for being so insensitive to her privacy, Jill refused to forgive me. To her I had committed the ultimate in betrayal. I had shared her personal feelings with another without her consent. Years later, Jill and I still are not the friends we once were. My actions had forever changed this relationship.

Three Kinds of Friends. Most of the time you can divide the people you call your friends into three categories. One group is the *fairweather* friends. They are happy to be with you and support you unless you have problems of some kind. The *fairweather* friends vanish at the first sign of trouble.

Then there are the *me first* friends. They need something from you, like someone to go to the movies with when no one else is available. Your "friendship" caters to their needs, never yours.

Thankfully, there are also people who are *faithful* friends. They won't tell your secrets to everyone else, and they will let you be angry with them and still love you. They believe the best about you, even if other people are putting you down. They have probably seen you at your worst, but they still think you are the best.

Jesus had all of these people in His life. A good friend betrayed Him for his own selfish reasons, and when Jesus needed relational support at the cross, His other disciples vanished. But He also had faithful friends, including Joseph of Arimathea and Nicodemus, who defied the majority of the religious leaders and took care of Jesus' body after His crucifixion (John 19:38-42).

The Monkey Traps. What would lead someone to betray his or her best friend? Scripture reveals that Satan prompted Judas to betray Jesus. How did Satan do it? Perhaps the story of the monkey traps would help us understand what happened.

Monkey trappers in North Africa set out a number of gourds filled with nuts and firmly fastened to the branch of a tree. Each gourd has a hole in it just large enough for the unwary monkey to stick his forepaw into it. When the hungry monkey discovers the nuts, he quickly grasps a handful, but the hole is too small for him to withdraw his clinched fist. And he doesn't have enough sense to open up his hand and let go in order to escape, so he is easily taken.

Whatever motive Judas had for betraying Jesus, he later tried to repent and give back the money—but it was too late. Judas had already been caught in Satan's "monkey trap." When the devil's devices ensnare us, we often hold our own key to escape. We can change our actions or just say no, but then the devil says, "Don't let go! You can't stop now!" Too often we don't.

THE LORD'S SUPPER

BACKGROUND SCRIPTURE: Luke 22:7-30

DEVOTIONAL READING: John 13:1-15

KEY VERSES: "This is my body, which is given for you. Do this in remembrance of me. . . . This cup that is poured out for you is the new covenant in my blood." Luke 22:19b-20.

KING JAMES VERSION

LUKE 22:7 Then came the day of unleavened bread, when the passover must be killed.

8 And he sent Peter and John, saying, Go and prepare us the passover, that we may eat.

9 And they said unto him, Where wilt thou that we prepare?

10 And he said unto them, Behold, when ye are entered into the city, there shall a man meet you, bearing a pitcher of water; follow him into the house where he entereth in.

11 And ye shall say unto the goodman of the house, The Master saith unto thee, Where is the guestchamber, where I shall eat the passover with my disciples?

12 And he shall shew you a large upper room furnished: there make ready.

13 And they went, and found as he had said unto them: and they made ready the passover.

14 And when the hour was come, he sat down, and the twelve apostles with him.

15 And he said unto them, With desire I have desired to eat this passover with you before I suffer:

16 For I say unto you, I will not any more eat thereof, until it be fulfilled in the kingdom of God.

17 And he took the cup, and gave thanks, and said, Take this, and divide it among yourselves:

18 For I say unto you, I will not drink of the fruit of the vine, until the kingdom of God shall come.

19 And he took bread, and gave thanks, and brake it, and gave unto them, saying, This is my body which is given for you: this do in remembrance of me.

20 Likewise also the cup after supper, saying, This cup is the new testament in my blood, which is shed for you.

21 But, behold, the hand of him that betrayeth me is with me on the table.

22 And truly the Son of man goeth, as it was determined: but woe unto that man by whom he is betrayed!

23 And they began to enquire among themselves, which of them it was that should do this thing.

NEW REVISED STANDARD VERSION

LUKE 22:7 Then came the day of Unleavened Bread, on which the Passover lamb had to be sacrificed. 8 So Jesus sent Peter and John, saying, "Go and prepare the Passover meal for us that we may eat it." 9 They asked him, "Where do you want us to make preparations for it?" 10 "Listen," he said to them, "when you have entered the city, a man carrying a jar of water will meet you; follow him into the house he enters 11 and say to the owner of the house, 'The teacher asks you, "Where is the guest room, where I may eat the Passover with my disciples?"' 12 He will show you a large room upstairs, already furnished. Make preparations for us there." 13 So they went the found everything as he had told them; and they prepared the Passover meal.

14 When the hour came, he took his place at the table, and the apostles with him. 15 He said to them, "I have eagerly desired to eat this Passover with you before I suffer; 16 for I tell you, I will not eat it until it is fulfilled in the kingdom of God." 17 Then he took a cup, and after giving thanks he said, "Take this and divide it among yourselves; 18 for I tell you that from now on I will not drink of the fruit of the vine until the kingdom of God comes." 19 Then he took a loaf of bread, and when he had given thanks, he broke it and gave it to them, saying, "This is my body, which is given for you. Do this in remembrance of me." 20 And he did the same with the cup after supper, saying, "This cup that is poured out for you is the new covenant in my blood. 21 But see, the one who betrays me is with me, and his hand is on the table. 22 For the Son of Man is going as it has been determined, but woe to that one by whom he is betrayed!" 23 Then they began to ask one another, which one of them it could be who would do this.

Monday, March 8	Luke 22:7-13	*The Disciples Prepare the Passover Meal*
Tuesday, March 9	Luke 22:14-18	*Jesus Eats with the Disciples*
Wednesday, March 10	Luke 22:19-23	*Do This in Remembrance of Me*
Thursday, March 11	John 13:1-5	*Jesus Washes the Disciples' Feet*
Friday, March 12	John 13:6-10	*Peter Protests*
Saturday, March 13	John 13:11-15	*Jesus Sets an Example*
Sunday, March 14	Luke 22:24-30	*Jesus Teaches about Greatness*

BACKGROUND

Matthew, Mark, and Luke clearly tie the Last Supper to celebrating the Passover. This festival was one of three that all Jews came to Jerusalem to observe, the other two being the Feasts of Pentecost and Tabernacles (Exod. 23:14-17).

The Passover commemorated the Hebrews being "passed over" by the angel of death in Egypt when they marked the doorposts of their houses with the blood of a lamb (12:13). A separate but related observance, the festival of unleavened bread (Lev. 23:6), was held for the seven days following Passover. By New Testament times, the two celebrations had come to be spoken of as one festival (Luke 22:1).

God specified that the Passover meal was to be eaten on the fourteenth day of the first month of the Jewish calendar (Lev. 23:5). Since the Jewish calendar is based on the cycles of the moon, the date for Passover varies; therefore, our date for Easter does as well.

Luke says that the day of the Passover meal was the same as that of the Lord's Supper (Luke 22:7), and Matthew and Mark also imply that the Lord's Supper involved Jesus celebrating the Passover meal with His disciples. John, however, says that the Last Supper was before the Passover meal (John 13:1). Many attempts have been made to explain this time difference, such as the Lord's Supper being a separate fellowship meal, but regardless of the time of the supper, it had elements of the Passover meal attached to it, including the bread and the wine.

Bread and wine were just two of the items that Peter and John would have obtained as they prepared the Passover for the rest of their group (Luke 22:13). At Passover time, a lamb was sacrificed at the temple for each Jewish family group; the disciples and Jesus may have been considered such a "family."

An unblemished lamb would be selected prior to Passover, then killed and roasted in the afternoon before the meal that evening. The lamb was to be eaten with the bread, wine, and a sauce made with bitter herbs. The lamb would remind the Jews of the blood on the doorposts in Egypt, the unleavened bread of their haste in leaving Egypt, and the bitter herbs of their suffering as Pharaoh's slaves (Exod. 12:8-20, 39).

Sometime in the centuries after the Exodus, the Jews had added the drinking of at least four cups of diluted wine to the Passover meal. Each of these cups related to one of God's four promises to His people found in 6:6-7. The head of the household would pronounce special blessings over the bread and wine during the meal and be responsible for explaining to the family the significance of the feast (13:8). The whole reason for having the meal was to remember that God had led His people out of slavery. In Jesus' day, the people were looking for a new Moses to lead them out of bondage to Rome. Instead, Jesus became the new sacrificial Lamb for the sins of the world (John 1:29).

NOTES ON THE PRINTED TEXT

It was the week of the festival of *Unleavened Bread* (Luke 22:1, 7), another name for Passover, and Luke says that Jesus wished to celebrate the traditional Passover meal with His disciples. Only Luke names the two disciples Jesus sent to make preparations for the meal—*Peter and John* (22:8). Jerusalem may have been crowded with as many as 100,000 pilgrims for the festival, all of whom needed to celebrate Passover within the city itself. Therefore, any person who had an extra room was obliged to let someone from out of town use it, with payment being the skins of the sheep sacrificed for the Passover.

Jesus sent Peter and John to Jerusalem from Bethany, where He and His group were staying (Mark 11:11; John 12:1). In the city they would meet "*a man carrying a jar of water*" (Luke 22:10) who would show them "*a large room upstairs, already furnished*" (22:12). Here they would make preparations for the meal (22:9, 13).

Large enclosed rooms on a house roof existed as far back as Old Testament days (2 Kings 1:2). A man carrying water would have been unusual, since that was what women normally did in those days. Some scholars have suggested this man was an Essene, since men in that religious sect did carry water. Others have speculated that "*the owner of the house*" (Luke 22:11) was the father of John Mark, since the disciples later met at John Mark's home (Acts 12:12). The unusual phrase "*The teacher asks you*" (Luke 22:11) seems to indicate that the owner was a follower of Jesus who had made some prearrangements with the Lord, such as providing furnishings in the room. These would have included cushions or couches for reclining and a low table. While the Passover meal was originally eaten standing up, reclining had become the usual posture for eating a festival meal.

Luke's description of the meal itself is longer than the descriptions in Matthew and Mark, and Jesus uses the occasion to teach the disciples about the Kingdom and about His coming sacrifice. When the meal began after sundown, Jesus *took his place at the table* (Luke 22:14), probably at the head end, and possibly with John and Judas on either side of Him. Jesus had "*eagerly desired to eat this Passover*" (22:15) with His disciples, because it was the last time He would eat a Passover meal with them on this earth, and because He was giving important new meanings to a meal they would always eat after His death. The Jews often made vows at special occasions such as "*I will not eat it until it is fulfilled*" (22:16), and the host would normally give *thanks* (22:17) for bread and wine at any meal.

According to Jewish tradition, the first cup at the meal was a blessing on the day and the wine, followed by ritual washings, and servants bringing in the food. Jesus' saying *"I will not drink of the fruit of the vine until the kingdom of God comes"* (22:18) emphasizes that this meal foreshadows the great messianic banquet at the end of time (Rev. 19:9).

The exact order of the Passover meal is not completely clear from Luke's description, since there would be at least four cups at Passover, but *the loaf of bread* (Luke 22:19) would be the unleavened bread like the Hebrews made when they left Egypt. However, the bread that Jesus now broke represented His body, which would be broken on the cross. Thus the Passover meal itself was representational, and Jesus gave its elements new meanings.

Therefore, the cup of wine that Jesus took *after supper* (22:20) would now remind His followers of His blood shed for the forgiveness of sin. Covenants in Old Testament times were typically sealed by the blood of a sacrifice, and now Jesus would be that sacrifice. The *"new covenant"* refers to the one promised by God centuries earlier through the prophet Jeremiah (Jer. 31:31-34) to replace the one given to Moses on Mount Sinai. The sacrificial system of that covenant would be replaced by the one-time, once-for-all sacrifice of the Lamb of God on the cross.

Sadly, this meal that Jesus' followers so often would observe *"in remembrance"* (22:19) of Him was marred by the presence of a traitor. Jesus announced that one of them would betray Him *"as it has been determined"* (22:22)—as the prophets said would happen. This is all the more horrifying because it was unthinkable for a guest at *"the table"* (22:21) to turn against his or her host. The disciples all asked themselves who would do such a thing, each one hoping that he was not the guilty person; but no one seems to have suspected Judas (22:23).

SUGGESTIONS TO TEACHERS

Your students may have *observed* the Lord's Supper many times in their lives, but how many times have they celebrated it? This is not necessarily a celebration in the sense of a party with hats and balloons. The apostle Paul warned the Corinthians not to observe the Lord's Supper *in an unworthy manner* (1 Cor. 11:27). However, that does not mean we should miss the joy that comes with remembrance. We have so many things that we need to remember about God each time we eat the bread and drink the cup.

1. GOD LOVES US—REGARDLESS. We come to the Lord's Supper as people unworthy of God's love, but He loves us anyway. No one comes to the table as a perfect person; but no one will be rejected from the table either who comes with a repentant heart. We should remember that the same unconditional love God shows us is the same sort of love we need to show to others, even if they have wronged or injured us.

2. GOD GAVE HIS BEST FOR US—HIS SON. Because God loves us, He gave His very own Son to die for us on the cross. We struggle to find other expressions of love that come anywhere close to what God did. We should remember to give Him the very best as well. God does not honor half-hearted discipleship.

3. GOD GIVES US BLESSINGS EVERY DAY. God's blessings for us did not come just at the cross. The Lord's Supper should remind us that we have so much to be thankful for now. If we can celebrate nothing else, we can rejoice that this is another day that the Lord has made, and that we are here to enjoy it together.

4. GOD HAS A WONDERFUL PLAN FOR OUR LIVES, TODAY AND FOREVER. Jesus' sacrifice is the key part of His plan for all of those who will trust in Him. He wants His followers to have an abundant life, both now and with Him in eternity. We may not like the way our lives are going at some particular point, but we can always know that Jesus is looking out for us in a way that no one else can.

FOR ADULTS	■ **TOPIC:** Celebration and Anticipation ■ **QUESTIONS:** 1. What did Jesus ask the disciples to do to prepare for His last meal with them? 2. Why was Jesus eager to share the

meal with His disciples? 3. What new significance did Jesus give the bread and the cup at the Passover meal? 4. What shocking revelation did He make at the meal? 5. What is the importance of the Lord's Supper to each of us today?

■ **ILLUSTRATIONS:**

Slow Down and Celebrate. Rose has a chronic illness: lupus. She is always careful about not overextending herself, especially around times of family celebrations or holidays. That is because the anticipation and preparation needed for these times can cause her to use up too much energy and become sick. Lupus can cause her fatigue, skin rashes, flu-like symptoms, and all kinds of aches and pains. Therefore, lupus forces Rose to slow down and focus on what is important for her to spend time and energy doing.

That is a lesson we all can benefit from whether we are dealing with an illness or another life situation. When we participate in the Lord's Supper, we need to view it as an opportunity to slow down and take time to internalize the impact of this event in our everyday lives. We shouldn't want this moment to pass without celebrating it. Remembering what Jesus' sacrifice and love have meant for each of us can deepen our relationship with Him.

The Santa Collection. Christmas was always a special time at our house. Mom loved to celebrate Christmas and enjoyed collecting Santa Clauses. She had a family room full of hundreds of them to prove it. Although they were displayed all year long, at Christmas Mom would rearrange them and put them throughout the house.

Over the years, we always enjoyed finding Mom that perfect new Santa to add to her collection. After Mom died, for a time those Santas brought sadness instead of joy to me, and I found it hard to put up any Christmas decorations at all. However, now after the passing of a few years, those Santas bring joy to me again. When I see them, I remember Mom and her love of celebrating the season.

That is what Jesus wants us to do when we celebrate the Lord's Supper. While it may be sad to remember His suffering in His sacrifice for us, we can experience joy through remembering His love for us.

Don't Enjoy It. A man had his annual physical exam and was waiting for the physician's initial report. After a few minutes the physician came in with his charts and said, "There's no reason why you can't live a completely normal life as long as you don't enjoy it."

That statement could be a description of how some of us think about the Lord's Supper. We are afraid to let this be a time of celebration for what God did for us through Jesus. A "normal" believer rejoices in Christ's sacrifice and wants to tell the whole world how it has changed his or her life for the better—eternally.

FOR YOUTH

■ TOPIC: Preparing to Remember

■ QUESTIONS: 1. What instructions did Jesus give Peter and John about preparing for the Passover meal? 2. Why would Jesus want to share a meal with His disciples, rather than just talk to them? 3. How did Jesus want the disciples to view the bread and the cup after He was gone? 4. What do you think Judas may have been thinking when Jesus said one of them would betray Him? 5. When your church observes the Lord's Supper, what do you understand to be going on?

■ ILLUSTRATIONS:

Yearbook Memories. Have you bought a yearbook for each year you have been in school? You might think it is not that important right now. You may still remember clearly who your friends were last year, how many games the football team won, and who was the valedictorian of the graduating class. Years from now those clear memories will become fuzzy, and you will have only a few pictures in a yearbook to help you remember that year of your life.

The disciples didn't understand everything Jesus was saying and doing that night of the first Lord's Supper, but later those representations He gave them took on greater significance for them. Like snapshots in a yearbook the bread and the cup brought back to mind Jesus and the sacrifice He made. In the same way those representations connect us to that night in the Upper Room when Jesus shared a special Passover meal with His disciples—and with everyone who would ever follow Him.

Little Things Mean a Lot. Children remember vividly those times when they work on special projects with their parents. Biff, Willy Loman's son in the play *Death of a Salesman,* said this about his deceased father as he remembered a time when they poured concrete together: "There were a lot of nice days. When he'd come home from a trip; or on Sundays, making the stoop; finishing the cellar; putting on the new porch; when he built the extra bathroom; and put up the garage. You know something, Charley, there's more of him in that front stoop than in all the sales he ever made." The "little thing" of remembering Jesus when we partake of the bread and the cup can change us forever. There is a lot of Jesus we need to remember in those two simple, everyday objects.

Good to the Last Drop. In her book *Strength for Today,* Sharon Broyles tells about preparing her children for Easter communion at her husband's hometown church. It was the practice at this church to allow children to take part in the Lord's Supper. When Sharon gave her preschooler the little cup out of the tray, saying, "Jesus loves you, Christian," he took it and inspected it carefully. When everyone was told to drink, Christian did—eagerly. While everyone else was putting the cup down, he was still busy trying to get every last drop of juice by poking his tongue deep into the tiny cup. It was as if that little taste only left him wanting more. That is what Jesus hopes for each of us as we remember Him through the enactment of the Lord's Supper. He doesn't want the Lord's Supper to be just for the moment; He wants us to take this experience to heart and want more of Him.

Have You Studied? Do you ever remember getting ready for a big history exam? Did you put in the time memorizing the facts needed for the test? So many times we are guilty of wanting to do well on a test, but failing to apply ourselves and study the material beforehand. We cannot remember what we have never bothered to learn. The Lord's Supper only means something to us if we know who Jesus is and what He did. A person prepared for the Lord's Supper is someone who best knows the Lord. Then remembering how much He suffered and sacrificed for us touches our hearts in the way He meant it to.

PRAYER AND ARREST

BACKGROUND SCRIPTURE: Matthew 26:36-50
DEVOTIONAL READING: John 12:27-36

3

KEY VERSE: "My Father, if it is possible, let this cup pass from me;
yet not what I want but what you want." Matthew 26:39b.

KING JAMES VERSION

MATTHEW 26:36 Then cometh Jesus with them unto a place called Gethsemane, and saith unto the disciples, Sit ye here, while I go and pray yonder.

37 And he took with him Peter and the two sons of Zebedee, and began to be sorrowful and very heavy.

38 Then saith he unto them, My soul is exceeding sorrowful, even unto death: tarry ye here, and watch with me.

39 And he went a little farther, and fell on his face, and prayed, saying, O my Father, if it be possible, let this cup pass from me: nevertheless not as I will, but as thou wilt.

40 And he cometh unto the disciples, and findeth them asleep, and saith unto Peter, What, could ye not watch with me one hour?

41 Watch and pray, that ye enter not into temptation: the spirit indeed is willing, but the flesh is weak.

42 He went away again the second time, and prayed, saying, O my Father, if this cup may not pass away from me, except I drink it, thy will be done.

43 And he came and found them asleep again: for their eyes were heavy.

44 And he left them, and went away again, and prayed the third time, saying the same words.

45 Then cometh he to his disciples, and saith unto them, Sleep on now, and take your rest: behold, the hour is at hand, and the Son of man is betrayed into the hands of sinners.

46 Rise, let us be going: behold, he is at hand that doth betray me.

47 And while he yet spake, lo, Judas, one of the twelve, came, and with him a great multitude with swords and staves, from the chief priests and elders of the people.

48 Now he that betrayed him gave them a sign, saying, Whomsoever I shall kiss, that same is he: hold him fast.

49 And forthwith he came to Jesus, and said, Hail, master; and kissed him.

50 And Jesus said unto him, Friend, wherefore art thou come? Then came they, and laid hands on Jesus, and took him.

NEW REVISED STANDARD VERSION

MATTHEW 26:36 Then Jesus went with them to a place called Gethsemane; and he said to his disciples, "Sit here while I go over there and pray." 37 He took with him Peter and the two sons of Zebedee, and began to be grieved and agitated. 38 Then he said to them, "I am deeply grieved, even to death; remain here, and stay awake with me." 39 And going a little farther, he threw himself on the ground and prayed, "My Father, if it is possible, let this cup pass from me; yet not what I want but what you want." 40 Then he came to the disciples and found them sleeping; and he said to Peter, "So, could you not stay awake with me one hour? 41 Stay awake and pray that you may not come into the time of trial; the spirit indeed is willing, but the flesh is weak." 42 Again he went away for the second time and prayed, "My Father, if this cannot pass unless I drink it, your will be done." 43 Again he came and found them sleeping, for their eyes were heavy. 44 So leaving them again, he went away and prayed for the third time, saying the same words. 45 Then he came to the disciples and said to them, "Are you still sleeping and taking your rest? See, the hour is at hand, and the Son of Man is betrayed into the hands of sinners. 46 Get up, let us be going. See, my betrayer is at hand."

47 While he was still speaking, Judas, one of the twelve, arrived; with him was a large crowd with swords and clubs, from the chief priests and the elders of the people. 48 Now the betrayer had given them a sign, saying, "The one I will kiss is the man; arrest him." 49 At once he came up to Jesus and said, "Greetings, Rabbi!" and kissed him. 50 Jesus said to him, "Friend, do what you are here to do." Then they came and laid hands on Jesus and arrested him.

HOME BIBLE READINGS

BACKGROUND

Judas had betrayed Jesus to the religious leaders, but Judas was not the only one who failed Jesus the night He was arrested. At the end of the Lord's Supper, Jesus and His disciples sang the traditional Passover hymns, including the great Hallel (Ps. 136; Matt. 26:30). They then crossed over the Kidron Valley from the city of Jerusalem to the Mount of Olives.

According to Matthew, somewhere during that walk, Jesus told the disciples that they would all desert Him that night—fulfilling the prophecy of Zechariah 13:7 that the flock would scatter when the shepherd was struck down (Matt. 26:31). Peter, of course, said he would never desert his Lord, but Jesus said Peter's desertion would be the worst: three times the disciple would deny he even knew Jesus (26:33-34). Peter and the rest of the disciples protested that they would never leave Jesus (26:35), but within a few hours, all the disciples would desert Him in fear for their own lives (26:56).

Concerning the Mount of Olives, it is a ridge about a mile long running north to south across the valley of the Kidron Brook from Jerusalem. On the eastern side of the ridge is the village of Bethany, home of Mary, Martha, and Lazarus; beyond Bethany is the arid Wilderness of Judea and the lonely road to Jericho. For centuries extensive olive groves had grown in the rich limestone soil of the ridge, giving it its name. The slopes rise 200 feet higher than the city itself, so even today a person can stand on the Mount of Olives for a panoramic view of Jerusalem.

Jesus had such a view on the day of His triumphal entry, when He stopped on the Mount and wept over the city (Luke 19:41-44). The Gospels say Jesus and His disciples went to the Mount of Olives often (Luke 22:39; John 18:1). Matthew says that it was here that Jesus explained to His disciples the future and the end of the age (Matt. 24:3), a highly significant place to do so in light of what Zechariah 14:1-5 says about the return of the Lord. Both Jews and Muslims see the Mount of Olives as the place of final judgment in the last days, so there are large Jewish and Muslim cemeteries on the slopes today.

Also, on the Mount of Olives at the time of Jesus was *a place called Gethsemane* (Matt. 26:36), which in Hebrew means "olive press." Here was likely an oil mill, a large grinding stone turned by two people that crushed the olives so that their oil could be collected for baking and frying. The use of the Greek word translated *place* indicates that it was an enclosed piece of ground, probably not a "garden" of flowers and trees, but an olive grove that Jesus and His disciples had permission to enter and use.

Jesus came to Gethsemane to pray to the Father that He might completely yield Himself to God's will. Jesus was filled with a sorrow so great that He was almost unable to bear it. He would be bearing the weight of the whole world's sins on His shoulders. He asked His three closest disciples to share His time of anguish, but they instead fell asleep. As Jesus finished praying, He no doubt looked back across the Kidron Valley toward Jerusalem and watched the torches of the mob led by Judas coming up to Gethsemane to arrest Him. *"The hour [was] at hand"* (26:45) when everyone would forsake Him.

NOTES ON THE PRINTED TEXT

The account of Jesus' prayer time and arrest focuses on a sharp contrast— the obedient Jesus paralleled with the unfaithful disciples. When Jesus arrived at *Gethsemane* (Matt. 26:36), He left eight of His disciples at the entrance to the garden and took *Peter and the two sons of Zebedee* (26:37; James and John)—His three closest followers—further into the grove with Him. Jesus implored these three, who had stood with Him on the mountain when He was transfigured and watched Him bring Jairus's daughter back from the dead, to *stay awake* (26:38) with Him as He agonized over the prospect of His death on the cross. The depth of Jesus' anguish over what was about to happen is shown when He said *"I am deeply grieved, even to death."* Why He felt this way is not specifically stated, but His words echo the sorrowful language of many of the Psalms (Pss. 42:5-6, 11; 43:5; 142:3-6; 143:3-4). How awful it was for Jesus to face being made sin and a curse for all humanity (2 Cor. 5:21; Gal. 3:13)!

In His hour of pain, Jesus wanted His friends to support Him. They should *"stay awake"* (Matt. 26:38) with Jesus to pray for Him—and also to pray for the trial they would face themselves (26:41). Jesus wanted their visible support as He went nearby and *threw himself on the ground and prayed, "My Father, if it possible, let this cup pass from me, yet not what I want but what you want"* (26:39). The cup may refer to the Old Testament cup of judgment given to all the nations (for example, Pss. 60:3; 75:8; Isa. 51:17-23; Jer. 25:15-29), or to imagery from the recent Passover meal, or to the cross (Mark 10:38), or to all of these concepts.

When Jesus finished praying, He came back to find His disciples not keeping watch or praying, but sleeping. He singled out Peter—who had just told Jesus that night *"I will never desert you"* (Matt. 26:33) and *"I will not deny you"* (26:35)— for failing to obey even Jesus' simple command (26:40). It was customary to stay awake late at night after the Passover meal and to talk about God's redemption, but on this night they could not stay awake. Jesus clearly described the struggle most people feel when they are faced with the temptation to disobey God: *"the spirit indeed is willing, but the flesh is weak"* (26:41). This distinction between a weak body and a spirit that wants to be obedient is later echoed in Paul's writing (see, for example, Rom. 7:14-25).

Two more times Jesus returned to pray to the Father about His own *"time of trial"* (Matt. 26:41). The temptation to not suffer crucifixion (and thus disobey the Father) was real. It was as real as the temptations Jesus faced in the wilderness after His baptism (see Heb. 5:7-10). Would He save Himself, or others? What He had taught other people to do, He now did Himself. Jesus said to the Father for a second time, *"your will be done"* (Matt. 26:42), an echo of the words of the Lord's Prayer. Jesus had no doubt that the Father could save Him from the cross, but Jesus also knew that *"if [the cup] cannot pass unless I drink it,"* He would endure the crucifixion. That was His reason for coming to earth: *"it is for this reason that I have come to this hour"* (John 12:27). While the disciples could not—or would not—obey, Jesus reaffirmed His obedience to the Father (Matt. 26:43-44).

Even now *"the hour [was] at hand"* (26:45) for Jesus to be *"betrayed into the hands of sinners."* The time of His passion had arrived (26:46). He had spent the last hours together with His disciples that He would spend with them before His resurrection, and they had failed Him. Now a *crowd* (26:47) of the temple guards, representing the Sanhedrin, and others was coming to arrest Jesus. The Prince of Peace, the man who had told the people to *"love your enemies and pray for those who persecute you"* (5:44), was confronted by a mob carrying *swords and clubs* (26:47). Perhaps they feared that Jesus' disciples would try to defend Him.

Matthew emphasized that leading this mob was *one of the twelve,* Judas. The person who was most disobedient to God now kissed the one who was willingly giving His life for a world of sinners (26:48). A kiss was a sign of affection between family members and close friends, and a devoted disciple often gave his *Rabbi* (26:49) a kiss of honor. In the pitch darkness of Gethsemane, the mob must be sure by a kiss that they were arresting the right man.

Jesus' statement, *"Friend, do what you are here to do"* (26:50) has been read in several ways. Some have seen irony here, especially in Jesus calling Judas His friend, but that greeting was not uncommon in the ancient world. Was Jesus sarcastic or resigned in telling Judas to *"do what you are here to do"?* Perhaps the statement indicates Jesus' final disappointment in the actions of Judas and also a final submission to God's will for Him on the cross.

SUGGESTIONS TO TEACHERS

Jesus not only gave us a Model Prayer (Matt. 6:9-13), but also He modeled how to pray. As we read about His anguished prayers in Gethsemane, we see in Him how we should pray to the Father ourselves.

1. PRAY EARNESTLY. Notice that Jesus expressed His deep grief to the Father three times. Matthew does not mention it, but Luke says that Jesus prayed so earnestly that *his sweat became like great drops of blood falling down on the* *ground* (Luke 22:44). While we will likely not pray that fervently, we need to take prayer seriously. Prayer should be more that just the "zipper" that opens and closes meetings, and it should not be an afterthought in our day either.

2. PRAY DIRECTLY. Jesus' prayer comes right to the point—if it is possible to avoid the cross, then let that happen. Jesus warned us not to pray long, flowery prayers to impress others (Matt. 6:5, 7). "Learning" how to pray does not involve mastering a new vocabulary full of archaic sounding language. We can talk to God much as we would talk to a friend.

3. PRAY EXPECTANTLY. Jesus expected an answer to His prayer, or He wouldn't have prayed. The answer He received is clear from what happened next. Sometimes we receive the answer we want, sometimes we don't, but we can always expect God to answer our prayers in His way and in His time.

4. PRAY HUMBLY. Jesus' prayer in Gethsemane echoes the words of the Lord's Prayer: *your will be done* (26:42), not mine. As Alan Redpath has said, "Before we can pray, 'Thy Kingdom come,' we must be willing to pray, 'My Kingdom go.'" We cannot order God to do anything, or presume He has to do what we ask. Instead, we must come to Him with a humble and contrite heart, for such an attitude He *will not despise* (Ps. 51:17).

| FOR ADULTS | ■ TOPIC: Praying During Tough Times ■ QUESTIONS: 1. How do you think Jesus was feeling that night as He prayed? 2. What did He ask the disciples to do for Him? |

3. What did Jesus ask the Father to do? 4. Who came to arrest Jesus in Gethsemane and why? 5. Do you pray to God constantly, or just when you are in trouble or need something? Why?

■ **ILLUSTRATIONS:**

Drop to Your Knees. A kindergarten class went to the fire station for a tour and some instruction in fire safety. The firefighter was explaining what to do in case of a fire. He said, "First go to the door and feel the door to see if it's hot." Then he said, "Fall to your knees. Does anyone know why you ought to fall to your knees?" One of the children said, "Sure, to start praying to ask God to get us out of this mess!"

There are many situations in our lives that can knock us to our knees. Tough times are plentiful in our society. We are attacked by personal problems, social problems, and spiritual problems. What a blessing it is to know that as we pray to God, He is always there to help us deal with our messes—large and small.

Cancer Is a Scary Word. As we left the physician's office on that Friday afternoon, my husband and I were stunned and afraid. The physician said that Ed had prostate cancer at the young age of 46, and would definitely need to have surgery or radiation treatment. It was up to us to choose which one. Each option had its advantages and disadvantages. We found it hard to rejoice at either prospect.

That following Sunday we were still searching for guidance from God about what to do and what to think about all of this. Naturally, the sermon that morning at church was just what we needed to hear. Our pastor's message was on the power of prayer. He used several passages from Psalms and the parable of the persistent widow in Luke 18:1-8 to help us see that we needed to pray boldly for what we wanted and needed. These were some of the same passages we had read together the day before; this message confirmed to us that God was there listening and that He would lead us to the right decisions. Not only did He help us decide on surgery, but He also helped the whole process go extremely well. The surgery removed all the cancer, and no other treatment was needed. Ed and I were reminded to trust God to help us through a bad situation, and He was faithful.

A Mother's Faithful Prayer. Dwight Moody's father died when Dwight was only four. A month later Mrs. Moody gave birth to twins; she now had nine children to feed and no income. Creditors hounded the widow, claiming everything they could get their hands on.

As if Mrs. Moody didn't have enough troubles, her eldest boy ran away from home. Certain that her son would return, Mrs. Moody placed a light for him in the window each night. Young Dwight was inspired by her faith and prayers. He wrote, "I can remember how eagerly she used to look for tidings of that boy; how she used to send us to the post office to see if there was a letter from him. . . . The voice of my mother was raised in prayer for that wanderer."

Mrs. Moody's many prayers were finally answered when her prodigal son eventually returned. Dwight Moody remembered, "While my mother was sitting at the door, a stranger was seen coming toward the house, and when he came to the door he stopped. My mother didn't know her boy. He stood there . . . his tears trickling down his face. When my mother saw those tears, she cried, 'Oh, it's my lost son?' and asked him come in. 'No mother,' he answered, 'I will not come in until I hear first that you have forgiven me.'" Mrs. Moody was eager to forgive him. She rushed and threw her arms around him. After all her struggles, her prayers were finally answered.

FOR YOUTH

■ TOPIC: Too Tired

■ QUESTIONS: 1. Why do you think Jesus wanted to spend time with His heavenly Father in prayer? 2. Why did Jesus want His disciples to stay awake with Him? 3. Why didn't His disciples stay awake? 4. Why did Judas greet Jesus with a kiss? 5. Why is it important for us to remain faithful to Jesus?

He Is Always There for You. Do you have a parent, a special friend, a relative, or a teacher in your life who takes time to listen when you are trying to make an important decision, but need a sounding board? As a schoolteacher, Carol always has teenagers coming to her to discuss the latest disaster in their lives. She never tells them exactly what they should do, but she tries to help them see all sides of a situation before they make their decision. From discussing boyfriends to which college they should attend, she says, "I try to be there when the kids need to talk, because I care so much about each one of them."

That is the kind of role God also wants to play in your life. He wants you to talk to Him—share your heartfelt dreams, sorrows, and joys. But unlike Carol, God will always be there when you need to talk. God is never too tired or too busy to listen, because He is someone who truly loves you, and wants to help you make the best choices for your life.

Wake Up to Prayer. If you think you don't have the time to pray, consider this experiment. When Danny was in college, he never seemed to have the time to pray for one reason or another, so he tried this. He put one of his favorite Christian cassettes in his alarm clock radio/cassette player. Each morning when it was time for the alarm to go off, instead of blaring music from the local radio station or a buzzer, he was greeted with soft, worshipful music. This music helped him awaken and focus on God. Then he was able to give himself time to pray before he started his busy day.

JESUS ON TRIAL

BACKGROUND SCRIPTURE: Mark 14 and 15
DEVOTIONAL READING: John 10:22-30

KEY VERSES: "Are you the Messiah, the Son of the
Blessed One?" Jesus said, "I am." Mark 14:61b-62a.

KING JAMES VERSION

MARK 14:55 And the chief priests and all the council sought for witness against Jesus to put him to death; and found none.

56 For many bare false witness against him, but their witness agreed not together.

57 And there arose certain, and bare false witness against him, saying,

58 We heard him say, I will destroy this temple that is made with hands, and within three days I will build another made without hands.

59 But neither so did their witness agree together.

60 And the high priest stood up in the midst, and asked Jesus, saying, Answerest thou nothing? what is it which these witness against thee?

61 But he held his peace, and answered nothing. Again the high priest asked him, and said unto him, Art though the Christ, the Son of the Blessed?

62 And Jesus said, I am: and ye shall see the Son of man sitting on the right hand of power, and coming in the clouds of heaven.

63 Then the high priest rent his clothes, and saith, What need we any further witnesses?

64 Ye have heard the blasphemy: what think ye? And they all condemned him to be guilty of death. . . .

15:1 And straightway in the morning the chief priests held a consultation with the elders and scribes and the whole council, and bound Jesus, and carried him away, and delivered him to Pilate.

2 And Pilate asked him, Art though the King of the Jews? And he answering said unto him, Thou sayest it. . . .

12 And Pilate answered and said again unto them, What will ye then that I shall do unto him whom ye call the King of the Jews?

13 And they cried out again, Crucify him.

14 Then Pilate said unto them, Why what evil hath he done? And they cried out the more exceedingly, Crucify him.

15 And so Pilate, willing to content the people, released Barabbas unto them, and delivered Jesus, when he had scourged him, to be crucified.

NEW REVISED STANDARD VERSION

MARK 14:55 Now the chief priests and the whole council were looking for testimony against Jesus to put him to death; but they found none. 56 For many gave false testimony against him, and their testimony did not agree. 57 Some stood up and gave false testimony against him, saying, 58 "We heard him say, 'I will destroy this temple that is made with hands, and in three days I will build another, not made with hands.'" 59 But even on this point their testimony did not agree. 60 Then the high priest stood up before them and asked Jesus, "Have you no answer? What is it that they testify against you?" 61 But he was silent and did not answer. Again the high priest asked him, "Are you the Messiah, the Son of the Blessed One?" 62 Jesus said, "I am; and 'you will see the Son of Man seated at the right hand of the Power,' and 'coming with the clouds of heaven.'" 63 Then the high priest tore his clothes and said, "Why do we still need witnesses? 64 You have heard his blasphemy! What is your decision?" All of them condemned him as deserving death. . . .

15:1 As soon as it was morning, the chief priests held a consultation with the elders and scribes and the whole council. They bound Jesus, led him away, and handed him over to Pilate. 2 Pilate asked him, "Are you the King of the Jews?" He answered him, "You say so.". . .

12 Pilate spoke to them again, "Then what do you wish me to do with the man you call the King of the Jews?" 13 They shouted back, "Crucify him!" 14 Pilate asked them, "Why, what evil has he done?" But they shouted all the more, "Crucify him!" 15 So Pilate, wishing to satisfy the crowd, released Barabbas for them; and after flogging Jesus, he handed him over to be crucified.

Monday, March 22	Mark 14:46-52	*Jesus Is Arrested, the Disciples Desert*
Tuesday, March 23	Mark 14:53-59	*Jesus Is Taken to the High Priest*
Wednesday, March 24	Mark 14:60-65	*Jesus Declares He Is the Messiah*
Thursday, March 25	John 10:22-30	*The Father and I Are One*
Friday, March 26	Mark 15:1-5	*Jesus Goes before Pilate*
Saturday, March 27	Mark 15:6-11	*The Crowd Wants Barabbas Released*
Sunday, March 28	Mark 15:12-15	*The Crowd Shouts for Jesus' Death*

BACKGROUND

After Jesus was arrested in Gethsemane, He was taken to a series of trials, both religious and civil, supposedly to determine His guilt or innocence on some kind of charges. Only the Gospel of John records Jesus' questioning before Annas, the former high priest (John 18:12-14, 19-23). Though the Romans had deposed Annas as the high priest in A.D. 14, he still influenced the politics of his day. Caiaphas, the current high priest, was his son-in-law, while five of Annas' sons, and his grandson, all became high priest as well.

Once Annas had questioned Jesus, he sent Him on to Caiaphas and members of the Sanhedrin, who held an unusual, if not illegal, nighttime trial (see Acts 4:3, 5). If *the whole council* (Mark 14:55) was indeed present, there would have been 70 people. However, to have a legal decision only a quorum was needed. Normally the Sanhedrin would have met in the temple and not in the high priest's house. According to later Jewish law, no trials were allowed on the Sabbath or at festival times, but this did not seem to bother those present. Nor did their requirement that a day must pass before a verdict could be rendered in a capital case, which this one was. That this was a "rigged" trial is shown by the presence of witnesses in the middle of the night. (It was probably already very early Friday morning when the trial started.) However, the witnesses could not agree in their testimonies, a point that should have invalidated the charges (Deut. 19:15-21). In fact, a person could not be put to death unless two witnesses agreed in their testimony (17:6). Jesus remained *silent and did not answer* (Mark 14:61) while the witnesses contradicted themselves and misquoted Him. With the case against Jesus in shambles, the high priest finally got Jesus to say He was *"the Messiah, the Son of the Blessed One."* The high priest and the council were thus satisfied that Jesus had condemned Himself, so they mocked and abused Him before taking Him to the next stage of the trial process (14:62-65).

Sometime just before dawn on Good Friday, the council reached a final, "legal" decision. Since the Romans would not consider blasphemy a crime punishable by death, the Jews had to convince the Roman governor, Pilate, that Jesus was guilty of treason against Caesar. Ironically, the man who had refused to become king and begin a revolt against Rome (John 6:15) was now charged with being a political revolutionary. Pilate, who normally stayed in the Roman capital of Caesarea, was in Jerusalem for the Passover to keep a lid on any celebrating that might turn against Rome. Now he was faced with a man who did not look or act like a traitor, but who was lumped together with someone who definitely was—Barabbas. In an incredible, almost impossible reversal of what should have happened, Pilate released the true revolutionary and sent the man who had done no evil to be crucified (18:28—19:16).

NOTES ON THE PRINTED TEXT

Jesus had been betrayed by one of His disciples and was now in the hands of His bitterest enemies, those religious leaders who were jealous of His power and angered by His criticism of them. We do not know exactly how many were part of the kangaroo court convened in the house of *the high priest* (Mark 14:54), Caiaphas, that night, but at least Joseph of Arimathea (Mark 15:43; Luke 23:50-51) was not part of the group that gathered to condemn Jesus.

Caiaphas, however, could have called this gathering in his house an "inquiry" into the facts, not a trial. The size and wealth of the house of Caiaphas is shown by the fact that the council group met in a large upstairs room above a courtyard while the servants were below (Mark 14:66). As a Sadducee, Caiaphas was kept in office by the Romans because he could keep the people under control. It was Caiaphas who first suggested that Jesus should die for the good of the nation (John 11:49-53), and he was determined to carry out that plan.

As the religious leaders *look[ed] for testimony against Jesus to put him to death . . . they found none* (Mark 14:55). The parade of false witnesses gave testimony that did not agree (14:56-57). When they tried to remember what Jesus had said about destroying and rebuilding the temple in three days (14:58), they could not correctly quote Him (14:59). Their statements sound like a garbled combination of Mark 13:2 and John 2:19.

With no credible witnesses to make a case against Jesus, the high priest then badgered Him to say something in self-defense (Mark 14:60), *but he was silent* (14:61; see Isa. 53:7; 1 Pet. 2:23). To try to get Jesus to incriminate Himself, the high priest put Jesus *"under oath"* (Matt. 26:63) and asked Him if He was *"the Messiah, the Son of the Blessed One"* (Mark 14:61). Calling God *"the Blessed One"* kept the high priest from using God's sacred name, something Caiaphas instead wanted Jesus to do. Jesus replied *"I am"* (14:62) the Messiah, but went on to say He was *"the Son of Man,"* combining in His reply ideas from Daniel 7:13 and Psalm 110:1. While Caiaphas and the Sanhedrin were sitting in judgment of Jesus at that moment, He was looking to the future, when He would sit in judgment on them at His return (Mark 14:62).

Now Caiaphas *tore his clothes* (14:63), an official indication from the high priest that he had heard someone commit *"blasphemy"* (14:64). Those present now all *condemned* Jesus to death, though they themselves could not carry out that sentence. Instead they spit on Him and humiliated Him (14:65).

Early the next morning (15:1), the council and religious leaders took Jesus to the Roman procurator, Pontius Pilate, to convince him that he should execute Jesus, since the Jews could only execute someone for profaning the temple. Also, the Jews stoned people to death, but they wanted Jesus cursed forever by being crucified (Gal. 3:13).

Pilate held trials between dawn and noon, so the leaders were quick to bring Jesus to him. Pilate had been appointed to the post of procurator, a kind of governor, in A.D. 26. He ruled Judea in the service of the Roman governor of the province of Syria, who could have Pilate removed at any time and sent back to Rome. Other contemporary writings tell us that Pilate had seriously offended the Jews at least twice since he had been appointed, which means he did not want more "incidents" that could cost him his job. Therefore, he immediately questioned Jesus on the only charge that really mattered to Rome: *"Are you the King of the Jews?"* (Mark 15:2). Jesus' saying *"You say so"* seems to mean that He is a king, but not in the way that Pilate thinks. The Gospel of John expands on that idea in Jesus' further reply to Pilate (John 18:33-37). While Pilate did not want to antagonize the Jews, he was not interested in doing them any favors either, and he knew they had brought Jesus to him *out of jealousy* (Mark 15:10).

To both satisfy the Jews and keep from executing an innocent man, Pilate proposed letting one prisoner, Jesus or Barabbas, free in honor of the Passover. While this particular custom is not found in writings outside the Gospels, other Roman documents mention similar practices. Pilate presumed that the crowd that had gathered for the trial would want Jesus released to them instead of Barabbas, who was in prison because of being involved with murderers and an *insurrection* (15:7). The leaders, however, had *stirred up the crowd* (15:11) against Jesus, and the crowd was shouting, *"Crucify him!"* (15:13). Though Pilate knew Jesus had done no *"evil"* (15:14), and though Pilate had been warned by his own wife not to harm Jesus (Matt. 27:19), Pilate sent Jesus to be crucified in order to satisfy *the crowd* (Mark 15:15).

SUGGESTIONS TO TEACHERS

How do you react when someone accuses you of something that you did not do? Most of what we would do is just the opposite of what Jesus did. We know from last week's lesson that even before Jesus was arrested, He spent time in prayer with His Father, keeping His focus on what His Father wanted to happen in the coming events.

1. JESUS DID NOT GET ANGRY AND YELL. Despite the midnight arrest and false accusations, Jesus did not say anything. He did not argue. He also did not accuse His accusers of lying and false arrest. Instead, He peacefully responded to their charges. Too often we respond first with anger and later repent of what we said. Sometimes we can wind up being as sinful as the ones who attacked us.

2. JESUS DID NOT SEEK REVENGE. Jesus did not call down 10,000 angels or strike the high priest dead. Jesus allowed them to do what they were going to do. Sometimes we will not even pause when attacked. We will speak or act automatically, and make the situation worse. Instead, as someone once said, "It is better to suffer an injustice than to commit one."

3. JESUS DID NOT SINK INTO SELF-PITY. Jesus did not cry to His Father, or anyone else, about how unfair this whole ordeal was becoming. Jesus did not allow Himself the luxury of this emotion. We, on the other hand, can easily think *Why is everybody always picking on me?*

4. JESUS DID NOT RUN AWAY. Although Jesus had the ability to avoid the situation entirely, He didn't. We can all learn from that. Whenever times get tough, we can be assured that Jesus is there, helping us face whatever is happening.

FOR ADULTS	■ **TOPIC:** Falsely Accused ■ **QUESTIONS:** 1. What was the testimony the witnesses gave

against Jesus? 2. What was Jesus' response to the witnesses and the high priest? 3. What did the religious leaders claim Jesus was guilty of doing? 4. What happened when Jesus was turned over to Pilate? 5. When we are falsely accused of something, how should we respond?

■ **ILLUSTRATIONS:**

No Greater Opportunity. James C. Dobson has said, "There is no greater opportunity to influence our fellowman for Christ than to respond with love when we have been unmistakably wronged. Then the difference between Christian love and the values of the world are most brilliantly evident."

Jesus was "unmistakably wronged" by the religious leaders, high priests, and Pilate. Jesus had every right to respond in any way except with love. But what an impact Jesus made in this world when He showed love instead of hatred, revenge, anger, or bitterness to those who so wrongfully accused and abused Him. We need to remember Jesus' response when we are faced with those who try to harm us, either intentionally or unintentionally.

The Fugitive. A popular U.S. television series of the 1960s was *The Fugitive*. Richard Kimball, wrongfully sentenced to die for his wife's murder, was running from the law in pursuit of the one-armed man he saw murder her. Week after week the only focus was to find the criminal and clear Kimball's name. The concluding episode when Kimball finally found the one-armed man was one of the highest rated shows in television history. The story was so powerful that it was made into a movie and another television series in 2000.

Unlike Jesus, who was willing to die for our sins, Kimball would not die for something he did not do. Jesus allowed Himself to be falsely accused for the benefit of all who would trust in Him.

Under the Gallows. Back in 1738, London's main prison was called Newgate. Charles Wesley (later to be the great Christian hymn writer) frequently went there, preaching to those prisoners sentenced to death. On one occasion Charles was even locked in overnight in order to pray with and comfort prisoners.

In his *Journal*, Wesley tells about a poor man who was condemned to die. Wesley told him of "one who came down from heaven to save the lost and him in particular." Wesley led this man to faith in Christ. After Wesley served this man Communion, he accompanied the man to the gallows. The assurance of salvation was etched on the new convert's face. Because of his new friend's faith, Wesley penned, "That hour under the gallows was the most blessed hour of my life!"

FOR YOUTH

■ TOPIC: Falsely Accused

■ QUESTIONS: 1. What did the witnesses accuse Jesus of saying? 2. How did the witnesses and the high priest respond to Jesus' silence? 3. Who did Jesus say He was? 4. Why did Pilate release Barabbas instead of Jesus? 5. How have you benefited from Jesus' willingness to go to the cross?

■ **ILLUSTRATIONS:**

Stuck in the Middle. Being the middle child is just asking to be wrongly accused, especially according to many middle children. Sometimes parents will unconsciously believe the oldest child would just know better than to do anything wrong, and the youngest child would just be too innocent to do anything wrong, leaving the middle child to be accused.

As a middle child myself, I remember many occasions when that was the case. When the cookie jar lid got cracked, when there was a piece of cake missing, or when someone let the bathtub overflow, I always seemed to be the one blamed— even when I was not home at the time! I could have held grudges against my parents and my brothers, but instead I have forgiven them. However, in fun I do enjoy reminding them of all the things my parents did catch my brothers doing wrong when I was totally innocent.

Being wrongly accused is just part of life at times; however, how we decide to deal with it speaks volumes on our relationship with God. Jesus was able to endure false accusations and forgive those who hurt Him. That is not always easy for us to do, but it should be a goal we all strive to reach.

The Magical Mr. McBeevee. In an episode of the classic television series *The Andy Griffith Show,* Opie told his father about meeting a magical Mr. McBeevee in the woods who walked in the treetops, while jingling and blowing smoke out of his ears. Andy tried to get Opie to admit that this man was just in Opie's imagination, but Opie refused to change his story about the man being real. Opie was even willing to be punished for lying and have his father angry at him, because he knew he was telling the truth. Thankfully, Andy came to the point where he was going to believe his son no matter how fabulous Opie's story seemed, because he believed in his son. In the end, Andy and Opie both learned lessons about believing in people from the miraculous telephone lineman who walked in the treetops with extra hands and had a shiny silver hat.

Although Opie was only a small boy, he had already learned the value of standing up for the truth when others falsely accused him of lying. Jesus also told the truth about Himself to the religious leaders, high priest, and Pilate, none of whom believed Him. In fact, Pilate asked Jesus *"What is truth?"* (John 18:38) without realizing that the answer was standing right in front of him.

The Stolen Wallet. Have you ever had a friend who was falsely accused of something and you hesitated to help or even refused to help? That is what happened to Angie. Angie and Kim, who were best friends, were going to have lunch together when Angie noticed she had forgotten her money. Telling Kim to wait a minute, Angie rushed back to the art room and grabbed her money. She hurried back down to the cafeteria, passing the art teacher, Miss James, to meet Kim in the lunchroom. Kim laughed and told Angie she had never seen anyone move so fast!

After lunch, when Angie and Kim went back to the art room, Miss James informed them that, while the class had been gone, her wallet had been taken; however, she kept glancing at Angie the whole time she said it. After class Miss James asked Angie to stay behind and started to ask her about why she had been in the art room while everyone else was gone. Angie explained why she had been in the room, and didn't even know where Miss James kept her purse. Angie, hurt that her teacher thought she would have done such a thing, appealed to Kim to go and talk to Miss James and verify her story, but Kim didn't want to get involved. Although Kim eventually went to Miss James to explain, and another person confessed to have stolen the wallet earlier that day, the friendship between Kim and Angie had been strained.

There were many people who did nothing to help Jesus on the way to the cross. Pilate's biggest crime was not so much what he did, but what he did not do. He knowingly sent a falsely accused, innocent man to His death, because Pilate was afraid to do otherwise.

JESUS' CRUCIFIXION

BACKGROUND SCRIPTURE: John 19:16b-42
DEVOTIONAL READING: John 10:11-18

KEY VERSES: So they took Jesus; and carrying the cross by himself, he went out to what is called The Place of the Skull, which in Hebrew is called Golgotha. There they crucified him. John 19:16-18.

KING JAMES VERSION

JOHN 19:16b And they took Jesus, and led him away.

17 And he bearing his cross went forth into a place called the place of a skull, which is called in the Hebrew Golgotha:

18 Where they crucified him, and two other with him, on either side one, and Jesus in the midst.

19 And Pilate wrote a title, and put it on the cross. And the writing was JESUS OF NAZARETH THE KING OF THE JEWS.

20 This title then read many of the Jews: for the place where Jesus was crucified was nigh to the city: and it was written in Hebrew, and Greek, and Latin.

21 Then said the chief priests of the Jews to Pilate, Write not, The King of the Jews; but that he said, I am King of the Jews.

22 Pilate answered, What I have written I have written.

23 Then the soldiers, when they had crucified Jesus, took his garments, and made four parts, to every soldier a part; and also his coat: now the coat was without seam, woven from the top throughout.

24 They said therefore among themselves, Let us not rend it, but cast lots for it, whose it shall be: that the scripture might be fulfilled, which saith, They parted my raiment among them, and for my vesture they did cast lots. These things therefore the soldiers did. . . .

26 When Jesus therefore saw his mother, and the disciple standing by, whom he loved, he saith unto his mother, Woman, behold thy son!

27 Then saith he to the disciple, Behold thy mother! And from that hour that disciple took her unto his own home.

28 After this, Jesus knowing that all things were now accomplished, that the scripture might be fulfilled, saith, I thirst.

29 Now there was set a vessel full of vinegar: and they filled a spunge with vinegar, and put it upon hyssop, and put it to his mouth.

30 When Jesus therefore had received the vinegar, he said, It is finished: and he bowed his head, and gave up the ghost.

NEW REVISED STANDARD VERSION

JOHN 19:16b So they took Jesus; 17 and carrying the cross by himself, he went out to what is called The Place of the Skull, which in Hebrew is called Golgotha. 18 There they crucified him, and with him two others, one on either side, with Jesus between them. 19 Pilate also had an inscription written and put on the cross. It read, "Jesus of Nazareth, the King of the Jews." 20 Many of the Jews read this inscription, because the place where Jesus was crucified was near the city; and it was written in Hebrew, in Latin, and in Greek. 21 Then the chief priests of the Jews said to Pilate, "Do not write, 'The King of the Jews,' but, 'This man said, I am King of the Jews.'" 22 Pilate answered, "What I have written I have written." 23 When the soldiers had crucified Jesus, they took his clothes and divided them into four parts, one for each soldier. They also took his tunic; now the tunic was seamless, woven in one piece from the top. 24 So they said to one another, "Let us not tear it, but cast lots for it to see who will get it." This was to fulfill what the scripture says, "They divided my clothes among themselves, and for my clothing they cast lots." . . .

26 When Jesus saw his mother and the disciple whom he loved standing beside her, he said to his mother, "Woman, here is your son." 27 Then he said to the disciple, "Here is your mother." And from that hour the disciple took her into his own home. 28 After this, when Jesus knew that all was now finished, he said (in order to fulfill the scripture), "I am thirsty." 29 A jar full of sour wine was standing there. So they put a sponge full of the wine on a branch of hyssop and held it to his mouth. 30 When Jesus had received the wine, he said, "It is finished." Then he bowed his head and gave up his spirit.

5

Monday, March 29	Isaiah 53:1-6	*Isaiah's Prophecy about the Suffering Servant*
Tuesday, March 30	Isaiah 53:7-12	*The Servant Bore the Sins of Many*
Wednesday, March 31	John 19:16-20	*Jesus Is Crucified*
Thursday, April 1	John 19:21-25a	*The King of the Jews*
Friday, April 2	John 19:25b-30	*It is Finished*
Saturday, April 3	John 19:31-37	*The Spear Pierces Jesus' Side*
Sunday, April 4	John 19:38-42	*Joseph and Nicodemus Take Jesus' Body*

BACKGROUND

Depending on where Pilate was staying in Jerusalem during the Passover, Jesus' trial may have taken place either at the Fortress Antonia, a castle-like fort built by Herod the Great that overlooked the temple, or at Herod's palace near the western wall of the city. Traditionally, Christians have said that Jesus was tried at the Fortress Antonia, then carried His cross (or just the horizontal crossbeam) to Golgotha, *The Place of the Skull* (John 19:17), for His crucifixion. The Bible describes Golgotha as *outside the city gate* (Heb. 13:12) and *near the city* (John 19:20). The spot has been identified for centuries at the location of the Church of the Holy Sepulchre, which in Jesus' day was outside the city walls near a Jewish cemetery. John says a garden and tomb were *in the place where [Jesus] was crucified* (19:41); so some believe that a rocky hill that looks like a skull near the present-day Damascus Gate is the site of Golgotha, and that the so-called Garden Tomb nearby is where Jesus was buried.

The Romans crucified criminals in prominent places, such as the city gate, as a warning to other potential offenders. Crucifixion was so repulsive that the Romans reserved it only for slaves and foreigners. Often several poles, about 10 feet high, remained upright in the ground at the crucifixion site so that the crimi-nals could have the crossbeams they carried to their execution quickly nailed to the poles. Near the top of the poles, the soldiers cut grooves into which the cross-beams could be inserted after the prisoners' wrists had been nailed or tied to the beams. Above each crossbeam was often a *titulus,* a tablet stating the person's crime. A small seat or block of wood could be nailed into the pole to hold the pris-oner's feet up. That way he would occasionally be able to catch his breath, and his death would take longer. In fact, a crucified person could take days to die from either a loss of blood circulation and coronary failure or a lung collapse. To speed the process along, the Roman soldiers would break the victim's legs below the knees with a club. The Jews were especially anxious to have the bodies of Jesus and the two criminals who were executed with Him taken down before the Sabbath began on Friday night (19:31-33).

Under Roman law, the soldiers who carried out Jesus' crucifixion were entitled to His clothes, since a person was crucified naked or nearly naked. They divided His clothing (perhaps His headdress, sandals, outer cloak, and girdle) *into four parts, one for each soldier* (19:23). The Roman army was divided into units of eight men who shared a tent, but sometimes four-person squads were assigned special tasks, such as executions. Since Jesus had a *seamless* tunic, they *cast lots for it* (19:24), in fulfillment, John says, of Psalm 22:18. This psalm, describing a man in agony, was a key passage of Scripture for early Christians, who saw in it a righteous man suffering at the hands of his enemies (John 19:16).

NOTES ON THE PRINTED TEXT

John's Gospel makes no mention of Simon of Cyrene carrying Jesus' cross, or crossbeam (Mark 15:21), but instead says that Jesus carried His cross *by himself* (John 19:17) to His crucifixion. John may be making a theological emphasis here, showing that Jesus completed His saving work without the help of others. Much as Isaac did, Jesus carried the materials to His own sacrifice (Gen. 22:6).

The site of Jesus' sacrifice was probably in view of the place where Isaac was almost sacrificed (the temple). The location of *The Place of the Skull, which in Hebrew is called Golgotha* (John 19:17) is disputed. Its name may have come from the many skulls found there from previous executions, or because it was the place where (one tradition says) Adam's skull was buried. Wherever the site was, it lay outside the city walls of that time, at a busy spot where *those who passed by* (Mark 15:29) could mock Jesus. He was crucified with two others, *one on either side* (John 19:18). The word used to describe the other two in Mark 15:27 could indicate someone who was part of a rebellion, not just a thief. The charge against Jesus, written on a piece of board nailed above His head, was that He was *"the King of the Jews"* (John 19:19), a crime of treason against Caesar. Outraged, the religious leaders demanded of Pilate that the inscription read *"This man said, 'I am King of the Jews'"* (19:21), but Pilate refused to change the wording (19:22).

That the board with Jesus' crime was written in at least three languages—*Hebrew, Latin,* and *Greek* (19:20)—shows the three cultures of His day in the Holy Land. Greek was the almost universal language of the time, the language in which the New Testament was first written.

Crucifixion was a slow, painful, humiliating method of death. Suspended above the ground, with His wrists nailed to His crossbeam, Jesus' body would have sagged from its own weight, but that would have sent pain shooting through His body. As Jesus tried to pull Himself up, He would have felt the intense pain of the nail or nails driven through His feet. Cramps would have set in, making it even more difficult to pull Himself up, and if He could not do that, He could not exhale air, which threatened to suffocate Him. Crucifixion victims could linger for days like this, but Jesus' body was weak from the flogging He had already endured. He would not last that long.

While this agony went on around them, the soldiers of the execution squad *took [Jesus'] clothes and divided them into four parts* (19:23), then *cast lots* (19:24) for His seamless tunic. Casting lots may have been something like throwing dice to determine the "winner" of the tunic—the ankle-length garment that Jesus wore next to His skin. The other items divided up would have been His outer garments. John saw here a fulfillment of Old Testament prophecy from Psalm 22:18—*"They divided my clothes among themselves, and for my clothing they cast lots"* (John 19:24). This is one of many details John told his readers that linked Jesus' death to Old Testament prophecies about the Messiah (see also 19:28, 36-37).

Besides the soldiers and a jeering crowd, John mentioned the women near the cross, including Jesus' mother and Mary Magdalene (19:25). While John was there too (*the disciple whom he loved,* 19:26), the ones who stayed closest to Jesus at His time of greatest suffering were His female followers. Did they feel less frightened for their lives than the other disciples, or were they more open with their feelings for Jesus? Mary, Jesus' mother, must have been devastated as she watched her son die. Perhaps that is one reason why Jesus said to John, *"Here is your mother"* (19:27). John, in turn, *took [Mary] into his own home.*

After this . . . Jesus knew that all was now finished (19:28). With the work that He had been sent to do now done, He asked for a drink and was given some of the wine vinegar mixed with water (*sour wine,* 19:29) that was popular with Roman soldiers. John said the drink was given to Jesus on a *branch* of the *hyssop* plant, one variety of which has a stalk over three feet long. Hyssop is connected with the symbolism of the slaughtered Passover lamb (Exod. 12:22). With the slight refreshment of this drink, Jesus could cry out with His last breath, *"It is finished"* (John 19:30). This exclamation, which is one word in Greek (*tetelestai*), was not a cry of defeat, but rather a proclamation of triumph. The work Jesus had been sent to do was completed. It is almost unbelievable that a person in so much pain and suffering could still be so in control of Himself that He decided when it was finally time to *[give] up his spirit.*

SUGGESTIONS TO TEACHERS

On Palm Sunday we celebrate Jesus' triumphal entry into Jerusalem, a time of waving branches and shouting "Hallelujah!" The next Sunday is Easter, when we sing praises for His resurrection. But in all the celebrating, we must not miss Good Friday and the horror of the crucifixion. Jesus had to go to Golgotha, and He told His disciples that many times. Some phrases from an old hymn, "'Man of Sorrows,' What a Name," by Philip Bliss, help explain why the Cross is essential to every Christian.

1. IN MY PLACE CONDEMNED JESUS STOOD. We are the sinful people who deserve death, *the wages of sin* (Rom. 6:23), not the sinless Son of God. But if He had not stood in our place and received our punishment, we would all die in our sin, separated from God forever.

2. SEALED MY PARDON WITH JESUS' BLOOD. Jesus said that He came *to give his life a ransom for many* (Mark 10:45). We all owe a debt we cannot pay, and Jesus paid a debt He did not owe. His death was a pardon, a reprieve from a sentence of execution, for each one who will trust in Him.

3. 'LIFTED UP' WAS JESUS TO DIE. Jesus also said, *Just as Moses lifted up the serpent in the wilderness, so must the Son of Man be lifted up, that whoever believes in him may have eternal life* (John 3:14-15). Those who want to be spiritually "healed" must look up in faith to the crucified Jesus. No other complete solution to your own problems or to the problems of humanity exists. There is no eternal life except through Jesus, *"the way, and the truth, and the life"* (14:6).

4. 'IT IS FINISHED' WAS JESUS' CRY. Jesus' final words from the cross put an end to any religion or theology that says you can work your way to God. Jesus did everything that had to be done to bridge the gap between humanity and God. You cannot build your own bridge to God; He has built a bridge to you. It is sad to see how people will not cross it.

FOR ADULTS	▪ TOPIC: Putting Your Life on the Line

▪ QUESTIONS: 1. What inscription did Pilate have placed on the cross? 2. Why did this inscription upset the Jewish leaders? 3. What fulfillments of Old Testament prophesies does John point out in his Gospel? 4. Who was at the cross as Jesus died? 5. How does Jesus' saying, *"It is finished"* (John 19:30) apply to you now?

▪ **ILLUSTRATIONS:**

A High Price. Anna was a Jew fleeing the German Gestapo in France during World War II. She knew she was close to being caught, and she wanted to give up. She came to the home of a French Huguenot. A widow lady came to that home to say that it was time to flee to a new place. Anna said, "It's no use; they will find me anyway. They are so close behind." The Christian widow said, "Yes, they will find someone here, but it's time for you to leave. Go with these people to safety. I will take your identification and wait here."

Anna then understood the plan: the Gestapo would come and find this Christian widow and think she was Anna. When Anna protested to the widow, the widow replied, "It's the least I can do; Christ has already done that and more for me."

The widow was caught and imprisoned in Anna's place, allowing time for Anna to escape safely. Within six months, the widow died in a concentration camp. Anna never forgot this ultimate sacrifice. In fact, Anna became a Christian herself because she met God through the greatest love a person can give—to lay down one's life for a friend. During the rest of Anna's life, she strove to do all she could for the less fortunate saying, "That's the least I can do considering what great sacrifices Christ has already made for me."

A Half-Hearted Prayer. Sometimes we do not take Jesus and His sacrifice for us seriously. He was willing to pay the price for us, but how do we respond in return?

While this prayer has an element of humor, sadly it is also one we can too easily identify with.

I love thy church, O God! Her walls before me stand,
But please excuse my absence, Lord; this bed is simply grand!
A charge to keep I have; a God to glorify,
But Lord, don't ask for money from me; the glory comes too high.
Am I a soldier of the cross, a follower of the Lamb?
Yes! Though I seldom pray or pay, I still insist I am.
Must Jesus bear the cross alone, and all the world go free?
No! Others, Lord, should do their part, but please don't count on me.
Praise God from whom all blessings flow, praise Him, all creatures here below!
Oh, loud my hymns of praise I bring, because it doesn't cost to sing!

A Reminder in the Register. A sermon by A. Leonard Griffith tells the story of a London restaurant owner named Emil Mettler who would never allow a mission worker to pay for a meal in his restaurant. One day Mettler happened to open his cash register in the presence of a minister, who was surprised to see with the bills and coins a six-inch nail. When the minister asked Mettler what the nail was for, Mettler said it was a reminder to him of the price that Christ had paid for his salvation and of what he owed Jesus in return.

We all need to be reminded of how Christ put His life on the line that day at Calvary. What love it took for Him to endure crucifixion for each one of us!

| FOR YOUTH | ■ TOPIC: Paying the Price |
| | ■ QUESTIONS: 1. Where was Jesus crucified and with whom? 2. Why was Jesus' inscription written in three different languages? |

3. What payment did the soldiers receive for crucifying Jesus? 4. What did Jesus do for His mother just before He died? 5. Jesus paid with His life for you to have eternal life. How should you respond to that?

■ **ILLUSTRATIONS:**
The Scarred Hands. A small orphaned boy lived with his grandmother. One night their house caught fire. The grandmother perished in the smoke and flames as a crowd gathered around the burning house. The boy's cries for help were heard above the crackling blaze. No one seemed to know what to do, for the front of the house was engulfed in flames.

Suddenly a stranger rushed from the crowd and went to the back of the house, where he spotted an iron pipe that reached an upstairs window. He climbed up and disappeared into the house, then reappeared with the boy. Amid the cheers of the crowd, the stranger climbed down the hot pipe with the boy holding on to his neck.

Weeks later a public hearing was held in the town to determine who would get custody of the boy. Each person wanting the boy spoke. One was a farmer who needed help on his farm and could offer a healthy life for the boy. Another was a teacher, who wanted to educate the boy. Still another was a rich man, who could give the boy everything.

Finally the chairperson asked, "Anyone else like to say a word before I make my decision?" From the back rose a stranger. He walked toward the front and stood directly in front of the little boy. Slowly the stranger removed his hands from his pockets. A gasp went up from the crowd. The little boy, whose eyes had been focused on the floor until now, looked up. The man's hands were terribly scarred. Suddenly the boy recognized the man. This was the man who had saved his life! The man's hands were scarred from climbing up and down the hot pipe. It was obvious to everyone who should get custody of the boy—the one willing to pay the price for his life. Those scarred hands said it all.

Not Pretending. Someone asked the following question in an advice column:

"An atheist I heard on TV said that Jesus just swooned on the cross and that the disciples nursed Him back to health. What do you think?"

Here was the response:

"Believe me, if that atheist was beaten with a barbed whip with 39 heavy strokes, nailed to a cross, hung in the sun for six hours, had a spear run through his side, and was put in an airless tomb for 36 hours, he would change his mind!"

Jesus did not just pretend to pay the price for us. He really did it. He was willing to give up His life for you and everyone else who would trust in Him.

Those Who Pay a Price. In each war or conflict the United States has ever fought, self-sacrifice has always been required. Men and women have understood that sometimes the loss of life or limb is unavoidable for a greater good. My Uncle Bill is like that. He has lived the past 60 years with a mangled leg. The physicians saved it after combat during World War II, but it has continued to give him many problems and pain ever since. Even with the pain and suffering, I have never heard my uncle complain, or say he was sorry he put his life on the line for his country. He wanted to keep America free, so his children could grow up feeling safe and secure.

Jesus also willingly gave His life as a sacrifice for us. In William Barclay's commentary on the Book of John, he says, "Jesus was not helplessly caught up in a mesh of circumstances from which he could not break free. Apart from any divine power he might have called in, it is quite clear that to the end he could have turned back and saved his life. He did not lose his life; he gave it. The Cross was not thrust upon him; he willingly accepted it."

THE EMPTY TOMB

BACKGROUND SCRIPTURE: Matthew 28:1-15
DEVOTIONAL READING: Luke 24:1-12

KEY VERSES: "Do not be afraid; I know that you are looking for Jesus who was crucified. He is not here; for he has been raised, as he said. Come, see the place where he lay." Matthew 28:5-6

6

KING JAMES VERSION

MATTHEW 28:1 In the end of the sabbath, as it began to dawn toward the first day of the week, came Mary Magdalene and the other Mary to see the sepulchre.

2 And, behold, there was a great earthquake: for the angel of the Lord descended from heaven, and came and rolled back the stone from the door, and sat upon it.

3 His countenance was like lightning, and his raiment white as snow:

4 And for fear of him the keepers did shake, and became as dead men.

5 And the angel answered and said unto the women, Fear not ye: for I know that ye seek Jesus, which was crucified.

6 He is not here: for he is risen, as he said. Come, see the place where the Lord lay.

7 And go quickly, and tell his disciples that he is risen from the dead; and, behold, he goeth before you into Galilee; there shall ye see him: lo, I have told you.

8 And they departed quickly from the sepulchre with fear and great joy; and did run to bring his disciples word.

9 And as they went to tell his disciples, behold, Jesus met them, saying, All hail. And they came and held him by the feet, and worshipped him.

10 Then said Jesus unto them, Be not afraid: go tell my brethren that they go into Galilee, and there shall they see me.

11 Now when they were going, behold, some of the watch came into the city, and shewed unto the chief priests all the things that were done.

12 And when they were assembled with the elders, and had taken counsel, they gave large money unto the soldiers,

13 Saying, Say ye, His disciples came by night, and stole him away while we slept.

14 And if this come to the governor's ears, we will persuade him, and secure you.

15 So they took the money, and did as they were taught: and this saying is commonly reported among the Jews until this day.

NEW REVISED STANDARD VERSION

MATTHEW 28:1 After the sabbath, as the first day of the week was dawning, Mary Magdalene and the other Mary went to see the tomb. 2 And suddenly there was a great earthquake; for an angel of the Lord, descending from heaven, came and rolled back the stone and sat on it. 3 His appearance was like lightning, and his clothing white as snow. 4 For fear of him the guards shook and became like dead men. 5 But the angel said to the women, "Do not be afraid; I know that you are looking for Jesus who was crucified. 6 He is not here; for he has been raised, as he said. Come, see the place where he lay. 7 Then go quickly and tell his disciples, 'He has been raised from the dead, and indeed he is going ahead of you to Galilee; there you will see him.' This is my message for you." 8 So they left the tomb quickly with fear and great joy, and ran to tell his disciples. 9 Suddenly Jesus met them and said, "Greetings!" And they came to him, took hold of his feet, and worshiped him. 10 Then Jesus said to them, "Do not be afraid; go and tell my brothers to go to Galilee; there they will see me."

11 While they were going, some of the guard went into the city and told the chief priests everything that had happened. 12 After the priests had assembled with the elders, they devised a plan to give a large sum of money to the soldiers, 13 telling them, "You must say, 'His disciples came by night and stole him away while we were asleep.' 14 If this comes to the governor's ears, we will satisfy him and keep you out of trouble." 15 So they took the money and did as they were directed. And this story is still told among the Jews to this day.

Monday, April 5	John 11:20-27	*I Am the Resurrection*
Tuesday, April 6	Luke 24:1-5	*The Stone Is Rolled Away*
Wednesday, April 7	Luke 24:6-12	*The Women Remembered Jesus' Words*
Thursday, April 8	Matthew 28:1-6	*Jesus Has Been Raised*
Friday, April 9	Matthew 28:7-15	*Go Quickly and Tell*
Saturday, April 10	John 20:19-23	*Jesus Stood among the Disciples*
Sunday, April 11	Romans 6:4-11	*Death No Longer Has Dominion*

BACKGROUND

After Jesus died, Joseph of Arimathea, a rich man who was a secret disciple of Jesus and likely a member of the Sanhedrin (Luke 23:50-51; John 19:38), asked Pilate for Jesus' body. Since Joseph was able to have an audience with Pilate in the evening (Matt. 27:57-58), after Pilate's normal "business" hours, Joseph must have been a fairly influential person.

Normally, the bodies of crucifixion victims were thrown into common graves, but family members could petition for the body. For some reason, Pilate granted Joseph's request, and so Joseph, with the help of Nicodemus (John 19:39), prepared Jesus' body for burial with spices and then placed it in Joseph's *own new tomb* (Matt. 27:60). Even if the Sabbath had already begun that Friday evening, the immediate burial of a body in the hot Judean climate was still allowed. Wrapping Jesus' body in *a clean linen cloth* (27:59) showed respect for Jesus that a common criminal would not have received. However, not all of the normal procedures to treat the body were possible at this late hour. Therefore, when Joseph and Nicodemus had finished preliminary preparations, they laid Jesus' body in the rock-cut tomb and *rolled a great stone* (27:60) in front of the entrance to keep out animals and grave robbers.

Also at the burial were *Mary Magdalene, and Mary the mother of James and Joseph* (27:56), who had watched Jesus die on the cross. Normally, women took care of burial preparations, but this was a special circumstance. The women instead gathered other spices to complete the burial, and they planned to come to the tomb after the Sabbath to use them (Luke 23:56—24:1). Matthew may have mentioned their presence at the burial to show that they indeed knew which tomb they were going to on Easter morning and did not visit some other empty tomb.

Only Matthew tells about how *the chief priests and the Pharisees* (Matt. 27:62) hurried to Pilate on the Sabbath, the day after Jesus' crucifixion, and demanded that Pilate secure the tomb *until the third day* (27:64). The Jews believed at this time that a person could still be found alive three days after death (presumably having awakened from a coma), so they were going to make sure that Jesus was truly dead. Further, they did not want His disciples to steal the body and tell people that Jesus had risen from the grave. Interestingly, unlike Jesus' own disciples, the authorities remembered Jesus saying that He would rise after three days.

Pilate, perhaps wondering why all this fuss was being made over a dead man, told them to *"Go, make it as secure as you can"* (27:65), and gave them a guard of soldiers to put at the tomb. The religious leaders also sealed the tomb, probably by fastening a cord to the rock and to the tomb with seals.

Thus, Jesus' enemies had done everything they could to keep Him in the grave. They were finally done with Jesus of Nazareth, who had been a thorn in their sides for so long. He was dead, buried, and gone—or so they thought.

NOTES ON THE PRINTED TEXT

At dawn on the morning after the Sabbath, as soon as there was enough light to see, the two women who had watched Jesus' burial (Matt. 27:61) *went to see the tomb* (28:1). Mark and Luke say they were taking spices to the tomb to finish anointing Jesus' body (Mark 16:1; Luke 24:1). Only Matthew mentions the dramatic events of that morning: a great earthquake, an angel descending from heaven, and the great stone suddenly rolled back from the tomb (Matt. 28:2).

As if in triumph, the angel dressed in *clothing white as snow* (28:3) sat on the stone and spoke to the women (28:4-5). It would be incorrect to conclude that the angel rolled away the stone to let Jesus out of the tomb. Instead, the stone was rolled away to let the rest of the world see that Jesus was already resurrected. *"He is not here; for he has been raised, as he said. Come, see the place where he lay"* (28:6). Both Mark and Luke say the women went into the tomb and saw that the place where they had seen His body laid was now empty (Mark 16:5-6; Luke 24:3). The Gospel of John mentions that the grave clothes were still in place, as if Jesus had risen right through them (John 20:5-7).

The angel had a job for the women. They were to tell Jesus' disciples that He would go ahead of them to Galilee, where He would appear to them. The words *he is going ahead of you* (Matt. 28:7) is a biblical phrase that connotes a shepherd leading his flocks (John 10:4). During Jesus' earthly ministry, Galilee was the place where He was better received by the people.

The women were to proclaim this incredible eyewitness message about Jesus' resurrection to the other disciples. While this fact may not seem unusual to us, in Jesus' time the witness of women was discounted and considered unreliable. If the Gospel testimonies were made up, they would not have chosen to have women give this crucial testimony, especially if they wanted to be readily accepted and believed. The women's presence gives a definite ring of authenticity to the account.

For their testimony, the women did not have to rely solely on what the angel said and what they saw in the empty tomb. As they were hurrying to tell the disciples what had happened, the risen *Jesus met them and said, "Greetings!"* (Matt. 28:9). This everyday welcome may have been intended to calm the women, who were both afraid and joyful at the same time. This was not some other-worldly

Jesus they were seeing, but the person whom they knew and immediately recognized. Out of reverence for the risen Son of God, the women *took hold of his feet, and worshiped him.* Sensing their fear, Jesus said, *"Do not be afraid"* (28:10). He then repeated what the angel had said. The women were to tell the disciples the incredible things they had seen and heard.

Jesus' body being gone was something the religious leaders had most feared and now had to explain. Of course, the easiest thing for them to have done was to produce the body themselves, especially if they had it or knew where it was. That would have immediately ended any nonsense about a person rising from the dead. However, what the authorities did shows that they knew for certain the tomb was empty.

When the guards went back to the city and told *the chief priests* (28:11) what had happened, they gathered with the elders and invented the necessary story (28:12). The authorities bribed the soldiers to agree with what they said: *"His disciples came by night and stole him away"* (28:13) while the guards were sleeping. Ironically, the authorities were now calling true the same lie they had earlier said the disciples were going to use to prove a false resurrection (27:64). It was a serious offense, punishable by death in some cases, for a Roman soldier to be found negligent in his duties; so the religious authorities would make sure that *"if this comes to the governor's ears, we will satisfy him and keep you out of trouble"* (28:14). The leaders had bribed Judas to betray Jesus; now they would give money to the soldiers to lie about Jesus' resurrection.

When Matthew said *this story is still told among the Jews to this day* (28:15), he meant that this was the account that was circulating at the time he when was writing his Gospel. Amazingly, it is still one of the explanations that people give in our time for what happened that first Easter. But the deceit of the authorities proves that Jesus' body was not in the tomb. Also, the eyewitness testimony of the women, and later of the doubting disciples, proves exactly what really happened. Christ had risen from the dead!

SUGGESTIONS TO TEACHERS

Someone has said about Easter, "Though each step to the cross was a step of agony, it was also a step of victory." Jesus was victorious over the enemy that all of us finally face—death. What happened that first Easter morning has profound implications for all Christians today. Four truths stand out.

1. THE EMPTY TOMB. There is no greater hope in this life than what comes from Jesus' resurrection. Because He lives, we can live too after the end of this lifetime. Note what Paul said: *If for this life only we have hoped in Christ, we are of all people most to be pitied. But in fact Christ has been raised from the dead, the first fruits of those who have died* (1 Cor. 15:19-20). Jesus was but the "advance party" of those who will follow Him.

2. THE ETERNAL DESTINATION. Christ rose from the dead to return to heaven and to reign eternally. Heaven is also the destination of all believers. As Paul said, *We have a building from God, a house not made with hands, eternal in the heavens* (2 Cor. 5:1). That home is waiting for us even now.

3. THE DEFEATED ENEMY. While Satan may have believed that he had triumphed over the Son of God on the cross, the opposite was true. Jesus defeated Satan, and we can have victory over him as well. He cannot keep us from doing God's will unless we let him. If you *resist the devil . . . he will flee from you* (Jas. 4:7).

4. THE EASTER MESSAGE. The good news about Easter is most of all a message that must be shared. It is, Paul told the Corinthians, a message *of first importance* (1 Cor. 15:3). Every person needs to hear that Jesus rose from the dead and offers those who trust in Him eternal life. Will everyone believe the truth? No. But that does not mean we should not share it, and especially share what it means to us personally.

FOR ADULTS

■ TOPIC: Changing Defeat into Victory

■ QUESTIONS: 1. Who came to Jesus' tomb on Easter morning? Why? 2. What happened at Jesus' tomb very early on Easter morning? 3. What message did the angel have for the women? 4. What message did Jesus give them? Why? 5. How would you respond to someone who said that Jesus never rose from the dead?

■ **ILLUSTRATIONS:**

The Limits of Cancer. When my mother was diagnosed with cancer, we were given this poem that tells about spiritual victory that can be found even in the worst situations. We have since discovered that it was written by Dan Richardson, a believer who, like my mom, eventually lost his battle with cancer. But that did not daunt their spirits or change their eternal destination with the Lord.

> Cancer is so limited . . .
> It cannot cripple love,
> It cannot shatter hope,
> It cannot corrode faith,
> It cannot eat away peace,
> It cannot destroy confidence,
> It cannot kill friendship,
> It cannot shut out memories,
> It cannot silence courage,
> It cannot invade the soul,
> It cannot reduce eternal life,
> It cannot quench the Spirit,
> It cannot lessen the power of the resurrection.

The Power in a Seed. In a cemetery in Hanover, Germany, there is a grave where huge slabs of granite and marble are cemented together and fastened with heavy steel clasps. It belongs to a woman who did not believe in the resurrection of the dead. Yet strangely, she directed in her will that her grave be made so secure that, if there were a resurrection, it would not include her. On the marker were inscribed these words: "This burial place must never be opened." In time, a seed covered over by the stones began to grow. Slowly it pushed its way through the soil and out from beneath them. As the trunk enlarged, the great slabs were gradually shifted so that the steel clasps were wrenched from their sockets. A tiny seed had become a tree that had pushed aside the massive stones.

The power seen at the Resurrection is the same power that can change a hardened heart toward God. The power seen at the Resurrection is the same power that will raise those who die in Christ to eternal life with Him.

The Only Answer. Some of the hardest questions in life all have the same answer: What is it that gives a widow courage as she stands beside a fresh grave? What is the ultimate hope of the amputee, the abused, or the burn victim? How can the parents of a brain-damaged or physically handicapped child keep from living their lives totally depressed? Where do the thoughts of a young couple go when they finally recover from the grief of losing their newborn child? How about when a family receives the news that their dad was killed in a terrorist attack? How about when a son or daughter dies due to an overdose? What is the final answer to pain, mourning, senility, insanity, terminal diseases, sudden calamities, and fatal accidents? By now, hopefully, you have guessed the correct answer: the hope of our coming resurrection!

For Youth

■ **Topic:** Alive!

■ **Questions:** 1. What did Mary Magdalene and the other Mary find when they reached the tomb? 2. Who spoke to these women at the tomb? 3. What reaction did the women have to seeing the angel? 4. What did the women do with Jesus' message? 5. What do you think is the importance of these women being the first ones to proclaim the Easter message?

■ **Illustrations:**

Alive! Not long ago, one of the oldest members in our congregation passed away. At the funeral, our pastor refused to speak about Mabel in the past tense with phrases such as "she was" or "she had been." He pointed out that she *is* in heaven and that she *is* in the presence of the Lord and that she *is* alive! Our pastor reminded us of the Scripture that assures us that when we are absent from our earthly bodies we are present with the Lord (2 Cor. 5:8).

Though I had always believed this truth, I had never thought of speaking about a deceased person in the present tense. This added a whole new dynamic for me in thinking about our loved ones who have already left this life here on earth. How exciting it is to think about them as being *alive* right now. In addition, as believers, we all have that same assurance that death is not the final chapter for us. It is the new beginning that we all are waiting for and believing in.

Surprise! A two-year-old girl could hardly wait for Easter to come. She had a new dress to wear and new shoes to go with it, but her father wondered whether she knew the true meaning of the holiday.

"Kara," he asked, "do you know what Easter means?"

"Yes, I do," she smiled.

"What does it mean then?"

With a smile on her face and her arms raised, she cried, "Surprise!"

What better word could there be to describe Easter? No one expected a crucified person to rise from the dead. Even the religious leaders, who put a guard on the tomb, did not do so because they expected a resurrection. The women came that morning to anoint a body, not find an empty grave. No one expected Jesus to be alive, but He was—and He still is! Surprise!

Empty! What is the biggest difference between the world's great religions? Look at the founders of each one. You can find the tomb of Muhammed in Saudi Arabia, and his body is there. You can find the tomb of Buddha in India, and his body is there. Look for the tomb of Jesus in Jerusalem, and even if you were certain of the site, you would find it empty. That He is alive today makes the difference in each one of our lives. It reminds us of the old hymn that begins, "I serve a risen Savior. He's in the world today." No other religion can dare make that claim.

THE THESSALONIANS' FAITH

BACKGROUND SCRIPTURE: 1 Thessalonians 1—3
DEVOTIONAL READING: 1 Thessalonians 2:13-20

KEY VERSES: We always give thanks to God for all of you and mention you in our prayers, constantly remembering before our God and Father your work of faith and labor of love and steadfastness of hope in our Lord Jesus Christ. 1 Thessalonians 1:2-3.

KING JAMES VERSION

1 THESSALONIANS 1:2 We give thanks to God always for you all, making mention of you in our prayers;

3 Remembering without ceasing your work of faith, and labour of love, and patience of hope in our Lord Jesus Christ, in the sight of God and our Father;

4 Knowing, brethren beloved, your election of God.

5 For our gospel came not unto you in word only, but also in power, and in the Holy Ghost, and in much assurance; as ye know what manner of men we were among you for your sake.

6 And ye became followers of us, and of the Lord, having received the word in much affliction, with joy of the Holy Ghost:

7 So that ye were ensamples to all that believe in Macedonia and Achaia.

8 For from you sounded out the word of the Lord not only in Macedonia and Achaia, but also in every place your faith to God-ward is spread abroad; so that we need not to speak any thing.

9 For they themselves shew of us what manner of entering in we had unto you, and how ye turned to God from idols to serve the living and true God;

10 And to wait for his Son from heaven, whom he raised from the dead, even Jesus, which delivered us from the wrath to come. . . .

3:6 But now when Timotheus came from you unto us, and brought us good tidings of your faith and charity, and that ye have good remembrance of us always, desiring greatly to see us, as we also to see you:

7 Therefore, brethren, we were comforted over you in all our affliction and distress by your faith:

8 For now we live, if ye stand fast in the Lord.

9 For what thanks can we render to God again for you, for all the joy wherewith we joy for your sakes before our God;

10 Night and day praying exceedingly that we might see your face, and might perfect that which is lacking in your faith?

NEW REVISED STANDARD VERSION

1 THESSALONIANS 1:2 We always give thanks to God for all of you and mention you in our prayers, constantly 3 remembering before our God and Father your work of faith and labor of love and steadfastness of hope in our Lord Jesus Christ. 4 For we know, brothers and sisters beloved by God, that he has chosen you, 5 because our message of the gospel came to you not in word only, but also in power and in the Holy Spirit and with full conviction; just as you know what kind of persons we proved to be among you for your sake. 6 And you became imitators of us and of the Lord, for in spite of persecution you received the word with joy inspired by the Holy Spirit, 7 so that you became an example to all the believers in Macedonia and in Achaia. 8 For the word of the Lord has sounded forth from you not only in Macedonia and Achaia, but in every place your faith in God has become known, so that we have no need to speak about it. 9 For the people of those regions report about us what kind of welcome we had among you, and how you turned to God from idols, to serve a living and true God, 10 and to wait for his Son from heaven, whom he raised from the dead—Jesus, who rescues us from the wrath that is coming. . . .

3:6 But Timothy has just now come to us from you, and has brought us the good news of your faith and love. He has told us also that you always remember us kindly and long to see us—just as we long to see you. 7 For this reason, brothers and sisters, during all our distress and persecution we have been encouraged about you through your faith. 8 For we now live, if you continue to stand firm in the Lord. 9 How can we thank God enough for you in return for all the joy that we feel before our God because of you? 10 Night and day we pray most earnestly that we may see you face to face and restore whatever is lacking in your faith.

7

Monday, April 12	1 Thessalonians 1:1-5	*Paul Remembers the Thessalonians' Faith*
Tuesday, April 13	1 Thessalonians 1:6-10	*You Have Become an Example*
Wednesday, April 14	1 Thessalonians 2:1-8	*Paul's Coming Was Not in Vain*
Thursday, April 15	1 Thessalonians 2:9-13	*You Received God's Word*
Friday, April 16	1 Thessalonians 2:14-20	*You Have Suffered for Christ*
Saturday, April 17	1 Thessalonians 3:1-5	*Paul Sends Timothy to Encourage*
Sunday, April 18	1 Thessalonians 3:6-13	*Timothy Brings Back Good News*

BACKGROUND

Thessalonica was a prime place to start a church. It was the capital and largest city of the Roman province of Macedonia (in what is now northern Greece). Thessalonica was both an important seaport and a major stopover on the Egnatian Way, the overland highway from Rome to the eastern provinces of the empire. The city was founded in 315 B.C. by the Macedonian general Cassander, who named it after his wife, the stepsister of the most famous Macedonian, Alexander the Great. When the Thessalonians supported Augustus in the Roman civil war that made him emperor, he rewarded the town by making it a free city. That meant it remained a mostly Greek city, unlike nearby Philippi, which prided itself on being a Roman colony. The Thessalonians chose their own rulers, who went by the title of politarchs. This is the Greek name translated as *city officials* in Acts 17:8. This unusual title is not found in earlier Greek literature, but was used correctly by Luke as he described Paul's visit to the city. The title has since been found on one of the ancient Roman gates to the city.

Paul came to Thessalonica on his second missionary journey after being beaten and jailed in Philippi and then miraculously released. With Paul came Timothy and Silas; it's likely that they left Luke in Philippi with the successful church there. In Thessalonica Paul spoke in the synagogue on at least three successive Sabbaths (17:2), arguing from Old Testament Scriptures that Jesus is the Messiah (17:3). Paul's arguments convinced not only some of the Jews in the synagogue, but also some God-fearing Greeks who attended and some important women from the community (17:4). That angered the rest of the Jews, who attacked the house where the evangelists were staying and tried to drag them to court (17:5). When the Jews couldn't find Paul, Timothy, and Silas, they instead took Jason, the owner of the house, and some other believers before the city rulers, saying, *"These people who have been turning the world upside down have come here also"* (17:6). They accused the Christians of promoting *"another king named Jesus"* (17:7). Under the cover of darkness, Paul, Timothy, and Silas escaped from Thessalonica to Beroea, where they again were favorably received in the local synagogue, until some of the Jews from Thessalonica appeared in Beroea and incited the people against the Christians. Paul left for Athens and then

Corinth, while Timothy and Silas stayed in Beroea (17:8-16).

Timothy and Silas later caught up with Paul in Corinth (18:5), bringing him a good report about the church in Thessalonica, but also saying the Thessalonians were worried about Paul not returning to see them. That prompted Paul to write a letter back to the church, our 1 Thessalonians. We can date the letter to Paul's first visit in Corinth, which was about A.D. 51. Many scholars have thus argued that 1 Thessalonians is the earliest letter of Paul's that we have in the Bible. In this letter Paul reviewed his initial reception in Thessalonica (1:2-10) and his continuing concern for the people there (2:1—3:13). Paul then repeated some teaching he had already given them on the return of Jesus (4:1—5:11) and how they should build up one another in their fellowship (5:12-22).

NOTES ON THE PRINTED TEXT

The *We* of 1 Thessalonians 1:2 refers to the senders of the letter, *Paul, Silvanus, and Timothy* (1:1). *Silvanus* is the Greek version of Silas, who is prominently featured with Paul on his second missionary journey. Silas was a leader in the Jerusalem church (Acts 15:22), a prophet (15:32), and a Roman citizen (16:37). Silas and Timothy both helped found the Thessalonian church (17:14). While these two are mentioned in the salutation of 1 Thessalonians, Paul is likely the main writer (see 2:18).

It was common in ancient letters to wish well being to the recipients of the epistle, but Paul more specifically says that *We always give thanks to God for all of you and mention you in our prayers* (1:2). The reason was the Thessalonians' *work of faith and labor of love and steadfastness of hope* (1:3). The praises Paul gave to the church were all the more remarkable when we remember that Paul was writing this probably just a few months after the founding of the church. Already he had heard from Timothy's report that the Thessalonians' new faith was showing itself in action, as faith should do (Jas. 2:17). One of those actions was their *labor of love* (1 Thess. 1:3), a phrase showing the energy they devoted to showing Christian love. Also, their hope was firmly placed in *our Lord Jesus Christ*, whose Gospel message they had heard and believed.

Paul, Silas, and Timothy had brought the Thessalonians that powerful message, and the three knew that the church had been *chosen* (1:4) by God for a special relationship with Him (see also Col. 3:12; 2 Thess. 2:13). Not only was this relationship evidenced in the faith, hope, and love of the church, but also the Holy Spirit had shown great *power* (1 Thess. 1:5) and brought *full conviction* when the church was started.

Of course, the Gospel message came to the Thessalonians through the words that Paul, Silas, and Timothy spoke, but it also came through the actions of the three: *the kind of persons we proved to be among you for your sake* (1:5). Actions always speak as loud as words, and the Thessalonians *became imitators* of Paul, Silas, and Timothy and, consequently, of *the Lord* Himself. Paul knew the church had a rough start, but despite persecution (1:6; 2:14; 3:3) from some in the community, the church had survived. The Holy Spirit had brought power to the preaching of the Gospel there, but He had also inspired *joy* (1:6) in those who received the message and persevered.

Any church with such a dynamic testimony draws attention, and therefore the Thessalonians were a well-known *example to all the believers in Macedonia and in Achaia* (1:7). Thessalonica was the capital of the northern Roman province of Macedonia, and Achaia was the southern province, which included Athens and Corinth. In other words, the whole region knew about this church, and those people outside of Thessalonica had made good reports about the congregation to Paul. *The word of the Lord [had] sounded forth* (1:8) from Thessalonica almost like a thunderclap, but in a quieter way people had also heard about Paul, Silas, and Timothy's warm *welcome* (1:9) there. The most compelling testimony of any church may be the one heard by word of mouth.

In the case of the Thessalonians, the testimony also showed how they *turned to God from idols, to serve a living and true God* (1:9). It is hard for us now to comprehend how dramatic it was for this group of Thessalonians to turn their back on their own culture. They could see snow-capped Mount Olympus, the supposed home of the Greek gods, some 50 miles south of them. But Zeus had not died for them and been *raised from the dead* (1:10) to save them. Jesus had. The dramatic change in the Thessalonians showed in three actions: they had turned from idols, they were serving God, and they were waiting for the return of Jesus, who would rescue them *from the wrath that is coming,* which God will pour out on the wicked at the end of the age.

Paul then reminded the Thessalonians about how he, Silas, and Timothy had tried to be good witnesses to them, and how much he wanted to come back to see them (2:1-20). However, instead of personally returning, the apostle had sent Timothy to find out firsthand how the church was doing (3:1-5). Timothy brought Paul good news of the Thessalonians' *faith and love* (3:6). That news had *encouraged* (3:7) Paul, especially during his own recent times of *distress and persecution* (probably in Beroea, Athens, and Corinth). How could these new Christians encourage Paul so much that he could hardly *thank God enough* (3:9) for them? It's because his life and witness was wrapped up in theirs. If they could *continue to stand firm in the Lord* (3:8), so could Paul. Even so, he would try to return to the church and teach them whatever was still *lacking* (3:10) in their faith so that they could be completely mature believers.

SUGGESTIONS TO TEACHERS

Three powerful words described the Thessalonian church: faith, love, and hope (1 Thess. 1:3). Those three qualities were so evident in the congregation that Paul himself was uplifted and encouraged by that young parish. Not only that, but also virtually the whole region, *every place* (1:8), had heard about this incredible body of believers. Their testimony should be the testimony of every church—and every believer—that wants to change the world for Christ. Here is a closer look at what the Thessalonian believers possessed that caught the attention of others and encouraged so many people.

1. A LIVING FAITH. The Thessalonians had no doubts about the Gospel, and they built their lives on it. Because of their faith, they could *stand firm in the Lord* (3:8). They did not doubt that Jesus had died and rose again to save them. They served a living God, not one of the dead idols at the temples they saw all around them. Is your faith rooted in a living, dynamic God, or in something else, such as a building or a long church history?

2. AN OUTREACHING LOVE. Faith is not complete until it is shared, and that's where love comes in. The Thessalonians loved God, but they also loved each other and those around them, even those who were persecuting them. That kind of love is not often seen, then or now. Would those around you, who know your church well, describe it as a "loving" church?

3. A FOREVER HOPE. Whenever the world turned against them, the Thessalonians remembered that this world was not their home. Jesus is coming again, and whatever happened, they could count on a home in heaven. This future focus kept them going when they felt discouraged and dismayed. Is your focus more on the temporary troubles of today or on the eternal promises of tomorrow?

FOR ADULTS

■ TOPIC: Encouraging Faith

■ QUESTIONS: 1. How often did Paul, Silas, and Timothy pray for the Thessalonians? 2. What kind of witnesses were the Thessalonians to others? 3. What kind of things did others say about the Thessalonians? 4. How did Paul receive encouragement from the Thessalonians? 5. How has someone been an encouragement to you during a difficult time in your life?

■ **ILLUSTRATIONS:**

Three Kinds of Faith. Evangelist D. L. Moody said that there are three kinds of faith in Christ: 1). *Struggling faith,* like a person in deep water desperately swimming; 2). *Clinging faith*, like a person hanging to the side of a boat; and, 3). *Resting faith*, like a person safely within the boat (and able to reach out with a hand to help someone else get in).

The Thessalonians had the third kind of faith. They were not only able to survive despite persecution, but they were also a shining example to other Christians throughout the region. They were even an encouragement to Paul during his own distress and persecution. By resting in God's hands and placing their faith in Him, the Thessalonians were able to "reach out their hands" to others, giving them hope, encouragement, and faith.

God Shaped. During the depression, Tom lost his job, his fortune, his wife, and his home, but he tenaciously held on to his faith—the only thing he had left.

One day Tom stopped to watch some men building a stone church. One of them was chiseling a triangular piece of rock. "What are you going to do with that?" asked Tom. The workman said, "Do you see that little opening way up there near the spire? Well, I'm shaping this down here so that it will fit up there."

Heart-broken, Tom walked away with his eyes filling with tears. It seemed that God had spoken through the workman to explain the ordeal through which he was passing. All of these awful circumstances of his life were teaching him the importance of looking to the Lord for help and strength. Tom realized that God had used a simple workman doing his everyday job to speak to his hurting heart.

Paul says that the Thessalonians were able to endure persecution because they believed the Gospel message he had shared with them. Besides believing this message, they also chose to demonstrate their faith by standing firm in the Lord. God "shaped" them to be examples of encouraging faith to everyone who knew them or heard about them.

The Faithful Nobodies. Author and pastor Chuck Swindoll encourages people to take this quiz about famous Christians:

1. Who taught Martin Luther his theology and inspired his translation of the New Testament?

2. Who financed William Carey's ministry in India?

3. Who was the elderly woman who prayed faithfully for Billy Graham for over 20 years?

4. Who helped Charles Wesley get underway as a composer of hymns?

5. Who was the wife of Charles Haddon Spurgeon?

How did you do? Did you get at least two right? Only one? None? Before you excuse your inability to answer the questions, stop and think. Had it not been for those unknown people who faithfully did what the Lord led them to do—those "nobodies"—a huge chunk of church history would be missing.

While we don't know the specific names of any of the Thessalonians either, their record of enduring and encouraging faith has inspired untold numbers of Christians through the centuries.

FOR YOUTH

■ **TOPIC:** Get the Message?

■ **QUESTIONS:** 1. How can you tell that Paul, Silas, and Timothy loved the Thessalonian believers? 2. What did the Thessalonians learn from Paul, Silas, and Timothy? 3. How were the Thessalonians a good Christian example to others? 4. What did Timothy say that concerned the Thessalonians about Paul? 5. What people in your life regularly pray for you or want the best for you?

A Grocery Store Blessing. Sarah was busily doing her weekly food shopping in a crowded, noisy grocery store. However, she noticed that she regularly crossed paths with an elderly gentleman in a wheelchair, with only a few necessities in his basket, throughout the store.

When Sarah finally made it to the checkout counter, the elderly gentleman was in the next line over. She had almost finished getting checked out, when all other noise in the store seemed very distant to her. She heard clearly the clerk in the next aisle tell the elderly gentleman that he was $8.32 short of having enough money for his groceries, and they were trying to decide what he could put back. Sarah quickly told her clerk to tell the other that she would pay the difference for the gentleman's groceries. Not only was the elderly gentleman touched by Sarah's kindness, the clerks could not believe Sarah would be so generous. In fact, Sarah's clerk began to cry. She simply could not believe that Sarah would do this for someone she did not know personally.

Sarah felt she was only being obedient to what the Spirit's message had been in her heart. She merely had taken the opportunity the Lord had provided for her to help another. She was not only used by God to bless the elderly gentlemen, but also the clerks, who were so amazed at her unselfish act of kindness. Just by doing what she knew God wanted her to do, she became a positive example of the Gospel in action to so many in the store. Beyond that, she said she got that "good deep down feeling" that she would have missed out on if she hadn't given a few dollars to help out the elderly gentleman.

What a lesson for each of us! Not only should we be open to God's leading, but we also should be open to act upon it.

A Message from God. Have you noticed those billboards, church marquees, and even key chains that have messages from God on them? A couple of years ago a Fort Lauderdale, Florida, advertising agency created a billboard campaign that promoted being sensitive to God's messages. Since then some of these messages have cropped up in many towns and cities around our country:

"Let's meet at My House . . . Sunday, before the game." —God
"That 'Love Thy Neighbor' thing—I meant it!" —God
"What part of 'Thou shalt not' didn't you understand?" —God
"We need to talk." —God

Even without billboards, God is trying to communicate with us. He wants us to know that He loves us, but more than that, He wants us to realize that our actions, or lack of actions, are an example to everyone around us. In a way we are our own "billboards" to everyone we come in contact with. The actions and words of the Thessalonians communicated God's love to the whole country. How well are you communicating?

A Sad Parable. Fred Somebody, Thomas Everybody, Peter Anybody, and Joe Nobody were neighbors. All four belonged to the same church. Sadly, though, none of them took their membership seriously.

Everybody went fishing on Sunday or stayed home to sleep. Anybody wanted to worship, but was afraid Somebody would talk badly about him behind his back. So only one went to church. Nobody. In addition, Nobody did all the visitation, and any other need that came up.

One time the church was looking for a Sunday school teacher. Everybody thought Anybody would do it, and Anybody thought Somebody would do it. There was only one who would do it: Nobody!

Then a new person (a non-believer) moved into their neighborhood. Everybody thought Somebody should try to share Christ with him. Anybody could have made an effort, but the only one who finally did was Nobody!

The Thessalonians did not wait for someone else to speak the message of Christ. They were willing and eager to share the Good News with others, and it showed.

COMING OF THE LORD

BACKGROUND SCRIPTURE: 1 Thessalonians 4—5
DEVOTIONAL READING: 1 Thessalonians 5:12-24

KEY VERSE: God has destined us not for wrath but for obtaining salvation through our Lord Jesus Christ. 1 Thessalonians 5:9.

KING JAMES VERSION

1 THESSALONIANS 4:13 But I would not have you to be ignorant, brethren, concerning them which are asleep, that ye sorrow not, even as others which have no hope.

14 For if we believe that Jesus died and rose again, even so them also which sleep in Jesus will God bring with him.

15 For this we say unto you by the word of the Lord, that we which are alive and remain unto the coming of the Lord shall not prevent them which are asleep.

16 For the Lord himself shall descend from heaven with a shout, with the voice of the archangel, and with the trump of God: and the dead in Christ shall rise first:

17 Then we which are alive and remain shall be caught up together with them in the clouds, to meet the Lord in the air: and so shall we ever be with the Lord.

18 Wherefore comfort one another with these words. . . .

5:2 For yourselves know perfectly that the day of the Lord so cometh as a thief in the night.

3 For when they shall say, Peace and safety; then sudden destruction cometh upon them, as travail upon a woman with child; and they shall not escape.

4 But ye, brethren, are not in darkness, that that day should overtake you as a thief.

5 Ye are all the children of light, and the children of the day: we are not of the night, nor of darkness.

6 Therefore let us not sleep, as do others; but let us watch and be sober.

7 For they that sleep sleep in the night; and they that be drunken are drunken in the night.

8 But let us, who are of the day, be sober, putting on the breastplate of faith and love; and for an helmet, the hope of salvation.

9 For God hath not appointed us to wrath, but to obtain salvation by our Lord Jesus Christ,

10 Who died for us, that, whether we wake or sleep, we should live together with him.

11 Wherefore comfort yourselves together, and edify one another, even as also ye do.

NEW REVISED STANDARD VERSION

1 THESSALONIANS 4:13 But we do not want you to be uninformed, brothers and sisters, about those who have died, so that you may not grieve as others do who have no hope. 14 For since we believe that Jesus died and rose again, even so, through Jesus, God will bring with him those who have died. 15 For this we declare to you by the word of the Lord, that we who are alive, who are left until the coming of the Lord, will by no means precede those who have died. 16 For the Lord himself, with a cry of command, with the archangel's call and with the sound of God's trumpet, will descend from heaven, and the dead in Christ will rise first. 17 Then we who are alive, who are left, will be caught up in the clouds together with them to meet the Lord in the air; and so we will be with the Lord forever. 18 Therefore encourage one another with these words. . . .

5:2 For you yourselves know very well that the day of the Lord will come like a thief in the night. 3 When they say, "There is peace and security," then sudden destruction will come upon them, as labor pains come upon a pregnant woman, and there will be no escape! 4 But you, beloved, are not in darkness, for that day to surprise you like a thief; 5 for you are all children of light and children of the day; we are not of the night or of darkness. 6 So then let us not fall asleep as others do, but let us keep awake and be sober; 7 for those who sleep sleep at night, and those who are drunk get drunk at night. 8 But since we belong to the day, let us be sober, and put on the breastplate of faith and love, and for a helmet the hope of salvation. 9 For God has destined us not for wrath but for obtaining salvation through our Lord Jesus Christ, 10 who died for us, so that whether we are awake or asleep we may live with him. 11 Therefore encourage one another and build up each other, as indeed you are doing.

8

Monday, April 19	1 Thessalonians 4:1-7	*Live to Please God*
Tuesday, April 20	1 Thessalonians 4:8-12	*Live Quietly*
Wednesday, April 21	1 Thessalonians 4:13-18	*The Lord Will Return*
Thursday, April 22	1 Thessalonians 5:1-5	*He Will Come as a Thief*
Friday, April 23	1 Thessalonians 5:6-11	*Be Alert*
Saturday, April 24	1 Thessalonians 5:12-18	*Encourage the Fainthearted*
Sunday, April 25	1 Thessalonians 5:19-28	*Prayer for Blamelessness at Christ's Coming*

BACKGROUND

While the Thessalonian church was an inspiration and encouragement to Paul, he still had three major concerns for them. One was that they could endure the persecutions that they faced on a regular basis (1 Thess. 3:2-5). The second concern was that they would keep Christian morals, especially abstaining from the sexual immorality that was a part of their culture (4:1-8). Finally, they were confused about the subject of Jesus' return, especially when He was coming. And what happened if believers died before He came (4:13—5:11)?

The Thessalonians had some of the same concerns Christians still have. What happens to people when they die? Will we see them again? What will happen to people who are still here when Jesus returns? Paul likely had taught the Thessalonians what Jesus Himself said: He could come at any time. Paul's wording in his letter makes it highly doubtful that he gave them any precise timetable for Christ's return (5:2).

Some of the Thessalonians, however, may have quit working in expectation of Jesus' imminent return (5:14). To set the record straight for the idlers, and to encourage those who had lost loved ones, Paul repeated some of the truths he had already taught, and he added some other instructions, perhaps in answer to direct questions Timothy had brought him. The issues were so important to the Thessalonians that Paul addressed them again in his second letter to the church.

What is the importance of even discussing Jesus' return? We do not know when it will occur, and Christians have embarrassed themselves through the centuries by announcing specific times and places. More than one generation of Christians has believed that Jesus just had to come in their lifetime, only to be proven wrong.

Paul, in his lifetime, did not witness Christ's return; however, Paul knew that the certainty of Jesus' return undergirds the Christian faith with a unique hope. The apostle specifically separated the Thessalonian believers from those living around them, namely, those *who have no hope* (4:13). Some of the Egyptian cults of Paul's day were popular because they promised an afterlife. Most people had an idea of a shadowy afterlife, but they generally did not see the afterlife in a positive way, and they had no concept of the resurrection of the dead. For many people, death was simply the end. As a popular Roman tomb inscription said: "I was not; I was; I am not; I care not." Therefore, intense grief and mourning seemed appropriate, for that person would never be seen by friends or loved ones again. Many ancient cultures had extensive mourning rituals.

That was not how Christians should view life and death. Jesus had conquered death, and those who believed in Him would conquer death as well, whether they died before His return or were alive at the time of His return. *So that whether we are awake or asleep* (5:10) when we meet Jesus, we have the certainty of living forever with Him.

NOTES ON THE PRINTED TEXT

The problem the Thessalonians seemed most concerned about was whether believers who had recently died would miss out on the benefits of the resurrection of the dead. Paul did not want them *to be uninformed* (1 Thess. 4:13)—that is, in the dark—about such matters, because they had a *hope* that non-Christians did not have. Paul did forbid his readers from grieving; that was not his point. While we may celebrate at a Christian funeral, we do so through the tears of personal sorrow. But since Christians *believe that Jesus died and rose again* (4:14), *through Jesus* we know that we have an eternal home and future.

Like many first-century Jews, Paul would have believed that the soul lived in heaven after death until *the resurrection on the last day* (John 11:24). The soul and body would be reunited at the resurrection, as Paul told the Corinthians (2 Cor. 5:1-10). Paul had *the word of the Lord* (1 Thess. 4:15) on how the resurrection of the dead would take place. We know from the Gospels and Acts (Matt. 24:30-31; Mark 13:24-37; Luke 21:27; Acts 1:11) that Jesus said He *will descend from heaven* (1 Thess. 4:16) at His return. Further, Paul said that *we who are alive, who are left until the coming of the Lord* (4:15) will not be taken by Jesus ahead of *those who have died*. The Greek word Paul used for *coming of the Lord* is *parousia*, which was a term for the official visit of a king or royal dignitary. The *cry of command* (4:16), *the archangel's call,* and *the sound of God's trumpet* are all part of the irresistible summons of the Lord to His people. They are linked to Old Testament imagery of the mighty God who will defeat His enemies and reign over the earth (Isa. 27:13; 42:13; Joel 2:1; Amos 2:2; Zech. 9:14; 14:3-4).

At Jesus' return, the Thessalonians would be encouraged to know that *the dead in Christ will rise first* (1 Thess. 4:16). After that, *we who are alive, who are left, will be caught up in the clouds together with them* (4:17). That Paul mentions himself in the present tense has caused some to say that Paul believed he would live to see Jesus' return, but that does not take into account the rest of Paul's comments about not knowing the time of the Lord's return. Paul simply emphasized to the Thessalonians (and in turn to us) that since he was still alive, he could, at any time, physically see the Lord's return, and therefore he must be prepared to meet Jesus. To be *caught up . . . together* with Jesus translates the Greek verb *harpazo* ("to snatch"), which in Latin is *rapere,* the word from which some Christians have derived the term Rapture. The *clouds* are a symbol in the Bible for the presence of God—for example, on Mount Sinai, in the tabernacle, and at Jesus' baptism, transfiguration, and ascension.

Paul's description of Jesus' return ended with the ultimate words of comfort: *we will be with the Lord forever.* The apostle had given his readers enough eternal hope—Jesus' return and their resurrection and reunion—that the Thessalonians could indeed *encourage one another with these words* (4:18).

Paul had already told the church not to speculate on *times* (5:1; particular dates) or *seasons* (certain conditions) of the Lord's return. Rather, *the day of the Lord will come like a thief in the night* (5:2), when people least expect Him. The day of the Lord is an Old Testament concept (Isa. 2:9-19; Amos 5:18-20) referring to a time when the Lord comes in judgment. In 1 Thessalonians it is at the end of the age. In a sense, the day of the Lord that Paul was describing began with Jesus' first coming and will end when He comes again, for at that time all His blessings and promises will be fulfilled.

Since we do not know the exact date and time, we must beware of people who say *"There is peace and security"* (5:3). The Roman emperors promised peace and security in the inscriptions on their coins, but not for eternity. Christians know Jesus will return, just as a pregnant woman knows that she will have a baby, but the *labor pains* still start unexpectedly.

In a series of metaphors, Paul urged the Thessalonians to be watchful and ready, the *children of light* (5:5) and *the day* and not of the *darkness* (5:4). The thief comes in the night, when people *asleep* (5:6) and get *drunk* (5:7), but Christians are to be *sober* (5:8) and ready, like soldiers on guard, as implied by *the breastplate of faith and love* and the *helmet* of the *hope of salvation.* Those who trust in Christ should not be involved in the darkness of this world, which brings God's *wrath* (5:9), but instead look forward to living *with him* (5:10), regardless of whether His return comes while we are awake or asleep. Faith, love, and hope were qualities Paul had already said the Thessalonians had. Therefore, they already had a good start on *encourag[ing] one another* (5:11) until Jesus' return.

SUGGESTIONS TO TEACHERS

Some Christians believe we are living in the "last days," and there is considerable false teaching about this topic. Therefore, Paul's message to the Thessalonians is one we need to hear clearly today. We do not need to speculate *concerning the times and the seasons* (1 Thess. 5:1) of Jesus' return, but we certainly need to *keep awake and be sober* (5:6), that is, be ready at all times for His coming, whenever it may be. How can we be ready? Some of the same things we do to get ready for a trip apply to being ready for Jesus' return.

1. BE FISCALLY READY. We look at our finances before a trip to be certain we have the money we need and have made the proper financial arrangements. In a similar way, we are to give to God that which is God's to support His work here until Jesus comes. Jesus said that where our treasure is, that's where our heart will be too (Matt. 6:21).

2. BE PHYSICALLY READY. For a trip there is usually the physical preparation of packing. While we cannot "pack" for our trip to heaven, physically we should always be aware of who we are with and what we are doing in light of Jesus' return. In other words, if Jesus came today, would there be things I do now I wouldn't want Him to find me doing? Am I being His witness to those around me, or would they never guess I'm a Christian by my words and actions?

3. BE EMOTIONALLY READY. Trips can be emotional experiences, something you are either "up" for or not. As a Christian, would your emotions at this time say, "This world is not my home," or "I am both in the world and of the world. I'm too tied to things here to even think about leaving"?

4. BE SPIRITUALLY READY. You may pray before a trip, asking God to watch over your travels. Of course, you first need *salvation through our Lord Jesus Christ* (1 Thess. 5:9) for your final, heavenly trip; but beyond that, like the Thessalonians, is your life characterized right now by faith, love, and hope? Paul finished chapter 5 with a virtual checklist of "spiritual" things we should all be doing every day as we wait for Jesus to return. That should be our checklist as well.

FOR ADULTS

■ TOPIC: Getting Ready

■ QUESTIONS: 1. What did Paul want the Thessalonians to be informed about? 2. What will happen to Christians who have already died when Jesus comes again? 3. What will happen to Christians who are still alive when Jesus returns? 4. How should Christians act as they wait for Jesus' return? 5. If you are preparing yourself for Jesus' return, what are you doing?

■ **ILLUSTRATIONS:**

Wait and Watch. The Lord has given special commendation to those who not only *wait* for His return, but also earnestly *watch* for Him. The difference between these terms can be illustrated by the story of a fishing vessel returning home after many days at sea. As they neared the shore, the sailors eagerly watched the dock where a group of their loved ones had gathered. The skipper looked through his binoculars and identified some of the wives he saw waiting there.

One man became concerned because his wife was not on the dock. Later, he left the boat sadly and trudged up the hill to his home. As he opened the door, his wife ran to meet him saying, "I have been waiting for you!" Quietly, he replied, "Yes, but the other men's wives were watching for them." While this man's wife obviously loved him, she had not been actively watching for his homecoming as he had hoped.

In the same way, sometimes I am so anxious for my husband to return home from work, I find myself walking to the front door several times to check and see if he has turned up the street toward home. Other times I am surprised by him suddenly walking in the door. Though I knew he would be coming, I had gotten preoccupied with other things—which at the time I thought were important. That is what happens when we fail to be ready for Jesus to return at any time; this is not a good time to be "surprised."

Ready or Not. The wreckage of the luxury liner *Titanic,* thought to have been "unsinkable," now rests 13,120 feet down on the Atlantic Ocean floor. In its day, the *Titanic* was the world's largest ship, weighing over 46 tons, being 882 feet long, and rising 11 stories high. The vessel employed a crew and staff of almost 1,000 and could carry nearly 2,500 passengers. The ship was ready for its passengers with a complete gymnasium, heated pool, squash court, and the first miniature golf course.

Even for all the elegant and luxurious extras this ship had, it still lacked some basic equipment needed for survival if something "unthinkable" happened. It was short the needed number of lifeboats for all of its passengers and crew, and on its first voyage it was short a simple pair of binoculars needed for the lookouts to spot icebergs. On its first trip, the ship received at least seven warnings about dangerous icebergs in its path; however, the captain and others were more concerned with getting to America in record time instead of watching out for the safety of the ship and its passengers.

The night of April 14, 1912, the "unthinkable" happened to the "unsinkable." Near midnight, the great *Titanic* struck an iceberg, ripping a 300 foot hole through 5 of its 16 watertight compartments. It sank in 2 1/2 hours, killing 1,513 people.

Sometimes we act as if Jesus is never coming back, despite the knowledge that He is. The *Titanic* supplies a lesson for us all. If the people in charge would have been more watchful and more diligent in doing the right things, many lives would have been saved, and possibly the entire ship would have made it to its destination on time. Jesus wants us to be ready and expectantly waiting for what He will bring us today or tomorrow.

Now Instead of Later. President John F. Kennedy once said, "The time to repair the roof is when the sun is shining." My grandfather said somewhat the same thing when he told me, "The time to shut the barn door is not after the cow is already gone." The time to get ready for Jesus to come is not when He has returned. Now is the time to get ready for Jesus. We all need to be doing things every day to help us prepare to meet Him, whether that meeting is at the Second Coming or when we die. Don't put off reading your Bible, or saying your prayers, or talking to someone who is lonely, or sharing the Gospel with someone who is lost. Every day we can be getting ready to meet Jesus, in small and big ways.

<table>
<tr><td>

FOR YOUTH

</td><td>

■ **TOPIC:** It's Your Life!

■ **QUESTIONS:** 1. Who will Jesus bring with Him when He returns?
2. How will we know that it is Jesus when He returns? 3. First

</td></tr>
</table>

Thessalonians 5:2 says that Jesus will come *like a thief in the night*. What does that mean? 4. What should you tell someone who says that Jesus is coming back soon? 5. What is one thing you are currently doing that tells others you are ready for Jesus to come back?

■ **ILLUSTRATIONS:**

I Can Sleep. A young man applied for a job as a farmhand. When the farmer asked for his qualifications, the young man said, "I can sleep when the wind blows." This puzzled the farmer, but he took a liking to the young man and hired him. A few days later, the farmer and his wife were awakened in the night by a violent storm. They quickly began to check things out to see if all was secure. They found that the shutters of the farmhouse had been securely fastened. A good supply of logs had been set next to the fireplace. The farm implements had been safely placed in the storage shed. The tractor had been moved into the garage. The barn had been properly locked. All was well. Even the animals were calm. It was then that the farmer grasped the meaning of the young man's words: "I can sleep when the wind blows." Because the farmhand had performed his work loyally and faithfully when the skies were clear, he was prepared for the storm when it broke. Consequently, when the wind blew, he had no fear. He was able to sleep in peace.

This is your life. You need to live it in order to be ready to meet your daily responsibilities and obligations. And as a Christian, one of your responsibilities is to be ready to meet Jesus. Do those things that the Lord asks of you so that you too may sleep in peace.

"Fish" for Life. A young boy stood idly on a bridge watching some fishermen. Seeing one of them with a basket full of fish, he said, "If I had a catch like that, I'd be happy."

"I'll give you that many fish if you do a small favor for me," said the fisherman. "I need you to tend this line a while. I've got some business down the street."

The young boy gladly accepted the offer. After the man left, the trout and bass continued snapping greedily at the baited hook. Soon the boy forgot everything else, and was excitedly pulling in a large number of fish. When the fisherman returned, he said to the young boy, "I'll keep my promise to you by giving you everything you've caught. And I hope you've learned a lesson. You mustn't waste time daydreaming and merely wishing for things. Instead, get busy and cast in a line for yourself."

This young boy made the most of his time, not realizing that he was really going to benefit the most from the amount of energy he put into catching the fish. He could have just as easily put out only enough effort to catch one or two fish. It's your life. What you get out of it depends greatly on what you put into it. As you think about being prepared for the Second Coming of Christ, "fish" as if your heavenly reward depends on it.

Stay Awake. Eight-year-old Peter Sweeney of Rockville Centre, New York, wrote a get-well letter to President Reagan after the President had been shot. Mr. Reagan decided to use the letter in the middle of an economic address to a joint session of Congress, which was being televised. Sadly, Peter was in bed asleep when the speech was broadcast. Peter slept through his big moment and had to be told about it the next day.

How many significant moments do we lose because we are asleep spiritually? Paul urged the Thessalonians to stay awake. He wanted them to be about the Lord's business at all times, for no one knows when the Lord will return. Paul wanted everyone's life to reflect his or her love of the Lord. As you live your life, remember to stay awake and make the most of the opportunities the Lord gives you.

CHOSEN TO OBTAIN GLORY

BACKGROUND SCRIPTURE: 2 Thessalonians 1—3
DEVOTIONAL READING: Ephesians 1:3-14

KEY VERSE: But we must always give thanks to God for you, brothers and sisters beloved by the Lord, because God chose you as the first fruits for salvation through sanctification by the Spirit and through belief in the truth. 2 Thessalonians 2:13.

KING JAMES VERSION

2 THESSALONIANS 1:3 We are bound to thank God always for you, brethren, as it is meet, because that your faith groweth exceedingly, and the charity of every one of you all toward each other aboundeth; 4 So that we ourselves glory in you in the churches of God for your patience and faith in all your persecutions and tribulations that ye endure: . . .

11 Wherefore also we pray always for you, that our God would count you worthy of this calling, and fulfil all the good pleasure of his goodness, and the work of faith with power: 12 That the name of our Lord Jesus Christ may be glorified in you, and ye in him, according to the grace of our God and the Lord Jesus Christ. . . .

2:13 But we are bound to give thanks alway to God for you, brethren beloved of the Lord, because God hath from the beginning chosen you to salvation through sanctification of the Spirit and belief of the truth: 14 Whereunto he called you by our gospel, to the obtaining of the glory of our Lord Jesus Christ. 15 Therefore, brethren, stand fast, and hold the traditions which ye have been taught, whether by word, or our epistle.

16 Now our Lord Jesus Christ himself, and God, even our Father, which hath loved us, and hath given us everlasting consolation and good hope through grace, 17 Comfort your hearts, and stablish you in every good word and work.

3:1 Finally, brethren, pray for us, that the word of the Lord may have free course, and be glorified, even as it is with you: 2 And that we may be delivered from unreasonable and wicked men: for all men have not faith. 3 But the Lord is faithful, who shall stablish you, and keep you from evil. 4 And we have confidence in the Lord touching you, that ye both do and will do the things which we command you.

NEW REVISED STANDARD VERSION

2 THESSALONIANS 1:3 We must always give thanks to God for you, brothers and sisters, as is right, because your faith is growing abundantly, and the love of everyone of you for one another is increasing. 4 Therefore we ourselves boast of you among the churches of God for your steadfastness and faith during all your persecutions and the afflictions that you are enduring. . . .

11 To this end we always pray for you, asking that our God will make you worthy of his call and will fulfill by his power every good resolve and work of faith, 12 so that the name of our Lord Jesus may be glorified in you, and you in him, according to the grace of our God and the Lord Jesus Christ. . . .

2:13 But we must always give thanks to God for you, brothers and sisters beloved by the Lord, because God chose you as the first fruits for salvation through sanctification by the Spirit and through belief in the truth. 14 For this purpose he called you through our proclamation of the good news, so that you may obtain the glory of our Lord Jesus Christ. 15 So then, brothers and sisters, stand firm and hold fast to the traditions that you were taught by us, either by word of mouth or by our letter.

16 Now may our Lord Jesus Christ himself and God our Father, who loved us and through grace gave us eternal comfort and good hope, 17 comfort your hearts and strengthen them in every good work and word.

3:1 Finally, brothers and sisters, pray for us, so that the word of the Lord may spread rapidly and be glorified everywhere, just as it is among you, 2 and that we may be rescued from wicked and evil people; for not all have faith. 3 But the Lord is faithful; he will strengthen you and guard you from the evil one. 4 And we have confidence in the Lord concerning you, that you are doing and will go on doing the things that we command.

9

HOME BIBLE READINGS

BACKGROUND

Perhaps a few weeks or a few months after Paul and his companions wrote their first letter to the Thessalonians, they wrote a second letter. The same senders are listed—*Paul, Silvanus, and Timothy* (2 Thess. 1:1)—as in the first letter, and the greeting *to the church of the Thessalonians in God our Father and the Lord Jesus Christ* is virtually the same as in 1 Thessalonians. This has led some commentators to suggest that someone besides Paul wrote the letter, using the first as a model and borrowing Paul's name and reputation to deal with a crisis that occurred in this church (or another church) some time after Paul's death. They also point to supposed differences in the theology of the Second Coming in the two letters. In the first letter, Jesus is coming as *a thief in the night* (1 Thess. 5:2), so that no one knows when He could come. However, in the second letter Paul specifically says that Jesus *will not come unless the rebellion comes first and the lawless one is revealed* (2 Thess. 2:3). Therefore, these commentators argue, while the first letter seems to say that the Second Coming could occur at any time, the second letter says it cannot happen at just any moment.

It seems more logical to say, however, that 2 Thessalonians is addressing the same subject as the first letter, but in a different way. Paul had tried to impress upon the church that Jesus could come at any time and that the believers should be faithfully and obediently watching for His return; nevertheless, either from what Paul said or from what some other *word* (2:2) or *letter* said, the Thessalonians were convinced *that the day of the Lord is already here*. Paul then reminded them about truths he had told them when he was still with them that should have shown them how Christ could not possibly have come yet (2:5).

It may be that increasing persecution in the Thessalonian church had convinced the believers that Jesus must be coming soon. Persecutions and struggles were seen as signs of the end of the age (see, for example, Mark 13:19-27), so it would be not be unusual for the congregation to think that the end must be at hand.

The Thessalonians may have been asking questions about their ordeal such as why they were suffering so much. Paul did more than just encourage them with this letter. He showed them "the big picture": *This is evidence of the righteous judgment of God, and is intended to make you worthy of the kingdom of God, for which you are also suffering* (2 Thess. 1:5). God is in control of history, and ultimately His justice will prevail, no matter what we may see or believe at any given time. In fact, the Lord had specifically chosen the Thessalonians *as the first fruits for salvation* (2:13) because they had accepted and believed the Gospel. Paul himself knew about persecution for the sake of the Gospel, but he also knew that the Lord is faithful and will watch over His people.

NOTES ON THE PRINTED TEXT

Paul had given thanks for the Thessalonians in his first letter, and here again he praised them because *your faith is growing abundantly, and the love of everyone of you for one another is increasing* (2 Thess. 1:3). Paul had prayed in his first letter that the Thessalonians would *increase and abound in love for one another and for all* (1 Thess. 3:12), and that was happening. In fact, the verbs Paul used in 2 Thessalonians 1:3 picture their faith *growing* like a healthy, luxurious plant and their love *increasing* like water flooding over a field. This is how faith and love should always be—expanding, not static, the natural byproduct of a growing relationship with the Lord.

Because of the Thessalonians' increasing faith and love, Paul could happily *boast* about them *among the churches* (1:4), the kind of boasting that encourages but is not prideful. The Thessalonians' faith and love have been especially evident during all of the *persecutions* and *afflictions* that the congregation had been *enduring*. They had "steadfast-faith"; the two words are treated as one concept in the Greek. That was the only way the church could endure its trials.

Paul reiterated that he *always* (1:11) remembered the Thessalonians in his prayers, especially as he thought about the future glorification of Christ in His people. The Thessalonians would not be separated from God as the nonbelievers would be at the final judgment (1:6-10); instead Paul prayed that they would be found *worthy of his call* (1:11). Believers do not accumulate worth and thereby merit God's favor. Rather, as Paul told the Ephesians, we are to *lead a life worthy of the calling* (Eph. 4:1) that God has on our lives. Paul also prayed that the Thessalonians, by God's power, would *fulfill . . . every good resolve and work of faith* (2 Thess. 1:11). Every work of faith comes out of a life of faith and is carried to completion through faith. Paul would not have to say to the Thessalonians what he said to the Galatians: *You were running well; who prevented you from obeying the truth?* (Gal. 5:7).

The purpose of completing these works of faith was not for the Thessalonians' glory but *that the name of our Lord Jesus* (2 Thess. 1:12) would be *glorified* in the Thessalonians. God will be glorified in His obedient people in the present, but ultimately He will be glorified at the last day (1:10). *Grace* (1:12) and glory go together; you cannot have one without the other. Grace is the standard for measuring glory. In fact, it is only by God's grace that we can receive glory at all, though ultimately we will throw our crowns of glory at His feet before His throne (Rev. 4:9-10).

After describing what will happen to the world when the man of lawlessness comes prior to Christ's return (2 Thess. 2:1-12), Paul repeated his words from the opening of the letter: *We must always give thanks to God for you* (2:13). Paul then returned to the idea from the first letter that God *chose* the Thessalonians for His purposes (1 Thess. 1:4-5). That implies a special relationship with God, much as Israel had in the Old Testament (see Isa. 41:8-10). Paul defined God's purposes in two steps: first, God chose the Thessalonians through the sanctification of the *Spirit* (2 Thess. 2:13), then He called them through their hearing of the Gospel to share in Christ's glory (2:14). In other words, the Spirit works, and people believe. When they believe, they can participate in Christ's glory.

Paul encouraged the Thessalonians to *stand firm and hold fast to the traditions that you were taught by us* (2:15). Since the New Testament had not yet been written, it was very important for the early church to remember what the apostles said. Another word for *traditions* could be "teachings." These apostolic truths are worth holding fast to during the storms of persecution.

After exhorting the Thessalonians to stand firm, Paul then prayed for them, asking the *Lord Jesus Christ* (2:16) and *God our Father* to give the church *comfort* and *good hope*. It is worth noting that Paul not only talked about Jesus and the Father together as one (together they give *eternal comfort and good hope*), but the apostle also put Jesus first. The *good hope* we will have until Jesus' return, but the *comfort* will last into eternity because Christ is eternal. The Thessalonians' inner strength would overflow into good works and words (2:17).

Paul had prayed for the Thessalonians, but he also asked them for prayer for himself and the others with him. These missionaries must spread the *word of the Lord* (3:1) as effectively to others as they had to the Thessalonians. The missionaries would encounter people just as *wicked and evil* (3:2) as those who were persecuting the Thessalonians. Paul had already said that Satan was hard at work in the world, using *all power, signs, lying wonders, and every kind of wicked deception* (2:9-10) to keep the Good News from spreading. But the Thessalonians had a faithful Lord who would strengthen and protect them from Satan's schemes (3:3). Therefore, Paul had *confidence in the Lord* (3:4) that He would guide the congregation through the troubles it was enduring, and it would continue to be a beacon of the Gospel in a hostile world.

SUGGESTIONS TO TEACHERS

The glory of God is not a subject overly familiar to most Christians. Further, many Christians would not immediately associate themselves with God's glory in any way; yet this is part of what Paul taught the Thessalonians. Those whom God has chosen, those who believe the Gospel message, will *obtain the glory of our Lord Jesus Christ* (2 Thess. 2:14). Glory, as Paul described it to the Thessalonians, has three aspects.

1. GLORY TO JESUS' NAME. Like the Thessalonians, we should bring glory to Jesus and His name through the positive witness of our lives. If we do, others will notice. The steadfastness and faith that the Thessalonians showed should be characteristic of all believers and their churches. What is our congregational and individual witness to others right now?

2. GLORY TO JESUS' PEOPLE. At the end of the age, we will be glorified. That is a reason to have hope. The Thessalonians endured all varieties of hardships and persecutions because they knew they would one day receive the glory of our Lord Jesus Christ. How often do we forget our glorious future and focus on our troubles now, so much so that our witness suffers?

3. GLORY TO JESUS' MESSAGE. As the Gospel message spreads, it is received and honored by those who accept it. The Gospel is glorified when it is accepted by true faith, so that in a sense it then "crowns" the lives of believers. That is what happened with the believers in Thessalonica, Paul said, and it can happen elsewhere. Do we still see the glory of the Gospel, or has it become so familiar that it has lost its "luster" for us? A message we no longer value is one we are less likely to share as much as we need to. After all, what person does *not* need the Gospel?

FOR ADULTS

■ **TOPIC:** Reflecting the Glory

■ **QUESTIONS:** 1. Why did Paul boast about the Thessalonians among the other churches? 2. How would the Thessalonians glorify the name of God? 3. For what did God choose the Thessalonians? 4. Why did Paul and the other missionaries need the Thessalonians' prayers? 5. In what ways does your life reflect God's glory?

■ **ILLUSTRATIONS:**

Seeing the Big Picture. Three people were part of a construction crew working on a large building project. A passerby asked each, "What are you doing?" "I'm mixing mortar," one said. Another said, "I'm helping put up this big stone wall." The third person responded, "I'm building a cathedral to the glory of God."

Those on the construction crew could just as well have been working in a factory, managing a retail store, or doing any one of a variety of jobs. Most people work to earn a living so they can provide for themselves and their families, and be successful. However, these reasons should not be the only ones for why Christians work. Like the third person in our story, we need to see that what gives work eternal value is not the product or service, but doing the job faithfully to the glory of the Lord. God's glory can not only be reflected in what we do, but also how we do it.

Seeing the Person Within. When I was in high school, I was shy and usually not noticed. However, I had a sophomore English teacher, Miss Lowe, who made me feel noticed and appreciated. She took the time to get to know me by asking me to be her student assistant. During those times when we were working together, she shared about herself and her Christian faith, knowing I was a new Christian. I have always been thankful that she helped me become more confident and open. By the next school year I became more self-assured and more involved in school activities. I even was elected president of one of the school's clubs. Now, looking back at those days, I can see how Miss Lowe successfully reflected God to not only me, but also to the rest of her students. Though she did not talk about God in class, her students certainly saw His reflection in her speech and actions.

Seeing a New Life. Carl had led a hard life. After his wife left him, his drinking became worse and began to consume his life. He thought there was no more reason for living, but in his time of desperation he turned to God. Carl prayed for God to intervene in some way in his life, and God led him to a church with loving people. Carl was not sure that God or the people in the church would accept him and help him, but they did. A few years later, Carl was a changed man. While not everyone in town would forget his past, he allowed God to help him clean up, and he allowed others to teach him about repentance, forgiveness, and unconditional love. By the time my husband and I met him, he had become someone people looked up to and admired. He reflected what it means to have a new life in Christ. Without his past, he never would have shone so brightly. Carl reminds us of a poem by J. Sidlow Baxter:

What God chooses, He cleanses.
What God cleanses, He molds.
What God molds, He fills.
What God fills, He uses.

FOR YOUTH

■ **TOPIC:** Steadfast Faith

■ **QUESTIONS:** 1. What did the Thessalonian church have to endure? 2. In what ways would the Thessalonians be a part of God's glory? 3. How were the Thessalonians able to stay steadfast in their faith? 4. Why did Paul have confidence in the Thessalonians? 5. What makes your faith strong? How can it become stronger?

■ **ILLUSTRATIONS:**

Faithful or Fizzled. A skyrocket is lovely to watch, but its beauty doesn't last long. There are people who have Christian experiences as brilliant as skyrockets or like giant Roman candles. They certainly can dazzle our eyes for a while. But then they sputter and go out. Their lives become sad, sick, and disappointing. People who faithfully maintain a spiritual glow over the years, through good times and bad, help us believe in the faithfulness of God. Their devotion to Christ is deep and constant because it is real.

I think about my aunt who for years has prayed for her brothers and sisters and their families, read and studied her Sunday school lesson each week, and generally thought of others more than herself. When I decided to go to seminary, she was one of the first persons I told, because I knew she would understand my desire to serve the Lord—and she did. Every young person should have someone like my aunt to look up to as a shining example of how a steadfast faith is lived out in everyday life.

Persistence Pays Off. Harold Sherman wrote a book entitled *How To Turn Failure Into Success.* In it he includes a "Code of Persistence" :

1. I will never give up so long as I know I am right.
2. I will believe that all things will work out for me if I hang on until the end.
3. I will be courageous and undismayed in the face of odds.
4. I will not permit anyone to intimidate me or deter me from my goals.
5. I will fight to overcome all physical handicaps and setbacks.
6. I will try again and again and yet again to accomplish what I desire.
7. I will take new faith and resolution from the knowledge that all successful men and women had to fight defeat and adversity.
8. I will never surrender to discouragement or despair no matter what seeming obstacles may confront me.

Persistence is a major ingredient in faithfulness, because faithfulness means to stick with God even when things are not going your way. Life will not always go your way, but God will.

Get Back on the Bus. Patsy Clairmont shares the following true story about her son Jason on the tape *God Uses Cracked Pots:*

"When he was 7, I sent him off to school one day and a little while later there was a knock at the door and I opened the door and it was Jason. I said 'Jason, what are you doing here?'

"He said, 'I've quit school!'

"I said, 'Why have you quit school?'

"He said, 'Well, it was too long, it was too hard, and it was too boring.'

"I said, 'Jason, you have just described life; get back on the bus!'"

Everyone wants to get off the bus at one time or another, but steadfast faith means you stay on for the ride. You may not know exactly where the bus is going, but you have faith in the Driver.

WORTHY IS THE LAMB

BACKGROUND SCRIPTURE: Revelation 4—5

DEVOTIONAL READING: Revelation 4:1-11

KEY VERSE: "Worthy is the Lamb that was slaughtered to receive power and wealth and wisdom and might and honor and glory and blessing!" Revelation 5:12.

10

KING JAMES VERSION

REVELATION 5:1 And I saw in the right hand of him that sat on the throne a book written within and on the backside, sealed with seven seals.

2 And I saw a strong angel proclaiming with a loud voice, Who is worthy to open the book, and to loose the seals thereof?

3 And no man in heaven, nor in earth, neither under the earth, was able to open the book, neither to look thereon.

4 And I wept much, because no man was found worthy to open and to read the book, neither to look thereon.

5 And one of the elders saith unto me, Weep not: behold, the Lion of the tribe of Juda, the Root of David, hath prevailed to open the book, and to loose the seven seals thereof.

6 And I beheld, and, lo, in the midst of the throne and of the four beasts, and in the midst of the elders, stood a Lamb as it had been slain, having seven horns and seven eyes, which are the seven Spirits of God sent forth into all the earth.

7 And he came and took the book out of the right hand of him that sat upon the throne.

8 And when he had taken the book, the four beasts and four and twenty elders fell down before the Lamb, having every one of them harps, and golden vials full of odours, which are the prayers of saints.

9 And they sung a new song, saying, Thou art worthy to take the book, and to open the seals thereof: for thou wast slain, and hast redeemed us to God by thy blood out of every kindred, and tongue, and people, and nation;

10 And hast made us unto our God kings and priests: and we shall reign on the earth.

NEW REVISED STANDARD VERSION

REVELATION 5:1 Then I saw in the right hand of the one seated on the throne a scroll written on the inside and on the back, sealed with seven seals; 2 and I saw a mighty angel proclaiming with a loud voice, "Who is worthy to open the scroll and break its seals?" 3 And no one in heaven or on earth or under the earth was able to open the scroll or to look into it. 4 And I began to weep bitterly because no one was found worthy to open the scroll or to look into it. 5 Then one of the elders said to me, "Do not weep. See, the Lion of the tribe of Judah, the Root of David, has conquered, so that he can open the scroll and its seven seals."

6 Then I saw between the throne and the four living creatures and among the elders a Lamb standing as if it had been slaughtered, having seven horns and seven eyes, which are the seven spirits of God sent out into all the earth. 7 He went and took the scroll from the right hand of the one who was seated on the throne. 8 When he had taken the scroll, the four living creatures and the twenty-four elders fell before the Lamb, each holding a harp and golden bowls full of incense, which are the prayers of the saints. 9 They sing a new song:

"You are worthy to take the scroll
  and to open its seals,
for you were slaughtered and by your blood
    you ransomed for God
  saints from every tribe and language and people
    and nation;
10 you have made them to be a kingdom and priests
    serving our God, and they will reign on earth."

Monday, May 3	Revelation 1:4-8	*Jesus Is Coming with the Clouds*
Tuesday, May 4	Revelation 2:1-7	*Jesus Holds the Seven Stars*
Wednesday, May 5	Revelation 2:18-29	*Words of the Son of God*
Thursday, May 6	Revelation 3:14-21	*Jesus Has Conquered*
Friday, May 7	Revelation 4:1-11	*Holy Is the Lord God Almighty*
Saturday, May 8	Revelation 5:1-5	*Who Is Worthy?*
Sunday, May 9	Revelation 5:6-14	*The Lamb Is Worthy*

BACKGROUND

For the first 30 years or so after Jesus' crucifixion and resurrection, Christianity was tolerated in the Roman Empire as a sect of Judaism, which was an officially recognized religion. While missionaries faced antagonism and even persecution in many of the towns they visited, this came mainly from the local citizens and some of the Jewish leaders, not from the Roman authorities.

This official toleration changed dramatically, however, during the reign of emperor Nero (A.D. 54–68). After a great fire burned Rome in A.D. 64, Nero accused the Christians of starting it, then had many of them tortured and killed many in the capital. Peter and Paul are both said to have died during Nero's persecutions. Nero encouraged the growing belief that Christians were a threat to traditional Roman religion and also to the emperor, who was more and more being worshiped as a divine being.

The emperor Domitian (A.D. 81–96) is credited with starting the first widespread persecution of Christians because he demanded worship as "Lord and God," and Christians refused to comply. While this persecution was short-lived, it set the stage for other widespread persecutions in the next two centuries.

Tradition says that John was exiled to the island of Patmos, about 35 miles off the western coast of modern-day Turkey, sometime during Domitian's reign. In the Roman province of Asia (which included Patmos and the city of Ephesus), emperor worship was very popular. Emperors as far back as Augustus (31 B.C.–A.D. 14) had given permission for people to erect temples to honor Caesar. John wrote *to the seven churches that are in Asia* (Rev. 1:4), encouraging them to stay strong during times of persecution, for he had been given the *revelation of Jesus Christ* (1:1). The Lord had shown Himself to John so that the apostle might tell the churches *"what is to take place after this"* (1:19).

In 1:1, John used the Greek word *apokalypsis*, which is usually translated "revelation," to describe the contents of his book. For this reason scholars have grouped the Book of Revelation with similar books of the Bible, putting them in the genre of apocalyptic literature. Like portions of Isaiah, Ezekiel, Daniel, and Zechariah, Revelation is characterized by extraordinary visions and symbols. Also, like these Old Testament writers, John used graphic imagery, promises, and warnings to describe the magnificent struggle between God and His adversaries.

Many believe the apostle used several direct and indirect references to the Old Testament to reveal that the events of Revelation would fulfill the apocalyptic predictions of the ancient biblical prophets.

NOTES ON THE PRINTED TEXT

After giving messages (Rev. 2—3) to seven present-day churches in Asia, John described a series of visions he had received about the future. Then, in chapter 4, John was transported *in the spirit* (4:2) to heaven. In a vision reminiscent of the throne room scenes in Isaiah 6, Ezekiel 1, and Daniel 7, John saw God's throne and listened to the singing of four living creatures, who praised God day and night (Rev. 4:8).

John also saw 24 elders who likewise worshiped God and said, *"You are worthy, our Lord and our God, to receive glory and honor and power"* (4:11). Some think these elders are exalted angels who served God in His heavenly court. Others think they are glorified saints in heaven. Still others think the number 24 is a symbolic reference to the 12 tribes of Israel in the Old Testament and the 12 apostles in the New Testament. In this case, all the redeemed of all time (both before and after Christ's death and resurrection) are represented before God's throne and worship Him in His heavenly sanctuary.

The vision continues in Revelation 5, where John sees *the one seated on the throne* (5:1) holding a scroll written on both sides and *sealed with seven seals*. That a scroll would have writing on both sides of it would be highly unusual, showing that the writer had much to say. The seven seals, which were pieces of wax or clay, would make it difficult to open except by an authorized person, someone who was *"worthy to open the scroll and break its seals"* (5:2). The seals would also ensure utmost secrecy for the document. What was on the scroll is not said; most likely, it was God's final plan for the end of the world.

An angel cried out for someone to come forward who was worthy enough to open the scroll, but no one did (5:3). At that point, John *began to weep bitterly* (5:4). Then one of the elders pointed to someone who was indeed *worthy to open the scroll*. He was Jesus, *the Lion of the tribe of Judah, the Root of David* (5:5). Both of these metaphors are familiar Old Testament titles, and together summed up Israel's hope for the coming Messiah (see Gen. 49:9-10; Isa. 11:1, 10; Jer. 23:5).

When Jesus came forward, the image of Him changed from a lion to *a Lamb standing as if it had been slaughtered* (Rev. 5:6). In Revelation, Jesus is described many times as the Lamb, indicating His sacrificial role on the Cross and linking Him to the Passover lamb (Isa. 53:7; John 1:29). The Lamb's *seven horns and seven eyes* (Rev. 5:6) represent perfection, for in Scripture seven was considered the perfect number. The horns symbolize kingly power, while the eyes show the Lamb's divine omnipresence and omniscience. John explained further that the seven eyes were *the seven spirits of God sent out into all the earth*. This is a reference to the perfection of the Spirit. His basic ministry is to exalt Christ and make Him alive and real to all who trust in Him.

Once the Lamb took the scroll, the four living creatures and the 24 elders began to worship Him with harp music (5:8). Like priests, the elders also held *golden bowls full of incense,* representing *the prayers of the saints* (Rev. 5:8; see Ps. 141:2). The worshipers began to sing *a new song* (Rev. 5:9), for this was a momentous occasion when a whole new order of reality was about to begin. Once again the elders and the living creatures said that Jesus is *worthy,* and that His worthiness came from His atoning sacrifice. The graphic word *slaughtered* again brings up the image of the Passover lamb, but the reason for Jesus' sacrifice is clear. He died so that His blood would ransom believers *"from every tribe and language and people and nation."* The Greek verb translated *ransomed* was used to describe the freeing of a slave by the payment of a price. Thus everyone who puts his or her trust in Christ can have freedom from the bondage of sin and death.

Jesus' atoning sacrifice created a new *kingdom* (5:10) of believers who are all *priests*. No longer would the Jews need a priest to go into the Holy of Holies in the temple to sacrifice for them; and no longer would the Gentiles be forced to stay in the outer temple courts to praise God. Access to the Lord had come to believers through Christ, and their priestly function would be to offer sacrifices of praise and thanksgiving to their heavenly Father (Heb. 13:15). Now it was time for God's kingdom to come *"on earth"* (Rev. 5:10); thus the seven seals had to be broken.

SUGGESTIONS TO TEACHERS

In John's vision of the heavenly throne room, all honor, praise, and worship is given to Jesus, the Lamb who was slain. Why is He worthy of praise? The reasons He is praised in heaven are the same reasons why we should praise Him now with our own songs of celebration.

1. JESUS DIED FOR US. Though He did not have to, Jesus willingly died on the cross for the sake of those in *"every tribe and language and people and nation"* (Rev. 5:9) who would put their trust in Him. The Greek verb rendered *slaughtered*, which was used to describe His death, reminds us just how much Jesus suffered for us. Whenever we think we have suffered too much ourselves, we should remember His suffering.

2. JESUS SAVED US. Jesus died for a purpose. His death was not an accident of history. His blood *ransomed* (5:9) us from the slavery into which sin has put us. We cannot save ourselves. We have been purchased with a price, Jesus' blood. Any time we think we are worthy ourselves of praise, we must remember who we are without Christ.

3. JESUS ADOPTED US. God loved us so much that He brought us who have trusted in Christ into His kingdom. One day we *"will reign on earth"* (5:10) with Jesus. But what does that mean for us today? It means that Jesus has overcome the world (John 16:33), so we can as well. The more we live for Him, the more His kingdom will come and His will be done, on earth as it is in heaven (Matt. 6:10).

As an echo of the praise Jesus receives in heaven, we should sing the old hymn of grace and praise—and mean what it says: "Were the whole realm of nature mine, that were a present far too small; love so amazing, so divine, demands my soul, my life, my all."

FOR ADULTS   ■ **TOPIC:** Who Is Worthy?
■ **QUESTIONS:** 1. What was the angel's question to John? 2. Who could open the scroll? Why? 3. Who worshiped the Lamb? 4. What did the Lamb do for people from all nations? 5. Jesus is the only one worthy of worship. What does this mean to you?

■ **ILLUSTRATIONS:**

Who Is Worthy? Is Jesus more worthy of worship than any of the other great teachers and philosophers of history? Frederick Buechner, in his book titled *Now and Then,* compares the teachings of Buddha and Christ.

"Buddha sits enthroned beneath the Bo tree in the lotus position. His lips are faintly parted in the smile of one who has passed beyond every power in earth or heaven to touch him. 'He who loves fifty has fifty woes, he who loves ten has ten woes, he who loves none has no woes,' he has said. His eyes are closed.

"Christ, on the other hand, stands in the garden of Gethsemane, angular, beleaguered. His face is lost in shadows so that you can't even see his lips, and before all the powers in earth or heaven he is powerless. 'This is my commandment, that you love one another as I have loved you,' he has said. His eyes are also closed."

Beneath his tree Buddha is shutting out the world and its suffering, while Christ is taking the world and its people into His heart and loving them. In fact, He died for all people—including you. As Revelation 5:9 says, by Jesus' blood He "*ransomed for God saints from every tribe and language and people and nation.*" Jesus alone is worthy of our worship.

Only Jesus. An anonymous author made this striking comparison: "Socrates taught for 40 years, Plato for 50, Aristotle for 40, and Jesus for only 3. Yet the influence of Christ's 3-year ministry infinitely transcends the impact left by the combined 130 years of teaching from these men who were among the greatest philosophers of all antiquity. Jesus painted no pictures; yet some of the finest paintings of Raphael, Michelangelo, and Leonardo da Vinci received their inspiration from Him. Jesus wrote no poetry; but Dante, Milton, and scores of the world's greatest poets were inspired by Him. Jesus composed no music; still Haydn, Handel, Beethoven, Bach, and Mendelssohn reached their highest perfection of melody in the hymns, symphonies, and oratorios they composed in His praise. Every sphere of human greatness has been enriched by this humble Carpenter of Nazareth.

"His unique contribution is the salvation of the soul! Philosophy could not accomplish that. Nor art. Nor literature. Nor music. Only Jesus Christ can break the enslaving chains of sin and Satan. Jesus alone can speak peace to the human heart, strengthen the weak, and give life to those who are spiritually dead."

What's Wrong with Me? My grandparents had only daughters, and when their first grandchild—my older brother—was born, he became the apple of their eye. So when I came along 4 years later—a girl—they were less than excited.

Once, when I was about six, my family was visiting and my grandma had a present for my brother, for no special reason. It was one of those huge antique car models complete with working doors, because they knew he loved to put models together. Naturally, I assumed I would get a present too, so I asked where my present was. It was obvious, even to a six year old, Grandma hadn't even thought about giving one to me. She left the room for a few minutes and returned with a box of pink tissues, saying "This is for you." I was devastated, but having been taught to always say thank you, I did. I thought to myself, *What was so wrong with me that I didn't get a present?* Although my mother tried to make up for this by getting me a doll I had been wanting after we got home, the damage was done. I have never forgotten the feeling of not being worthy of a special gift.

So often we do this to Jesus. We will give our time and money to sports, shopping, or other things, leaving little for Him. Whether we realize it or not, what we end up giving Him shows how much we think He is worth.

■ TOPIC: Worthy of What?

■ QUESTIONS: 1. Where was John in his vision? 2. Why was John crying? 3. What did John say the Lamb looked like? 4. Why were people worshiping the Lamb? 5. How do you worship Jesus?

■ ILLUSTRATIONS:

Who's All Wet? In the years 1014–1035, there ruled over England a Danish king named Canute. King Canute grew tired of hearing his servants flatter him with extravagant praises about his greatness, power, and invincibility. He decided to give his people an object lesson. He ordered his throne to be set down on the seashore, where he commanded the waves not to come in and soak him. No matter how forcefully he ordered the tide not to come in, however, his order was not obeyed. Soon the waves lapped around his throne.

One historian says that King Canute never wore his crown again, but hung it on a statue of the crucified Christ. Now his people understood who was really worthy of praise and worship.

Who Gets the Praise? In Anne Graham Lotz's book titled *The Vision of His Glory,* she says, "If Jesus alone is worthy of all praise—and He is!—why do we seek praise for ourselves? Why are we offended when others don't give us credit for what we have done?"

Lotz goes on to tell a true story about a person who spoke dynamically for one hour and 45 minutes—about herself! When she finished, those present applauded politely (and thankfully) as she went to her seat. When the master of ceremonies stepped to the microphone, she gestured for the audience to stand for the closing prayer. The woman did not see this and she thought the audience was giving her a standing ovation! Quickly she stepped back up to the microphone to thank them!

We are all guilty of doing something like this, even if it is on a smaller scale. We want the praise and attention for ourselves, when in fact, we simply don't deserve it without recognizing who gave it to us. We need to remember that whether we achieve our goals on the athletic field or in the classroom, the one who makes it possible for us to accomplish these things is Jesus.

Keeping Our Minds on Worship. We were members at a church where the youth helped the adults worship better each Sunday. The youth made a group decision to sit up front each week, so they would be more accountable in paying attention to the service and message. However, a more important thing happened. After a few weeks, they found themselves actually worshiping.

When I had a conversation with one of the girls, Kara, she told me that it was very powerful how they found the words in the songs to have more meaning, and the message to really speak to their hearts. They had put themselves in a position where they had fewer distractions, and they were less tempted to talk to each other, pass notes, or fall asleep. They actually felt like the Lord was present with them during worship. Kara said she was amazed that, when she took the focus off herself and her friends, she began to realize more of who Jesus is and what He had done in her life. Kara also knew others in the youth group who were beginning to feel the same way.

This made a big impact on the adults in our church. The youths' example helped us all to see the need to focus on Jesus, and not something else during times of worship. Their behavior challenged us to not write out our grocery lists or think about where we were eating lunch when church was over. We were on our way as a church community to take seriously the task of being "*a kingdom and priests serving our God*" (Rev. 5:10).

SALVATION BELONGS TO GOD

BACKGROUND SCRIPTURE: Revelation 7
DEVOTIONAL READING: Revelation 3:7-13

KEY VERSE: "The Lamb at the center of the throne will be their shepherd, and he will guide them to springs of the water of life, and God will wipe away every tear from their eyes." Revelation 7:17.

KING JAMES VERSION

REVELATION 7:1 And after these things I saw four angels standing on the four corners of the earth, holding the four winds of the earth, that the wind should not blow on the earth, nor on the sea, nor on any tree.

2 And I saw another angel ascending from the east, having the seal of the living God: and he cried with a loud voice to the four angels, to whom it was given to hurt the earth and the sea,

3 Saying, Hurt not the earth, neither the sea, nor the trees, till we have sealed the servants of our God in their foreheads. . . .

9 After this I beheld, and, lo, a great multitude, which no man could number, of all nations, and kindreds, and people, and tongues, stood before the throne, and before the Lamb, clothed with white robes, and palms in their hands;

10 And cried with a loud voice, saying, Salvation to our God which sitteth upon the throne, and unto the Lamb.

14b These are they which came out of great tribulation, and have washed their robes, and made them white in the blood of the Lamb.

15 Therefore are they before the throne of God, and serve him day and night in his temple: and he that sitteth on the throne shall dwell among them.

16 They shall hunger no more, neither thirst any more; neither shall the sun light on them, nor any heat.

17 For the Lamb which is in the midst of the throne shall feed them, and shall lead them unto living fountains of waters: and God shall wipe away all tears from their eyes.

NEW REVISED STANDARD VERSION

REVELATION 7:1 After this I saw four angels standing at the four corners of the earth, holding back the four winds of the earth so that no wind could blow on earth or sea or against any tree. 2 I saw another angel ascending from the rising of the sun, having the seal of the living God, and he called with a loud voice to the four angels who had been given power to damage earth and sea, 3 saying, "Do not damage the earth or the sea or the trees, until we have marked the servants of our God with a seal on their foreheads. . . . "

9 After this I looked, and there was a great multitude that no one could count, from every nation, from all tribes and peoples and languages, standing before the throne and before the Lamb, robed in white, with palm branches in their hands. 10 They cried out in a loud voice, saying, "Salvation belongs to our God who is seated on the throne, and to the Lamb!"

14b "These are they who have come out of the great ordeal; they have washed their robes and made them white in the blood of the Lamb.

15 For this reason they are before the throne of God, and worship him day and night within his temple, and the one who is seated on the throne will shelter them.

16 They will hunger no more, and thirst no more; the sun will not strike them, nor any scorching heat;

17 for the Lamb at the center of the throne will be their shepherd, and he will guide them to springs of the water of life, and God will wipe away every tear from their eyes."

Monday, May 10	Psalm 3:1-8	Deliverance Belongs to the Lord
Tuesday, May 11	Psalm 25:1-5	The God of My Salvation
Wednesday, May 12	Psalm 62:1-6	My Rock and My Salvation
Thursday, May 13	Psalm 62:7-12	On God Rests My Deliverance
Friday, May 14	Acts 13:32-39	Through Jesus Is Forgiveness of Sins
Saturday, May 15	Revelation 7:1-10	Salvation Belongs to Our God
Sunday, May 16	Revelation 7:11-17	Before the Throne of God

BACKGROUND

The Book of Revelation begins and ends with Christ. Though filled with magnificent visions and symbols that may be difficult to understand, first and foremost the book is about Jesus—His character, His mission, and His final goal of bringing all things into subjection to His Father's perfect will. In Revelation we learn many things about Christ that we cannot find anywhere else in Scripture—at least not in such intricate detail.

Admittedly, a lot of mystery surrounds Revelation. Perhaps no other book of the Bible is more difficult to interpret than this one. Its abundant figures and intriguing symbols have stimulated many different explanations about the book's message. And certainly the unusual imagery of the book has caused numerous disagreements among interpreters.

Despite the enigma surrounding Revelation, however, this book is primarily characterized by hope. The writer declared that Christ will one day return to vindicate the righteous and judge the wicked and unbelieving. Revelation is also known for its warnings. Throughout this spectacular vision, Jesus calls believers to commit themselves to live in righteousness and integrity by the power of the Spirit. Jesus also admonishes the wicked to turn away from their sin and trust Him for their salvation.

As we learned last week, chapter 5 of the book reveals that only the Lamb is worthy to open the scroll with the seven seals. In chapter 6, He breaks four seals and unleashes judgments in the form of four horsemen, who bring war, famine, disease, and death to the earth. When the fifth seal is broken, it reveals those who had been martyred for the faith and are awaiting vengeance on the enemies of God. The opening of the sixth seal brings a great earthquake, signaling the beginning of the day of the Lord and the outpouring of His wrath on the wicked.

In chapter 7, however, God's judgment is held back until protection is given to the servants of God who are still on the earth so that they will not perish in the horrible time that is coming. Those who are to be sealed number 144,000, *sealed out of every tribe of the people of Israel* (7:4). The number represents 12,000 from each of the tribes of Israel.

The identity of the 144,000 saints mentioned in Revelation 7:4-8 is debated. They could be a select group of people from the literal 12 tribes of Israel; or they could be a specific number of believers whom God will in some way shield during a final period of distress. It could be that 144,000 (calculated using 12 as a multiple of 12) is a symbolic number for the fullness of the people of God. In other words, the Lord will bring all His followers safely to Himself. He will protect them either by removing them from the earth or by giving them the strength they need to endure persecution and remain loyal to Him.

NOTES ON THE PRINTED TEXT

In heaven, John had already seen angels, elders, and other creatures worshiping God on His throne. John had also seen Jesus, identified as the Lamb who was slain, open the seals on the great scroll in God's right hand to initiate judgment on the earth. This judgment, preceded by an earthquake and terrifying signs in the skies, is so overwhelming that those on earth cry out to the mountains and the rocks, *"Fall on us and hide us from the face of the one seated on the throne and from the wrath of the Lamb"* (Rev. 6:16).

There then occurs a pause in the proceedings, perhaps to show that God is in control. Although judgment is inevitable, it comes at His time and under His direction. *Four angels standing at the four corners of the earth* (7:1) are told to stop *the four winds* from blowing and bringing destruction on the earth. The four angels may be similar to the four horsemen mentioned in Revelation 6. In the biblical world the wind could bring good rains off the ocean, hot blasts from the desert that would kill the crops, or plagues of locusts.

The judgment will not go on until another angel has come with *the seal of the living God* (7:2) to mark *"the servants of our God with a seal on their foreheads"* (7:3). Kings in John's time usually used a signet ring as their seal to authenticate official documents. The seal on the believers would be a mark of ownership signifying the special protection of the Lord. In Ezekiel 9:4, it is suggested that God's mark of ownership and protection is the Hebrew letter *taw*, which looks like the English letter "X." Revelation 3:12, 14:1, and 22:4 suggest that God's name is the imprint He places on the foreheads of His servants.

John next saw in heaven *a great multitude* (7:9) that was too large to count. This throng was made up of people from every nation, tribe, people, and language, and they stood before the throne of God and before the Lamb. Many ideas have been suggested regarding the identity of this host of believers. They could be the saved of all ages, only Gentile believers, or martyrs killed during a final period of great distress, to name three common views.

One remarkable aspect of the scene John saw in heaven is the position of the believers before God's throne, a place of safety and security. The early readers of Revelation might have associated *white* robes with the garb of Roman generals, who dressed in this fashion when celebrating their triumphs. The clothing worn by the saints in heaven represent the purity, righteousness, and glory of Christ. The *palm branches* they carry represent total victory and unending joy.

Everything about the scene points to the acceptance of these believers before God. They are celebrating triumph in a place of honor before the Lord and the Lamb. This truth is reflected in the chorus the multitude in heaven shouted before the throne. They acknowledged that salvation comes only from God the Father, and the Lamb, His Son (7:10).

John learned that the vast multitude had *"washed their robes and made them white in the blood of the Lamb"* (7:14). Thus, like all believers, they are saved on the basis of Christ's sacrifice. It is a paradox of the Christian faith that we must be washed in Jesus' blood to be as white as snow. Only then can we, as believers, worship *"before the throne of God . . . day and night within his temple"* (7:15), so that He can *shelter* us. The Greek word translated *shelter* comes from an Old Testament term meaning "tent" and pictures God dwelling with His people, sheltering and protecting them (see Lev. 26:11; Ezek. 37:27).

Those who are in God's very presence will not *hunger* (Rev. 7:16) or *thirst* any more (Rev. 7:16), nor will they be baked by the desert *heat*. At God's throne believers will find the *"springs of the water of life"* (7:17). The imagery is that of a shepherd guiding his sheep to a freshwater spring in the desert. Salvation from the death that sin brought into the world will be complete. In heaven, the righteous will enjoy unending life. The elder told John that God will wipe away all tears from the eyes of His people. They will never experience pain, suffering, sickness, grief, or death. In some way, the Lord will cause their past never to bring them remorse in the coming age.

SUGGESTIONS TO TEACHERS

What will heaven be like? Will we just be sitting on clouds all day playing harps and singing? We do not have all the answers to our questions that we wish we did, but the Book of Revelation tells us what rewards believers will find when they reach paradise. Three stand out in this passage.

1. NO MORE SEPARATION FROM GOD. Revelation pictures believers standing by the throne of God, worshiping Him *"day and night within his temple"* (7:15). There will be no barriers in heaven between God and His people, and no separation between believers due to nations, tribes, or languages. While we cannot exactly have that now, remind your students that we can see some of the glory of God reflected in our own lives when we faithfully serve Him, and we should work toward breaking down those barriers that separate believers here on earth.

2. NO MORE HUNGER OR THIRST. All our basic physical needs will disappear in heaven. We will no longer be hungry or hot or thirsty. As the Good Shepherd who leads His sheep to the greenest pasture, Jesus will guide us to the *"springs of the water of life"* (7:17), where we will not want. While physical needs may be paramount in our lives today, they will be nonexistent in heaven.

3. NO MORE SUFFERING. The Scripture that has comforted millions of believers who have lost loved ones tells us that one day *"God will wipe away* *every tear"* (7:17). The suffering of this life, and our heart-breaking separation from other believers who have died, will end in heaven one day. While it is sometimes hard for us to remember, our life today is only temporary. The everlasting joys of eternity are really just around the corner.

<table>
<tr><td>

FOR ADULTS

</td><td>

■ **TOPIC:** The Faithful Are Rewarded

■ **QUESTIONS:** 1. Why did God tell the angels to hold back the four winds from the earth? 2. Who did John see in the great multitude

</td></tr>
</table>

worshiping God in heaven? 3. Who are the people wearing the white robes? 4. What are the differences between heaven and earth? 5. How do you become one of the faithful worshiping at God's throne?

■ **ILLUSTRATIONS:**

The Smallest Loaf. There was once a rich baker who sent for 20 of the poorest children in town and said to them, "In this basket is a loaf of bread for each of you. Take one and come back every day and I'll give you more." Immediately the youngsters began quarreling about who would get the largest loaf. Snatching from the basket, they left without even thanking the baker.

Gretchen, a poorly dressed little girl, patiently waited until the others had left. She then took the smallest loaf, which remained in the basket, kissed the old man's hand, and went home.

The next day the scene was repeated. But when Gretchen's mother sliced this loaf, she found many shiny gold coins inside. Gretchen took the money back to the baker, thinking there had been some mistake, but he said, "No, my child, it was not a mistake. I put them into the smallest loaf knowing you would be rewarded."

Faithfulness is shown in many character traits, including honesty and humility as little Gretchen showed the baker. Just as the baker felt compelled to bless Gretchen for her sweet spirit, our God wants to bless each of us for our actions and thoughts that are pure and unselfish. In this world we may not see a reward for every good thing we do, but we can be assured that God will not forget to reward us when we get in heaven.

More Than Just Oranges. Our reward does not always depend on whether we accomplish a task perfectly. I remember a time when I was working for an advertising agency, and we had a big mailing of oranges to send to our clients as part of a promotion we were doing for the Orange Bowl. The people who were responsible for this to get done dropped the ball (or the orange!), and I tried to step in and get everything organized. However, I was not able to accomplish this on my own, but the president of the agency, who also attended my church, was very impressed that I had taken the initiative to help solve the problem of mailing the oranges. He then personally stepped in and helped me finish the job. He knew that even though I had failed to do the job perfectly on my own, my motive was to help the agency succeed, and he told me how proud he was of me.

Even if something we felt led to do does not go exactly as we thought it would, we can be assured that Jesus knows the motive and desire of our hearts, especially as we serve Him (see Matt. 25:31-46).

Thank You. A few years back Ray Boltz, a Christian musician, had a hit song called "Thank You." The song tells the story of someone who goes to heaven and meets a long line of people his life personally touched because he was faithful in doing what the Lord asked of him. Each person in the line says, "Thank you for giving to the Lord. I am a life that was changed. Thank you for giving to the Lord. I am so glad you gave." Eventually he meets Jesus, who tells him to look at those around him, for great is his reward.

The song helps us realize that sometimes we are totally unaware that our actions and words affect so many others. That is why it is important for us to be faithful to the Lord in our everyday lives, for we really have no idea how the little things we do impact eternity.

FOR YOUTH

■ TOPIC: Try a New Life!

■ QUESTIONS: 1. Who brought the seal of God, and what did he say? 2. Where did the great multitude come from? 3. How did the robes come to be white? 4. What will believers be doing or experiencing in heaven? 5. When you think about heaven, is this what you had pictured? Why or why not?

■ ILLUSTRATIONS:

A Tug at the Heart. A teenager became a Christian during a revival. The next week at school his friends questioned him about the experience. "Did you see a vision?" asked one friend. "Did you hear God speak?" asked another. The teenager answered no to all these questions. "Well, how did you know you were saved?" they asked. He searched for an answer and finally he said, "It's like when you catch a fish. You can't see the fish or hear the fish; you just feel him tugging on your line. I just felt God tugging on my heart."

Have you felt God tugging at your heart? Maybe it is something that your pastor or Sunday school teacher said. Maybe it is the changed life you saw one of your friends leading. Maybe it was something you felt God speak to you during personal prayer or Bible reading. God does not approach everyone in the same way, but the results of trusting in Him are the same. No matter how He calls us, we are all invited to live a life committed to following Him, and "catching" His love, direction, and opportunities for our lives. Finally, when we get to heaven and have the honor of worshiping at His throne, we will be very glad that there was that special day in our lives when He first tugged at our heart.

The Life You Save. Author Frederick Buechner once said, "Car inspection stickers used to have printed on the back 'Drive carefully—the life you save may be your own.' That is the wisdom of men in a nutshell.

"What God says, on the other hand, is 'The life you save is the life you lose.' In other words, the life you clutch, hoard, guard, and play safe with is in the end a life worth little to anybody, including yourself; and only a life given away for love's sake is a life worth living. To bring his point home, God shows us a man [Jesus] who gave his life away to the extent of dying a national disgrace without a penny in the bank or a friend to his name. In terms of men's wisdom, he was a perfect fool, and anybody who thinks he can follow him without making something like the same kind of fool of himself is laboring under not a cross but a delusion."

Sometimes we are guilty of hanging on to our lives, somehow thinking that, if we "give it away" for Jesus, we will lose something worthwhile. Jesus wants to give everyone who trusts in Him a new life that is infinitely better than any other kind of life we could try to live. Trust Him, and give your life away to Him.

Don't Get Lost. Grandpa decided to take his grandsons, ages four and six, to spend the day at Disney World. While in one of the stores, he bought each of them a little flag to carry. Several times they stopped to watch the marching band dressed as toy soldiers, and each time the boys would be fascinated as the band marched by. Suddenly, Grandpa realized that the four-year-old was missing. He searched all about, calling his grandson's name, as he made his way through the crowd. As Grandpa sat down to catch his breath and to decide what to do next, he looked up to see the marching band of toy soldiers go by. There, at the end of the line, smiling and waving his flag, was his grandson, having the time of his life, completely unaware that he was lost!

Are you aware of which parade you are following? One parade may take you on to a life of self-indulgence, where what you think you want determines what you do. Another parade may take you on to a life of being moral, but without you really knowing why. Still another parade may be just following your friends wherever they go. Many people have fallen behind a parade like the little boy in this story, going on their own merry way, totally unaware of a loving Father's concern that they are lost. Don't get lost. Find the right parade, the one that leads to the throne of God and the multitudes praising Him for eternity.

A CALL FOR ENDURANCE

BACKGROUND SCRIPTURE: Revelation 14
DEVOTIONAL READING: 2 Timothy 2:3-13

KEY VERSE: Here is a call for the endurance of the saints, those who keep the commandments of God and hold fast to the faith of Jesus. Revelation 14:12.

KING JAMES VERSION

REVELATION 14:6 And I saw another angel fly in the midst of heaven, having the everlasting gospel to preach unto them that dwell on the earth, and to every nation, and kindred, and tongue, and people,

7 Saying with a loud voice, Fear God, and give glory to him; for the hour of his judgment is come: and worship him that made heaven, and earth, and the sea, and the fountains of waters.

8 And there followed another angel, saying, Babylon is fallen, is fallen, that great city, because she made all nations drink of the wine of the wrath of her fornication.

9 And the third angel followed them, saying with a loud voice, If any man worship the beast and his image, and receive his mark in his forehead, or in his hand,

10 The same shall drink of the wine of the wrath of God, which is poured out without mixture into the cup of his indignation; and he shall be tormented with fire and brimstone in the presence of the holy angels, and in the presence of the Lamb:

11 And the smoke of their torment ascendeth up for ever and ever: and they have no rest day nor night, who worship the beast and his image, and whosoever receiveth the mark of his name.

12 Here is the patience of the saints: here are they that keep the commandments of God, and the faith of Jesus.

13 And I heard a voice from heaven saying unto me, Write, Blessed are the dead which die in the Lord from henceforth: Yea, saith the Spirit, that they may rest from their labours; and their works do follow them.

NEW REVISED STANDARD VERSION

REVELATION 14:6 Then I saw another angel flying in midheaven, with an eternal gospel to proclaim to those who live on the earth—to every nation and tribe and language and people. 7 He said in a loud voice, "Fear God and give him glory, for the hour of his judgment has come; and worship him who made heaven and earth, the sea and the springs of water."

8 Then another angel, a second, followed, saying, "Fallen, fallen is Babylon the great! She has made all nations drink of the wine of the wrath of her fornication."

9 Then another angel, a third, followed them, crying with a loud voice, "Those who worship the beast and its image, and receive a mark on their foreheads or on their hands, 10 they will also drink the wine of God's wrath, poured unmixed into the cup of his anger, and they will be tormented with fire and sulfur in the presence of the holy angels and in the presence of the Lamb. 11 And the smoke of their torment goes up forever and ever. There is no rest day or night for those who worship the beast and its image and for anyone who receives the mark of its name."

12 Here is a call for the endurance of the saints, those who keep the commandments of God and hold fast to the faith of Jesus.

13 And I heard a voice from heaven saying, "Write this: Blessed are the dead who from now on die in the Lord." "Yes," says the Spirit, "they will rest from their labors, for their deeds follow them."

12

Monday, May 17	John 16:29-33	*In the World You Face Persecution*
Tuesday, May 18	Matthew 10:16-22	*Endure to the End*
Wednesday, May 19	Matthew 24:9-14	*Many Will Fall Away*
Thursday, May 20	Matthew 24:45-50	*Be Faithful to the Task*
Friday, May 21	1 Corinthians 15:12-20	*Our Hope in the Risen Lord*
Saturday, May 22	1 Corinthians 15:54-58	*We Have Victory through Christ*
Sunday, May 23	Revelation 14:6-13	*A Call for Endurance*

BACKGROUND

How should readers interpret Revelation as a whole? What do all of the numbers and symbols tell us about the future, or even about the world we are living in right now? Over the centuries, at least four major "schools" of interpretation have developed to try to explain what Revelation means. The four generally agree that the seven churches mentioned in Revelation 2—3 were real first-century congregations who were the first recipients of John's message. Beyond that, there is wide disagreement.

One group believes that the prophecies of Revelation have already been finished. Known as the preterists, this group sees the fall of the Roman Empire and the destruction of Jerusalem in A.D. 70 as the main events behind the symbols. In this view, the book had the most meaning for its original readers; it gave them hope through the persecutions of the church that were to increase soon after John wrote. This group additionally thinks chapters 4—19 symbolize conditions contemporary to John's time, while chapters 20—22 represent heaven and the victory of good over evil.

A second group believes that Revelation 6—18 is an overview of the course of church history from the first century until the return of Christ. This group, called the historicists, sees events in Revelation 4—19 being fulfilled in such events as the Protestant Reformation or the two world wars, with chapters 20—22 being about the final judgment and a new heaven and earth that are still to come.

A third group—known as the futurists—believe most of the prophecies of Revelation will occur in a period of final crisis just before the return of Christ. Though many in this group think the seven churches mentioned in chapters 1—3 were real congregations that existed during the time of John, others maintain the seven parishes symbolize seven stages of church history. This group generally thinks chapters 4—19 concern a time of future tribulation. They maintain that God will judge an apostate church as well as Antichrist and his followers. Those who hold to this view say this time of judgment will end with the return of Christ.

A fourth group is called the idealists. They believe the symbols and prophecies in Revelation represent principles of spiritual warfare that apply to all ages. Revelation is thus a kind of theological poem that describes the eternal conflict between good and evil in the world. Any evil person through the ages (such as

Hitler) could be seen as a kind of antichrist who eventually would be defeated. In this approach, then, chapters 4—19 are regarded as representing the conflict of good and evil, while chapters 20—22 are said to symbolize the triumph of good.

The imagery in Revelation is colorful, intense, and capable of being understood in a variety of ways. That is why some believers prefer to use a combination of approaches when interpreting the book.

NOTES ON THE PRINTED TEXT

U p until this point in John's unfolding vision, he recounted a series of seal and trumpet judgments being unleashed on humankind. After the blowing of the seventh trumpet, the apostle presented such key symbolic characters as the woman, the dragon, the beast, the false prophet, and the 144,000. Then, as John watched, he saw an angel flying *in midheaven* (Rev. 14:6). God gave this celestial being *an eternal gospel* to proclaim to all the people of the earth. Some think this is the saving message of Jesus' death and resurrection. More likely the announcement recorded in 14:7 denotes the content of the good news the angel proclaimed.

The angel directed all earth's inhabitants to *"Fear God and give him glory."* This emphasis on revering and honoring the Lord was made in light of the fact that the time for Him to judge the wicked had come. The angel also urged humanity to worship the Creator of heaven and earth. This has been God's will for earth's inhabitants throughout history. Some think the angel's message is only a declaration that judgment is about to fall, with no appeal being made for the wicked to repent. The context, however, suggests that the Lord was making a final call for the people of the world to abandon their sin and acknowledge Him as their God.

John next saw another angel following the first one across the sky and announcing that the great city of Babylon is *fallen* (14:8). The celestial being explained that Babylon had seduced the nations of the world like a prostitute and made them drunk on *"the wine of the wrath of her fornication."* The reference to Babylon echoes terminology found in Daniel 4:30. In fact, there are numerous similar literary correspondences between Daniel and Revelation. This suggests that what is anticipated in Daniel concerning the end times comes to final fulfillment in Revelation.

The identity of Babylon in Revelation is disputed. Some think it is a code name for Rome, which in John's day was the epitome of opposition to God and His people. Others maintain that some notorious ancient city—such as Babylon, Rome, Tyre, or Jerusalem—will be rebuilt in the end times as the capital of a great world empire headed up by Antichrist. Still others think Babylon represents the corrupt political, commercial, social, and religious systems of the world.

John next saw a third *angel* (Rev. 14:9) following the first two across the sky. This creature announced that those who worshiped the beast that came out of the sea or the *image* made to represent it will experience God's judgment. The same end was true for those who are branded on their forehead or hand with the distinctive *mark* of the beast.

Then a third angel followed the other two, crying out to those with the mark of the beast on earth that they would drink the undiluted *"wine of God's wrath"* (14:10). The cup of God's wrath being poured out is an Old Testament image of His judgment (Ps. 75:8; Isa. 51:17; Jer. 25:15-17). The angel added to that image a picture of how those who worship the beast will suffer for all eternity, *day [and] night* (Rev. 14:11), *tormented with fire and sulfur in the presence of the holy angels and in the presence of the Lamb* (14:10). John could not have painted a more horrible picture for those of his time who might be tempted to renounce Jesus and be "marked" as worshipers of the beast.

Instead of caving in to the world, believers were urged to steadfastly endure the trials and tribulations of this world, to *keep the commandments of God and hold fast to the faith of Jesus* (14:12). Reliance on Jesus is the only way to remain faithful in the face of all the world does to compromise, demoralize, or destroy Christians and Christianity. In fact, John heard a voice from heaven saying that those who die faithfully following Jesus will be *blessed* (14:13), an announcement so important that it must be written down. It is the second of seven blessings found in Revelation (see 1:3; 16:15; 19:9; 20:6; 22:7, 14). To that message the Spirit Himself added, *"They will rest from their labors, for their deeds follow them"* (14:13). God will remember all that the faithful have endured in remaining loyal to Him.

SUGGESTIONS TO TEACHERS

John described two different groups of people that we see around us today—those who give in to the world and are marked as the devil's slaves, and those who faithfully follow Christ and serve Him for eternity. While John called on *the saints* (Rev. 14:12) to endure and resist becoming one with the world, he also recorded how much God longed for those who are caught in the world's snares to come over to His side. God even sent an angel to urge all the people of the world who did not serve Him to worship Him and spend eternity with Him, their Creator (14:7). These people are not only the enemies of God and Christians, but also the captives of Satan and his schemes. They are "prisoners of war" (POWs) in a cosmic struggle between good and evil, prisoners that all Christians can help release and repatriate to the "good" side. Why should we call them POWs? This acronym describes their current condition.

1. POWERLESS. Without the power of the Holy Spirit in their lives, the unsaved remain Satan's prisoners. Can they receive God's power and be released? Certainly, but we must help them, by explaining the Gospel to them and by showing them how wonderful a regenerate life in Christ can be.

2. OPPRESSED. What keeps people as slaves to Satan? Paul said they have a disobedient spirit that keeps them following the desires of the flesh (Eph. 2:2-3), rather than the Holy Spirit. The unsaved are oppressed by the desire to always serve themselves and do whatever their hearts desire. Leading them to trust in Christ can lift that burden from their lives and bring them into a relationship with the one who bears our burdens for us.

3. WITHOUT HOPE. People with no hope have nothing to live for except today. They do not see a future outside the fence of Satan's confinement. They need Christians who will show them that there is an eternal side to life, and that a grand and glorious future awaits those who will be with the Lord forever. Whether they realize it or not, in this life they are making eternal choices, and we need to help them see the right choices to make.

FOR ADULTS	■ **TOPIC:** A Call for Endurance ■ **QUESTIONS:** 1. What was message of the first angel? 2. What had happened to the great city of Babylon? 3. What will those who

worship the beast receive? 4. How should the saints live in light of eternity? 5. How is endurance important in living the Christian life?

■ **ILLUSTRATIONS:**

Victory Takes Endurance. So many things in our lives happen instantly, from Internet connections to our morning coffee. However, when we are building our lives with Christ, certain things like faith, trust, hope, and love take time to grow and strengthen.

In his book titled *Seeds of Greatness*, Dennis Waitley points out examples of how long it took some major companies to make their first billion dollars. McDonald's took 22 years, IBM took 46 years, and Xerox took 63 years. The climb to success was not without problems and disappointments for these companies. The people in charge showed patience and endurance in building the companies' reputations and fortunes over a period of decades.

As we go through our lives, we need to be building our patience and endurance, too. Though we could easily be discouraged by losses, conflicts, or criticisms, God wants to help us stay focused on Him and the final victory before us.

Through It All. Walter Winchell, an American journalist, once stated, "A friend is one who walks in when others walk out." When I read this quote, I thought about our good friends Lynn and Alan. They often remind us that my husband, Ed, and I have stuck by them when few others did. A few years ago they had to undergo a farm bankruptcy, and suddenly people who they thought were their friends didn't have much of anything to do with them. It never occurred to us to walk away from them during this difficult time. They needed someone to talk to, cry with, and pray with.

While Ed and I may not have had something as public as a bankruptcy to deal with, Lynn and Alan have helped us through many difficult situations in our own lives. We have not only shared the sorrow of losing parents, but also the joy that comes from sharing our faith and love in the Lord.

This kind of friendship is an excellent example of endurance. While we may know that the Lord will stick with us through all the good and bad times of our lives, we also need earthly friends who remind us of this enduring love. He is beside us through it all—whether we are unpopular, suffering, or rejoicing.

Keep Focused on the Purpose. A man bought a new hunting dog and could hardly wait to see how the dog would perform. First, he took him out to track a bear. No sooner had they gotten into the woods than the dog picked up the scent. Suddenly the dog stopped, sniffed the ground, and headed in a new direction. He had caught the scent of a deer that had crossed the bear's path. A few moments later the dog halted again, this time smelling a rabbit that had crossed the path of the deer. On and on this continued until the breathless hunter finally caught up with his dog, only to find him barking triumphantly down the hole of a field mouse.

Sometimes we, as Christians, are like that. We may start out with high goals of keeping Christ first in our lives, but soon our attention is diverted to less important things. Only *those who keep the commandments of God and hold fast to the faith of Jesus* (Rev. 14:12) will endure through this life and into the next one.

FOR YOUTH

■ Topic: Where Do I Belong?

■ Questions: 1. How many angels did John see? 2. What message did each angel bring? 3. Who will receive God's wrath? Why? 4. What is the goal of endurance? 5. Do you see yourself as being committed to Christ no matter what happens? Explain.

■ Illustrations:

Part of the Family. Being close to Christ, and Him to you, is something like living in a small town. My husband and I lived in town of about 3,000 people for over 12 years. The town was basically a mile square, with one stoplight on Main Street. Just like the joke says, we really didn't need to use our turn signal while driving because everyone knew where we were going. And if I forgot to use my seatbelt, the children I taught at school would tell me about it the next day. If we missed Sunday morning church, we would receive a call that afternoon, asking if we were OK.

This kind of closeness helped us feel like we belonged there. We were members of the family, and our actions were noticed by everyone. Christ wants us to belong to Him, and be part of His spiritual family. He wants our lives to reflect Him now, and He wants us to be among those who are blessed at the end of time.

Life Is like a Deck Chair. In a *Peanuts* comic strip, there was a conversation between Lucy and Charlie Brown. Lucy said that life is like a deck chair. Some place it so they can see where they are going; some place it so they can see where they have been; and some place it so they can see where they are at present. Charlie Brown's reply: "I can't even get mine unfolded."

Do you need help unfolding your "deck chair" and placing it where you belong? In other words, have you found your purpose and direction in life? When we put our lives in God's hands, we may not know everything that will happen to us in this life, but we can be assured that He will stay beside us now and that we will be with Him throughout eternity.

How Can I Find God? There is an ancient tale from India about a young man who was seeking God. He went to a wise old sage for help. "How can I find God?" he asked the old man. The old man took him to a nearby river. Out they waded into the deep water. Soon the water was up just under their chins. Suddenly the old man seized the young man by the neck and pushed him under the water. He held the young man there until the young man was fighting for his life.

Finally the old man released his grip and allowed the young man to surface. Coughing water from his lungs and still gasping for air, the young man asked the old man indignantly, "What did that have to do with my finding God?"

The old man asked him quietly, "While you were under the water, what did you want more than anything else?" The young man thought for a minute and then answered, "I wanted air. I wanted air more than anything else." The old man replied, "When you want God as much as you wanted air, you will find Him."

Those who have found God know how strong the desire is to want more of Him. He becomes as much a part of our lives as the air that we breathe. A relationship this close helps develop feelings of belonging.

A New Heaven and Earth

Background Scripture: Revelation 21:1—22:5
Devotional Reading: Revelation 22:1-5

Key Verse: "See, the home of God is among mortals. He will dwell with them; they will be his peoples, and God himself will be with them." Revelation 21:3.

KING JAMES VERSION

REVELATION 21:1 And I saw a new heaven and a new earth: for the first heaven and the first earth were passed away; and there was no more sea.

2 And I John saw the holy city, new Jerusalem, coming down from God out of heaven, prepared as a bride adorned for her husband.

3 And I heard a great voice out of heaven saying, Behold, the tabernacle of God is with men, and he will dwell with them, and they shall be his people, and God himself shall be with them, and be their God.

4 And God shall wipe away all tears from their eyes; and there shall be no more death, neither sorrow, nor crying, neither shall there be any more pain: for the former things are passed away.

5 And he that sat upon the throne said, Behold, I make all things new. And he said unto me, Write: for these words are true and faithful.

6 And he said unto me, It is done. I am Alpha and Omega, the beginning and the end. I will give unto him that is athirst of the fountain of the water of life freely.

7 He that overcometh shall inherit all things; and I will be his God, and he shall be my son. . . .

22 And I saw no temple therein: for the Lord God Almighty and the Lamb are the temple of it.

23 And the city had no need of the sun, neither of the moon, to shine in it: for the glory of God did lighten it, and the Lamb is the light thereof.

24 And the nations of them which are saved shall walk in the light of it: and the kings of the earth do bring their glory and honour into it.

25 And the gates of it shall not be shut at all by day: for there shall be no night there.

26 And they shall bring the glory and honour of the nations into it.

27 And there shall in no wise enter into it any thing that defileth, neither whatsoever worketh abomination, or maketh a lie: but they which are written in the Lamb's book of life.

NEW REVISED STANDARD VERSION

REVELATION 21:1 Then I saw a new heaven and a new earth; for the first heaven and the first earth had passed away, and the sea was no more. 2 And I saw the holy city, the new Jerusalem, coming down out of heaven from God, prepared as a bride adorned for her husband. 3 And I heard a loud voice from the throne saying,

"See, the home of God is among mortals. He will dwell with them; they will be his peoples, and God himself will be with them;

4 he will wipe every tear from their eyes. Death will be no more; mourning and crying and pain will be no more, for the first things have passed away."

5 And the one who was seated on the throne said, "See, I am making all things new." Also he said, "Write this, for these words are trustworthy and true." 6 Then he said to me, "It is done! I am the Alpha and the Omega, the beginning and the end. To the thirsty I will give water as a gift from the spring of the water of life. 7 Those who conquer will inherit these things, and I will be their God and they will be my children." . . .

22 I saw no temple in the city, for its temple is the Lord God the Almighty and the Lamb. 23 And the city has no need of sun or moon to shine on it, for the glory of God is its light, and its lamp is the Lamb. 24 The nations will walk by its light, and the kings of the earth will bring their glory into it. 25 Its gates will never be shut by day—and there will be no night there. 26 People will bring into it the glory and the honor of the nations. 27 But nothing unclean will enter it, nor anyone who practices abomination or falsehood, but only those who are written in the Lamb's book of life.

13

Monday, May 24	Revelation 19:6-10	*The Lord Almighty Reigns*
Tuesday, May 25	Revelation 21:1-7	*A New Heaven and Earth*
Wednesday, May 26	Revelation 21:9-14	*John Sees the Holy City*
Thursday, May 27	Revelation 21:22-27	*God's Glory Is Its Light*
Friday, May 28	Revelation 22:1-5	*There Will Be No More Night*
Saturday, May 29	Revelation 22:6-10	*I Am Coming Soon!*
Sunday, May 30	Revelation 22:12-17	*I am the Alpha and Omega*

BACKGROUND

John noted that he saw the new Jerusalem as a bride made ready for her husband (Rev. 21:2). In the ancient Near East, the wedding ceremony usually took place after dark at the bride's house. Prior to the wedding ceremony, the groom and his friends would form a procession and walk to the home of the bride. After the couple was officially married, the procession would return to the home of the groom or his father.

As the procession journeyed along a planned route, friends of the groom would join the group and participate in singing, playing musical instruments, and dancing. The bride would wear an ornate dress, expensive jewelry (if she could afford it), and a veil over her face. The groom typically hung a garland of flowers around his neck.

Once the procession arrived at its destination, a lavish feast, lasting up to seven days, would begin. Friends would sing love ballads for the couple and share stories about them. Everyone would consume food and drink in generous quantities. At the end of the first day's festivities, the bride and groom would be escorted to their private wedding chamber.

NOTES ON THE PRINTED TEXT

In John's unfolding vision, the condemnation of the wicked (Rev. 20:11-15) is followed by the new creation that awaits believers. The apostle related that he saw *a new heaven and a new earth* (21:1). These are total replacements for the their old counterparts, *the first heaven and the first earth,* which God had destroyed. He evidently did this to eliminate any corrupting presence or influence of sin (2 Pet. 3:7, 10-13).

What John saw is consistent with Isaiah's reference to the *new heavens and a new earth* (Isa. 65:17). The apostle, however, was not thinking of merely a world free of sin and hardness of heart. John's vision was of a creation new in all its qualities.

God will also eliminate the vast and mysterious seas. In the Old Testament, the sea was a symbol for the agitation and restlessness associated with evil (Isa. 57:20; Jer. 49:23). In Revelation, the sea is the source of the satanic beast and a burial site for the dead (Rev. 13:1; 20:13). In the eternal state, there can be no physical and symbolic place for this seething cauldron of wickedness.

The apostle's attention quickly passed from the creation to the new heaven and earth and to *the holy city, the new Jerusalem* (21:2), which God sent down out of heaven. The Lord magnificently adorned the new Jerusalem (the bride) for her husband (the groom). The implication here is that the city surpassed the beauty of everything else God had made.

Some think the new Jerusalem is a symbol of the Christian community in heaven; however, based on the detailed information recorded in verses 10-21, others maintain the new Jerusalem will be a literal city where God's people dwell for all eternity. In either case, a new world is coming and it will be glorious beyond imagination.

John then heard *a loud voice from the throne* (21:3) declare that God Himself had come to *dwell* with *his peoples*. In contrast to the past, when God's presence left both the tabernacle in the wilderness and the first temple, God now permanently tabernacled with all believers (see Ezek. 37:26). While God dwells in the church now by the Holy Spirit, the faithful will all one day see Him face to face. Then tears, death, mourning, and pain will all cease (Rev. 21:4). The old order of things will pass away because of *the one who was seated on the throne* (21:5).

This is one of several places in Revelation where the throne of God is mentioned. In ancient times thrones were symbols of power, sovereignty, and majesty. The throne in heaven serves as reminder of the just reign of God over the course of history. Also, the Lamb's constant presence near, around, and on the throne makes it the focal point for His exercise of power. God's presence blazes forth from the celestial throne (4:2-3). The image is one of a transparent jewel radiating the splendor of the divine. It is interesting to note that throughout Revelation John did not describe the details of God's appearance. This reminds us that the Lord's greatness and glory are beyond our ability to comprehend.

God promised to make *"all things new"* (21:5). He has the power to do so, for because He is *"the Alpha and the Omega"* (21:6). This expression, which is emphatic in the original, draws upon the first and last letters of the Greek alphabet. It's as if the divine were saying, "I and no other." It is similar in meaning to the expressions *"the beginning and the end"* and *"the first and the last"* (1:17; 22:13). The idea behind these statements—which are applied interchangeably to both the Father and the Son—is one of totality. In other words, the Lord is the beginning and ending of all things. Also, His rule encompasses the past, the present, and the future. Furthermore, He is sovereign over all that takes place in human history and is directing its course to a final and proper conclusion (Col. 1:17; Heb. 1:3).

God then promised to give *water* (Rev. 21:6) from the life-giving fountain to everyone who was *thirsty*. This pledge is a vivid reminder of the refreshment and satisfaction believers will enjoy in heaven. In the eternal state, God will satisfy the yearnings of the soul. This assurance is grounded in the Lord's own nature.

Those who overcome in this life will receive an eternal inheritance and an eternal relationship. They will be the eternal people of the eternal God (21:7). Virtue and purity will characterize life for the redeemed in heaven; and the Lord will ban from heaven all who are characterized by the vices listed in 21:8.

In Revelation 21:9-21, John gave a stunning description of the new Jerusalem, which is the final dwelling place for God's people. The city sparkles like a precious gem and radiates the majesty of the Lord. The city also resembles a gigantic cube and the same shape as the Most Holy Place in the tabernacle and temple. Unlike the Jerusalem of Bible times, however, the new Jerusalem will have *no temple* (21:22) in it. The reason is that *the Lord God the Almighty and the Lamb* are the city's temple. Similarly, the new Jerusalem will have no need for the sun or the moon, for *the glory of God* (21:23) illuminates the city and *the Lamb* is the city's source of light.

All *the nations* (21:24) will walk in the city's *light*. Likewise, *the kings of the earth* will bring their glory and honor to it. The new Jerusalem will truly be the center of life for the redeemed in eternity. It will be such a safe and secure haven that during the day its gates will *never be shut* (vs. 25). Even *night*, with all the fears and uncertainties connected with it, will be eliminated.

In the new Jerusalem, God will be worshiped face-to-face. The city will be a cosmopolitan place, where redeemed humanity in all its cultural diversity will live together in peace. In fact, *the glory and the honor of the nations* (21:26) will stream into the new Jerusalem. God will vindicate the faith of the redeemed by not permitting any immoral or wicked people to enter the holy city. The inhabitants of the new Jerusalem will only be those whose names are recorded in *the Lamb's book of life* (21:27).

SUGGESTIONS TO TEACHERS

What will increase the sales of almost any product on the market? Add to the product's name the words "New and Improved!" People seem to be fascinated by new things, so John's vision of a new heaven, a new earth, and a new Jerusalem probably intrigues us. There are at least three reasons for our fascination, and these three reasons can also help us rethink our Christian lives on this side of eternity:

1. NEW THINGS ARE UNTARNISHED. The *new heaven* (Rev. 21:1) and the *new earth* that are coming will only faintly resemble what exists now. None of the problems that are here now will be found in eternity. In much the same way, Paul said, when we trust in Christ for salvation, we become new creations— *everything old has passed away; see, everything has become new!* (2 Cor. 5:17). God wants to always be at work in our lives through the Holy Spirit, creating in us new people who are genuinely *transformed* (Rom. 12:2).

2. NEW THINGS ARE FRESH. New life in springtime brings fresh leaves and plants, not a recoloring or reworking of what was there last year. The old fall leaves, for example, do not suddenly change color and reattach themselves to the branches. Thus, a plant always has new opportunities to grow and flourish. Similarly, people should always grow in Christ, continually looking for new opportunities to serve Him and to be more like Him.

3. NEW THINGS ARE UNCLUTTERED. Though the Holy Spirit makes us new creations in Christ, it's hard to be a completely new person in Him because we carry with us the "clutter" of what we once were or are still trying not to be. Thankfully, in the new heaven and new earth, the past will not even be a memory. The slate will be wiped clean. Though we have a start on that process now, we can only fully complete it with Christ in eternity, for when we leave this earth to be with Him, we will "leave our baggage at the terminal before departing."

FOR ADULTS	■ TOPIC: A New Homecoming

■ **QUESTIONS:** 1. What did John see that was new? 2. What will happen when God dwells with His people? 3. Why does God call Himself *"the Alpha and the Omega"* (Rev. 21:6)? 4. Why will there be no temple or sun in the new Jerusalem? 5. Does this eternal city appeal to you? Why?

■ **ILLUSTRATIONS:**

Home Where I Belong. My husband and I were settled into our lives in western Kansas. We thought we had found our "hometown." We had lots of friends and ministry opportunities that made us feel wanted and loved. However, we both felt God calling us into full-time ministry. For us that meant we had to move away to a large city in another state to attend seminary. We left our nice home to live in a small two-bedroom apartment on the seminary campus. We left friends who knew all of our strengths and weaknesses to be with people we did not know. We left good-paying jobs with lots of benefits to work five part-time jobs between us with no benefits.

Even with all of the losses, we found a wonderful new home. God blessed us with new friends, wonderful professors, and exciting challenges. God always provided for our needs—even if it was at the last minute! God also helped us grow spiritually in ways we never had imagined. We both felt we had finally come home to a place we had always needed to be.

I think we experienced just a small taste of what our new home in the eternal city will be like. Although everything will be new, we will feel like we have come home to the place where we belong.

Let's Go to Your House. Tom was elderly, and for many years he had enjoyed taking long walks with the Lord each evening. On these walks, he and the Lord would talk about all kinds of things, especially about many of the important times in Tom's life, such as when he met his wife, the birth of his children, and special Christmases.

One day, while Tom was out walking with the Lord for an especially long time, Tom sensed the Lord conveying to him, "We are closer to My house than we are to yours. Why don't you just come home with Me?" Tom was glad to go.

I think that is the way God would like for all of us to view His house. In Revelation 21:7 God said, *"I will be their God and they will be my children."* Going to heaven is going home to be part of the everlasting family of God.

The Definition of Heaven. Robert Capon, author of *The Parables of the Kingdom,* says, "'Heaven' or 'heavenly' in the New Testament bear little relation to the meanings we have so unscripturally attached to them. For us, heaven is an unearthly, humanly irrelevant condition in which bed-sheeted, paper-winged spirits sit on clouds and play tinkly music until their pipe-cleaner halos drop off from boredom. But in Scripture, it is a city with boys and girls playing in the streets; it is buildings . . . that use amethysts for cinder blocks and pearls as big as the Ritz for gates; and indoors, it is a dinner party to end all dinner parties at the marriage supper of the Lamb. It is, in short, earth wedded, not earth jilted. It is the world as the irremovable apple of God's eyes."

This new city that God is creating for us will be more than we could ever hope for or imagine. God is eagerly awaiting the time when all believers will be gathered together at His table, having come to His house to stay.

■ TOPIC: A New World Coming!

■ QUESTIONS: 1. What happened to the first earth and sea? 2. What will the new Jerusalem look like? 3. Why will there be no more death or sorrow in the new Jerusalem? 4. Who will be allowed in the holy city? 5. Why do you think it is important to have your name in the Lamb's book of life?

■ ILLUSTRATIONS:

Leaving the Old Behind. During my growing up years, my family moved around a lot because of my dad's job. I was in six different school systems by the time I graduated from high school. While going to someplace new was scary and hard on me, my mom always tried to help my brothers and me see the good things that could come from all things being new. She told us it was our golden opportunity to change a bad habit or attitude we did not like about ourselves. No one would know all of our past faults, and the new people would not be able to throw our past mistakes up in our face.

I especially remember our move during my middle school years. I came from a school with about 300 students to one with over 900 students. I decided I was going to be more outgoing and not as shy in this new school. It was fun to create a "new world" for myself. I was still true to myself—with the same likes, dislikes, and morals, for example—but I was "allowed" to talk more freely in class and to be more adventurous. I even tried out for the school play and joined several clubs!

As we look ahead to the new world God will create for believers in heaven, we can be excited to know that all old things will pass away. No one will care about the past mistakes and failures in our lives if our name is written in the Lamb's book of life.

A Happy Ending. Katie was offered the opportunity to select a dog for her birthday present. At the pet store, she was shown a number of puppies. From them she picked the one whose tail was wagging furiously. When Katie was asked why she chose that particular dog, she said, "I wanted the one with the happy ending."

Everyone will share in the ultimate "happy ending," if they make the choice now to follow the living Christ as Lord and Savior. Revelation promises us that a new world is coming for all believers and what a happy "beginning" it will be!

What Will Heaven Be Like? Billy Graham once said, "Just as there is a mystery to hell, so there is a mystery to heaven. Yet I believe the Bible teaches that heaven is a literal place. Is it one of the stars? I don't know. I can't even speculate. The Bible doesn't inform us. I believe that out there in space where there are one thousand million galaxies, each a hundred thousand light years or more in diameter, God can find some place to put us in heaven. I'm not worried about where it is. I know it is going to be where Jesus is. Christians don't have to go around discouraged and despondent with their shoulders bent. Think about it—the joy, the peace, the sense of forgiveness that He gives you, and then heaven, too."

HOLD FAST TO THE FAITH

THE REASON TO BE FAITHFUL

BACKGROUND SCRIPTURE: Hebrews 1:1—2:4
DEVOTIONAL READING: Colossians 1:15-20

KEY VERSE: "[God's Son] is the reflection of God's glory and the exact imprint of God's very being." Hebrews 1:3a.

KING JAMES VERSION

HEBREWS 1:1 God, who at sundry times and in divers manners spake in time past unto the fathers by the prophets,

2 Hath in these last days spoken unto us by his Son, whom he hath appointed heir of all things, by whom also he made the worlds;

3 Who being the brightness of his glory, and the express image of his person, and upholding all things by the word of his power, when he had by himself purged our sins, sat down on the right hand of the Majesty on high;

4 Being made so much better than the angels, as he hath by inheritance obtained a more excellent name than they.

5 For unto which of the angels said he at any time, Thou art my Son, this day have I begotten thee? And again, I will be to him a Father, and he shall be to me a Son?

6 And again, when he bringeth in the firstbegotten into the world, he saith, And let all the angels of God worship him.

7 And of the angels he saith, Who maketh his angels spirits, and his ministers a flame of fire.

8 But unto the Son he saith, Thy throne, O God, is for ever and ever: a sceptre of righteousness is the sceptre of thy kingdom. . . .

9 Thou hast loved righteousness, and hated iniquity; therefore God, even thy God, hath anointed thee with the oil of gladness above thy fellows.

2:1 Therefore we ought to give the more earnest heed to the things which we have heard, lest at any time we should let them slip.

2 For if the word spoken by angels was stedfast, and every transgression and disobedience received a just recompence of reward;

3 How shall we escape, if we neglect so great salvation; which at the first began to be spoken by the Lord, and was confirmed unto us by them that heard him;

4 God also bearing them witness, both with signs and wonders, and with divers miracles, and gifts of the Holy Ghost, according to his own will?

NEW REVISED STANDARD VERSION

HEBREWS 1:1 Long ago God spoke to our ancestors in many and various ways by the prophets, 2 but in these last days he has spoken to us by a Son, whom he appointed heir of all things, through whom he also created the worlds. 3 He is the reflection of God's glory and the exact imprint of God's very being, and he sustains all things by his powerful word. When he had made purification for sins, he sat down at the right hand of the Majesty on high, 4 having become as much superior to angels as the name he has inherited is more excellent than theirs.

5 For to which of the angels did God ever say,
"You are my Son;
today I have begotten you"?
Or again,
"I will be his Father,
and he will be my Son"?
6 And again, when he brings the firstborn into the world, he says,
"Let all God's angels worship him."
7 Of the angels he says,
"He makes his angels winds,
and his servants flames of fire."
8 But of the Son he says,
"Your throne, O God, is forever and ever,
and the righteous scepter is the scepter of your kingdom.
9 You have loved righteousness and hated wickedness;
therefore God, your God, has anointed you
with the oil of gladness beyond your companions."

2:1 Therefore we must pay greater attention to what we have heard, so that we do not drift away from it. 2 For if the message declared through angels was valid, and every transgression or disobedience received a just penalty, 3 how can we escape if we neglect so great a salvation? It was declared at first through the Lord, and it was attested to us by those who heard him, 4 while God added his testimony by signs and wonders and various miracles, and by gifts of the Holy Spirit, distributed according to his will.

HOME BIBLE READINGS

Monday, May 31	Acts 4:5-12	*Christ Is the Cornerstone*
Tuesday, June 1	Colossians 1:15-20	*Christ Is the Image of God*
Wednesday, June 2	Colossians 1:21-27	*Christ in You, Hope of Glory*
Thursday, June 3	Colossians 2:1-6	*In Christ Are Treasures of Wisdom*
Friday, June 4	Hebrews 1:1-5	*Christ, the Reflection of God's Glory*
Saturday, June 5	Hebrews 1:6-13	*You Established the Universe*
Sunday, June 6	Hebrews 1:14—2:4	*Salvation Declared through Christ*

BACKGROUND

Although this book is usually called "The Letter to the Hebrews," it does not read much like an epistle. Rather than a letter, we might more aptly call Hebrews "a published sermon." Most ancient letters, such as the epistles Paul wrote, began by identifying both their writers and recipients. However, the author of Hebrews did not follow that pattern. The unknown writer jumped immediately into his topic. Also, Hebrews contains few references to its readers. We may continue the tradition of calling it a letter, but it reads more like a sermon.

We have quickly alluded to a puzzling question—"Who wrote Hebrews?" Regrettably, no one knows. It might have been Paul, Apollos, Barnabas or some-one else. Thankfully, our uncertainty regarding the book's author does not dra-matically affect its interpretation.

The opening verses of Hebrews, as well as the epistle as a whole, are packed solid with quotations from and allusions to the Old Testament. This fact, at least indirectly, gave Hebrews its title. You can easily follow the logic behind this con-clusion. The letter contains much Old Testament material. Therefore, the writer must have assumed this type of content would strongly influence his readers. Also, the readers must have been people who knew and valued the Old Testament. Therefore, the readers were likely Jews, or "Hebrews," as they are sometimes called.

Through roughly the first two-thirds of the epistle, the writer made his point— that God's people should worship Jesus, their Savior—by means of contrasts. Within these contrasts, the writer repeatedly pointed out that Jesus is superior to any other entity. In the first chapter, the author laid out two such contrasts: God's revelation in Jesus surpasses what we read in the Old Testament (1:1-3). Likewise, the stature of Jesus Himself is higher than the position angels hold (1:4—2:4).

As we continue our study of Hebrews, we will see similar contrasts. The con-tent within these contrasts offers further support to the idea that this epistle was written for Jews, more specifically Jewish Christians. Each of the contrasts high-lights Jesus' superiority to some person or system the Jews valued (for example, the Old Testament itself, Moses, or the temple sacrificial system). By means of these contrasts, the writer sought to prevent Jewish Christians from forsaking

Jesus to return to traditional Jewish ways.

The writer of Hebrews finished this first section of the book with strong words of warning. If *every transgression or disobedience* [of the law] *received a just penalty, how can we escape if we neglect so great a salvation?* (2:2-3). You can find similar warning passages in 3:7—4:13; 5:11—6:12; 10:19-39; and 12:14-29.

What factors necessitated these warnings? Evidently readers of this book were facing persecution (see 10:32-34). Jewish Christians might have been caught in a ferocious middle ground, receiving painful exclusion, both from pagans and from non-Christian Jews. A retreat into the relative safety of Judaism might have tempted some Hebrew believers. And so the writer began this letter by reminding these Christians why they came to Jesus in the first place: The Son, *the reflection of God's glory* (1:3), offers a far better way.

Notes on the Printed Text

The writer to the Hebrews opened his symphony with strong verbal notes. *Long ago God spoke . . . by the prophets, but in these last days he has spoken to us by a Son* (1:1-2). The writer saw God's first words as valuable, but His more recent words as priceless. At the same time, no New Testament author ever negated the value of God's prior revelation. The entire Bible contains words that *God spoke*. All Old Testament writers, here collectively described as *the prophets* (1:1), authoritatively and accurately spoke God's mind, particularly for their times.

Before going on, note the significance of the words *in these last days* (1:2). Frequently, the prophets had looked forward to "the last days" (for example, Isa. 2:2; Hos. 3:5; Mic. 4:1), or as we might say, "the end times." As the writer used the past tense in reference to the *last days* (Heb. 1:2), he announced that, in one important sense, the end times had begun. They had been inaugurated with the coming of God's *Son*. Wise Christians do not neglect what God had spoken through His previous messengers, but *pay greater attention* (2:1) to that which God accomplished *by* [His] *Son* (1:2).

God's new revelation surpasses His prior words. Having stated that foundational premise, the writer moved toward his next point: Jesus' superiority to the angels. Before stating that idea, however, the writer offered several key summaries of Jesus' person and work. God *appointed* His Son *heir of all things*. These words likely allude to Psalm 2:8, where the Lord had promised to give His Son the nations as His heritage. *Through* (Heb. 1:2) His Son, God *created the worlds*. Not only will Jesus receive all things in the end, but also He participated in their origin.

The Son *is the reflection of God's glory* (1:3). Some translators prefer the stronger word "radiance." Jesus not only reflects God's light; the light of God Himself shines out from His Son. The Son is *the exact imprint of God's very being*. Jesus was more than a rough representation of the Father. Jesus forever is

God. The Son *sustains all things by his powerful word.* Is it possible that Jesus might tell each daffodil to grow, each heart to beat, and gravity to hold us safely on earth? Perhaps Jesus is the one that holds all molecules together. Those thoughts may be a bit whimsical, but our universe certainly would change dramatically if the Son withdrew His hand from it.

The Son *made purification for sins.* As you will see, Jesus' self-sacrifice forms a major theme later in the epistle (chapters 8 through 10). Here the writer foreshadowed his subsequent writing on the Son's act of power and love. The Son *sat down at the right hand* (1:3) of God. When the Son finished the work the Father sent Him to do, the Father invited the Son to the place of greatest honor.

The writer, having laid out this description of who Jesus is and what He had done, offered his next major premise: Jesus had *become as much superior to angels as the name he has inherited is more excellent than theirs* (1:4). What name had Jesus received? The Old Testament quotations in 1:5 (Ps. 2:7 and 2 Sam. 7:14) answer that question. Jesus is called God's Son. As the writer pointed out, God had never called any angel *my Son* (Heb. 1:5).

To any readers tempted to worship angels, the author gave this reminder. The angels are not divine beings, for they join humanity in worshiping the Son (1:6, quoting Deut. 32:43). But their lower status did not make them valueless (just as Jesus' superior revelation did not negate the Old Testament). The writer merely wanted his readers to see angels in the right perspective—as God's *servants* (Heb. 1:7, quoting Ps. 104:4.) Hebrews 1:8 and 9 continue in the same vein. Jesus may have seen Himself as a servant (for example, Mark 10:45), but in comparison to the angels, He is a King! Words like *throne* (Heb. 1:8), *scepter,* and *anointed* (1:9) all point to Jesus' royalty.

This week's lesson text passes over the rest of Hebrews 1. It moves to the opening verses of the second chapter, verses that further developed and applied the unfolding logic of the epistle. If Jesus' revelation is more complete than what anyone could read in the Old Testament, then everyone *must pay greater attention to* (2:1) His truth. This verse includes a reference to the writer's concern for his readers—he feared that they might *drift away* from that truth.

Words in 2:2 tie together the first chapter's two contrasts: Jesus is superior both to the Old Testament and the angels. A tradition had developed (seen in Scripture in Deut. 33:2 and Gal. 3:19) that, on Mount Sinai, angels had transmitted God's law to Moses. Even so, the message God gave through His Son clearly surpasses any earlier message delivered by mere angels. If God rebuked those who neglected the earlier, partial revelation, how can anyone escape who rejects the later final word of *salvation* (Heb. 2:3)? So, in effect, the writer asked his readers to choose between temporary pain combined with eternal reward, or comfort in this life followed by God's far greater eternal punishment.

The writer finished this paragraph by offering support for his claims. On what basis could readers trust his warning? First, the writer placed himself in line with *the Lord* and *those who* [had] *heard him* (2:4). In effect, the author pointed out that rejecting his message involved turning back from God's Son, whom the writer had so gloriously portrayed in 1:2-3. Second, God the Father Himself *added his testimony* (2:4) to the validity of the new covenant by means of *signs, wonders,* and the *gifts of the Holy Spirit.* Perhaps some of this book's readers had been visiting Jerusalem at the time of the first Pentecost, when signs and miracles substantiated the apostles' preaching. In any case, the readers' own transformed lives served as a great miracle of God's power.

SUGGESTIONS TO TEACHERS

As the writer to the Hebrews opened his epistle, he must have been thinking that the most alluring temptations his readers faced did not involve obvious evils such as murder or adultery. Instead, they were tempted to overvalue the good (such as Old Testament and angels) by elevating them to the level of the perfect (namely, God's Son). Christians today face similar temptations. Encourage your students to see the truth of the following statements.

1. ALL GOD'S GIFTS ARE VALUABLE. Just as the writer to the Hebrews valued the divine gifts of the Old Testament and the angels, so God's people today can appropriately enjoy all the good gifts God has given us. When God looked down on the world He had just made, He called it all very good.

2. BUT GOD'S GREATEST GIFT IS HIMSELF. God has given His people gifts such as natural beauty, the Scriptures, family and friends, and churches, but none of them can compare with His greatest gift—God Himself coming to earth in the form of His Son, Jesus Christ.

3. ALONG WITH HIS GIFTS, GOD GIVES A WARNING. God instructs His people to worship Him, the Giver. They become guilty of idolatry when any of even God's best gifts takes first priority in their lives.

4. WE CAN ENJOY GOD AND HIS GIFTS. The writer wanted his readers to avoid worshiping the Old Testament and the angels. He thus instructed them to obey the teaching of the Old Testament and follow the example of the angels in worshiping the one true God (Father, Son, and Holy Spirit), the giver of all good gifts. The writer knew that, when God's people worship Him alone, they can best enjoy both God and all His many gifts.

FOR ADULTS

■ TOPIC: The Reason to Be Faithful

■ QUESTIONS: 1. Why do you think some believers might have given too high a priority to the Old Testament and angels? 2. What were the dangers of drifting away from the true faith? 3. By what reasoning did the writer try to argue that Jesus is superior? 4. What are some of God's good gifts that Christians might be tempted to overvalue? 5. By what means can we catch ourselves when, in our loyalties, one of God's gifts is rivaling God Himself?

■ **ILLUSTRATIONS:**

Unusual Gifts Used for God. The opening paragraph of Hebrews offered its readers a wonderful example of using the Greek language with great stylistic effect. We don't know who wrote this epistle, but we do know that he must have been a highly educated person. When the writer became a Christian, God did not ask him to leave his education and talents behind. Instead, God called him to use his thinking and writing abilities for the glory of God and the growth of the church. Perhaps you know people who offer their skills and experience to God for His use.

Joy piloted a casino boat in Baton Rouge, Louisiana, before she heard God's call on her life. Today she gives her time ministering to riverboat captains and crews. Joy knows what it's like to spend entire months away on the river. From her experience, she can minister empathetically to others who face that situation.

Barb was a computer web genius. She now gives half her time to building and maintaining a Christian website. Her site offers all kinds of information enabling Christians to minister better to nearby people of other ethnic groups.

The New Surpasses the Old. While in third grade, I typed my first research paper. On my mother's manual typewriter, I pecked away at the keys. Beginning with that ancient model, I can remember several typewriters I have known—my own first manual that helped me through college, the electric typewriter my bride owned that took us through seminary, and a later model we bought while pastoring. That last typewriter printed by means of a ball rather than keys. In their time, typewriters served me well. On rare occasions, when filling in hard copy forms, I still wish I owned one. But typewriters have now been surpassed. When I consider all a computer enables me to do, do I ever consider discarding my word processor for even the best of typewriters? Not for a moment!

Drifting Away. Several years before I met her, my wife Kathy helped lead a church youth group. One youth group trip took several leaders and teens to Atlanta. While there, everyone spent an afternoon at Stone Mountain Lake. Kathy had never sailed before but decided she would take this opportunity. She pooled money with one of the kids and rented a small sailboat. The owner gave instructions he thought adequate.

Looking back, across many years, my wife insists that the boat had problems and that the owner had no right to rent them a defective sailboat. Perhaps the problem lay with the boaters rather than the boat. We will never know for sure.

In any case, you have already figured out what happened. Out on the lake, a good breeze was blowing, but not taking Kathy in the direction she wanted. Can you imagine how the rest of the group must have laughed as they watched Kathy and Harold being towed back to shore? They had no intention of drifting away, but that's what they had done. Hebrews 2:1 exhorts, *we must pay greater attention to what we have heard, so that we do not drift away from it.*

■ **TOPIC:** Why Be Faithful?

■ **QUESTIONS:** 1. How do you think the writer of Hebrews felt about the Old Testament? 2. What opinion might he have held of angels? 3. How might Jesus have felt when some of His Jewish followers gave more honor to their traditions than they did to Him? 4. What reasoning do you see in the logic behind the question asked in 2:2-3? 5. What components of your life might cause you to *drift away* (2:1) from loyalty to God?

■ **ILLUSTRATIONS:**

The Brilliant Light. Some of you have been blessed enough to observe a complete solar eclipse. During these events, the moon passes directly between the earth and the sun, blocking the sun's light. But even under these unusual circumstances, wise friends warned you not to look directly at the sun. Why? The sun still shines so brightly that even when its rays are blocked, you can be blinded by its radiance. Through the middle part of each typical sunny day, our eyes cannot distinguish the sun from its brilliance. In a similar way, we cannot separate God the Father and God the Son. Hebrews 1:3 reminds us that Jesus shines with the same brilliance of His Father.

Twins. We have since moved across the country, but when we resided in western New York, we lived next door to Jack and Mary. They had three young children: Hannah, Helen, and Mark. I could easily distinguish Mark, for he was a boy and a bit smaller than his sisters. But the two girls were identical twins. Maybe I should have tried harder, but I never could tell the two of them apart. I miss this family, but we recently heard news that would have made living next to them even more confusing. Mary is expecting another set of twins!

You may have had similar problems with distinguishing twins you know. Even if you are not a twin, you may look similar enough to one of your siblings that other people confuse the two of you.

The first readers of Hebrews were forgetting who Jesus was. Some of them somehow thought angels more impressive than Jesus Himself. But when the writer of this letter called Jesus *the exact imprint of God's very being* (1:3), he helped them see that the Father and the Son are more alike even than identical twins could be.

Even Losers Have Great Value. During the 2001 season, the Seattle Mariners baseball team did not win the World Series. In fact, they did not even play in the World Series. The New York Yankees had already defeated the Mariners in the American League Championship Series. When it really counted, the Mariners did not win their last few big games. But all baseball fans recognized that the Mariners still had a great team. In fact, the 2001 Mariners won more regular season games than any team had won in several decades. One of their players, Ichiro

Suzuki, won the league batting title, Rookie of the Year, and Most Valuable Player awards. And many feel that Ichiro was not even the most significant player on the team! In the end, the Mariners did not win. At least in the playoffs, they were not the best team. But, over the season, they still played very well.

The writer to the Hebrews wanted his readers to see Jesus as the ultimate winner. In value, He surpassed the Old Testament and the angels. Even so, when this writer came to chapter 11, his "Hall of Faith," he pointed out the value of the great examples from the Old Testament. Wise Christians do not neglect the Old Testament, for it offers great teaching to us all.

JESUS FULFILLS THE PLAN OF SALVATION

2

BACKGROUND SCRIPTURE: Hebrews 2:5-18
DEVOTIONAL READING: Philippians 2:5-11

KEY VERSE: "Therefore [Jesus] had to become like his brothers and sisters in every respect, so that he might . . . make a sacrifice of atonement for the sins of the people." Hebrews 2:17.

KING JAMES VERSION

HEBREWS 2:5 For unto the angels hath he not put in subjection the world to come, whereof we speak. 6 But one in a certain place testified, saying, What is man, that thou art mindful of him? or the son of man, that thou visitest him? 7 Thou madest him a little lower than the angels; thou crownedst him with glory and honour, and didst set him over the works of thy hands: 8 Thou hast put all things in subjection under his feet. For in that he put all in subjection under him, he left nothing that is not put under him. But now we see not yet all things put under him. 9 But we see Jesus, who was made a little lower than the angels for the suffering of death, crowned with glory and honour; that he by the grace of God should taste death for every man.

10 For it became him, for whom are all things, and by whom are all things, in bringing many sons unto glory, to make the captain of their salvation perfect through sufferings. 11 For both he that sanctifieth and they who are sanctified are all of one: for which cause he is not ashamed to call them brethren, 12 Saying, I will declare thy name unto my brethren, in the midst of the church will I sing praise unto thee. 13 And again, I will put my trust in him. And again, Behold I and the children which God hath given me.

14 Forasmuch then as the children are partakers of flesh and blood, he also himself likewise took part of the same; that through death he might destroy him that had the power of death, that is, the devil; 15 And deliver them who through fear of death were all their lifetime subject to bondage. 16 For verily he took not on him the nature of angels; but he took on him the seed of Abraham. 17 Wherefore in all things it behoved him to be made like unto his brethren, that he might be a merciful and faithful high priest in things pertaining to God, to make reconciliation for the sins of the people. 18 For in that he himself hath suffered being tempted, he is able to succour them that are tempted.

NEW REVISED STANDARD VERSION

HEBREWS 2:5 Now God did not subject the coming world, about which we are speaking, to angels. 6 But someone has testified somewhere,

"What are human beings that you are mindful of them,
    or mortals, that you care for them?
7 You have made them for a little while lower than
    the angels;
    you have crowned them with glory and honor,
8 subjecting all things under their feet."

Now in subjecting all things to them, God left nothing outside their control. As it is, we do not yet see everything in subjection to them, 9 but we do see Jesus, who for a little while was made lower than the angels, now crowned with glory and honor because of the suffering of death, so that by the grace of God he might taste death for everyone.

10 It was fitting that God, for whom and through whom all things exist, in bringing many children to glory, should make the pioneer of their salvation perfect through sufferings. 11 For the one who sanctifies and those who are sanctified all have one Father. For this reason Jesus is not ashamed to call them brothers and sisters, 12 saying,

"I will proclaim your name to my brothers and
    sisters,
    in the midst of the congregation I will praise you."
13 And again,

"I will put my trust in him."
And again,

"Here am I and the children whom God has given
    me."

14 Since, therefore, the children share flesh and blood, he himself likewise shared the same things, so that through death he might destroy the one who has the power of death, that is, the devil, 15 and free those who all their lives were held in slavery by the fear of death. 16 For it is clear that he did not come to help angels, but the descendants of Abraham. 17 Therefore he had to become like his brothers and sisters in every respect, so that he might be a merciful and faithful high priest in the service of God, to make a sacrifice of atonement for the sins of the people. 18 Because he himself was tested by what he suffered, he is able to help those who are being tested.

313

Monday, June 7	Acts 2:32-36	*God Has Made Jesus Messiah*
Tuesday, June 8	Acts 2:37-41	*Forgiveness of Sins through Christ*
Wednesday, June 9	Colossians 2:8-12	*Raised with Christ through Faith*
Thursday, June 10	Philippians 2:5-11	*Jesus Christ Is Lord*
Friday, June 11	Hebrews 2:5-9	*Jesus Tasted Death for Everyone*
Saturday, June 12	Hebrews 2:10-18	*Jesus Is the Pioneer of Salvation*
Sunday, June 13	Hebrews 3:1-6	*Christ, the Son, Was Faithful*

BACKGROUND

Hebrews 2:5-18, the second major section of the epistle, built on what preceded it. Chapter 1:1-14 clearly stated that God's Son is far greater than angels. Then 2:1-4 applied that truth to the letter's readers. If God had offered a revelation that surpassed the commandments previously given through the angels, then God's people would be fools to ignore the superior word.

The Scripture text for this week's lesson continues the comparison between Jesus and the angels. But in 2:5-18 the writer to the Hebrews interjected a third party—humanity—into his rankings. Jesus is undoubtedly higher than the angels, but where do people fit into this comparison? At least in some senses, they fall into third place, a level lower than the angels held (2:7). By right, the hierarchy of God's order is set: Jesus belongs to the highest honor, the angels come next, and humanity falls into third position.

But as the epistle continues, the writer highlighted Jesus' unbelievable humility. He who had eternally occupied first place willingly, for a time, gave up that position. He stooped not merely to second place—the level of the angels—but accepted an even lower position, equality with human beings (2:11, 14, 17).

If some wanted to argue that, in the overall structure of things, humanity held a fairly high position, the writer freely agreed. When God created human beings, He *crowned them with glory and honor* (2:7). God placed all other visible creation under their authority (2:8). But humanity had not lived up to God's expectations. People did not rule the world. No, it appeared that the world had people under its control (2:8).

While God intended people to live and govern the world under His authority, they had rejected that position, choosing instead to go the way of sin, following the plan of God's enemy, the devil. As a result, people found themselves no longer free, but enslaved to the masters they had chosen: sin and the devil (2:14, 17). Those two brought humanity into further subjection to death (2:14-15).

But did humanity's fallen state hinder the Son from accepting unity with people? No. Their plight did not prevent Christ from becoming a human being. In fact, it was precisely their need that motivated Him to move toward them (2:16). Jesus became one with humanity—in every way but one. Unlike the rest of us, Jesus followed God's plan. He rejected the ways of sin. In doing so, He showed

Himself stronger than Satan and death. In Jesus' sufferings and death, He dealt directly with Satan and death, beating them down (2:14). In doing so, Jesus blazed a new trail for people. He became the *pioneer of their salvation* (2:10).

NOTES ON THE PRINTED TEXT

Hebrews 2:5 picks up the theme of *angels* right where 1:14 left it. The latter verse pointed out that God never saw angels as equals, but as servants. God had not given His angelic servants control over *the coming world, about which* the writer had been *speaking* (2:5). Of which world had he been speaking? It was the present world in which his readers lived, the new age that Christ had inaugurated (earlier portrayed in 1:2 as *these last days*).

If God had chosen not to delegate world control to angels, to whom had God given this great authority? The writer answered this question by quoting Psalm 8:4-6. These verses described those to whom God gave authority over creation. A quick reading of the KJV text might lead one to mistake the identity of this person or group. The NRSV clarifies this potential confusion. Where the KJV uses the phrase "son of man" as the subject for Psalm 8:4, the NRSV offers *mortals*. Because Jesus frequently described Himself as "the Son of Man," many people see Psalm 8 as a prophecy referring only to Jesus. While "Son of Man" is a title Jesus adopted, the Old Testament writers often used this phrase to describe any human being.

Yes, despite the fact that God made *human beings* (Heb. 2:6) for *a little while lower than the angels,* He *crowned them with glory and honor* (2:7). How? *By subjecting all things under their feet* (2:8). He *left nothing* in the created universe *outside their control.* With these words, the writer celebrated the great privilege God gave humanity. But the writer's joyful thought quickly turned to dejection as he remembered that the world did not reflect God's original plan: *we do not yet see everything in subjection to them,* to humankind. The small but significant word *yet* hinted, however, that the writer had not given up hope.

What was the source of hope? *Jesus* (2:9), God's Son, who became one with humanity (*made lower than the angels*). He has *now* been *crowned with glory and honor.* Note that last phrase is repeated from 2:7 and Psalm 8. Why is Jesus' incarnation a source of hope? Why has Jesus been so highly rewarded? It is *because of the suffering of death* (Heb. 2:9). *By the grace of God,* Jesus has tasted *death,* not merely for Himself, but *for everyone* (2:9). The rest of the chapter more fully explains the new way of *salvation* (2:10) of which Christ has become the *pioneer.*

God, who ultimately rules both the world and humanity (those to whom He delegated authority over the world), chose the most *fitting* way to bring *many children to glory.* His own Son became one with humanity and finished His work through His *sufferings.*

Why is this way most *fitting?* It is because both Jesus (*the one who sanctifies,* 2:11) and believers (*those who are sanctified*) all have one Father; that is, they come from the same divine source. Not only do they come from the same divine source, but also they have a common bond in their humanity—*Jesus is not ashamed to call them brothers and sisters.*

Further Old Testament quotations support and build on these ideas. The writer saw Psalm 22:22 as an example of Jesus seeing believers as His *brothers and sisters* (Heb. 2:12). The latter part of that verse (Ps. 22:22), as well as Isaiah 8:17 (*"I will put my trust in him,"* Heb. 2:13) are quoted as evidence that Jesus, in contrast to the rest of humanity, completely followed God's plan. As a result, God gave believers to Jesus as God's own *children.*

Returning from Old Testament quotations to his own voice, the writer repeated and expanded these thoughts. Jesus did not merely claim to be the spiritual brother of the redeemed; He shared humanity's *flesh and blood* (2:14). With one major exception, Jesus shared the same human existence with all people. As 2:12-13 noted, He lived as God had intended. So, though death held power over all others, it stood defenseless before God's Son. When He faced death, He destroyed *the one who has the power of death, that is, the devil* (2:14). Jesus defeated death itself. Not only did He pioneer a new way, Jesus offered freedom to *those who all their lives were held in slavery by the fear of death* (2:15).

Who did Jesus deliver into freedom? Not *angels,* but those whose flesh and blood He shared, *the descendants of Abraham* (2:16). In this reference to Jewish readers, the writer did not exclude Gentiles; he merely highlighted Jesus as the only source of salvation for all people, including the Jews.

Hebrews 2:17 introduced yet another image for Jesus' work of salvation. Just as priests within the old covenant offered sacrifices to cover people's sins, Jesus also did so. He became a *high priest,* offering His own body as *a sacrifice of atonement for the sins of the people.*

The writer closed the chapter by moving from the past tense to the present tense. Not only did Jesus offer salvation to humanity by His past sacrifice, He also offers present help to believers, *who are being tested* (2:18). Their past sins, their present temptations, and their fear of future death—Jesus, in His perfect life and obedient death, defeated them all.

SUGGESTIONS TO TEACHERS

Y ou may wish to use this week's lesson time as an invitation to salvation. None of us can ever assume that all our class members truly know Jesus. This week's Scripture text reflects this outline of the salvation message.

1. GOD'S FIRST PROGRAM. In creating a world and people with whom He was pleased, God established a good program. Humanity would live in good relationship with Him. Within the context of that relationship, He would guide people in their role as governors of that world.

2. GOD'S FIRST PROGRAM RUINED. God's first program could have worked well. God deserves no blame for its failure. The people whom the Lord made used their God-given power to turn from Him. In rejecting God's good plan, they hoped to set up a better plan, one that would elevate themselves. Instead, they had fallen into Satan's trap and his plan would destroy humanity.

3. GOD'S SECOND PROGRAM. God could have let people go their own way. Instead, He demonstrated His power, love, and wisdom, by devising another plan that could bring humanity back to Him. His own Son would become human. Jesus, united with both God and people, could enable humanity to return to the life God originally intended.

4. GOD'S SECOND PROGRAM EFFECTED. As God wished, in Jesus' life and death, the Savior blazed the new trail for humanity. Jesus defeated humanity's enemy. Jesus became the priest and sacrifice humanity needed.

5. THE RESULT OF GOD'S SECOND PROGRAM. The salvation trail is open for people to walk. People no longer need to live as slaves to sin; they can freely receive salvation by putting their trust in Christ. No one else needs to offer any new sacrifices; Jesus has offered Himself, the perfect sacrifice.

FOR ADULTS

■ TOPIC: Partners in Suffering

■ QUESTIONS: 1. By what principles do you think God originally intended humanity to govern the world? 2. In contrast to what God originally planned, how have people treated God, each other and the natural world? 3. In what sense do you see Jesus as the *pioneer of . . . salvation* (Heb. 2:10)? 4. What factors made Jesus uniquely qualified to be God's instrument in bringing humanity back to God's original plan? 5. How should we respond to Jesus' provision of salvation?

■ **ILLUSTRATIONS:**

A Creative Inventor. We all remember the name Thomas Edison for his successes, the invention of over a thousand devices we all have known and loved. These include the incandescent electric light bulb, the phonograph, the motion-picture projector, and key components of the first telephones. But behind any of these or other successes stood a number of failures.

Edison received his first patent for an electric vote recorder. But no one wanted to buy such a machine. Officials rejected his better way, choosing to stay with the tradition of paper ballots. Did Edison despair? He then began living the philosophy he later summarized, "Every wrong attempt discarded is a step forward." Each new insight and skill he gained contributed to his amazing record as an inventor.

Living in New York City to be near the center of action, Edison was there ready to help when the local Gold Exchange's telegraphic price indicator failed. He not only fixed the machine, but also found ways to improve it. Soon the Western Union Company asked him to refine their new, but primitive stock ticker machine.

These successes started Edison on his way to fame. Yet none of his successes came without many preliminary failures.

In a similar but even greater way, our God met people's rejection of His first plan with creativity and determination. He went on to offer salvation in Christ.

A Twentieth Century Hero of Freedom. Nelson Mandela stands as one of the great heroes of the past century. Did you know that Mandela received some of his first education at a school run by British missionaries? In time, Mandela earned a law degree. Along with two partners, Mandela established South Africa's first black law firm. In the hopes of fighting South Africa's rigid racial discrimination system (known as apartheid), the three colleagues soon set up the African National Congress Youth League, of which Mandela became president six years later.

Within another few years, Mandela and others were arrested for alleged plots to overthrow the South African government. Mandela and seven associates were convicted of treason and sentenced to life in prison. Mandela spent the next 27 years behind bars, most of that time in a harsh maximum security island prison. Negotiations with government officials finally brought Mandela's release.

In his new freedom, Mandela did not quietly retire but resumed his work with the African National Congress (A.N.C). Tempered by his years in prison, Mandela became a respected leader of groups fighting apartheid. He toured the world, winning friends for his cause. Likewise, he interacted with white national leaders. Under his leadership, the A.N.C. gave up its weapons in exchange for recognition as a legitimate political party. At the next election, Mandela became president of the country that had imprisoned him. During his tenure, he led South Africa in relative peace through the transition toward equality of people of all races.

Another earlier leader brought His people to freedom from Satan's even more tyrannical regime.

Pioneers. The writer to the Hebrews portrayed Jesus as a pioneer, one who entered new territory for the first time, making it possible for others to follow Him. In American history, Lewis and Clark deserve the title of *Pioneers Extraordinaire*. Soon after President Thomas Jefferson's Louisiana Purchase doubled the land controlled by the United States government, Congress approved an expedition to explore this territory and travel on to the Pacific. Jefferson appointed his own secretary, Meriwether Lewis, and Lewis's friend, William Clark, to lead what became a four-year, 2500 mile continental adventure. At the time Lewis, Clark, and company headed west, only four roads crossed the entire Appalachian ridge. With the help of Sacagawea, a Native American woman (now featured on American dollar coins), this small brave corps of people traveled all the way to the Oregon coast. The knowledge they gained laid the foundation for the great westward movement of the American nation.

**FOR
YOUTH**

■ TOPIC: Help with Suffering

■ QUESTIONS: 1. What are some of the ways that human beings compare and contrast with angels? 2. In order to bring salvation to people, why did Jesus become one of us (as opposed to becoming an angel)? 3. What did Jesus give up in becoming a human being? 4. How did Jesus' life and death result in victory over Satan, sin, and death? 5. Is belief in the fact of Jesus' victory enough to save us or does God want us to make a more personal response?

■ **ILLUSTRATIONS:**

My Father's Good Plan. During my college years, my father handed me the keys to a bright red, brand-new Camaro. I was shocked. What was the story? My older sister, Evelyn, had graduated from college and left home to work in New York City. But for her first new cars, Evelyn still depended on Dad to do the dickering. Although we had moved a couple hours from Dad's friend's Chevy dealership, Dad still received good deals from him that made the drive worthwhile. When Dad took the call reporting that the new car was ready, my sister made plans to come home to Elmira for the weekend. But first she needed someone to pick the car up for her to drive her new car back to the city. Dad, of course, took charge. But he needed a second driver in order to get both cars home.

As we drove up to Williamson, I had no doubt but what I would drive the old car home, while Dad drove the sports car for its first hundred miles. I never dreamed Dad would hand me the new car keys. Maybe my dad's father had once let him drive a new tractor across their farm. In any case, with a mere "Take it easy" from Dad, I was soon driving the sportiest, most powerful vehicle I could imagine. I had been trained to pay attention to speed limit signs. But some stretches of road were straight and wide open. I quickly figured out that this car could beat speed limits if I did much more than touch the gas pedal. I quickly left Dad behind.

Dad had devised a good plan. "We will get Evelyn's car safely to our house. Phil has proven to be a good driver. I will give him the thrill of driving the new car home." Did I follow Dad's good plan? Well, yes and no. Two hours later, I did stop the car safely in our driveway. But when Dad arrived several minutes later, Dad asked Mom how long I had been there. He did some quick calculations, then sat me down for a few words about my driving speed. I could have ruined Dad's good plan by wrecking my sister's car even before she saw it. Thankfully, I didn't.

Sadly, humanity's rejection of God's good plan cost our heavenly Father an overwhelming amount.

A Costly Sacrifice. Marcia is a student at a Christian college. At least she was a student there until several months ago. Did she drop out? Was she expelled? No, her health forced her to drop out for a semester. In this case, Marcia's generosity brought the health problems on herself, and she stands as an amazing example to us all.

Marcia's friend Dorothy struggled with life-threatening kidney failure. She faced one of several possibilities: death, three times a week kidney dialysis, or the hope for a kidney transplant. Many people in Dorothy's circumstances face no choice but dialysis. The physicians find no readily available person with a compatible kidney. Dorothy's parents and siblings were willing, but none could offer a compatible organ. Marcia too was willing, but saw little possibility that her kidney would be helpful when Dorothy's own flesh and blood could not give her what she needed. To everyone's surprise, Marcia's blood and tissue types matched Dorothy's closely. Marcia willingly postponed her college education, and even risked her own life, to give Dorothy an opportunity at a normal, healthy life.

Months have now gone by. Progress has not been as quick as everyone might have hoped, but both Marcia and Dorothy are moving toward health, all because of Marcia's free sacrifice.

The Best Coaches. Many young people play on athletic teams at their schools or in community leagues. If you have such experience, think about some of the people who have served as your coaches. Which ones have done the best job? It is likely the ones who both knew the game well and how to handle people.

What experience does it take to know a game well? Reading books in a library doesn't provide adequate training. Most of the best coaches played the game themselves.

What experience does it take to handle people well? You'd think that the best players might make good coaches. Sometimes they do, but more often, the best coaches are not the Hall of Fame players, but those who have struggled, who perhaps spent time sitting on the bench.

As a boy, I cheered for the Baltimore Orioles. Their manager, Earl Weaver, may have had a hot temper, but he led the team to several championships. What experience did Weaver bring to his role? It was years as a baseball player, but all in the minor leagues, where he struggled unsuccessfully to make it to the majors.

What qualifies Jesus to help us in our times of testing? He has lived in our world as a human being just like us. He is God, but that did not necessarily make His life easier. He struggled. He suffered. His facing the same kinds of testing and pain we face enables Him to offer us the instruction and strength we need.

BE FAITHFUL: OBEY!

BACKGROUND SCRIPTURE: Hebrews 3:12—4:13
DEVOTIONAL READING: 2 Corinthians 5:16—6:2

KEY VERSE: For we have become partners of Christ,
if we only hold our confidence firm to the end. Hebrews 3:14.

KING JAMES VERSION

HEBREWS 3:12 Take heed, brethren, lest there be in any of you an evil heart of unbelief, in departing from the living God.

13 But exhort one another daily, while it is called To day; lest any of you be hardened through the deceitfulness of sin.

14 For we are made partakers of Christ, if we hold the beginning of our confidence stedfast unto the end;

15 While it is said, To day if ye will hear his voice, harden not your hearts, as in the provocation.

16 For some, when they had heard, did provoke: howbeit not all that came out of Egypt by Moses.

17 But with whom was he grieved forty years? was it not with them that had sinned, whose carcases fell in the wilderness?

18 And to whom sware he that they should not enter into his rest, but to them that believed not?

19 So we see that they could not enter in because of unbelief.

4:1 Let us therefore fear, lest, a promise being left us of entering into his rest, any of you should seem to come short of it.

2 For unto us was the gospel preached, as well as unto them: but the word preached did not profit them, not being mixed with faith in them that heard it. . . .

9 There remaineth therefore a rest to the people of God.

10 For he that is entered into his rest, he also hath ceased from his own works, as God did from his.

11 Let us labour therefore to enter into that rest, lest any man fall after the same example of unbelief.

12 For the word of God is quick, and powerful, and sharper than any twoedged sword, piercing even to the dividing asunder of soul and spirit, and of the joints and marrow, and is a discerner of the thoughts and intents of the heart.

13 Neither is there any creature that is not manifest in his sight: but all things are naked and opened unto the eyes of him with whom we have to do.

NEW REVISED STANDARD VERSION

HEBREWS 3:12 Take care, brothers and sisters, that none of you may have an evil, unbelieving heart that turns away from the living God. 13 But exhort one another every day, as long as it is called "today," so that none of you may be hardened by the deceitfulness of sin. 14 For we have become partners of Christ, if only we hold our first confidence firm to the end. 15 As it is said,

"Today, if you hear his voice,
do not harden your hearts as in the rebellion."

16 Now who were they who heard and yet were rebellious? Was it not all those who left Egypt under the leadership of Moses? 17 But with whom was he angry forty years? Was it not those who sinned, whose bodies fell in the wilderness? 18 And to whom did he swear that they would not enter his rest, if not to those who were disobedient? 19 So we see that they were unable to enter because of unbelief.

4:1 Therefore, while the promise of entering his rest is still open, let us take care that none of you should seem to have failed to reach it. 2 For indeed the good news came to us just as to them; but the message they heard did not benefit them, because they were not united by faith with those who listened. . . .

9 So then, a sabbath rest still remains for the people of God; 10 for those who enter God's rest also cease from their labors as God did from his. 11 Let us therefore make every effort to enter that rest, so that no one may fall through such disobedience as theirs.

12 Indeed, the word of God is living and active, sharper than any two-edged sword, piercing until it divides soul from spirit, joints from marrow; it is able to judge the thoughts and intentions of the heart. 13 And before him no creature is hidden, but all are naked and laid bare to the eyes of the one to whom we must render an account.

HOME BIBLE READINGS

BACKGROUND

This week's lesson text reveals a fascinating pattern of God using previously written Scripture to speak to His people. Of course, God frequently uses the Bible to speak to us in the twenty-first century. But this week's lesson text makes it obvious that even in ancient times, God was already using His inspired records to help His people hear and respond to the truth.

The pattern works like this: First, God has spoken to His people in the past. Second, God still speaks to His people today through the Word He has revealed in the past. In this week's lesson text, we see this dual truth occurring in at least two "generations." The author of Hebrews, throughout chapters 3 and 4 of the epistle, looked back to Psalm 95, the writer of which looked back to the Pentateuch. Reversing the ancient sequence gives a clearer view of the pattern.

As the Israelites trekked from Egypt across the wilderness to the promised land, God had assured them that He would provide all they needed. Yet repeatedly, God's people doubted His power to provide. On at least two significant occasions, they complained of thirst (see Exod. 17:1-7 and Num. 20:1-13 for the original accounts). Ultimately, their lack of trust and obedience prevented the exodus generation from settling in their new homeland.

Centuries later, the psalmist heard God speaking to him through His earlier word to the wandering Israelites. The psalmist used the already ancient divinely inspired record to issue a fresh wakeup call to his contemporaries. Then, in a still later era, the writer to the Hebrews heard God speaking to him through the psalmist's reference to the yet earlier wilderness incidents. At least one result of God's repetitive speaking was the material recorded in Hebrews 3 and 4.

What common themes do these chapters share with Psalm 95, Exodus 17, and Numbers 20? We have alluded to two such themes already. First, God speaks to His people. Second, God promises His blessings to those who heed His Word; but those who reject God's Word do so at their own risk.

To the ancient Israelites, God opened the way to the promised land—if only they would follow Him and His way toward and into it. To those singing psalms in the Jerusalem temple, God hinted that a "rest" still stood in His people's future, if they would follow Him in a way their forefathers had not (Ps. 95:11). The writer to the Hebrews picks up these same themes: *Therefore, while the promise of enter-*

ing his rest is still open, let us take care that none of you should seem to have failed to reach it. . . . Let us therefore make every effort to enter that rest, so that no one may fall through such disobedience as theirs (4:1, 11).

NOTES ON THE PRINTED TEXT

Hebrews 3 opens with a comparison between Moses and Jesus. Although the writer was careful not to criticize Moses, he sought clearly to show that God's people should follow Jesus, God's Son, not Moses, God's servant (3:5-6). If the writer could praise Moses for his faithful service, he offered little affirmation for Moses' original followers. Hebrews 3:7-11 gives the writer's longest quotation from Psalm 95, in which God stated His anger at those who rebelled against Him.

This week's lesson text begins with the writer directly applying his ancestors' experiences to each of his readers: *Take care, brothers and sisters, that none of you may have an evil, unbelieving heart that turns away from the living God* (Heb. 3:12). After encouraging them as individuals to follow God's plan, the writer suggested that believers should support one another as they jointly faced temptation. *Exhort one another every day* (3:13). Then he turned to God's most recent revelation of Himself in Jesus Christ. In effect, the writer was answering questions raised by the previous two verses: What does following the living God mean for us today? To what faithfulness should we be exhorting one another? God called us to *become partners of Christ* (3:14). God now calls us to *hold* that *first confidence firm to the end*.

In 3:15, we learn that the Word of God had spoken on some previous occasion. The Lord then proclaimed again through the writer of Hebrews to the Jewish believers in the early church. To them, the author of the letter issued the same warning God had offered through the psalmist—"*Today, . . . do not harden your hearts.*" Indeed, the author of the epistle wished for his readers to remain pliable before God and His Word.

A series of hypothetical questions follows. Each demanded reflection on the wilderness wanderers. The Israelites had failed. Those who consider their experiences and their failures are less likely to fall into similar errors. The questions in 3:16 revolve around "Who?" Were those who failed, being ignorant of God's power and faithfulness? No, they were the very ones who saw God perform miracle after miracle as they *left Egypt under the leadership of Moses.*

Then the writer turned his attention to "What?" Those people who had seen God work *sinned* (3:17) in rebelling against their faithful God. The next question was "Why?" Why did God become *angry* with them? Why did God forbid these people from entering *his rest* (3:18) in the promised land? It was not because they were ignorant; no, they were blatantly *disobedient.* And then digging a bit further, the writer stated that the deeper cause of the Israelites' disobedience was *unbelief* (3:19).

As Hebrews 4 opens, the writer turned his attention from the past to the present. As God spoke to His people in ancient times, God was still speaking to His people in the first century. The writer built his argument well. At this point, he could hint at many relevant comparisons between ancient times and the present.

Just as the Israelites had seen God give them freedom from Egyptian slavery, so the readers of Hebrews had experienced the freedom God had given them in Christ. The ancient Israelites rejected their God through unbelief and disobedience. The writer saw his readers at that moment facing eternity-changing choices: belief in and obedience to God in Jesus versus the real possibility of turning away from the living God. And, of course, if they were to reject God, they would face an even deadlier exclusion from God's rest. *Therefore, while the promise of entering his rest is still open, let us take care that none of you should seem to have failed to reach it* (4:1).

What did the writer mean as he used the word *rest*? Throughout Hebrews 4, he used this word with at least three connotations. At points he was looking back to the promised land—rest God had promised His people. In 4:9 and 10, the writer alluded to an even earlier time, when God had rested after the six days of creation. But what *rest* did the writer intend for his readers to enter and enjoy?

Hebrew 4:2 seems to answer that question. *The good news* has come *to us.* The writer distinguished this word from *the message* [the ancient Israelites] *heard.* Perhaps the opening verses of his letter had returned to his mind. *Long ago God spoke to our ancestors . . . by the prophets, but in these last days he has spoken to us by a Son* (1:1-2). The rest for the readers involved the peace they experienced in relationship with Jesus, as well as the eternal heavenly reward still awaiting them. Many of them had experienced God's rest in the present; some of them could miss that treasure in the present and future.

Hebrews 4:9-11 continues the writer's exhortation. Just as God promised a rest to His people in days past, *a sabbath rest still remains for the people of God* (4:9). Those who enter that *rest also cease from their labors as God did from his* (4:10). These words possibly allude to the believers' dependence on grace *(rest)* rather than their own works *(labors).* At the same time, living in God's plan did not involve an aimless drifting, but rather a sincere *effort* (4:11) to continue in faith and in obedience to God's Word, as He had spoken it in Jesus.

Why should God's people heed His Word, as spoken in the past or the present? Hebrews 4:12-13 answers that question. First, God's Word, no matter how ancient, is still *living and active* (4:12). Scholars and students still read the works of Plato, but few, if any, groups of philosophical lay people gather for weekly Plato study. But millions come together every week to allow God's *two-edged sword . . . to judge the thoughts and intentions of* their *hearts.* People heed God's Word because of its living power, and also because they will someday stand before the God who has spoken. *All are naked and laid bare to the eyes of the one to whom we must render an account* (4:13). Their God will judge; wise people pay attention to His truth while it is still *called "today"* (3:13).

SUGGESTIONS TO TEACHERS

God spoke to the Israelites. A psalmist, centuries later, sensed the voice of God in what He had previously spoken. Much later, the writer to the Hebrews remembered these Old Testament accounts and knew that God was speaking through His ancient Word. As you have worked through Hebrews 3 and 4, you have likely already seen the next step: God still speaks today through Exodus, Numbers, Psalms, and Hebrews! Help your students see these steps in responding to what God says. Wise twenty-first century people still . . .

1. HEAR GOD'S WORD. Jesus often referred to those who have ears to hear. He recognized that some people do not "tune" their ears to listen to the voice of God. He has spoken in the past. He continues to speak through His inspired Word. Do we take time and do we quiet ourselves so that we can hear Him speak?

2. BELIEVE GOD'S WORD. Hearing is a good step, but by itself is inadequate. Picture someone who receives a letter informing her of an unexpected inheritance. If she reads the words, but cannot believe the letter was intended for her, she may forfeit what belongs to her. Likewise we can imagine someone who sits in a church service every week, hears the Bible read, but cannot believe that the good news applies to him or her. God offered the promised land to His people, but *they were unable to enter because of unbelief* (Heb. 3:19).

3. OBEY GOD'S WORD. It's hard to imagine someone who believes, but does not act on what she knows. But isn't that a good definition of procrastination? She knows that her car needs its oil changed regularly, but finds herself too busy. She then wonders why her car does not run smoothly. He knows that if he does not study for the test, he will not pass the course. But other activities distract him and he flunks out of college. *Let us therefore make every effort to enter that rest, so that no one may fall through such disobedience as theirs* (4:11).

4. SPEAK GOD'S WORD. God's people not only enjoy the privilege of hearing Him through His Word, but also can pass that good news along to others. Each of us can be an instrument through whom God speaks to others. *Exhort one another every day* (3:13). You can be the means by which others enter and mature as a part of God's family.

FOR ADULTS

■ TOPIC: Be Faithful: Obey!

■ QUESTIONS: 1. What factors might have hindered first century Jews from becoming Christians or remaining devoted to the Savior? 2. By what means does the writer of Hebrews argue that Christians should remain faithful to Jesus? 3. What would have been the benefits of the Jewish Christians encouraging one another in their faith? 4. What do you feel the writer meant by the *rest* (4:1) he encouraged his hearers to enter? 5. Which of these four—hearing, believing, obeying, or sharing God's Word—causes you greatest struggle? Why?

Old Truths Are Still Truths. An old truth may be as relevant as any sentence recently composed. My grandfather, who would now be about 110 years old, hated the practice of gossip. In the small Pennsylvania community where the Bence clan lived, news could travel quickly. When school friends narrated tales about common acquaintances to my dad, Jim, he often brought the stories home. Around the fire that evening, my dad would recite what he had heard. When the accounts reflected poorly on people, his father would reprimand Jim. "But Dad, I know this story is true." "That does not matter, Jim. You should always tell the truth, but you should not always be telling it."

My father died in his eighties last summer. I couldn't tell you how many times I heard him repeat my grandfather's proverbial statement. It came out of the 1920's. But that does not matter. The old truth is still just as true today as it was then.

My wife still uses recipes her grandmother used. Kathy has passed some of these on to our daughters. That's fine with me. The old boiled custard recipe from Tennessee still tastes great in Seattle!

Crossing the Jordan. I occasionally pull out my old recording of spirituals. Why do these anonymous songs communicate so powerfully? Despite their origin in the most tragic circumstances, when one person believed he or she had the right to own another person, so many of them offer hope to us when we face pain today.

My favorite spirituals all involve the theme of hope—"All my trials, Lord, soon be over," "There is a balm in Gilead," and "Going to cross over into campground." We still can feel the plaintive cry of slaves as they anticipated a time of relief, of rest. Occasionally, a spiritual's imagery came directly from the exodus and wanderings of the Israelites, biblical people just released from slavery.

The following quatrain's writing precedes the eras of spirituals, but fits their ethos well. "On Jordan's stormy banks I stand, and cast a wishful eye to Canaan's fair and happy land, where my possessions lie." Nothing in the present could ever distract believing slaves from their hope for the future.

Words Are Powerful. Words change people's lives. Some adults struggle all their lives with the effects of cruel words thoughtlessly spoken by a parent or teacher like, "You will never amount to anything." Child psychologists tell us that young people need to hear 10 statements of affirmation to compensate for one strong word of condemnation. God's message is even more powerful than that of any earthly parent. We can rejoice that His Word bears repeating, that it offers good news of hope, not sentiments that destroy.

Grandfather Clock. For several days, my wife and I have been trying to correct my old grandfather clock. For some reason, it has gotten into its head that it should chime the hour 15 minutes early. Just this afternoon, Kathy was working with the clock. She not only maneuvered its hands; she actually spoke to the clock. But then what happened at 2:45? The stubborn timepiece chimed 3 o'clock. We have done our best. We have patiently worked with the clock. But it continues to go its own way. Not only that, but unless it chimes more accurately, it will mislead others.

FOR YOUTH

■ TOPIC: Stay Faithful

■ QUESTIONS: 1. Why did the writer of Hebrews see value in referring to the old accounts of God's people in the wilderness? 2. In what ways was hearing about Jesus *good news* (4:2), especially for Jews? 3. In what sense had the readers of this letter become *partners of Christ* (3:14)? 4. What did the writer mean by the phrase *as long as it is called "today"?* (3:13)? 5. What difference has the Word of God made in your life?

■ ILLUSTRATIONS:

A Hearing Problem. Many years ago, my wife and I were driving from New York to Florida. Several times during the trip, Kathy, from the passenger's seat, told me I was not listening to her as carefully as I should. While in Florida, we discovered that I could only hear when Kathy was speaking to me from my right side.

To make a long story short, physicians eventually discovered that a tumor deep within my inner ear was blocking transmission of sound between my right ear and my brain. Regrettably, major surgery was the only way to remove the tumor. In that process, the surgeons found it necessary to sever my nerve of hearing. Now it's even harder for me to hear Kathy when we are out in the car. But at least Kathy no longer accuses me of not listening to her. It's not my fault!

What factors within or outside your control could prevent you from submitting to the voice of God, as found recorded in His Word?

Do You Hear Me? Can you remember, when you were younger, your parents asking whether you could hear them? Maybe they have spoken those words to you recently. What is the true intent of their question? They are not actually doubting your hearing ability, are they? No. They are asking why you have not responded to what they said.

Our younger daughter was a well-behaved child. She rarely rebelled against us in any blatant way. But she was nowhere near perfect. When she was in junior high, we assigned her the task of washing the dishes. She never said, "No, I will not do the dishes." But she did have a sneaky way of finding almost anything that would enable her to put off her chore. "I need to call Wendy first. I would rather do my homework right now. I will wait until after my favorite TV show, OK?" Sometimes we allowed her to postpone the chore for a few minutes, but when that time was up, she often tried another set of excuses. We knew she had heard our command, but she did not want what she had heard to interrupt her plans.

Obeying the Authority. Our friend Jean Louis was spending some time in France. Late one night, he called a taxi. As the driver was taking him across the city, he hardly slowed the car before going straight through a red light. Startled into alertness, Jean Louis quickly asked, "What were you doing? Did you not see that light?" The driver calmly replied, "It's the middle of the night. When no one else is on the road, why should I give in to that silly little machine hanging in the air? I know better than it does." In telling the story, Jean Louis admitted that the driver's example has influenced him. Driving alone late at night, Jean Louis questions himself at deserted intersections, "Do I have to wait until this light turns green?"

JESUS: THE HIGH PRIEST

BACKGROUND SCRIPTURE: Hebrews 4:14—5:10
DEVOTIONAL READING: Hebrews 7:1-18

KEY VERSE: Since, then, we have a great high priest . . . , Jesus, the Son of God, let us hold fast to our confession. Hebrews 4:14.

4

KING JAMES VERSION

HEBREWS 4:14 Seeing then that we have a great high priest, that is passed into the heavens, Jesus the Son of God, let us hold fast our profession.

15 For we have not an high priest which cannot be touched with the feeling of our infirmities; but was in all points tempted like as we are, yet without sin.

16 Let us therefore come boldly unto the throne of grace, that we may obtain mercy, and find grace to help in time of need.

5:1 For every high priest taken from among men is ordained for men in things pertaining to God, that he may offer both gifts and sacrifices for sins:

2 Who can have compassion on the ignorant, and on them that are out of the way; for that he himself also is compassed with infirmity.

3 And by reason hereof he ought, as for the people, so also for himself, to offer for sins.

4 And no man taketh this honour unto himself, but he that is called of God, as was Aaron.

5 So also Christ glorified not himself to be made an high priest; but he that said unto him, Thou art my Son, to day have I begotten thee.

6 As he saith also in another place, Thou art a priest for ever after the order of Melchisedec.

7 Who in the days of his flesh, when he had offered up prayers and supplications with strong crying and tears unto him that was able to save him from death, and was heard in that he feared;

8 Though he were a Son, yet learned he obedience by the things which he suffered;

9 And being made perfect, he became the author of eternal salvation unto all them that obey him;

10 Called of God an high priest after the order of Melchisedec.

NEW REVISED STANDARD VERSION

HEBREWS 4:14 Since, then, we have a great high priest who has passed through the heavens, Jesus, the Son of God, let us hold fast to our confession. 15 For we do not have a high priest who is unable to sympathize with our weaknesses, but we have one who in every respect has been tested as we are, yet without sin. 16 Let us therefore approach the throne of grace with boldness, so that we may receive mercy and find grace to help in time of need.

5:1 Every high priest chosen from among mortals is put in charge of things pertaining to God on their behalf, to offer gifts and sacrifices for sins. 2 He is able to deal gently with the ignorant and wayward, since he himself is subject to weakness; 3 and because of this he must offer sacrifice for his own sins as well as for those of the people. 4 And one does not presume to take this honor, but takes it only when called by God, just as Aaron was.

5 So also Christ did not glorify himself in becoming a high priest, but was appointed by the one who said to him,

"You are my Son,
today I have begotten you";

6 as he says also in another place,

"You are a priest forever,
according to the order of Melchizedek."

7 In the days of his flesh, Jesus offered up prayers and supplications, with loud cries and tears, to the one who was able to save him from death, and he was heard because of his reverent submission. 8 Although he was a Son, he learned obedience through what he suffered; 9 and having been made perfect, he became the source of eternal salvation for all who obey him, 10 having been designated by God a high priest according to the order of Melchizedek.

HOME BIBLE READINGS

BACKGROUND

Perhaps as well as any passage in Scripture, this week's lesson text from the Letter to the Hebrews highlights the value of having a Savior who is both divine and human. That unique combination of two natures in one person enables Jesus to be our *great high priest* (4:14).

What does it mean to be a priest? A priest acts as an intermediary between people and God, and between God and His people. Aaron and his descendants filled that role during the Old Testament period. God ordained them, setting them apart from others to act as His priests. The humanity of these priests enabled them to stand in place of the people. And their commission enabled them to approach God with the people's sacrifices and prayers. For a period of time, these priests' God-ordained service was adequate, but it could be neither permanent nor complete.

God always knew the better plan He would subsequently establish. His later strategy would still involve a human mediator. Like the Old Testament priests, this person would experience all testing common to humanity (4:15). This human priest could sympathize with the weaknesses people endure (4:15). But the ministry of one more merely human priest would offer no improvement over the service the Levites had offered (see 7:11). God's better plan involved a priest who was both human and divine. The God-man, Jesus Christ, would not only experience temptation, but also, unlike all other human priests, completely conquer it.

Throughout His life, Christ's thoughts and actions were characterized by *obedience* (5:8). He was *without sin* (4:15). And, as the Son of God, Christ's earthly life ended, not with a physical body decaying in a grave, but rather with the risen Lord victoriously passing *through the heavens* (4:14). Thus, Jesus' life, death, and resurrection qualify Him to be *the source of eternal salvation* (5:9).

God, through the writer to the Hebrews, used yet another image to describe Jesus Christ. The Father declared His Son to be "*a priest forever, according to the order of Melchizedek*" (5:6). In order better to understand this unusual analogy, we should refer to Genesis 14:18-20. These three Old Testament verses show Melchizedek's primary appearance on the stage of Scripture. This came after the patriarch Abraham had won a significant battle. At that time, King Melchizedek of Salem brought bread and wine in order to bless God's chosen leader. Abraham, in turn, gave the king a tenth of the battle's spoils. The Genesis narrative describes

Melchizedek as *priest of God Most High* (14:18).

So how does this enigmatic figure relate to the ministry of Jesus? The main Scripture reading for this week's lesson does not specifically deal with this issue. But a look at Hebrews 7:1-18 further develops the Melchizedek analogy. Verses 2 and 3, in particular, draw several comparisons between Melchizedek, the ancient king-priest, and Jesus Christ, who centuries later served in a similar role.

It's helpful to note that the name "Melchizedek" means "my king is righteous," a title most appropriate for Jesus who lived a perfect life. The fact that Melchizedek served as king of Salem (meaning "king of peace") also fits Christ well. Perhaps the reference to Salem foreshadows Jerusalem and Jesus who conquered death outside that city.

The writer to the Hebrews additionally noted that New Testament believers know little about Melchizedek. The writer actually used that lack of information to his advantage. Just as Melchizedek seemingly appeared and disappeared without record of parents, birth, or death, so too the existence of the Son of God is without beginning or end. Thus, as the eternal one taking on humanity, Jesus undoubtedly is best qualified to serve as our *great high priest* (4:14).

NOTES ON THE PRINTED TEXT

This week's Scripture passage opens by offering reassurance to those who had just read the warning in Hebrews 4:13. People who stand alone and open before God have little hope. But, if *a great high priest* (4:14) has preceded them *through the heavens,* they can rest assured as a result of putting their trust in Him.

This great high priest is none other than *Jesus,* the Son of man who ministered for a time on earth. But this priest-prophet is also *the Son of God.* The last line of 4:14 implies a strong rhetorical question—"Who could bear to stand before God without the assistance of such a priest?" Obviously, no one. Therefore the writer exhorted his readers not to forsake Jesus to return to Judaism. Instead, they should *hold fast to* the *confession* of Jesus Christ that they had previously made.

In case someone might object, "Why would a divine one want to stand with weak little me?" the writer continued. *We do not have a high priest who is unable to sympathize with our weaknesses, but we have one who in every respect has been tested as we are, yet without sin* (4:15). Because Jesus existed in a body as fully human as ours, and because He had faced the same types of temptations that challenged His contemporaries, He understands human frailty. As a result, He is fully qualified to serve as the great High Priest, standing before God to represent believers.

Because of the assistance Christ offers to His followers, saved humanity need not feel terror before God; instead, they can approach His throne *of grace with boldness* (4:16). As believers do so, they can *receive mercy* for past sins and *find grace to help in* every current and future *time of need.*

The writer next stepped back from his exhortation to lay some background. He described the role human high priests play in order to draw comparisons and contrasts to Jesus' high priesthood. First the writer offered similarities. *Every high priest chosen from among mortals is put in charge of things pertaining to God on their behalf, to offer gifts and sacrifices for sins* (5:1).

With these words, the writer broadly defined the role of priests, both those who served in the Jerusalem temple and the one who offered His sacrifice outside the holy city. Any human priest, because he is *subject to weakness* (5:2) himself, can *deal gently* with his fellow sinners. Christ, too, deals gently with sinners. That comparison, however, led right into the major contrast between Jesus and all other priests. While a typical human priest was himself a sinner (needing to *offer sacrifice for his own sins;* 5:3), Jesus, being *without sin* (4:15), needed to make no offering for Himself.

The writer next discussed the similarities between the Jewish high priests and our *great high priest* (4:14). Both receive their position through divine appointment. Human high priests *take this honor . . . only when called by God, just as Aaron was* (5:4). No one would dare assume the role as a high priest unless God willed that step. Likewise, Christ Himself took on His High Priesthood only when *appointed by the one who said to him, "You are my Son . . . You are a priest forever"* (5:5-6). The quote in 5:5 comes from Psalm 2:7, while the quote in Hebrews 5:6 comes from Psalm 110:4.

The rest of this week's lesson text returns to the effective ministry of Jesus as high priest. In the garden of Gethsemane, the night before He would offer His own body as a sacrifice for humanity's sins, Jesus *offered up prayers and supplications* (Heb. 5:7) to God. This verse's allusion to Jesus' *loud cries and tears* supports the writer's claim that even God's Son had endured the worst of human testing (4:15).

Amazingly, the Son *learned obedience through what he suffered* (5:8). You might wonder, "How could the all-knowing Christ learn?" This does not mean Christ turned from disobedience to obedience; rather, it means that He obeyed God in a way He had never done before. The Son obeyed the Father as a human being. Each victory over temptation gave Jesus experiential insight. He conquered temptation all of the time, and His continual *obedience* sets a great example for His followers. Thus, 5:9 calls on us to *obey him* as He obeyed His Father.

This verse raises another puzzling question, namely, in what sense could the Son of God be *made perfect?* This does not mean that Christ was ever imperfect. The writer was stressing that Jesus' human experience entered a new dimension of fullness and completion as a result of overcoming temptations and dying on the cross.

Consequently, Jesus *became the source of eternal salvation for all who obey him.* This sacrifice, being offered by the person *designated by God a high priest according to the order of Melchizedek* (5:10), was completely and permanently effective. Why then would anyone want to turn back to their old ways?

SUGGESTIONS TO TEACHERS

In his commentary on the Letter to the Hebrews, entitled *Christ above All*, Raymond Brown uses four adjectives to describe the portrayal of Jesus' high priesthood. You can profitably use this material to take your students through this week's lesson text.

1. CHRIST'S PRIESTHOOD WAS VICTORIOUS. All other high priests offered their sacrifices in the Jerusalem temple. They then returned home, only to go back to the sanctuary on other days to offer still more sacrifices. In contrast, Jesus offered one eternally perfect sacrifice. After His resurrection, He *passed through the heavens* (4:14), returning to His eternal home. The other priests' sacrifices may have had some effect, but any benefit was temporary. In offering His sacrifice, Jesus defeated Satan, sin, and death once and for all.

2. CHRIST'S PRIESTHOOD WAS COMPASSIONATE. Perhaps God could have designed a world where a mere snap of His fingers offered forgiveness and salvation to people. Also, He who had created the world through His Word possibly could have redeemed it merely by speaking. But God willingly chose the costlier method that more fully revealed Himself, particularly His love for humanity. Hebrews 4:15 especially portrays how the God-man, Jesus Christ, made Himself vulnerable to demonstrate His compassion for the lost.

3. CHRIST'S PRIESTHOOD WAS SUBMISSIVE. Hebrews 5:7-8 describes how Jesus willingly accepted and fulfilled the Father's plan of redemption. Christ humbled Himself by taking on the role of a humble servant who learned obedience through the things He suffered. As a human being, He pled with His Father for some relief from the trauma He faced, but, when there was no other way to offer salvation, Jesus fully submitted to the Father's will.

4. CHRIST'S PRIESTHOOD WAS EFFECTIVE. Jesus achieved the goal of redemption. By offering Himself as a sacrifice in the manner the Father wished, Jesus *became the source of eternal salvation for all who obey him* (5:9). His submissive expression of love and obedience enabled a host of lost people down through the centuries to find new life in Him. We are wise to devote every aspect of our lives in adoration and service to Him.

FOR ADULTS

■ **TOPIC:** Approach in Boldness

■ **QUESTIONS:** 1. How does this week's Scripture passage highlight the divinity of Jesus Christ? 2. How does this week's lesson text unveil the humanity of Jesus Christ? 3. In what ways does the high priesthood of the divine-human Jesus eliminate the need for subsequent human priests? 4. On what basis do God's people boldly approach His throne of grace? 5. With what needs can we boldly approach God's throne today? Why is it imperative that we do so?

Holding Fast to His Confession. When Martin Luther posted for public debate his first list of Reformation ideas, the church authorities initially did not do anything. They hoped Luther's ideas would disappear on their own. Then after three years, one prominent leader felt he needed to respond. He labeled many of Luther's ideas heretical. When the reformer received the official document, he burned the decree on a public bonfire. "If they are going to burn my writings, I can burn theirs."

The other prominent church leader then took further action by excommunicating Luther. Luther faced the possibility of being burned at the stake, which was the end of others who suggested new theological ideas. While on trial before the authorities, Luther was asked to recant. He steadfastly refused. "My conscience is captive to the will of God," he announced. "I will not recant anything, for to go against conscience is neither honest nor safe. Here I stand; I cannot do otherwise. God help me."

Appointing Myself? One might argue that, out of all American citizens, the nine members of the United States Supreme Court have more power than anyone, with the possible exception of the President. The members of the Court cannot enact new laws, but they have the power to review laws established by any state legislature or the U.S. Congress itself. With the U.S. Constitution as their only superior, they can overturn laws or decisions of lower courts. Over the years, their rulings have impacted the lives of millions of people.

Perhaps some of us might think that we could make wiser, fairer decisions than the nine present justices. But who among us would ever be foolish enough to appoint ourselves to the Supreme Court? That would be nothing short of ridiculous. Only the President of the United States can appoint new justices, and he can do so only when a current member retires or dies.

Completing the Task. At the end of the 2000 college football season, the University of Miami team was left out of the national championship game. A most complicated Bowl Championship Series formula determines which two teams play for the national title. The University of Miami players felt cheated, for earlier in the season, they had defeated Florida State, one of the two teams that did play for the championship.

At the beginning of the 2001 season, the proud Miami players told each other that they would not be cheated again. If they had to win all their games, they would do just that, so that no other team could claim greater right to play in the big season-ending game. They not only established that commitment, but also followed through with it. At the end of the regular season, the University of Miami stood as the only undefeated major college football team in America. Without dispute, they had earned the right to play in the biggest game. They not only walked on the Rose Bowl field, but also walked off as overwhelming winners of the game and that year's national title.

FOR YOUTH

■ **TOPIC:** Who Cares for Me?

■ **QUESTIONS:** 1. In what ways did Jesus need to learn obedience? 2. What kinds of strain would Jesus have faced as He prayed the night before His death? 3. What are some of the temptations that Jesus faced that people still face today? 4. What did it mean for the first readers of the Letter to the Hebrews to *hold fast to* (4:14) their *confession?* 5. In what areas of your life do you need the grace and support of Jesus?

■ **ILLUSTRATIONS:**

The Need for an Intermediary. When I was younger, professional athletes negotiated their own contracts with team owners. Today that practice is quite rare. Most of the players feel they will end up with a better deal if an agent represents them.

Andrew Jones, after enjoying his first few years with the Atlanta Braves, wanted to stay with this team. He was even willing to sacrifice larger salaries he might have received from other teams to stay where he was. Because he knew the Braves would offer what he considered a fair amount of money, he did not employ an agent to work with him in his contract renewal. Only after signing a new contract did he realize that the new agreement omitted one crucial factor. It did not include a no-trade clause. Jones had sacrificed money out of loyalty to his team, but his team had made no similar agreement of strong loyalty to him. In this case, perhaps Jones would have been much better off had he worked through an intermediary.

Approaching Boldly. Perhaps you have seen or read Charles Dickens's *Oliver Twist.* Early in the story, Oliver's single mother had died. He ended up as an inmate of a barely livable Victorian orphanage. The children there received little love. Each child was allotted adequate food to survive, but never enough to fill his or her stomach.

After one meal of nothing more than oatmeal porridge, Oliver did what no child in memory had done before him. He bravely approached the master of the dining hall. As Oliver did so, he held his empty bowl before him, and asked, "May I have some more, sir?" The rest of the boys watched in utter amazement. Oliver's master reacted with rage, blatantly rejecting Oliver's wish. The writer to the Hebrews encouraged us to approach our heavenly Father boldly, knowing that He loves us and will give us what is best.

Faithful to the End. Throughout the last 63 years of their lives, my parents remained loyal to the wedding vows they had spoken to each other the day of my father's college graduation. During those years, they faced all kinds of challenges, but they did so together. One son, born prematurely, lived only a few days. Another son, just short of his eighth birthday, chased a ball into the road, only to be struck and killed by an oncoming car. They lived in big houses and small houses. They pastored churches that loved them and some where relationships were not quite so pleasant.

On Flag Day of 1999, my mother suffered a crippling stroke. My father, always an on-the-go, keep-moving sort of guy, patiently sat with her nearly every day, despite the fact that her communication powers were greatly diminished. But no matter what came their way, they had promised to be faithful to each other until death separated them. They kept that promise. They offered a wonderful example to the thousands whose lives they touched. Perhaps your grandparents or some other older couple you know have been equally loyal to each other.

BE FAITHFUL TO TEACHING

BACKGROUND SCRIPTURE: Hebrews 5:11—6:12
DEVOTIONAL READING: Psalm 119:97-106

KEY VERSE: Therefore let us go on toward perfection. Hebrews 6:1a.

KING JAMES VERSION

HEBREWS 5:11 Of whom we have many things to say, and hard to be uttered, seeing ye are dull of hearing. 12 For when for the time ye ought to be teachers, ye have need that one teach you again which be the first principles of the oracles of God; and are become such as have need of milk, and not of strong meat. 13 For every one that useth milk is unskilful in the word of righteousness: for he is a babe. 14 But strong meat belongeth to them that are of full age, even those who by reason of use have their senses exercised to discern both good and evil.

6:1 Therefore leaving the principles of the doctrine of Christ, let us go on unto perfection; not laying again the foundation of repentance from dead works, and of faith toward God, 2 Of the doctrine of baptisms, and of laying on of hands, and of resurrection of the dead, and of eternal judgment. 3 And this will we do, if God permit. 4 For it is impossible for those who were once enlightened, and have tasted of the heavenly gift, and were made partakers of the Holy Ghost, 5 And have tasted the good word of God, and the powers of the world to come, 6 If they shall fall away, to renew them again unto repentance; seeing they crucify to themselves the Son of God afresh, and put him to an open shame. 7 For the earth which drinketh in the rain that cometh oft upon it, and bringeth forth herbs meet for them by whom it is dressed, receiveth blessing from God: 8 But that which beareth thorns and briers is rejected, and is nigh unto cursing; whose end is to be burned.

9 But, beloved, we are persuaded better things of you, and things that accompany salvation, though we thus speak. 10 For God is not unrighteous to forget your work and labour of love, which ye have shewed toward his name, in that ye have ministered to the saints, and do minister. 11 And we desire that every one of you do shew the same diligence to the full assurance of hope unto the end: 12 That ye be not slothful, but followers of them who through faith and patience inherit the promises.

NEW REVISED STANDARD VERSION

HEBREWS 5:11 About this we have much to say that is hard to explain, since you have become dull in understanding. 12 For though by this time you ought to be teachers, you need someone to teach you again the basic elements of the oracles of God. You need milk, not solid food; 13 for everyone who lives on milk, being still an infant, is unskilled in the word of righteousness. 14 But solid food is for the mature, for those whose faculties have been trained by practice to distinguish good from evil.

6:1 Therefore let us go on toward perfection, leaving behind the basic teaching about Christ, and not laying again the foundation: repentance from dead works and faith toward God, 2 instruction about baptisms, laying on of hands, resurrection of the dead, and eternal judgment. 3 And we will do this, if God permits. 4 For it is impossible to restore again to repentance those who have once been enlightened, and have tasted the heavenly gift, and have shared in the Holy Spirit, 5 and have tasted the goodness of the word of God and the powers of the age to come, 6 and then have fallen away, since on their own they are crucifying again the Son of God and are holding him up to contempt. 7 Ground that drinks up the rain falling on it repeatedly, and that produces a crop useful to those for whom it is cultivated, receives a blessing from God. 8 But if it produces thorns and thistles, it is worthless and on the verge of being cursed; its end is to be burned over.

9 Even though we speak in this way, beloved, we are confident of better things in your case, things that belong to salvation. 10 For God is not unjust; he will not overlook your work and the love that you showed for his sake in serving the saints, as you still do. 11 And we want each one of you to show the same diligence so as to realize the full assurance of hope to the very end, 12 so that you may not become sluggish, but imitators of those who through faith and patience inherit the promises.

5

Monday, June 28	Galatians 1:6-12	*There Is No Other Gospel*
Tuesday, June 29	Galatians 5:1-10	*Stand Firm in Christ's Freedom*
Wednesday, June 30	Hebrews 10:32-39	*Don't Abandon Your Confidence*
Thursday, July 1	Psalm 119:97-101	*Your Decrees Are My Meditation*
Friday, July 2	Psalm 119:102-106	*Your Word Is a Light*
Saturday, July 3	Hebrews 5:11—6:3	*Move On to Solid Food*
Sunday, July 4	Hebrews 6:4-12	*Do Not Become Sluggish*

BACKGROUND

In the opening chapters of Hebrews, we have encountered a skilled theologian at work. The writer carefully explained the superiority of faith centered on Jesus Christ and the overwhelming value of Christ's life, death, and resurrection. As we read the last verses of chapter 5 and the opening half of chapter 6, we see not only a theologian's mind, but also a pastor's heart. He has turned his attention from proclaiming truth to encouraging an appropriate response to truth. He sensed that, in the realm of spiritual learning, a hearer needed both to understand and believe. This insight into the writer's character informs our understanding of the letter as a whole. He explained important truth not merely for its own sake, but also for the power God's truth contains, power to eternally change the lives of believers.

At the same time, our understanding of the letter as a whole informs our understanding of this week's lesson text. We can better understand this passage's strong warnings when we remember that the readers of the epistle faced persecution that threatened their ongoing loyalty to Jesus (see, for example, 12:7 and 13:3, 12-13). Fear of suffering, or even loss of life, was potentially frightening some Jewish Christians back into Judaism, a position that looked safer at least in the short run. But forsaking Christ involved moving away from salvation, and thus entailed a much greater risk for all eternity.

Picture some overwhelming contemporary danger, let's say, a house on fire. Those who first discover the blaze do and say almost anything to warn those at risk to bring everyone to safety. If people spoke with the same vehemence to invite children out to view a flower or to eat a meal, we might regard their tone of voice as unnecessarily extreme. But, at a point of life-threatening danger, when others do not realize the risk, hardly any warning can be too strong and any speaking volume too loud.

In this week's Scripture passage, the writer saw the great danger some of his readers faced: the danger of *crucifying again the Son of God* (6:6), of being cursed, and of being spiritually *burned over* (6:8). Were his readers aware of their plight? Apparently not. The writer saw them as *dull in understanding* (5:11). Behind that English phrase stands a single Greek word that could be translated "sluggish," a word the NRSV translators used later in 6:12.

Understandably, then, the writer issued as stern a warning as possible. His words remain true for all times; but, as we seek to understand them, we benefit by remembering their original context.

NOTES ON THE PRINTED TEXT

In the verses immediately preceding the opening of this week's lesson text, the writer of Hebrews portrayed Jesus as *the source of eternal salvation* (5:9) and *a high priest according to the order of Melchizedek* (5:10). Concerning these weighty topics, the writer knew he had *much to say that is hard to explain* (5:11).

That may be an understatement, since the greatest of Christian thinkers have never fully understood all the outworkings of the salvation God offers through Jesus. Yet, the writer did not criticize his readers for failing in their best efforts to understand, but that they had ceased all effort to develop a further awareness of foundational Christian doctrine. They had become *dull in understanding*. In other words, they had willingly chosen to turn their attention away from eternal truths to focus their thought on less important matters.

This choice not only hurt the readers, but also others. When they should have reached a level of spiritual competence that enabled them to be *teachers* (5:12) helping others, they were still requiring the time of other instructors *to teach* them *again the basic elements of the oracles of God*. Thus, in failing to teach others, and also in taking the time of someone who could have been teaching others, the slackard believers were doubly hindering the spread of the truth.

Hebrews 5:13-14, by means of a simple image, reaffirms the failure of the readers. They had not yet reached the point of spiritual weaning. They still needed *milk* (5:13), the most easily digested spiritual truth, rather than solid food appropriate for those who have, through diligent *practice* (5:14), become *mature* in distinguishing *good from evil*, or separating the central from the less important.

What was the solution to the readers' failure to grow? *Let us go on toward perfection* (6:1), the writer encouraged them. Behind the Greek word rendered *perfection* stands no absolute score, but the hope for a steady growth toward spiritual maturity. This would involve moving beyond *the basic teaching about Christ* (6:1). Then, as they moved beyond the elementary principles of the faith, they would not reject the *foundation* of knowledge they had gained. Also, they would be able to build on that foundation a deeper, richer understanding of their heritage.

The rest of 6:1-2 alludes to the knowledge the readers had gained early in their Christian lives: *repentance from dead works and faith toward God* (the need to turn from their past sinful lives to a new life in Christ), instruction about *baptisms* (the first ritual confirming their new birth), *laying on of hands* (a means of transferring spiritual blessing and power), *resurrection of the dead* and *eternal judgment* (the basic belief that life extended beyond physical death).

The writer never negated the value of these truths; he merely wanted his readers to go beyond the basic foundation of Christian faith. He hoped they would build superstructures on those foundations. He briefly stated that hope in 6:3—

And we will do this, if God permits.

In 6:4-8, the writer issued a sobering warning about the perils of not going forward to Christian maturity. While there are differing views regarding how to properly understand these verses, it remains clear that turning away from Christ results in spiritual disaster.

The author's desire was not to discourage his readers, but to spur them on to greater levels of faithfulness and Christlikeness. He realized that only Jesus can save people from their sins and make them holy and righteous in God's eyes; and only Jesus can enable believing sinners to become members of God's family and the recipients of His eternal blessings.

By bearing spiritual fruit in their lives, the readers would demonstrate that they had truly received and appreciated the blessings of God's salvation in Christ; of course, they had to make a decisive break with their present spiritual sluggishness.

The writer not only felt deep concern for his *beloved* (6:9) friends, but also was *confident* that they would remain loyal to their faith. He was assured that God would continue reaching out to them. *God is not unjust; he will not overlook your work and the love that you showed for his sake in serving the saints, as you still do* (6:10).

In a metaphorical sense, the "coach," at "halftime" in the spiritual event, felt some concern about how things were going for his fellow team members. But he confidently believed that they would rise up to the challenges facing them. We can benefit from considering the closing words of the writer's "halftime" exhortation—*We want each one of you to show the same diligence so as to realize the full assurance of hope to the very end, so that you may not become sluggish, but imitators of those who through faith and patience inherit the promises* (6:11-12).

SUGGESTIONS TO TEACHERS

We know few specifics about the people involved in the Letter to the Hebrews. The precise identity of the writer and the recipients remains unknown. But this week's Scripture passage does indicate the writer's strong concern for the spiritual condition of his readers and for the major choice they had to make regarding to their eternal future. There may be people in your class facing similar dangers. Feel free to echo the writer's emphasis on both diagnosis and available options.

1. THE READERS LIVED IN A STATE OF IGNORANCE. They had been taught the basics of the Christian faith, but had not even taken in that information well. They continually needed someone to start all over again with them at square one. They should have mastered that knowledge and then have been able to move on to greater depths of knowledge. The readers passively received truth, but had exerted little effort toward greater intimacy with God.

2. THE READERS LIVED IN A STATE OF IMMATURITY. Because of what they did not know, they were not able to grow. Increase in knowledge does not guarantee growth in maturity, but willful rejection of further insight almost always results in stunted personal development.

3. THE READERS LIVED IN A STATE OF INCONSISTENCY. They had committed themselves to Christ. They indicated their wish to move forward in their faith. But their circumstances, their fear of persecution or personal loss, was hindering them from firmly holding to their confession. They were trying to hang onto two incompletely incompatible systems. The writer asked them to make their choice. Between which options could they (and your students) choose?

4. THE READERS COULD CHOOSE THEIR OWN CONTINUED IMPOVERISHMENT. If they chose to live and follow Christ only sluggishly, they could never swallow anything more substantial than spiritual milk, they would never progress beyond the most basic teachings of the faith, and they could risk even further eternal loss.

5. THE READERS SHOULD CHOOSE TO MOVE TOWARD IMPROVEMENT. God remained faithful to them. He had not changed. If they would more diligently follow Him, they would move on to more solid spiritual food, substantial knowledge, and the hope of a blessing from God. The choice was theirs and ours.

FOR ADULTS

■ TOPIC: A Call to Higher Faith

■ QUESTIONS: 1. How might the fact that these believers were living under the threat of persecution affect the way we interpret the Letter to the Hebrews? 2. To what degree were the readers of this epistle responsible for their own spiritual dullness (5:11)? 3. How do you think the writer intended for his readers to *be trained by practice to distinguish good from evil* (5:14)? 4. How do you think the writer would have defined the word *perfection* (6:1)? 5. What specific steps can we take to move us in the direction of spiritual maturity?

■ ILLUSTRATIONS:

Crucifying Christ Again. Despite the fact that the following story about the apostle Peter does not appear in Scripture, members of the early church came to cherish this narrative. We can't be sure the story is true, but the meaning behind it has motivated many Christians, ancient and modern.

In the seventh decade of the first century A.D., Nero ruled the Roman Empire. He was a cruel emperor, known for lighting up his garden parties with torches made of the burning bodies of crucified Christians. When Nero's soldiers nearly caught one of the biggest prizes, Peter himself, the apostle managed to escape. Peter ran for his life.

As the story goes, while Peter was getting away, a figure stopped him in the road. Jesus had appeared once again to the leader of the disciples. Peter spoke first. "Lord, where are you going?" Jesus quietly replied, "Peter, I am walking into Rome. There I will be crucified again, this time specifically in your place." Peter realized what was happening. He turned around, returned to Rome, and died as a martyr for his Lord.

The Easy Way. During summer orientation, all staff in training stopped at the camp pool. In order to enter the pool's deep end any time during that summer, we each needed to demonstrate to the lifeguard's satisfaction that we could handle water over our heads. She did not care what we did as long as she watched us maneuver the deep end for two minutes without drowning.

Looking for the easiest way out, I asked if I could merely tread water for two minutes. The lifeguard said that would be fine. So for 120 seconds, I floated on my back. I passed the swimming test, but during that time went absolutely nowhere. I exerted little energy while I lazed away. For two minutes, I avoided drowning. I thought I was smart, but how much wiser I would have been if I had used even that short time to build muscles by swimming more energetically.

Eat for Your Health. I have always found it amazing how I can train my appetite. You would think it would be the other way around, but if I move into a pattern of eating more, I find my body craving more. If I decrease my daily consumption, my body settles into that routine and is more easily satisfied.

When I was a kid, Mom made a meat and potatoes meal nearly every day. A day without meat? As a young man, I thought that an absurd thought. After marriage and two daughters, I went back to school for three years. We cut our budget to the core. Our grocery budget would not permit much red meat. So we ate fruit and vegetables, and ended up becoming quite fond of healthier food. That was nearly 15 years ago, but we never returned to anything close to our earlier meat consumption. I go for days without eating meat and think nothing of it.

The readers of the Letter to the Hebrews had trained their spiritual appetites for only spiritual milk. If that was all they took in, their souls learned to live on that meager diet. But their spiritual health suffered, too.

FOR YOUTH

■ TOPIC: Growing Stronger

■ QUESTIONS: 1. What do you think the writer meant when he pointed out that by this time, his readers should have become *teachers* (Heb. 5:12)? 2. On what basis do you think the writer might have chosen his particular list of basic teachings about Christ (6:1-2)? 3. How do you think he would have defined the benefits of the Christian life (6:4-5)? 4. About whom might the writer have been speaking when he mentioned the group he wished his readers to imitate: *those who through faith and patience inherit the promises* (6:12)? 5. How would you evaluate your movement toward spiritual maturity in Christ?

Evaluating Maturity. I remember a day when I took my 18 month old daughter to visit Florence. Florence was an elderly member of the congregation I pastored. Because of severe arthritis, she rarely escaped the prison of her third floor apartment. She could have moved to a nearby building with an elevator, but felt safe in the apartment she had occupied for years. Florence received few visitors and rarely saw children. Whenever I could, I took little Elizabeth along for my pastoral visits. Elizabeth enjoyed the big bowls of ice cream Mrs. Lind gave her. Mrs. Lind enjoyed Elizabeth. I had a great time watching the two of them smile.

On this particular day, Elizabeth had new knowledge to show off. She had been learning some basic anatomy. "OK, Elizabeth, where is your nose?" She quickly pointed to it. "Your knee? Your neck? Your belly?" Elizabeth received a perfect score on this test. Everyone smiled. I was the proud father of my intelligent baby. But how would I have felt if, two years later, Elizabeth's awareness of the world had progressed no further? Of course, long before that we would have taken her to a physician to see what was stunting her development. Capabilities that demonstrated her maturity at one age would be woefully inadequate years or even months later.

Need for a Choice. A *Seattle Times* front page article featured Eli. Eli is a troubled youth whose mother cannot handle him. Eli needs help, but the state has not yet found anyone with the patience to keep him for long. He has spent time in juvenile detention, in psychiatric hospitals, and in foster homes. When all else fails, he spends long days being watched by strangers in social service offices, then nights with strangers at new foster homes, which accept him for one night only.

Several years ago, when Eli was 9, there was a glimmer of hope. Specially trained foster parents took him in. Concerning that situation, a social worker at first wrote, "Eli has responded beautifully. The child is a handsome, somewhat stocky lad responding well to the organic diet followed by the foster parents." But then within months, Eli was expelled from the neighborhood school for throwing chairs. Eli then, in another fit of anger, attacked the home in which he lived. He bashed walls and a television set, then tore down curtains at the windows. When asked what had caused this rampage, Eli replied that the home had too many rules.

Eli was most recently released from a detention center (to which he had been sentenced for attempting to stab a helper with a pen). Obviously Eli needs help. He needs people who will love him and guide him in the right direction. But people have offered Eli all they can. Eli also needs to make some choices of his own. He can learn to control his rage or his rage will continue to control him.

Greater than Expected Maturity. One look at Sondra Clark would lead you to think she's a typical kid. Her hair is fixed in pigtails. She bounces around like lots of twelve year olds. What makes her unusual? It's her concern for children dying of AIDS in Africa.

After visiting orphans in Kenya and Uganda a year ago, Sondra has become national "spokeschild" for Childcare International, an interdenominational relief organization. During the last months, she has helped raise $30,000 to help needy children. She has recruited 85 families to financially sponsor young people overseas. Starting this summer, she and her parents are taking a full year out of their routines to travel across the United States, speaking in churches for Childcare International.

At age 12, Sondra is showing more mature concern for others than many people ever show!

JESUS BRINGS A NEW COVENANT

BACKGROUND SCRIPTURE: Hebrews 8—9
DEVOTIONAL READING: Hebrews 10:10-18

KEY VERSE: Jesus has now obtained a more excellent ministry,
and to that degree he is the mediator of a better covenant. Hebrews 8:6.

KING JAMES VERSION

HEBREWS 8:6 But now hath he obtained a more excellent ministry, by how much also he is the mediator of a better covenant, which was established upon better promises.

7 For if that first covenant had been faultless, then should no place have been sought for the second.

8 For finding fault with them, he saith, Behold, the days come, saith the Lord, when I will make a new covenant with the house of Israel and with the house of Judah:

9 Not according to the covenant that I made with their fathers in the day when I took them by the hand to lead them out of the land of Egypt; because they continued not in my covenant, and I regarded them not, saith the Lord.

10 For this is the covenant that I will make with the house of Israel after those days, saith the Lord; I will put my laws into their mind, and write them in their hearts: and I will be to them a God, and they shall be to me a people:

11 And they shall not teach every man his neighbour, and every man his brother, saying, Know the Lord: for all shall know me, from the least to the greatest.

12 For I will be merciful to their unrighteousness, and their sins and their iniquities will I remember no more.

NEW REVISED STANDARD VERSION

HEBREWS 8:6 But Jesus has now obtained a more excellent ministry, and to that degree he is the mediator of a better covenant, which has been enacted through better promises. 7 For if that first covenant had been faultless, there would have been no need to look for a second one.

8 God finds fault with them when he says:
"The days are surely coming, says the Lord,
    when I will establish a new covenant with the
        house of Israel
    and with the house of Judah;
9 not like the covenant that I made with their
        ancestors,
    on the day when I took them by the hand to lead
        them out of the land of Egypt;
for they did not continue in my covenant,
    and so I had no concern for them, says the Lord.
10 This is the covenant that I will make with the
        house of Israel
    after those days, says the Lord:
I will put my laws in their minds,
    and write them on their hearts,
and I will be their God,
    and they shall be my people.
11 And they shall not teach one another
    or say to each other, 'Know the Lord,'
for they shall all know me,
    from the least of them to the greatest.
12 For I will be merciful toward their iniquities,
    and I will remember their sins no more."

BACKGROUND

Both Hebrews 5 and subsequently 7:11—8:5 portray Jesus as a high priest superior to the Old Testament (that is, the old covenant's) priesthood. As the writer of the epistle penned these words, he never came close to saying the old Levitical priesthood was worthless, for God Himself had given Moses the model for that priesthood as one part of the Mount Sinai covenant. Through Moses, God had carefully instructed the Israelites how they should live. He wanted Moses and the people to follow precisely this divine model (8:5). That model, the Mount Sinai covenant, and its priesthood centered around the tabernacle and its successor, the Jerusalem temple.

It makes sense that the old God-given priesthood could be greatly modified only if the Mount Sinai covenant were also replaced. Could that happen? Yes! It has happened! That is precisely the message of this week's lesson text. Not only is Jesus a new and superior high priest, but also *he is the mediator of a better covenant* (8:6).

On what basis could Jesus make the first covenant *obsolete* (8:13)? To answer that question, the writer of Hebrews quoted the prophet Jeremiah at length (8:8-12). In effect, the writer pointed out that Jeremiah, a God-inspired representative of the old covenant, had foretold that the first covenant was only temporary. In time, it would be replaced by a superior covenant.

The quote from Jeremiah 31:31-34 would have spoken powerfully to the Jewish readers of the Letter to the Hebrews. They would have known and trusted the old covenant from their earliest days. Perhaps Jewish friends or family members had criticized them for leaving the traditional ways to follow Jesus as their new high priest. Such a move would make more sense if the new priest had established a new and better covenant, one foretold within the old covenant itself.

In what ways was the new covenant superior? Under the inspiration of God, Jeremiah had foreseen the new covenant's advantages. Rather than being a covenant written on stone tablets, God promised to write the principles of the new covenant on people's *hearts* (8:10). Instead of God revealing Himself as a relatively remote figure, living behind an imposing curtain in the Jerusalem temple, under the new covenant, God's interaction with the redeemed would become more personal and intimate.

Whereas before, God's people had struggled to know Him, within the new covenant, they would gain a much clearer understanding of their Lord (8:11). Although within the old covenant, God had made provision for the pardoning of the sins of His people, the new covenant sharpened their awareness of His eternal forgiveness in Christ (8:12). God would establish this new covenant forever (8:9). It would never need replacement. Without doubt, it was the stronger of the two covenants.

Thus, as the writer of Hebrews penned chapter eight of his epistle, he was in effect asking, "Why would you Jewish Christians want to return to the second best way, even though it was a good way? God has offered a far better way; God has offered Himself in Christ!"

NOTES ON THE PRINTED TEXT

This week's Scripture passage, which quotes from Jeremiah 31:31-34, begin's with the contrastive *but* (Heb. 8:6). With that word, the writer of the epistle drew a sharp distinction with what preceded. The Jerusalem temple, set up as *a sketch and shadow of the heavenly one* (8:5), formed part of the old way. *But Jesus has now obtained a more excellent ministry* (8:6), one in which he serves *exalted above the heavens* (7:26). To the degree that the heavenly ministry surpasses the earthly one, *he is the mediator of a better covenant* (8:6).

What makes the new covenant superior to the old? The second covenant *has been enacted through better promises*. The content of these better promises can be found in the words of Jeremiah, which the writer of Hebrews proceeded to cite verbatim (8:8-12).

Even within itself, the old covenant anticipated something new and better (8:7-9). *For if that first covenant had been faultless, there would have been no need to look for a second one* (8:7). The first covenant had its limitations. As the writer of Hebrews continued, he did not specifically identify those shortcomings. Instead, he focused on the benefits of the new covenant. Jeremiah's quotation moved closest to stating a weakness of the old system by noting that God's people "*did not continue in* [that] *covenant*" (8:9). For reasons Jeremiah did not state, the people of Israel continually struggled to follow God within the Mosaic covenant.

God, of course, did not absolve the previous generations of their rebellious ways. In fact, God found *fault with them* (8:8), not with his first covenant. At the same time, in His grace, God promised to offer, and subsequently in Jesus did offer, His new and superior covenant. Through Jeremiah, God had committed Himself to this promise. "*The days are surely coming . . . when I will establish a new covenant with the house of Israel and with the house of Judah.*"

Hebrews 8:9 specifies that the new covenant would differ from the previous *covenant* made with the *ancestors* of both Jeremiah's hearers and the first century Jews. Those ancestors had lived during the period of the Exodus—"*the day when* [God] *took them by the hand to lead them out of the land of Egypt."* Because God's people had not remained loyal to Him and His first covenant, He *"had no concern for them"* (8:9).

Perhaps these last words sound harsh to us. Did God cease loving His people? Of course not! Despite His eventually allowing them to be carried off into exile, God even then was planning to restore a remnant of the people to their homeland. Better yet, God promised that He would inaugurate for them a new covenant.

In 8:10, we see this new covenant described. *"This is the covenant that I will make with the house of Israel after those days, says the Lord."* From that intro- duction, God through Jeremiah offered a fuller picture of the new covenant and its overwhelming advantages.

Whereas God had given the old covenant largely in an external form, with the new covenant He would now place His divine word within His people. *"I will put my laws in their minds, and write them on their hearts."* Not only would God in Jesus incarnate the new covenant before His people, but also through His Spirit's indwelling, God would enable all people who followed Him to know Him inti- mately. In a sense far greater than human beings had ever known, God would ful- fill His ancient promise, which was spoken to Moses and the generation of the Exodus (Exod. 6:7), that *"I will be their God, and they shall be my people"* (Heb. 8:10).

Because God would place His living Word within His people, they would enjoy greater opportunity for intimate fellowship with Him and thus experience less need for teachers. *"And they shall not teach one another . . . for they shall all know me, from the least of them to the greatest"* (8:11). God intended His people to enjoy that level of intimacy with Him and personal knowledge of Him. Sadly, the original readers of this letter were slipping dangerously away from God's ideal (see 5:11-14).

Not only did God offer the promise of increased fellowship with and knowl- edge of Him, but also the new covenant would include a greater gift of mercy toward His people's *iniquities* (8:12). He would *"remember their sins no more."* The reality is that, when God speaks of *"a new covenant"* (8:13), it implies He has made *the first one obsolete.* In a sense, the old covenant is out of date and *will soon disappear.*

SUGGESTIONS TO TEACHERS

As you work with your students, remind them that we live today under the provisions of the new covenant. We continue to enjoy all its advantages. As you highlight these, you might want to contrast our present interac- tion with God with the less extensive level of fellowship enjoyed by those who lived under the earlier covenant. Lead your students in gratitude for God's gen- erosity. One good way we can show gratitude for God's new covenant gifts is to enjoy them to the fullest! In particular, there is . . .

1. GREATER INTIMACY WITH GOD. Through God's Spirit, all new covenant believers can know the Lord in a manner similar to, and even more personally, than we know one another. In the days before Jesus came, the nation of Israel collectively could know God, but, with rare exceptions, individuals tended to know about God only through what they had heard. Under the new covenant, God has come to live not only with but also in His people.

2. GREATER KNOWLEDGE OF GOD. Through the incarnation of Jesus and the indwelling of the Holy Spirit, first century Christians could know more about God and also know God Himself. In addition to these blessings, later generations of Christians also gained access to the complete written New Testament (which only gradually was collected and distributed). From this we see that God has given us many ways to know Him.

3. GREATER FORGIVENESS FROM HIM. God offered forgiveness to Old Testament people, but the associated ritual of animal sacrifice dreadfully complicated the process. Now through Jesus, God's people have more direct access to Him and to His grace. Not only do we receive forgiveness, but through the Spirit, we can receive assurance of that forgiveness and our resulting relationship with God.

4. GREATER CERTAINTY OF GOD'S ETERNAL FAITHFULNESS. During the period of the old covenant, the Israelites struggled to know God. As the prophets began to speak about a new day coming, their hearers might have rejoiced in what God was going to do, but generations died, not seeing that new day. They might have heard God's promise of a new covenant, but they died under the old covenant. Today, we know we live in the days of God's new covenant. The covenant established through Christ will never change!

FOR ADULTS

■ TOPIC: Call to Perfection

■ QUESTIONS: 1. What weaknesses do you see in the old covenant? 2. Under the old covenant, did the greater problem lie with the covenant or the people who did not keep it? Why? 3. Within the new covenant, what laws has God placed in His people's minds and hearts? 4. In what sense do new covenant Christians not need teachers (Heb. 8:11)? 5. What greater responsibilities do we, as new covenant Christians, bear?

■ ILLUSTRATIONS:

Eternal Students. Have you heard the phrase "eternal student?" My parents used those words to describe people who seemingly never left school. Eternal students used one educational diploma merely as a stepping stone toward another. My parents laughed, implying that such people should finally leave school and enter the real world. Probably they laughed at me, for beyond high school, I spent 10 years gaining more education. I felt comfortable in school; I performed well there.

Finally having received one last diploma, I returned to school, but this time to sit on the other side of the teacher's desk.

The longer I spend in school, the more I sense that quality teachers seek to work themselves out of their jobs. They teach not only particular subjects, but, more importantly, the process of learning. Their students reach the point where they know enough about a subject and about learning to go on teaching themselves. At the same time, all skilled learners, either formally or informally, become teachers and models for others. In at least a spiritual sense, God wants all of us to remain eternal students, coming to know Him well enough to teach His truth to others, for when we are sharing Christ with others, we ourselves grow at an even faster rate.

A New Potential. At church recently, my elderly Uncle Bob briefly fell unconscious. To be safe, friends called an ambulance, which took him to the local hospital. After some tests, the physicians sensed that my uncle's heart was not functioning well. They recommended heart bypass surgery.

Over the last couple decades, most of us have come to take such operations for granted. We forget how limited surgeons were before scientists invented the artificial heart pump. Surgeons can remove and repair human hearts, but only because, for the duration of the procedure, a machine can efficiently circulate a patient's blood throughout his or her body.

Fifty years ago, no such machine was available. Open heart surgery was little more than a dream. People like Uncle Bob would not have survived long. But now, with the help of new technology, he was able to come home within a few days, with the same sense of humor he has always had.

Open Now to All. Boston's Museum of Fine Arts includes a display unlike any I have seen in several major world art museums. When construction for a new shopping mall was about to condemn Oak Hill, a lovely home built in 1800, it needed to come down. The mall owners could have carefully photographed the mansion and displayed huge pictures throughout their new business establishment. That would have been one way to preserve the memory of the old place and allow people to experience it continually.

Curators at the museum decided they could do much better. They moved, and completely reconstructed within their museum, several entire rooms from the house. The original carpets, drapes, door jambs, fireplaces—everything but the space which these rooms had occupied—was moved to make a unique museum display. This is much better than photographs. People can see Oak Hill in three dimensions. The museum experience now, in effect, enables all people to walk into old Oak Hill itself.

God declared the need for a new covenant. And, through His grace, He opened a new and better covenant with the redeemed.

FOR YOUTH

■ TOPIC: A Spiritual Pact

■ QUESTIONS: 1. What does the biblical word "covenant" mean? 2. What do you think it would have been like living under the old covenant and then hearing that a better covenant was coming? 3. In what way under the new covenant is our relationship with God potentially better? 4. In what sense do new covenant Christians know God today? 5. Which of the new covenant privileges do you most enjoy? Why?

■ ILLUSTRATIONS:

Laws in Our Minds and Hearts. Do you remember learning how to ride a bicycle? One of your parents, or perhaps an older sibling, placed you on the bike seat. They then gave you a long list of how-to rules. "Pedal. Maintain your balance. Use the handle bars to steer and help maintain your balance. Stay away from trees and walls."

You tried to remember all those rules as you began moving forward. How far did you go the first time? Most of us fell within just a few feet. Why? We could not remember and follow all the rules at the same time. Even if we could remember them, we could not communicate them to our hands, feet, and torso quickly enough. We hit the ground repeatedly.

But finally the moment came. We successfully rode the bike. And, with perhaps only minor problems, you have been riding a bike ever since. How often do you need to remind yourself of the bike-riding rules? Probably never. They have become part of who you are.

Back to the Old Apartment? My wife and I recently moved to a new apartment. Moving is a lot of trouble. Why didn't we stay where we were? We asked that question too, during the many trips between the two houses. We felt particular frustration the afternoon when we realized there was no way our couch would fit through the doors of our new place. (Strong friends somehow pushed and pulled the couch onto a second floor deck. We then took down double glass doors and moved the couch in with ease.) We liked our old apartment. It offered plenty of space and a wonderful view. So why did we move?

Our new apartment has many wonderful advantages. I have already mentioned one deck; we actually have two! The old place had only a bathtub; here we have a nice warm shower. There's a dishwasher, our own washer and drier, newer, tighter windows—and the list goes on. And the rent is actually less than at our previous home. Would we want to move back to our old apartment? Not for a moment! We are happy with our new agreement.

Declaration of Independence. Not long ago was the 227th anniversary of the signing of the American Declaration of Independence at the Continental Congress in Philadelphia. For decades, Great Britain had governed the people of the 13 colonies. Many within those locales thought it wisest for the people of Pennsylvania, Massachusetts, Georgia, and the other colonies to remain in agreement with King George III. Even if British rule restricted Americans' freedom a bit, some felt that economic advantages and the danger of war argued against moving toward freedom.

But as the representatives deliberated, they finally reached agreement. They would establish a new agreement, not with Britain, but with each other, among the colonies. They committed themselves, even if it required their death, to break free from the old ways and establish a brand new system. Aren't we glad that Jesus, at the cost of His death, chose to fulfill the old covenant and establish a new, better one?

ROLL CALL OF THE FAITHFUL

BACKGROUND SCRIPTURE: Hebrews 11
DEVOTIONAL READING: 1 Peter 4:12-19

KEY VERSE: Without faith it is impossible to please God, for whoever would approach him must believe that he exists and that he rewards those who seek him. Hebrews 11:6.

KING JAMES VERSION Faith shows confidence in God

HEBREWS 11:1 Now faith is the substance of things hoped for, the evidence of things not seen. 2 For by it the elders obtained a good report. *Faith pleases God*

4 By faith Abel offered unto God a more excellent sacrifice than Cain, by which he obtained witness that he was righteous, God testifying of his gifts: and by it he being dead yet speaketh. 5 By faith Enoch was translated that he should not see death; and was not found, because God had translated him: for before his translation he had this testimony, that he pleased God. 6 But without faith it is impossible to please him: for he that cometh to God must believe that he is, and that he is a rewarder of them that diligently seek him. 7 By faith Noah, being warned of God of things not seen as yet, moved with fear, prepared an ark to the saving of his house; by the which he condemned the world, and became heir of the righteousness which is by faith. *Faith takes us into unknown territory*

8 By faith Abraham, when he was called to go out into a place which he should after receive for an inheritance, obeyed; and he went out, not knowing whither he went. 9 By faith he sojourned in the land of promise, as in a strange country, dwelling in tabernacles with Isaac and Jacob, the heirs with him of the same promise: 10 For he looked for a city which hath foundations, whose builder and maker is God. 11 Through faith also Sara herself received strength to conceive seed, and was delivered of a child when she was past age, because she judged him faithful who had promised. 12 Therefore sprang there even of one, and him as good as dead, so many as the stars of the sky in multitude, and as the sand which is by the sea shore innumerable. 13 These all died in faith, not having received the promises, but having seen them afar off, and were persuaded of them.

NEW REVISED STANDARD VERSION

HEBREWS 11:1 Now faith is the assurance of things hoped for, the conviction of things not seen. 2 Indeed, by faith our ancestors received approval. . . .

4 By faith Abel offered to God a more acceptable sacrifice than Cain's. Through this he received approval as righteous, God himself giving approval to his gifts; he died, but through his faith he still speaks. 5 By faith Enoch was taken so that he did not experience death; and "he was not found, because God had taken him." For it was attested before he was taken away that "he had pleased God." 6 And without faith it is impossible to please God, for whoever would approach him must believe that he exists and that he rewards those who seek him. 7 By faith Noah, warned by God about events as yet unseen, respected the warning and built an ark to save his household; by this he condemned the world and became an heir to the righteousness that is in accordance with faith.

8 By faith Abraham obeyed when he was called to set out for a place that he was to receive as an inheritance; and he set out, not knowing where he was going. 9 By faith he stayed for a time in the land he had been promised, as in a foreign land, living in tents, as did Isaac and Jacob, who were heirs with him of the same promise. 10 For he looked forward to the city that has foundations, whose architect and builder is God. 11 By faith he received power of procreation, even though he was too old—and Sarah herself was barren—because he considered him faithful who had promised. 12 Therefore from one person, and this one as good as dead, descendants were born, "as many as the stars of heaven and as the innumerable grains of sand by the seashore."

13 All of these died in faith without having received the promises, but from a distance they saw and greeted them.

7

Monday, July 12	Romans 4:13-22	*Abraham Did Not Weaken in Faith*
Tuesday, July 13	Hebrews 11:1-6	*Abel and Enoch Had Faith*
Wednesday, July 14	Hebrews 11:7-12	*By Faith Noah Built an Ark*
Thursday, July 15	Hebrews 11:13-19	*They Desired a Heavenly Country*
Friday, July 16	Hebrews 11:20-26	*Isaac, Jacob, and Joseph Had Faith*
Saturday, July 17	Hebrews 11:27-31	*By Faith Moses Led the Israelites*
Sunday, July 18	Hebrews 11:32-40	*Others Commended for Their Faith*

BACKGROUND

For many Christians, Hebrews 11 is the most familiar chapter of the epistle. In the past, it has helpfully reminded them of their need to "hang in there" in faith. Placing this chapter in its context in the letter as a whole may give it even greater meaning for us.

For whom was the unknown writer penning these words? It was for Jewish believers who were in danger of forsaking their faith in Christ to return to the more familiar ways of Judaism. Thus whom did the writer use as his greater models of faithfulness? They were several Old Testament followers of God, men and women who have long stood as mentors of God's people. Since the readers of Hebrews were Jewish Christians, the use of the great Old Testament examples was doubly appropriate.

In what particular way did Abel, Enoch, Noah, Abraham, and others serve as examples to this letter's original readers? Each one believed God, having heard His promises, despite the fact that none of them saw anything close to their complete fulfillment. Abel, Enoch, Noah, and Abraham, all from the early pages of Genesis, faced great temptation. They must have asked themselves why they should believe in a God who committed Himself in word, but seemed to make His people wait years, decades, or longer, before fulfilling His pledges. But they refused to yield to this temptation; they continued to trust God.

The readers of Hebrews had chosen to follow Christ in what others had promised would be a better way. But life was not working out that way. They had already faced rejection and even persecution for their faith (10:32-33). Undoubtedly at times they felt confused. Among their non-believing peers, they likely felt treated as *strangers and foreigners* (11:13). They too must have wondered, "Where is the better way God has pledged to us?"

And so, by offering both a description of faith and the example of their faith-filled ancestors, the writer encouraged his readers to continue on the Christian way. Even if life seemed treacherous at the time, in the end, God would prove Himself faithful. How did the writer know this? It was with his eyes of faith. As Hebrews 11 indicates, he gave many more examples of those who believed despite not seeing the fulfillment of God's promises. Then at that chapter's end, and in the opening verses of chapter 12, the writer pulled back the curtain to give his readers a glimpse of God's great finale—the heavenly reward that His past followers had received.

NOTES ON THE PRINTED TEXT

The context of this week's Scripture passage helps us to see Hebrews 11:1 in its full brightness. *Now faith is the assurance of things hoped for, the conviction of things not seen.* Christians must exercise faith in God, especially when they do no have sight either of God Himself or of all the gifts He promised to give them.

Indeed, by faith our ancestors received approval (11:2). This verse should be regarded as the chapter's thesis statement. God approved the great Old Testament noteworthies precisely for their faith, their believing what they could not see. Hebrews 11:4-38 then recounts many of these episodes of faith.

Why did the writer of the epistle include Hebrews 11? Was it so that the Jewish Christians would honor their ancestors? Perhaps, but that was certainly not his primary purpose. Was it so that believers would cherish the concept of faith? That possibility stands closer to the truth, but it does not yet hit the target (so to speak). The writer was urging his readers to hang tightly to God Himself. In this chapter, faith is understood as simply the means to the end of each reader's ongoing relationship with God, the ultimately faithful one.

After briefly alluding to God's creation activity (11:3), the writer offered the first example in his "Hall of Faith." *By faith Abel offered to God a more acceptable sacrifice than Cain's* (11:4). In what way did Abel's sacrifice surpass his brother's offering? Perhaps it was not so much the form of their gifts to God, but rather the attitude behind their gifts. Cain may have given his offering out of duty, while Abel was truly seeking a relationship with God.

In any case, Abel received no immediate visible reward from God; instead, he received his brother's deadly attack. But through the sacrifice offered in faith, Abel, despite his untimely death, received what was most important—God's approval. What was the writer of Hebrews hoping his readers would see in Abel's example? It's that, even if faithfulness to God results in their premature death through persecution, they should not let the fear of death shake them from their loyalty to God. Through the words of Scripture, Abel *still speaks.*

The writer chose Enoch as his second example. Enoch was a man who walked with God; then *"he was not found, because God had taken him"* (11:5). Enoch, someone might say, received his reward. He saw God's promise instantly fulfilled when God transferred him to heaven, even though he did not experience death. Yes, because Enoch had pleased God, the Lord enabled him to bypass death. But, like Abel, Enoch did not see the fulfillment of God's promises until after he left this life. Enoch's move to heaven was extraordinary. At the same time, his life had no known unusual features, except that he faithfully walked with God. With this example, the writer encouraged his readers to continue walking with God, even when they could not see all they longed for.

If Enoch pleased God, how could first century Christians do that? What did it mean for them to walk with Him? *Without faith it is impossible to please God, for whoever would approach him must believe that he exists and that he rewards those who seek him* (11:6). To please God, people must believe what they cannot see. God calls His people to believe, as Abel and Enoch did, that He exists and that He is good, even when the circumstances cause believers to doubt God's existence and blessing.

Noah offers a slightly different example of faith. God called him to active obedience, to undertake a task for which his contemporaries mocked him. Evidently Noah had previously seen neither a flood nor a huge boat, but God *warned* (11:7) him to build *an ark to save his household* in the face of an upcoming deluge. Noah demonstrated his faith through obedience.

Noah's actions not only offered physical rescue from the waters, but also served as the opportunity for him to please God and become *an heir to the righteousness that is in accordance with faith.* Perhaps the writer of Hebrews sensed that God wanted this group of first-century Jewish Christians not merely to endure persecution, not merely to walk faithfully with God, but also, like Noah, to take steps of active obedience that would reveal their faith in God to the world.

Abraham, the ancestor of the Jewish nation, receives the largest share of attention in Hebrews 11. The writer highlighted three major faith moments in the life of the patriarch. Two of them appear in this week's lesson text: Abraham's obedience in moving to a new and unknown country and his faith in believing that God would enable Sarah to bear a son, even in her old age.

God called Abraham to leave his home and country to move to a new land the patriarch had never seen, a land still totally unknown to him. *By faith Abraham obeyed* (11:8). God directed him to live in that new *land he had been promised,* although Abraham never owned a bit of it except a cave in which he buried his deceased wife. Though God promised this land to Abraham and his descendants, the patriarch lived there *as in a foreign land, living in tents* (11:9), never able to put down lasting roots.

What enabled Abraham to make such sacrifices? He looked beyond place and possession in this world; instead *he looked forward to the city that has foundations, whose architect and builder is God* (11:10). The first readers of the Letter to the Hebrews would easily have deciphered the writer's intent; he wanted them also to keep their eyes primarily on God and the future world He was preparing for them.

When God promised Abraham and Sarah a son in their old age and in Sarah's barrenness, Abraham *considered him faithful who had promised* (11:11). God did keep this promise during Abraham's lifetime. Sarah gave birth to Isaac, but not until years after the promise had first been given. The writer of Hebrews described the greater fulfillment of God's promises to Abraham. God gave him descendants, *"as many as the stars of heaven and as the innumerable grains of sand by the seashore"* (11:12; see Gen. 15:5 and 22:17).

Before moving on to another episode of faith in the life of Abraham, as well as many more from the lives of other Old Testament heroes of faith, the writer of Hebrews paused to offer a summary thought. All the faithful ones *died in faith* (11:13) without receiving what God had promised them. Instead, they saw the fulfillment of these divine pledges *from a distance* and welcomed them. These stalwarts of faith agreed that *they were strangers and foreigners on the earth*. Their example lives on in the pages of Scripture for us to contemplate and follow.

SUGGESTIONS TO TEACHERS

In this week's lesson text, the writer of Hebrews set forth his description of faith, emphasized its necessity, and offered historical examples his readers would have known well. In doing so, he sought to motivate them to become examples of faith in God and its accompanying trait, obedience to God. As the writer noted in 11:13, these believers did trust God, but never lived on earth long enough to see God's promises fulfilled. The writer called his first readers and us to consider these noteworthy examples of trust and obedience.

1. THE EXAMPLE OF ABEL. In faith, Abel offered his animal sacrifice to the God he could not see. Perhaps Abel sensed that the sacrifice represented all he was and owned. In his sacrifice, he dedicated himself to God. Perhaps your students have previously given themselves to God. Are they ready, in faith, to reaffirm that previous commitment?

2. THE EXAMPLE OF ENOCH. In faith, Enoch walked with God. Enoch's relationship with God went beyond any number of individual encounters with the Lord; that relationship seemingly dominated who Enoch was. You may want to take the opportunity to ask your students for evidence that they are more than Sunday morning Christians, but those who truly walk with God.

3. THE EXAMPLE OF NOAH. In faith, Noah built an ark. Like Enoch, Noah walked with God. The strength of their relationship enabled Noah to trust and obey the Lord and His instructions. Had it not been for that faith, Noah probably would have agreed with his neighbors that boat-building was a strange hobby. God today still commands the redeemed to do what our world thinks is foolish. In what ways are your students called to live as if they were aliens in this world, as those who are citizens of God's future kingdom?

4. THE EXAMPLE OF ABRAHAM. In faith, Abraham left everything he had ever known to follow God to a new home. Even there, God never allowed Abraham to settle completely. God does not call all His spiritual children to leave their homelands, but God does call some. Gently find a way to measure the strength of your students' faith. How far would they go, if God called them? What would the challenges be for them? How would they handle these, especially if hints of doubt might creep in?

■ **TOPIC:** Living Faith

■ **QUESTIONS:** 1. What for you is the significance of the description of faith in Hebrews 11:1? 2. Why do you think our faith in Christ so pleases God? 3. Why do you think God preferred Abel's sacrifice over Cain's? 4. What enabled various Old Testament examples of faith to maintain strong trust in and obedience to the Lord? 5. To what step of faith might God be calling you?

■ **ILLUSTRATIONS:**

A Chain of Faith. Many of us have gained spiritual benefit, either directly or indirectly, from the ministry and writings of John Wesley. On what occasion did Wesley first exercise faith in Jesus? Wesley did so while attending a small group where the leader was reading aloud from the writings of Martin Luther. Martin Luther, in turn, moved toward salvation while reading the Book of Romans. (It was Luther's commentary on Romans that Wesley heard on the night of his "heart-warming" salvation experience.)

In a similar chain, the writer of Hebrews found his faith increased as he thought about Old Testament figures such as Abel, Enoch, Noah, and Abraham. The writer shared their accounts with his readers, hoping that the ancient examples of faith would inspire first-century believers. Today, our faith can be strengthened as we read the Letter to the Hebrews. Models from the past have always motivated God's people.

Not Living to See the Dream. Abraham Lincoln was assassinated on a Good Friday evening. Just five days before, on Palm Sunday morning, Robert E. Lee and Ulysses Grant met in a small house at Appomattox Courthouse to sign the agreement that ended the Civil War. The President had led the United States through the most traumatic period in its history. His primary goal was to reunite his country, to show the world that a government of the people and by the people could survive.

Lincoln came close, but never saw that day. Soldiers on both sides had laid down their guns, but then a gunman tragically shot Lincoln down. As Moses could see, but not enter the promised land, as the other heroes of faith mentioned in Hebrews 11 died before seeing the fulfillment of God's promises to them, Lincoln died before seeing his dream—the nation's wounds gradually being healed.

Running the Marathon. Running the 26 miles of a marathon requires a high level of dedication. Some of us have given thought to trying such a race, but few of us have put our feet to the pavement for that long. I recently read a story that inspired me to at least think about trying one more time. At least this account took away any excuse I ever had. Fenya Brown, at age 88, still gets her sneakers out for the long run. She called it "a form of insanity, but a very wonderful one." Even after three bouts with breast cancer in the last 10 years, she continually believes that she can do what perhaps no other woman her age has ever done. Her faith causes me to marvel!

FOR YOUTH   ■ TOPIC: Faith Alive
■ QUESTIONS: 1. Why does God call people to put their faith in what they cannot see? 2. If you were Noah, how do you think you would you have felt when God commanded you to build an ark? 3. In what ways is righteousness connected to faith? 4. In what sense is obedience connected with faith? 5. What is the most difficult command God has given you?

■ **ILLUSTRATIONS:**

Marriage Proposal. When I asked my wife, Kathy, to marry me, I asked two questions, not one. The second question was the obvious one. But her answer to the first was equally essential. "If I ask you to marry me, will you go with me anywhere that God leads me?" Thankfully, Kathy replied positively to the first question, so I could go on to the second. And thankfully for me, Kathy gave a "yes" to that question, too.

During our wedding ceremony, Kathy recited to me Ruth's words to Naomi, which are recorded in Ruth 1:16. Little did either of us dream what those words might entail. We first pastored in Pennsylvania and New Jersey, not all that far from Kathy's Kentucky roots. But the next step? God took us to Saint Andrews, Scotland, for three wonderful years.

Far enough? Not yet. From there, we moved to Melbourne, Australia, where we taught at a missionary Bible college for six years. After that period, God took us for a while back closer to our original homes in the eastern U.S. But, one more time we packed our gear in a rental truck and headed for Seattle, Washington. We think we are settled here for good, but if once again, God asks us, like Abraham, to move to some other unknown location, we will be ready to go.

Honeymoon Adventure. When she married me, Kathy thought she knew me well. But I had managed to keep a few secrets. Our February honeymoon took us to Gatlinburg, Tennessee. Neither of us are skiers, but Kathy suggested that, merely for the view, we ride the gondola up to the ski lodge. She never gave a thought to the safety of this ride. She, without a doubt, believed that the car would be safe and it would give us a great experience. I also moved on faith, but I could "see" much less certainty than Kathy felt. You see, Kathy had not yet become aware of my fear of heights.

As the car began its journey through the air, Kathy was running from side to side taking in all the snowy mountain vistas. Meanwhile, I was turning green. Thankfully, Kathy had chosen to exercise her strong faith and I, my weaker version, in a trustworthy operation. We returned safely to the ground, her with disappointment that the adventure was over, and I with great relief for the same reason.

Daniel's Faith. Daniel was a wallpaper hanger in China. But that was not his life. He found his true meaning in his relationship with Jesus. Daniel risked his safety as he pastored an illegal underground church. Daniel knew the danger well. His parents had previously spent years in prison for refusing to forsake Jesus. Daniel continued to obey God's call even when that meant leaving his wife and parents in China while he traveled to Australia to receive more Bible training.

Although Daniel had no steady source of income, he believed God would provide. And God did. In time, Daniel's wife and even his parents were allowed to join him. Has Daniel given up on China? By no means! He plans to return as often as he can to offer his encouragement to his fellow Christians there.

FAITHFULNESS AND DISCIPLINE

BACKGROUND SCRIPTURE: Hebrews 12
DEVOTIONAL READING: 1 Peter 4:12-19

KEY VERSE: Endure trials for the sake of discipline. Hebrews 12:7a.

KING JAMES VERSION

HEBREWS 12:1 Wherefore seeing we also are compassed about with so great a cloud of witnesses, let us lay aside every weight, and the sin which doth so easily beset us, and let us run with patience the race that is set before us, 2 Looking unto Jesus the author and finisher of our faith; who for the joy that was set before him endured the cross, despising the shame, and is set down at the right hand of the throne of God. 3 For consider him that endured such contradiction of sinners against himself, lest ye be wearied and faint in your minds.

4 Ye have not yet resisted unto blood, striving against sin. 5 And ye have forgotten the exhortation which speaketh unto you as unto children, My son, despise not thou the chastening of the Lord, nor faint when thou art rebuked of him: 6 For whom the Lord loveth he chasteneth, and scourgeth every son whom he receiveth. 7 If ye endure chastening, God dealeth with you as with sons; for what son is he whom the father chasteneth not? 8 But if ye be without chastisement, whereof all are partakers, then are ye bastards, and not sons. 9 Furthermore we have had fathers of our flesh which corrected us, and we gave them reverence: shall we not much rather be in subjection unto the Father of spirits, and live? 10 For they verily for a few days chastened us after their own pleasure; but he for our profit, that we might be partakers of his holiness. 11 Now no chastening for the present seemeth to be joyous, but grievous: nevertheless afterward it yieldeth the peaceable fruit of righteousness unto them which are exercised thereby. 12 Wherefore lift up the hands which hang down, and the feeble knees; 13 And make straight paths for your feet, lest that which is lame be turned out of the way; but let it rather be healed.

NEW REVISED STANDARD VERSION

HEBREWS 12:1 Therefore, since we are surrounded by so great a cloud of witnesses, let us also lay aside every weight and the sin that clings so closely, and let us run with perseverance the race that is set before us, 2 looking to Jesus the pioneer and perfecter of our faith, who for the sake of the joy that was set before him endured the cross, disregarding its shame, and has taken his seat at the right hand of the throne of God.

3 Consider him who endured such hostility against himself from sinners, so that you may not grow weary or lose heart. 4 In your struggle against sin you have not yet resisted to the point of shedding your blood. 5 And you have forgotten the exhortation that addresses you as children—

"My child, do not regard lightly the discipline of the Lord,
  or lose heart when you are punished by him;
6 for the Lord disciplines those whom he loves,
  and chastises every child whom he accepts."

7 Endure trials for the sake of discipline. God is treating you as children; for what child is there whom a parent does not discipline? 8 If you do not have that discipline in which all children share, then you are illegitimate and not his children. 9 Moreover, we had human parents to discipline us, and we respected them. Should we not be even more willing to be subject to the Father of spirits and live? 10 For they disciplined us for a short time as seemed best to them, but he disciplines us for our good, in order that we may share his holiness. 11 Now, discipline always seems painful rather than pleasant at the time, but later it yields the peaceful fruit of righteousness to those who have been trained by it.

12 Therefore lift your drooping hands and strengthen your weak knees, 13 and make straight paths for your feet, so that what is lame may not be put out of joint, but rather be healed.

8

361

BACKGROUND

It should be clear by now that the Letter to the Hebrews sets out to show that the new covenant is superior to the old covenant because of the person of Christ. He stands at the peak of revelation, being superior to angels (1:1—2:9) and to Moses (3:1-6). Jesus is the outshining of God's glory and the very character and essence of the divine (1:3). Whatever revelations appeared before Jesus were but shadows or outlines of what He disclosed.

Christ is the supreme and exalted High Priest (4:14). Whereas earthly priests inherited their office, Jesus was appointed by the direct call of God (5:5-6). Whereas earthly priests followed in the lineage of Aaron, Christ, who has no successors, is a priest forever, according to the order of Melchizedek (7:17). Whereas earthly priests ministered within humanly made temples, Christ ministers within the true sanctuary, namely, the eternal house of God (8:2; 9:24). Whereas earthly priests offered animal sacrifices for their sins as well as for those of the people, Jesus offered the one perfect sacrifice that never needs to be offered again—His sinless self (5:3; 10:4-14).

As the unique Son of God who made the supreme sacrifice of Himself to God, Jesus is described by the writer of Hebrews as the *pioneer of their salvation* (2:10), the *perfecter of our faith* (12:2), and the *great shepherd of the sheep* (13:20). Christ saves His people from sin and death, and He saves them for fellowship with God. In Hebrews, salvation is metaphorically called the *rest* (4:1) of God, *eternal inheritance* (9:15), and the *Holy Place* (9:12).

The author's three main emphases—namely, Jesus as Son, High Priest, and Savior—are drawn together in 5:8-10. In light of Christ's preeminence, the author urged his readers to hold fast to the true confession and endure whatever suffering or reproach was necessary on its behalf (4:14; 6:18; 13:13).

The exhortation to persevere in the pilgrimage of faith is grounded in the writer's proof that the Old Testament itself testified to the imperfection of the covenant at Sinai and its sacrificial system, thereby pointing ahead to a new High Priest—Jesus Christ. He is better than the mediators, sanctuary, and sacrifices of the old order. In association with Christ, there is greater grace and glory, as well as greater accountability, which now have arrived in the new covenant mediated by Jesus.

Unlike the earthly and external aspects of the Old Testament sanctuary, Christ sanctifies believers for the true worship of God, so that they can draw near to heaven itself with clean consciences. Christ is the guarantee of this better covenant bond, for He links believers inseparably with the Lord of grace.

NOTES ON THE PRINTED TEXT

Hebrews 11 mentioned a number of Old Testament saints who lived by faith. They were the great *cloud of witnesses* (12:1) who encouraged the Hebrews to remain loyal to Jesus. The imagery is that of athletes running a race in an amphitheater filled with people. Those in the stands were motivating examples of faithfulness.

The term rendered *witnesses* is loaded with significance. The Greek word is *martus* and it comes from the verb *martureo*, which means "to testify" or "to bear witness." The idea is one of affirming what we have seen or experienced. The New Testament writers sometimes applied *martus* to those believers in Christ who were attesting to their faith while enduring persecution. Some of them died as a result of their witness. Thus, in time, such Christians came to be known as martyrs, that is, those who voluntarily suffered death as the penalty for their allegiance to Christ.

The writer compared his readers to athletes competing in a long-distance race. In ancient Greece, runners would strip themselves of anything that might weigh them down or entangle their arms and legs. Similarly, believers were to rid themselves of every *sin* that might prevent them from living for Christ.

Jesus was the supreme example of faith in the race; in fact, He was the *pioneer and perfector* (12:2) of the believers' faith. Thus, as they lived for Christ, they were to focus their attention on Him. His single-minded devotion to the Father's will enabled Him to disregard the shame of the cross. Jesus allowed Himself to be executed because of the joy that God had put before Him; and now Jesus is sitting at God's right hand.

Knowing that his readers would sometimes feel weary and lose heart because of opposition, the writer of Hebrews urged them to *consider* (12:3) Jesus. The Lord had to endure terrible opposition from *sinners*, and yet He persevered until He won the victory. Christ would also enable believers to persevere no matter what obstacles they faced. The Hebrews had endured persecution; and though they were tempted to return to their former way of life, the writer urged them not to give up. He reminded them that none of them had died for their faith (12:4).

The writer next drew an extended comparison between loving parents who discipline their children and God who allows believers to suffer—because He loves them and wants them to grow. The writer, in 12:5-6, established the validity of this analogy by quoting from Proverbs 3:11-12. These verses teach that discipline in the lives of believers is evidence that we are God's children. He uses sufferings and hardships to purify our lives and deepen our faith in Him.

The author assured his readers that they could trust in their heavenly Father, who treated them as His *children* (Heb. 12:7). He would continue to discipline them to strengthen their commitment to Him. In Bible times parents routinely disciplined their children. Similarly, God disciplines His spiritual *children* (12:8); in fact, those who have not experienced His discipline are *illegitimate*.

The Hebrews respected their earthly *parents* (12:9) for disciplining them. They were also to appreciate the discipline they received from their heavenly *Father*. When He corrected them, His purposes were wise and loving in nature.

Sometimes human parents are motivated by the wrong reasons when they discipline their children. God, however, *disciplines* (12:10) His children because He wants them to be holy, as He is. By enduring trials, they learn to share in His *holiness*.

Hebrews 12:11 admits that it is never fun to be corrected; yet the griefs that spring from tragedies, persecutions, and conflicts prepare God's children to be at peace in all situations and to respond properly to God and other people in the face of difficulties.

The writer, perhaps returning to the running imagery, exhorted his readers to strengthen their limp *hands* (12:12) and enfeebled *knees*. Hebrews 12:13 extends the imagery by quoting from Proverbs 4:26. The Hebrews were to smooth out the racetrack so that even the *lame* (Heb. 12:13) could get around it without falling and hurting themselves. The idea is that, as we are running our own race, we should look out for our fellow believers and try to help them succeed in their races as well. By God's grace the Christian life is one in which we all can eventually wear the wreath of victory—no matter what disabilities we start with.

SUGGESTIONS TO TEACHERS

The readers of the Letter to the Hebrews faced persecution. Many students in your class are also facing hard times of their own. The writer of the epistle used both historical facts and helpful analogies to encourage his followers toward steadfastness. Today, you can use these same images to encourage others to maintain hope and progress.

1. GOD'S PEOPLE BEFORE THEM HAD STRUGGLED AND WON. The writer opened Hebrews 12 by reminding his readers of the *great . . . cloud of witnesses* (12:1) that *surrounded* them. These witnesses were God's people from the past who had heard His promises and remained faithful to Him, despite not seeing the fulfillment of these pledges. But by the time Hebrews was written, all these witnesses had moved up into the grandstands of heaven. God's faithful people ultimately would join them in victory.

2. JESUS HIMSELF HAD STRUGGLED AND WON. *Jesus . . . endured the cross, disregarding its shame* (Heb. 12:2). Because of His complete obedience to the Father, even to death, Jesus *has taken his seat at the right hand of the throne of God*. Contemporary believers find comfort in the fact that their God empathizes with their pain. God's Son faced it at its worst, and He enables Christians to be victorious today.

3. VICTORIOUS ATHLETES WILLINGLY STRUGGLE IN ORDER TO WIN. The writer of Hebrews used an athletic analogy to stress this point. The runners persevere in *the race that is set before* (12:1) them. Even when they sense themselves drooping, they forge on toward the finish line. They willingly challenge themselves. If their contest is worth all their energy and effort, how much more important is it for Christians to remain faithful to Jesus, especially as they press on toward their heavenly goal?

4. CHILDRENS' STRUGGLES WITH DISCIPLINE ENABLE THEM TO GROW. The middle portion of this week's Scripture passage employs the analogy of parents discipling their children. As loving parents allow their children to be stretched, they protect their children from anything that would truly harm them. Likewise, God always monitors our circumstances. If He chooses not to protect us from suffering, He allows only that testing that enables us to become holy as He is holy.

■ **TOPIC:** Maturing Faith through Obedience

■ **QUESTIONS:** 1. What is the significance of the statement that Jesus is *the pioneer and perfecter of our faith* (Heb. 12:2)? 2. What incentive does the fact of Jesus' suffering offer to His followers? 3. Why does the Lord discipline *those whom he loves* (12:6)? 4. In what ways did the first readers of Hebrews experience *drooping hands* (12:12) and *weak knees*? 5. Which of this chapter's images gives you the most encouragement to keep going even through difficult times? Why?

■ **ILLUSTRATIONS:**

A Parent's Discipline. My father undoubtedly believed in discipline. His word ruled the house. All seven of his children knew that his belt did more than hold his pants up. On occasion, when he felt our behavior merited punishment, we felt his belt in an appropriate place on our backside just below our own beltline. I can remember two specific occasions when Dad literally "belted" me. Looking back, I am not sure I deserved that severe a punishment on either occasion. But, in any case, Dad let me know that I did not rule the world. And because of or perhaps despite Dad's discipline, I have turned out fine.

I became a parent myself. My two daughters have reached adulthood. I never used a belt, but they both experienced my discipline. Like my father did, I disciplined them because I loved them. I wanted them to turn out well. And because of (or despite) my discipline, they have both turned out well. It won't be long before they will be showing their love for my grandchildren by disciplining them.

Personal Victory. The runners in the first Olympic Women's Marathon were entering the stadium at the end of the race. The year was 1984 and the location was Los Angeles. On a hot day, the women had run a course through the streets of the city. For the hours they had been running, the heat had been radiating off the pavement. As they entered the Olympic Coliseum, participants needed to run a full lap around the track before crossing the finish line. An American won the race that year, but her victory is not what people remember about this particular Olympic event.

Well out of the medals, a Swiss runner, Gabriella Anderson-Schiess, came through the stadium tunnel and into view. Everyone immediately sensed that Gabriella might not make it to the end. Rather than running directly around the track, she was staggering right and left. She dragged one of her legs as if she had suffered a stroke. Gabriella had given her all, but was suffering from exhaustion and heat stroke.

Immediately, Gabriella's coach, accompanied by a paramedic team, rushed over to help her. The paramedics wanted to put her on a stretcher and carry her off the field. Gabriella could not speak, but could motion that she wished to be left to finish the race on her own. Had anyone offered any assistance other than a drink, she would have been disqualified from the race. She had run 26 miles; she wanted to finish the event.

The crowd rose to its feet and cheered Gabriella. They had warmly supported the American winner during her last lap, but that greeting was nothing compared to the exuberant support everyone offered Gabriella. Despite her pain and exhaustion, she pulled her body around the track and collapsed across the finish line. With perseverance, she ran her race to the very end. She won no medal, but she won the greatest of personal victories.

The Barracuda. Eleanor recently retired at age 80. But her retirement has nothing to do with slowing down or even giving up her cause. Eleanor merely gave up her position as executive director of WAMI, Washington Advocates for the Mentally Ill. WAMI is the country's largest state mental-health advocacy group of its kind.

Thirty years ago, her own family tragedy moved Eleanor and some acquaintances to form this new advocacy group. Eleanor's own son John, until that point a normal teenager, was diagnosed with schizophrenia. He had moved into a box in the basement, hung a noose for decoration, and demonstrated other patterns of abnormal behavior. Eleanor's feelings of helplessness triggered her determination. Since then she and other WAMI members have lobbied the state legislature, the University of Washington, and other government institutions on behalf of the mentally ill and their families. Determination? She's got it. Despite her small size, and age, she is still known among colleagues as "the barracuda." Will mere retirement slow her down? Not in the least!

■ **TOPIC:** Accepting Discipline

■ **QUESTIONS:** 1. In your opinion, what is the relationship between Hebrews 11 and 12? 2. What *weight* (12:1) do you think prevents believers from running their race well? 3. Why is it appropriate for God to discipline us as His spiritual children? 4. In what ways has God disciplined you? How have you responded? 5. What can you do to help other believers run their race of faith better?

■ **ILLUSTRATIONS:**

Strengthen Your Weak Knees. Perhaps you remember the name of Picabo (Peek-a-boo) Street. (Once you've heard the name, it's a hard one to forget.) This American skier won a gold medal in the 1998 super-G and a silver in the 1994 downhill. No matter how she performs in future events, she deserves a medal just for her perseverance.

Between the two medals she presently holds, Street overcame a severe knee injury. Then less than a month after the 1998 Nagano Games, while racing in another event, Street crashed on the slopes, breaking her left femur and tearing major ligaments in her right knee. Street did not race for over two years after that injury. But she returned not only to skiing, but to world class form. Her first performances revealed how out of shape she was. But she has been able to strengthen her weak knees to the point of entering Olympic competition once again.

The Discipline of Study Skills. I teach an introduction to college life course for a group of first term technical school students. The topic for tonight's class is study skills. Some of them don't need this evening's session. I hope they will pick up one or two helpful hints, but the quality and the promptness of the assignments they have already given me demonstrate the quality of their previous learning.

Has the discipline some previous teacher instilled in these students had a positive effect? Undoubtedly. Did they like that discipline when they received it? Probably not. But now that they have reached the level of college work, they have built habits that will make them a success at any level of study.

Still on the Job. A recent newspaper article informed me that *The Weekly Reader* is celebrating its one hundredth birthday. I had forgotten all about this newspaper, but now easily remember the impact it had on me. Although I haven't stepped foot in my elementary school for over 30 years, I can still remember the excitement I felt when Miss Clarke, my third grade teacher, gave each of us the latest copy of *The Weekly Reader*. It was full of fun puzzles, feature stories, as well as a third grade level accounting of some recent news event. That four-page paper shaped me. It instilled in me a love for news and newspapers that I hold to this day. I had great fun discovering that *The Weekly Reader*'s editors were still doing their job, shaping third graders across the United States even in the new century.

Skittles's Trek. People aren't the only creatures with perseverance. The *Seattle Times* reported the amazing story of Skittles, a two-year-old orange tabby cat. The Sampsons, Skittles's family, took him on a Labor Day weekend trip from their home in northeastern Minnesota to southern Wisconsin. As the Sampsons were packing their car to return home, Skittles was nowhere to be seen.

The family needed to return home to pick up work the next day, so they left. They hoped and prayed that Skittles would return to their temporary Wisconsin headquarters. They would gladly make the return trip to retrieve their loved pet. Skittles never returned to that spot, but three months later, the Sampsons heard a cat at their back door. You guessed it—Skittles had somehow found his way across 350 miles. For 13 weeks, he persevered, through who knows what adventures, to find his way home.

SELECT GOOD LEADERS

BACKGROUND SCRIPTURE: 1 Timothy 3:1-13; 5:17-19
DEVOTIONAL READING: Acts 20:17-28

KEY VERSE: Hold fast to the mystery of the faith with a clear conscience. 1 Timothy 3:9.

KING JAMES VERSION

1 TIMOTHY 3:1 This is a true saying, If a man desire the office of a bishop, he desireth a good work. 2 A bishop then must be blameless, the husband of one wife, vigilant, sober, of good behaviour, given to hospitality, apt to teach; 3 Not given to wine, no striker, not greedy of filthy lucre; but patient, not a brawler, not covetous; 4 One that ruleth well his own house, having his children in subjection with all gravity; 5 (For if a man know not how to rule his own house, how shall he take care of the church of God?) 6 Not a novice, lest being lifted up with pride he fall into the condemnation of the devil. 7 Moreover he must have a good report of them which are without; lest he fall into reproach and the snare of the devil.

8 Likewise must the deacons be grave, not double-tongued, not given to much wine, not greedy of filthy lucre; 9 Holding the mystery of the faith in a pure conscience. 10 And let these also first be proved; then let them use the office of a deacon, being found blameless. 11 Even so must their wives be grave, not slanderers, sober, faithful in all things. 12 Let the deacons be the husbands of one wife, ruling their children and their own houses well. 13 For they that have used the office of a deacon well purchase to themselves a good degree, and great boldness in the faith which is in Christ Jesus. . . .

5:17 Let the elders that rule well be counted worthy of double honour, especially they who labour in the word and doctrine. 18 For the scripture saith, Thou shalt not muzzle the ox that treadeth out the corn. And, The labourer is worthy of his reward. 19 Against an elder receive not an accusation, but before two or three witnesses.

NEW REVISED STANDARD VERSION

1 TIMOTHY 3:1 The saying is sure: whoever aspires to the office of bishop desires a noble task. 2 Now a bishop must be above reproach, married only once, temperate, sensible, respectable, hospitable, an apt teacher, 3 not a drunkard, not violent but gentle, not quarrelsome, and not a lover of money. 4 He must manage his own household well, keeping his children submissive and respectful in every way— 5 for if someone does not know how to manage his own household, how can he take care of God's church? 6 He must not be a recent convert, or he may be puffed up with conceit and fall into the condemnation of the devil. 7 Moreover, he must be well thought of by outsiders, so that he may not fall into disgrace and the snare of the devil.

8 Deacons likewise must be serious, not double-tongued, not indulging in much wine, not greedy for money; 9 they must hold fast to the mystery of the faith with a clear conscience. 10 And let them first be tested; then, if they prove themselves blameless, let them serve as deacons. 11 Women likewise must be serious, not slanderers, but temperate, faithful in all things. 12 Let deacons be married only once, and let them manage their children and their households well; 13 for those who serve well as deacons gain a good standing for themselves and great boldness in the faith that is in Christ Jesus. . . .

5:17 Let the elders who rule well be considered worthy of double honor, especially those who labor in preaching and teaching; 18 for the scripture says, "You shall not muzzle an ox while it is treading out the grain," and, "The laborer deserves to be paid."
19 Never accept any accusation against an elder except on the evidence of two or three witnesses.

9

Monday, July 26	Acts 6:1-7	*Select Those Full of the Spirit*
Tuesday, July 27	Acts 20:17-24	*Paul Didn't Shrink from His Ministry*
Wednesday, July 28	Acts 20:25-31	*Keep Watch over the Flock*
Thursday, July 29	Hebrews 13:7-17	*Remember Your Leaders*
Friday, July 30	1 Timothy 3:1-7	*A Bishop Must Be above Reproach*
Saturday, July 31	1 Timothy 3:8-13	*Deacons Must Be Serious*
Sunday, August 1	1 Timothy 5:17-22	*Good Leaders—Worthy of Double Honor*

BACKGROUND

Together, 1 and 2 Timothy, as well as Titus, are known as the "Pastoral Letters." Paul, of course, wrote all his letters from his position as a church leader, a pastor. But these three letters find uniqueness in that their recipients were also acting as pastors. With one other exception (Philemon—a letter written to a layman), Paul sent his other epistles to entire churches.

Paul wrote the three Pastoral Letters near the end of his life, in a period that extends beyond the record found in the Book of Acts. The account Luke wrote in Acts describes Paul's life to and through his first imprisonment in Rome, a jail term during which he wrote letters to churches at Philippi, Colossae, and Ephesus. Bible scholars then surmise that Paul was released from that imprisonment and engaged in another period of traveling ministry. During what we might call Paul's fourth missionary journey, he wrote 1 Timothy and Titus. Roman authorities then arrested Paul once again. During the time of this last imprisonment (that led up to the apostle's execution), Paul wrote 2 Timothy.

Paul sensed that his earthly ministry was coming to an end. So he focused his last days on equipping others to lead various local congregations after his death. Thus his letters during this period instructed two of Paul's own co-workers in matters relating to their own ministry. As he did so, Paul held a long-range view. Not only did the apostle sense his own death coming, but also he knew that Timothy and Titus would eventually join him in heaven. Thus, Paul counseled them not only in their own relationships with the churches they pastored, but also in how to select and train leaders who would ultimately carry on their work.

First Timothy, which is the focus of this week's lesson, provides the longest description in the New Testament on the qualifications for elders (3:2-7), comments about supporting and rebuking elders (5:17-20), and the only explicit description in the New Testament of the qualifications for deacons (3:8-13). Paul's specific directives to Timothy also contain much practical advice on how a church leader should function.

This letter is noteworthy for its emphasis on sound doctrine (1:10; 3:9; 4:6; 6:3). There are affirmations of salvation by grace (1:13-16), Christ as the one Mediator between God and humanity (2:5), and the substitutionary atonement of Christ (2:6). The epistle includes a poetic meditation on the work of Christ, which affirms His incarnation, resurrection, and ascension (3:16), an anticipation of the second coming of Christ (6:14), a marvelous doxology (vss. 15-16), and evidence of the expansion of the concept of Scripture beyond the Old Testament to include elements of the New Testament revelation (5:18).

Also distinctive about 1 Timothy are its comments about women (2:9-15), which include a lengthy section on proper care for widows in the church (5:3-16). There is even background information about Timothy, including probable references to both his baptism (6:12) and his ordination (1:18; 4:14).

NOTES ON THE PRINTED TEXT

What Paul had to say about selecting church leaders was worthy of trust. For example, those who wanted to become a bishop had noble aspirations. *Bishop* (1 Tim. 3:1) means overseer and refers to the pastor of the church. Not everyone could be a pastor, for certain preconditions had to be met. These are listed in 3:2-7.

Overseers had to be blameless, meaning above *reproach* (3:2) among non-Christians. The mention of this requirement should prompt us to evaluate the quality of our witness before the unsaved. Pastors also had to be *married only once*. The emphasis here is on being faithful to one's spouse, and the mention of it should spur us who are married to never compromise our wedding vows.

Pastors had to be *temperate* and earnest in the discharge of their duties. They also had to be *respectable* in their conduct to others. How vigilant and sincere are we in serving the Lord? How well behaved are we among others? These are tough questions to answer, especially if we desire to minister for Christ. Overseers were to be *hospitable*, that is, willing to provide for the needs of traveling Christians. They also had to be skilled in teaching God's Word. Only those who had such an ability would do well as a shepherd of God's people.

Pastors could not be addicted to wine; otherwise how could they feed and lead the people of God? Overseers had to be *gentle* (3:3), not violent and argumentative. Their affections were to be on God, not money. They were to be patient, not belligerent or covetous, reasonable and approachable, not contentious and greedy. Which of these qualities would be true of our lives? Which of the vices do we struggle with? Hopefully the Lord is helping us to be more virtuous in our treatment of others.

Pastors had to *manage* (3:4) their families *well*. This means their children had to be well-behaved and obedient, not unruly and rebellious. Otherwise, how could ministers maintain an orderly church if their home was chaotic and out of control (3:5)? We should take a few moments to consider how well we manage our homes. Are our loved ones respectful or rebellious? Do they love God or despise Him?

Those who minister the Gospel must not be new converts to the faith. This is because they could become easily inflated with *conceit* (3:6) and invite the kind of judgment that God imposed on *the devil* when he became prideful. What is our attitude toward church leadership? Do we want to minister the Gospel so that we might receive the attention and praise of others? If so, our motivation is wrong.

Finally, Paul stated that those who were chosen as overseers should have the respect of the unsaved people in the community; otherwise, they would fall under heavy criticism and be disgraced by Satan (3:7). What is our reputation among the unsaved? Do they see us as being genuine or phony in our witness? The answer to this question suggests a lot about what kind of church leader we would make.

The qualifications of deacons were quite similar to those of pastors. Deacons traditionally have been charged with the physical care and well-being of the church. This is an awesome responsibility and so should not be taken lightly.

Deacons needed to be reverent and deserving the respect of others. They also needed to be sincere in their speech, unaddicted to *wine* (3:8), and not eager to get rich by cheating others. Deacons should cling tenaciously to *the mystery of the faith* (3:9), that is, the revealed truth of the Gospel, without any element of doubt. Those who did not have a *clear conscience* were unqualified to serve in this noble office.

Recent converts were poor candidates for the office of deacon. Before serving in this capacity, the genuineness of their faith had to be examined. Only those whose conduct and beliefs were above reproach could *serve as deacons* (3:10).

In 3:11, Paul said the *women* should be *serious*, that is, reverent and dignified. This verse could be a reference either to the wives of deacons or women who served in the office of deaconess. The *women* also were to exercise self-control and be worthy of trust. When godly Christian women faithfully serve, the church is greatly blessed.

Paul said that *deacons* (3:12) were to be utterly faithful to their mates. Deacons also had to manage their children and home in a godly manner. The work of a deacon, although difficult at times, was commendable. Those who faithfully discharged their responsibilities enjoyed a *good standing* (3:13) among their fellow believers and had the assurance that their *faith* in *Christ* was genuine.

Elders (5:17) were overseers whose duties included feeding and leading God's people. Paul said the leaders who did an exceptional job in fulfilling their pastoral duties (especially, *preaching and teaching* sound doctrine) were worthy of receiving *double honor*. This refers both to the respect associated with being a pastor and additional financial compensation.

Paul defended his position by first quoting Deuteronomy 25:4, which teaches that the ox was allowed to eat from the grain it walked over in the process of separating the chaff from the kernels. The apostle meant that hardworking Christian ministers deserved to be paid fairly for their work. The apostle then cited Luke 10:7. In other words, those who minister the Gospel should be compensated accordingly.

Paul was familiar with the tendency of some disgruntled believers to bring false charges against overseers. Perhaps in light of his own experiences, the apostle cautioned Timothy not to immediately accept an *accusation* (1 Tim. 5:19) against a church leader. Allegations only were to be entertained when a minimum of *two or three* credible *witnesses* had ample evidence to back up their claims of wrongdoing.

SUGGESTIONS TO TEACHERS

Paul knew that the future of the church depended, to a great degree, on the quality of its leaders. Thus he selected others (such as Timothy and Titus) who could serve as good leaders. But beyond that, Paul described the type of people that ministers should desire as their successors. Can the standard in today's churches be any lower? God calls all of us, as believers, to evaluate our lives by these criteria so that we can serve Him in any way He sees fit.

1. QUALITY OF RELATIONSHIP WITH JESUS. Paul intended that church leaders not be new converts and that they be those whom the church had had adequate time to test. The apostle wanted pastors and deacons to be those who had matured in their faith. No one can change the quantity of time that he or she has known Jesus. But each of us can seek, as time passes, to ensure that our relationships with Him not merely grow older, but deeper.

2. QUALITY OF RELATIONSHIP WITH FAMILY. Paul specifically stated that church leaders should be chosen from those who served first as good family leaders. Paul recognized that those who abused their spouse or their children would also abuse the church. All Christians need to live in faithfulness to Christ not only before their broader communities, but also before those who see them the most and know them the best. If our spouses or children would not nominate us for church office, then perhaps we should not serve.

3. QUALITY OF RELATIONSHIP WITH FELLOW CHRISTIANS. Perhaps you have known people who moved into ministry for selfish reasons. Do such people serve God or His church fruitfully? Thankfully a person's human sinfulness does not prevent God from working through him or her, but the Lord works through people far more easily when they seek to live as servants, not bosses.

4. QUALITY OF RELATIONSHIP WITH THE NON-CHRISTIAN COMMUNITY. The church can neither let the world choose its leaders nor set the criteria by which good church leaders are known. But how can non-believers respect the church if its leaders do not live by the high standards the congregation itself proclaims? From this we see that even the world holds high expectations for church leaders.

FOR ADULTS

■ **TOPIC:** Foundations for Effective Leadership
■ **QUESTIONS:** 1. Why do you think Paul saw quality church leadership as being so important? 2. In what way is a person's rela-

tionship with his or her family a good test of his or her potential for church leadership? 3. Do you feel the standards for church leaders should be higher than those of other church members? Why or why not? 4. Why did Paul recommend giving even an otherwise highly qualified new Christian a time of testing before being given a leadership position? 5. What other virtues do you think are essential for quality church leadership?

■ ILLUSTRATIONS:

Whitefield's Power. In the years just before the American Revolution, God used George Whitefield, an associate of John Wesley, to help bring revival to the colonies. Like Wesley, Whitefield possessed an amazing mind, a convincing preaching style, and most importantly, a heart for God.

On one occasion, Whitefield was preaching in Philadelphia. Benjamin Franklin, the great American statesman, chose to attend the service. Near the end of his sermon, Whitefield asked his hearers to make a contribution to an orphanage he had founded in Savannah, Georgia.

The appeal first upset Franklin. He thought to himself, "Why should I give money for children who live a thousand miles from here when there are plenty of poor children here in Philadelphia?" Whitefield continued to speak. Franklin felt moved and decided to put his copper coins in the offering plate. Whitefield continued. Franklin felt so convinced that he gave his silver coins, then a gold coin, and finally emptied his pockets for Whitefield's worthy cause!

What motivated Franklin to give? Whitefield certainly was *an apt teacher* (1 Tim. 3:2). But was he a *lover of money* (3:3)? No, none of the offerings he collected went into his own pocket. Whitefield was known and respected even among people outside the church (such as Benjamin Franklin). Whitefield lived a life *above reproach* (3:2).

A Little Maturity. When I was born, my dad was a pastor. Ten years later, he was elected district superintendent. One year Dad asked me to serve as a page at the annual district business meeting. The pastors and elected lay delegates carried out their business in good form. I knew then I was headed for the pastorate, and dreamed of the day when I would have the right to speak at such events.

The day came. Fresh out of seminary, I was a pastor of my own church. I could hardly wait for district conference when I could be seated within the official body, cast my ballot, and even speak. The first couple years, I must have driven other people crazy. I felt a need to speak (or at least ask a question) on nearly every issue. That was my right, and nothing was going to hinder me from exercising it! I look back and recognize how foolish I must have looked.

Paul told Timothy to be wary of giving too much power to spiritual rookies. The apostle knew they weren't ready for it. A little maturity goes a long way.

A Surprise for Your Pastor. *"Truly I tell you, it will be hard for a rich person to enter the kingdom of heaven"* (Matt. 19:23). Have you known some lay people who did their best to help their pastor enter the kingdom—by keeping him or her poor? One church decided to surprise their pastor. Its people saw how faithfully their leader served. They sensed that he deserved a reward he could receive before he reached heaven. Behind his back, they chose to double his small salary. That step of faith stretched the church, but God rewarded their generosity. Their numbers grew. Their offerings increased. They met that year's budget. Is your pastor ready for such a surprise?

FOR YOUTH

■ TOPIC: Who Me, Lead?
■ QUESTIONS: 1. What is the importance of self-control? 2. What characteristics make a person a good teacher? 3. What type of parents command the respect of their children? 4. Why did Paul emphasize the need for church members to honor their parish leaders? 5. What steps can young people take to prepare themselves for effective and faithful church leadership?

■ ILLUSTRATIONS:

The Leader Sets the Pattern. For decades, athletes and scientists agreed that no human being would ever run a mile in less than four minutes. And their predictions proved accurate. No one did. But one young man believed that he could go beyond that limit. Fifty years ago this past spring, on May 6, 1954, Roger Bannister broke the four-minute barrier. Now, among world class male runners, several athletes beat Bannister's one-time record in nearly every mile race. But it took someone of Bannister's determination to be the first. He set the pattern. He became a great leader whose example others follow.

Habitat for Humanity. Nearly 30 years ago, in rural Georgia, Millard and Linda Fuller founded Habitat for Humanity. The Fullers had dreamed of ways to help poor people own their own homes. Their final idea caught on, for Habitat for Humanity chapters have sprung up around the world. Habitat partners volunteer time to build houses inexpensively. The future homeowners often work alongside the volunteers. Together they construct a home that even low income earners can afford to buy.

How did the idea catch on so well? In the early years of their organization, the Fullers came up with a brilliant idea. Within 10 miles of their home lived a man known and respected throughout the world. If they could recruit him as a spokesman, others would help make their dream reality. So they made contact with former President Jimmy Carter, a man known for his Christian character. President Carter not only agreed to speak in behalf of this project, but also recruited a group, picked up his own hammer, boarded a Trailways bus, and traveled to

Brooklyn, where he led a group in a home construction project. The media coverage that resulted gave Habitat for Humanity a boost into the national spotlight, which is just what it needed to catch people's attention.

Why don't you investigate the possibility of donating your time to a worthy cause such as Habitat? The Fullers and President Carter acted as leaders. Thousands of others of all ages have since joined their team. You could not only join, but also recruit others to do the same!

The Infection from a False Leader. In his book, *The 17 Indisputable Laws of Teamwork,* John Maxwell relates the story of how incorrect leadership can drag people down. At a football game, five people came to a first aid station feeling ill. The attending physician asked questions and found out that all five had bought drinks from the same stadium vendor. He quickly diagnosed food poisoning.

Just as quickly, the physician sent a messenger to the public address announcer to tell the entire crowd to avoid all stadium drinks. The physician thought his announcement would help reduce the problem, but, before too long, people all over the stadium were falling ill. They had heard the announcement and assumed that they too had consumed a tainted drink.

But further investigation revealed that the stadium drinks were harmless. The first five victims had each eaten a salad at the same problem restaurant on the way to the game. As soon as the public address system announced that people could return to purchasing drinks, a stadium full of people felt physically better. False information, spread even accidentally by one "false leader," infected thousands of people.

BE MINISTERS OF GODLINESS

BACKGROUND SCRIPTURE: 1 Timothy 4:7-16; 5:1-8
DEVOTIONAL READING: 2 Peter 1:3-11

KEY VERSE: Godliness is valuable in every way, holding promise for both the present life and the life to come. 1 Timothy 4:8b.

KING JAMES VERSION

1 TIMOTHY 4:7 But refuse profane and old wives' fables, and exercise thyself rather unto godliness. 8 For bodily exercise profiteth little: but godliness is profitable unto all things, having promise of the life that now is, and of that which is to come. 9 This is a faithful saying and worthy of all acceptation. 10 For therefore we both labour and suffer reproach, because we trust in the living God, who is the Saviour of all men, specially of those that believe. 11 These things command and teach. 12 Let no man despise thy youth; but be thou an example of the believers, in word, in conversation, in charity, in spirit, in faith, in purity. 13 Till I come, give attendance to reading, to exhortation, to doctrine. 14 Neglect not the gift that is in thee, which was given thee by prophecy, with the laying on of the hands of the presbytery. 15 Meditate upon these things; give thyself wholly to them; that thy profiting may appear to all. 16 Take heed unto thyself, and unto the doctrine; continue in them: for in doing this thou shalt both save thyself, and them that hear thee. . . .

5:1 Rebuke not an elder, but intreat him as a father; and the younger men as brethren; 2 The elder women as mothers; the younger as sisters, with all purity.

3 Honour widows that are widows indeed. 4 But if any widow have children or nephews, let them learn first to shew piety at home, and to requite their parents: for that is good and acceptable before God. 5 Now she that is a widow indeed, and desolate, trusteth in God, and continueth in supplications and prayers night and day. 6 But she that liveth in pleasure is dead while she liveth. 7 And these things give in charge, that they may be blameless. 8 But if any provide not for his own, and specially for those of his own house, he hath denied the faith, and is worse than an infidel.

NEW REVISED STANDARD VERSION

1 TIMOTHY 4:7 Have nothing to do with profane myths and old wives' tales. Train yourself in godliness, 8 for, while physical training is of some value, godliness is valuable in every way, holding promise for both the present life and the life to come. 9 The saying is sure and worthy of full acceptance. 10 For to this end we toil and struggle, because we have our hope set on the living God, who is the Savior of all people, especially of those who believe.

11 These are the things you must insist on and teach. 12 Let no one despise your youth, but set the believers an example in speech and conduct, in love, in faith, in purity. 13 Until I arrive, give attention to the public reading of scripture, to exhorting, to teaching. 14 Do not neglect the gift that is in you, which was given to you through prophecy with the laying on of hands by the council of elders. 15 Put these things into practice, devote yourself to them, so that all may see your progress. 16 Pay close attention to yourself and to your teaching; continue in these things, for in doing this you will save both yourself and your hearers. . . .

5:1 Do not speak harshly to an older man, but speak to him as to a father, to younger men as brothers, 2 to older women as mothers, to younger women as sisters—with absolute purity.

3 Honor widows who are really widows. 4 If a widow has children or grandchildren, they should first learn their religious duty to their own family and make some repayment to their parents; for this is pleasing in God's sight. 5 The real widow, left alone, has set her hope on God and continues in supplications and prayers night and day; 6 but the widow who lives for pleasure is dead even while she lives. 7 Give these commands as well, so that they may be above reproach. 8 And whoever does not provide for relatives, and especially for family members, has denied the faith and is worse than an unbeliever.

10

HOME BIBLE READINGS

BACKGROUND

Helpful background information for this week's lesson can be found in 1 Timothy 4:1-7. A careful study of the letter indicates that religious frauds had infiltrated the Ephesian assembly and turned some away from the faith. The presence of corrupt teaching at Ephesus was a harbinger of what would take place in later times as the appearing of Christ for His church drew near (4:1).

The Spirit clearly revealed to Paul that some would depart from the truths of the Christian faith. They would pay attention to *spirits* that lie and the *teachings of demons*. Although they appeared to be well-intentioned, these religious frauds dispensed lies upon lies without feeling the slightest twinge of conscience. It was as if someone had *seared* their sense of right and wrong with a branding *iron* so that they were insensitive to the truth (4:2).

The false teachers at Ephesus promoted a rigid asceticism. For example, they claimed that followers of God must not marry and barred them from eating certain kinds of food. Paul declared, however, that the things *God created* (4:3) were to be welcomed with gratitude by those who knew and embraced *the truth*.

A number of people at Ephesus were being misled by the notion that asceticism gained God's favor. Paul wanted Timothy to combat this error with the truth. The apostle explained that everything *created by God* (4:4) was *good*, or wholesome, in His eyes. Therefore, *nothing* He made was to be *rejected*, especially if it was welcomed with a thankful attitude. The idea is that, when believers sit down to eat a meal, they should recognize God has provided the food and express gratitude to Him for it.

Paul said that what we eat is *sanctified* (4:5), or set apart, for our use *by God's word and by prayer.* What is meant by *God's word*? Perhaps this signifies quoting Scripture verses when we pray before eating. It also might mean keeping in mind the biblical teaching about our liberty in Christ. Regardless of the meaning, it is clear that believers should thank God at mealtimes for the food He has graciously provided.

Paul said Timothy would be a good minister, or *servant* (4:6), of *Christ Jesus* if he taught the believers at Ephesus the truths about marriage and eating. By emphasizing the doctrines of the Christian *faith*, Timothy would demonstrate that they *nourished* him. He also would show that he was strengthened by the *sound teaching* he received and carefully *followed.*

NOTES ON THE PRINTED TEXT

Once again Paul stressed to Timothy the importance of embracing sound doctrine and rejecting the falsehoods taught by spiritual charlatans. Specifically, he was to have nothing to do with the worldly *myths and old wives' tales* (1 Tim. 4:7) being spread by some at Ephesus. Instead, he was to make *godliness* his life pursuit. We too should make this our goal, for God is honored when our lives are characterized by holiness and an abiding reverence for Him.

Practically everywhere you look there are people spending lots of time and money to improve their physical health. Sadly, there are far fewer people devoted to enhancing their spiritual health. Paul said that bodily exercise was slightly helpful for a short period of time. In contrast, training oneself to be godly was eternally profitable in all areas of life. A person reaped spiritual blessings in the *present* (4:8) and also in the future. How ironic it is that we give so little attention and time to that which is so eternally beneficial.

Paul's statements about godliness were *sure and worthy of full acceptance* (4:9). He and other ministers of the Gospel were willing to do their utmost to promote spiritual and eternal values. They willingly labored to the point of exhaustion and endured the reproach of antagonists for the cause of Christ (4:10). Very few of us would be able to make the same statement about our level of commitment to the Gospel. Perhaps the Lord would have us to reevaluate how much we are actually doing for Him.

Why would Paul and others like him labor so intensively to promote the cause of godliness? The apostle explained that he and his associates had placed their *hope* in *the living God*, the one who alone could save the lost. His representatives were confident that all who believed in Him for eternal life would be saved. As those who have trusted in Christ, let us be as diligent as Paul was in proclaiming the Gospel to others.

Paul clearly told Timothy what he was to *insist on and teach* (4:11). For instance, he was to direct the Christians at Ephesus to believe the truth and apply it to their lives. Of course, the congregation needed a godly *example* (4:12) to follow as well as sound doctrine to obey. That is why Paul urged Timothy to be an example to believers in the compassion he showed, the attitude he displayed, the *faith* he demonstrated, and the virtuous way he lived. Such a godly lifestyle would undercut the efforts of those who questioned his leadership and authority because he was a younger man.

Paul urged Timothy to give his fullest *attention* (4:13) to his ministerial duties. This especially included the *public reading*, preaching, and *teaching* of the Word. Such an emphasis would be in keeping with the declarations that were made by various church leaders to Timothy at the time of his public ordination (4:14). We may not be called by God to serve as a pastor of a church; nevertheless, each of us has at least one spiritual gift we can faithfully use in the building up of Christ's body (see 1 Pet. 4:10-11).

Timothy was to think seriously about what Paul said and to give himself entirely to his ministerial duties. This included preaching the Gospel and leading the flock of believers at Ephesus. If Timothy faithfully discharged his pastoral responsibilities, the growth of his spiritual life and the *progress* (1 Tim. 4:15) of his ministry would be evident to everyone in the church. As we remain true to the Gospel and diligent in serving the Lord, others will see our growth and development as Christians.

As Timothy remained faithful to his calling, he would *save* (4:16) both himself and those who heard him preach. Paul meant that as his spiritual child pursued godliness and emphasized sound Bible doctrine, many people would come to know the truth and be saved. We know from Scripture that God saves a person; nevertheless, He graciously uses devout believers to lead people to trust in Christ. May we willingly allow Him to use us for such a noble purpose.

In 5:1-2, Paul talked about the proper treatment of various age groups. He told his spiritual child not to rebuke the older men in the congregation; rather, Timothy was to be as respectful and considerate to them as he would his own *father* (5:1). Similarly, he was to treat *younger men as brothers, older women as mothers*, and *younger women as sisters*. Paul summarized by saying that Timothy's behavior was to be characterized by *absolute purity*.

In 5:3-10, Paul talked about the proper treatment of older *widows*. In the early church, the death of a woman's husband could leave her in an abandoned and helpless state. Also, widowhood was viewed with reproach by many in Greco-Roman society. Thus, a widow without legal protection was often vulnerable to neglect or exploitation. If a woman's husband died when her children were adolescents, they were considered orphans. Regrettably, it was far too common for greedy and unscrupulous agents to defraud a destitute widow and her children of whatever property they owned.

There were three primary ways a widow could provide for the financial needs of herself and her children. First, she could return to her parents' house; second, she could remarry, especially if she was young or wealthy; or third, she could remain unmarried and obtain some kind of employment. The last prospect was rather bleak, for it was difficult in ancient times for a widow to find suitable work that would meet the economic needs of herself and her family.

Paul said it was the responsibility of the church to care for truly destitute *widows* (5:3). Not every widow, of course, was homeless and helpless. Some had *children or grandchildren* (5:4) who could supply their material needs. In such an instance, the widow's immediate family should demonstrate their devotion to Christ by helping out their needy family members. Such a charitable response was *pleasing* to God. This means that if we have destitute loved ones, it is our responsibility to care for their material needs.

There were widows who had no family or means of financial support. Many trusted in God and devoted themselves to continual and fervent prayer (5:5). They were the ones the church should support. Other widows, however, indulged themselves in the pleasures of the world. They were spiritually *dead* (5:6) even though they were enjoying life. Timothy was to exhort such people to abandon their sinful ways and live in a manner that was *above reproach* (5:7). This reminds us that our conduct needs to be blameless, for living for the moment is senseless and displeases God.

Paul made it clear that any family member who failed to help out loved ones in need had practically *denied the faith* (5:8). By their selfish and uncaring actions, the ungrateful Christians were behaving in a way that was worse than the unsaved. The apostle's words should prompt us to do whatever we can to ensure that the financial needs of our parents and grandparents are being met.

SUGGESTIONS TO TEACHERS

Paul wrote 1 Timothy from a distance. He cared about both Timothy and the church he led. In the apostle's concern, he wrote to Timothy, and through Timothy to each member of that congregation. Today, Paul's epistle still offers instructions for each of us, but also, through us, Paul offers his teaching to everyone we know. You can apply the following thoughts to your own role as a teacher, or the perhaps less formal role your students serve as their lives and words instruct others.

1. INSTRUCTIONS CHRISTIANS SHOULD HEAR. Paul wanted there to be no likelihood that Timothy would miss any of the apostle's important teaching. For that reason, Paul included sentences such as this one: *The saying is sure and worthy of full acceptance* (4:9). If this teaching was that important for a church leader thousands of years ago, then we need to hear it today. We cannot teach others what we ourselves do not know.

2. INSTRUCTIONS CHRISTIANS SHOULD FOLLOW. Hearing is the necessary first step, but in itself, hearing is inadequate. We must go on to *put these things* [the biblical truths we have heard] *into practice* (4:15). Can we teach others what we do not do? If we try, our negative actions will always speak louder than our positive words.

3. INSTRUCTIONS CHRISTIANS SHOULD ENABLE OTHERS TO HEAR. Teachers are called to listen to the truth, to live the truth, and to lead others into the truth. *These are the things* [the truth of God we are supposed to hear and heed] *you must insist on and teach* (4:11). A Bible teacher learns in order to teach. A teacher instructs, not to hear herself or himself talk, but that others might learn. In your life and in your words, how can you best communicate the truth of God our Savior?

4. INSTRUCTIONS CHRISTIANS SHOULD HELP OTHERS FOLLOW. Paul not only gave Timothy instructions for himself and for him to share with others, and Paul not only wanted Timothy to *give these commands* (5:7), but also to hold hearers accountable for what they had been taught. Paul relieved Timothy of the need to honor widows who chose to ignore God's plan. Paul's desire was not merely that widows be physically fed, but also that widows and all others be nourished in the way of godliness.

FOR ADULTS

■ **TOPIC:** Exercise and Sacrifice

■ **QUESTIONS:** 1. Why did Paul instruct Timothy to stay away from godless myths and tales? 2. Why did Paul place greater emphasis on godliness than on physical exercise? 3. Why was Paul so emphatic that Timothy follow the apostle's instructions? 4. To what end did Paul want Timothy to *toil and struggle* (1 Tim. 4:10)? 5. To what degree do you devote yourself to scriptural teaching?

■ **ILLUSTRATIONS:**

The Kid Professor. The setting for my first college teaching assignment was not in a traditional American college where the students were all younger than I. Instead many of the students at the Australian Bible college were mature, second career, ministry candidates.

I especially remember some members of my first preaching class. Roughly half of them were surprised to discover that their professor was younger than they were. In time, Judy, along with her husband, John, became co-pastors of the college church my family attended. Thang, who had escaped to Australia as a Vietnamese boat person, became a skillful preacher both in English and Vietnamese. Andrew continued as a skilled youth pastor. I count it a privilege to have taught them.

In order to adjust to this situation of teaching my elders, I needed to remember that God had called me there and that He had given me both rich education and experience. As the semester continued, we all forgot about my age. We grew together, both in knowledge and in friendship.

Stirring Up Their Gifts. Wayne and Bonnie are ones whose God-given gifts have helped so many people. Wayne and Bonnie came as short-term missionaries to the Australian Bible college where my wife and I taught.

Wayne's gifts lay in the areas of leadership and administration. During the short time Wayne was on campus, he helped improve many college business practices. More visibly, his skills enabled the college to replace its telephone system with a more efficient one, saving the college money at the same time. While there, Wayne was able to raise money adequate to brick face the only clapboard buildings on campus. A stranger merely walking on to campus could easily see the benefits of Wayne using his gifts for the community good.

Bonnie was not a business manager, a college teacher, or even a builder. With two young children at home, she was unable to take on many public tasks. But Bonnie still found ways to use her abilities. Her apartment became a student retreat. Bonnie brought people together. She organized formal events. Or, wherever Bonnie was, an informal fun time soon developed. Even the pranks she concocted helped bring us all together.

Several years later, Wayne and Bonnie volunteered to return to the college as career missionaries. Did the campus leaders welcome Wayne and Bonnie back? They sure did!

First to the South Pole. John Maxwell, in his *The 21 Irrefutable Laws of Leadership,* tells the story of two groups who simultaneously wanted to be the first to reach the South Pole. The year was 1911.

One group was lead by Robert Falcon Scott, a British naval officer with some experience in the Antarctic. Scott chose to move as quickly as he could, without adequate preparation and testing of equipment. He assumed that motorized sleds would be more efficient, but had not adequately prepared for the possibility of mechanical breakdown. Plan B involved ponies dragging the sleds. Regrettably, the temperatures dropped too low and the ponies had to be killed. Struggling with frostbite and dehydration, the men themselves ended up dragging the sleds for the last weeks of the pilgrimage. When the "hare" (in a manner of speaking) finally reached the finish line, he found a note from the "turtle" who had accomplished a trip of the same length in roughly half the time.

What made the difference? Ronald Amundsen, the leader of the other team, had listened to the advice of experts. He consulted with Eskimos who had experience living and traveling in frigid temperatures. Their wisdom led him to use dogsleds, and to travel only six hours a day, leaving everyone time for adequate rest. Amundsen listened to those who described the equipment he and his team would need. Following the counsel of more experienced individuals, Amundsen and his team reached the South Pole on schedule. Their only problem of any size was a painful cavity in one team member's mouth.

When in doubt, listen to the advice of the experts who have been there before.

FOR YOUTH

■ **TOPIC:** Faith Training

■ **QUESTIONS:** 1. What does it mean to have one's *hope set on the living God* (1 Tim. 4:10)? 2. For what reasons might Paul have been so insistent on the *public reading of scripture* (4:13)? 3. What do you think would have happened in Timothy's ministry if he had allowed people to despise his youth? 4. Why did Paul give Timothy instructions for dealing with specific age and gender groups (5:1-2)? 5. If you were to become a quality Christian leader among your peers, which of Paul's instructions to Timothy would be most relevant in your situation? Why?

■ ILLUSTRATIONS:

Life-Saving Instructions. Jason and Walt, along with a group of other friends, were mountain climbing. They had made it high enough on the mountain that they were climbing, which was covered with snow and ice. The summit was in sight, when Jason completely lost his footing. He slid a hundred feet or more before coming to a stop.

The rest of the group descended carefully, but quickly, to check on their friend, to make sure he was fine. They hoped they would together resume and complete their ascent. Physically, Jason was fine, but his long fall had shaken him emotionally. He'd moved into a state close to shock. He'd had lost all desire of starting back up the mountain, but felt equally uncomfortable about making his way down.

Figuratively, Jason felt frozen where he was. He would literally have frozen where he was if not for the loving concern and guidance of his fellow climbers. Walt took charge. He guided his friend back down the mountain. Giving instructions detailed almost to the point of telling Jason where on each step to place his feet, Walt led his friend to safety. To this day, Jason gives Walt credit for saving his life.

Paul told Timothy to pass quality instruction along to his hearers, for in doing so, he would save both himself and his hearers (1 Tim. 4:16).

The Public Reading of Scripture. Twice while I was in seminary, the same Salvation Army officer couple spoke in chapel. Both times, the husband preached the main sermon. Interestingly, I remember nothing about him or what he said. Both times, before he preached, his wife came to the pulpit and began quoting Scripture. Nothing unusual about that, you say? Perhaps not, except for the fact that she was quoting from memory entire chapters of the Bible. Her love for the Bible and the Lord about whom it spoke shone through the woman's face and radiated in her voice.

Taking In a Widow. Near the end of World War II, in a rural area of Tennessee, a wife received the dreaded news. Her husband had died in battle. That would have been disaster for any wife, but for Dona, this word shattered her life. Her husband had been her only living relative. Dona had no occupational skills. She saw no way to earn a living. Without her husband's paycheck, she could not continue to pay her rent. Where would she go?

My wife's grandparents, Walter and Hattie, attended the same church Dona did. They saw this widow's plight and chose to act. Their own children were grown.

They had space to spare in their old farmhouse. So Hattie invited Dona to come live with them. Dona gratefully accepted the offer. She was able to help with farm chores and house cleaning.

One day Walter suffered a heart attack while driving the tractor on a hillside. He lost consciousness. The tractor rolled and crushed him underneath. Dona was there to support Hattie through her tragedy. They grew into old age as two widows offering each other strength.

Today, the government does more to support widows. But many Christians still seek to follow the spirit of Paul's instructions to Timothy by adopting orphans from international refugee camps, financially supporting children in other countries, or some other means of gracious love for the truly needy.

HANDLE GOD'S WORD RIGHTLY

BACKGROUND SCRIPTURE: 2 Timothy 2
DEVOTIONAL READING: Psalm 119:9-16

KEY VERSE: Do your best to present yourself to God as one approved by him, a worker who has no need to be ashamed, rightly explaining the word of truth. 2 Timothy 2:15.

KING JAMES VERSION

2 TIMOTHY 2:1 Thou therefore, my son, be strong in the grace that is in Christ Jesus. 2 And the things that thou hast heard of me among many witnesses, the same commit thou to faithful men, who shall be able to teach others also. 3 Thou therefore endure hardness, as a good soldier of Jesus Christ. 4 No man that warreth entangleth himself with the affairs of this life; that he may please him who hath chosen him to be a soldier. 5 And if a man also strive for masteries, yet is he not crowned, except he strive lawfully. 6 The husbandman that laboureth must be first partaker of the fruits. 7 Consider what I say; and the Lord give thee understanding in all things.

8 Remember that Jesus Christ of the seed of David was raised from the dead according to my gospel: 9 Wherein I suffer trouble, as an evil doer, even unto bonds; but the word of God is not bound. 10 Therefore I endure all things for the elect's sakes, that they may also obtain the salvation which is in Christ Jesus with eternal glory. 11 It is a faithful saying: For if we be dead with him, we shall also live with him: 12 If we suffer, we shall also reign with him: if we deny him, he also will deny us: 13 If we believe not, yet he abideth faithful: he cannot deny himself.

14 Of these things put them in remembrance, charging them before the Lord that they strive not about words to no profit, but to the subverting of the hearers. 15 Study to shew thyself approved unto God, a workman that needeth not to be ashamed, rightly dividing the word of truth.

NEW REVISED STANDARD VERSION

2 TIMOTHY 2:1 You then, my child, be strong in the grace that is in Christ Jesus; 2 and what you have heard from me through many witnesses entrust to faithful people who will be able to teach others as well. 3 Share in suffering like a good soldier of Christ Jesus. 4 No one serving in the army gets entangled in everyday affairs; the soldier's aim is to please the enlisting officer. 5 And in the case of an athlete, no one is crowned without competing according to the rules. 6 It is the farmer who does the work who ought to have the first share of the crops. 7 Think over what I say, for the Lord will give you understanding in all things.

8 Remember Jesus Christ, raised from the dead, a descendant of David—that is my gospel, 9 for which I suffer hardship, even to the point of being chained like a criminal. But the word of God is not chained. 10 Therefore I endure everything for the sake of the elect, so that they may also obtain the salvation that is in Christ Jesus, with eternal glory. 11 The saying is sure:

If we have died with him, we will also live with him;
12 if we endure, we will also reign with him;
if we deny him, he will also deny us;
13 if we are faithless, he remains faithful—
for he cannot deny himself.

14 Remind them of this, and warn them before God that they are to avoid wrangling over words, which does no good but only ruins those who are listening. 15 Do your best to present yourself to God as one approved by him, a worker who has no need to be ashamed, rightly explaining the word of truth.

HOME BIBLE READINGS

Monday, August 9	Psalm 119:1-6	*Keep God's Precepts Diligently*
Tuesday, August 10	Psalm 119:9-16	*Treasure God's Word in Your Heart*
Wednesday, August 11	Acts 18:24-28	*Believers Encourage Apollos in the Word*
Thursday, August 12	2 Timothy 2:1-7	*Entrust Teachings to Faithful People*
Friday, August 13	2 Timothy 2:8-13	*God's Word Is Not Chained*
Saturday, August 14	2 Timothy 2:14-19	*Rightly Explain the Word of Truth*
Sunday, August 15	2 Timothy 2:20-26	*The Lord's Servant, an Apt Teacher*

BACKGROUND

The second time Paul wrote to Timothy, the apostle continued several themes begun in his first epistle. For instance, he wanted Timothy not to be discouraged or intimidated by those who did not respect him as the leader of the church. Paul also wanted Timothy to know how to confront and correct the false teachers who were causing confusion and dissension in the congregation and be courageous enough to stand against them (2 Tim. 2:25; 3:12-14; 4:3-5).

Paul was writing from a Roman prison and seemed to know that the end of his life was near. This was not the first time Paul had been detained by the authorities. He had been held in prison in a number of places. Earlier in Rome he had been kept under house arrest. Paul had always eventually been released. This time, however, he sensed that the outcome would be different. He spoke about how he had finished his work and completed the race. However, he did not intend that this letter to Timothy would be his last contact with him. Instead, the apostle hoped Timothy would be able to come visit him in Rome.

Church tradition states that Paul was executed by the emperor Nero near the end of his reign of terror. Nero committed suicide in A.D. 68, so Paul probably wrote this last epistle around A.D. 67.

Second Timothy reveals some of Paul's personal concerns. In it he opened his heart to his younger colleague in the faith, expressing sorrow and anger about those who had turned their backs on the apostle and left the truth of the Gospel. In some ways Paul felt completely abandoned (1:15; 4:10). The apostle thus poured out his heart to Timothy. The bleak prison walls had cut Paul off from those he longed to be with. The lonely echoes of the dungeon heightened the intensity of his desire to see Timothy as soon as possible (1:8; 2:3; 4:9).

Despite Paul's hardships, the Holy Spirit used him to minister greatly to others. The apostle's words are now part of Scripture and have continued to strengthen and encourage church leaders throughout the centuries. Pastors and lay leaders who have struggled against opposition—either from within the church or from without—have found comfort in Paul's words to Timothy as he ministered at Ephesus.

With respect to the first chapter of 2 Timothy, four important truths are stressed related to Paul's overall purpose. First, he was confident that Timothy would devotedly serve the Lord at Ephesus. Second, God had given him all he needed to be an effective minister. Third, Timothy was to rekindle the spiritual gift he originally received from the Lord. Fourth and finally, he had excellent examples to follow in remaining loyal to Christ.

NOTES ON THE PRINTED TEXT

Timothy's father was Greek, and his mother—Eunice—was a devout Jewish Christian. Timothy's mother and grandmother—Lois—diligently instructed Timothy in the Hebrew Scriptures from his earliest childhood. Luke wrote that the young man had a good reputation in both Lystra and Iconium (Acts 16:1-2).

Paul met Timothy while in Lystra on his first missionary journey. Apparently Timothy made a good impression on the apostle, for he selected him for service right away. Timothy must have been quite young when he first joined Paul on his second missionary journey—especially considering Paul's exhortation in 1 Timothy 4:12, which was written at least 10 years after Timothy began itinerating with the apostle.

Timothy accompanied Paul on numerous segments of his missionary journeys. Eventually the young man became one of the apostle's most devoted companions. This might explain why Paul planned to send Timothy to Corinth during a time of great tension and division. The breaks in his accompanying the apostle occurred when Timothy was instructed to minister at churches in such areas as Ephesus and Corinth. The testimony of Scripture is that Paul's co-worker enjoyed a long and fruitful ministry in evangelism and teaching.

In 2 Timothy 2, Paul exhorted his younger co-worker to remain faithful to Christ despite the prospect of suffering. The apostle used three analogies from everyday life to make his point. Paul also underscored the importance of being a courageous witness (2:1-2), a faithful follower (2:3-7), and a heavenly citizen (2:8-13). We discover from this chapter that God wants His people to be strong in faith and stalwart in character as they labor for Christ in the midst of persecution.

Paul began by urging his younger colleague in the faith to be spiritually strong in the *grace* (2:1) of God that was available to all who trusted *in Christ Jesus*. The Lord's grace would enable the apostle's co-worker to face stiff opposition from antagonists. Timothy was also to *entrust* (2:2) to others the biblical doctrines Paul had taught him. Timothy's disciples were to be dependable and reliable Christians who would also be qualified *to teach others* the same things (vs. 2). God has called us to train and equip others to serve Him. We should be diligent and committed to the task of making disciples.

Paul wanted to prepare Timothy for the possibility of being persecuted as a Christian. The apostle urged his friend to put up with adverse circumstances as a *good soldier* (2:3) of the Messiah. Paul related that a soldier on active duty would not enmesh himself in *everyday affairs* (2:4); rather, he would remain wholly devoted to his commanding *officer.* The Savior is our Leader and we exist to please Him.

Paul noted that a champion *athlete* (2:5) had to obey the *rules* in order to be qualified to win. As we proclaim the good news, we must heed God's Word. The apostle finally observed that the hardworking *farmer* (2:6) was entitled to the *first share* of the harvest. This suggests that God will eternally bless us for diligently serving Him.

Paul urged Timothy to seriously consider what he said. The apostle was convinced that God would help his co-worker to understand the significance of these truths (2:7). As we grasp and apply what Paul wrote, the Lord will powerfully use us to be an agent of dramatic change in the lives of others.

As Timothy encountered hardship, he was to remember *Jesus* (2:8). As *a descendant of David,* Christ was fully human. The Savior's resurrection from the dead validated His claim to be God the Son. These were the truths Paul declared in his gospel message, and he was imprisoned as a *criminal* (2:9) for his efforts. Nevertheless, the good news was unchained and fully able to transform lives. We have the assurance of knowing that the Gospel we proclaim cannot be shackled by any human power.

For *the sake of the elect* (2:10), that is, God's special people, Paul was willing to *endure* all sorts of hardships. He desired that all people would hear the good news, be liberated from sin, and become partakers of eternal glory through faith in *Christ Jesus.* What a wonderful privilege we have of telling others this wonderful message about salvation in the Lord!

Paul quoted a fragment from an early Christian hymn to underscore the eternal glory that awaits all believers. The apostle said that those who are spiritually united with Jesus in His death enjoy eternal life both now and in the future (2:11). Also, if Christians *endure* (2:12) suffering now, they will *reign* with Jesus in His kingdom. Those who *deny* ever knowing Him, however, will in turn be denied by Him. If believers are sometimes *faithless* (2:13), Christ will still remain *faithful* to them, for He *cannot deny* who He is. It is good to know that our salvation ultimately rests in the hands of the Lord, not us.

Timothy was to *remind* (2:14) the believers at Ephesus about the truths of the Gospel. As he called on the Lord as his witness, Paul's friend was to exhort the Ephesian Christians to avoid senseless arguments that ruin the participants. Instead, Timothy was to please God through his diligent study and accurate exposition of *the word* (2:15). Timothy would never need to be ashamed of carefully handling this repository *of truth.* We also should not be embarrassed to teach the message of truth to others.

For most of us the prospect of suffering for Christ is not very pleasant. Yet the Bible teaches that at some point in our lives we will experience hardship as believers (Acts 14:22; 2 Tim. 3:12). Instead of being depressed or enraged when we experience adversity, we should recognize the good things the Lord is trying to produce in our life. He is seeking to develop our character and make us more Christlike (Rom. 8:28-30; Jas. 1:2-4).

As this week's lesson makes clear, God wants us to be strong in faith and resolute in our commitment to the Lord. We also discover from the Scripture text that we cannot avoid experiencing hardship as followers of Christ. Instead of shunning this prospect, we should make the best of it by remaining close to the Lord and single-minded in our devotion to Him. We also should proclaim the good news, disciple new converts, and shun all associations with evil. When we courageously suffer and diligently labor for Christ, we have the assurance of knowing that God is well pleased and will eternally bless us.

SUGGESTIONS TO TEACHERS

Suffering is an unpleasant subject for most of us—even more so for those who are currently enduring it or are close to those who are. How many of us enjoy relating the details of one of our painful ordeals? How many of us want to contemplate the death of someone dear to us? Not many would.

Suffering also affects our outlook on life and ourselves. The film *Schindler's List* is a good example of how the visual depiction of extreme suffering can impact our views about our own human nature. How many of us would be like Oscar Schindler in his attempt to save people from suffering, or be like most people who closed their eyes to the hardships of others?

As believers, we cannot ignore the suffering that Christ went through for us. We also cannot disregard the trials His apostles and disciples of the early church endured for our ultimate benefit. As your class members discuss the material in this week's lesson, be sure to stress that God summons believers to courageously suffer and labor for Christ.

1. THE ANALOGY OF THE SOLDIER. How many Christians do you know who serve Jesus only for what they receive from Him? How strong is their faith? Compare them to soldiers. Now admittedly some people do enter military service primarily for what they will receive: pay, other financial benefits, and the opportunity to grow as individuals. But the best soldiers move beyond selfish motivation. They seek to serve others in their units. They seek to serve the nation they represent. Paul saw the Christian life, not as a vacation or an escape, but as participation in the greatest of spiritual battles. Good Christians follow the pattern set by good soldiers.

2. THE ANALOGY OF THE ATHLETE. Athletes love to excel. They love to climb on podiums and receive rewards for victory. They use all legitimate means to place their bodies in ultimate condition. But we have all heard stories of athletes taking illegal drugs to give them an even further edge. When their cheating is exposed and when their victories are taken from them, they experience public shame. Why did Paul compare the rule-keeping athlete with the quality Christian? What rules might Christians be tempted to break? Paul by no means was suggesting a return to the legalism of his earlier days. No, he sought to remind Timothy and all of us of the greatest principle—remain loyal to Jesus no matter what. You cannot win if you move away from Jesus.

3. THE ANALOGY OF THE FARMER. Paul saw no problem with motivating Timothy and others with the thought of future eternal reward. But do notice the analogy Paul used as he brought the promise of heavenly blessings into the picture. Farmers do not live for instant rewards, but, instead, work faithfully for months before they see their crop bear fruit. Likewise, Christians look not for short-term comfort, but for the eternal reward that comes in its season after long periods of faithfulness.

4. THE ANALOGY OF PAUL'S OWN MINISTRY. In the midst of various analogies, Paul threw in another real-life comparison. The apostle asked Timothy to consider the example of Paul's own ministry. It's as if the apostle were saying, "I have fought as a good soldier, but for now the only reward I have is this prisoner of war camp. I have kept all the rules as a good athlete, but for now the only crown I receive is made of thorns. But I am remaining faithful, as a good farmer does, so that I can receive my true reward at the time God has set." *I endure everything for the sake of the elect* (2 Tim. 2:10). Paul set his own life as an example for Timothy and us to follow.

5. THE ANALOGY OF THE WORKER. In 2:15, Paul implied a comparison between two types of workers, those that end their workweeks with shame and those who can look back with feelings of legitimate pride. The latter have done their work to the best of their ability, in contrast to those who knowingly have offered shoddy labor. Some workers do only enough to get by. Faithful workers produce a quality product. Paul reminded Timothy and us that both in what we say and do, we cannot cut any corners. We need to offer our best to God and His people.

FOR ADULTS

■ TOPIC: Grace for God's Workers

■ QUESTIONS: 1. In what ways does grace make a Christian strong? 2. Why would Timothy need to *think over* (2 Tim. 2:7) what Paul had written? 3. In what sense could Paul believe that the Word of God was *not chained* (2:9)? 4. Over what types of words might Timothy and his congregation be tempted to wrangle? 5. Which of Paul's analogies seems most appropriate for you? Why?

■ ILLUSTRATIONS:

My Father's Will. My dad died one summer on the last Sunday of July, just as Mom had died the previous summer on that same day. By the evening of Dad's death, my six siblings and I had gathered from around the country for a funeral, to support each other, and to begin caring for household details. At one poignant moment the next day, my oldest sister, the executor for the estate, called us all into the living room for the reading of the will. At first there were no great surprises. After gifts to Christian institutions that my parents had valued, their worldly goods were to be divided as equally as possible among the seven of us. But at the end of the document, my dad spoke powerfully to us one last time.

"I desire to leave the following message with my beloved children: 'The material inheritance which I have left you is small and insignificant. However, I trust that I have left you the memory of a faithful father, who honored Christ in his ministry and in his daily life. I would direct you "To an inheritance incorruptible, and undefiled, which fadeth not away, reserved in Heaven for you," which your Heavenly Father hath provided for you, "according to His abundant mercy," and "hath begotten us again into a lively hope by the resurrection of Jesus Christ from the dead." Don't miss it.'"

As Rachel read those words, with tears in our eyes, we remembered the most important legacy our parents had left us.

Remembered as a Teacher. People who have done any reading on World War I (or have closely followed *Peanuts* cartoons) know the name of Baron Manfred von Richthofen, the great German air force ace. Far fewer people have heard about Oswald Boelcke, who may have had far more impact on the tactics used by fighter pilots to this day.

William Cohen, in his volume, *The New Art of the Leader,* tells Boelcke's story. Boelcke was himself a skilled fighter. But his goal went beyond winning glory for himself. Today he is remembered as a strategist and team-builder. He would not allow any pilot newly assigned to his squadron to fly with him until the rookie had adequately learned the system. What system did Boelcke develop? Planes should fly together in squadrons supporting and protecting one another.

Oswald Boelcke himself was shot down and killed in 1916, quite early in the war. Yet, his careful concern for training others has given him his own place in military history.

Workers without Shame. My wife and I have furnished our house as much as possible with antiques. Even as I speak, my wife sits at her "desk," an oak library table her parents gave her. I first fell in love with our bed when I saw it in Kathy's grandparents' bedroom. These older items have so much more history and personality.

But that's not the only reason we prefer older items. We have also found that we can buy what others consider "second-hand" furniture at a far lower cost. But even that's not their best trait. We have found that furniture built 50 or a 100 years ago was made far more solidly! In contrast to much of what is manufactured today, our older furniture will last us our entire lifetimes. Workers today may be doing the best they can with the materials and machines they have, but I will take solid old handcrafted woodwork any day. The workers from the past need feel no shame over the quality of their work.

<table>
<tr><td>

FOR YOUTH

</td><td>

■ TOPIC: Working for God

■ QUESTIONS: 1. In what ways is the Christian life like a battle? 2. Why was the image of a patient farmer a good one for Paul to

</td></tr>
</table>

use? 3. Despite the fact that he was a prisoner, what factors enabled Paul to retain his own spiritual and emotional strength? 4. What did Paul mean when he wrote that the Savior *cannot deny himself* (2 Tim. 2:13)? 5. What does God need to change in your life so that you can be *a worker who has no need to be ashamed* (2:15)?

■ ILLUSTRATIONS:

Playing by the Rules. An article in a recent issue of *Baseball Digest* highlighted the value of knowing and playing by the rules of the game. On one play a batter passed a baserunner and thus was called out. How could the batter do something so silly? When the batter hit a long drive, the baserunner thought an opposing fielder caught the ball and returned to first base. The batter correctly saw that the fielder had missed the ball, so he ran full speed ahead, assuming that the baserunner was well ahead of him.

On another day, a player knew the rules well and used them to his advantage. A batter hit a ball sharply to the pitcher. The ball then became stuck in the pitcher's glove, so he threw his glove to the first baseman in time to beat the runner. The umpire rightly called the batter out.

The Patient Farmer. Almost all of us know some young child who struggled to wait for seeds to sprout. The story almost always happens with a similar script. The child, with the help of a parent or older sibling, excitedly planted seeds in a pot. Following the older person's instructions, the child watered the dirt and set the pot in the sun where it would receive the necessary warmth.

The child watched all that day. The next morning, she was sure the seedling would have poked its head through the soil, but it had not. By the third day, most young children decide that the seed has died. They pull it out to see what went wrong. By that time, they can see that the seed had begun to sprout, but when they try then to place it back in the soil, it's too late. Patient farmers wait for their crop to mature. Then they receive their reward.

Father and Son. Paul was not Timothy's biological father, but their relationship was perhaps as close as most sons enjoy with their fathers. Can you think of some adult, other than your own parents, who has had a significant positive influence on your development as a person? In an article in the *Seattle Times,* King County

Executive Ron Sims gave loads of credit to a childhood Sunday school teacher and his wife. When Sims reflected on the influence of Sylvester and Pauline Lake, he ran out of words. "Mr. Lake helped make me. How do you measure the contribution of a person who helped shape your values, who helped teach me to be kind and to care? It's immeasurable."

What specifics does Sims remember? The Lakes had him to their home for meals. After an auto accident, Sims was housebound with a fractured skull, so the Lakes often brought him stacks of books to read. Lake not only taught his Sunday school class with words, but also with his life. Sims looks back and summarizes the Lakes's ministry as "a magnificent gesture of caring."

REMAIN FAITHFUL

BACKGROUND SCRIPTURE: 2 Timothy 3:1—4:8
DEVOTIONAL READING: 1 John 5:1-5

KEY VERSE: As for you [Timothy], always be sober, endure suffering,
do the work of an evangelist, carry out your ministry fully. 2 Timothy 4:5.

KING JAMES VERSION

2 TIMOTHY 3:1 This know also, that in the last days perilous times shall come. 2 For men shall be lovers of their own selves, covetous, boasters, proud, blasphemers, disobedient to parents, unthankful, unholy, 3 Without natural affection, trucebreakers, false accusers, incontinent, fierce, despisers of those that are good, 4 Traitors, heady, highminded, lovers of pleasures more than lovers of God; 5 Having a form of godliness, but denying the power thereof: from such turn away. . . .

12 Yea, and all that will live godly in Christ Jesus shall suffer persecution. 13 But evil men and seducers shall wax worse and worse, deceiving, and being deceived. 14 But continue thou in the things which thou hast learned and hast been assured of, knowing of whom thou hast learned them; 15 And that from a child thou hast known the holy scriptures, which are able to make thee wise unto salvation through faith which is in Christ Jesus. 16 All scripture is given by inspiration of God, and is profitable for doctrine, for reproof, for correction, for instruction in righteousness: 17 That the man of God may be perfect, throughly furnished unto all good works.

4:1 I charge thee therefore before God, and the Lord Jesus Christ, who shall judge the quick and the dead at his appearing and his kingdom; 2 Preach the word; be instant in season, out of season; reprove, rebuke, exhort with all longsuffering and doctrine. 3 For the time will come when they will not endure sound doctrine; but after their own lusts shall they heap to themselves teachers, having itching ears; 4 And they shall turn away their ears from the truth, and shall be turned unto fables. 5 But watch thou in all things, endure afflictions, do the work of an evangelist, make full proof of thy ministry.

NEW REVISED STANDARD VERSION

2 TIMOTHY 3:1 You must understand this, that in the last days distressing times will come. 2 For people will be lovers of themselves, lovers of money, boasters, arrogant, abusive, disobedient to their parents, ungrateful, unholy, 3 inhuman, implacable, slanderers, profligates, brutes, haters of good, 4 treacherous, reckless, swollen with conceit, lovers of pleasure rather than lovers of God, 5 holding to the outward form of godliness but denying its power. Avoid them! . . .

12 Indeed, all who want to live a godly life in Christ Jesus will be persecuted. 13 But wicked people and impostors will go from bad to worse, deceiving others and being deceived. 14 But as for you, continue in what you have learned and firmly believed, knowing from whom you learned it, 15 and how from childhood you have known the sacred writings that are able to instruct you for salvation through faith in Christ Jesus. 16 All scripture is inspired by God and is useful for teaching, for reproof, for correction, and for training in righteousness, 17 so that everyone who belongs to God may be proficient, equipped for every good work.

4:1 In the presence of God and of Christ Jesus, who is to judge the living and the dead, and in view of his appearing and his kingdom, I solemnly urge you: 2 proclaim the message; be persistent whether the time is favorable or unfavorable; convince, rebuke, and encourage, with the utmost patience in teaching. 3 For the time is coming when people will not put up with sound doctrine, but having itching ears, they will accumulate for themselves teachers to suit their own desires, 4 and will turn away from listening to the truth and wander away to myths. 5 As for you, always be sober, endure suffering, do the work of an evangelist, carry out your ministry fully.

12

Monday, August 16	Luke 6:20-26	*Rejoice in Persecution*
Tuesday, August 17	Luke 21:12-19	*By Endurance You Will Gain*
Wednesday, August 18	2 Timothy 3:1-9	*Avoid Lovers of Pleasure*
Thursday, August 19	2 Timothy 3:10-15	*Continue in What You Have Believed*
Friday, August 20	2 Timothy 3:16—4:4	*Be Persistent in Proclaiming the Word*
Saturday, August 21	2 Timothy 4:5-10	*I Have Kept the Faith*
Sunday, August 22	2 Timothy 4:11-18	*The Lord Gave Me Strength*

BACKGROUND

The pastoral letters clearly show the love and concern of Paul as a pastor and administrator of several local churches. The apostle wrote these epistles to maintain the faith of God's people and to insure the faithfulness of the church. The purpose of his writing was to deal with the care and organization of the church. Paul charged Timothy and Titus to avoid heresy, hold to sound doctrine, and maintain a pure and godly life. The apostle also included instruction on how to appoint qualified officials, how to conduct proper worship, and how to maintain corporate discipline in the church.

With respect to 2 Timothy, the style of this letter is urgent, for Paul faced death alone in a dungeon. His epistle is a document of sharp contrasts. There are strong and passionate warnings laced with insightful wisdom and firm resolve. Yet in other places there are wearisome feelings, quiet and honest reflections, and even a few candid admissions of decisions made in years gone by.

Paul wrote this letter with two purposes in mind. First, he directed Timothy to come to Rome (4:9, 21) and provided instructions on who and what to bring with him (4:11-13). Second, the apostle wanted to leave Timothy with a final letter of personal encouragement in his ministry (1:5-14; 2:1-16, 22-26; 3:10—4:5).

This epistle has an intensely personal nature and tone. One senses Paul's strong love and concern for Timothy. The apostle encouraged his close friend to use his spiritual gifts. Paul wrote to strengthen Timothy's loyalty to Christ in the face of the suffering and persecution that would come. The apostle challenged Timothy to handle the Word of God accurately, and to faithfully instruct others in the truths of the faith. Paul gave warnings and instructions about how a believer should relate to the world in times of apostasy.

Like the earlier letter, 2 Timothy exhibits a strong concern for sound doctrine (1:13-14; 2:2; 4:3) and contains sound instruction concerning the grace of God (1:9-11), the faithfulness of Christ (2:11-13), and the nature and function of the Scriptures (3:15-17). There are affirmations of salvation by grace (1:9), election (1:9; 2:10, 19), and the divine inspiration of Scripture (3:16). This letter also affirms the resurrection (2:8) and second coming of Christ (4:1, 8). In the closing chapter, Paul exhorted Timothy to preach the Word, whether in season or out of season. This had been the apostle's life mission, and he wanted to encourage his beloved son in the faith to do the same.

Though Paul's life would soon end, he remained confident. He was not ashamed of the Gospel (1:12), and he was willing to endure everything for the sake of believers (2:10). He knew that he had been faithful to Christ (4:7) and that Jesus Himself was faithful (1:12; 2:13). Paul had confidence that the one who in the past had rescued him from death (3:11; 4:17) would bring him through death and enable him to inherit eternal life (4:8, 18).

Throughout Paul's letter to Timothy, the apostle underscored the importance of remaining faithful to the Gospel. Many regrettably teach that the good news is faith in Christ plus something else. For example, some groups claim that the practice of some external rite or ceremony is needed in addition to faith for someone to be saved.

Such a notion is false and to be rejected, for it subtly adds works to the clear and simple condition for salvation set forth in the Word of God. Unbelievers, in order to avail themselves of the salvation offered in Christ, must only trust in Jesus as their own personal Savior, believing that His death for sin on the cross was final and sufficient forever. Salvation includes both eternal deliverance from the penalty of sin and the new life believers have in Christ. Biblical redemption has no reality, validity, or meaning apart from faith in the Lord.

NOTES ON THE PRINTED TEXT

Paul said that in *the last days* (2 Tim. 3:1) troubling *times* would come. He was referring to the church era, which began with Christ's first advent and will end when He returns for His holy people. As this age drew to close, people would increasingly become *lovers* (3:2) of themselves and *money*. They would be boastful, haughty, slanderous, *disobedient to their parents*, unappreciative, and impious. The Lord wants us to be godly in what we think and do. As we clothe ourselves with the love and virtue of Christ, our lives will be pleasing to Him.

As the coming of Christ approaches, people will be increasingly heartless and detestable, verbally abusive, without self-control, cruel, and *haters* (3:3) of all that is *good*. They will betray others, act rashly, be filled with arrogance, and love sensual pleasures more than *God* (3:4). As we think about the vices listed in these verses, we should seriously examine our own lives to see whether any of them are present in us. If so, we should turn to the Lord and His grace for cleansing and renewal.

Paul's comments especially applied to the false teachers at Ephesus. They outwardly seemed to be godly; however, they denied the *power* (3:5) of Christ that was necessary for all true piety and devotion. The apostle urged his co-worker and the rest in the church to have no dealings with such spiritual frauds. We likewise will not want to have anything to do with people who seem to be religious but do not truly follow Christ and His teachings.

In 3:11, Paul testified that the Lord repeatedly delivered him from life-threatening danger. He knew, of course, that God would soon allow him to be martyred for the faith. The apostle soberly declared that all who were united to Christ by faith would suffer persecution (3:12). This truth also applies to us. As we witness for Christ, we might be mistreated by others.

Paul related that, as the coming of Jesus for His church drew closer, *wicked people* (3:13) and spiritual *impostors* would grow increasingly more numerous and *worse* in their behavior. They would deceive others and in turn be deceived themselves. The apostle urged Timothy, however, to remain faithful to the truths he *learned* (4:14), *believed*, and knew to be absolutely valid. He could have full confidence in them, for he received them from a trustworthy source, Paul. We likewise should wholeheartedly embrace and endorse what the apostle taught.

The doctrine Timothy received from Paul agreed with what his Jewish mother and grandmother taught him from the Old Testament when he was a young child. These same Scriptures gave the apostle's friend the wisdom that would eventually lead to *salvation through faith in Christ Jesus* (3:15). As we tell others about the Lord, we too must rely on God's Word to communicate His message of redemption.

Paul declared that *all Scripture* (3:16) originated with *God*; in fact, He is the ultimate Author of the written Word. Because the Bible is *inspired,* it is immeasurably profitable for instruction in sound doctrine, for rebuking the unruly, for correcting moral errors, and for *training* people to live in an upright manner. The servants of *God* (3:17) who heed His Word will be thoroughly prepared and equipped to do all kinds of *good* deeds. As we commit our lives in service to God, we should make the Bible the foundation for our beliefs, endeavors, and long-term goals.

Paul was about to issue a command to Timothy. To help him regard it with the utmost seriousness, the apostle summoned *God* (4:1) the Father and *Christ Jesus* as his witnesses. Christ is the one who would *judge the living and the dead*. He is also the one who would one day return and establish His *kingdom*. In light of these important truths, we should live in anticipation of our Lord's appearing. We should also be more faithful in our service to Him.

Timothy's prime objective was to *proclaim the message* (4:2). He was to be ready and willing regardless of whether *the time* seemed right or wrong, or whether it might be the popular or unpopular thing do to. He was to use God's Word to correct and censure the transgressor and exhort and encourage the wayward. His efforts were to include tremendous amounts of *patience* and painstaking instruction. We will also want to be patient and diligent as we minister the Gospel to others.

Paul explained that *the time* (4:3) was coming when people would not consent to the teaching of *sound doctrine*. Instead, they would listen to religious experts who would please them by telling them what they wanted to hear. Rather than embrace *the truth* (4:4) of Scripture, people in coming days would eagerly welcome senseless *myths*. There are many in our day who gravitate toward ideas that seem ridiculous and inane. The best defense against this tendency, of course, is to preach the Word.

Paul urged Timothy to remain level-headed and calm as he endured afflictions. Despite the prospect of *suffering* (4:5), he was to evangelize the lost and fulfill his God-given *ministry*. He could do so knowing that Paul had gone before him. The apostle admitted that he would soon be executed. His life was like a drink offering being poured out on the altar (4:6). Throughout his years of Christian service, he fought well, *finished the race* (4:7), and remained faithful to the Savior. Hopefully when we look back on our lives, we will be able to say that we did all we could for the cause of Christ.

SUGGESTIONS TO TEACHERS

We have learned that times of peril await believers as the church age draws to a close. The end of the age will be characterized by self-love, a flagrant disregard for others, and an appalling hypocrisy. We have been encouraged to heed the truth of God's Word despite the presence of ungodliness and persecution. We cannot go wrong with such a policy. After all, Scripture will help us to combat false teaching, learn the ways of the Lord, and minister for Him. There is no other infallible beacon to guide us to an eternally safe harbor.

1. THE PRIORITY OF SCRIPTURE. *All scripture is inspired by God* (2 Tim. 3:16). In contrast, the itching ears of sinful humanity freely revel in myths that offer pleasure, but no truth. Likely your students, if offered the choice, would argue that Scripture takes priority. Encourage them, however, to compute the time they gave to the study and application of God's Word; then have them do the same with the hours given to other non-work-related pursuits.

2. THE NEED FOR SCRIPTURE. Christ will *judge the living and the dead* (4:1). In 3:2-5, Paul described those who do not know or have rejected God's plan. Their attitude and actions demonstrate their broken relationship with Him. Neither these people nor those with whom they associate can be happy. Worse than that, they will sometime face Jesus, *who is to judge the living and the dead* (4:1). Without the teachings of the Scripture, they live without hope. Remind your students that believers never outgrow their need for divine truth. Paul thus encouraged Timothy to *continue in what* (3:14) he had *learned* from the Word.

3. THE POWER OF SCRIPTURE. In contrast to others, Timothy and his fellow-believers had come to know *the sacred writings* (3:15) that were *able to instruct* them *for salvation through faith in Christ Jesus.* The Lord, through His Word, could transform people from being *lovers of themselves* (3:2) to *lovers of God* (3:4). In this regard, Scripture is *useful for teaching, for reproof, for correction, and for training in righteousness* (3:16). Help your students remember that the equipping the Lord gives for *every good work* (3:17) is not a one-time event, any more than exercising, eating, or sleeping satisfy our bodies' needs on one occasion and for all time thereafter.

4. THE MINISTRY OF THE SCRIPTURE. *From childhood* (3:15), Timothy had *known the sacred writings*. His grandmother and mother had guided him in God's ways from childhood (1:5). Paul had continued that Word-directed ministry to Timothy. In turn, Paul instructed Timothy to carry on that same ministry to others (4:2, 5). Likewise, encourage your students to pass along to family members and acquaintances the spiritual truths they have received. As we faithfully *proclaim the message* (4:2), we prepare our world for Christ's *appearing and his kingdom* (4:1).

FOR ADULTS	■ **TOPIC:** Remaining Steadfast ■ **QUESTIONS:** 1. What happens to society when authority is ignored and people treat each other brutally? 2. Why are some people

easily led astray by spiritual frauds? 3. How can our example of godliness and devotion make a difference in the lives of other Christians? 4. Why is proclaiming the Gospel so important? 5. How can we use God's Word to teach others the right way to live?

■ **ILLUSTRATIONS:**

A Message More Important than Comfort. I recently heard Eugene Peterson describe how he began work on his Bible paraphrase, *The Message*. Peterson was pastoring a church in suburban Baltimore. A period of racial rioting broke out in the city. Several leading church members proudly showed their pastor the guns they had bought for self-protection. Peterson noted that his people felt more concern for their own safety than for the needs of their city. He chose to focus his Sunday school teaching on the Letter of Paul to the Galatians. Peterson's goal was to help people see their God-given freedom, rather than the need to set up procedures by which they could ensure their own comfort.

The first few Sundays, as Peterson taught from Galatians, the class members gave their usual friendly smiles all through the lesson. They drank their coffee as usual. Peterson felt frustrated that they could not see the revolutionary nature of Paul's letter.

Peterson thus decided to try restating the truth of this epistle in contemporary words, paragraph by paragraph. He made copies of his editing and offered it the next Sunday. Catching a fresh glimpse of the power of the Gospel, the class woke up to the truth. One Sunday soon after that, Peterson was cleaning up the room after the teaching hour had ended. He noticed that the coffee cups still held all their contents. His group had so come alive to the Word of God that they forgot all about their coffee!

An Actor. The speaker at my Christian college graduation ceremony was the newly elected president of another college. He spoke eloquent words encouraging graduates and all in attendance to work hard, to follow Christ, and to be His instruments for changing the world.

As the speaker received an honorary doctorate that day, he looked like the model of Christian leadership. Unfortunately, a few years later, a board member at the other college received an anonymous tip that encouraged a study of the college president's personal history. What did that study discover? That this man had lied about his previous academic experience and that his life was a sham. He evidently held the form of godliness, but not its power.

Desire for God's Word. In a book entitled *The Wonders of the Word of God,* Robert Sumner tells the story of a new Christian who was injured in an explosion at work. As a result of the tragic incident, he lost both hands, the use of many facial muscles, and his sight.

As the man began to regain his strength, he found great disappointment in losing his ability to read his Bible, even by means of Braille. He drew some hope when he heard the story of a woman who read a Braille Bible by means of her lips. But when a Braille Bible came in the mail, the man discovered that his lips had not retained enough feeling for him to distinguish the letters. Just then, he stuck his tongue out. In the process, he discovered he could feel the Braille raised letters with his tongue. At last count, he had read the Bible through four times.

An Example? Timothy learned the right way, God's way, as a child. Timothy's mother and grandmother evidently both spoke and lived in a godly manner. In all ages, some speak well, but don't live the life.

The story is told of a father and young son who entered a bank so that the father could cash a large check. As the pair were leaving the bank, the man discovered that he had received one too many 100-dollar bills. He turned to his son, remembering lessons of honesty he had taught the boy. As he thought about the error, he hissed, "You know, Al, we have a decision to make here. Should we, or should we not, tell your mother about this?"

 FOR YOUTH

■ TOPIC: Facing Hard Times

■ QUESTIONS: 1. Why do people tend to love themselves more than the Lord? 2. How can ministers combat false teachers who try to mislead church members by spreading bogus doctrines? 3. Why would any believer choose to endure suffering for the cause of Christ? 4. What motivates people to reject the truth of God's Word for the lies of Satan? 5. How can the grace of God sustain us in the difficult times we face?

■ ILLUSTRATIONS:

Thawed For Immortality. The Ice Man toy is an object that is put together and then has water poured over it before being frozen. The child then melts the Ice Man with warm water syringes and scalpels to remove the "organs." *Time Magazine* asked whether this might not encourage belief in immortal life through cryogenics. (Cryogenics is a branch of physics concerned with the production and maintenance of extremely low temperatures, and with the effects that occur under such conditions.)

As Christians, we know that immortality does not come through cryogenics. Rather, eternal life comes through faith in Christ. Nothing we do as humans can ever alter that truth.

Besieged by Choices. We who live in the United States are besieged by an estimated 600 to 1,200 choices each day through advertising. For instance, when we visit a mall or a supermarket, we are confronted by dozens of commercial messages. And it isn't going to change.

Beginning in 2001, the advertising industry grew domestically to become a $200 billion-a-year business. Five blimps float over the Super Bowl, in addition to the once-extraordinary Goodyear blimp. Direct-mail videos and CD-ROMS began to promote political candidates in 1992, and are now used to entice people to buy everything from insurance policies to fitness programs. Movie advertisements appear at ATMs, and fast sound bites and video clips play while people wait for their money. Some gasoline stations have fitted gas-pump islands with video screens that run a stream of advertisements.

In such an environment, how do we choose wisely? The key is to give Jesus foremost priority in our lives.

Changed Lives. Thirty years ago, Pablo was a 14-year-old street kid in Manila, the capital of the Philippines. In order to survive, Pablo joined a gang of thieves. At least he thought the gang would help him live to become an adult. In 1971, members of a rival gang stabbed Pablo twice with an ice pick. Somehow this boy did live to be an adult.

Eventually Pablo fathered a child, Jorlan. But did adulthood or the experience of being a father change Pablo? No. He continued life as an arrogant brute. With that kind of father, Jorlan did not stand much of a chance, did he? He ended up hating his father and living on the streets.

But, in time for them both, an organization called Urban Street Ministries began offering Jesus to the people of their Manila neighborhood. Today, Pablo, Jorlan, and their entire family are attending a small urban congregation. Pablo still can point to the scars he and others have inflicted on his body. But God, through His Word and faithful witnesses, has changed the lives of this entire family for time and eternity.

Proclaim the Message. In his book, *Developing the Leaders around You,* John Maxwell referred to a seminary professor who liked to tell this story. A woman looking for companionship chose to buy a parrot. She hoped to carry on conversations with her new pet. But the bird remained silent.

The woman returned to the store and asked advice. An attendant asked whether the bird cage included a mirror. So the woman bought a mirror, hoping it would cheer up her parrot into talking. But the bird spoke no words. The woman went back to the store again. This time another salesperson told her parrots liked ladders to climb. So the parrot was soon climbing up and down his ladder. But his silence continued.

Finally, the woman went to the store a last time. She told the sad story of her parrot's death. The sales crew gathered around her to mourn with her. One asked, "Did the bird ever say anything before it died?" "Yes," she replied. "He thanked me for the mirror and ladder, but then asked why I'd never bought him any food."

DO GOOD WORKS

BACKGROUND SCRIPTURE: Titus 2:1—3:11
DEVOTIONAL READING: James 1:19-25

KEY VERSE: Show yourself in all respects a model
of good works, and in your teaching show integrity. Titus 2:7.

KING JAMES VERSION

TITUS 2:7 In all things shewing thyself a pattern of good works: in doctrine shewing uncorruptness, gravity, sincerity, 8 Sound speech, that cannot be condemned; that he that is of the contrary part may be ashamed, having no evil thing to say of you. . . .

11 For the grace of God that bringeth salvation hath appeared to all men, 12 Teaching us that, denying ungodliness and worldly lusts, we should live soberly, righteously, and godly, in this present world;
13 Looking for that blessed hope, and the glorious appearing of the great God and our Saviour Jesus Christ; 14 Who gave himself for us, that he might redeem us from all iniquity, and purify unto himself a peculiar people, zealous of good works. . . .

3:1 Put them in mind to be subject to principalities and powers, to obey magistrates, to be ready to every good work, 2 To speak evil of no man, to be no brawlers, but gentle, shewing all meekness unto all men. 3 For we ourselves also were sometimes foolish, disobedient, deceived, serving divers lusts and pleasures, living in malice and envy, hateful, and hating one another. 4 But after that the kindness and love of God our Saviour toward man appeared, 5 Not by works of righteousness which we have done, but according to his mercy he saved us, by the washing of regeneration, and renewing of the Holy Ghost; 6 Which he shed on us abundantly through Jesus Christ our Saviour; 7 That being justified by his grace, we should be made heirs according to the hope of eternal life. 8 This is a faithful saying, and these things I will that thou affirm constantly, that they which have believed in God might be careful to maintain good works. These things are good and profitable unto men.

9 But avoid foolish questions, and genealogies, and contentions, and strivings about the law; for they are unprofitable and vain. 10 A man that is an heretick after the first and second admonition reject.

NEW REVISED STANDARD VERSION

TITUS 2:7 Show yourself in all respects a model of good works, and in your teaching show integrity, gravity, 8 and sound speech that cannot be censured; then any opponent will be put to shame, having nothing evil to say of us. . . .

11 For the grace of God has appeared, bringing salvation to all, 12 training us to renounce impiety and worldly passions, and in the present age to live lives that are self-controlled, upright, and godly, 13 while we wait for the blessed hope and the manifestation of the glory of our great God and Savior, Jesus Christ. 14 He it is who gave himself for us that he might redeem us from all iniquity and purify for himself a people of his own who are zealous for good deeds. . . .

3:1 Remind them to be subject to rulers and authorities, to be obedient, to be ready for every good work, 2 to speak evil of no one, to avoid quarreling, to be gentle, and to show every courtesy to everyone. 3 For we ourselves were once foolish, disobedient, led astray, slaves to various passions and pleasures, passing our days in malice and envy, despicable, hating one another. 4 But when the goodness and loving kindness of God our Savior appeared, 5 he saved us, not because of any works of righteousness that we had done, but according to his mercy, through the water of rebirth and renewal by the Holy Spirit. 6 This Spirit he poured out on us richly through Jesus Christ our Savior, 7 so that, having been justified by his grace, we might become heirs according to the hope of eternal life. 8 The saying is sure.

I desire that you insist on these things, so that those who have come to believe in God may be careful to devote themselves to good works; these things are excellent and profitable to everyone. 9 But avoid stupid controversies, genealogies, dissensions, and quarrels about the law, for they are unprofitable and worthless. 10 After a first and second admonition, have nothing more to do with anyone who causes divisions.

13

Monday, August 23	2 Corinthians 9:10-15	*Generosity Glorifies God*
Tuesday, August 24	Matthew 5:11-16	*Let Your Light Shine Before Others*
Wednesday, August 25	Titus 2:1-5	*Elders Should Teach Younger*
Thursday, August 26	Titus 2:6-10	*Be a Model of Good Works*
Friday, August 27	Titus 2:11-15	*Be Zealous for Good Deeds*
Saturday, August 28	Titus 3:1-6	*Be Ready for Every Good Work*
Sunday, August 29	Titus 3:7-11	*Good Works Are Excellent and Profitable*

BACKGROUND

Titus was a Gentile believer who often served as Paul's emissary. When Judaizers infiltrated the church at Antioch, Titus accompanied Paul on his trip to Jerusalem to confer with the other apostles about the matter. The fact that Titus was not required to become circumcised became part of Paul's argument to the Galatians in defense of the Gospel (Gal. 2:1-3).

Titus acted as Paul's liaison to the Corinthian church, where he was well received (2 Cor. 2:12-13; 7:5-7, 13-15). Titus brought word about the conditions in Corinth to the apostle in Macedonia and returned to Corinth with 2 Corinthians (7:6). Titus was also instrumental in seeing to it that the Corinthians followed through on their commitment to contribute to the relief fund for the believers in Jerusalem (8:6-24; 12:18). Paul's choice of Titus for this mission may have been based both on his Greek heritage and the genuine affection he had for the people of the city (7:15).

At some point during Paul's ministry, he and Titus traveled to Crete. Finding that the church needed to be organized, Paul left Titus behind to *put in order what remained to be done, and [to] appoint elders in every town* (Titus 1:5). Later, Paul asked Titus to join him in Nicopolis, but only after he had been received by either Artemas or Tychicus (3:12).

Titus was apparently with Paul during his imprisonment in Rome, but by the time 2 Timothy was written, the pair had separated. While others, like Demas, had deserted Paul for selfish reasons, the absence of Titus is evidence of his faithfulness in ministry. Titus probably would have preferred to stay with Paul during his imprisonment. Instead, he went to Dalmatia on another mission (2 Tim. 4:10).

Although there is no way to be certain, some have conjectured that Titus was slightly older than Timothy and less timid in nature. In any case, Titus was capable of handling difficult assignments, perhaps because of his affection for those to whom he ministered. His ministry record was one of faithful and unselfish service. Titus is a prime example of the New Testament ideal of servant leadership. He was as capable of leading as he was following.

The Letter of Paul to Titus was prompted both by the need to appoint suitable leaders in Crete and by the encroachment of false teaching there. The content of the epistle indicates that false teachers had been dwelling on fables instead on the

Scriptures. False teaching had corrupted the morals of Cretan believers, who were also in danger of being influenced by their unbelieving neighbors. In addition, legalism threatened to distort the saving message of grace as the unmerited gift of God.

The epistle is grouped with Paul's two letters to Timothy under the category of Pastoral Epistles because of its emphasis on the local church. Its similarity in content with Paul's First Letter to Timothy suggests that Titus was probably written about the same time, while Paul was still at liberty between A.D. 62–66.

This letter, like 1 Timothy, emphasizes sound doctrine (Titus 1:9; 2:8, 10) and challenges believers to good works (1:16; 2:14; 3:14). In particular, Paul stressed the quality of sober-mindedness (1:8; 2:2, 4-6, 12) and the importance of charitable Christian conduct (2:7, 14; 3:1, 8, 14). The epistle contains two excellent theological meditations on the grace that God has extended in Christ (2:11-14; 3:4-7). Titus also affirms the deity of Christ in a striking manner. The title "Savior" is applied in the same contexts to both the Father (1:3; 2:10; 3:4) and the Son (1:4; 2:13; 3:6). In fact, 2:13 speaks of *our great God and Savior, Jesus Christ.*

Titus contributes to our understanding of the work of the Spirit in salvation and the Christian life (3:5). The letter is also a key New Testament document for church organization, being filled with guidelines for elders, pastors, and other believers. Paul included practical instruction about the roles of men, women, and servants (2:1-10). He also wrote about how to deal with false teaching (1:9-16; 2:1, 7-8, 12, 15; 3:2, 8-11, 14). A church needs organization, sound doctrine, and good teaching to survive; and in this letter, Paul gave Titus a succinct overview on how to achieve this delicate balance.

NOTES ON THE PRINTED TEXT

In Paul's Letter to Titus, the apostle reminded his co-worker in the faith that, as he reached out to others, he was to be earnest and dignified, not indifferent and crass. Sincerity, not hypocrisy, was to characterize his *teaching* (2:7). Paul urged Titus to remain godly in all that he said and did. For example, he was to offer doctrinally correct and spiritually uplifting instruction. His teaching was to be so wholesome and pure that no one would be able to justly criticize or censure it. Despite their efforts to discredit the Gospel, the opponents of Titus would be unable to do so and ashamed for even trying (2:8).

In 2:11, Paul noted that that the *grace of God* was the basis for behaving in an upright manner. When Jesus came to earth as a human being, the grace of God *appeared* to humankind. The Lord's intent was that all people, regardless of their gender, age, or social status, might have an opportunity to trust in Christ for *salvation*. The grace of the Lord did not just concern salvation; it also declared that believers should *renounce* (2:12) all forms of irreverence and impiety as well as wanton and forbidden desires. Christians were to replace their sinful ways with self-control, rectitude, and piety.

The present age in which believers live is known for its wickedness and rebellion. The coming age of the Messiah, however, will be known for its goodness and righteousness. As we pursue godly living, we look with anticipation and joy to the glorious return of Christ. Paul referred to Jesus as *our great God and Savior* (2:13).

When Christ came to the earth the first time, He died on the cross for our misdeeds. He willingly became our atonement for sin so that we might be set free from enslavement to every form of wickedness. He also sought to spiritually purify us as His own special *people* (2:14). In gratitude, we should enthusiastically search for ways to do *good* works in His name.

Paul first instructed Titus that the believers on Crete were to submit to and readily obey the *authorities* (3:1) on the island, whether kings, magistrates, or local officials. The Christians also were to participate in *good*, or constructive, deeds on the island. Corruption may have been widespread among the governing authorities on Crete. The believers on the island, however, could not use this as an excuse for slandering their civic officials. Titus was to direct his congregates to malign no one, to promote peaceful relations, to be kind and thoughtful to others, and to display a humble disposition to all people (3:2).

What would motivate the believers on Crete to be kind to others who might be harsh in return? Their salvation in Christ would provide strong incentive. Before trusting in the Lord, the Cretans were spiritually senseless, rebellious, morally deluded, and enslaved to all sorts of forbidden *passions* (3:3). They were characterized by evil and jealous emotions; others hated them and they likewise hated others.

The believers on Crete, like all people, stood condemned before God; yet He showed His *kindness* (3:4) and love by sending His Son to earth to redeem sinners from their dismal plight. The advent of Christ was not due to any good things humanity *had done* (3:5); rather, the Lord saved people like the believers on Crete because of His great *mercy*. In love He cleansed them from the defilement of sin and made them new people through *the Holy Spirit*.

The Father abundantly provided the *Spirit* (3:6) to the believers on Crete when they trusted in *Christ*, their *Savior*. Thus, they were declared righteous by God's *grace* (3:7), made inheritors of fabulous eternal blessings, and became recipients of *eternal life*. The Cretan believers could confidently set their hope on these truths.

What Paul stated in Titus 3:4-7 was valid and worthy of constant affirmation. By keeping *these things* (3:8) in mind, the believers on Crete would have strong motivation to invest their lives in performing *good* deeds. Paul said the performance of wholesome activities was useful and helpful *to everyone*.

Regrettably, some on Crete were preoccupied with mythical Jewish stories and fabricated Old Testament genealogies. They not only rejected the Gospel but also urged others to abide by their humanly devised ceremonies and restrictions. Paul urged Titus to avoid *stupid* (3:9) speculations concerning the nature of *genealogies* and the keeping of *the law*. A preoccupation with these things would lead to squabbles and divisions among the churches on Crete. That is why they were a *worthless* and futile waste of God-given energy. Titus was to warn the divisive

Cretans to stop their harmful activities. If they refused to do so, he was to warn them again. If they ignored this *admonition* (3:10), he was to have *nothing* to do with them.

SUGGESTIONS TO TEACHERS

God has redeemed us from a life of sin so that we might faithfully serve Him. We do this by humbly submitting to earthly authorities, promoting the general well-being of our community, and combating false doctrines. As we make every effort to perform good deeds, we reflect the love and concern of Christ. Be sure to stress to the class that . . .

1. GOOD WORKS ARE NEVER THE BASIS OF SALVATION. God *saved us, not because of any works of righteousness that we had done, but according to his mercy* (Titus 3:5). How many people do we know who are convinced they are going to heaven on the basis of their own goodness? We can never despise the good that such people do for their families, for others, or for us. At the same time, we must find opportunities where we can graciously remind them that no one is good enough to earn God's love.

2. GOOD WORKS APPEAR ALWAYS AS THE RESULT OF SALVATION. We should also stress that the fruit of salvation is good works. Now, of course, no wise Christian rules out the possibility of deathbed conversions, where a person may not have opportunity, in this life, to demonstrate the transformation that Christ brings. But in other cases, salvation produces a change not only in a person's relationship with God, but also in the way he or she lives. Again, we need to be careful not to expect absolute perfection. None but Christ attain that ideal. But if an inner transformation truly has occurred, visible changes will appear as well.

3. GOOD WORKS MAY BE A HELPFUL INSTRUMENT TO THE SALVATION OF OTHERS. Paul urged Titus to live as *a model of good works* (2:7). It was so that others might see his own transformation and give glory to his heavenly Father. The best way to deal with opponents of the Gospel is to melt their opposition, to lead them by word and deed in the way of truth (2:8).

4. ALONG WITH SALVATION, GOOD WORKS SHOULD BE A MAJOR FOCUS WITHIN THE CHURCH. Paul encouraged Titus to proclaim both salvation and good works to believers. Paul wanted all people to experience both. In our churches today, we need to help people both to enter the Kingdom and become its loyal, obedient citizens. If we neglect either of these emphases (or stray too far from them toward other secondary matters), we fail rightly to proclaim God's entire message.

FOR ADULTS

■ **TOPIC:** Do the Right Thing

■ **QUESTIONS:** 1. How do salvation and good works relate to each other? 2. Why are the experience of salvation and the subsequent transformed life both so important? 3. In the transformed life, why are good *words* and good *works* both so important? 4. In the church, which controversies are worth discussing? 5. What are some of the unprofitable and worthless controversies that have caused unnecessary division in local churches?

■ ILLUSTRATIONS:

A Contemporary Model. The respect that even non-Christians give to Billy Graham stands as a great testimony to his character. Throughout his ministry, he truly has shown himself to be a model of *good works* (Titus 2:7) and *sound speech* (2:8). Even those who disagree with him can cast no slurs on his character.

Stop Being So Generous! In the wake of the World Trade Center bombings in September 2001, the American people gave generously to meet the needs of those who had suffered loss. In fact, so much was given that the authorities finally asked people to stop giving. What would it take for a church leader today to feel that he or she had to stop Christians from doing so much good?

No Divisions among Us. When my wife, Kathy, and I first became parents, we vowed to each other that we would never challenge each other in front of one of the children. When one of us made a decision, particularly about discipline, the other would stand behind the decision maker. Our children quickly learned that they could not go to Mom, when Dad had spoken, or to Dad, when Mom had laid down the law.

Schindler's Mercy. Perhaps you remember the movie *Schindler's List*. During World War II, as the Nazis were gathering Jews to send them to the gas chambers, a businessman named Oscar Schindler chose to take action. Although not otherwise known for his morality, before the war was over, Schindler had given his large fortune to save the lives of all the Jews he could. He established a factory near a work camp. In that factory, he provided food, health care, and ultimately safety for hundreds of Jews. He wished he could have rescued more, but he did what he could.

Did the particular Jews whose lives he protected do anything to earn Schindler's mercy? They had little, if anything, to offer. Yet after the war, none of them ever forgot the man who had saved them from death. They repaid his kindness by showering him with many kindnesses and supporting him with material objects he needed.

Love for the Homeless. One day, I walked a mile or so to our local public library. In just that short walk, I was approached twice by homeless men, asking me for money. As a believer committed to loving others as Christ loves them, I never know quite how to respond.

In one similar situation a few years ago, I gave money, but later regretted my choice. A man approached me in a gas station asking for money supposedly for gas. He gave me a long story about taking his wife home after surgery and his leaving his wallet at the hospital. His story sounded so convincing that I gave him $10. As I drove on, I realized that details in his story did not fit together well. He had "taken me." Regrettably, that one bad experience has skewed my vision of all people asking for money. At least some of these people truly are needy. How would Christ have us respond?

My cynical self suggests that I should tell beggars to go get a job, to work as I do. But then I know that many of them have mental and emotional issues that hinder them from living a normal life. What should I do? Perhaps I could at least go with these people to a fast food restaurant and buy them a hamburger. In that situation, I would know that money was not being dreadfully abused. But I would also receive the joy of obeying God's Word. I would, in this manner, devote myself to *good works* (Titus 3:8).

FOR YOUTH	■ **TOPIC:** Do the Right Thing

■ **QUESTIONS:** 1. What are some appropriate ways a pastor can encourage the congregation to be more godly in their behavior? 2. What can believers do to be an example of godliness and virtue to others? 3. How can believers fully appropriate God's grace? 4. How can believers avoid getting involved in foolish arguments and petty quarrels? 5. How can believers tactfully handle those who are divisive in their beliefs and actions?

■ **ILLUSTRATIONS:**

A Model Mom. Who served as the greatest model for Theo Ratliff, a 1995 first round NBA draft choice and center for the Atlanta Hawks? It was his mother. When her boys were young, she supported the family by driving an hour each way to her job in a garment factory. When she came home each evening, she spent time, alongside her children, doing her own homework—toward a college degree. She reached her goals—providing food and shelter for her children, her own college graduation, and raising her sons well.

Theo said, "Without that type of influence from within their families, a lot of our friends went astray." Even today, Camillia Ratliff could probably live off her son's income. But she did not earn that college degree for nothing. She currently manages elder-care programs in 10 Alabama counties.

Communicating Positively. During the Korean War, many Americans died perhaps unnecessarily while prisoners of war. The conditions in which they lived were horrible, but not in themselves deadly. What killed these men? In solitary confinement, they lost the will to live.

In contrast, many men facing similar tragedy during the Viet Nam War managed to survive. What made the difference? Again, many captured soldiers were placed in solitary confinement. Sometimes they went weeks, months, or even years without face-to-face contact with each other. But, secretly, they developed a code that enabled them to stay in touch with each other.

The American prisoners invented a language that involved tapping on the walls between cells. Through this means, they could communicate news, offer encouragement, and even pray together. Despite physical separation, they focused on remaining a team. Do you think they wasted much of their "conversations" in quarreling? Of course not! Instead, they focused on "speaking" that which would help one another survive.

Avoid Speaking Needless Criticism. People, young and old, derive some strange pleasure by putting other people down. A couple listened one evening as their daughters, over dinner, said all kinds of less than ideal things about their friends. They got together on the same person, Marsha, calling her "strange," "odd," and many worse things.

Mother, who knew the young woman in question, finally had enough. "You know," she remarked, "I too think Marsha is strange and odd." The girls felt stunned. Mother never entered in the name-calling conversations. But then she continued, "I think she's strange because I have never heard her speak negatively about anyone else." Mom's subtle comment quieted her girls through the rest of that meal!

Enough Points? On a jet, a pastor found himself sitting next to a man convinced he could get into heaven by the good things he had done. For the sake of the argument, the pastor decided to play along for a while. "OK," the pastor said. "Let's say you needed 10,000 points to get into heaven. How do you think you would have earned those points?"

The man thought. He started out, "I have been married to the same woman for 30 years. I have not cheated on her once." The pastor answered quickly, "That would give you two points." "Two points; is that all? Well, I go to church every Sunday and place something in the offering every week." "That's great, but that would be worth only two more points. How are you going to come up with the other 9,996 points you need to get into heaven?"

"Well, at the rate you are awarding points, I will never get into heaven by the good things I have done!" The pastor smiled and quietly remarked, "Yes, that's the truth."

NOTES

NOTES

NOTES

NOTES

NOTES